P9-CQD-214

IMAGINING SOCIOLOGY

AN INTRODUCTION WITH READINGS

Catherine Corrigall-Brown

Second Edition

OXFORD
UNIVERSITY PRESS

OXFORD
UNIVERSITY PRESS

Oxford University Press is a department of the University of Oxford.
It furthers the University's objective of excellence in research, scholarship,
and education by publishing worldwide. Oxford is a registered trade mark of
Oxford University Press in the UK and in certain other countries.

Published in Canada by
Oxford University Press
8 Sampson Mews, Suite 204,
Don Mills, Ontario M3C 0H5 Canada

www.oupcanada.com

Copyright © Oxford University Press Canada 2020

The moral rights of the author have been asserted

Database right Oxford University Press (maker)

First Edition published in 2016

All rights reserved. No part of this publication may be reproduced, stored in
a retrieval system, or transmitted, in any form or by any means, without the
prior permission in writing of Oxford University Press, or as expressly permitted
by law, by licence, or under terms agreed with the appropriate reprographics
rights organization. Enquiries concerning reproduction outside the scope of the
above should be sent to the Permissions Department at the address above
or through the following url: www.oupcanada.com/permission/permission_request.php

Every effort has been made to determine and contact copyright holders.
In the case of any omissions, the publisher will be pleased to make
suitable acknowledgement in future editions.

Library and Archives Canada Cataloguing in Publication

Title: Imagining sociology : an introduction with readings / Catherine Corrigall-Brown.
Names: Corrigall-Brown, Catherine, author.
Description: Second edition. | Includes index.
Identifiers: Canadiana (print) 20190096659 | Canadiana (ebook) 20190096667 | ISBN 9780199031085
(softcover) | ISBN 9780199031139 (EPUB)
Subjects: LCSH: Sociology—Textbooks. | LCSH: Canada—Social conditions—Textbooks. | LCGFT: Textbooks.
Classification: LCC HM586 C68 2019 | DDC 301—dc23

Cover image: © iStock/olaser
Cover and interior design: Laurie McGregor

Oxford University Press is committed to our environment.
Wherever possible, our books are printed on paper which comes from
responsible sources.

Printed and bound in Canada

2 3 4 — 21 20 19

Contents

Part III   The Role of Institutions   195

10 Work and Rationalization 278

11 Health 303

Publisher's Preface

Oxford University Press is delighted to present the second edition of Catherine Corrigall-Brown's *Imagining Sociology: An Introduction with Readings*. This exciting new edition brings sociology to life through a fresh, lively treatment of core topics that incorporates important readings in the field and ample opportunities for applied learning. This innovative approach empowers students to see how sociology can help them make sense of the world—and is sure to spark their sociological imaginations!

Key Features

Integrated Readings

The *only* **introductory sociology text to integrate readings**, this book allows students to engage directly with classic and contemporary sociological works. With **thirteen new integrated readings**, the second edition of *Imagining Sociology* combines both classic and contemporary readings to illuminate concepts and theories under discussion and highlight the discipline's roots as well as its current findings.

READINGS

Critical reading questions draw out key points and encourage students to develop their own conclusions about sociological ideas and issues.

CRITICAL READING QUESTIONS

1. How is this article an example of labelling theory? How did the diagnosis of "insane" lead to the symptoms observed by the staff?
2. Why does a false positive diagnosis of mental illness generally have more serious repercussions than a false positive diagnosis of physical illness?
3. What is the significance of the fact that many patients, but none of the staff, managed to detect pseudopatients?
4. What can this study teach us about why people engage in deviant acts and/or crime? How can it help us to better deal with people labelled deviant?

Thought-provoking activities in each chapter facilitate applied learning and help readers connect sociological concepts to everyday life.

The History and Biography of Higher Education in Canada 10
Suicide in Canada 21
How Do Toys Socialize Us? 46
Performing the Self Online 59
The Changing Social Construction of Deviance 66
Calculating Crime Rates 83
Social Status Markers 115
Creating Low-Income Cut-Offs (LICOs) 124
Defining and Calculating Racial Groups 134
Canadian Citizenship Test 160
Performing Gender in Music 169
Gender Associations 176
The Reality of Reality TV 220
Using Media Literacy with Alcohol and Tobacco Ads 223
Comedy and the TV Family 229

Increasing or Decreasing Fertility in Quebec and China 241
How Can We Measure the "College or University Experience"? 257
Critically Analyzing School Curriculum 269
The Commodification of Love 287
Training Employees for Emotional Labour 300
The Freshman 15 and Binge Drinking: Health as a Personal Trouble or Public Issue 309
Accessibility in Everyday Life 326
The Ecological Footprint 336
Commodity Chains and Global Inequality 338
Micro-financing and Global Inequality 349
The Truth and Reconciliation Commission of Canada 375
Civil Society on Campus and among the Young 388

ACTIVITY

Highlight boxes are updated throughout the book and discuss relevant topics such as social determinants of health, racial and gender inequality, social media, and automation in the workplace, providing students with deeper insight into the issues, themes, and theories explored in each chapter.

HIGHLIGHT

Contemporary and Canadian coverage—including examples from recent events and popular culture, the latest research in the field, and Canadian cases and data—gives students a current and relevant overview of the discipline.

---

16   PART I Understanding Society

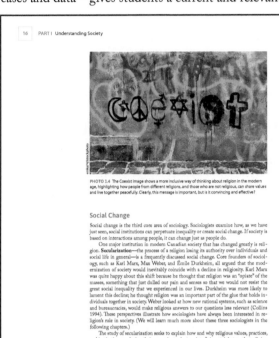

PHOTO 1.4 The Coexist image shows a more inclusive way of thinking about religion in the modern age, highlighting how people from different religions, and those who are not religious, can share values and live together peacefully. Clearly, this message is important, but is it convincing and effective?

Social Change

Social change is the third core area of sociology. Sociologists examine how, as we have just seen, social institutions can perpetuate inequality or create social change. If society is based on interactions among people, it can change just as people do.

One major institution in modern Canadian society that has changed greatly is religion. **Secularization**—the process of a religion losing its authority over individuals and social life in general—is a frequently discussed social change. Core founders of sociology, such as Karl Marx, Max Weber, and Émile Durkheim, all argued that the modernization of society would inevitably coincide with a decline in religiosity. Karl Marx was quite happy about this shift because he thought that religion was an "opiate" of the masses, something that just dulled our pain and senses so that we would not resist the great social inequality that we experienced in our lives. Durkheim was more likely to lament this decline; he thought religion was an important part of the glue that holds individuals together in society. Weber looked at how new rational systems, such as science and bureaucracies, would make religious answers to our questions less relevant (Collins 1994). These perspectives illustrate how sociologists have always been interested in religion's role in society. (We will learn much more about these three sociologists in the following chapters.)

The study of secularization seeks to explain how and why religious values, practices, and institutions are losing their power in modern society. It is certainly true that religion is currently less integral to many functions of Canadian society than it was in the past. For example, traditionally, many schools were run by religious institutions. You can still attend a religious school, but most schools in Canada are now operated by the state and are non-religious. Religious institutions were also once the main provider of charitable and welfare services, running orphanages, soup kitchens, and hospitals. Now the government primarily performs such functions. Many religious institutions are still involved in these activities and raise money for these causes; however, the control of these services rests mostly in the hands of the state.

---

1 The Sociological Imagination   15

Institutions are important because they generally help society to run smoothly. They do so in part by socializing us and thereby teaching us the rules of our society. When you first go to school, you learn that you must sit quietly in class and raise your hand when you want to speak. These rules are important and help later schooling and other social interactions to function. Imagine if everyone just wandered around the room during your university classes—the result would certainly be a chaotic environment.

However, institutions can also serve a negative function by maintaining and reinforcing inequality. In fact, one of the main reasons that inequality tends to persist is the role of social institutions. Because standardized methods become routine, they can reinforce some of the differences between people. For example, if your university or college has very high tuition, students of lower social classes might not be able to attend the school. In this way, the institution is partly responsible for people from lower social classes being less likely to get the degrees that would allow them to increase their social standing.

Institutions can also be an avenue for social change. We know that individuals from lower social classes are much less likely to get a university or college degree than those from higher social classes. Many social programs instituted by the Government of Canada have tried to address this imbalance. The Veterans Rehabilitation Act (VRA), passed in 1944, included a program that helped World War II veterans receive a post-secondary education by paying their full tuition and living expenses for up to four years. The idea was that helping soldiers to get an education would help them to return to civilian life. More than 120,000 veterans—mostly men—received this support. Research estimates that as a result of the program, men of the postwar period had an average of 0.2 to 0.4 more years of education and had higher wages over the course of their lives than they otherwise would have had (Lemieux and Card 1998).

PHOTO 1.3 Prime Minister Justin Trudeau meets with the File Hills Qu'Appelle Tribal Council. This meeting between a governing body (the Tribal Council) and the head of another governing body (the prime minister of Canada) highlights the complexity and multifaceted nature of institutions such as governments.

---

13 Change through Policy and the Law   367

The TRC worked for six years, collecting documents and more than 6000 accounts from those who funded the schools, officials of the institutions that operated the schools, survivors, their families, communities, and anyone else personally affected by the residential school experience. The TRC's final report, released on 2 June 2015, includes 94 recommendations, such as legislation for education, child welfare, and Aboriginal languages and the implementation of the UN's Declaration on the Rights of Indigenous Peoples (Watters 2015).

In the following reading, we will learn about the important work of the Truth and Reconciliation Commission in Canada. How is this commission an example of reparations, and how is it being implemented in Canada?

READING

TRC Principles of Reconciliation and "The Canadian Reconciliation Landscape: Current Perspectives of Indigenous Peoples and Non-Indigenous Canadians"

The Truth and Reconciliation Commission of Canada Principles of Reconciliation

The Truth and Reconciliation Commission of Canada believes that in order for Canada to flourish in the twenty-first century, reconciliation between Aboriginal and non-Aboriginal Canada must be based on the following principles.

1. The *United Nations Declaration on the Rights of Indigenous Peoples* is the framework for reconciliation at all levels and across all sectors of Canadian society.
2. First Nations, Inuit, and Métis peoples, as the original peoples of this country and as self-determining peoples, have Treaty, constitutional, and human rights that must be recognized and respected.
3. Reconciliation is a process of healing of relationships that requires public truth sharing, apology, and commemoration that acknowledge and redress past harms.
4. Reconciliation requires constructive action on addressing the ongoing legacies of colonialism that have had destructive impacts on Aboriginal peoples' education, culture and languages, health, child welfare, the administration of justice, and economic opportunities and prosperity.
5. Reconciliation must create a more equitable and inclusive society by closing the gaps in social, health, and economic outcomes that exist between Aboriginal and non-Aboriginal Canadians.
6. All Canadians, as Treaty peoples, share responsibility for establishing and maintaining mutually respectful relationships.
7. The perspectives and understandings of Aboriginal Elders and Traditional Knowledge Keepers of the ethics, concepts, and practices of reconciliation are vital to long-term reconciliation.
8. Supporting Aboriginal peoples' cultural revitalization and integrating Indigenous knowledge systems, oral histories, laws, protocols, and connections to the land into the reconciliation process are essential.

Truth and Reconciliation Commission of Canada. 2015. *What We Have Learned: Principles of Truth and Reconciliation, pp. 3–4. Reconciliation Canada.* The Canadian Reconciliation Landscape, 2017.

Reconciliation Canada. 2017. The Canadian Reconciliation Landscape. http://reconciliationcanada.ca/staging/wp-content/uploads/2017/05/NationalNarrativeReport-ReconciliationCanada-ReleasedMay2017_2.pdf.

Indigenous content discusses recent events related to Indigenous relations in Canada, including integrated readings on reconciliation.

6 Gender at the Intersections   183

and political rights. Instead, it tends to work in cultural arenas—for example, challenging gender depictions in the media, sexist language, and gendered norms around sexuality.

Intersectionality

The concept of **intersectionality**—the study of how various dimensions of inequality can combine—is one product of feminism's third wave. Kimberlé Williams Crenshaw coined the term in 1989 and explains it with the following metaphor:

> Discrimination, like traffic through an intersection, may flow in one direction, and it may flow in another. If an accident happens in an intersection, it can be caused by cars traveling from any number of directions and, sometimes, from all of them. Similarly, if a Black woman is harmed because she is in an intersection, her injury could result from sex discrimination or race discrimination. But it is not always easy to reconstruct an accident. Sometimes the skid marks and the injuries simply indicate that they occurred simultaneously, frustrating efforts to determine which driver caused the harm. (149)

The theory came out of Crenshaw's research on work and discrimination in the 1980s. Crenshaw (1989) studied a group of black women in the United States who had filed a workplace discrimination lawsuit. A round of layoffs at their workplace had resulted in all the black women being fired. The trial judge ruled against these women—he said that there was no gender discrimination because white women were not fired and there was no racial discrimination because black men were not fired. As the law saw only two types of discrimination (discrimination against women based on their sex or discrimination against racial minorities based on their race), there was no discrimination in this case.

These black women and Crenshaw understood that the former's experience was rendered invisible by intersectionality. The fact that they were both black and women made

PHOTO 6.6 At the 2014 MTV Video Music Awards, Beyoncé performed in front of a large sign that said "Feminist." Some praised her performance as a political statement and argued that it raised feminism's profile among young women. Others were more critical of the word being used by a performer who often uses her sexuality to sell her music. Do you think that Beyoncé is a feminist? How does this performance fit into (or challenge) our ideas of what a feminist is?

Theory integrated throughout the text helps students easily relate theoretical concepts to the various sociological issues discussed in each chapter.

A lively and accessible writing style grabs students' attention and helps them easily understand concepts under discussion.

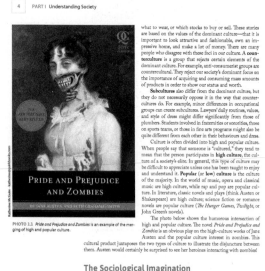

4   PART I Understanding Society

PHOTO 1.1 *Pride and Prejudice and Zombies* is an example of the merging of high and popular culture.

what to wear, or which stocks to buy or sell. These stories are based on the values of the dominant culture—that it is important to look attractive and fashionable, own an impressive home, and make a lot of money. There are many people who disagree with these foci in our culture. A **counterculture** is a group that rejects certain elements of the dominant culture. For example, anti-consumerist groups are countercultural. They reject our society's dominant focus on the importance of acquiring and consuming mass amounts of products in order to show our status and worth.

Subcultures also differ from the dominant culture, but they do not necessarily oppose it in the way that countercultures do. For example, minor differences in occupational groups can create subcultures. Lawyers' daily routines, values, and style of dress might differ significantly from those of plumbers. Students involved in fraternities or sororities, those on sports teams, or those in fine arts programs might also be quite different from each other in their behaviours and dress.

Culture is often divided into high and popular culture. When people say that someone is "cultured," they tend to mean that the person participates in **high culture**, the culture of a society's elite. In general, this type of culture may be difficult to appreciate unless one has been taught to enjoy and understand it. **Popular (or low) culture** is the culture of the majority. In the world of music, opera and classical music are high culture, while rap and pop are popular culture. In literature, classic novels and plays (think Austen or Shakespeare) are high culture; science fiction or romance novels are popular culture (*The Hunger Games*, *Twilight*, or John Green's novels).

The photo below shows the humorous intersection of high and popular culture. The novel *Pride and Prejudice and Zombies* is an obvious play on the high-culture works of Jane Austen and the popular culture interest in zombies. This cultural product juxtaposes the two types of culture to illustrate the disjuncture between them. Austen would certainly be surprised to see her heroines interacting with zombies!

The Sociological Imagination

In Canadian society, most people believe that individuals shape their own destiny. To a certain extent, this is true—we, as individuals, make decisions every day that shape the kind of life we lead. For example, you made decisions about whether to attend university or college, how hard to work in your classes, where to live when attending school, and what type of summer job you want. But, of course, many factors influence these decisions.

Let's examine your decision about a summer job. If your parents are willing and able to help pay for your education, you might not have to work in the summer, or you might choose to take an unpaid internship, which would be impossible if you needed to pay your own tuition. In this way, your individual choice of whether you work and what type of job you get is, to some degree, structured by the wealth and support of your parents. The reason we might be interested in how your individual choices are constrained is that it might shape later outcomes for you. For example, students who have completed an unpaid internship might find it easier to get a good job after graduation because

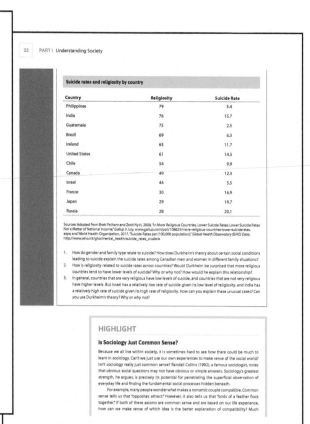

22   PART I Understanding Society

Suicide rates and religiosity by country		
Country	Religiosity	Suicide Rate
Philippines	79	3.4
India	76	15.7
Guatemala	75	2.5
Brazil	69	6.3
Ireland	63	11.7
United States	61	14.3
Chile	54	9.9
Canada	49	12.3
Israel	44	5.5
France	30	16.9
Japan	29	19.7
Russia	28	20.1

Sources: Adapted from Brett Pelham and Zsolt Nyiri, 2008, "In More Religious Countries, Lower Suicide Rates: Lower Suicide Rates Not a Matter of National Income," Gallup 3 July, www.gallup.com/poll/108625/more-religious-countries-lower-suicide.aspx and World Health Organization, 2017, "Suicide Rates per (100,000 population)," *Global Health Observatory (GHO) Data,* http://www.who.int/gho/mental_health/suicide_rates_crude/e

1. How do gender and family type relate to suicide? How does Durkheim's theory about certain social conditions leading to suicide explain the suicide rates among Canadian men and women in different family situations?
2. How is religiosity related to suicide rates across countries? Would Durkheim be surprised that more religious countries tend to have lower levels of suicide? Why or why not? How would he explain this relationship?
3. In general, countries that are very religious have low levels of suicide, and countries that are not very religious have higher levels. But Israel has a relatively low rate of suicide given its low level of religiosity, and India has a relatively high rate of suicide given its high rate of religiosity. How can you explain these unusual cases? Can you use Durkheim's theory? Why or why not?

HIGHLIGHT

Is Sociology Just Common Sense?

Because we all live within society, it is sometimes hard to see how there could be much to learn in sociology. Can't we just use our own experiences to make sense of the social world? Isn't sociology really just common sense? Randall Collins (1992), a famous sociologist, notes that obvious social questions may not have obvious or simple answers. Sociology's greatest strength, he argues, is precisely its potential for penetrating the superficial observation of everyday life and finding the fundamental social processes hidden beneath.

For example, many people wonder what makes a romantic couple compatible. Common sense tells us that "opposites attract." However, it also tells us that "birds of a feather flock together." If both of these axioms are common sense and are based on our life experience, how can we make sense of which idea is the better explanation of compatibility? Much

A research methods icon flags whether a study presented in the text involved a survey, experiment, interview, or participant observation, helping students to readily see how core quantitative and qualitative methods are used by sociologists.

 **RESEARCH METHOD**
SURVEY

 **RESEARCH METHOD**
EXPERIMENT

 **RESEARCH METHOD**
INTERVIEW

 **RESEARCH METHOD**
PARTICIPANT
OBSERVATION

A vibrant four-colour design—featuring an array of photos, maps, tables, and graphs—reflects the vitality of the field and helps students visualize data trends and essential issues and concepts.

PART
II Social Inequality

Photo credit: artur maia de carvalho/Shutterstock

4   Social Inequality
and Social Class

Chapter Outline

Introduction
Karl Marx and Social Class
    Class Struggles
    Reading: "Manifesto of the Communist Party," by
        Karl Marx and Friedrich Engels
Class Consciousness
Max Weber and Social Status
    Activity: Social Status Markers
Income Inequality in Canada

Reading: Nickel-and-Dimed: On (Not) Getting by in
    America, by Barbara Ehrenreich
Poverty
    Activity: Creating Low-Income Cut-Offs (LICOs)
Summary
Key Terms
For Further Reading
References

Photo credit: Khoroshvili Ilya/Shutterstock

3 Deviance, Law, and Crime   83

than the rate for non-Aboriginal adults in Canada. This number has continued to grow in the last decade, increasing by 6 per cent in this period (Correctional Services Canada, 2017).

Conflict theorists argue that the higher crime rates in these populations could be the result of low socio-economic status (SES) and lack of education, as well as high rates of victimization, substance abuse, and gang participation in Aboriginal and African-Canadian communities (Latimer and Foss 2004). In this way, the real predictor of engagement in

Calculating Crime Rates

The Government of Canada and the criminal justice system calculate the crime rate to give us a sense of the amount of types of crimes that occur in Canada. However, official statistics do not necessarily report actual rates of crime because not every criminal activity is reported and some activities reported to police are not crimes. Instead, these statistics are collected by using particular methods with particular limitations, constraints, and complications. Go to this book's companion website to access Samuel Perreault's "Police-Reported Crime Statistics in Canada, 2012." Read the article, and then answer the following questions:

1. How is the crime rate calculated? What is good about this traditional crime rate and what is missed?
2. How is the CSI better or worse than the traditional crime rate that Canada has used? (See Statistics Canada's "Section: 1 The Crime Severity Index," available at this book's companion website.)
3. Beyond the traditional crime rate and CSI, what other methods could be used to construct as comprehensive a crime rate as possible?
4. What are the benefits of using **victimization surveys** instead of a traditional crime rate? Why do victimization surveys usually show evidence of higher crime rates than do official statistics?

ACTIVITY

Helpful pedagogical features, including chapter outlines, lists of key terms, and further readings, enhance student comprehension and offer avenues for learning beyond the classroom.

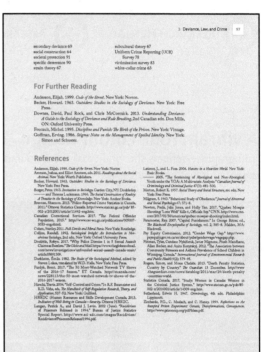

Ancillary Resource Center

Resources for Instructors and Students

Imagining Sociology is supported by an outstanding array of additional materials for both instructors and students, all available on the book's Ancillary Resource Centre, at **www.oup.com/he/CorrigallBrown2e**.

- Access to this collection is free for instructors who have assigned this book for their course. For access, speak to your OUP sales representative, or visit www.oupcanada.com/SocVideos.

For Instructors

- **An instructor's manual** includes learning objectives, chapter overviews, lists of key concepts, sample answers to critical reading questions and activities, discussion topics, and classroom activities.
- **A test generator** allows instructors to sort, edit, import, and distribute hundreds of questions in multiple-choice, short-answer, and true/false format.
- **PowerPoint slides** summarize key points from every chapter and incorporate figures and tables from the text.
- **OUP's sociology streaming video collection** provides easy and immediate access to a variety of videos, both feature-length and curated clips, with an accompanying video guide that includes learning objectives, suggested clips, discussion questions, and assignment suggestions for each video.

- **OUP Canada's sociology streaming video library** Over 20 award-winning feature films and documentaries of various lengths (feature-length, short films, and clips) are available online as streaming video for instructors to either show in the classroom or assign to students to watch at home. An accompanying video guide contains summaries, suggested clips, discussion questions, and related activities so that instructors can easily integrate videos into their course lectures, assignments, and class discussions.

Additional Materials for Students

- **A comprehensive online study-guide** provides chapter summaries, self-assessment quizzes, annotated lists of readings and web resources, as well as other material designed to enhance student learning.
- **A list of relevant web links for in-chapter activities** allows students to easily access online activity components.

Preface

I remember signing up for my first sociology course. I needed one more course to complete my schedule in my first year of university, and a friend suggested that I take sociology. Even though I had never heard of sociology and did not know what it would entail, I took the course. I was forever changed.

That course fundamentally altered the way I think about the world around me. Sociology provided me with a lens to understand our complex society. I learned that while we all have a lifetime of experiences within society, the importance of that society is often hard to understand because we are so immersed in it. Sociology helped me to understand how society as a whole shaped my life and the world around me.

By teaching sociology for many years, I have had the pleasure of helping students to discover their sociological imagination, the key lens we use to understand the connection between individuals and society. It is a delight to see them start to use the theories, ideas, and research in our discipline to help make sense of the world around them. We can use these ideas to answer pressing questions such as "Why is there poverty?" "Why do men and women earn different amounts of money?" "How do race and ethnicity shape our lives?" "How does social change happen?"

This book aims to bring sociology to life. Original readings by the founders of the discipline and today's top sociologists illuminate the concepts and theories in the text. These readings highlight the discipline's roots as well as its current foci and findings. Critical thinking questions, which follow every reading, facilitate further thought and will help you to apply the reading's main concepts. The book also includes highlight boxes, which explore various theories and issues and provide deeper insight into the concepts discussed in each chapter. Key terms are defined in a glossary.

Each chapter also contains activities that will help you to connect the theories and ideas of sociology to your life. For example, what can you learn about socialization by looking at the toys you played with as a child? How can comparing your grandparents' education with your own help you to understand the larger social changes in educational attainment in Canada? What do the curricula of your high-school classes tell you about the values of society and how they are changing? How are protest events depicted in the media, and how does this portrayal shape how you think about protesters?

As the systematic study of human society, sociology covers a lot of ground. This book is divided into four sections. Part I introduces the sociological imagination, the process of socialization, and how we learn to fit into society and develop a sense of identity. Part II focuses on social inequality, a core area of sociology. This section examines social class, social status, race, ethnicity, gender, and sexuality. We also discuss global inequality between countries. Understanding how inequalities between people and countries arise, perpetuate, and can be reduced is fundamental to sociology and is a primary theme of this book. Part III assesses several core institutions of society, including the media, family, education, work, and health. Sociology as a discipline encourages us to understand how individual choices can be structured or limited by larger social forces. Institutions are one such force that can shape the kind of lives we lead and larger patterns of social inequality.

We end the book by examining social change. It is clear that there is much inequality in society and a myriad of social problems in Canada and around the world. In Part IV, we learn about the role of the state, social movements, and other avenues for creating social change. It is certainly possible to make a more equal and just world. In fact, social change is a constant phenomenon that has helped us to address many social problems. The diversity of people in your sociology class is a testament to how society can change and become more equal. However, much more can be done! Learning about social change will conclude this book and, I hope, ignite your sociological imagination.

Acknowledgements

My sociological imagination has been shaped by the many wonderful professors who taught me at the University of Victoria, Western University, and the University of California, Irvine. My colleagues at the University of British Columbia have helped me to build on this foundation and deepened my interest and enjoyment of sociology. They have all shaped my understanding of and fascination with the discipline, which I hope to pass on to sociology students.

I am indebted to the wonderful people at Oxford University Press who have helped this project come to fruition. Liz Ferguson, Rhiannon Wong, Dorothy Turnbull, Ian Nussbaum, and Lisa Ball have deftly guided this project through its many stages, and their hard work is much appreciated. This book has also been strengthened by the wonderful work of four students who helped me to make it as accessible and animated as possible. I thank Mabel Ho, Kevin Hennessy, Joseph Jamil, and Paige Lougheed for their invaluable assistance.

Most important, I thank my wonderful husband, Steve Weldon, for his endless support of this project and all my work. I also gratefully acknowledge my parents, Melodie and Hans, for their encouragement and my sister, Sarah, for her inspiration.

This book is dedicated to my son, Leo. He was born into a challenging world but one filled with possibilities. May it become more equal and just as he grows.

For Leo

PART I

Understanding Society

Photo credit: Ryoji Iwata/Unsplash

1

The Sociological Imagination

Chapter Outline

Photo credit: Erik Eastman/Unsplash

Introduction

The word *sociology* was coined by Auguste Comte, who believed that this new discipline had the potential to bring together all the sciences and to improve society. Comte was, in part, inspired to create this new area of study because he lived in a period of rapid social change (1798–1857). Industry was replacing agricultural ways of life, democracies were emerging from dictatorships, and populations were migrating from the countryside to the cities. Wanting to make sense of this immense social change, Comte sought to understand how society worked and the effect of these larger processes on society and the people living in it.

Before and after Comte, individuals from all disciplines have been interested in explaining how society operates and why it sometimes does not work as well as we think it could. For example, philosophers as far back as Socrates and Plato wondered what makes a good society. But sociology is different in that it studies society in a systematic way. In fact, what defines sociology as a discipline is that it focuses on the systematic study of human society. This definition begs the question, "What is society?"

Society is the largest-scale human group that shares a common geographic territory and common institutions. Societies are not necessarily the same as states. In fact, many states contain a number of different societies. For example, Canada is sometimes thought to contain two distinct societies, with Quebec reflecting a society different from that of the rest of Canada. This idea is reinforced by the existence of many distinct institutions in the province. For example, Quebec's legal system is based on the Napoleonic code, whereas the other provinces and territories use the British system of common law.

Society is based on and requires social interaction among its members. These interactions can occur in a variety of settings and on a number of different levels, such as in neighbourhoods, schools, or workplaces. Such connections are important because they create shared understandings and are the basis of continued cooperation between the members of a society. These interactions also work to socialize newcomers, either those who emigrated from other parts of the world or young people who are learning how to act within our society. Through this socialization, we teach others the written and unwritten rules and values of our society. We also use this interaction among members to monitor and regulate each other, making sure that we all follow the society's rules and expectations.

Interactions within society happen in patterned ways—for example, most people go to the same coffee shop every morning and have the same conversation with the barista. These routines, expectations, and behaviours are established over time so that ongoing cooperation between people is possible (Charon 2012). Imagine if you replied to the barista's question of "How are you?" with a long story about your new sociology course or your indecision about whether to go on another date with someone. He would probably be quite surprised at your unusual behaviour in this situation because the routine is that you simply say, "Fine, thank you." By responding in an unexpected way, you challenge the common expectations of how this social interaction should take place. The fact that most interactions in society are predictable establishes a common set of understandings of how our society works and how we are supposed to behave in it.

Interactions in society are also shaped by culture. **Culture** is a system of behaviour, beliefs, knowledge, practices, values, and materials. Cultures shape how we act and the physical elements of our society. Our culture affects a myriad of elements of our lives, from how we set up cities to how we dress. It is clear from this definition that culture is contested—we certainly don't all agree on how we should act or what we should believe. These distinctions can exist between the dominant culture and subcultures or countercultures.

The **dominant culture** is able to impose its values, beliefs, and behaviours on a given society because of its political and economic power. Think about the "human interest" stories discussed on "The View," "The Social," or "Good Morning America." They tend to be of interest to the people with a lot of money or power: how to decorate a home,

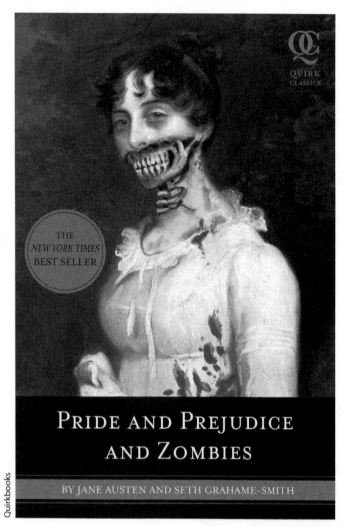

Quirkbooks

PHOTO 1.1 *Pride and Prejudice and Zombies* is an example of the merging of high and popular culture.

what to wear, or which stocks to buy or sell. These stories are based on the values of the dominant culture—that it is important to look attractive and fashionable, own an impressive home, and make a lot of money. There are many people who disagree with these foci in our culture. A **counterculture** is a group that rejects certain elements of the dominant culture. For example, anti-consumerist groups are countercultural. They reject our society's dominant focus on the importance of acquiring and consuming mass amounts of products in order to show our status and worth.

Subcultures also differ from the dominant culture, but they do not necessarily oppose it in the way that countercultures do. For example, minor differences in occupational groups can create subcultures. Lawyers' daily routines, values, and style of dress might differ significantly from those of plumbers. Students involved in fraternities or sororities, those on sports teams, or those in fine arts programs might also be quite different from each other in their behaviours and dress.

Culture is often divided into high and popular culture. When people say that someone is "cultured," they tend to mean that the person participates in **high culture**, the culture of a society's elite. In general, this type of culture may be difficult to appreciate unless one has been taught to enjoy and understand it. **Popular** (or **low**) **culture** is the culture of the majority. In the world of music, opera and classical music are high culture, while rap and pop are popular culture. In literature, classic novels and plays (think Austen or Shakespeare) are high culture; science fiction or romance novels are popular culture (*The Hunger Games*, *Twilight*, or John Green's novels).

Photo 1.1 shows the humorous intersection of high and popular culture. The novel *Pride and Prejudice and Zombies* is an obvious play on the high-culture works of Jane Austen and the popular culture interest in zombies. This cultural product juxtaposes the two types of culture to illustrate the disjuncture between them. Austen would certainly be surprised to see her heroines interacting with zombies!

The Sociological Imagination

In Canadian society, most people believe that individuals shape their own destiny. To a certain extent, this is true—we, as individuals, make decisions every day that shape the kind of life we lead. For example, you made decisions about whether to attend university or college, how hard to work in your classes, where to live when attending school, and what type of summer job you want. But, of course, many factors influence these decisions.

Let's examine your decision about a summer job. If your parents are willing and able to help pay for your education, you might not have to work in the summer, or you might choose to take an unpaid internship, which would be impossible if you needed to pay your own tuition. In this way, your individual choice of whether you work and what type of job you get is, to some degree, structured by the wealth and support of your parents. The reason we might be interested in how your individual choices are constrained is that it might shape later outcomes for you. For example, students who have completed an unpaid internship might find it easier to get a good job after graduation because they will have gained skills and social contacts while working. Students who have wealthy parents (and therefore don't need a summer job) are more likely than other students to have time to do an internship, which can perpetuate inequality in society over time.

This example illustrates how individual choices (sometimes called agency) are structured in society. We have the ability to make decisions, but our choices are often shaped or limited by larger social forces, such as our family, our social class, the economy, the education system, and gender norms. Many sociologists have tried to make sense of this complicated relationship between an individual's agency and society's constraints. Marx famously said that "[people] make their own history, but they do not make it as they please; they do not make it under self-selected circumstances, but under circumstances existing already, given and transmitted from the past" (in Tucker 1978, 595).

C. Wright Mills (1959/2000) also tried to tackle these complicated issues with what he called the **sociological imagination**. Mills called on us to try to see the connections between our individual lives and the larger society in which we live. He argued that we can only understand our own lives and biographies if we understand the larger history of our society. Once we make these connections, we will be able to see the relationship between our own **personal troubles** (problems that we face as individuals) and larger **public issues** (social problems that arise in society).

First published in 1959, Mills's *The Sociological Imagination* is one of the most widely read sociology books of all time. The sociological imagination is at the core of sociology. In fact, it is the inspiration for the title of this textbook. The following excerpt, from Chapter 1 of the book, discusses the links between the personal and the public.

PHOTO 1.2 C. Wright Mills, the author of *The Sociological Imagination*, is pictured here on his motorcycle. Using the sociological imagination, we can see how society as a whole can shape our individual experiences and how our own personal biographies are related to larger historical processes.

Estate of C. Wright Mills

From *The Sociological Imagination*

C. Wright Mills

Nowadays men often feel that their private lives are a series of traps. They sense that within their everyday worlds, they cannot overcome their troubles, and in this feeling, they are often quite correct: what ordinary men are directly aware of and what they try to do are bounded by the private orbits in which they live; their visions and their powers are limited to the close-up scenes of job, family, neighbourhood; in other milieux, they move vicariously and remain spectators. And the more aware they become, however vaguely, of ambitions and of threats which transcend their immediate locales, the more trapped they seem to feel.

Underlying this sense of being trapped are seemingly impersonal changes in the very structure of continent-wide societies. The facts of contemporary history are also facts about

Mills, C. Wright. 1959. *The Sociological Imagination*, 3–24. Oxford: Oxford University Press.

the success and the failure of individual men and women. When a society is industrialized, a peasant becomes a worker; a feudal lord is liquidated or becomes a businessman. When classes rise or fall, a man is employed or unemployed; when the rate of investment goes up or down, a man takes new heart or goes broke. When wars happen, an insurance salesman becomes a rocket launcher; a store clerk, a radar man; a wife lives alone; a child grows up without a father. Neither the life of an individual nor the history of a society can be understood without understanding both.

Yet men do not usually define the troubles they endure in terms of historical change and institutional contradiction. The well-being they enjoy, they do not usually impute to the big ups and downs of the societies in which they live. Seldom aware of the intricate connection between the patterns of their own lives and the course of world history, ordinary men do not usually know what this connection means for the kinds of men they are becoming and for the kinds of history-making in which they might take part. They do not possess the quality of mind essential to grasp the interplay of man and society, of biography and history, of self and world. They cannot cope with their personal troubles in such ways as to control the structural transformations that usually lie behind them.

Surely it is no wonder. In what period have so many men been so totally exposed at so fast a pace to such earthquakes of change? That Americans have not known such catastrophic changes as have the men and women of other societies is due to historical facts that are now quickly becoming "merely history." The history that now affects every man is world history. Within this scene and this period, in the course of a single generation, one-sixth of mankind is transformed from all that is feudal and backward into all that is modern, advanced, and fearful. Political colonies are freed; new and less visible forms of imperialism installed. Revolutions occur; men feel the intimate grip of new kinds of authority. Totalitarian societies rise, and are smashed to bits—or succeed fabulously. After two centuries of ascendancy, capitalism is shown up as only one way to make society into an industrial apparatus. After two centuries of hope, even formal democracy is restricted to a quite small portion of mankind. Everywhere in the underdeveloped world, ancient ways of life are broken up and vague expectations become urgent demands. Everywhere in the overdeveloped world, the means of authority and of violence become total in scope and bureaucratic in form. Humanity itself now lies before us, the super-nation at either pole concentrating its most coordinated and massive efforts upon the preparation of World War III.

The very shaping of history now outpaces the ability of men to orient themselves in accordance with cherished values. And which values? Even when they do not panic, men often sense that older ways of feeling and thinking have collapsed and that newer beginnings are ambiguous to the point of moral stasis. Is it any wonder that ordinary men feel they cannot cope with the larger worlds with which they are so suddenly confronted? That they cannot understand the meaning of their epoch for their own lives? That—in defence of selfhood—they become morally insensible, trying to remain altogether private men? Is it any wonder that they come to be possessed by a sense of the trap?

It is not only information that they need—in this Age of Fact, information often dominates their attention and overwhelms their capacities to assimilate it. It is not only the skills of reason that they need—although their struggles to acquire these often exhaust their limited moral energy.

What they need, and what they feel they need, is a quality of mind that will help them to use information and to develop reason in order to achieve lucid summations of what is going on in the world and of what may be happening within themselves. It is this quality, I am going to contend, that journalists and scholars, artists and publics, scientists and editors are coming to expect of what may be called the sociological imagination.

1

The sociological imagination enables its possessor to understand the larger historical scene in terms of its meaning for the inner life and the external career of a variety of individuals. It enables him to take into account how individuals, in the welter of their daily experience, often become falsely conscious of their social positions. Within that welter, the framework of modern society is sought, and within that framework the psychologies of a variety of men and women are formulated. By such means the personal uneasiness of individuals is focused upon explicit troubles and the indifference of publics is transformed into involvement with public issues.

The first fruit of this imagination—and the first lesson of the social science that embodies it—is the idea that the individual can understand his own experience and gauge his own fate only by locating himself within his period, that he can know his own chances in life only by becoming aware of those of all individuals in his circumstances. In many ways it is a terrible lesson; in many ways a magnificent one. We do not know the limits of man's capacities for supreme effort or willing degradation, for agony or glee, for pleasurable brutality or the sweetness of reason. But in our time we have come to know that the limits of "human nature" are frighteningly broad. We have come to know that every individual lives, from one generation to the next, in some society; that he lives out a biography, and that he lives it out within some historical sequence. By the fact of his living he contributes, however minutely, to the shaping of this society and to the course of its history, even as he is made by society and by its historical push and shove.

The sociological imagination enables us to grasp history and biography and the relations between the two within society. That is its task and its promise. To recognize this task and this promise is the mark of the classic social analyst. . . . And it is the signal of what is best in contemporary studies of man and society.

No social study that does not come back to the problems of biography, of history, and of their intersections within a society has completed its intellectual journey. Whatever the specific problems of the classic social analysts, however limited or however broad the features of social reality they have examined, those who have been imaginatively aware of the promise of their work have consistently asked three sorts of questions:

(1) What is the structure of this particular society as a whole? What are its essential components, and how are they related to one another? How does it differ from other varieties of social order? Within it, what is the meaning of any particular feature for its continuance and for its change?

(2) Where does this society stand in human history? What are the mechanics by which it is changing? What is its place within and its meaning for the development of humanity as a whole? How does any particular feature we are examining affect, and how is it affected by, the historical period in which it moves? And this period—what are its essential features? How does it differ from other periods? What are its characteristic ways of history-making?

(3) What varieties of men and women now prevail in this society and in this period? And what varieties are coming to prevail? In what ways are they selected and formed, liberated and repressed, made sensitive and blunted? What kinds of "human nature" are revealed in the conduct and character we observe in this society in this period? And what is the meaning for "human nature" of each and every feature of the society we are examining?

Whether the point of interest is a great power state or a minor literary mood, a family, a prison, a creed—these are the kinds of questions the best social analysts have asked. They are the intellectual pivots of classic studies of man in society—and they are the questions inevitably raised by any mind possessing the sociological imagination. For that imagination is the capacity to shift from one perspective to another—from the political to the psychological; from examination of a single family to comparative assessment of the national budgets of the world; from the theological school to the military establishment; from considerations of an oil industry to studies of contemporary poetry. It is the capacity to range from the most impersonal and remote transformations to the most intimate features of the human self—and to see the relations between the two. Back of its use there is always the urge to know the social and historical meaning of the individual in the society and in the period in which he has his quality and his being.

That, in brief, is why it is by means of the sociological imagination that men now hope to grasp what is going on in the world, and to understand what is happening in themselves as minute points of the intersections of biography and history within society. In large part, contemporary man's self-conscious view of himself as at least an outsider, if not a permanent stranger, rests upon an absorbed realization of social relativity and of the transformative power of history. The sociological imagination is the most fruitful form of this self-consciousness. By its use men whose mentalities have swept only a series of limited orbits often come to feel as if suddenly awakened in a house with which they had only supposed themselves to be familiar. Correctly or incorrectly, they often come to feel that they can now provide themselves with adequate summations, cohesive assessments, comprehensive orientations. Older decisions that once appeared sound now seem to them products of a mind unaccountably dense. Their capacity for astonishment is made lively again. They acquire a new way of thinking, they experience a transvaluation of values: in a word, by their reflection and by their sensibility, they realize the cultural meaning of the social sciences.

2

Perhaps the most fruitful distinction with which the sociological imagination works is between "the personal troubles of milieu" and "the public issues of social structure." This distinction is an essential tool of the sociological imagination and a feature of all classic work in social science.

Troubles occur within the character of the individual and within the range of his immediate relations with others; they have to do with his self and with those limited areas of social life of which he is directly and personally aware. Accordingly, the statement and the resolution of troubles properly lie within the individual as a biographical entity and within the scope of his immediate milieu—the social setting that is directly open to his personal experience and to some extent his willful activity. A trouble is a private matter: values cherished by an individual are felt by him to be threatened.

Issues have to do with matters that transcend these local environments of the individual and the range of his inner life. They have to do with the organization of many such milieux into the institutions of a historical society as a whole, with the ways in which various milieux overlap and interpenetrate to form the larger structure of social and historical life. An issue is a public matter: some value cherished by publics is felt to be threatened. Often there is a debate about what that value really is and about what it is that really threatens it. This debate is often without focus if only because it is the very nature of an issue, unlike even widespread trouble, that it cannot very well be defined in terms of the immediate and everyday environments of ordinary men. An issue, in fact, often involves a crisis in institutional arrangements, and often too it involves what Marxists call "contradictions" or "antagonisms."

In these terms, consider unemployment. When, in a city of 100,000, only one man is unemployed, that is his personal trouble, and for its relief we properly look to the character of the man, his skills, and his immediate opportunities. But when in a nation of 50 million employees, 15 million men are unemployed, that is an issue, and we may not hope to find its solution within the range of opportunities open to any one individual. The very structure of opportunities has collapsed. Both the correct statement of the problem and the range of possible solutions require us to consider the economic and political institutions of the society, and not merely the personal situation and character of a scatter of individuals.

Consider war. The personal problem of war, when it occurs, may be how to survive it or how to die in it with honour; how to make money out of it; how to climb into the higher safety of the military apparatus; or how to contribute to the war's termination. In short, according to one's values, to find a set of milieux and within it to survive the war or make one's death in it meaningful. But the structural issues of war have to do with its causes; . . . with its effects upon economic and political, family and religious institutions, with the unorganized irresponsibility of a world of nation-states.

Consider marriage. Inside a marriage a man and a woman may experience personal troubles, but when the divorce rate during the first four years of marriage is 250 out of every 1,000 attempts, this is an indication of a structural issue having to do with the institutions of marriage and the family and other institutions that bear upon them.

Or consider the metropolis—the horrible, beautiful, ugly, magnificent sprawl of the great city. For many upper-class people, the personal solution to "the problem of the city" is to have an apartment with private garage under it in the heart of the city, and 40 miles out, a house by Henry Hill, garden by Garrett Eckbo, on a hundred acres of private land. In these two controlled environments—with a small staff at each end and a private helicopter connection—most people could solve many of the problems of personal milieux caused by the facts of the city. But all this, however splendid, does not solve the public issues that the structural fact of the city poses. What should be done with this wonderful monstrosity? Break it all up into scattered units, combining residence and work? Refurbish it as it stands? Or, after evacuation, dynamite it and build new cities according to new plans in new places? What should those plans be? And who is to decide and to accomplish whatever choice is made? These are structural issues; to confront them and to solve them requires us to consider political and economic issues that affect innumerable milieux.

In so far as an economy is so arranged that slumps occur, the problem of unemployment becomes incapable of personal solution. In so far as war is inherent in the nation-state system and in the uneven industrialization of the world, the ordinary individual in his restricted milieu will be powerless—with or without psychiatric aid—to solve the troubles this system or lack of system imposes upon him. In so far as the family as an institution turns women into darling little slaves and men into their chief providers and unweaned dependents, the problem of a satisfactory marriage remains incapable of purely private solution. In so far as the overdeveloped megalopolis and the overdeveloped automobile are built-in features of the overdeveloped society, the issues of urban living will not be solved by personal ingenuity and private wealth.

What we experience in various and specific milieux, I have noted, is often caused by structural changes. Accordingly, to understand the changes of many personal milieux we are required to look beyond them. And the number and variety of such structural changes increase as the institutions within which we live become more embracing and more intricately connected with one another. To be aware of the idea of social structure and to use it with sensibility is to be capable of tracing such linkages among a great variety of milieux. To be able to do that is to possess the sociological imagination. . . .

CRITICAL READING QUESTIONS

1. What does Mills mean by "neither the life of an individual nor the history of a society can be understood without understanding both"? How could you understand your own life better by knowing more about history? How do individual biographies shape history? Think of a concrete example of this connection between individual biography and larger social history.

2. What do the terms *personal troubles* and *public issues* mean? How could we understand the issues of gender inequality, poverty, and crime as either a personal trouble or a public issue? How does labelling these problems a personal trouble or a public issue shape the kinds of solutions we would propose to solve them?

3. Mills questions the role of the physical and natural sciences in this chapter. He says that in some cases "they have raised more problems . . . than they have solved, and the problems that they have raised lie almost entirely in the area of social not physical affairs" (Mills 1959/2000, 15). How could the problem of climate change illustrate this point? What are the social ways by which we could prevent or ameliorate the effects of climate change?

ACTIVITY

The History and Biography of Higher Education in Canada

C. Wright Mills emphasized how individual biographies and the history of society are inextricably linked. With this idea in mind, let's examine higher education in Canada. By examining your own personal biography, we can see how you came to higher education. Mills, however, pushed us to understand our own personal biographies as they relate to the history of society as a whole. We can begin to see this connection between biography and history by comparing your personal story with the biographies of your parents and grandparents and with the Canadian population as a whole. Through these comparisons, we can gain insight into how access to higher education has changed and how larger historical changes in society might have affected you and your family. Throughout this activity, keep in mind Mills's distinction between the role of history and biography.

1. Begin by tracing the educational attainment of your family. What are your parents' and grandparents' highest levels of education, either in Canada or elsewhere? Compare the educational pathways of the males and females in your family. Do both sides of your family have similar types and amounts of education? Try to explain why the different people in your family (parents and grandparents, male and female, both sides of your family) attained the education that they did.

2. The following figures outline the percentage of males and females enrolled in American and Canadian universities in the 1960s (roughly when your grandparents might have gone to university) and in recent years (your generation's university attendance). The second figure shows the male and female rates of attendance over time. Looking at the overall statistics of university enrolment in Canada and the United States, how has the number and type of people attending university changed? What major trends do you observe in the charts? What types of larger historical changes in society have led to these changes in university enrolment? How have larger social processes created these changing patterns?

3. How does knowing the larger historical trends in Canadian society help you to better understand the biographies of your family members? How does knowing your own family's biography help you to better understand the historical trends you observe in the data on Canadian society?

Understanding the connection of your own biography to the history of society is a fundamental part of Mills's sociological imagination. As did many sociologists before and since him, Mills strived to see the connection

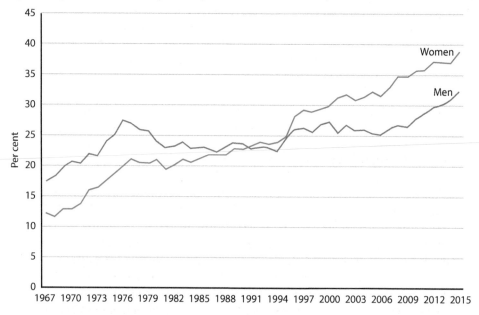

FIGURE 1.1   Percentage of the US population 25 years and older with a bachelor's degree or higher by sex, 1967–2015

Source: C.L. Ryan and K. Bauman, 2016, "Population Characteristics: Current Population Reports," *Educational Attainment in the United States: 2015,* United States Census. https://www.census.gov/content/dam/Census/library/publications/2016/demo/p20-578.pdf

between individual experiences and the structure of society as a whole. Throughout this book, keep these ideas in mind, and try to see how your own life and experiences are shaped by the society in which you live.

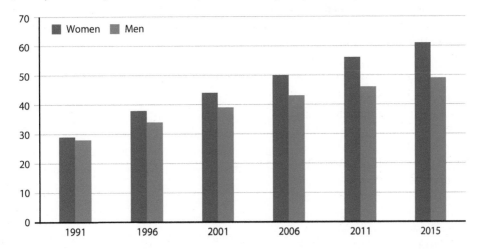

FIGURE 1.2   **Full-time undergraduate university enrolment, Canada, by sex, 2001–16**

Source: Statistics Canada, 2016, "Labour Force Survey, Annual Average, 1991, 1996, 2001, 2011, and 2015," Catalogue no. 89-503-X, Ottawa: Statistics Canada, https://www150.statcan.gc.ca/n1/pub/89-503-x/2015001/article/14640/c-g/c-g01ab-eng.htm

Three Core Foci of Sociology

As we learned earlier, sociology is the systematic study of human society. Sociologists can study a wide variety of things; in fact, almost anything in human society can be examined with a sociological perspective. However, most of sociology focuses on three core areas: the study of social inequality, the role of social institutions, and the study of social change.

Social Inequality

The study of **social inequality** is at the core of sociology. Generally, inequality is the gap between the advantaged and disadvantaged in society. More precisely, inequality is based on the "differences between people . . . that are *consequential* for the lives they lead, most particularly for the rights and opportunities they exercise and the rewards or privileges they enjoy" (Grabb 2006, 2; emphasis in original).

RESEARCH METHOD
INTERVIEW

People differ from one another in an almost infinite number of ways. For example, humans have different eye colours, are different heights, and write with either their right or left hand (or both). While these are all differences among people, they are not particularly consequential in a person's life. Differences that are more important, and that have been the basis of most sociological inquiry, include social class, gender, race, and ethnicity. These topics have been of interest to sociologists since the beginning of the discipline. More recently, sociologists—and society in general—are starting to see the importance of other differences, such as sexual orientation, age, immigration status, disability, and ability. All these differences can be very important for the lives that individuals lead.

Characteristics such as our gender, race, or age can shape the rights, opportunities, rewards, or privileges that individuals enjoy. Examples include the right to vote and

HIGHLIGHT

When Social Patterns Are Broken—Harold Garfinkel and Breaching Experiments

Harold Garfinkel (1991) was interested in the unexamined ways by which we follow the rules of our society. He argued that people unknowingly create and recreate the rules of society every day. He thought that we could not really see or understand these rules until they are broken. Individuals are constantly interacting with one another, guided by a set of expectations regarding how they should act in a given situation. However, we are not always able to articulate, or even notice, these rules because they are taken for granted. To examine these accepted ways of producing social order in society, Garfinkel developed what he called **breaching experiments**. In a breaching experiment, the researcher breaks a social rule to reveal the unrecognized way by which all individuals cooperate to maintain the smooth functioning of social interactions and social order. Garfinkel—or, more often, his graduate students—would break a social rule and then see how people reacted. By creating disorder, he hoped to demonstrate how social order is usually maintained.

In one experiment, Garfinkel instructed his students to act as guests in their parents' homes during their holiday visit. The students were to be excessively polite, ask permission to use the restroom, and pretend not to know the people in the household.

By behaving like strangers, the students undermined the expectations of how children should act toward their parents. Students reported that parents were upset and confused by the behaviour—some were even quite angry at being treated so formally.

Garfinkel also did many experiments in grocery stores. He had students take items from other people's carts. Shoppers initially assumed that a mistake had been made. Perhaps the students thought the cart was their own? However, the students would tell the other shopper that they simply found it easier to take items from another cart instead of walking the aisles. This behaviour is not explicitly forbidden—grocery stores have no signs saying not to take things from someone else's cart, and the items have not yet been purchased. However, the shoppers often were angry at having their carts raided.

Although many people find encounters with rule-breakers frustrating, it is a long-standing part of comedy. The movie *Borat* is essentially one long breaching experiment. The titular character, a native of Kazakhstan, travels across the United States, breaking social norms. In one scene, he walks the streets of New York City and starts talking to strangers. Some of them get so unnerved that they literally run away from him. Television shows such as *The Big Bang Theory* and *Just for Laughs: Gags* are also based on the humour in seeing other people break social rules. When Sheldon from *The Big Bang Theory* does something unusual, such as not allowing anyone to sit in his seat on the couch, we find it humorous because social rules dictate

the opportunity to attend university or college. Women were not afforded the right to vote in federal elections in Canada until 1921, and First Nations people did not get the right to vote in Canada until 1960. Therefore, being female or being First Nations had important consequences for the political rights that these individuals received. Rewards and privileges include access to good jobs and safe housing. We know, for example, that Canadians who are of a lower social class are much less likely than those in a higher class to live in a safe neighbourhood with good amenities (e.g., parks and schools nearby).

Inequality between people exists in all societies. When sociologists look at inequality, they are interested in a number of key questions. Why does inequality exist? How is inequality generated, maintained, and reproduced? What are the implications of inequality? How can inequality be reduced? These and other important questions form the basis of the sociological study of inequality.

While the existence of inequality is universal, the type and amount differ across societies and over time. Different societies exhibit varying levels of inequality, with some societies much more unequal than others. For example, the traditional caste system that existed in India, which made it almost impossible for people to move out of the social status of their birth, was much more unequal than modern Indian or Canadian society. Inequality also increases and decreases within a single society. For example, India's rigid caste system has been challenged over time. The Indian government passed legislation to fight the discrimination experienced by the lowest

AF archive/Alamy Stock Photo

Socially "awkward" behaviours can inspire sociologists to ask what we consider "normal" or "acceptable" behaviours. What are some of the unspoken social rules that you must follow in your life as a student to appear normal?

that we allow guests to sit wherever they please. It is only by breaking the social rule, or seeing others do so, that we can see what the social rule is and why following it makes society run smoothly.

What kinds of experiments could you conduct that would breach the social order? How could you act differently in your day-to-day life to show the unexamined rules that we usually follow in society?

caste group, the untouchables. There has also been a rise in marriage between castes, which was historically unthinkable but has reduced prejudice and inequality between groups. In fact, in India there is very high representation of people from traditionally lower castes in government, showing how inequality can change over time. Finally, inequality is based on different factors across societies—some societies have a lot of racial inequality but little class differentiation, while others have little racial inequality but strict class hierarchies.

Many people wonder if our society is becoming more or less equal. This question is extremely difficult to answer because it depends on the kind of inequality being examined and on the measures used. For simplicity's sake, we will examine income and assess whether inequality based on this factor is increasing or decreasing across social class, race, and gender groups.

There is a great deal of evidence that class inequality is increasing in Canada. We can see this trend if we compare the richest 20 per cent of families with the poorest 20 per cent (each called a quintile). In a totally equal society, each group would earn 20 per cent of the society's entire income. We know that this is certainly not the case because some people are much richer than others in this country. This inequality increased from the 1970s to the 1990s and has remained relatively high ever since. In 1999, the top 20 per cent of Canadians earned almost 12 times as much as the bottom 20 per cent. Thirteen years later, in 2012, the top 20 per cent were making almost 13.5 times the income of the bottom 20 per cent (Uppal and LaRochelle-Cote 2012).

The growing divide between Canada's rich and poor does not tell the whole story of inequality in this country. Other types of inequality are declining. For example, if we compare the earnings of individuals based on their ethnicity or race, there is less inequality now than there was in the past. Let's compare visible minorities with non-visible minorities. **Visible minorities** are defined by the Government of Canada as "persons, other than Aboriginal peoples, who are non-Caucasian in race or non-white in colour" (Government of Canada 1995, 2). The use of the word *visible* is significant because Canada has important historical political divisions based on language (English vs French) and religion (Catholics vs Protestants), which are "invisible" traits. Some people suggest that we move away from the term "visible minority" and encourage the use of other terms, such as racialized people.

In 2011, visible minorities born in Canada made 26.6 per cent less income than did Canadians who are not visible minorities (Statistics Canada 2011). While the situation is certainly not equal, it is better than it was in 1990 when the figure was 29.9 per cent. In other words, the inequality between the incomes of Canadian-born visible minorities and non-minorities is declining. Although the imbalance is improving, we clearly have a long way to go before such inequality is eradicated.

Income inequality based on gender has both increased and decreased. In 1991, Canadian women working full-time made 68.7 per cent of what their male counterparts did. This number increased to 72.3 per cent in 1996 but then dropped to 68.8 per cent in 2015 (Samuel and Basavarajappa 2006; Statistics Canada 2015). This example shows the challenges of reducing inequality. The task would be even more difficult if we looked beyond simple income to experiences of discrimination and prejudice or educational and work opportunities. It is no surprise, then, that so many sociologists are concerned with such an important and elusive topic.

In addition to measuring and assessing social inequality, sociologists often study why and how inequality persists. We know that all societies have inequality. But why is this the case? How does inequality endure? How can it be reduced? This book examines all these questions. In particular, we will learn more about inequality that arises from social class, race, ethnicity, and gender.

Social Institutions

Social institutions are the norms, values, and rules of conduct that structure human interactions. Institutions are not just physical places or buildings but also the social arrangements for how things are done. For example, the institution of education is not just a school or classroom; it is a set of larger arrangements that organize how people will receive education and what they will learn. There are five core institutions in modern Canadian society: the family, education, religion, the economy, and government. Other institutions, such as the mass media, medicine, science, and the military are also important parts of Canadian society.

Institutions are standardized ways of doing something. In institutions, actions become regularized, patterned, and reproduced. When you consider education, you might think of your specific teachers, your class experience, or the schools you attended. Such details are certainly important aspects of your education. However, the institution of education is far more than these parts. It is based on the routine and patterned ways that education is delivered and assessed. For example, the material that you learned in elementary and secondary school was not simply the choice of your teachers. The institution of education sets a curriculum and decides, for example, that all students in Grade 9 will read Shakespeare's *Romeo and Juliet*. Our education system is also based on teaching students from roughly 8:30 to 3:00 five days a week for 10 months of the year. All these routines are established by the institution of education in Canada and structure how education functions across the country.

Institutions are important because they generally help society to run smoothly. They do so in part by socializing us and thereby teaching us the rules of our society. When you first go to school, you learn that you must sit quietly in class and raise your hand when you want to speak. These rules are important and help later schooling and other social interactions to function. Imagine if everyone just wandered around the room during your university classes—the result would certainly be a chaotic environment.

However, institutions can also serve a negative function by maintaining and reinforcing inequality. In fact, one of the main reasons that inequality tends to persist is the role of social institutions. Because standardized methods become routine, they can reinforce some of the differences between people. For example, if your university or college has very high tuition, students of lower social classes might not be able to attend the school. In this way, the institution is partly responsible for people from lower social classes being less likely to get the degrees that would allow them to increase their social standing.

Institutions can also be an avenue for social change. We know that individuals from lower social classes are much less likely to get a university or college degree than those from higher social classes. Many social programs instituted by the Government of Canada have tried to address this imbalance. The Veterans Rehabilitation Act (VRA), passed in 1944, included a program that helped World War II veterans receive a post-secondary education by paying their full tuition and living expenses for up to four years. The idea was that helping soldiers to get an education would help them to return to civilian life. More than 120,000 veterans—mostly men—received this support. Research estimates that as a result of the program, men of the postwar period had an average of 0.2 to 0.4 more years of education and had higher wages over the course of their lives than they otherwise would have had (Lemieux and Card 1998).

Adam Scott/Prime Minister's Office

PHOTO 1.3 Prime Minister Justin Trudeau meets with the File Hills Qu'Apelle Tribal Council. This meeting between a governing body (the Tribal Council) and the head of another governing body (the prime minister of Canada) highlights the complexity and multifaceted nature of institutions such as governments.

emka74/istockphoto

PHOTO 1.4 The Coexist image shows a more inclusive way of thinking about religion in the modern age, highlighting how people from different religions, and those who are not religious, can share values and live together peacefully. Clearly, this message is important, but is it convincing and effective?

Social Change

Social change is the third core area of sociology. Sociologists examine how, as we have just seen, social institutions can perpetuate inequality or create social change. If society is based on interactions among people, it can change just as people do.

One major institution in modern Canadian society that has changed greatly is religion. **Secularization**—the process of a religion losing its authority over individuals and social life in general—is a frequently discussed social change. Core founders of sociology, such as Karl Marx, Max Weber, and Émile Durkheim, all argued that the modernization of society would inevitably coincide with a decline in religiosity. Karl Marx was quite happy about this shift because he thought that religion was an "opiate" of the masses, something that just dulled our pain and senses so that we would not resist the great social inequality that we experienced in our lives. Durkheim was more likely to lament this decline; he thought religion was an important part of the glue that holds individuals together in society. Weber looked at how new rational systems, such as science and bureaucracies, would make religious answers to our questions less relevant (Collins 1994). These perspectives illustrate how sociologists have always been interested in religion's role in society. (We will learn much more about these three sociologists in the following chapters.)

The study of secularization seeks to explain how and why religious values, practices, and institutions are losing their power in modern society. It is certainly true that religion is currently less integral to many functions of Canadian society than it was in the past. For example, traditionally, many schools were run by religious institutions. You can still attend a religious school, but most schools in Canada are now operated by the state and are non-religious. Religious institutions were also once the main provider of charitable and welfare services, running orphanages, soup kitchens, and hospitals. Now the government primarily performs such functions. Many religious institutions are still involved in these activities and raise money for these causes; however, the control of these services rests mostly in the hands of the state.

HIGHLIGHT

How Would Different Disciplines Study Your Classroom?

One way to think about how sociology is distinct as a discipline is to compare it with other academic areas of study. For example, how would a sociologist study your classroom? How might an engineer, biologist, or historian study it differently?

An engineer might be interested in the classroom's acoustics and whether those sitting in the back can hear the professor. She might also study the airflow, the materials used for the furniture or fixtures, and the insulation. A biologist would be much less interested in these issues and would probably focus on the students' genetic diversity, the other organic material in the room (not bugs or rodents, we hope!), and the spread of bacteria from person to person.

A historian would be more similar to a sociologist than either the engineer or biologist, but he would still study very different elements of the classroom. He might be interested in the growth of universities over the past 100 years, the history of a school, and perhaps larger histories of migration that brought the students in this classroom to this particular school.

While sociologists share some of these interests (for example, they are also interested in migration patterns), they would be much more likely to emphasize the three core foci of sociology. Sociologists might ask, "Who is in this classroom and who is not?" They would examine how different genders, different ethnicities and religions, and different social classes are represented in the classroom and try to understand the social processes that make some people more likely to attend university than others. They would also be interested in how the institution of education shapes young people: Who decides what is covered in a university education? What material is not covered? How does going to university socialize us? Finally, when examining social change, a sociologist might ask how the university has changed. Do different types of people attend? Are different things taught? How does the relationship between the university and other institutions in society differ over time? While all the disciplines have important and interesting questions to ask about this classroom, each has a particular and distinct perspective on how they make sense of the social world.

Who is in this classroom and who is not? To what extent does this photo depict the ethnic, class, and gender makeup of your class?

Canadians are also becoming less religious. In 1967, 50 per cent of Canadians reported attending religious services weekly. This number had decreased to less than 10 per cent by 2015 (General Social Survey 2015). This decline is fairly typical of the general secularization occurring across North America and Europe. However, some sociologists have questioned whether it is a universal trend or just a tendency in a certain set of countries that also share other characteristics, such as level of development.

In fact, **religiosity** (a measure of how religious a person is) is increasing in many parts of the world. Scott M. Thomas, a British scholar who looks at trends in religiosity, finds that religion is actually quite healthy around the world (Bibby 2011). Between 1950 and 2013, the number of Catholics in the world doubled from fewer than 500 million to more than 1.2 billion (BBC News 2013). There is also a dramatic increase in the spread of evangelical Protestantism, which now has 700 million adherents worldwide (Bibby 2011).

The discussion of religion's changing role illustrates a number of key elements in the study of sociology. Religion is an important institution in society whose set of organized beliefs establishes how we, as a society, will attempt to meet our basic social needs. It provides norms, values, and rules of conduct for individuals and helps to structure human interactions. Religion's changing role shows the larger social transformations that are at the heart of the study of sociology. Finally, the changing nature of religion depends on the social context in which it is examined.

Three Core Aims of Sociology

When looking at sociology's core areas, sociologists aim to do three main things. They try to see general themes in everyday life. They seek to assess critically what seems familiar and common sense. And they examine how individuals both shape society and are shaped by society.

Everyone has a lifetime of experiences in society. From all these experiences, we come to generalize about how society functions and how people behave in it. However, sometimes this familiarity can be a challenge—it can be difficult to study society because it is all around us. It is like a fish trying to study water. However, sociology, as the systematic study of human society, pushes us to make sense of all our experiences and what we see around us and to come up with general ideas about how society functions.

In *Invitation to Sociology*, Peter Berger (1963) calls on us to see "the general in the particular." Put another way, sociologists should look for general patterns in particular people's behaviour. We may know some women who are very successful in large companies and have a great deal of responsibility in their jobs, but we see that most CEOs and members of Parliament are men. This information suggests that there is a general pattern of women being less likely than men to hold positions of power. We can now ask ourselves why this might be the case: Is it that fewer women choose to enter business or politics, or is there discrimination in these professions? Through systematic study, we can answer these types of questions.

The final goal of sociology is to see the dual process of how we shape society and how society shapes us. People create institutions in society in many ways, such as by passing laws and electing leaders who decide how some of these institutions will run. The institutions then influence individuals and the society in which they live. Émile Durkheim's famous study of suicide illustrates this relationship.

Émile Durkheim and the Study of Suicide

Although Comte coined the term *sociology*, no universities offered courses or did research in sociology during his lifetime. Émile Durkheim, who was born in France in 1858, was one of the original proponents of creating a field of sociology that would have a significant presence at universities. He argued that sociology was different from philosophy, a popular discipline at the time, because it would focus on empirical research. He claimed that sociology was distinct from psychology, another well-established discipline of the period, because it prioritized the social over the individual. To help establish this new discipline, Durkheim created *L'Année sociologique*, an annual review of French sociology that became the country's most influential publication of its kind. He also wrote a number of significant books using the sociological perspective and method he was advocating, including *The Division of Labour in Society* (1893), *The Rules of the Sociological Method* (1895), *On the Normalcy of Crime* (1895), *Suicide* (1897), and *The Elementary Forms of Religious Life* (1912).

For Durkheim, sociology was a unique discipline because it was to be based on the study of **social facts**, the external social structures, norms, and values that shape individuals' actions. As Durkheim (1897/1951, 37–8) explained, the "sociological methods as we practice it rests wholly on the basic principle that social facts must be studied as things, that is, as realities external to the individual." He believed that society is something more than just a group of individuals and that the individual in society is "dominated by a moral reality greater than himself" (38).

To illustrate his concept of social facts and the way the sociological method could work, Durkheim conducted a study of suicide. The topic was chosen quite deliberately. At first glance, suicide seems like an obviously individual act; a person's choice to take his own life is often explained in terms of the person's own psychology. For example, we often think that people commit suicide because they are depressed or unhappy. While Durkheim acknowledged that psychology might matter, he argued that psychology alone cannot explain suicide. "Admittedly," he wrote, "under similar circumstances, the degenerate is more apt to commit suicide than the well man; but he does not necessarily do so because of his condition" (Durkheim 1897/1951, 81). He asked the following question: If suicide is strictly an individual psychological decision, why are suicide rates different for men and women, for Protestants and Catholics, and across countries? These differences can be explained only by social facts, elements of society that are beyond the individual.

Durkheim began his study not by looking at an individual's decision to commit suicide but by comparing the rates of suicide across groups of people. This systematic study of suicide led him to argue that there are four **types of suicide**, which differ based on the level of integration or regulation in a society as a whole. Societies differ in individuals' integration into the society. In societies with extremely low levels of integration, individuals commit egoistic suicide, whereas in societies with extremely high levels of

HIGHLIGHT

Getting to Know Émile Durkheim

- Durkheim was part of the Army of Justice, a group of intellectuals who fought what they considered the unfair execution of a French captain accused of treason.
- Durkheim's early death was attributed to his "loss of spirit and well-being" after his son's death in World War I.
- Durkheim wrote three of sociology's most influential works (*Suicide, The Rules of Sociological Method,* and *The Division of Labor in Society*) within a five-year period.
- Durkheim did not make it into the École normale supérieure until his third attempt.

integration, they commit altruistic suicide. Societies also differ in their level of regulation, the degree of external constraint on individuals. When regulation is excessively low, individuals commit anomic suicide; when it is excessively high, they commit fatalistic suicide. In essence, Durkheim argued that the conditions of society as a whole are so powerful that they influence even this most personal decision for individuals.

Durkheim believed that the best part of individuals—their morals, values, and sense of purpose—comes from society. When individuals do not feel integrated into society, this can lead to egoistic suicide. Being a part of society can give their lives meaning, and participating in religion is one way that many people derive such meaning. Despite this important potential function, not all religions are equally effective at integrating individuals. For example, Durkheim found that Protestants were much more likely than Catholics to commit suicide, despite the fact that the two religions prohibit and condemn suicide with equal fervour. He argued that this difference was partly because the Protestant Church is less effective than the Catholic Church at integrating its members. Protestantism focuses on individual faith, and adherents are encouraged to read and interpret the Bible on their own. Catholicism, however, places more emphasis on participating in church activities that are run by a clearly defined hierarchy of leaders. This feature encourages Catholics to interact with one another and to rely on the church to interpret religious teachings for them, both of which increase the amount of social interaction between members and the integration they feel.

In order to support this argument, Durkheim compared countries that were mostly Protestant (Prussia, Denmark, and Saxony) with those that were mostly Catholic (Spain, Portugal, and Italy). He found that the average suicide rate in the Protestant countries was 190 per million persons, whereas it was only 58 per million persons in the Catholic countries (Durkheim 1897/1951, 152). The larger social context of Protestantism was associated with a suicide rate almost four times higher than the social context of Catholicism. However, some might argue that other differences between these countries might account for the different suicide rates. In order to test this claim, Durkheim compared the rates across regions of Switzerland, a nation with both Catholic and Protestant areas. Even within this one country, the suicide rate of Protestants was four to five times higher than that of Catholics (155). These data support Durkheim's argument that those who are less integrated are more likely to commit suicide and that some religions are more effective at integrating their adherents than others.

While a lack of integration in society can lead to suicide, Durkheim argued that excessively integrated societies can also have high suicide rates. Highly integrated societies can include cults in which adherents sometimes commit mass suicide. For example, a mass suicide of 39 Heaven's Gate members occurred in California in 1997. Terrorists who martyr themselves for a cause are also examples of how being excessively integrated into a society, so much so that a person thinks only about the group's needs, can be associated with suicide.

According to Durkheim, levels of regulation in society are also associated with suicide. In a society with very little regulation, individuals can come to feel anomic, a term Durkheim used to refer to a feeling of rootlessness or normlessness. When the rules and regulations of society are weak or unclear, individuals feel free to do anything they please. While this freedom sounds good, a lack of regulation can reduce an individual's feeling of meaning and connection to others. Durkheim argued that a lack of regulation can occur in either good times, such as economic booms, or bad times, such as economic depressions. Any temporary disruption in the social order makes the collectivity unable to exercise its authority over the individual. In these times, the old rules and standards for behaviour no longer apply, but new rules and standards have not yet been created. This situation can lead to anomic suicide.

The final type of suicide discussed by Durkheim, fatalistic suicide, occurs when there is excessive regulation in society. Durkheim named this type of suicide but did not spend much time discussing it in his work. He did say, however, that it occurs among "persons with futures pitilessly blocked and passions violently choked by oppressive discipline" (1857/1951, 276). For example, a slave might commit suicide because she feels she has no other option and her life is totally controlled by another.

The brilliance of Durkheim's study is in the way it shows how a phenomenon that is generally thought of as a psychological process, the decision to commit suicide, is shaped by the structure of the society in which a person lives. By examining the integration and regulation in a society, we can predict its suicide rate. Or, by comparing across groups of people, we can predict who will be more or less likely to commit suicide based on the propensity of their group to be integrated into or regulated by society. For example, Durkheim compared the suicide rates of men and women and found that men are more likely to commit suicide in part because they tend to be less integrated into society. In the same way, he found that unmarried individuals are more likely to commit suicide because they are less integrated into families.

Durkheim's work, while highly influential, has sparked criticism and debate. Some later researchers argue that there is a logical error in the research: Durkheim explained micro-level individual behaviour (the act of suicide) with macro-level country statistics (suicide rates). Despite this potential problem, the work illuminates the connection between individuals and the society in which they live, which is at the heart of sociology.

Suicide in Canada

Can we still use Durkheim's insights to understand suicide rates today? The first chart shows suicide rates in Canada by gender and family type. The second chart lists countries by their level of religiosity and suicide rates. Examine the data, and answer the following questions.

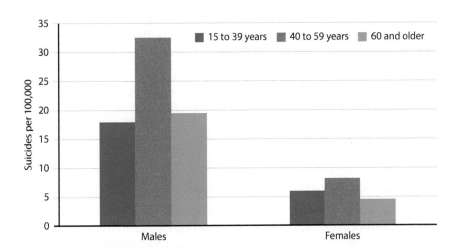

FIGURE 1.3   Suicide rates per 100,000, Canada, 2009

Source: Statistics Canada, 2012, *Canadian Vital Statistics Death Database*, CANSIM, table 051-0010, Ottawa: Statistics Canada, https://www.statcan.gc.ca/pub/82-624-x/2012001/article/chart/11696-02-chart4-eng.htm

ACTIVITY

Suicide rates and religiosity by country

Country	Religiosity	Suicide Rate
Philippines	79	3.4
India	76	15.7
Guatemala	75	2.5
Brazil	69	6.3
Ireland	63	11.7
United States	61	14.3
Chile	54	9.9
Canada	49	12.3
Israel	44	5.5
France	30	16.9
Japan	29	19.7
Russia	28	20.1

Sources: Adapted from Brett Pelham and Zsolt Nyiri, 2008, "In More Religious Countries, Lower Suicide Rates: Lower Suicide Rates Not a Matter of National Income," *Gallup* 3 July, http://www.gallup.com/poll/108625/more-religious-countries-lower-suiciderates .aspx; and World Health Organization, 2017, "Suicide Rates per (100,000 population)," *Global Health Observatory (GHO) Data*, http://www.who.int/gho/mental_health/suicide_rates_crude/e

1. How do gender and family type relate to suicide? How does Durkheim's theory about certain social conditions leading to suicide explain the suicide rates among Canadian men and women in different family situations?
2. How is religiosity related to suicide rates across countries? Would Durkheim be surprised that more religious countries tend to have lower levels of suicide? Why or why not? How would he explain this relationship?
3. In general, countries that are very religious have low levels of suicide, and countries that are not very religious have higher levels. But Israel has a relatively low rate of suicide given its low level of religiosity, and India has a relatively high rate of suicide given its high rate of religiosity. How can you explain these unusual cases? Can you use Durkheim's theory? Why or why not?

HIGHLIGHT

Is Sociology Just Common Sense?

Because we all live within society, it is sometimes hard to see how there could be much to learn in sociology. Can't we just use our own experiences to make sense of the social world? Isn't sociology really just common sense? Randall Collins (1992), a famous sociologist, notes that obvious social questions may not have obvious or simple answers. Sociology's greatest strength, he argues, is precisely its potential for penetrating the superficial observation of everyday life and finding the fundamental social processes hidden beneath.

For example, many people wonder what makes a romantic couple compatible. Common sense tells us that "opposites attract." However, it also tells us that "birds of a feather flock together." If both of these axioms are common sense and are based on our life experience, how can we make sense of which idea is the better explanation of compatibility? Much systematic research has been conducted in sociology to answer just this question, and this research comes to a clear consensus that while it may seem like opposites attract, most couples share similar characteristics. In fact, the **homophily** principle structures social relationships of every type, including marriage, friendship, and work relationships. Most people have personal networks that are very homogeneous, which is partly why most romantic partners are similar to one another. They are most likely to be similar in race and ethnicity, with age, religion, education, and occupation following, in roughly that order. In addition, couples are also most often similar in terms of their attitudes and values.

There are many reasons that most people romantically couple with and marry people who are similar to them. The most important reason is simple geography. Most people have more contact with those who are like them. For example, one of the main reasons that people tend to date and marry others of similar age is because of the age-based structure of schooling. The fact that schools group ages together into classrooms induces homophily. Because many people meet romantic partners and select mates while they are attending school and are most likely to meet and interact with others of their age group in these settings, it is not surprising that they are most likely to choose a partner in their age group.

Partners are also most likely to come from the same social class or status. This is, in part, because our social class often determines the neighbourhood where we grow up and live. People with more money and higher-status occupations tend to live in more expensive neighbourhoods where other upper-class people live. They are also more likely to attend elite private schools where they meet others of their social class. And they are more likely to work in fields such as the law, business, or medicine where other people of their class are located. These social networks bring people of the same class into contact with one another and provide opportunities to create friendships.

The finding that most relationships, be they romances, friendships, or acquaintances, tend to be between people who are similar can be very important for understanding how society works. If people tend to know others like themselves, they might be less likely to be open or tolerant of people who are different from them. It also might limit the amount and diversity of information people receive, since they are generally in contact just with people who have the same opinions and experiences. Considering what we think we know about society and examining it in a systematic way can help us to better understand the world around us. This is what sociology is all about.

gpointstudio/iStockphoto

According to the homophily principle, friends and romantic partners tend to have similar interests and to come from similar backgrounds. This group of friends at a music festival shares an interest in music and fashion and probably comes from similar ethnic and class backgrounds. What similarities and dissimilarities can you find between you and your friends?

Research Methods: How Do Sociologists Study Society?

Sociologists conduct research to understand how society operates in a systematic way. They use this information to answer questions about individual behaviour and the functioning of society as a whole.

When sociologists look at a social issue, one of the first things they do is posit a research question. **Research questions** focus on the relationship between two variables. **Variables** are any construct that can take on different values—that can vary. For example, age can be a variable because people are different ages. There are two main types of variables, independent variables and dependent variables. **Independent variables** are the ones that *affect* other variables. By nature they have to come before a dependent variable. **Dependent variables** are *affected by* independent variables. Research questions look at the relationship between independent and dependent variables, how the former affect the latter. For example, if we are asking, "what is the relationship between ethnicity and income?" ethnicity is the independent variable, and income is the dependent variable. We are testing to see whether your ethnicity affects how much money you make. We would not expect that the amount of money that you make would change your ethnicity. Once sociologists have a research question and know the variables upon which they will focus, they decide on the research method that is most appropriate for answering this question.

Sociology and the other social sciences include two major types of research: qualitative and quantitative (although many researchers use both types of methods). **Quantitative research** focuses on things that can be counted. This research examines how variables relate to one another and tests these relationships with statistical models. For example, a quantitative researcher interested in education might focus on the educational outcomes of different groups of people. They could record the age, sex, and ethnicity of each person who graduates from university and use statistical models to generalize about what types of people are more or less likely to get degrees. Quantitative research focuses on measuring social phenomena and using statistical models to assess the patterns of association among these variables. Because these types of techniques require a large number of cases to test for the relationships between variables effectively, quantitative research often must examine relationships at a more general level.

One of the major ways that quantitative research is conducted is with surveys. **Survey research** involves giving questionnaires to a large number of people to learn about their characteristics, attitudes, or behaviours. The census, collected by Statistics Canada for the Government of Canada, is an example of a survey. In the census, Statistics Canada asks Canadians about themselves, including their age, gender, and income. We can use this data to examine many types of questions. For example, we can study whether men make more money than women do, how this discrepancy might differ across professions, and whether it is increasing or decreasing over time. This information is quite important for understanding gender inequality and for choosing a career.

Experiments are another major quantitative method. In experiments, the researcher looks at the effect of some factor, sometimes called a treatment, on individual behaviour. This approach involves comparing two groups—the experimental group and the control group. The experimental group is given the treatment, while the control group is not. If we wanted to understand the effect of money as an incentive for learning, for example, we could bring two groups of students to a lab. We would have all the students learn a list of words. Half of the students would be paid money for each correct word they learned; the others would receive nothing. Presuming that the students in each group were the same in terms of important characteristics (such as their intelligence), if the students who were told they would be paid for correct answers did better on the task than those not given this incentive, we would conclude that paying students to achieve was a useful way to improve performance.

Qualitative research tends to examine a smaller number of cases in more detail and emphasizes social processes. Instead of focusing on counting phenomena, qualitative researchers often examine the meaning of action for individuals and groups. Sociologists use a variety of qualitative techniques. Two major qualitative methods in sociology are interviewing and participant observation. **Interviewing** is a qualitative method in which a researcher asks each participant the same set of questions and records his or her responses. Interviews allow the researcher to ask questions that require longer answers and to ask follow-up questions to get more detail. For example, interviews might be quite useful if you are interested in how going to university or college changes the way young people see themselves. To understand how various elements of university life, such as living in a dorm, taking classes, joining campus groups, and making friends, can shape an individual's identity, you might want to give individuals more time to explain these complicated changes and to ask follow-up questions to probe for more information.

Participant observation (or **ethnography**) is another core qualitative method. The researcher actively engages with a group of individuals and works to understand their lives and experiences through intensive involvement with them over an extended period of time. For example, if you wanted to understand how young people pick up others in a bar, you might go to the same bar every Saturday night and watch as young people introduce themselves to one another. By observing them, you could see what types of people are the most likely to approach others or be approached. You could also see how couples interact with one another in the context of the bar. While you could, of course, survey or interview people about their pick-up practices, you could certainly learn additional things by watching these interactions happen in person. In fact, as a researcher you might gain insights that the people had not considered (we might not be the best assessors of our own pick-up techniques).

Additional research techniques are also used by sociologists. For example, many sociologists use content analysis to study documents such as newspapers, historical letters, Tweets, or other texts. Some sociologists also use focus groups, which are interviews conducted with larger groups of people. The diversity of our discipline allows for a wide range of research methods, which are appropriate for answering different types of research questions.

These four core sociological methods are all good ways to understand the social world. No one method is the best method of research. All these techniques are simply tools. Just as it would be ridiculous to argue that a hammer is a better tool than a saw (it depends on whether you want to join things together or cut something in half), it does not make sense to argue which method is the best. Each method is more or less useful for understanding different types of phenomena, and it is always useful to have as many tools in our toolkit as possible.

Throughout this book, we will learn about studies using each of these core methods. A marginal icon ⚲ indicates the specific method. When you come across these studies in this class and others, think about how another method might be more or less able to answer the same questions and about what else we might learn through another method of research.

HIGHLIGHT

Doing Sociology: Making Use of the Sociological Toolkit

The four main sociological methods are useful for answering different types of research questions. If you are interested in studying crime, for example, surveys could help you to answer many questions. In Canada, the government conducts a survey of victimization every five years as part of the General Social Survey. In this survey, individuals are asked a whole series of questions about crime and being a victim of crime. Using this data, you could answer research questions such as "who is most likely to be a victim of crime?" or "who is most likely to report a crime to the police?" By comparing across ethnicities, older and younger people, and those who live in cities with those who live in rural areas, you could better understand who is most likely to experience crime and who is most likely to report that crime to the police when it happens.

Experiments could also help you to better understand crime, albeit answering different specific questions. An experiment would not be very effective at helping you to understand who is most likely to be a victim of a crime because the group of people who you would have come to your laboratory to engage in your experiment would probably not accurately reflect the experiences of the Canadian population as a whole. However, experiments could help you to answer different types of questions. For example, you could create an experiment to better understand how we perceive different perpetrators of crime. Your research subjects would be told to read a story of a crime, perhaps a theft of a pair of jeans from a store. They would all read the same story, except that half would be told that the thief was a woman and half would be told that the thief was a man. You could then ask each group how serious they thought the crime was. Through this type of experiment, you could better understand whether people see the severity of a crime differently depending on who they think committed it. Are we more likely to see a male perpetrator as a "real criminal" but a female perpetrator as a "casual shoplifter"? Would we think differently of a 15-year-old perpetrator as opposed to one who is 50?

Interviews could also be effective ways to understand crime. They are most appropriate for unpacking complex thought processes because the interviewer has longer to talk with the respondent and is able to get more in-depth answers. We could use interviews to answer a research question such as "how do people come to engage in criminal behaviour?" To answer this, we could go to a prison and interview inmates about how they first got involved in crime. By talking with them about how this happened, we could come to better understand how their family background, friends, neighbourhood, and other factors did (or did not) relate to their entry into criminal activity. While you could, of course, ask how inmates got involved in crime through a survey, respondents would then be forced to answer from a set of fixed categories (perhaps you would have a list of five or six reasons they could check off), and you would not be able to ask for more detail about this complicated process.

Finally, you could engage in participant observation of crime. If you were interested in how police enforce crime, for example, you could engage in participant observation and ride along with police officers to see how they interact with people who are suspected of committing crimes. Police have a lot of discretion to stop people or not. And when they stop someone they think has committed a crime, they can decide to give them a warning or a ticket or take them to the police station and charge them with a crime. How do police officers make these decisions? It would be possible to conduct a survey or interviews of police officers. However, some of these processes are unconscious and may be better observed in real time.

All of these methods, and other methods used by sociologists, can help us to understand the complex issues surrounding crime and criminality. Each is able to address slightly different research questions and provide different types of data. In order to really understand any social phenomenon, it is useful to have sociologists working with all of these different research techniques and sharing their findings.

We end this chapter by considering the pivotal concern of reconciliation among Indigenous and non-Indigenous people in Canada. Sociologists, and all Canadians, must actively consider how reconciliation can inform our understandings of the society in which we live and the possibilities for a more just and equal society in the future. The following reading, by Susan O'Donnell and David Perley, examines the idea of reconciliation, taking into account the sometimes conflicting desires that groups have in this process. Consider how taking these issues into account challenges our traditional understanding of society and how sociologists can make reconciliation central in their work.

Toward a Sociology of the Reconciliation of Conflicting Desires

Susan O'Donnell and David Perley

We believe that sociological research can contribute to justice for Indigenous peoples; however, the focus of the research needs to change. The starting point for our contribution is the analysis by Eve Tuck (2009) of the need to suspend damage-centered research in Indigenous communities. According to Tuck (2009), damage-centered research documents everything that is broken or wrong in Indigenous communities. The result is that Indigenous people see themselves as damaged. Much of the current and past sociological research on Indigenous communities is damage centered. The research can look at historical and political causes such as colonization to explain poverty, ill health, and social dysfunction in Indigenous communities but the result is the same: we understand Indigenous communities and people to be broken, needing to be fixed. The damage in Indigenous communities has also been documented extensively in reports from the Truth and Reconciliation Commission of Canada (TRC; 2015), the United Nations Special Rapporteur on the Rights of Indigenous Peoples (Anaya 2014), and the Royal Commission on Aboriginal Peoples (RCAP; 1996). The mass media also reports regularly on the damage, loss, pain, and deficits. Every Canadian is aware of the "Indigenous problem."

Tuck (2009) believes there was a need for damage-centered research in the past, to document the stories, but now it is time to shift, to craft research so that it focuses on desire instead of damage. Desire-based research captures the complexity and contradictions of everyday lives. It documents not only the painful elements but also the wisdom and hope, because Indigenous communities are so much more than broken. It remains important to expose ongoing structures of inequity; desire-based research does not ignore oppression but rather makes good choices available for people.

Tuck (2009) explains that many Indigenous communities participate in damage-centered research in the hope that it will bring about change. However, this approach is based on a flawed theory of social change: by establishing harm or injury, reparation will be achieved; by testifying that damage was caused, the perpetrators will be forced to be accountable. The flaw in this theory of social change is that reparation has never been achieved. We will add that at the time of writing, the newest federal government has stated its intention to enact all the recommendations of the TRC. It is good to hope that the government will make the changes required to achieve justice for Indigenous peoples; however, a review of the history of government action strongly suggests otherwise. Indigenous people desire to make decisions for themselves rather than have them made for them by the Department of Indigenous

Susan O'Donnell and David Perley. 2016. "Toward a Sociology of the Reconciliation of Conflicting Desires." *Canadian Review of Sociology* 54(3): 474–81.

READING

Affairs and Northern Development. Indigenous people desire to determine their own destiny and shape their own future. Fulfilling this particular desire requires colonial structures to be replaced with structures that recognize the principle of self-determination.

Crucially for our analysis, Tuck (2009) also makes the point that desires can be conflicting. We can desire to be critically conscious and also desire something that maintains oppressive social structures. Our contribution expands from that point: we believe that sociology has a unique role to play by doing research on these conflicting desires. All groups of people have desires that may conflict internally. How we as a society reconcile these desires will determine the extent to which true justice for all Indigenous peoples will be achieved. We propose a sociology of the reconciliation of conflicting desires and suggest some practical ways that this type of research could move forward.

Our Conflicting Desires

Indigenous authors working across Canada are leading the analysis of settler colonialism, including Taiaiake Alfred (2005, 2009), Marie Battiste (2013), Jeff Corntassel (2012), Glen Coulthard (2014), Pamela Palmater (2011), Leanne Simpson (2014), and Eve Tuck and K. Wayne Yang (2012), among others. A settler colonialism lens sees that Canadian state policies are designed to remove Indigenous peoples from their traditional lands so that the resources can be extracted for economic gain. For millennia, the Indigenous people in the regions where resources are extracted survived as hunters and gatherers with strong connections to the land and all that it provides; it is only in recent history that they are living on small reserve lands with limited access to the resources needed to develop their communities.

One way to ensure unfettered access to natural resources in Canada is to weaken the communities in those regions by removing the children and putting them into residential schools. Another way is to make living conditions in the communities so difficult that many people will want to leave and move to the cities. Underfunding for Indigenous education, health, social services, housing, and so on, have been well documented by Indigenous organizations over the years. As the housing manager in a remote Indigenous community interviewed recently said: "We receive just enough to fail" (Beaton et al. 2015:110). Tuck and Yang (2012) have argued persuasively that decolonization is not a metaphor: it is about land.

If decolonization is about land, then reconciliation is also about land. Resources taken from Indigenous lands maintain the Canadian economy. The unrestrained extraction of resources from Indigenous lands is directly responsible for the high standard of living experienced by most Canadians, the majority of whom live in cities. The fact that resource extraction is carried out with little regard for the environment is directly responsible for the relatively low prices we pay for consumer goods, especially petroleum-based products. We all have many desires. Below we list six that are central to our argument.

- Desire 1: We want Indigenous communities to be healthy, strong, and thriving. This includes options for community members to live, learn, work, and play in Indigenous languages; follow Indigenous cultural practices; and create new ways of seeing and being Indigenous.
- Desire 2: We want all development of lands and resources to be respectful, environmentally sound, and sustainable. This includes meaningful consent with Indigenous communities and nations in whose traditional territories the development is proposed.
- Desire 3: We want a safe and secure home for everyone in our families and communities. This includes having the choice to stay where we are currently living for as long as we want.
- Desire 4: We want stolen lands to be returned to their rightful owners. This includes supporting the development of a process to repatriate unceded and unsurrendered Indigenous traditional territories as well as those recognized by treaty.

- Desire 5: We want to be able to buy fresh fruits and vegetables out of season that are grown far away and transported to local grocery stores and sold as inexpensively as possible; and/or we want a vehicle, preferably a new one, to be able to use whenever we want and we want fuel to be inexpensive; and/or we want to be able to take inexpensive flights to visit friends or family or to have fun in warm places when we need a break; and/or at Christmas we want to be able to buy things for our families that they do not really need; and/or at any time we want to be able to buy things for ourselves we do not need, including fashionable clothes and home furnishings and the latest electronic devices, and we want everything we buy to be at the lowest possible price.
- Desire 6: We want a strong Canadian economy and to maintain a high standard of living so that we have enough money to afford Desire 5; and/or we want all Canadians and citizens of other countries to experience a similar standard of living if that is their desire.

Readers can see where we are going with this: most of us have conflicting desires, non-Indigenous people and Indigenous people. First, the way resource extraction occurs in Canada, with little or no respect for the land and the people who live there, gives most of us the level of wealth we desire (Desire 6). At the same time, we may also desire many material goods at inexpensive prices (Desire 5), which is also possible because of the way resource extraction occurs in Canada. However both these desires conflict with Desire 2, because the way resource extraction occurs in Canada does not have meaningful consent by and sharing the benefits with Indigenous peoples and is not respectful of the land, environmentally sound, and sustainable. They also conflict with Desire 1.

Second, most of us live on stolen land. Tuck and Yang (2012) and others have stated that decolonization (and therefore, reconciliation) will involve settling the land question, which is Desire 4 for some of us. Whether or not we have Desire 4, we believe most Canadians want Indigenous communities to be healthy, strong, and thriving (Desire 1), which in practice requires respectful and sustainable resource extraction (Desire 2) and stolen land returned to its rightful owners (Desire 4). This potentially presents a big conflict of desires, especially again for non-Indigenous Canadians who want to be secure in the knowledge that they can continue to live where they are currently living for as long as they want to (Desire 3).

At the same time, it is important to analyze privilege and the ability to actually act on our desires: for example, the desire to buy fresh produce out of season at inexpensive prices should be understood differently for a person of privilege living in downtown Toronto and a person living in a remote First Nation or Inuit community where fresh produce is always prohibitively expensive and poverty levels are high. However, all of us have a stake in ensuring that these desires are reconciled in the best way possible to make justice for all Indigenous peoples a reality.

Doing Sociological Research on Conflicting Desires

Research on desires and conflicting desires can take many approaches; we can see avenues for quantitative researchers although our own research methods are qualitative and we believe qualitative methods will offer the most results. What follows are points researchers should consider when embarking on this adventure; we see them as guidelines without being prescriptive. As this is a new research area for us, it is important to be as thoughtful and creative as possible with our approaches and be open to new possibilities. We believe all research toward justice for Indigenous peoples must support capacity building so Indigenous communities can participate meaningfully in the research and conduct the research themselves if they so desire.

1. Research questions: There are many possibilities although we suggest the core focus of this research is to understand the desires people have for lands and resources that conflict with their desire to want Indigenous communities to be healthy,

strong, and thriving, and how they reconcile their desires. The high-level aim of this research is to develop a sociological analysis of the reconciliation of conflicting desires that can inform action. The different contexts of privilege and material wealth and geography and the ability to act on our desires will be an important part of the analysis.

2. Research participants: These can be people who identify as Indigenous or non-Indigenous; however, a good starting point would be to focus on non-Indigenous people who likely have the most conflicting desires. An obvious source of participants would be the non-Indigenous people who actively demonstrate their support for Indigenous rights, such as activists. In New Brunswick, for example, many non-Indigenous people supported the antifracking protests and continue to provide support for those who were arrested and their families.

3. Research partners: When doing research with Indigenous communities, our experience suggests the best approach is to develop long-term partnerships with regional organizations that support local Indigenous community development. These partners may or may not be interested in the research with non-Indigenous people unless the benefits to Indigenous communities are clear.

4. Research team: Work with your research partners on a vision for increasing research capacity in rural and remote communities. This includes using technologies effectively to build and maintain relationships with rural and remote communities. Plan research projects so that the primary objective is to support the development of local community research capacity. Find ways to build local capacity whenever possible. Invest in the local community infrastructure and businesses—when visiting the community, pay for the use of facilities such as broadband networks, meeting rooms, local caterers, local accommodations, and other local facilities. Include the regional partners and community leadership in the development of research projects and plans. Hire community researchers to work as research assistants and liaisons with local community members. Hire other community people whenever possible for ongoing research activities, for example, to develop Web sites, transcribe interviews, and organize events; pay them well.

5. Data collection: Use appropriate data-collection protocols. Design research data collection so that the information collected will benefit a wider range of purposes in Indigenous communities, such as information that can be used by community development staff for funding applications. When conducting research with Indigenous participants, develop and sign research agreements with community political leaders, with expectations and contributions of both parties clearly articulated. The community should own the data collected: learn from the OCAP protocol (Assembly of First Nations 2007) and Article 31 of the United Nations Declaration on the Rights of Indigenous Peoples (UN General Assembly 2007). If they do not have their own research ethics protocols, inform community leaders and members about the ethical requirements of research in the TCPS2 (Canadian Institutes of Health Research, Natural Sciences and Engineering Research Council of Canada and Social Sciences and Humanities Research Council of Canada 2014), so that they will always demand high ethical standards from us and future researchers.

6. Publications: Always include at least one Indigenous co-author in any publication about Indigenous people. When discussing a particular Indigenous community, a community member should be a co-author of all publications coming from that community. Figure out a way to provide financial support so that community co-authors can travel to conferences to deliver presentations about the community. Recognize that publications other than academic articles would be useful in

communities, such as posters, information sheets, and articles in community news-letters and Indigenous media.

7. Action: The findings about reconciliation of conflicting desires should lead to strategies to remove the conflicts with the central desire: healthy, strong, and sustainable Indigenous communities. This may involve being a public intellectual, using the position of privilege of being a university-affiliated sociologist to speak out against injustice to Indigenous people and communities and removing the conflicts we have to making things right.

Conclusion: Toward Reconciliation

We have argued that to contribute to justice for Indigenous peoples, the focus of sociological research needs to shift from documenting the damage in Indigenous communities to understanding how Canadians have conflicting desires. In his preface to the challenging book by Paulette Regan, *Unsettling the Settler Within*, Taiaiake Alfred observes that, in relation to settler colonialism, "Canadians are in denial, *in extremis*" (Regan 2010, ix). We agree and suggest that our denial can be largely explained by our failure to reconcile our conflicting desires: we want self-determination for Indigenous nations and we also want to own many things we do not need and to buy them at the lowest possible cost, fueling an economic system that requires unsustainable exploitation of resources on stolen Indigenous lands. Glen Coulthard (2014) writes, "For Indigenous nations to survive, capitalism must die" (p. 174). Perhaps this is the answer, perhaps not. We believe that a better understanding of how people reconcile their conflicting desires is part of the solution. How we reconcile these desires will determine our collective future.

CRITICAL READING QUESTIONS

1. What is a damaged-centred approach to studying Indigenous issues in Canada? Why is this approach problematic?
2. What is a desire-based approach, as proposed in this article? How might this type of approach help us to understand how different groups of people can come together towards reconciliation?
3. What is the sociology of reconciliation of conflicting desires? How do the authors suggest that we can all participate in doing this?

Summary

We began this chapter, and this book, by introducing sociology as a discipline focused on the systematic study of human society. Sociologists focus on three core areas of study: social inequality, social institutions, and social change. When looking at these three areas, sociologists aim to see general themes in everyday life, critically examine the familiar world around them, and understand how society shapes individuals while individuals also shape society. We have come to better understand these ideas through examining C. Wright Mills's concept of the sociological imagination, Harold Garfinkel's breaching experiments, and Émile Durkheim's study of suicide. Mills encourages us to connect our own individual biography with the history of society and to see how our personal troubles are connected to larger public issues. Through this lens of the sociological imagination, we can make sense of how society works and how the individual is connected to the society in which she or he lives. Finally, we learned some of the major qualitative and quantitative ways that sociologists conduct research—something that will be highlighted throughout the book.

Key Terms

breaching experiments 12
counterculture 4
culture 3
dependent variable 24
dominant culture 3
experiment 24
high culture 4
homophily 23
independent variable 24
interview 25
participant observation (ethnography) 25
personal troubles 5
popular (or low) culture 4
public issues 5
qualitative research 25

quantitative research 24
religiosity 18
research question 24
secularization 16
social fact 19
social inequality 11
social institutions 14
society 3
sociological imagination 5
sociology 3
subcultures 4
survey research 24
types of suicide 19
variable 24
visible minority 14

For Further Reading

Berger, Peter. 1963. *Invitation to Sociology*. Garden City, NY: Doubleday.
Collins, Randall. 1992. *Sociological Insight: An Introduction to Non-obvious Sociology*, 2nd edn. New York: Oxford University Press.
Durkheim, Émile. 1897/1951. *Suicide: A Study in Sociology*. New York: Free Press.
Kuhn, Thomas S. 1995. *The Structure of Scientific Revolutions*. Chicago: University of Chicago Press.
Mills, C. Wright. 1959/2000. *The Sociological Imagination*. New York: Oxford University Press.

References

Alfred, T. 2005. *Wasáse: Indigenous Pathways of Action and Freedom*. Toronto: Broadview Press.
——— 2009. "Colonialism and State Dependency." *Journal of Aboriginal Health* 5(2): 42–60.
Anaya, Jalf. 2014. Report of the Special Rapporteur on the Rights of Indigenous Peoples, James Anaya on the Situation of Indigenous Peoples in Canada. Human Rights Council, Twenty-Seventh Session, A/HRC/27/52/Add.2. New York: United Nations General Assembly.
Battiste, M. 2013. *Decolonizing Education: Nourishing the Learning Spirit*. Saskatoon: Purich Publishing.
BBC News. 2013. "How Many Roman Catholics Are There in the World." 14 March. http://www.bbc.com/news/world-21443313.
Beaton, B., T. Burnard, A. Linden, and S. O'Donnell. 2015. "Keewaytinook Mobile: An Indigenous Community-Owned Mobile Phone Service in Northern Canada." In L. Dyson, S. Grant, and M. Hendricks, eds, *Indigenous People and Mobile Technologies*, 109–25. New York: Routledge.
Berger, Peter. 1963. *Invitation to Sociology*. Garden City, NY: Doubleday.
Bibby, Reginald. 2011. *Beyond the Gods and Back: Religion's Demise and Rise and Why It Matters*. Lethbridge, AB: Project Canada Books.
Canadian Institutes of Health Research, Natural Sciences and Engineering Research Council of Canada and Social Sciences and Humanities Research Council of Canada. 2014. "Tri-council Policy Statement:

Ethical Conduct for Research Involving Humans." http://www.pre.ethics.gc.ca/pdf/eng/tcps2-2014/TCPS_2_FINAL_Web.pdf.
Charon, Joel M. 2012. *Ten Questions: A Sociological Perspective*. Belmont, CA: Wadsworth Publishing.
Collins, Randall. 1994. *Four Sociological Traditions: Selected Readings*. New York: Oxford University Press.
Corntassel, J. 2012. "Re-envisioning Resurgence: Indigenous Pathways to Decolonization and Sustainable Self-Determination." *Decolonization: Indigeneity, Education & Society* 1(1): 86–101.
Courthald, G.S. 2014. *Red Skin, White Masks: Rejecting the Colonial Politics of Recognition*. Minneapolis: University of Minnesota.
Durkheim, Émile. 1897/1951. *Suicide: A Study in Sociology*. Glencoe, IL: Free Press.
——— 1956. *Education and Sociology*. Glencoe, IL: Free Press.
——— 1960. *The Division of Labour in Society*. Glencoe, IL: Free Press.
——— 1982. *The Rules of the Sociological Method*, edited by Steven Lukes, translated by W.D. Halls. New York: The Free Press.
Garfinkel, Harold. 1991. *Studies in Ethnomethodology*. Malden, MA: Polity Press/Blackwell Publishing.
General Social Survey. 2015. "Religious Affiliation and Attendance in Canada." http://www.intrust.org/Magazine/Issues/New-Year-2016/Religious-affiliation-and-attendance-in-Canada.

Government of Canada. 1995. Employment Equity Act. http://laws-lois .justice.gc.ca/eng/acts/E-5.401.

Grabb, Edward. 2006. *Theories of Social Inequality*, 5th edn. Toronto: Nelson.

Lemieux, Thomas, and David Card. 1998. "Education, Earnings, and the 'Canadian GI Bill.'" NBER Working Paper Series, Working Paper 6718. Cambridge, MA: National Bureau of Economic Research. http://www.nber.org/papers/w6718.pdf.

Mills, C. Wright. 1959. *The Sociological Imagination*. Oxford: Oxford University Press.

Palmater, P. 2011. "Stretched beyond Human Limits: Death by Poverty in First Nations." *Canadian Review of Social Policy* 65(66): 112–27.

Regan, P. 2010. *Unsettling the Settler Within: Indian Residential Schools, Truth Telling, and Reconciliation in Canada*. Vancouver: UBC Press.

Royal Commission on Aboriginal Peoples (RCAP). 1996. The Report of the Royal Commission on Aboriginal Peoples. Ottawa: Minister of Supply and Services Canada.

Samuel, John, and Kogalur Basavarajappa. 2006. "The Visible Minority Population in Canada: A Review of Numbers, Growth and Labour Force Issues." *Canadian Studies in Population* 33(2): 241–69.

Simpson, L. 2014. "Land as Pedagogy: Nishnaabeg Intelligence and Rebellious Transformation." *Decolonization: Indigeneity, Education & Society* 3(3): 1–40.

Statistics Canada. 2011. "National Household Survey." Ottawa: Statistics Canada. https://www12.statcan.gc.ca/nhs-enm/2011/dp-pd/dt-td/Index-eng.cfm

——— 2015. CANSIM. http://www5.statcan.gc.ca/cansim/home -accueil?lang=eng.

Truth and Reconciliation Commission of Canada. 2015. "Honouring the Truth, Reconciling for the Future: Summary of the Final Report of the Truth and Reconciliation Commission of Canada." http://www.myrobust.com/websites/trcinstitution/File/Reports/Executive_Summary_English_Web.pdf.

——— 2015. "Truth and Reconciliation Commission: Call to Action Report." Winnipeg. http://www.trc.ca.

Tuck, E. 2009. "Suspending Damage: A Letter to Communities." *Harvard Educational Review* 79(3): 409–28.

——— and K.W. Yang. 2012. "Decolonization Is Not a Metaphor." *Decolonization: Indigeneity, Education, and Society* 1(1): 1–40.

Tucker, Robert C., ed. 1978. *The Marx-Engels Reader*. London: Norton.

UN General Assembly. 2007. United Nations Declaration on the Rights of Indigenous Peoples: Resolution/Adopted by the General Assembly, 2 October 2007, A/RES/61/295. http://refworld.org/docid/471355a82.html.

Uppal, Sharanjit, and Sebastien LaRochelle-Cote. 2012. "Changes in Wealth across the Income Distribution, 1999–2012." http://www.statcan.gc.ca/pub/75-006-x/2015001/article/14194-eng.htm#a3.

2 Socialization: Becoming a Member of Society

Chapter Outline

Photo credit: wavebreakmedia/Shutterstock

Introduction

Former British prime minister Margaret Thatcher famously declared, "There is no such thing as society . . . there are individual men and women, and there are families" (Keay 1987). This is a bold statement. While Thatcher was willing to admit that individuals do, at least, have families, she asserted that there is no higher level of organization or collectivity of importance beyond individuals and their immediate relatives.

Sociologists would argue that Thatcher missed something crucial. Most of us feel a loyalty to some society, be it our birthplace (e.g., Canada, China, Chile) or our ethnic group (e.g., Italian Canadians, Iraqi Canadians, Indonesian Canadians). We also feel society's constraints guiding our actions and beliefs. We can see that society shapes our behaviours, such as how to eat a meal or what to say when we meet a stranger. But how does society enable and constrain our actions?

The Individual and Society

Émile Durkheim, whose study of suicide was discussed in Chapter 1, said that society soars above us, exerts a constraining influence on us, and regulates collective activity. At the same time, society enables us to understand the rules that govern social behaviour and helps us to get along with one another. This chapter examines how we become a member of society through socialization, an important process that both facilitates our existence in society and constrains our actions. We will discuss how we, as individuals, come to fit into society through socialization, why this process is important, and how it happens throughout our lives.

Durkheim's first published article, excerpted in the following pages, was a review of the German sociologist Albert Schaeffle's *Bau und Leben des Sozialen Körpers: Erster Band* (which roughly translates as "the construction and life of the social body"). Written when Durkheim was 27 years old, the article lays the foundation for his influential theory of society, which he continued to develop over the course of his career. The review begins with a discussion of Jean-Jacques Rousseau's ideas of human nature. A famous philosopher and political theorist, Rousseau (1712–1778) began his theories of human nature by thinking about what humans would be like before society existed. Rousseau (2011) thought that humans could exist before there were societies and that they would be "happy savages" who did not interact with one another or have language. He asserted that the stage before society existed, between the primitive idea of humans as brute animals and the modern extreme of decadent civilization, was the best stage in human development. He imagined that

French Photographer / Bibliotheque Nationale, Paris, France / Bridgeman Images

PHOTO 2.1 Émile Durkheim is often considered one of the founding fathers of sociology. Here he sits, perhaps pondering society!

nothing is so gentle as man in his primitive state, when placed by nature at an equal distance from the stupidity of brutes and the fatal enlightenment of civil man. . . . The more one reflects on it, the more one finds that this state was the least subject to upheavals and the best for man, and that he must have left it only by virtue of some fatal chance happening that, for the common good, ought never to have happened. The example of savages, almost all of whom have been found in this state, seems to confirm that the human race had been made to remain in it always; that this state is the veritable youth of the world; and that all the subsequent progress has been in appearance so many steps toward the perfection of the individual, and in fact toward the decay of the species. (64, 74)

For Rousseau, society corrupts humans and leads to our "decay."

Durkheim fundamentally disagreed with these ideas for a number of reasons. First, he thought that humans could not exist without society or develop without interaction with other humans. In addition, he argued that society is good for people because it helps them to feel connected to one another. In fact, Durkheim's definition of what it means to be human is fundamentally social; he posited that part of what makes us human is our interactions with and dependence on one another. While Rousseau might have been able to imagine a world of humans before society, Durkheim claimed that it is impossible to have humans without society because society is what *makes* us human.

READING

Review of *Albert Schaeffle, Bau und Leben des Sozialen Körpers: Erster Band*

Émile Durkheim

I

... Society is not a simple collection of individuals, it is an entity which preceded those who comprise it at present and which will survive them, which acts more on them than they on it, which has its own life, own consciousness, own interests and destiny. But what is its nature? ...

We are not dealing with man as Rousseau conceived of him—that abstract being, born to solitude, renouncing it only very late and by a sort of voluntary sacrifice, and then only as the issue of a well-deliberated covenant. Every man is, on the contrary, born for society and in a society. What proves this is not only his marvelous aptitude for defining himself within it and, consequently, for uniting himself with it; still more, it is his inability to live in isolation. What remains if, from the sum of our knowledge, our sentiments, and our customs we take away all that comes to us from our ancestors, our masters, and the milieu in which we live? We will have removed at the same time all that makes us truly men. But aside from all that thus reaches us from outside, there is within us, or so it appears, something intimate and personal which is our own creation; this is our ideal. This is, in the final analysis, a world in which the individual reigns supreme and into which society does not penetrate. Doesn't the cult of the ideal presuppose an entirely internal life, a spirit turned inward on itself and detached from other things? Is idealism not at once the most elevated and the most prideful form of egoism? Quite the contrary, there is no more powerful link for uniting men to one another. For the ideal is impersonal; it is the common possession of all mankind. It is toward this dimly glimpsed goal that all the forces of our nature converge. The more we are clearly aware of it, the more we feel that we are in solidarity with each other. This is precisely what distinguishes human society from all others; it alone can be moved by this need for a universal ideal. ...

Durkheim, Émile. 1978. "Review of Albert Schaeffle, Bau und Leben des Sozialen Körpers: Erster Band by Durkheim." In *From Émile Durkheim on Institutional Analysis*, edited and translated by Mark Traugott, 93–114. Chicago: University of Chicago Press.

IV

There exists a social consciousness of which individual consciousness are, at least in part, only an emanation. How many ideas or sentiments are there which we obtain completely on our own? Very few. Each of us speaks a language which he has not himself created: we find it ready-made. Language is, no doubt, like the clothing in which thought is dressed up. It is not, however, everyday clothing, not flattering to everyone's figure, and not the sort that anyone can wear to advantage. It can adapt itself only to certain minds. Every articulated language presupposes and represents a certain articulation of thought. By the very fact that a given people speaks in its own way, it thinks in its own way. We take in and learn at the same time. Similarly, where do we get both the rules of reasoning and the methods of applied logic? We have borrowed all these riches from the common capital. Finally, are not our resolutions, the judgments which we make about men and about things, ceaselessly determined by public mores and tastes? That is how it happens that each people has its own physiognomy, temperament, and character. That is how it happens that at certain moments a sort of moral epidemic spreads through the society, one which, in an instant, warps and perverts everyone's will. All these phenomena would be inexplicable if individual consciousness were such independent monads.

But how are we to conceive of this social consciousness? Is it a simple and transcendent being, soaring above society? The metaphysician is free to imagine such an indivisible essence deep within all things! It is certain that experience shows us nothing of the sort. The collective mind (*l'esprit collectif*) is only a composite of individual minds. But the latter are not mechanically juxtaposed and closed off from one another. They are in perpetual interaction through the exchange of symbols; they interpenetrate one another. They group themselves according to their natural affinities; they coordinate and systematize themselves. In this way is formed an entirely new psychological being, one without equal in the world. The consciousness with which it is endowed is infinitely more intense and more vast than those which resonate within it. For it is "a consciousness of consciousness" (*une conscience de consciences*). . . .

We can, therefore, affirm that a collective consciousness is nothing but an integrated system, a harmonic consensus. And the law of this organization is the following: each social mass gravitates about a central point and is subject to the action of a directing force which regulates and combines the elementary movements. Schaeffle calls this force authority. The various authorities are subordinated one to another in their turn, and that is how a new life, at once unified and complex, arises out of all the individual activities.

Authority can be represented by a man or by a class or by a slogan. But whatever form it takes, it is indispensable. What would become of individual life without innervation? We would have chaos. Always and everywhere it is faith that provides the force of authority. If we obey when authority commands, it is because we believe in it. Faith can be freely given or imposed; with progress, it will no doubt become more intelligent and more enlightened, but it will never disappear. If, by the use of violence or trickery, it is suffocated for a time, either the society breaks apart or new beliefs are reborn without delay—beliefs less correct and worse than those which preceded them because they are less ripe and not so well tested, because, pressed by the necessity of living, we seize upon the first beliefs to happen along, without examining them. What's more, faith is nothing to be embarrassed about. We cannot know everything or do everything for ourselves; this is an axiom which every day becomes more true. It is, therefore, quite necessary that we address ourselves to someone else, someone more competent. Why stake our honour on being self-sufficient? Why not take advantage of the division of labour?

Authority is, nonetheless, a terrible thing if it is tyrannical. Everyone must be able to criticize it and need submit to it only voluntarily. If the masses are reduced to passive obedience, they will ultimately resign themselves to this humiliating role; they will become, little by little, a sort of inert matter which will no longer resist events, which can be moulded at will, but from which it will no longer be possible to wrest the slightest spark of life. Yet the basis of a people's force is the initiative of the citizens; it is the activity of the masses. Authority directs social life but neither creates it nor replaces it. It coordinates its movements, but presupposes their existence. . . .

A broad-minded individual can, almost at the same time, think one thing and its opposite; but he cannot at once act and abstain from acting. One must choose between two courses of action. It is, therefore, necessary that someone in the society be charged with choosing and deciding. Some authority is no doubt also necessary to coordinate individual intellects and sensitivities. But this authority has no precise organization; it is established here or there according to needs and circumstances. It is, moreover, only consultative. On the other hand, that authority which is charged with guarding the interests of the country is made to command and must be obeyed. That is why it is concentrated at certain determinate points of the territory and belongs only to certain clearly designated persons. In the same way, the principles which regulate collective activity are not indecisive generalizations or vague approximations but positive laws, the formulation of which is sharply delineated once and for all.

However, the role of the public is not purely passive submission: it participates in this activity even though it does not direct it. The laws do not owe their existence to the solitary will of the legislator. They are immanent in society just as the laws of gravity are immanent in physical bodies. The state does not create the former any more than the scientist creates the latter. Law and morality are simply the conditions of collective life; it is, therefore, the people who make them, so to speak, and the people who determine them just by living. The legislator states and formulates them. Moreover, he is not indispensable. If he does not intervene, the law nonetheless exists in the form of custom—half unconscious, it is true, but no less efficacious for that. It loses its precision, not its authority. Moreover, most collective resolutions are directly prepared and almost imposed by public opinion. Once a question becomes the order of the day, opposing sides are organized, engage in battle, and fight for the majority. To be sure, in well-constituted societies, this entire movement, once it arrives on the threshold of social consciousness, stops there. At that point, the organ of the will begins to function. But who cannot see that the matter has already been decided, just as the human will has already been predetermined, by the time that deliberation is cut off? It is the stronger side which triumphs.

But if we concede so large a role to individual wills, will they not impart to the social body all sorts of disordered movements? This fear would be legitimate if egoism was man's only natural sentiment. If everyone pursued only his personal ends, the society would be done for; torn in all directions, it would soon break apart. But at the same time that we love ourselves, we love others. We have a certain sense of solidarity (*Gemeinsinn*) which prevents us from ignoring others and which predisposes us without difficulty to devotion and sacrifice. Of course, if we believe that society is an invention of men, an artificial combination, then there is reason to fear that it will perpetually be torn apart. For so fragile a bond can be broken at any moment.

Man is free, Rousseau said, and yet everywhere he is in chains. If this is true, there is reason to fear that at any moment he will break his chains. But this savage individualism is not part of nature. The real man—the man who is truly a man—is an integral part of a society which he loves just as he loves himself, because he cannot withdraw from it without becoming decadent.

V

Social psychology can ultimately be reduced to the special study of the nervous system: it is a chapter of histology. Schaeffle passes from the tissues to the organs.

Every organ is formed by the combination of five functional tissues. . . . These five elements are combined in different ways and in different proportions, but they are all necessary and are found everywhere. The Church, whose ends are not of this world, still has its economic organization; the shop and the factory have their intellectual lives. . . .

Social life does not take place in the penumbra of the unconscious; everything happens in broad daylight. The individual is not led by instinct; rather, he has a clear conception of the group to which he belongs and the ends which it is appropriate to pursue. He compares, discusses, and yields only to reason. Faith itself is but the free submission of an intellect which comprehends the advantages and the necessity of the division of labour. That is why there is something free and willed about the social organization. Societies are not, to be sure, the product of a contract, and they cannot be transformed from one day to the next. But, on the other hand, they are not the product of a blind necessity, and their history is not a fatal evolution. Consciousness are perpetually open to ideas and, consequently, to change. They can, therefore, escape their first impulse and modify the given direction, or, at any rate, if they persist in the original course, it is because they wished to. Finally, what sets human societies entirely apart is their remarkable tendency toward universality. Animal societies never extend beyond a tiny space, and colonies of a single species always remain distinct, often even enemies. Human societies (*les nations*), on the contrary, become more and more confused with one another; national characteristics, races, and civilizations mix and interpenetrate. Already science, art, and religions have no country. Thus, little by little a new society emerges from all the isolated and distinct groups, a society in which all others will fuse, and which will end by one day including the entire human race. . . .

CRITICAL READING QUESTIONS

1. Durkheim begins his article by stating that society is not simply a collection of individuals; society has "its own life, own consciousness, own interests and destiny." What does he mean by society's consciousness and interests? Give examples of both.
2. Durkheim suggests that individuals have very few ideas that are completely their own. What does this statement mean?
3. How do ideas become the great truths of science, dogmas of religion, or prescriptions of fashion? How do these ideas become accepted as "true"?
4. Where do laws come from, according to Durkheim?

Socialization

While Durkheim and Rousseau might have disagreed about what humans would be like without society, they agreed that humans are shaped by their society. Current sociological work remains focused on how this shaping occurs. How do we come to learn how to fit into society? We gain this knowledge through **socialization**, the lifelong process of learning our society's norms, customs, and ideologies. This process also provides us with the skills necessary for participating in society, thereby helping us both to fit into society and to develop a sense of identity and self.

Socialization is understood differently depending on your theoretical perspective. Sociology has three classic theoretical perspectives that will be used throughout this book: structural functionalism, conflict theory, and symbolic interactionism. Feminist and post-modernist perspectives emerged later in the discipline but are also important lenses through which we can understand the social world.

Structural functionalism, which was particularly popular in the early years of the discipline, is mainly interested in explaining how society functions effectively. Sociologists working within the structural functionalist tradition look at how different structures or institutions in society work together to create consensus and social cohesion. A common analogy, popularized by structural functionalist Herbert Spencer, is that the parts of society are like organs in the human body. Just as the body is made up of various parts that need to function together properly for it to be healthy, the parts of society need to work well together for society to run smoothly. The body's purpose is to survive; therefore, its subsystems (e.g., the respiratory system or central nervous system) have to cooperate and maintain the system as a whole. For the structural functionalists, society's purpose is also to survive and reproduce itself. All the subsystems of society (e.g., the family or the education system) must work well together to keep society running smoothly.

Structural functionalists consider socialization an extremely significant part of how society functions effectively. From this perspective, socialization is a top-down process. When children internalize social rules and values through socialization and learn to conform to the **roles** (the behaviours, beliefs, and norms performed in social situations) and expectations of society, they learn how to be a part of society. Talcott Parsons, who was a prominent structural functionalist and was highly influenced by Durkheim, discussed the importance of socialization in his book *Family, Socialization, and Interaction Process*. According to Parsons (1955), we must all learn society's rules and values; when we all understand them, there is social conformity and consensus. The more thoroughly members of society accept and adopt the dominant rules and values, the more smoothly society will function.

Structural functionalists see socialization as a process that helps to create solidarity and cohesion. However, some sociologists argue that this perspective takes a rather rosy picture of how individuals are socialized into society. They claim that socialization is not always a harmonious process and that fitting into society as it is might not be such a great thing, given the inequality and social problems that exist. **Conflict theory** sees society and socialization in a very different way. Instead of focusing on cohesion as the foundation of society, conflict theorists suggest that human behaviour and social relations result from the underlying conflicts that exist between competing groups. Conflict theory was developed by Karl Marx, who understood society as being based on the conflict between social classes—particularly the clash between individuals who own the means of production (capitalists) and those who do not (workers). (We will learn more about Marx in Chapter 3, where we discuss social class and status.) A common theme in this perspective is that some individuals and groups have more power than others and that the struggle over power is a key element of social life.

Many later sociologists have extended Marx's theory and applied it to conflicts based on social differences beyond class. For example, feminist sociologists focus on gender relations. Feminist theorists argue that, in virtually every society, men (and things associated with men) are held in higher regard than women (Seidman 2008). And as a group with social power, men have an interest in maintaining their social privilege over women (Seidman 2008). In general, feminist theory focuses on **patriarchy**, the system of male domination in society. Feminist theorists argue that the patriarchy is at least as important as class inequality in determining a person's power in life. (We will learn more about feminist theory, and the different strains of this theory, in Chapter 6 on gender).

Both conflict theorists and structural functionalists agree that socialization helps to re-create society as it is now. But whereas structural functionalists see this re-creation as positive, conflict theorists see it as negative. They ask the following questions: Who has the power to shape how individuals are socialized? How does socializing people to fit into society as it is benefit some groups over others? How does socialization help or hinder social inequality?

Melvin Kohn's (1959) study of parental socialization and social class illustrates how conflict theorists might think about socialization. Kohn examined how parental social class shapes the values that parents encourage in their children. He argues that while

RESEARCH METHOD
INTERVIEW

HIGHLIGHT

Early Women of Sociology

It is not surprising that the founding figures of sociology were male. This reflects the fact that sociology as a discipline emerged in a time when women were not able to attain higher education and were expected to focus on family roles instead of engaging in paid work. Because of this, feminist scholars have argued that sociology has traditionally been organized around men—their experiences and their positions (Seidman 2008). In essence, men have been both the subjects and the authors of sociology, and the experiences of women have been (largely) ignored until recently (Smith 1987).

Despite their under-representation, there have been a few trail-blazing women active in early sociology. Harriet Martineau (1802–1876) is often called the first female sociologist. She translated Comte into English and wrote one of the first books on research methods. She also conducted studies of slavery and gender inequality, making a comparison between women and slaves in an essay titled "The Political Non-existence of Women."

Jane Addams (1860–1935) was also an important early female sociologist. She co-founded Hull House, a shelter for the poor in Chicago where many University of Chicago sociologists based their research. She was a campaigner for social reform, and her work challenged many taken-for-granted assumptions about the role of gender, class, and inequality in society. Her work was so ground-breaking, in fact, that FBI Director J. Edgar Hoover characterized Addams as being "the most dangerous woman in America" in the 1920s. She was awarded the Nobel Peace Prize in 1931 (Reardon 2006). That is some great sociology!

most parents agree that children should be taught a general set of values, their opinions on the most important values are shaped by their social class.

Kohn (1959) interviewed 400 families—half from the working class and half from the middle class. He found significant differences when comparing the values emphasized by the mothers from these two groups. Middle-class mothers were more likely to focus on the importance of internal feelings and self-direction. For example, they tended to value empathy, happiness, self-control, and curiosity for both their sons and daughters. Working-class mothers, however, were more likely to emphasize the importance of values that lead to conformity among their children. For example, neatness and obedience were much more likely to be highly valued by working-class mothers than by middle-class mothers. Working-class mothers also had very different expectations for boys and girls. For boys, they valued school performance and ambition highly; for girls, they tended to emphasize the importance of neatness and good manners.

How do these findings affect our understanding of socialization? A conflict theorist would highlight how the different values could reinforce the pre-existing inequality between these two social classes. Valuing curiosity and happiness instead of conformity and obedience has real implications for the types of jobs that these children will be prepared to do. Most professional jobs require ambition and curiosity and could not be done well by someone who is merely obedient. The working-class mothers also perpetuate gender inequality by encouraging their sons to perform well in school and their daughters to be polite. These different traits could certainly lead to different career outcomes for boys and girls.

Like structural functionalists, conflict theorists tend to think of socialization as mostly a top-down process. Some sociologists argue, however, that children also learn from one another and from their shared experiences. For example, kids on the playground learn songs and games from one another. **Symbolic interactionism** examines how socialization is negotiated through our connections with other people. Instead of seeing people as receptacles of socialization (as, some might say, structural functionalists and conflict theorists do), symbolic interactionists claim that we actively participate in our socialization. Furthermore, this group of sociologists does not believe that meanings naturally attach to things. Herbert Blumer (1969) elaborated on this theory in *Symbolic Interactionism: Perspectives and Methods*. In this book, he explains that symbolic interactionism contains three basic premises: humans act toward things based on the meanings they assign to them; the meaning of things is derived or arises from social interactions between people; and individuals use an interpretative process to understand and modify meanings.

Socialization not only teaches us how to interact with one another, but it also helps us to develop a sense of self. In fact, sociologists believe that even something as personal as our identity and sense of self comes from others. Our own name and our nickname are given to us by others; we think of ourselves with words and categories used and created by others; and our sense of self is assembled and constructed from the reactions of others. Symbolic interactionists are particularly interested in how we develop a sense of self through socialization.

RESEARCH METHOD
SURVEY

Two important symbolic interactionists who were interested in socialization and the development of self were George Herbert Mead and Charles Horton Cooley. Mead (1934) argued that children develop their sense of self through four **stages of role-taking**. In the first, or preparatory stage, children learn to use language and other symbols by imitating the **significant others** in their lives. Significant others are key individuals—primarily parents and, to a lesser degree, older siblings and close friends—after whom young children model themselves. Children in this stage simply copy other people's actions or behaviours. For example, when you smile at a baby, she will often smile back. Babies do not necessarily understand what you are doing or why; they simply imitate your actions. They also mimic their parents by wanting to hold the objects they see their parents using, such as keys, even though they don't understand how to use such items.

The second stage, in which children pretend to be other people, is called the role-taking stage. Children engage in role-playing games, thus exhibiting a number of behaviours they see performed by various people in their lives. For example, many children like to play house by performing the role of mother or father. In these roles, they might cook, clean, or care for children (in the form of dolls).

By about seven years of age, children move into the third stage, the game stage. Games are different from play because they involve complex rules and require children to take the role of several other people simultaneously. For example, if you are a pitcher in a baseball game, you have to think about what you are doing while simultaneously understanding what the batter, the shortstop, and the catcher are supposed to do. You also have to remember all the rules of the game, such as when a player is allowed to run from base to base, when a player is out, and when an inning is over. Understanding all these roles and rules at once is quite complicated.

The final stage involves taking the role of the generalized other. Children in this stage are able to think of how they generally appear to other people instead of how they appear to one specific significant other such as a parent or sibling. Do people tend to think of you as shy, smart, or mischievous? Understanding how a generalized other will think of you requires that you be able to take the perspective of people you may not know well or at all.

Through all these stages, individuals learn about themselves and the society in which they live. This development is not a simple matter of learning a list of rules. Instead, children have to interact with other people in order to understand the roles that these other people play, their own roles, and how they should fit into relationships with others.

They must negotiate how they see themselves and their place in society through interacting with other people.

Mead's theory highlights the importance of significant and generalized others in the process of socialization. Other theorists call these various groups of people **agents of socialization** because they guide us through the process of becoming a member of society and help to shape the people we become. There are many different agents of socialization, but we tend to consider the family, peer groups, the education system, the mass media, and religion to be the most important. Each of these groups teaches us how we are supposed to behave as adults in society, to perform different roles, and to function effectively within society and social groups. We sometimes learn from agents of socialization through direct teaching, such as when we learn math or reading in school. However, much socialization takes the form of latent learning, which occurs when we imitate role models, such as the people we see on TV.

Charles Horton Cooley (1902) said that our sense of self is assembled and constructed from the reactions of others. He called this process the **looking-glass self**. When we look at other people, they act as a mirror that helps us to understand how we appear. In essence, we look to others to better understand who we are.

The idea behind Cooley's theory is that we refine our sense of self in light of other's reactions. In fact, we develop a self-image based on the messages we get from others (as we understand them). This development occurs in three main steps: we imagine how others see us; we imagine how others judge our appearance; and we refine this appearance based on how we interpret such judgments. In other words, our understanding about who we are depends largely on how we see ourselves evaluated by others. Just as we see our physical body reflected in a mirror, we also see our social selves reflected in other people's reactions to us. And when we consider the judgments of others, this can cause an emotional reaction—we might feel pride or shame at how we think we are being judged.

PHOTO 2.2 What are these children emulating? Where might they have learned these behaviours? What other mimicking behaviours have you noticed among small children?

Jupiterimages/Thinkstock

This process might become problematic. Consider a person with an eating disorder. While this person might be a normal and healthy body weight, she might see herself as overweight and might think that others also see her in this way, even when they do not. Other people are clearly valuable sources of information about us, but we are not always good at reading what they think about us. For example, when people laugh after we say something, we cannot always tell if they are ridiculing us or if they think we just told a funny joke. As a result, we could respond to a false impression of how we appear to others. In addition, it is not always a good idea to let other people's opinions of us shape how we feel about ourselves.

Cooley's concept of the looking-glass self has all the hallmarks of the symbolic interactionist perspective. It focuses on how we attach meaning to things (including ourselves) through interacting with other people. This theory is based on the idea that we learn about ourselves through interacting with others in society. Think of how these processes were not possible for Anna and Genie (see p. 39). Children who do not interact with others cannot learn to be a member of society or develop a sense of self.

Socialization is a lifelong process. In its earliest stage, called **primary socialization**, we learn how to become a member of society by discovering the attitudes, values, and actions that are culturally and socially appropriate. It helps to think of primary socialization as the process by which individuals learn the unwritten rules of a society, such as how to have a conversation. Family members are very important in this primary socialization because they are the first people we encounter in our lives.

Much of what we learn at this stage is not explicitly taught. Instead, it is learned through observation and imitation. For example, no one specifically tells us how far we should stand from other people when we talk with them. We learn this information by observing how our parents and other adults engage in conversations. We might not even be able to say the specific acceptable distance between conversation partners—is it 20 or 40 centimetres? But we can definitely tell if someone is standing too close or too far away. People who stand too close seem aggressive and rude. People who stand too far away seem uninterested and pompous. Primary socialization teaches us these types of unwritten rules.

Next, we go through **secondary socialization**, when we learn the appropriate behaviours and attitudes of a subculture within our larger society. For example, secondary socialization could occur when individuals join a soccer team. When they join this smaller group, they cannot simply apply the rules they learned in primary socialization. They certainly could not seek the kind of nurturing relationship they

HIGHLIGHT

Applying the Core Theories

One of the challenges of sociology is seeing social phenomena from different theoretical perspectives. Think of theories as lenses. If you put on sunglasses with purple lenses, the world looks purple. If you change to a pair with green lenses, the same world looks green. When you look at an issue through a structural functionalist lens, you will see it in a different way from the way you would if you were looking through a lens of conflict theory, symbolic interactionism, or feminist theory. For example, the theories would understand sex work very different ways.

Structural functionalists often argue that if a structure in society no longer serves a function, it will be eliminated. The fact that sex work is a long-standing reality in society must mean, from a structural functionalist perspective, that it serves some function. For example, some suggest that sex work is a way for people to earn an income if they are not able to work in other professions. You could also argue that sex work might keep marriages together because spouses would not have to engage in long or numerous extra-marital affairs to satisfy their sexual interests (although this hypothesis is certainly controversial).

Although there is some logic to how structural functionalists might explain why sex work exists in society, this theory misses certain things. Conflict theory would try to understand sex work by

asking how the practice is rooted in conflict, power, and inequality. What types of people are most likely to turn to sex work to make money? Why are other forms of employment not available to them? What is the power relationship between the sex worker and the customer?

Feminist theorists would focus on how gender shapes and structures sex work. Why are most sex workers women and most people who hire sex workers men? How might the relations between clients and sex workers be different if the sex worker were male? What is the relationship between female sex workers and the (mostly) male pimps?

Symbolic interactionists would ask still different questions. How do sex workers use their clothing and behaviour to indicate that they are sex workers without actually saying so (which is illegal)? How do sex workers and customers negotiate the meaning of their sexual interaction and what that interaction means to each participant?

While these theories are presented as distinct and separate, sociological work often incorporates multiple theories when trying to understand the social world. For example, it is clear that sex work is based on power inequalities and that the interactions between sex workers and customers are negotiated. Moreover, sex work serves certain functions for some members of

have with their parents from their team members. Along with having to alter their behaviour to fit into this new group, they also have to learn new behaviours that will mark them as a member of the group. For example, they learn how to interact with teammates, do team cheers, wear the uniform, and playfully trash talk the other team. The main difference between primary and secondary socialization is one of scale. Primary socialization refers to the process of becoming a member of larger society, while secondary socialization refers to the process of socializing someone to be a member of a *smaller* group within that society.

Primary and secondary socialization usually occur during the early years of an individual's life. As we age, we have to learn to play new roles. Two types of socialization that occur later in life, when life changes such as entering a new profession or family situation require people to incorporate new roles, are anticipatory socialization and resocialization.

Anticipatory socialization refers to the process in which individuals "rehearse" potential roles that they may have to take on in the future, such as mother, father, or a new position at work. We can see this in Mead's theory of the development of the self—children play at being parents in order to rehearse for a role they might later perform. We continue to rehearse roles later in life. For example, medical students often practise interacting with patients to learn good bedside manner. Anticipatory socialization gives us a chance to prepare for a new role before we even begin to play it in real life. This way, we are ready for all the behaviours and responsibilities that the role will entail once we are expected to perform it.

microgen/iStockphoto

Sex workers use various strategies and physical habits to communicate to potential clients that they offer sexual services. These visual cues are important because they allow sex workers to attract customers without having to say explicitly that they are engaging in sex work.

society (while obviously serving as a dysfunction for others). The best way to understand the social world is to see how various theories and theoretical approaches can help us to make sense of phenomena.

People are also sometimes resocialized, whereby they take on new roles and discard former behaviours, attitudes, and values. In **resocialization**, we do not just add a new role to all the other roles we play, we replace an old role with a new one. For example, adults who retire face the prospect of resocialization when they have to discard their former patterns of working and the identity attached to their occupation and take on the new role of a retiree. Resocialization is sometimes a voluntary process, such as when a person has a religious conversion, moves to a new country, or joins the military. Other times, individuals are forced to change roles. Involuntary resocialization can include role changes such as leaving prison, being fired, or being forced to enter a rehab facility. A person does not have a choice about whether or not to leave prison, but he must discard the "prisoner" role for a new one in this situation.

The process of resocialization can be difficult, but many things can ease this transition. For example, ex-convicts sometimes move to halfway houses after they leave prison. Instead of having to manage on their own, they are assisted with reintegrating into society by having a structure that helps them to find work, re-establish an independent routine, and organize their time. They replace their old role as prisoners with a new role as regular members of society.

Helen Rose Fuchs Ebaugh (1988) both experienced and wrote about resocialization. Ebaugh was a Catholic nun who left the order and married later in life. This major transformation led her to think more critically about how people generally transition from one role to another. She argues that changing roles is a common experience in modern society. In earlier societies, individuals often spent their whole lives in the same town, with one partner, one job, and a very limited set of experiences. Today, people move from city to city, change jobs, partner and re-partner, and experience a multitude of other social role changes. To understand these changes, Ebaugh interviewed 185 people who were experiencing a wide range of social transformations, such as leaving jail, divorcing, leaving jobs as police officers or doctors, retiring, and changing sexual identity. Her research illustrates common stages of what she calls the "role exit process," regardless of the discarded role. Individuals move from being disillusioned with a particular identity to searching for alternative roles, experiencing a turning point that triggers their decision to exit a past role, and, finally, creating an "ex" identity. Think about what it means to become an ex-girlfriend or ex-boyfriend. It requires that you shed your old identity (as one half of a couple) and come to embrace a new role of being an "ex." How do we expect "exes" to act? Will they be happy to see their past partners move on, or do we expect that they will be jealous and bitter? The "ex" role in this context is clearly defined and shapes how people expect you to behave when you leave a relationship. This is why the public is often so skeptical of celebrities who "consciously uncouple" and remain friends after a divorce. They are challenging our taken-for-granted conceptions of what the "ex" role means in this context.

RESEARCH METHOD
INTERVIEW

ACTIVITY

How Do Toys Socialize Us?

Even things as innocuous as toys are important parts of socialization. You've probably noticed that many children play with gender-specific toys. Playing with dolls, action figures, or other gendered toys is part of how children become socialized into their gender roles. While sex (being male or female) is assigned at conception and involves physical trait differences, gender (ideas of femininity and masculinity) are learned. **Gender socialization** is the process of learning how to behave in a way that is consistent with the gender rules and norms of your society. The play that we engage in as children is an important part of our learning to act in ways that our society deems appropriately masculine or feminine.

For example, playing with Barbies or Disney princesses and G.I. Joes or superheroes teaches children something about what a boy or girl should be like in society. Think about what you do with a Barbie doll. Mostly, you simply dress her up, change her hair, and buy her accessories, such as cars and dream houses. This play reinforces the idea that physical appearance is very important for women and that material goods can help them to define and demonstrate who they are. Even the newer versions of Barbie, including Doctor Barbie and Astronaut Barbie, are only distinguishable from the original by clothing and accessories. Apparently, all it takes to be a doctor is a nice lab coat and a stethoscope! Other examples of gendered toys you might have played with include "Bratz" dolls, easy bake ovens, cabbage patch dolls, or my little ponies.

What about G.I. Joe, the "real American hero"? Do you dress him and change his hair, as you do with Barbie? No—you can't even change G.I. Joe's outfit because it is painted on. Instead, you fight with him, reinforcing the idea that men should be aggressive and strong and that they become heroes by being violent and physically powerful. It is important to note that there is much discussion about Barbie's physical shape being an unrealistic ideal for women (which is certainly true) but little discussion of G.I. Joe's physicality, which is also unrealistic (unless you have no neck and an upper body like an upside-down triangle). Toys like teenage mutant ninja turtles or toy guns also emphasize these sorts of traits for boys.

To see what toys today's children play with, visit websites such as Amazon.com, look at their toy section (www.amazon.com), and then answer the following questions:

1. What types of things are these toys teaching?
2. Are boys and girls encouraged to play with different types of toys? What might be the impact of such encouragement?
3. Do toys that were traditionally gender-neutral (such as Lego) now seem gendered? If so, how?

Jaime King/Instagram. Photo Karolina Henke

PHOTO 2.3 What types of clothes do we sell to boys and girls? Girls' shirts say "princess," "smile," and "happy" while boys' shirts have cars, trucks, and superheroes. Actress Jaime King released a line of gender-neutral clothing in 2016 to encourage children to dress the way they feel regardless of societal gender norms.

It is clear that socialization in general, and gender socialization in particular, starts very young.

However, we are taught and retaught how to act according to our gender throughout our lives. Think about the beauty products that you use. Deodorant, shampoo, and razors are essentially the same across brands, but they are marketed to and priced for men and women very differently. Using the following websites as starting points, explore the Internet and your local drugstore to look at these different products and their advertisements.

Deodorant Men: Old Spice (www.oldspice.ca/en-ca/pick-your-scent/pick-your-scent)
Women: Secret (www.secret.com)

Shampoo Men: American Crew (www.americancrew.com)
Women: Herbal Essences (www.herbalessences.com)

Razors Men: Gillette (www.gillette.com)
Women: Quattro (www.schick.com/schick-women)

Now answer these questions:

1. How are these products marketed to men and women differently?
2. What could these products and advertisements be teaching us about the ways women and men should act?
3. What products, if any, did you find that do not follow gender stereotypes?

Aging and Socialization

As we've discussed, the process of learning how to become a member of society and developing an identity is shaped by the society in which we live. While it may feel like growing up is just a natural biological process that remains unchanged, the culture and institutions of our society shape this process. The sociological study of aging focuses on both the social aspects of how individuals age and concerns with the general aging of the population as a whole. The experience of aging, and moving through the life-course, depends on social factors such as changes in public policies and programs, overarching cultural values, and norms. In addition, our understanding of the aging process, and its different stages, has changed over time.

One way that our cultural understanding of aging has changed is in the concept of childhood as a life-stage. The historian Steven Mintz (2004) explains that prior to the eighteenth century, there was no idea of childhood as a separate period of life—children were just small adults in waiting. By the middle of the century, "childhood was increasingly viewed as a separate stage of life that required special care and institutions to protect it" (3). For example, child labour laws emerged to protect children, as a group, from the harsh realities of working in factories. During the nineteenth century, the growing acceptance of this new ideal of childhood was evident among the middle class. Young people began living in the parental home for longer periods and were expected to obtain more formal schooling. This period also saw an increasing consciousness about young people's emotional and psychological development. These changes culminated in the development of the concept of adolescence around the beginning of the twentieth century.

The notion of adolescence as a period between childhood and adulthood, in which young people learn about themselves and form identities, is a historical invention. Our modern conception of adolescence is that it is a period when young people are rebellious, are prone to dramatic displays, and engage in violent and risky behaviour. Think of how television shows such as *"Riverdale," "Degrassi" or the movie Mean Girls* depict adolescents as impulsive, tempestuous, and emotional. This period is generally thought to be a time of "storm and stress" for young people (Hall 1904).

One of the first and most important scholarly works that challenged our current ideas about adolescence as a time of turmoil and stress was *Coming of Age in Samoa* (1928) by anthropologist Margaret Mead (no relation to our friend George Herbert). To see if our Western understanding of adolescence was a natural and biological phenomena or a social creation, she compared the transition to adulthood in American society with the same period in Samoan society. If young Samoans also experienced adolescence as a time of "storm and stress," Mead would have additional evidence that such turmoil was simply the natural experience of this period of life. However, if she found that adolescence was not such a stressful period in Samoa, it would lead us to question the assumption that young people will be dramatic, rebellious, and in search of their identity at this stage.

RESEARCH METHOD
PARTICIPANT
OBSERVATION

Mead (1928) engaged in participant observation in three villages in Samoa. She lived in these villages and (with the help of an interpreter) interviewed 68 young women between the ages of nine and 20. She found that, compared with Western societies, adolescence in Samoa was not a stressful time. She attributed this finding to cultural differences between Samoa and Western countries. While Mead's book on this research was very popular and generally well received, some argued that she failed to recognize the change that occurred in Samoan society. Despite these concerns, the research highlights how something that appears natural could be a product of the culture and institutions of our society.

Popular movies and television shows often focus on the struggles that young people have when transitioning to adulthood. Television shows such as *Friends* and *Master of None* focus on the prolonged period when young people are transitioning into adulthood. Sociologists have long been interested in how individuals move through life-stages and how larger institutions of society can shape these transitions. Frank Furstenberg and his colleagues (2004) focus particularly on the transition to adulthood in modern society. They argue that our ideas about becoming an adult have changed and that these changes are related to larger historical transformations in society.

As Furstenberg and colleagues (2004) explain:

> In the past several decades, a new life stage has emerged: early adulthood. No longer adolescents, but not yet ready to assume the full responsibilities of an adult, many young people are caught between needing to learn advanced job skills and depending on their family to support them during the transition.

What does it take to be considered an adult? Do you feel like an adult? Furstenberg argues that there are seven traditional markers of adulthood: completing education, financial independence, working full-time, being able to support a family, leaving the parental home, getting married, and having a child. With these markers in mind, a full 65 per cent of American men and 77 per cent of American women had reached adulthood and done all seven of these things by age 30 in 1960. By 2000, only 31 per cent of men and 46 per cent of women had completed these steps by that age (Furstenberg et al. 2004).

The trends are similar in Canada. In 1981, only 27 per cent of Canadians between the ages of 20 and 30 lived with their parents. By 2016, this had increased to 35 per cent. At the same time, the number of young people living in families (with a spouse, partner, or children and apart from their parents) in couples had decreased. While 52 per cent of those between 20 and 30 were in couples in 1981, this declined to 42 per cent in 2011. And, finally, the number of first children born to women over 30 has increased dramatically in this time, from 24 per cent in 1981 to 52 per cent in 2011. Clearly, moving out of the parental home, creating couples, and having children is happening later in Canada today than it did 30 years ago (see Table 2.1).

It is important to note, however, that our idea of adulthood and what it takes to be considered an adult has changed over time. While marriage and children were critical markers of adulthood in the 1950s, particularly for women, they are no longer seen in the same way. In fact, Furstenberg finds that only slightly more than half of Americans still

Gelatin silver print. Manuscript Division, Library of Congress (50a)

PHOTO 2.4 Margaret Mead (centre) poses for a photograph with two unidentified Samoan girls, c. 1926. Through her research, Mead found that adolescent Samoan girls were free of the "teen angst" experienced by Westerners. Think about how teenagers are currently depicted in the Western media. Do the media tend to depict this period as one of stress and anxiety?

TABLE 2.1	Percentage of Canadians aged 20 to 30 living with parents, in couples, and giving birth, 1981 and 2016		
		1981	2016
Living with parents		27	35
Living with spouse, partner, or child (apart from parents)		52	42
First-time births to mothers over 30		24	52

Sources: Adapted from Statistics Canada, 2017, *Census in Brief: Young Adults Living with Their Parents in Canada in 2016*, Ottawa: Statistics Canada 2016 Census, Ottawa. http://www12.statcan.gc.ca/census-recensement/2016/as-sa/98-200-x/2016008/98-200-x2016008-eng.cfm; and Cohn, D'Vera. 2013. "In Canada, most babies now born to women 30 and older." *Fact Tank*. July 10. http://www.pewresearch.org/fact-tank/2013/07/10/in-canada-most-babies-now-born-to-women-30-and-older/

see marriage and having children as important parts of what makes someone an adult (Furstenberg et al. 2004). Markers such as moving out of the parental home, completing education, and getting a job still remain important components of how we see adulthood in contemporary society. It is clear that these transitions are increasingly difficult for individuals to achieve and take longer to complete.

Why does the transition to adulthood take longer today than it did in the past? It is easy to argue that this results from the different character of young people today—sometimes people say that young people are simply not working hard enough or are entitled. These explanations see the problem of delayed adulthood as a personal trouble that young people face in modern times. Remember that C. Wright Mills saw personal troubles as problems that affect individuals. However, this delayed adulthood is also a public issue, a problem that exists on a social level and has social causes. For example, programs that helped young people who fought in World War II to attend university, which were discussed in Chapter 1, helped to make university more affordable for a whole cohort of young people. Higher tuition and expenses associated with going to university or college and the increased cost of housing also make it more difficult for young people to become financially independent. Finally, it takes longer to complete education and secure a full-time, good-paying job than it did in the past. For all of these reasons, it is simply not true that young people today are at fault for having trouble making the transition smoothly. Instead, the larger social structure is creating more barriers to this transition, and there are fewer programs to assist young people in overcoming these barriers in modern times.

How do we deal with the challenging circumstances of transitioning to adulthood in Canada today? Once we recognize that this is a public issue, not just a personal trouble, we must seek larger social solutions. Paul Kershaw, a UBC professor in the School of Population and Public Health, started the Generation Squeeze campaign in order to address some of these issues. He argues that young people today face increasingly challenging circumstances, including higher debt from school, a more difficult time finding a job and buying a house, and a less generous government to help them make the transition to adulthood. In order to change this, he suggests that young adults get together as a political lobby to try to shape government policy and make it friendlier to the needs of young people.

His organization, Generation Squeeze, is modelled after the Canadian Association of Retired People, a very powerful lobby of more than 300,000 Canadians over the age of 50 who push for policies that help older Canadians (Kershaw 2017). Generation Squeeze lobbies for affordable housing, reduced tuition, environmental protection, and childcare. Their slogan is a "Canada that works for all generations." Campaigns like this show how we have agency to change social policies and deal with large-scale social problems, like the delayed transition to adulthood in modern society.

As stated earlier, aging research is centrally concerned with different phases of the life-course and changes in our understanding of these phases. This research also examines the general aging of the population as a whole and its implications for society. It is clear

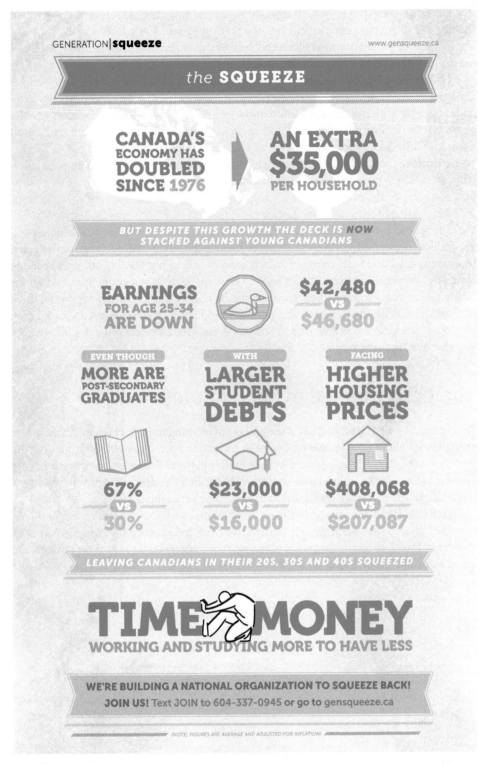

FIGURE 2.1   Generation Squeeze is a political advocacy group for Canadians under 40. They argue that there is generational inequality in this country, with most resources going to older Canadians at the expense of programs to help younger Canadians. This group calls for a "Canada that works for all generations." Would you consider joining a group like this?

Source: Dr Paul Kershaw. University of BC/ Generation Squeeze Lab. Available at: , https://d3n8a8pro7vhmx. cloudfront.net/gensqueeze/pages/136/attachments/original/1435709058/20150630_GS_Story1. pdf?1435709058

that Canadian society as a whole is aging; the number of older people is now greater than the number of younger people. In 1966, the median age for Canadians was 27.8 (meaning half of our population was older and half was younger than this age). By 2016, the mean age had risen to 41.0 years (Statistics Canada 2017).

The fastest-growing age group in the Canadian population is seniors. This trend is expected to continue for the next several decades, mainly because of low fertility rates and increasing life expectancies. In fact, at the end of 2016 the number of seniors over 65 exceeded the number of children 14 and under in Canada (Figure 2.2). The increase is so notable that by 2031, about 25 per cent of Canadians will be over the age of 65. This increase in older Canadians is occurring while the percentage of the Canadian population who are children remains the same, at around 16 per cent (see Figure 2.2).

The aging of the population as a whole has serious social and economic implications for both pensions and health care. For example, the Old Age Security (OAS) program and the Guaranteed Income Supplement (GIS) for low-income seniors cost $27.1 billion and $7.7 billion, respectively, in 2009 (Library of Parliament 2011). These figures are projected to quadruple by 2036. In terms of health care, an aging population can also be quite expensive. While seniors account for only 14 per cent of the population, they account for nearly 44 per cent of annual health care costs. As the population of seniors grows, these costs will rise. With the increased size of the over-65 group, there is also a decreased proportion of working-age individuals to support these social services. Figure 2.3 illustrates this changing age structure in Canada.

The Performance of Social Roles

An important part of socialization is the process of learning to perform roles. Shakespeare thought a lot about how people play roles in society. In *As You Like It*, he wrote: "All the world's a stage, And all the men and women merely players." Canadian sociologist Erving Goffman (1922–1982) shared this view when he created the **dramaturgical perspective**, seeing social life as a stage and individuals as actors portraying roles.

Goffman is considered one of the most influential sociologists of the twentieth century. He believed that when we meet others, we work to influence their impression of us (Goffman 1959). In essence, we want to manage the impression that we give to others. We can do this by changing our setting or appearance. And this process is iterative—while

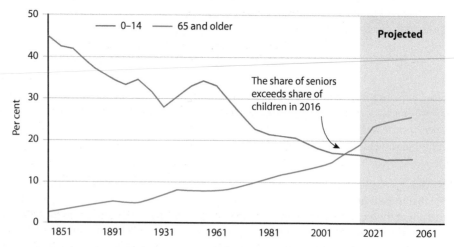

FIGURE 2.2   Proportion of children 14 years and under and people aged 65 and older in Canada, 1851–2061 (projected)

Source: *The Globe and Mail*, source: Statscan, 2017 Census.

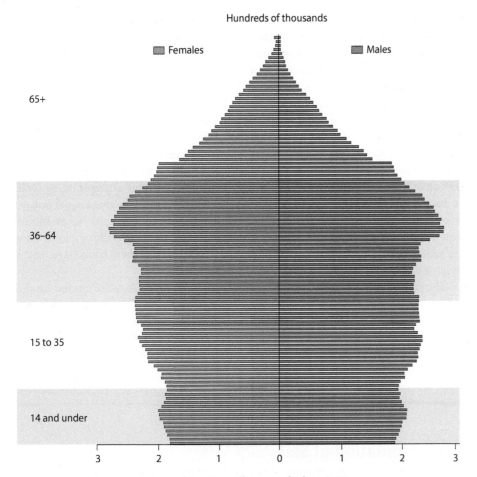

FIGURE 2.3 **The age structure of the Canadian population, 2016**

Source: Grant, Tavia and Jeremy Agius (2017). "Census 2016: The Growing Age Gap, Gender Ratios and other Key Takeaways." The Globe and Mail, source: Statscan, 2017 Census. https://www.theglobeandmail.com/news/national/census-2016-statscan/article34882462/

we try to shape our conversation partner's impression of us, she tries to form the most accurate impression possible. Like other symbolic interactionists, Goffman was interested in how individuals interact with others to create an impression and to gauge the impressions given off by others.

Goffman also believed that individuals try to "smooth out" social interaction to make it easier and more comfortable for everyone. In order to do this, we constantly work to avoid embarrassing others or ourselves. For example, if someone slips and falls down, we might help them up and then casually say, "It's quite an uneven floor, I find it slippery too," so that they feel less embarrassed. The challenge is that the behaviours that are appropriate or least likely to cause embarrassment differ across situations. For example, it is acceptable to yell and sing loudly at a football game but probably not in class. Therefore, we must learn to tailor how we act based on the situation. We must be able to take our stage of action into account when deciding how to behave and then modify our behaviour accordingly.

For example, if you have a job interview, you might practise parts of your performance in advance, thinking of how you would answer questions that might be asked. You would certainly think about your clothing and appearance, since you want to look like you would fit in the new workplace. If everyone wears a suit, perhaps you should too. If the interview is for a creative job, such as at an advertising agency or media company, you would perhaps choose to present a more artistic self with an interesting necklace or funky patterned socks. Clearly, you have to manage the impression you give, and the props you use to do so, based on the social situation.

In social interaction, as in the theatre, there is a front stage where we perform. This is where actors work to make a positive impression on others. But there is also a back stage that includes the private places where individuals do not feel they are being watched. Essentially, the back stage has no audience to try to impress.

The concepts of front stage and back stage are easy to see in many social settings. Think about restaurant workers. How are they different when they are front stage in the restaurant (where they are serving tables for patrons) versus back stage (in the kitchen or dishwashing area)? Workers tend to maintain a calm demeanour and a cheerful disposition in the front of the restaurant, while they might grumble and spit in the food in the back stage. Although we often prepare for the front stage by thinking about what impression we hope to make, we are sometimes caught out of "character" when someone unexpectedly sees us in our back stage. For example, a customer walking past a restaurant's kitchen to get to the washroom may see the servers in their back stage, perhaps having a drink or complaining about the customers.

The following reading is from Goffman's most famous book, *The Presentation of Self in Everyday Life* (1959). In this excerpt, Goffman explains the dramaturgical model, which has been very influential in many areas of sociology. As you read the following pages, consider what this theory tells us about social interaction and socialization. How do we learn to interact with others? How is this process like the theatre?

The Presentation of Self

Erving Goffman

When an individual enters the presence of others, they commonly seek to acquire information about him or to bring into play information about him already possessed. They will be interested in his general socio-economic status, his conception of self, his attitude toward them, his competence, his trustworthiness, etc. Although some of this information seems to be sought almost as an end in itself, there are usually quite practical reasons for acquiring it. Information about the individual helps to define the situation, enabling others to know in advance what he will expect of them and what they may expect of him. Informed in these ways, the others will know how best to act in order to call forth a desired response from him.

For those present, many sources of information become accessible and many carriers (or "sign-vehicles") become available for conveying this information. If unacquainted with the individual, observers can glean clues from his conduct and appearance which allow them to apply their previous experience with individuals roughly similar to the one before them or, more important, to apply untested stereotypes to him. They can also assume from past experience that only individuals of a particular kind are likely to be found in a given social setting. They can rely on what the individual says about himself or on documentary evidence he provides as to who and what he is. If they know, or know of, the individual by virtue of experience prior to the interaction, they can rely on assumptions as to the persistence and generality of psychological traits as a means of predicting his present and future behaviour.

Goffman, Erving. 1959. Introduction from *The Presentation of Self in Everyday Life*. Garden City, NY: Doubleday. Copyright © 1959 by Erving Goffman. Used by permission of Doubleday, an imprint of the Knopf Doubleday Publishing Group, a division of Penguin Random House LLC. All rights reserved.

However, during the period in which the individual is in the immediate presence of the others, few events may occur which directly provide the others with the conclusive information they will need if they are to direct wisely their own activity. Many crucial facts lie beyond the time and place of interaction or lie concealed within it. For example, the "true" or "real" attitudes, beliefs, and emotions of the individual can be ascertained only indirectly, through his avowals or through what appears to be involuntary expressive behaviour....

The expressiveness of the individual (and therefore his capacity to give impressions) appears to involve two radically different kinds of sign activity: the expression that he gives, and the expression that he *gives off*. The first involves verbal symbols or their substitutes which he uses admittedly and solely to convey the information that he and the others are known to attach to these symbols. This is communication in the traditional and narrow sense. The second involves a wide range of action that others can treat as symptomatic of the actor, the expectation being that the action was performed for reasons other than the information conveyed in this way. As we shall have to see, this distinction has an only initial validity. The individual does of course intentionally convey misinformation by means of both of these types of communication, the first deceit, the second feigning....

Let us now turn from the others to the point of view of the individual who presents himself before them. He may wish them to think highly of him, or to think that he thinks highly of them, or to perceive how in fact he feels toward them, or to obtain no clear-cut impression; he may wish to ensure sufficient harmony so that the interaction can be sustained, or to defraud, get rid of, confuse, mislead, antagonize, or insult them. Regardless of the particular objective which the individual has in mind and of his motive for having this objective, it will be in his interests to control the conduct of the others, especially their responsive treatment of him.[1] This control is achieved largely by influencing the definition of the situation which the others come to formulate, and he can influence this definition by expressing himself in such a way as to give them the kind of impression that will lead them to act voluntarily in accordance with his own plan. Thus, when an individual appears in the presence of others, there will usually be some reason for him to mobilize his activity so that it will convey an impression to others which it is in his interests to convey. Since a girl's dormitory mates will glean evidence of her popularity from the calls she receives on the phone, we can suspect that some girls will arrange for calls to be made, and Willard Waller's finding can be anticipated:

> It has been reported by many observers that a girl who is called to the telephone in the dormitories will often allow herself to be called several times, in order to give all the other girls ample opportunity to hear her paged.[2]

Of the two kinds of communication—expressions given and expressions given off—this report will be primarily concerned with the latter, with the more theatrical and contextual kind, the nonverbal, presumably unintentional kind, whether this communication be purposely engineered or not. As an example of what we must try to examine, I would like to cite at length a novelistic incident in which Preedy, a vacationing Englishman, makes his first appearance on the beach of his summer hotel in Spain:

> But in any case he took care to avoid catching anyone's eye. First of all, he had to make it clear to those potential companions of his holiday that they were of no concern to him whatsoever. He stared through them, round them, over them—eyes lost in space. The beach might have been empty. If by chance a ball was thrown his way, he looked surprised; then let a smile of amusement lighten his face (Kindly Preedy), looked round dazed to see that there *were* people on the beach, tossed it back with a smile to himself and not a smile *at* the people, and then resumed carelessly his nonchalant survey of space.

But it was time to institute a little parade, the parade of the Ideal Preedy. By devious handlings he gave any who wanted to look a chance to see the title of his book—a Spanish translation of Homer, classic thus, but not daring, cosmopolitan too—and then gathered together his beach-wrap and bag into a neat sand-resistant pile (Methodical and Sensible Preedy), rose slowly to stretch at ease his huge frame (Big-Cat Preedy), and tossed aside his sandals (Carefree Preedy, after all).

The marriage of Preedy and the sea! There were alternative rituals. The first involved the stroll that turns into a run and a dive straight into the water, thereafter smoothing into a strong splashless crawl towards the horizon. But of course not really to the horizon. Quite suddenly he would turn on to his back and thrash great white splashes with his legs, somehow thus showing that he could have swum further had he wanted to, and then would stand up a quarter out of water for all to see who it was.

The alternative course was simpler, it avoided the cold-water shock and it avoided the risk of appearing too high-spirited. The point was to appear to be so used to the sea, the Mediterranean, and this particular beach, that one might as well be in the sea as out of it. It involved a slow stroll down and into the edge of the water—not even noticing his toes were wet, land and water all the same to *him*!—with his eyes up at the sky gravely surveying portents, invisible to others, of the weather (Local Fisherman Preedy).[3]

The novelist means us to see that Preedy is improperly concerned with the extensive impressions he feels his sheer bodily action is giving off to those around him. We can malign Preedy further by assuming that he has acted merely in order to give a particular impression, that this is a false impression, and that the others present receive either no impression at all, or, worse still, the impression that Preedy is affectedly trying to cause them to receive this particular impression. But the important point for us here is that the kind of impression Preedy thinks he is making is in fact the kind of impression that others correctly and incorrectly glean from someone in their midst. . . .

There is one aspect of the others' response that bears special comment here. Knowing that the individual is likely to present himself in a light that is favourable to him, the others may divide what they witness into two parts; a part that is relatively easy for the individual to manipulate at will, being chiefly his verbal assertions, and a part in regard to which he seems to have little concern or control, being chiefly derived from the expressions he gives off. The others may then use what are considered to be the ungovernable aspects of his expressive behaviour as a check upon the validity of what is conveyed by the governable aspects. In this a fundamental asymmetry is demonstrated in the communication process, the individual presumably being aware of only one stream of his communication, the witnesses of this stream and one other. For example, in Shetland Isle one crofter's wife, in serving native dishes to a visitor from the mainland of Britain, would listen with a polite smile to his polite claims of liking what he was eating; at the same time she would take note of the rather rapidity with which the visitor lifted his fork or spoon to his mouth, the eagerness with which he passed food into his mouth, and the gusto expressed in chewing the food, using these signs as a check on the stated feelings of the eater. The same woman, in order to discover what one acquaintance (A) "actually" thought of another acquaintance (B), would wait until B was in the presence of A but engaged in conversation with still another person (C). She would then covertly examine the facial expressions of A as he regarded B in conversation with C. Not being in conversation with B, and not being directly observed by him, A would sometimes relax usual constraints and tactful deceptions, and freely express what he was "actually" feeling about B. This Shetlander, in short, would observe the unobserved observer.

Now given the fact that others are likely to check up on the more controllable aspects of behaviour by means of the less controllable, one can expect that sometimes the individual will try to exploit this very possibility, guiding the impression he makes through behaviour felt to be reliably informing.[4] . . . A specific illustration may be cited from Shetland Isle. When a neighbour dropped in to have a cup of tea, he would ordinarily wear at least a hint of an expectant warm smile as he passed through the door into the cottage. Since lack of physical obstructions outside the cottage and lack of light within it usually made it possible to observe the visitor unobserved as he approached the house, islanders sometimes took pleasure in watching the visitor drop whatever expression he was manifesting and replace it with a sociable one just before reaching the door. However, some visitors, in appreciating that this examination was occurring, would blindly adopt a social face a long distance from the house, thus ensuring the projection of a constant image. . . .

In everyday life, of course, there is a clear understanding that first impressions are important. . . . When the interaction that is initiated by "first impressions" is itself merely the initial interaction in an extended series of interactions involving the same participants, we speak of "getting off on the right foot" and feel that it is crucial that we do so. . . .

In stressing the fact that the initial definition of the situation projected by an individual tends to provide a plan for the co-operative activity that follows—in stressing this action point of view—we must not overlook the crucial fact that any projected definition of the situation also has a distinctive moral character. It is this moral character of projections that will chiefly concern us in this report. Society is organized on the principle that any individual who possesses certain social characteristics has a moral right to expect that others will value and treat him in an appropriate way. Connected with this principle is a second, namely that an individual who implicitly or explicitly signifies that he has certain social characteristics ought in fact to be what he claims he is. In consequence, when an individual projects a definition of the situation and thereby makes an implicit or explicit claim to be a person of a particular kind, he automatically exerts a moral demand upon the others, obliging them to value and treat him in the manner that persons of his kind have a right to expect. He also implicitly foregoes all claims to be things he does not appear to be[5] and hence foregoes the treatment that would be appropriate for such individuals. The others find, then, that the individual has informed them as to what is and as to what they *ought* to see as the "is."

One cannot judge the importance of definitional disruptions by the frequency with which they occur, for apparently they would occur more frequently were not constant precautions taken. We find that preventive practices are constantly employed to avoid these embarrassments and that corrective practices are constantly employed to compensate for discrediting occurrences that have not been successfully avoided. When the individual employs these strategies and tactics to protect his own projections, we may refer to them as "defensive practices"; when a participant employs them to save the definition of the situation projected by another, we speak of "protective practices" or "tact." Together, defensive and protective practices comprise the techniques employed to safeguard the impression fostered by an individual during his presence before others. It should be added that while we may be ready to see that no fostered impression would survive if defensive practices were not employed, we are less ready perhaps to see that few impressions could survive if those who received the impression did not exert tact in their reception of it.

In addition to the fact that precautions are taken to prevent disruption of projected definitions, we may also note that an intense interest in these disruptions comes to play a significant role in the social life of the group. Practical jokes and social games are played in which embarrassments which are to be taken unseriously are purposely engineered.[6] Fantasies are created in which devastating exposures occur. Anecdotes from the past—real, embroidered, or fictitious—are told and retold, detailing disruptions which occurred, almost occurred, or occurred and were admirably resolved. There seems to be no grouping which does not have a ready supply of these games, reveries, and cautionary tales, to be used as a source of humour, a catharsis for anxieties, and a sanction for inducing individuals to be modest in their claims and reasonable in their projected expectations. The individual may tell himself through dreams of getting into impossible positions. Families tell of the time a guest got his dates mixed and arrived when neither the house nor anyone in it was ready for him. Journalists tell of times when an all-too-meaningful misprint occurred, and the paper's assumption of objectivity or decorum was humorously discredited. Public servants tell of times a client ridiculously misunderstood form instructions, giving answers which implied an unanticipated and bizarre definition of the situation.[7] Seamen, whose home away from home is rigorously he-man, tell stories of coming back home and inadvertently asking mother to "pass the fucking butter."[8] Diplomats tell of the time a near-sighted queen asked a republican ambassador about the health of his king.[9]

To summarize, then, I assume that when an individual appears before others he will have many motives for trying to control the impression they receive of the situation. . . .

CRITICAL READING QUESTIONS

1. What is Goffman's distinction between expressions that one gives and expressions that one gives off? What is Goffman referring to when he uses the terms *face-to-face interaction*, *projective techniques*, *defensive practices*, and *protective practices/tact*?

2. a. Suppose you are about to visit or email your professor to ask a question about the upcoming exam. In terms of the expressions you give and expressions you give off, how could you ensure that your professor infers that you are a smart student?

    b. Suppose you are preparing for a date that you have been looking forward to for several days. Your goal is to have fun and to ensure that your partner infers that you are a cool person. How might you accomplish this goal?

    c. Is there a difference between how you would act in each situation? Why or why not? Which is the "real" you?

3. Goffman seems to imply that individuals have considerable control over how others perceive them and that these perceptions are largely the result of face-to-face interactions. What are some other factors that might influence the perceptions others have of an individual? For example, how might power, inequalities, or history influence perceptions?

NOTES

1. Here I owe much to an unpublished paper by Tom Burns of the University of Edinburgh. He presents the argument that in all interaction a basic underlying theme is the desire of each participant to guide and control the responses made by the others present. A similar argument has been advanced by Jay Haley in a recent unpublished paper, but in regard to a special kind of control, that having to do with defining the nature of the relationship of those involved in the interaction.

2. Willard Waller, "The Rating and Dating Complex," *American Sociological Review*, 2, 730.

3. William Sansom, *A Contest of Ladies* (London: Hogarth, 1956), 230–31.

4. The widely read and rather sound writings of Stephen Potter are concerned in part with signs that can be engineered to give a shrewd observer the apparently incidental cues he needs to discover concealed virtues the gamesman does not in fact possess.

5. This role of the witness in limiting what it is the individual has been stressed by Existentialists, who see it as a basic threat to individual freedom. See Jean-Paul Sartre, *Being and Nothingness*, trans. by Hazel E. Barnes (New York: Philosophical Library, 1956).

6. Goffman, op. cit., pp. 319–27.

7. Peter Blau, "Dynamics of Bureaucracy" (PhD dissertation, Department of Sociology, Columbia University, forthcoming, University of Chicago Press), pp. 127–29.

8. Walter M. Beattie, Jr, "The Merchant Seaman" (unpublished MA Report, Department of Sociology, University of Chicago, 1950), p. 35.

9. Sir Frederick Posonby, *Recollections of Three Reigns* (London: Eyre & Spottiswoode, 1951).

ACTIVITY

Performing the Self Online

Who are we in a social media age? Clara Dollar ponders this question in her essay "My (So Called) Instagram Life," published in the *New York Times* (2017). She describes meeting a man online and the "self" she displayed in this process:

> "You're like a cartoon character," he said. "Always wearing the same thing every day."
>
> He meant it as an intimate observation, the kind you can make only after spending a lot of time getting to know each other. You flip your hair to the right. You only eat ice cream out of mugs. You always wear a black leather jacket. I know you.
>
> And he did know me. Rather, he knew the caricature of me that I had created and meticulously cultivated. The me I broadcast to the world on Instagram and Facebook. The witty, creative me, always detached and never cheesy or needy.
>
> That version of me got her start online as my social media persona, but over time (and I suppose for the sake of consistency), she bled off the screen and overtook my real-life personality, too. And once you master what is essentially an onstage performance of yourself, it can be hard to break character.

Clara's story unpacks how she presents herself online and the thought that goes into this process. Is this Instagram self her "real" self? Or is her presentation of self face-to-face her "real" self? And what about the differences across her social media presentations—Facebook, Instagram, Twitter, Snapchat? In this activity, consider how you present your self online and how this relates to Goffman's dramaturgical model.

First, take a look at your online presence. Are you on Facebook, Instagram, Twitter, Snapchat, or other social media? If so, answer the following questions about yourself. If you are not on social media, find a celebrity or public figure, look at their various social media profiles, and answer the following questions about this person.

1. How do you (or your celebrity) appear online? How is this the same as or different from the way you are in "real" life face-to-face? Why might there be differences?
2. How can we use Goffman's dramaturgical model to understand the presentation of self online? What is front stage and what is back stage? How might people break character online? What are the impressions given and impressions given off online?
3. Are you (or your celebrity) different across your different profiles? Why are you consistent or different? What does this tell you about the complexity of the self?
4. Some people have "fake" profiles—profiles on these platforms that are not made under their real names. Why might someone do this? Does this tell us anything about their sense of self or their identity?

Summary

In this chapter, we have learned how socialization helps individuals become members of society. Socialization is important because it is the process of both learning the rules and norms of society and developing a sense of identity. Sociologists from different theoretical traditions look at this process in a variety of ways. Sociologists in the structural functionalist tradition, such as Durkheim and Parsons, tend to focus on how socialization helps society to run smoothly and creates social cohesion. Conflict theorists, such as Marx, focus on how socialization may reinforce the inequality in society. Feminist theory calls on us to consider how gender shapes the process of socialization. Symbolic interactionists, such as George Herbert Mead, Cooley, and Goffman, see socialization as something that is negotiated throughout social life.

Socialization is generally understood as a complicated, lifelong process that is shaped by a variety of individuals and institutions. For example, many different agents of socialization, such as the family and peer groups, help to form the people we become as adults. This process is also shaped by the culture and history of our society as a whole. Looking at the invention of adolescence and the changing transition to adulthood highlights how our understanding of the way that individuals become adults has changed.

Key Terms

agents of socialization 43

anticipatory socialization 45

conflict theory 40

dramaturgical perspective 52

gender socialization 46

looking-glass self 43

patriarchy 40

primary socialization 44

resocialization 46

roles 40

secondary socialization 44

significant others 42

socialization 39

stages of role-taking 42

structural functionalism 39

symbolic interactionism 42

For Further Reading

Blumer, Herbert. 1969. *Symbolic Interactionism: Perspective and Method.* Englewood Cliffs, NJ: Prentice-Hall.

Cooley, Charles Horton. 1902. *Human Nature and the Social Order.* New York: Scribner's.

Goffman, Erving. 1959. *The Presentation of Self in Everyday Life.* New York: Anchor Books.

Mead, George Herbert. 1934. *Mind, Self, and Society.* Chicago: University of Chicago Press.

Parsons, Talcott. 1955. *Family, Socialization, and Interaction Process.* Glencoe, IL: Free Press.

References

Blumer, Herbert. 1969. *Symbolic Interactionism: Perspective and Method.* Englewood Cliffs, NJ: Prentice-Hall.

Cohn, D'Vera. 2013. "Love and Marriage." Pew Research Social and Demographic Trends. http://www.pewsocialtrends.org/2013/02/13/love-and-marriage.

Cooley, Charles Horton. 1902. *Human Nature and the Social Order.* New York: Scribner's.

Dollar, Clara. 2017. "My (So Called) Instagram Life." *The New York Times* 5 May. https://www.nytimes.com/2017/05/05/style/modern-love-my-so-called-instagram-life.html.

Ebaugh, Helen Rose Fuchs. 1988. *Becoming an Ex: The Process of Role Exit.* Chicago: University of Chicago Press.

Furstenberg, Jr, Frank F., Sheela Kennedy, Vonnie C. McLoyd, Ruben G. Rumbaut, and Richard A. Setterstein, Jr. 2004. "Growing up Is Harder to Do" *Contexts* 3(3): 33–41.

Gaetz, Stephen, Jesse Donaldson, Tim Richter, and Tanya Gulliver. 2013. *The State of Homelessness in Canada 2013.* Toronto: Canadian Homelessness Research Network Press. http://www.homelesshub.ca/ResourceFiles/SOHC2103.pdf.

Goffman, Erving. 1959. *The Presentation of Self in Everyday Life.* New York: Anchor Books.

Government of Canada. 1995. *Employment Equity Act.* http://laws-lois.justice.gc.ca/eng/acts/E-5.401.

Hall, G.S. 1904. *Adolescence: Its Psychology and Its Relation to Physiology, Anthropology, Sociology, Sex, Crime, Religion, and Education* (Vols 1 & 2). Englewood Cliffs, NJ: Prentice-Hall.

Keay, Douglas. 1987. "Aids, Education and the Year 2000." *Woman's Own*, 31 October, 8–10. http://www.margaretthatcher.org/document/106689.

Kershaw, Paul. 2017. Generation Squeeze. http://www.generationsqueeze.ca.

Kohn, Melvin L. 1959. "Social Class and Parental Values." *American Journal of Sociology* 64 (4): 337–51.

Library of Parliament. 2011. "41st Parliament: Current and Emerging Issues." http://www.parl.gc.ca/content/lop/researchpublications/currentemergingissues-e.pdf.

Mead, George Herbert. 1934. *Mind, Self, and Society.* Chicago: University of Chicago Press.

Mead, Margaret. 1928. *Coming of Age in Samoa.* New York: W. Morrow.

Mintz, Steven. 2004. *Huck's Raft: A History of American Childhood.* Cambridge, MA: Belknap Press.

Parsons, Talcott. 1955. *Family, Socialization, and Interaction Process.* Glencoe, IL: Free Press.

Reardon, Patrick T. 2006. "Why You Should Care about Jane Addams." *Chicago Tribune* 11 June. http://articles.chicagotribune.com/2006-06-11/news/0606110193_1_jane-austen-abigail-adams-peace-and-freedom.

Rousseau, Jean-Jacques. 2011. "Discourse on the Origin of Inequality." In *The Basic Political Writings*, 2nd edn, translated by Donald A. Cress. Indianapolis: Hackett.

Seidman, Steven. 2008. *Contested Knowledge: Social Theory Today.* Wiley-Blackwell.

Smith, Dorothy. 1987. *The Everyday World as Problematic: A Feminist Sociology.* Boston: Northeastern University.

Statistics Canada. 2017. "Projected Life Expectancy at Birth by Sex, by Aboriginal Identity, 2017." Table 91-547-XIE. Ottawa: Statistics Canada.

3 Deviance, Law, and Crime

Photo credit: Burst/Pexels

Chapter Outline

Introduction

According to *ET Canada*, five of the top 10 top-rated shows in the 2016–17 season were related to crime or policing: *NCIS*, *Bull*, *Blue Bloods*, *NCIS: New Orleans*, and *NCIS: Los Angeles* (Furdyk 2017). It is not surprising that these shows are so popular, given that the public has always been captivated by crime and deviance. Sociologists have also been fascinated with this topic since the early days of the discipline. This chapter examines crime, law, and deviance and asks: Why do people commit crimes? How do we deal with criminals in our society? Why do some people deviate from accepted norms of behaviour despite the fact that we are all socialized to fit in and follow the rules?

What Is Deviance?

Deviance is any act that breaks an accepted social standard, from minor misdeeds to serious crimes. Many deviant acts break norms but are not punishable by the state. No Canadian goes to jail for cheating on a spouse, but most people consider adultery to be contrary to an important norm of behaviour (i.e., being faithful to our long-term romantic partner).

It is important to note that, just because deviance breaks a norm, it is not always unusual. Many norms are often broken. Put another way, not all norms are "normal." Take the example of jaywalking. Jaywalking certainly breaks both a norm and the law (you can be fined for doing it). However, engaging in this behaviour is "normal"—most people have, at some point, jaywalked. Perhaps you were on a quiet street in the middle of the night and darted across the road. While doing so might be "normal," it still breaks a norm of behaviour and is illegal.

Deviance varies in the severity of public response, perceived harmfulness, and degree of public agreement. Severity of public response refers to the public's reaction to the act, which can range from minor disapproval, such as a scowling look, to severe punishment, such as jail time. Perceived harmfulness is the amount of harm the perpetrator's behaviour is thought to have inflicted. An act could be a bit offensive or cause severe physical pain or death. Degree of public agreement indicates the extent to which the public agrees that the act is deviant or criminal. Certain acts may be considered seriously dangerous and deviant by some but may be dismissed as insignificant minor deviance by others. However, crimes such as sexual assault or incest are almost universally considered deviant and criminal.

Some acts of deviance are labelled as minor deviances. Acts of minor deviance are not crimes and are generally not seen as particularly harmful to society. Having a tattoo, for example, is not seen (even by your grandmother) as being particularly harmful to society as a whole; therefore, the general public response will be mild (in Canada, no one is sent to jail or fined for having a tattoo). Such acts are seen as minor ways of stepping outside the norms of society.

The next level of deviant acts are criminal but are thought of as **lesser crimes**. For example, petty theft and speeding are both illegal but are not usually seen as extremely serious violations of social norms. Many people have stolen something small when they were children. You probably do not think that someone who stole a candy bar when she was eight years old is a bad person, even though theft is bad behaviour and illegal. At some point, most people have also driven faster than the legal speed limit, and many people have received punishment for this act (in the form of a speeding ticket). Speeding is illegal; however, this crime's perceived harmfulness and severity of public response is moderate—you certainly get a ticket if you are caught, but you will not be sent to jail or judged harshly by others.

HIGHLIGHT

Polygamy in Canada

In most countries, marriage is traditionally understood as monogamous. The practice of polygamy, which is illegal in Canada and the United States, is an interesting challenge to our modern conception of this institution, including our ideas of devotion to one person to the exclusion of everyone else and the romantic love that we expect between two spouses. Polygamous unions are also difficult to align with Canadian ideas about families, household living arrangements, and parental responsibilities.

Because of its unconventionality, polygamy fascinates many people. Several television shows have examined polygamous marriages and families, such as the drama "Big Love" (2006–11) and the reality show "Sister Wives" (2010–present). Both focus on a polygamous family—one man, his wives, and their children—as it struggles with regular family issues (such as decisions about vacations and child-rearing) as well as problems specific to polygamous families (such as needing to hide the lifestyle for fear of legal repercussions).

The four women pictured above are all wives of Kody Brown, shown in the middle of this photograph. Their story of living a polygamous life is the focus of the TLC show *Sister Wives*. Why has television shown so much interest in this type of family?

The final category of deviant acts is called **consensus crimes**. Acts in this group are illegal, perceived to be very harmful to society as a whole, and have a high level of public agreement regarding their seriousness. Murder and sexual assault are typically categorized as consensus crimes. They are seen as extremely harmful to society, and the vast majority of individuals agree that they are very wrong. These crimes carry severe punishments, ranging from long jail sentences to (in some countries) capital punishment.

One form of deviance that has high social costs and a negative impact on society is **white-collar crime**. This type of crime often occurs in a work setting and is motivated by monetary gain; it does not involve intentional or direct acts of violence. White-collar crime can be small in scale, such as stealing from one's workplace. However, there are also more serious acts, such as the ones that helped to cause the 2008 housing market crisis in the United States. White-collar crime is discussed less often and involves less stigma than other types of crimes despite the fact that it has serious social consequences and is much more costly for society as a whole. Conflict theorists argue that the reason for this is that those who commit such crimes have a great deal of social and economic power and can thus avoid punishments or even prosecution.

Social Construction

The theory of **social construction** was developed by Peter L. Berger and Thomas Luckmann. In *The Social Construction of Reality* (1966), they argue that all knowledge is created and maintained by social interactions. When we interact with other people, we reinforce our common knowledge of reality as well as our understanding of how society is and should be. In this interaction, we also shape each other's definition of the situation.

These ideas might sound familiar. Social construction is based on the symbolic interactionist perspective, discussed in Chapter 2. Remember that the main basis of symbolic interactionist theory is that meanings do not naturally attach to things—we derive meaning and come to understand our society and our role in it through interacting with other people. Just like the symbolic interactionists Cooley and Mead, Berger and Luckmann argue that we internalize a predefined world. We learn about this world through the process of socialization and interaction with socializing agents, such as our parents and friends.

Berger and Luckman (1966) explain that social construction is a two-step process. First, people categorize experiences, then act on the basis of this information. Second, they forget the social origins of categories and classifications, seeing them as natural and unchanging. For example, different societies have arbitrarily categorized time in different ways throughout history—from 3- to 19-day weeks. Once we divided time into a seven-day week, as we have in our society, we set up practices such as market days and religious days that function within this particular configuration. These days become routine as we set up our lives around them—for instance, many of us do not work on the weekends because they are religious days. We have forgotten that the seven-day week is a somewhat random social creation that could be organized in another way. Instead, we have come to see it as a natural and unchangeable way of doing things.

The Social Construction of Deviance

Our ideas about deviance are socially constructed. The norms we define as important in our society are always changing and are different across cultures. Because these norms are always evolving, it is clear that there is nothing "natural" about what we consider deviant (or even criminal). What we label as deviant changes when the norms and values of a society change. Being gay was long considered deviant in Canada. In the early years after Confederation, homosexual activity was a crime that could lead to the death penalty (although there is no surviving record of any individuals being executed for it in Canada). In fact, homosexuality was not decriminalized in Canada until 1969. Upon repealing the law, then minister of justice Pierre Elliot Trudeau famously said, "There's no place for the state in the bedrooms of the nation."

In Canada and other countries, attitudes toward the LGBTQ community are becoming increasingly tolerant, with

ZUMA Press, Inc. / Alamy Stock Photo

PHOTO 3.1 In one of the more highly publicized cases of white-collar crime, businesswoman and tv personality Martha Stewart was convicted of insider trading in 2004. As part of her sentence, she served five months in federal prison. When you think about criminals, do you tend to think about people such as Stewart? Why or why not?

laws legalizing gay marriage, adoption, and other spousal rights and benefits for gay couples. It is now illegal to discriminate against individuals based on their sexual orientation or to promote hatred against any group based on colour, race, sexual orientation, religion, or ethnic group (which is known as a hate crime). However, simply decriminalizing homosexual activity does not mean that same-sex relationships are no longer considered deviant or are accepted by all members of the public. Furthermore, many countries still consider engaging in homosexual activity highly deviant and punish this behaviour with the death penalty (see Figure 3.1). The changing norms around homosexuality in Canada and around the world illustrate the socially constructed nature of crime and deviance.

Émile Durkheim thought about crime and deviance in a very unconventional way. Instead of portraying crime and deviance as a negative force in society, Durkheim (1982) suggested that these things are necessary, functional, and even good for a society. He noted that all societies have crime and deviance; that is, there is a **normality of crime**. In addition, he argued that deviance and crime cannot be eliminated because they are important and functional.

According to Durkheim (1982), deviance has four basic functions. First, it affirms cultural values and norms. When people commit an act of deviance, it helps others to understand the rules of society—we know that a rule is important if breaking it is labelled as deviant. In this way, deviance is needed to define and sustain morality in society. Second, society's response to a deviant act helps individuals understand what is right and what is wrong. We cannot learn what is and is not acceptable without illustrations of people breaking rules. Third, responding to deviance helps unite individuals in society. For example, when someone commits a mass murder, members of society feel shocked and alarmed. Seeing that others feel the same way affirms the severity of the deviance and brings people together. Finally, deviance can encourage social change. Durkheim argued that today's deviant can be tomorrow's beacon of morality. Important leaders of social movements, such as Louis Riel, Martin Luther King, Jr, and Rosa Parks, were considered deviant in their time because they broke norms. Now considered heroes, they are recognized for helping to change values and norms in their societies, particularly the acceptance of people from various ethnic and racial groups.

FIGURE 3.1   **Laws on criminalization of homosexuality and legalization of gay marriage by country, 2016**

Source: Adapted from Christina Nunez, 2016, "Map Shows Where Being LGBT Can Be Punishable by Law," *National Geographic* 16 July, http://news.nationalgeographic.com/2016/06/lgbt-laws-gay-rights-world-map. NG Maps.

Everett Collection Inc / Alamy Stock Photo

PHOTO 3.2 Television programs such as *Judge Judy* allow viewers to get a peek inside how the laws and rules of our society are applied (albeit in a very artificial forum). How is this "functional" for society as a whole?

Daytime talk shows such as *Maury, Dr. Phil, and Judge Judy* illustrate Durkheim's first three functions of deviance. Many consider the guests on such shows to be deviant—they cheat on their spouses, steal from their parents, or have children with men who deny being the father. The audience members, in the studio and at home, enjoy watching these shows partly because they get to sit in judgment of the people on the stage. By seeing people who are clearly breaking the norms of society, the audience feels a sense of solidarity because they believe that society's norms and rules are clear (and they get satisfaction from knowing that they follow those rules while the guests do not).

ACTIVITY

The Changing Social Construction of Deviance

Even within the same society, individuals have different ideas about what counts as deviance and the seriousness of various deviant acts. And it is clear that some people's definition of what is deviant is more influential than others. For example, people who make laws (elected officials) and who apply those laws (such as police officers) have more authority to define deviance in consequential ways. Consider the items in this list, and answer the following questions:

- downloading music without paying
- cheating on your romantic partner
- using steroids to improve athletic performance
- hitting a child as punishment
- taking Adderall to study late for an exam
- dating someone from a different ethnic group
- abstaining from alcohol in any context
- hitting your spouse
- getting a tattoo
- killing someone
- having sex before marriage
- punching someone in a fight
- driving after drinking alcohol

1. Rank these acts in terms of their severity. Which ones do you consider the most and least serious acts of deviance?
2. Which of these acts are illegal in Canada? Which are legal in Canada but illegal elsewhere?
3. What acts are now considered less serious than they were in the past? Which are considered more serious?
4. How do different groups of people vary in their attitudes about the seriousness of these acts? How would your grandparents, religious leader, friends, or other people in your life answer these questions differently?
5. How is power related to defining deviance? What groups have more power to define deviance and to make their definitions dominant in society as a whole? How is power related to deciding on the punishments for different deviant acts?
6. Would you answer these questions differently in a different context? If yes, give an example. Which deviant acts in the list might be acceptable in certain contexts?

Why Are People Deviant?

Scholars have developed many theories in an attempt to explain why people are deviant or commit crimes. Some of these theories look at individual-level explanations. Most of the theories that sociologists use, however, are based on broader social explanations for an individual's propensity to engage in deviance or break the law.

Individual Explanations of Deviance and Crime

Individual-level explanations of crime generally focus on the deviant or criminal's character (Collins 1992). The logic behind these explanations is, for example, that thieves steal because they are greedy and murderers kill because they are aggressive. Some arguments are grounded in biology, such as the theory that criminals are genetically defective, predisposed to crime, or have too much testosterone. The idea that criminals are "simply bad people" and their deviant propensities come from within generally leads to support for severe punishments, such as the death penalty or long jail sentences. After all, if criminals are just "bad apples," nothing can be done to rehabilitate them; therefore, we should reduce the potential harm they can do by removing them from society. However, as Collins notes, there is little empirical evidence to support the claim that more punitive reactions to crime significantly reduce crime rates. We will discuss punishment and its effects later in this chapter.

Social Explanations of Deviance and Crime

Unlike individual explanations, social explanations seek to understand criminal activity as a product of the criminal's environment, particularly how it shapes his actions. Sociologists use a wide variety of these explanations, which originate from the different theoretical perspectives we have discussed in this book.

Strain theory argues that some individuals' goals and opportunities for success do not match (Merton 1957). If, for example, criminals come from broken homes and low-income neighbourhoods and lack opportunities to change their social conditions, they may experience strain. An individual might want to make enough money to be self-sufficient but be unable to get a well-paying job. Thus, he could turn to crime to fulfill this aspiration.

Subcultural theory focuses on the role of culture in crime. Stanley Cohen (2011) argues that gangs and other criminal organizations are subcultures with norms and values different from those of the larger culture. As such, we can understand these gangs as a collective adaptation to social conditions and a rejection of the establishment's cultural goals. For example, beating someone up to defend a friend might be seen as both legitimate and necessary within gang subculture.

Tara Walton/Toronto Star via Getty Images

PHOTO 3.3 Participants at the Community Walk of Hope for Peace in Toronto bring attention to the death of Abshir Hassan and other victims of gun violence.

Elijah Anderson's famous study, *Code of the Streets* (1999), uses both strain and subcultural theories to explore the street-oriented subculture of American inner-city ghettos. Through participant observation, Anderson tries to understand how young minority men living in these ghettos search for respect and how this search can create the need for aggressive, violent, and criminal behaviour. He explains that the consequence of this relentless pursuit of respect is a vicious cycle that begins with the hopelessness and alienation many inner-city youth feel at the hands of joblessness and racism in mainstream culture and leads to violence as a means of gaining respect. This violence, in turn, reinforces the negative perceptions many whites and middle-class individuals have about the ghetto poor, thus legitimating the code of the streets in the eyes of the minority youths.

RESEARCH METHOD
PARTICIPANT
OBSERVATION

Anderson (1999, 9) writes that the code's basic requirement is "the display of a certain predisposition to violence" and "mayhem," which may include fighting, exacting revenge, or stealing "trophy" objects (such as clothes or girlfriends). Young men ascribing to the code of the streets often use violence and the threat of violence to "campaign for respect." Children from street-oriented homes, for example, spend a great deal of time "hanging" with their peers on the streets, thus making their primary social bonds and social interactions with their friends rather than their parents. The toughest person in this context is often the one who garners the most respect.

Consistent with subcultural theory, this important work highlights how the norms and values that groups follow can be quite different, even within the same society, and how the social context can influence individuals' behaviour. In many ways, it is rational for young minority men living in US ghettos to act violently and criminally if that is what it takes to survive. These same behaviours would be irrational in a middle-class suburban context.

Developed by Edwin Sutherland (1947), **learning theory** is an extension of strain and subcultural theories. Sutherland argued that different environments provide opportunities to learn to engage in deviance and crime. The saying "The best place to learn how to be a criminal is in jail" epitomizes the logic behind learning theory—if people interact with and are exposed to criminals, they learn to engage in criminal behaviour. Via the social interaction that occurs in jail, for example, individuals learn a new set of skills. Sitting in a prison cafeteria might lead to a conversation about how best to steal a car without getting caught or how to justify to oneself that committing crimes is acceptable. This argument is based on ideas about the importance of socialization (see Chapter 2).

Travis Hirschi's (2004) **control theory** also focuses on social context's role in deviant and criminal behaviour. He argues that weak social control can lead individuals to engage in deviant or criminal acts. A number of factors can result in weak control. An individual might not have close relationships with her parents, teachers, or peer group. Or individuals can have weak institutional involvement if they are not actively engaged in organizations such as religious institutions, schools, sports teams, or other groups. Individuals can also have weak beliefs in traditional values. Finally, individuals can have limited opportunities for success if, for example, there is high unemployment or a lack of access to education where they live. Most people are integrated in these four ways and thus are less likely to engage in deviance. This theory might remind you of Durkheim's theory of suicide. Remember, Durkheim argued that individuals who are well integrated into their community and peer groups are less likely to commit suicide, arguably an act of deviance because it breaks a social norm.

These social explanations of crime focus on why individuals might be more or less likely to commit crimes based on their social environment. **Labelling theory** (just like symbolic interactionist theory) explores how we respond to deviant or criminal acts and how this reaction (or label) can either increase or decrease an individual's propensity to engage in further deviance. This theory originated in the work of Howard Becker (1963), who argues that almost all young people engage in deviant behaviour but only some get caught. If a young person is apprehended by authorities and is actually arrested, charged, convicted, and sentenced, her life can be significantly affected in a negative way. It is not the deviant behaviour, per se, that leads to the later problems. Instead, being labelled deviant can create a deviant or criminal identity for the young person. Once an individual is labelled a criminal, she may find it difficult to get a job and may turn to illegitimate means, such as crime, to make money. Labelling involves a process by which identifying someone as a criminal can produce a self-fulfilling prophecy. Collins (1992, 99) explains that the response to deviance is critical in labelling theory:

> The labelling theory declares that crime is actually created by the process of getting caught. Unlike the previous types of theories that we looked at, the personal characteristics of the individuals, or their social class or ethnic or neighborhood background, is not a crucial point. It is assumed that all sorts of people violate the law. But only some of them get caught, are prosecuted, labeled and all the rest, thereby becoming full-fledged criminals. If criminals who go through the courts and the prisons are so often likely to be disproportionately poor, black, or otherwise fit someone's idea of "social undesirables" or the "socially deprived," it is because these are the types of people who are most likely to be apprehended and prosecuted.

In sum, labelling theory posits that when a person is caught and labelled as a deviant or a criminal, they become stigmatized and viewed as a criminal by others. This situation also creates a process of identity formation—people begin to adopt the identity of "deviant." As a result, individuals sometimes change the way they view themselves and engage in deviant or criminal behaviour to fulfill this social role or identity.

It is important, from a labelling theory perspective, to differentiate between primary and secondary acts of deviance. **Primary deviance** includes early, random acts of deviance. This sort of deviance is very common, and most people have, at some point, engaged in primary deviant activity. **Secondary deviance**, however, is much more serious. The result of persistent deviant behaviour, it can often cause an individual to organize his life and identity around being "deviant."

Take, for example, a young boy who gets into a fight at school. If this were his first act of deviance, labelling theory would encourage us not to label him a deviant or criminal. But if the boy were arrested for his behaviour, others would likely label him a deviant and a "bad kid." Over time, it would be hard for him to find a job or other opportunities because everyone knows he is a "bad seed." In this way, it is not so much the act of deviance but how we as a society respond to it that leads to more (or less) deviance.

HIGHLIGHT

Police Handling of Sexual Assault Allegations across Canada

When you report a crime to the police, usually a police officer will interview you and investigate. They are trying to find out if a crime occurred and if there is a good chance of successfully prosecuting this crime. There are many ways that a case can be closed without the police laying a charge. For example, the police might think there is not enough evidence to move forward, or the complainant may not want to proceed with pressing charges. However, police officers can also close a case by labelling it "unfounded." Closing a case as "unfounded" means that the police officer thinks that no crime was attempted or occurred.

A 20-month long investigation by *The Globe and Mail* shows that police dismiss one in five sexual assault claims as baseless, or "unfounded" (Doolittle 2017). This report is the result of data collected by journalist Robyn Doolittle, who gathered information from more than 870 police forces and exposed the ways that these decisions were made and the flaws in the process.

It is important to note that unfounded cases could, of course, occur as a result of malicious or mistaken reports. Between 2 and 8 per cent of sexual assault complaints are false, according to

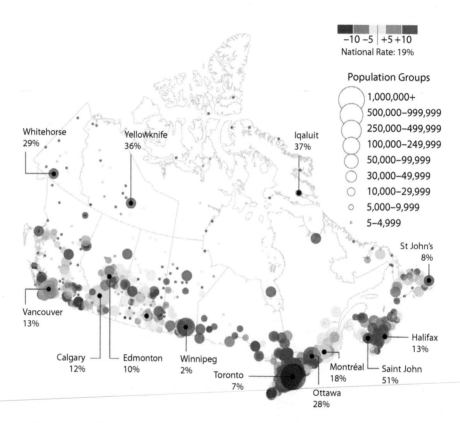

FIGURE 3.2   "Unfounded" sexual assault rate, by city

Source: Robyn Doolittle, 2017, "Unfounded: Why Police Dismiss 1 in 5 Sexual Assault Claims as Baseless," The *Globe and Mail* 3 February, https://www.theglobeandmail.com/news/investigations/unfounded-sexual-assault-canada-main/article33891309l. By permission of The Globe and Mail, source: Statscanada, 2016 Census.

The Canadian Youth Criminal Justice Act recognizes the importance of labelling. Under this act, it is illegal to publish the identity of a young offender. One of the purposes of this legislation is to help young people avoid being labelled as deviant and stigmatized. Keeping a young offender's identity private could help to prevent primary deviance from being translated into secondary deviance and increase the chance that youthful deviance will not lead to a life of crime.

research in North America, the UK, and Australia. This is similar to the rate of false reporting of other crimes. However, the 20 per cent rate of "unfounded" closures for sexual assault far exceeds this. And this rate is twice the rate of "unfounded" case closures for physical assault (which are "unfounded" only 10 per cent of the time).

It is also notable that the rate of "unfounded" is very different across police departments. In Toronto, you only have a 7 per cent chance of being "unfounded," whereas your chance of being categorized as "unfounded" is 51 per cent in Saint John. Essentially, half of all sexual assault claims made to the police in Saint John are closed because the police think that no crime has occurred. Imagine this happening with physical assault or some other crime.

Why might there be such different rates of "unfounded" across police departments? These differences could be the result of inadequate training for police officers, dated interviewing techniques that do not take into account the effect that trauma can have on memory, and the persistence of rape myths among law-enforcement officials.

It is important to note that this research has had important implications for how police deal with sexual assault complaints. For example, Ottawa once had very high rates of "unfounded" classifications for sexual assault—34 per cent in 2010. After much criticism, the police force instituted a set of new practices to address this high rate. They increased training for the police officers on how to classify cases, added additional oversight to catch mistakes, and increased training in how to interview claimants. By 2014, the "unfounded" rate had dropped to 12 per cent. However, police handling of sexual assault remains a significant problem and needs further investigation in order to better deal with potential victims, assailants, and the community as a whole.

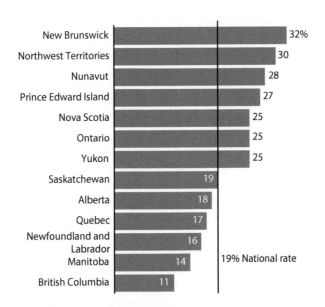

FIGURE 3.3   "Unfounded" rates by province

The national rate covers 89 per cent of Canada's population. The percentage of the population covered in each province is as follows. NB 95%, NT 100%, NU 100%, PE 73%, NS 99%, ON 99%, YT 100%, SK 97%, AB 66%, QC 73%, NL 100%, MB

Source: Robyn Doolittle, 2017, "Unfounded: Why Police Dismiss 1 in 5 Sexual Assault Claims as Baseless," The *Globe and Mail* 3 February, https://www.theglobeandmail.com/news/investigations/unfounded-sexual-assault-canada-main/article33891309. By permission of The Globe and Mail, source: Statscan, 2016 Census.

Social explanations generally advocate for rehabilitative punishments and crime prevention by focusing on contextual factors, such as reducing concentrated poverty and facilitating access to education and employment. Some of these theories, including labelling theory, shift the emphasis away from the offender and his environment and toward the response to the deviant act. Proponents of labelling theory tend to promote programs that divert youths caught engaging in criminal acts from the courts and into community service as a means to avoid labelling them as a criminal too hastily.

RESEARCH METHOD
EXPERIMENT

D.L. Rosenhan's article illustrates the process of labelling. Rosenhan had eight mentally and physically healthy volunteers admitted to a mental hospital to see how they would be treated once they were labelled insane as well as how long it would take for them to be labelled sane and released.

READING

On Being Sane in Insane Places

D.L. Rosenhan

If sanity and insanity exist, how shall we know them?

The question is neither capricious nor itself insane. However much we may be personally convinced that we can tell the normal from the abnormal, the evidence is simply not compelling. It is commonplace, for example, to read about murder trials wherein eminent psychiatrists for the defence are contradicted by equally eminent psychiatrists for the prosecution on the matter of the defendant's sanity. . . .

To raise questions regarding normality and abnormality is in no way to question the fact that some behaviours are deviant or odd. Murder is deviant. So, too, are hallucinations. Nor does raising such questions deny the existence of the personal anguish that is often associated with "mental illness." Anxiety and depression exist. Psychological suffering exists. But normality and abnormality, sanity and insanity, and the diagnoses that flow from them may be less substantive than many believe them to be.

At its heart, the question of whether the sane can be distinguished from the insane (and whether degrees of insanity can be distinguished from each other) is a simple matter: Do the salient characteristics that lead to diagnoses reside in the patients themselves or in the environments and contexts in which observers find them? . . .

Gains can be made in deciding which of these is more nearly accurate by getting normal people (that is, people who do not have, and have never suffered, symptoms of serious psychiatric disorders) admitted to psychiatric hospitals and then determining whether they were discovered to be sane and, if so, how. If sanity of such pseudopatients were always detected, there would be prima facie evidence that a sane individual can be distinguished from the insane context in which he is found. Normality (and presumably abnormality) is distinct enough that it can be recognized wherever it occurs, for it is carried within the person. If, on the other hand, the sanity of the pseudopatients were never discovered, serious difficulties would arise for those who support traditional modes of psychiatric diagnosis. Given that the hospital staff was not incompetent, that the pseudopatient had been behaving as sanely as he had been outside of the hospital, and that it had never been previously suggested that he belonged in a psychiatric hospital, such an unlikely outcome would support the view that psychiatric diagnosis betrays little about the patient but much about the environment in which an observer finds him.

This article describes such an experiment. Eight sane people gained secret admission to 12 different hospitals. . . .

Pseudopatients and Their Settings

The eight pseudopatients were a varied group. One was a psychology graduate student in his twenties. The remaining seven were older and "established." Among them were three psychologists, a pediatrician, a psychiatrist, a painter, and a housewife. Three pseudopatients were women, five were men. All of them employed pseudonyms, lest their alleged diagnoses embarrass them later. Those who were in mental health

Rosenhan, D.L. 1973. "On Being Sane in Insane Places." *Science*, 179 (19 January): 250–8.

professions alleged another occupation in order to avoid the special attentions that might be accorded by staff, as a matter of courtesy or caution, to ailing colleagues. With the exception of myself (I was the first pseudopatient and my presence was known to the hospital administrator and chief psychologist and, so far as I can tell, to them alone), the presence of pseudopatients and the nature of the research program was not known to the hospital staffs.

The settings were similarly varied. In order to generalize the findings, admission into a variety of hospitals was sought. The 12 hospitals in the sample were located in 5 different states on the East and West coasts. Some were old and shabby, some were quite new. Some were research-oriented, others not. Some had good staff–patient ratios, others were quite understaffed. Only one was a strictly private hospital. All of the others were supported by state or federal funds or, in one instance, by university funds.

After calling the hospital for an appointment, the pseudopatient arrived at the admissions office complaining that he had been hearing voices. Asked what the voices said, he replied that they were often unclear, but as far as he could tell they said "empty," "hollow," and "thud." The voices were unfamiliar and were of the same sex as the pseudopatient. The choice of these symptoms was occasioned by their apparent similarity to existential symptoms. Such symptoms are alleged to arise from painful concerns about the perceived meaninglessness of one's life. It is as if the hallucinating person were saying, "My life is empty and hollow." The choice of these symptoms was also determined by the absence of a single report of existential psychoses in the literature.

Beyond alleging the symptoms and falsifying name, vocation, and employment, no further alterations of person, history, or circumstances were made. The significant events of the pseudopatient's life history were presented as they had actually occurred. Relationships with parents and siblings, with spouse and children, with people at work and in school, consistent with the aforementioned exceptions, were described as they were or had been. Frustrations and upsets were described along with joys and satisfactions. These facts are important to remember. If anything, they strongly biased the subsequent results in favour of detecting sanity, since none of their histories or current behaviours were seriously pathological in any way.

Immediately upon admission to the psychiatric ward, the pseudopatient ceased simulating any symptoms of abnormality. In some cases, there was a brief period of mild nervousness and anxiety, since none of the pseudopatients really believed that they would be admitted so easily. Indeed, their shared fear was that they would be immediately exposed as frauds and greatly embarrassed. Moreover, many of them had never visited a psychiatric ward; even those who had nevertheless had some genuine fears about what might happen to them. Their nervousness, then, was quite appropriate to the novelty of the hospital setting, and it abated rapidly.

Apart from that short-lived nervousness, the pseudopatient behaved on the ward as he "normally" behaved. The pseudopatient spoke to patients and staff as he might ordinarily. Because there is uncommonly little to do on a psychiatric ward, he attempted to engage others in conversation. When asked by staff how he was feeling, he indicated that he was fine, that he no longer experienced symptoms. He responded to instructions from attendants, to calls for medication (which was not swallowed), and to dining-hall instructions. Beyond such activities as were available to him on the admissions ward, he spent his time writing down his observations about the ward, its patients, and the staff. Initially these notes were written "secretly," but as it soon became clear that no one much cared, they were subsequently written on standard tablets of paper in such public places as the dayroom. No secret was made of these activities.

The pseudopatient, very much as a true psychiatric patient, entered a hospital with no foreknowledge of when he would be discharged. Each was told that he would have to get out by his own devices, essentially by convincing the staff that he was sane. The psychological stresses associated with hospitalization were considerable, and all but one of the pseudopatients desired to be discharged almost immediately after being admitted. They were, therefore, motivated not only to behave sanely, but to be paragons of co-operation. That their behaviour was in no way disruptive is confirmed by nursing reports, which have been obtained on most of the patients. These reports uniformly indicate that the patients were "friendly," "co-operative," and "exhibited no abnormal indications."

The Normal Are Not Detectably Sane

Despite their public "show" of sanity, the pseudopatients were never detected. Admitted, except in one case, with a diagnosis of schizophrenia,[1] each was discharged with a diagnosis of schizophrenia "in remission." The label "in remission" should in no way be dismissed as a formality, for at no time during any hospitalization had any question been raised about any pseudopatient's simulation. Nor are there any indications in the hospital records that the pseudopatient's status was suspect. Rather, the evidence is strong that, once labelled schizophrenic, the pseudopatient was stuck with that label. If the pseudopatient was to be discharged, he must naturally be "in remission"; but he was not sane, nor, in the institution's view, had he ever been sane.

The uniform failure to recognize sanity cannot be attributed to the quality of the hospitals, for, although there were considerable variations among them, several are considered excellent. Nor can it be alleged that there was simply not enough time to observe the pseudopatients. Length of hospitalization ranged from 7 to 52 days, with an average of 19 days. The pseudopatients were not, in fact, carefully observed, but this failure speaks more to traditions within psychiatric hospitals than to lack of opportunity.

Finally, it cannot be said that the failure to recognize the pseudopatients' sanity was due to the fact that they were not behaving sanely. While there was clearly some tension present in all of them, their daily visitors could detect no serious behavioural consequences—nor, indeed, could other patients. It was quite common for the patients to "detect" the pseudopatient's sanity. During the first three hospitalizations, when accurate counts were kept, 35 of a total of 118 patients on the admissions ward voiced their suspicions, some vigorously. "You're not crazy. You're a journalist, or a professor [referring to the continual note-taking]. You're checking up on the hospital." While most of the patients were reassured by the pseudopatient's insistence that he had been sick before he came in but was fine now, some continued to believe that the pseudopatient was sane throughout his hospitalization. The fact that the patients often recognized normality when staff did not raises important questions.

Failure to detect sanity during the course of hospitalization may be due to the fact that physicians operate with a strong bias toward what statisticians call the type 2 error.[2] This is to say that physicians are more inclined to call a healthy person sick (a false positive, type 2) than a sick person healthy (a false negative, type 1). The reasons for this are not hard to find: it is clearly more dangerous to misdiagnose illness than health. Better to err on the side of caution, to suspect illness even among the healthy.

But what holds for medicine does not hold equally well for psychiatry. Medical illnesses, while unfortunate, are not commonly pejorative. Psychiatric diagnoses, on the contrary, carry with them personal, legal, and social stigmas.[3] It was therefore important to see whether the tendency toward diagnosing the sane insane could be reversed. . . .

The Stickiness of Psychodiagnostic Labels

Beyond the tendency to call the healthy sick—a tendency that accounts better for diagnostic behaviour on admission than it does for such behaviour after a lengthy period of exposure—the data speak to the massive role of labelling in psychiatric assessment. Having once been labelled schizophrenic, there is nothing the pseudopatient can do to overcome the tag. The tag profoundly colours others' perceptions of him and his behaviour. . . .

Once a person is designated abnormal, all of his other behaviours and characteristics are coloured by that label. Indeed, that label is so powerful that many of the pseudopatients' normal behaviours were overlooked entirely or profoundly misinterpreted. Some examples may clarify this issue. . . .

As far as I can determine, diagnoses were in no way affected by the relative health of the circumstances of a pseudopatient's life. Rather, the reverse occurred: the perception of his circumstances was shaped entirely by the diagnosis. A clear example of such translation is found in the case of a pseudopatient who had had a close relationship with his mother but was rather remote from his father during his early childhood. During adolescence and beyond, however, his father became a close friend, while his relationship with his mother cooled. His present relationship with his wife was characteristically close and warm. Apart from occasional angry exchanges, friction was minimal. The children had rarely been spanked. Surely there is nothing especially pathological about such a history. Indeed, many readers may see a similar pattern in their own experiences, with no markedly deleterious consequences. Observe, however, how such a history was translated in the psychopathological context, this from the case summary prepared after the patient was discharged.

> This white 39-year-old male . . . manifests a long history of considerable ambivalence in close relationships, which begins in early childhood. A warm relationship with his mother cools during his adolescence. A distant relationship to his father is described as becoming very intense. Affective stability is absent. His attempts to control emotionality with his wife and children are punctuated by angry outbursts and, in the case of the children, spankings. And while he says that he has several good friends, one senses considerable ambivalence embedded in those relationships also . . .

All pseudopatients took extensive notes publicly. Under ordinary circumstances, such behaviour would have raised questions in the minds of observers, as, in fact, it did among patients. Indeed, it seemed so certain that the notes would elicit suspicion that elaborate precautions were taken to remove them from the ward each day. But the precautions proved needless. The closest any staff member came to questioning those notes occurred when one pseudopatient asked his physician what kind of medication he was receiving and began to write down the response. "You needn't write it," he was told gently. "If you have trouble remembering, just ask me again."

If no questions were asked of the pseudopatients, how was their writing interpreted? Nursing records for three patients indicate that the writing was seen as an aspect of their pathological behaviour. "Patient engaged in writing behaviour" was the daily nursing comment on one of the pseudopatients who was never questioned about his writing. Given that the patient is in the hospital, he must be psychologically disturbed. And given that he is disturbed, continuous writing must be a behavioural manifestation of that disturbance, perhaps a subset of the compulsive behaviours that are sometimes correlated with schizophrenia.

One tacit characteristic of psychiatric diagnosis is that it locates the sources of aberration within the individual and only rarely within the complex of stimuli that surrounds him. Consequently, behaviours that are stimulated by the environment are commonly misattributed to the patient's disorder. For example, one kindly nurse found a pseudopatient pacing the long hospital corridors. "Nervous, Mr. X?" she asked. "No, bored," he said.

The notes kept by pseudopatients are full of patient behaviours that were misinterpreted by well-intentioned staff. Often enough, a patient would go "berserk" because he had, wittingly or unwittingly, been mistreated by, say, an attendant. A nurse coming upon the scene would rarely inquire even cursorily into the environmental stimuli of the patient's behaviour. Rather, she assumed that his upset derived from his pathology, not from his present interactions with other staff members. Occasionally, the staff might assume that the patient's family (especially when they had recently visited) or other patients had stimulated the outburst. But never were the staff found to assume that one of themselves or the structure of the hospital had anything to do with a patient's behaviour. One psychiatrist pointed to a group of patients who were sitting outside the cafeteria entrance half an hour before lunchtime. To a group of young residents he indicated that such behaviour was characteristic of the oral-acquisitive nature of the syndrome. It seemed not to occur to him that there were very few things to anticipate in a psychiatric hospital besides eating.

A psychiatric label has a life and an influence of its own. Once the impression has been formed that the patient is schizophrenic, the expectation is that he will continue to be schizophrenic. When a sufficient amount of time has passed, during which the patient has done nothing bizarre, he is considered to be in remission and available for discharge. But the label endures beyond discharge, with the unconfirmed expectation that he will behave as a schizophrenic again. Such labels, conferred by mental health professionals, are as influential on the patient as they are on his relatives and friends, and it should not surprise anyone that the diagnosis acts on all of them as a self-fulfilling prophecy. Eventually, the patient himself accepts the diagnosis, with all of its surplus meanings and expectations, and behaves accordingly.[4] . . .

CRITICAL READING QUESTIONS

1. How is this article an example of labelling theory? How did the diagnosis of "insane" lead to the symptoms observed by the staff?

2. Why does a false positive diagnosis of mental illness generally have more serious repercussions than a false positive diagnosis of physical illness?

3. What is the significance of the fact that many patients, but none of the staff, managed to detect pseudopatients?

4. What can this study teach us about why people engage in deviant acts and/or crime? How can it help us to better deal with people labelled deviant?

NOTES

1. Interestingly, of the 12 admissions, 11 were diagnosed as schizophrenic and 1, with the identical symptomatology, as manic-depressive psychosis. This diagnosis has a more favourable prognosis, and it was given by the only private hospital in our sample. On the relations between social class and psychiatric diagnosis, see A. deB. Hollingshead and F.C. Redlich, *Social Class and Mental Illness: A Community Study* (Wiley, New York, 1958).

2. T.J. Scheff, *Being Mentally Ill: A Sociological Theory* (Aldine, Chicago, 1966).

3. J. Cumming and E. Cumming, *Community Men. Health* 1, 135 (1965); A. Farina and K. Ring, *J. Abnorm. Psychol.* 70, 47 (1965); H.E. Freeman and O.G. Simmons, *The Mental Patient Comes Home* (Wiley, New York, 1963); W.J. Johannsen, *Ment. Hygiene* 53, 218 (1969); A.S. Linsky, *Soc. Psychiat.* 5, 166 (1970).

4. Scheff, *Being Mentally Ill*.

The Power of the Situation

On 30 January 2017, a man entered the Quebec Islamic Cultural Centre and opened fire. He was apprehended and pleaded guilty to six counts of first-degree murder and six attempted murder charges. This man was a student at Laval University and grew up in what was described as a happy home with both parents and a twin brother. He was not previously known to the police and had not been previously arrested. In the media coverage of the event, he was described as a "lone wolf" (Newton, Jones, and Yan 2017). How did this man go from what appears to be a "normal" life to committing such horrible hate crimes? And how might the fact that this man was white alter the type of media coverage this act received, particularly the fact that he was not described as a terrorist and his ethnicity and religion were not central to the coverage of his acts?

Two famous experiments have investigated why individuals who often have no past history of deviant or criminal behaviour can do such heinous things. Perpetrators sometimes justify their actions by saying that they were simply "following orders." In the 1960s, Stanley Milgram tested whether individuals are more likely to blindly follow orders from authority figures in certain conditions and, if so, how this behaviour affected people's treatment of one another. Ten years later, Philip Zimbardo conducted the Stanford Prison experiment, which explored how individuals' behaviours are shaped by the social context and social roles.

Milgram's (1963) experiment involved three people: an experimenter (an authoritative role), a volunteer (who acted as a teacher), and a learner (who was an actor paid by Milgram). The volunteer and the learner drew slips of paper to determine their roles; however, unknown to the volunteer, both slips said "Teacher." The actor would always play the learner role, and the volunteer would always be the teacher. Throughout the experiment, the learner and teacher were located in different rooms so that they could talk to but not see one another (see Photo 3.5). The teacher was instructed to teach the learner a list of word pairs. Each time the learner made a mistake, the teacher was to give him an electrical shock. The teacher was given a sample shock to get a sense of how strong it felt. After each wrong answer, the teacher was to increase the shock by 15 volts. In reality, there were no shocks. The learner set up a tape recorder integrated with the electroshock generator, which played pre-recorded sounds for each shock level. Partway through the experiment, after receiving several "shocks," the learner began to bang on the wall between him and the teacher. He then began complaining of a heart condition. Finally, there was silence from the learner's room.

As the learner demonstrated more serious signs of distress, most of the teachers wanted to stop the experiment. But the experimenter urged them to go on, saying, "The experiment requires that you continue"; "It is absolutely essential that you continue"; and "You have no other choice, you must go on." Milgram and his colleagues thought that most people would not continue to administer the shocks after hearing the distress of the learner, but 65 per cent (26 of 40) of the volunteers in the first set of the experiment administered the final, massive 450-volt shock, though many were very uncomfortable doing so. Milgram concluded that being assigned the role of teacher and having an authority figure giving instructions led many people to administer much stronger shocks than they would have otherwise.

In the Stanford Prison experiment, Zimbardo (Zimbardo, Maslach, and Haney 1999) recruited 24 mentally and physically healthy, middle-class, white males with no history of crime or emotional, physical, or social problems. Half of the participants were randomly assigned to the role of prisoner and half to the role of guard. Zimbardo placed these young men in a simulated prison in the basement of Stanford University to see how they would adapt to their assigned roles in this unfamiliar environment.

Zimbardo was astonished by the extent to which the participants adopted their roles. The guards enforced their authority over the prisoners, sometimes engaging in psychological torture. Many prisoners

RESEARCH METHOD EXPERIMENT

RESEARCH METHOD EXPERIMENT

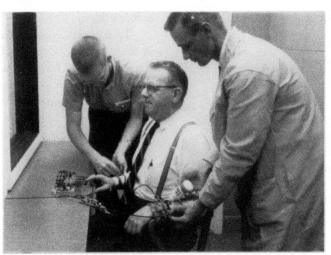

PHOTO 3.4 The Milgram experiment, "teacher" role. The teacher is being instructed in how to give electrical shocks to the "learner" (who is, unbeknown to them, an actor).

From the film Obedience (1968) by Stanley Milgram, renewed 1993 by Alexandra Milgram and distributed by Alexander Street Press

Philip G. Zimbardo, Inc.

PHOTO 3.5 Students in the roles of prisoner and guard in the Stanford Prison experiment.

passively accepted the abuse. Those who resisted the guards were harassed by the other prisoners. In fact, the treatment of the prisoners was so dire that two of the prisoners quit the experiment early and the experiment as a whole was stopped after only six days. As Zimbardo (in Aronson and Aronson 2011, 127) explains, "in less than a week the experience of imprisonment undid (temporarily) a lifetime of learning, human values were suspended, self-concepts were challenged and the ugliest, most base, pathological side of human nature surfaced."

These studies highlight how deviant behaviours are more likely and more severe in certain social settings. Both push us to understand that it is not just that some people are "bad" but that some situations can make people act in ways contrary to their usual selves. As Zimbardo (in Aronson and Aronson 2011, 128) argues, "individual behavior is largely under the control of social forces and environmental contingencies rather than personality traits, character, will power or other empirically unvalidated constructs." We thus expect that deviance is more likely in certain situations, such as when individuals enjoy anonymity (in Milgram's study, the volunteer is in a separate room from the person he is shocking; in Zimbardo's, the guards wear the same uniform and reflective glasses so that prisoners cannot see their eyes). Consider how the theories of crime and deviance we have learned about in this chapter support or contradict the findings of these studies.

Crime Rates

Crime has consequences at both the micro-individual level and the macro-social level. People who have been victims of crime are clearly affected by their experience; however, the existence of crime in a community can also affect residents' well-being and health (HRSDC 2013; Pittman et al. 2012). These serious implications are one reason that governments spend large amounts of money on trying to prevent and reduce crime.

To this end, governments must know how much and what types of crimes occur in their country. Conducted by Statistics Canada since 1962, the **Uniform Crime Reporting (UCR) Survey** collects information on all criminal incidents reported to, and substantiated by, Canadian police services. Using data from the UCR Survey, Figure 3.4 shows crime rates in Canada from 1962 to 2012. The crime rate is the incidence of a particular type of crime per 100,000 people in a population. The figure separates crimes that are violent, such as murder and sexual assault, from property crimes, such as robbery and breaking and entering. You will notice that crime rates were at their highest in 1991 and have been declining steadily since. Property crime experienced a particularly sharp drop; violent crimes decreased at a slower rate, although they have always occurred at much lower rates than property crime.

Measuring the severity of crime is also important. The **Crime Severity Index (CSI)** assigns each offence a weight based on the severity of the sentences handed down by the courts. For example, petty theft is less serious and results in shorter sentences than homicide. As shown in Figure 3.5, the CSI has declined every year since 2003 until 2015 when it increased for the first time in 12 years. Figures 3.6 and 3.7 show the rates of homicide (arguably the most severe crime) and break and enter/motor vehicle theft (less serious crimes). Although both offences are generally declining, the rate is much steeper for the property crimes.

RESEARCH METHOD
SURVEY

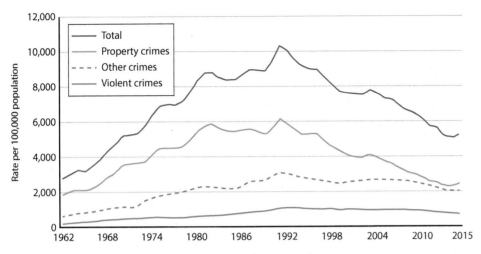

FIGURE 3.4 Police-reported crime rates, Canada, 1962–2015

Note: Information presented in this chart represents data from the UCR Aggregate (UCR1) Survey, and permits, historical comparisons back to 1962. New definitions of crime categories were introduced in 2009 and are only available in the new format back to 1998. As a result, numbers in this chapter will not match data release in the new UCR2 format. Specifically, the definition of violent crime has been expanded. In addition, UCR1 includes some different offences in the 'Other' crimes category. Populations are based upon July 1st estimates from Statistics Canada, Demography Division.

Source: Mary Allen, 2016, "Police-Reported Crime Statistics in Canada, 2015," *Juristat* 20 July, Catalogue no. 85-002-X, Ottawa, Statistics Canada, http://www.statcan.gc.ca/pub/85-002-x/2016001/article/14642-eng.htm

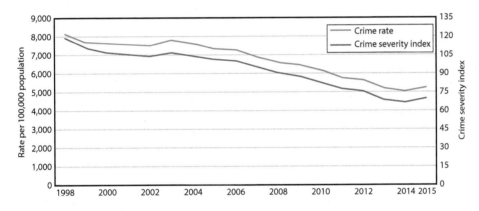

FIGURE 3.5   Police-Reported Crime Severity Indexes, 1998–2015

Note: Additional data are available on CANSIM (Tables 252-0051 and 252-0052). The crime rate is based upon Criminal Code incidents, excluding traffic offences. The Crime Severity Index (CSI) is based on Criminal Code incidents, including traffic offences, as well as other federal statute violations. For the CSI, the base index was set at 100 for 2006 for Canada. Populations are based upon July 1st estimates from Statistics Canada, Demography Division.

Source: Mary Allen, 2016, "Police-Reported Crime Statistics in Canada, 2015," *Juristat* 20 July, Catalogue no. 85-002-X, Ottawa: Statistics Canada, http://www.statcan.gc.ca/pub/85-002-x/2016001/article/14642-eng.htm

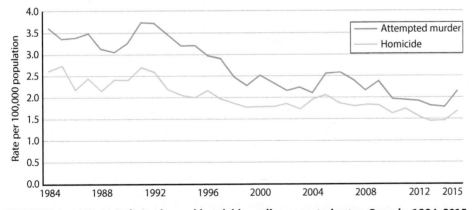

FIGURE 3.6   Attempted murder and homicide, police-reported rates, Canada, 1984–2015

Note: Additional data are available on CANSIM (Table 252–0051). Populations are based upon July 1st estimates from Statistics Canada, Demography Division.

Source: Mary Allen, 2016, "Police-Reported Crime Statistics in Canada, 2015," *Juristat* 20 July, Catalogue no. 85-002-X, Ottawa, Statistics Canada, http://www.statcan.gc.ca/pub/85-002-x/2016001/article/14642-eng.htm

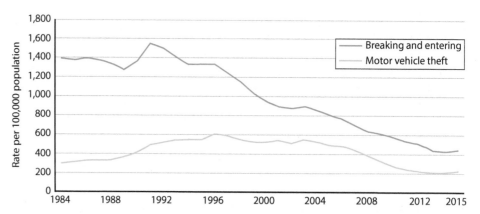

FIGURE 3.7   **Break and enter and motor vehicle theft, police-reported rates, Canada, 1984–2015**

Note: Additional data are available on CANSIM (Table 252–0051). Populations are based upon July 1st estimates fromStatistics Canada, Demography Division.

Source: Mary Allen, 2016, "Police-Reported Crime Statistics in Canada, 2015," *Juristat* 20 July, Catalogue no. 85-002-X, Ottawa: Statistics Canada, http://www.statcan.gc.ca/pub/85-002-x/2016001/article/14642-eng.htm

HIGHLIGHT

Comparing Crime around the World

Comparing crime rates across countries is difficult because laws, police practices, and crime classifications often differ. For example, marijuana possession is legal in the Netherlands, was legalized in Canada in 2018, and can lead to jail time in the United States. Murder is reported and tracked in all countries. The map shows that most of the Western world has relatively low murder rates compared to other regions. High murder rates tend to occur in countries with high levels

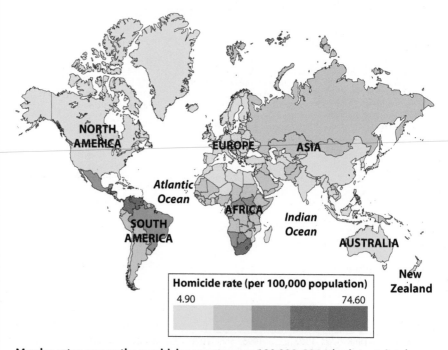

Murder rates across the world, by country, per 100,000, 2014 (or latest data)

Source: Kuang Keng Luek Ser, 2016, "Map: Here Are Countries with the World's Highest Murder Rates," *Pri's The World* 27 June, https://www.pri.org/stories/2016-06-27/map-here-are-countries-worlds-highest-murder-rates

of poverty, inequality, and discrimination. These differences partly account for the higher rates of murder in certain countries. Although this global comparison makes Canadian murder rates appear relatively low, many argue that comparing Canada with countries experiencing high levels of poverty and underdevelopment may not be a fair comparison. The first bar graph, "Homicide rate per 100,000, 2015," compares Canada's murder rate with that of some other industrialized countries. We can see that the Canadian murder rate, while much lower than the rate in the United States, is still relatively high when compared with that of some European countries and Australia.

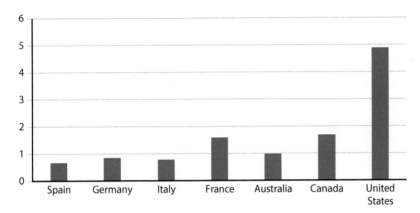

Homicide rate per 100,000, 2015

Source: Adaped from data from the United Nations Office on Drugs and Crime, 2015

The rate of gun ownership is another explanation given for higher crime rates in certain countries, particularly murder rates. Many more Americans than Canadians own guns—the number of guns per 100 people in the United States is about three times higher than it is in Canada (see bar graph, "Guns per 100 civilians"). The US murder rate is also about three times higher. While these statistics are interesting, we have to be cautious about drawing a connection between them. For example, gun ownership in the UK is about the same as it is in Canada; however, Britain's murder rate is much lower than ours.

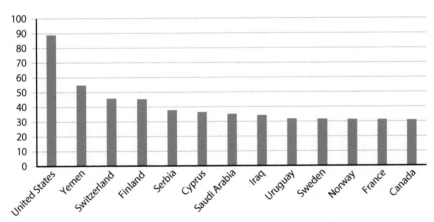

Guns per 100 civilians

Source: Adapted from CBC article on the Small Arms Survey, http://www.cbc.ca/news/world/small-arms-survey-countries-with-the-most-guns-1.3392204

It is also instructive to look at the prison population across countries. We can see in the final bar graph, "Prisoners per 100,000 population," that the Canadian prison population is similar to the rate in the UK and the Netherlands and much lower than that in the United States and Russia, which have around five times more prisoners per capita. Comparing rates across countries allows us to assess the extent to which Canada's laws, criminal justice system, and culture as a whole effectively handle and reduce crime.

Continued

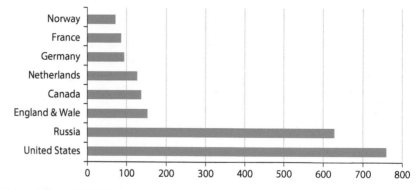

Prisoners per 100,000 population

Sources: Adapted from Ken MacQueen, 2009, "The Lowdown on Crime in Canada: We Have a Higher Murder Rate Than Germany and a Lower One Than Scotland," *Maclean's*, 1 July, http://www.macleans .ca/news/canada/the-lowdown-on-crime-in-canada-compared -to-other-countries; BBC News, 2018, *World Prison Populations*, http://news.bbc.co.uk/2/shared/spl/hi/uk/06/prisons/html/nn1page1 .stm; and Julie Reitano, 2016, "Adult Correctional Statistics in Canada, 2014/2015," *Juristat* 22 March, Catalogue no. 85-002-x, Ottawa: Statistics Canada, http://www.statcan.gc.ca/pub/85-002-x/2016001/ article/14318-eng.htm

PHOTO 3.6 Why are crimes such as shoplifting generally considered less serious? Would your opinion of someone change if you found out that she had shoplifted as a teenager? Why or why not?

Crime Rates by Group

Looking at a country's overall crime rate can demonstrate whether crime is increasing or decreasing and what types of crimes are most prevalent. However, these overall statistics mask some important differences between groups. Crime rates vary widely by age of the accused perpetrators. The peak age at which individuals commit crimes is 17, and individuals are most likely to commit crimes between the ages of 15 and 21 (see Figure 3.8). These youth crimes are usually acts of primary deviance and tend to be of low severity, such as drug use, shoplifting, and petty theft. In most cases, criminal behaviour ends with the onset of adulthood and adult responsibilities. After 60, people are highly unlikely to engage in criminal activity!

Crime rates also differ significantly by gender. In Canada, women account for only about 25 per cent of people accused of committing a Criminal Code offence (Statistics Canada 2017). This imbalance is most pronounced for violent crimes, such as homicide, for which women account for only about one-tenth of the accused. Women tend to be more evenly represented in crimes such as abduction, prostitution, and theft under $5000.

Interestingly, trends in crime for men and women have diverged over time. Crime by men has been declining for 20 years in Canada; however, crime by women has been increasing (Brennan 2013). Violent crime among women, in particular, has seen a notable increase. While the rate of male violent crime has decreased by 32 per cent since 1991, the rate of female violent crime has increased by 34 per cent. That said,

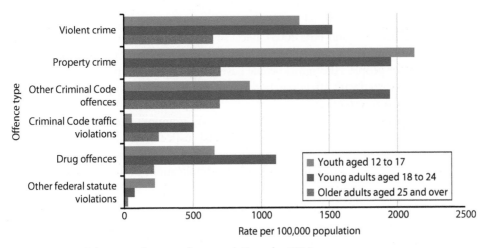

FIGURE 3.8   Crime rate by age of accused, Canada, 2014

Note: Rates are calculated on the basis of 100,000 population in each age group. Populations are based upon July 1st estimates from Statistics, Canada, Demography Division. Exudes accused where age is over 89.

Source: Statistics Canada, Mary K. Allen and Tamy Superle, 2014, "Youth Crime in Canada, 2014." *Juristat* 17 February, Catalogue no. 85-0020x, Ottawa: Statistics Canada, http://www.statcan.gc.ca/pub/85-002-x/ 2016001/article/14309-eng.htm

women have always been less likely than men to commit violent crimes, accounting for only 20 per cent of this type of crime in 2011.

Finally, there is a wide difference in crime rates by ancestry and race. A disproportionate number of Aboriginal and black Canadians are in the criminal justice system. Aboriginal people represent 4 per cent of the population but account for 23 per cent of federal inmates. The incarceration rate for Aboriginal adults is 10 times higher than the rate for non-Aboriginal adults in Canada. This number has continued to grow in the last decade, increasing by 6 per cent in this period (Correctional Services Canada, 2017).

Conflict theorists argue that the higher crime rates in these populations could be the result of low socio-economic status (SES) and lack of education, as well as high rates of victimization, substance abuse, and gang participation in Aboriginal and African-Canadian communities (Latimer and Foss 2004). In this way, the real predictor of engagement in

Calculating Crime Rates

The Government of Canada and the criminal justice system calculate the crime rate to give us a sense of the amount of types of crimes that occur in Canada. However, official statistics do not necessarily report *actual* rates of crime because not every criminal activity is reported and some activities reported to police are not crimes. Instead, these statistics are collected by using particular methods with particular limitations, constraints, and complications. Go to this book's companion website to access Samuel Perreault's "Police-Reported Crime Statistics in Canada, 2012." Read the article, and then answer the following questions:

1. How is the crime rate calculated? What is good about this traditional crime rate and what is missed?
2. How is the CSI better or worse than the traditional crime rate that Canada has used? (See Statistics Canada's "Section: 1 The Crime Severity Index," available at this book's companion website.)
3. Beyond the traditional crime rate and CSI, what other methods could be used to construct as comprehensive a crime rate as possible?
4. What are the benefits of using **victimization surveys** instead of a traditional crime rate? Why do victimization surveys usually show evidence of higher crime rates than do official statistics?

ACTIVITY

crime is poverty and other social problems, not race or ethnicity. Demographics could be another cause (Latimer and Foss 2005). Because Canada's Aboriginal population is significantly younger than its non-Aboriginal population and younger people commit more crime than older people, Aboriginal people have a higher probability of being in the age group most associated with offending. In this way, crime rates by group can indicate other inequalities between groups of Canadians.

The following reading from *Maclean's* magazine examines the inequality that Indigenous people face at every level of the criminal justice system. When reading this article, consider how larger issues of inequality are related to the high levels of incarceration among Indigenous people in Canada and the implications of this discrimination for Canadian society as a whole.

Canada's Prisons Are the New Residential Schools

Nancy Macdonald

PHOTO 3.E Canada's crime rate just hit a 45-year low. It's been dropping for years—down by half since peaking in 1991. Bizarrely, the country recently cleared another benchmark, when the number of people incarcerated hit an all-time high. Dig a little further into the data, and an even more disquieting picture emerges.

Source: Millar, Erin. 2016 "Survey indicates Indigenous people targeted by police in Prairie provinces." *The Discourse*. February 18.

Macdonald, Nancy. 2016. "Canada's Prisons Are the 'New Residential Schools.'" *Maclean's* 18 February. https://www.macleans.ca/news/canada/canadas-prisons-are-the-new-residential-schools.

While admissions of white adults to Canadian prisons declined through the last decade, Indigenous incarceration rates were surging: Up 112 per cent for women. Already, 36 per cent of the women and 25 per cent of men sentenced to provincial and territorial custody in Canada are Indigenous—a group that makes up just four per cent of the national population. Add in federal prisons, and Indigenous inmates account for 22.8 per cent of the total incarcerated population.

In the U.S., the go-to example for the asymmetric jailing of minority populations, black men are six times more likely to be imprisoned than white men. In Canada, the Indigenous incarceration rate is 10 times higher than the non-Indigenous population—higher even than South Africa at the height of apartheid. In Saskatchewan, if you're Indigenous, you're 33 times more likely to be incarcerated, according to a 1999 report, the most recent available.

This helps explain why prison guard is among the fastest-growing public sector occupations on the Prairies. And why criminologists have begun quietly referring to Canada's prisons and jails as the country's "new residential schools."

In some Prairie courtrooms, Indigenous defendants now make up 85 per cent of criminal caseloads, defence lawyers say. At Manitoba's Women's Correctional Centre in Headingley, as many as nine in 10 women were Indigenous, according to one recent count. At nearby Stony Mountain Institution, Indigenous men make up 65 per cent of the inmate population. Often, they're there because they failed to comply with a curfew or condition of bail. Or they're a low-level drug offender, caught up in Canada's harsh new mandatory-minimum sentences.

That's one reason for the upsurge. In the past decade, Stephen Harper's government passed more than 30 new crime laws, hiking punishment for a wide range of crimes, limiting parole opportunities and also broadening the grounds used to send young offenders to jail.

But the problem isn't just new laws. Although police "carding" in Toronto has put street checks, which disproportionately target minority populations, under the microscope, neither is racial profiling alone to blame. At every step, discriminatory practices and a biased system work against an Indigenous accused, from the moment a person is first identified by police, to their appearance before a judge, to their hearing before a parole board. The evidence is unambiguous: If you happen to be Indigenous, justice in Canada is not blind.

Chapter 1 – The street check

On Dec. 10, 2014, Simon Ash-Moccasin, a Regina teacher, actor and playwright, was walking to a holiday party for Briarpatch magazine, where he sits as a board member. He says officers began tailing him as he approached Casino Regina in the city's downtown core. Ash-Moccasin "fit a description," he was told after asking why he was being stopped. "I know which one that is," the Cree-Saulteaux 41-year-old later told Maclean's. "There's only one."

Ash-Moccasin has a good understanding of arrest protocol thanks to an acting gig with the Saskatchewan Police College, teaching trainee officers how not to collar a suspect. He plays the bad guy.

In real life, Ash-Moccasin initially refused to give his name. An officer threw him against a wall, he says. One attempted to cuff him without reading him his rights. He says he was shoved, headfirst, into the backseat. He was briefly detained until his record check came back clean. Before being released, officers told Ash-Moccasin, who was wearing a distinctive green camouflage jacket, that they were looking for an Indigenous man dressed all in black, with no front teeth, trying to hawk a TV.

Ash-Moccasin is among several Indigenous men and women in Prairie cities who allege they are being unfairly, and illegally, singled out.

To approach the issue from a different perspective, Maclean's and Discourse Media (with the support of Canadian Journalists for Free Expression) surveyed more than 850 post-secondary students in Regina, Saskatoon and Winnipeg, to see whether there was any difference in the likelihood of being stopped for Indigenous and non-Indigenous students.

Survey results show the odds of an Indigenous student from the sampled population being stopped by police were 1.6 times higher than a non-Indigenous student, holding all other explanatory variables (like gender and age) fixed. Indigenous students will be stopped more frequently, the study indicates; whether or not they were engaged in or close to an illegal activity when stopped by police had little influence in explaining the results. This suggests staying out of trouble does not shield Indigenous student from unwanted police attention.

The survey produced other unsettling data. Indigenous students were more likely to "disagree" or "strongly disagree" that their racial group is viewed positively by police. An Indigenous student had a 69 to 84 per cent chance of "disagreeing" or "strongly disagreeing," depending on their age; a non-Indigenous student had a 10 to 21 per cent chance of responding the same way. Students were also asked to share three words that they feel describe police officers. The most common words non-Indigenous students associate with police—"helpful," "authority"—differed dramatically from those chosen by Indigenous students: "racist," "scary."

Criminals, meanwhile, have learned to exploit biases. In Saskatchewan, non-Indigenous men and women are recruited to carry drugs and weapons for Indigenous gangs, says Robert Henry, a Saskatoon academic whose PhD research focused on Indigenous street gangs. "They use their whiteness to move around police stop checks."

Police say complaints of racial profiling are without substance. The Saskatchewan Public Complaints Commission, which investigates complaints against municipal police, says not a single allegation of racism by a civilian against an officer with any municipal police force in the province has ever been substantiated. Police say random street checks are necessary, acting as deterrents, helping solve crime and keeping the public safe.

There are signs tactics may be changing. The Winnipeg Police Service, under Chief Devon Clunis, who was raised in the city's troubled North End, is testing a new approach to policing in that neighbourhood. Dubbed the "Block-by-Block" program, it zeroes attention on a 21-block area, and brings families concentrated help from social service and health agencies, community groups and schools to try to tackle problems—like substance abuse or domestic violence—before police need to be called. "From day one, I said, 'We are going to dramatically change the way we police in this city,'" Clunis told Maclean's. He calls it "crime prevention through social development." Results are due in spring.

But for those repeatedly targeted by police attention, the impact can be profound. "It makes you feel like you're less human, like your life is worth less," says Bear, who was nine the first time he was first stopped, walking home from school in downtown Saskatoon. He's stopped every few months, he says: "When I was younger it made me ashamed—of having brown skin, of growing up where I did."

Chapter 2 – Bail denied

On a recent day, some 70 per cent of defendants who parade past a judge via video link from the Winnipeg Remand Centre are Indigenous, many dressed in jail-issue, baggy, grey sweatsuits. It is a grim cattle call: The Indigenous 18-year-old female accused of stealing meat from a Superstore, the 19-year-old man from Shamattawa, Man., given 25 days for missing a parole check-in. He's been homeless since aging out of foster care, where he was abused and repeatedly left out in the cold. When they pleaded out, their cases often wrapped up in under five minutes, sentencing included. This is bail court, and it is here, at this early stage ahead of trial—with its rigorous standards of due process and proof—that a criminal defendant is most vulnerable. For a majority of Indigenous accused, their case ends here, multiple front-line lawyers told Maclean's.

Maclean's spent two days observing the scene. Duty counsel lawyers in Toronto and Winnipeg admit they rarely spend more than 10 minutes with a defendant. Sometimes, it's as little as five. In Winnipeg, some met them in court: In hushed, hurried phone calls—their hands over their mouths to muffle their words—these lawyers rushed through the deal on offer from the Crown. It was unclear whether some of the accused, with intellectual disabilities and fetal alcohol spectrum disorder were equipped to understand proceedings. Repeated interruptions hammered home the point: "Miss, when can I go home?" a 53-year-old Cree man, who pleaded guilty to public intoxication, asked the judge immediately after his sentence was read out.

No province except P.E.I. denies bail more frequently than Manitoba: Just three of 10 inmates in the province's overcrowded jails have been sentenced to a crime; the rest are in remand custody, awaiting trial.

Charges for violating conditions like these are soaring. In B.C., fully 40 per cent of criminal court matters are now "administration of justice" offences, which include breaching conditions of bail or probation, according to a recent study. Alberta found that 52 per cent of Indigenous prisoners had been incarcerated for a breach, almost twice the rate for non-Indigenous prisoners, according to a 2011 report by the province's justice branch.

Two years ago, 19-year-old Jonathan Champagne (his name was changed because he was a minor at the time of his arrest) was granted bail after an arrest on a charge of sexual assault. He claims it never happened. A few months later, while walking down Portage Avenue in a favourite red T-shirt, police stopped him on suspicion he was wearing gang colours. Champagne has never been in a gang. He doesn't use drugs. Police searched him, finding a paring knife in his shorts pocket. He was arrested for carrying a concealed weapon. This time, the judge refused to let him out on bail. The 17-year-old, who was shuttled between 10 homes in four cities growing up, was devastated: A few months earlier, he'd been placed in a tough, but loving home with a corrections officer. He's come to trust the family, a first. But the nine-month wait to trial meant losing that placement.

His lawyer, Billy Marks, appealed the judge's decision. His foster parents were so convinced of Champagne's innocence they agreed to foot the $500 monthly cost of an ankle monitoring system to strengthen his case. But the judge refused to budge.

Behind bars, Champagne was vilified and targeted. After admitting to wanting to end his life, he was placed in segregation. He spent 23 hours a day in a tiny cell, fed through the door and released to "the cage," a tiny, enclosed exercise yard for an hour. He'd walk in circles until his time was up. "It got to the point where I didn't want to be alive anymore," he says.

These were his options: Spend nine months in jail and fight the charges, or plead out. The Crown had approached Marks to say they would agree to jointly recommend time served if his client pleaded guilty to sexual assault. The guilty plea broke Marks's heart. "But at the same time, I could see what was happening to him."

He is hardly alone. Many plead out, even when they're innocent, because they can't make bail, putting them at risk of losing jobs, housing, and custody of their children, defence lawyers told Maclean's. The simple act of having an Indigenous lawyer, meanwhile, can almost double the number of "not guilty" pleas at first appearance to 49 per cent, according to one federal study.

Chapter 4 – Segregation

In prison, Indigenous offenders serve much harder time than anyone else. Indigenous inmates are placed in minimum-security institutions at just half the rate of their non-Indigenous counterparts. They are more likely to be placed in segregation, accounting for 31 per cent of cases; and, once in isolation, they'll spend 16 per cent more time there. They account for 45 per cent of all self-harm incidents. Nine in 10 are held to the expiry of their sentence, versus two-thirds of the non-Indigenous inmate population. They are more likely to be restrained in prison, to be involved in use-of-force incidents, to receive institutional charges, to die there.

Many of these disparities are known because Howard Sapers, the correctional investigator of Canada, made a point of tracking race-specific corrections data. Two years ago, troubled by the surging growth of the Indigenous inmate population, he issued a special report on it in Parliament, blaming systemic racism and cultural bias. It was one of only two the office has ever issued, to "signal this was a very important matter requiring urgent action." It received "anything but," Sapers says now, bitterly. Last year, the federal government announced he was being replaced (a process interrupted by the election, which left him on the job).

An Indigenous offender's problems begin with intake, Sapers says, where their risk level is often consistently over-classified by the Custody Rating Scale; it determines whether they belong in minimum, medium or maximum security (and almost everything else about their time behind bars). For years, the federal government has been ignoring repeated demands to reform these and other assessment tools used on the Indigenous inmate population. The latest, in September, came in a blistering Federal Court ruling. Justice Michael Phelan ordered Correctional Service Canada (CSC) to stop using them on Indigenous offenders, arguing they are "susceptible to cultural bias," and can produce "junk" data.

"This is not an issue the CSC missed inadvertently," Justice Phelan wrote, noting the U.K., Australia and the U.S. have all studied such assessments to ensure they are reliable for cultural minorities. "It has been a live issue since 2000, on the CSC's 'radar screen,' and the subject of past court decisions. It is time for the matter to be resolved." CSC immediately appealed.

Part of the problem is that the marginalization experienced by some Indigenous peoples gets turned into "risk": intergenerational trauma, alcoholism, a history of abuse, a lack of education, employment, a bank account or even hobbies make it more likely an inmate will be housed in maximum, and classed "high risk."

Cruelties are built into the system. The main reason Indigenous women—who account for 78 per cent of all self-harm incidents in prison—are moved to higher security levels is due to self-harm, including suicide attempts, according to a 2008 report by the Ontario Women's Justice Network.

"There is a group in Canada that keeps mysteriously dying," says University of Toronto sociology professor Sherene Razack. "We have convinced ourselves that we are improving. The reality is systems are in place to keep reproducing this."

Since no data on the race of those dying in prison in Canada exists, Razack undertook a study of in-custody deaths in Saskatchewan; her study found that Indigenous men account for roughly 50 per cent of all male deaths, many from suicide, head-injury or fatal encounters with police. Many of these deaths occur because officials "will not touch, examine, or closely monitor Indigenous people in their care," Razack says. "This indifference kills."

Chapter 5 – A new start

"Courtroom's open," Judge Marion Buller-Bennett says with a wide smile, ushering everyone waiting in the corridor into the second-floor courtroom at the New Westminster Provincial Courthouse. As the gallery fills, Buller-Bennett, a member of the Mistawasis First Nation in Saskatchewan, leaves the judge's dais, pulls up a plastic chair, and asks everyone to introduce themselves. Several she greets with a few words in their language, thus opening B.C.'s First Nations Court, which operates unlike any other courtroom in the country.

Legal jargon is barred. Formalities are not observed. There is no prisoner's dock, no microphones. Babies, noisy kids, coffee, laughter—all are welcome. Elsewhere, a judge might threaten sanction after an interruption or outburst. Buller-Bennett encourages them.

During a hearing for a 28-year-old Cree man who pleaded guilty to a drug offence, a recovering crystal meth addict stood up to commend his progress. Someone else suggested he consider Warriors Against Violence, an anger management program geared to Indigenous men. Another piped up with the number of a bus that will take him directly to it. Before he left, the Sandy Lake First Nation man, choking back tears, thanked the judge for acknowledging him—a "first," he said. As he was leaving, someone grabbed him in a bear hug. "You're doing great man," he said. "Stick with it."

Indigenous offenders can only appear before B.C.'s First Nations Court if they are entering guilty pleas (and their charges must be minor, and without a mandatory minimum sentence). They then work with the judge and two courtroom elders to come up with a "healing plan," a 12-month suspended sentence, which generally includes a stay in a residential treatment facility, anger management and parenting classes, addictions and cultural programming.

Most appearing before Buller-Bennett on that day were intergenerational survivors of residential schools. Their stories rarely deviated from a grim narrative: harrowing childhood, substance abuse, incarceration—almost always for crimes fuelled by or to feed their addictions.

"Rather than apply another Band-Aid," Buller-Bennett explained to the court, the point is to "help deal with what's causing the problem, often addiction." To monitor progress, the offender is required to return every two months. A missed appearance triggers a bench warrant, as in regular court.

At the completion of sentences, Buller-Bennett holds "graduation ceremonies." Two elders blanket graduates in red and black fleece, among the highest honours in Coastal First Nations culture. Not one got through it dry-eyed.

Buller-Bennett has said recidivism rates in the eight-year-old court, based on Cree teachings, beliefs and values, are low. Similar courts in Australia have more than halved recidivism rates. As in the Australian courts, elders tend to say things a judge might not. "It's like being publicly scolded by your grandma," Rose Falla, an Indigenous magistrate who helped establish Koori Courts in Australia's Victoria state told Maclean's.

But Jonathan Rudin sums up the problem: Where these innovations are most needed—Manitoba, Saskatchewan and Alberta—is exactly where you see the "most intransigence, the fewest innovations."

These same critiques could also be levelled at Ottawa, which, for a decade, has been ignoring calls to reform biased correctional admissions tests, bail and other laws disproportionately impacting Indigenous offenders. Instead, it appears to be incarcerating as many Indigenous people as possible, for as long as legally possible, with far-reaching consequences for Indigenous families. "[Indigenous people] are not there because of a crime spree," says Sapers. "They're there because of the impact of social factors, government policy and mandatory minimum sentences."

This situation does not help increase public safety: incarceration has almost no effect on bringing down crime, and it increases the likelihood of reoffending, as any criminologist will argue. Indigenous communities complain offenders are being returned more hardened, hopeless, violent and angry.

"What we are doing is using our criminal justice system to defend ourselves from the consequence of our own racism," says Toronto criminal lawyer John Struthers, who cut his legal teeth as a Crown attorney in remote, northern communities. "Rather than treat alcoholism, addiction, trauma, we keep the doors closed."

"Once you're in the system, you never get out," says Dwight Monkman. Three of his four brothers have been incarcerated. The 26-year-old Winnipegger, a member of the Lake Manitoba First Nation, spoke to Maclean's late last summer from the Headingley Correctional Institution, where he was incarcerated for a weapons charge and breaching a condition of his release. Since turning 18, the longest stretch Monkman says he's spent on the outside was 15 months. "I'm actually scared to get out," he says, clutching the battered, black phone under his chin. "Because I know I'll end up right back here."

CRITICAL READING QUESTIONS

1. What factors account for the rise in the number of Indigenous people in Canadian prisons? How are new laws, racial profiling, and discrimination related to these rates?

2. Look at the word cloud that illustrates the feelings that Indigenous and non-Indigenous people have about the police and their interaction with the police. How are these word clouds different? What might account for these differences?

3. What is the impact of stopping Indigenous people at such a significantly higher rate than other groups? What might the implications of these frequent stops be for relations between Indigenous communities and the police, arrest rates, and other things?

4. How does inequality between Indigenous and non-Indigenous people occur at the time of arrest, in court, in sentencing, and in the experience of prison occur? How might we address some of these inequalities?

Punishment

Punishment is the penalty inflicted on someone for committing a transgression. In criminal law, penalties are decided upon by a judge and/or jury, depending on the severity of the crime. Punishments are a denial of certain privileges, abilities, or rights; in Canada, these can be fines, community service, imprisonment, or restorative justice measures. In other countries (and historically in Canada), penalties for transgressing the law also include torture and death.

Punishment has various functions. Perhaps the most basic is **retribution**. Retribution is based on the idea that a punishment should be comparable to the suffering caused by the crime (i.e., "an eye for an eye"). The thinking is that a crime upsets society's moral balance. By punishing the criminal in equal measure, this balance and moral order can be restored. Retributive justice must be proportionate to the crime committed so that criminals suffer the pain that they have inflicted on others. A murderer can be executed, but someone who commits robbery should not be. Proponents of retributive justice argue that it can help to satisfy the resentment felt by the victim or victim's family.

The second main function of punishment is **deterrence**, the process of dissuading someone from future wrongdoing by making the "cost" of punishment outweigh the "benefit" of committing the crime. Deterrence assumes that offenders conduct a rational cost–benefit analysis before committing an offence. There are two types of deterrence: general and specific. **General deterrence** involves making an example out of deviants to deter others from committing crimes. **Specific deterrence** aims to discourage specific individuals by convincing them that engaging in crime does not benefit them. For example, if an individual is charged with drug trafficking and sentenced to a long jail sentence, he may decide that remaining in the drug trade is not worth the risk of future (and longer) jail terms.

Many people consider the death penalty the ultimate deterrent. The idea is that the high cost of potentially being executed is greater than any benefit from committing a crime. Canada abolished the death penalty in 1976 but has not executed anyone since 1962. Many other countries have also abolished the death penalty, including the UK, France, and Germany. However, there are many countries that still use it: China, Iran, North Korea, Yemen, and the United States have the most executions per year (Rogers and Chalabi 2013). While many people support the death penalty, some believe that it is morally wrong to kill in all contexts. Others worry that some innocent people might be executed, which is particularly problematic given the strong evidence of bias, especially racial bias, in capital punishment. For example, studies show that blacks, and non-whites more generally, who are convicted of killing whites are more likely to get the death penalty than whites who kill other whites (Paternoster 2007).

The next major function of punishment is **rehabilitation**, a newer focus of the criminal justice system. Rehabilitation is not simply about punishing criminals but aims to reform, or "heal," them and help them to reintegrate into society so that they will not reoffend. If you believe, for example, that crime originates from the social environment, rehabilitation might be an

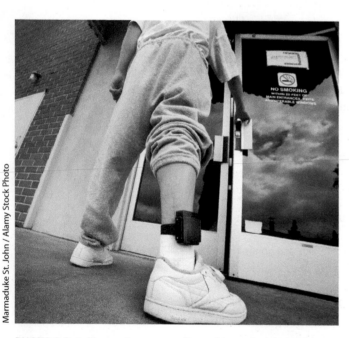

Marmaduke St. John / Alamy Stock Photo

PHOTO 3.7 Ankle monitors are usually used in conjunction with house arrest. How are they punishments, and how might they deter future crimes?

appropriate response to deviance. If offenders learn to be deviant, they can learn to conform. However, rehabilitation is needed to transform the "deviant" into this new identity. Rehabilitation does so by motivating constructive improvement on the part of the offender.

Parole, the supervised early release of a prisoner for such things as good behaviour, can be thought of as part of rehabilitation. Parole officers work with parolees to help them adjust to life outside prison and to ensure that they do not violate the conditions of their release. If they do breach those terms, they can be sent back to prison. **Probation** is a possibility for individuals who are convicted of less serious crimes. These individuals are released into the community under supervision and certain conditions, such as attending and completing a substance abuse program or having a curfew. If the offender does not adhere to these conditions or is arrested, the probation can be revoked.

Punishment is also about **societal protection**. When we incapacitate criminals, we physically prevent them from committing crimes. For example, when criminals are put in jail or are equipped with electronic monitoring devices, we limit their ability to commit crimes and try to protect other members of society from crime. Incapacitation can include imprisonment, the death penalty, or castration of sex offenders.

Punishment is also used for boundary-setting, education, and norm re-enforcement. The logic is that if wrongdoing goes unpunished, citizens will become demoralized and will not respect laws, thus ultimately threatening the "moral fabric" of society. Historically, societies pursued these goals by holding executions in public. Doing so reinforced the sovereign's power (i.e., the state's power to punish those who violate its laws) in the minds of the people. Punishment thus aided in boundary-setting by illustrating what the population is or is not allowed to do and publicly demonstrated that the state is the ultimate enforcer of power. A very effective way to increase solidarity in a society is to have its members collectively agree that something is wrong. For example, when people comment on what a "monster" a high-profile murderer is, they implicitly emphasize the collective opinion that murder is wrong and that those who commit murder are deviant and lie outside society's norms. This theory of punishment is consistent with Durkheim's argument about the functions of crime, which include creating solidarity and clarifying social norms.

Finally, punishment can lead to **restoration**. Offenders restore order by compensating or fixing the injustice caused by their crime. Restorative justice requires that the offender must first accept guilt. Examples of restorative justice include vandals cleaning up their graffiti and offenders participating in Aboriginal healing circles. In Chapter 13, we will learn about a recent and prominent incidence of restorative justice, the Truth and Reconciliation Commission of Canada.

Individuals who ascribe to individual-level explanations for crime tend to favour harsher punishments, while those who use social explanations tend to support less punitive responses. Regardless of whether the punishments are harsh or lenient, **recidivism rates** (the rates at which individuals reoffend) are generally quite high. For example, Langan and Levin (2002) found that approximately 67.5 per cent of released prisoners were rearrested within three years. This number should make us question how well the current system rehabilitates individuals who have entered the criminal justice system.

The following excerpt from Michel Foucault's *Discipline and Punish: The Birth of the Prison* examines two types of punishment: torture and incarceration. The comparison of the public torture of Robert-François Damiens, who was convicted of attempted murder in the mid-eighteenth century, with the daily routine of inmates in a nineteenth-century prison illustrates the dramatic changes that have occurred in punishment in Western societies. Foucault also discusses the reasons for these changes and the issue of the most humane way to punish a criminal.

The Body of the Condemned

Michel Foucault

On 2 March 1757 Damiens the regicide was condemned "to make the *amende honorable* before the main door of the Church of Paris," where he was to be "taken and conveyed in a cart, wearing nothing but a shirt, holding a torch of burning wax weighing two pounds"; then, "in the said cart, to the Place de Grève, where, on a scaffold that will be erected there, the flesh will be torn from his breasts, arms, thighs and calves with red-hot pincers, his right hand, holding the knife with which he committed the said parricide, burnt with sulphur, and, on those places where the flesh will be torn away, poured molten lead, boiling oil, burning resin, wax and sulphur melted together and then his body drawn and quartered by four horses and his limbs and body consumed by fire, reduced to ashes and his ashes thrown to the winds" (*Pièces originales . . .*, 372–4).

"Finally, he was quartered," recounts the *Gazette d'Amsterdam* of 1 April 1757. "This last operation was very long, because the horses used were not accustomed to drawing; consequently, instead of four, six were needed; and when that did not suffice, they were forced, in order to cut off the wretch's thighs, to sever the sinews and hack at the joints. . . .

"It is said that, though he was always a great swearer, no blasphemy escaped his lips; but the excessive pain made him utter horrible cries, and he often repeated: 'My God, have pity on me! Jesus, help me!' The spectators were all edified by the solicitude of the parish priest of St Paul's who despite his great age did not spare himself in offering consolation to the patient."

Bouton, an officer of the watch, left us his account: "The sulphur was lit, but the flame was so poor that only the top skin of the hand was burnt, and that only slightly. Then the executioner, his sleeves rolled up, took the steel pincers, which had been especially made for the occasion, and which were about a foot and a half long, and pulled first at the calf of the right leg, then at the thigh, and from there at the two fleshy parts of the right arm; then at the breasts. Though a strong, sturdy fellow, this executioner found it so difficult to tear away the pieces of flesh that he set about the same spot two or three times, twisting the pincers as he did so, and what he took away formed at each part a wound about the size of a six-pound crown piece.

"After these tearings with the pincers, Damiens, who cried out profusely, though without swearing, raised his head and looked at himself; the same executioner dipped an iron spoon in the pot containing the boiling potion, which he poured liberally over each wound. Then the ropes that were to be harnessed to the horses were attached with cords to the patient's body; the horses were then harnessed and placed alongside the arms and legs, one at each limb.

"Monsieur Le Breton, the clerk of the court, went up to the patient several times and asked him if he had anything to say. He said he had not; at each torment, he cried out, as the damned in hell are supposed to cry out, 'Pardon, my God! Pardon, Lord.' Despite all this pain, he raised his head from time to time and looked at himself boldly. The cords had been tied so tightly by the men who pulled the ends that they caused him indescribable pain. Monsieur Le Breton went up to him again and asked him if he had anything to say; he said no. Several confessors went up to him and spoke to him at length; he willingly kissed the crucifix that was held out to him; he opened his lips and repeated: 'Pardon, Lord.'

"The horses tugged hard, each pulling straight on a limb, each horse held by an executioner. After a quarter of an hour, the same ceremony was repeated and finally, after several attempts, the direction of the horses had to be changed, thus: those at the arms were made to pull towards the head, those at the thighs towards the arms, which broke the arms at the

Foucault, Michel. 1977. "Body of the Condemned." In *Discipline and Punish*. English Translation copyright © 1977 by Alan Sheridan. New York: Pantheon. Originally published in French as *Surveiller et Punir*. Copyright © 1975 by Editions Gallimard. Reprinted by permission of Georges Borchardt, Inc., for Editions Gallimard.

joints. This was repeated several times without success. He raised his head and looked at himself. Two more horses had to be added to those harnessed to the thighs, which made six horses in all. Without success.

"Finally, the executioner, Samson, said to Monsieur Le Breton that there was no way or hope of succeeding, and told him to ask their Lordships if they wished him to have the prisoner cut into pieces. Monsieur Le Breton, who had come down from the town, ordered that renewed efforts be made, and this was done; but the horses gave up and one of those harnessed to the thighs fell to the ground. The confessors returned and spoke to him again. He said to them (I heard him): 'Kiss me, gentlemen.' The parish priest of St Paul's did not dare to, so Monsieur de Marsilly slipped under the rope holding the left arm and kissed him on the forehead. The executioners gathered round and Damiens told them not to swear, to carry out their task and that he did not think ill of them; he begged them to pray to God for him, and asked the parish priest of St Paul's to pray for him at the first mass. . . .

Eighty years later, Léon Faucher drew up his rules "for the House of young prisoners in Paris":

Art. 17. The prisoners' day will begin at six in the morning in winter and at five in summer. They will work for nine hours a day throughout the year. Two hours a day will be devoted to instruction. Work and the day will end at nine o'clock in winter and at eight in summer.

Art. 18. *Rising*. At the first drum-roll, the prisoners must rise and dress in silence, as the supervisor opens the cell doors. At the second drum-roll, they must be dressed and make their beds. At the third, they must line up and proceed to the chapel for morning prayer. There is a five-minute interval between each drum-roll.

Art. 19. The prayers are conducted by the chaplain and followed by a moral or religious reading. This exercise must not last more than half an hour.

Art. 20. *Work*. At a quarter to six in the summer, a quarter to seven in winter, the prisoners go down into the courtyard where they must wash their hands and faces, and receive their first ration of bread. Immediately afterwards, they form into work-teams and go off to work, which must begin at six in summer and seven in winter.

Art. 21. *Meal*. At ten o'clock the prisoners leave their work and go to the refectory; they wash their hands in their courtyards and assemble in divisions. After the dinner, there is recreation until twenty minutes to eleven.

Art. 22. *School*. At twenty minutes to eleven, at the drum-roll, the prisoners form into ranks, and proceed in divisions to the school. The class lasts two hours and consists alternately of reading, writing, drawing and arithmetic.

Art. 23. At twenty minutes to one, the prisoners leave the school, in divisions, and return to their courtyards for recreation. At five minutes to one, at the drum-roll, they form into work-teams.

Art. 24. At one o'clock they must be back in the workshops: they work until four o'clock.

Art. 25. At four o'clock the prisoners leave their workshops and go into the courtyards where they wash their hands and form into divisions for the refectory.

Art. 26. Supper and the recreation that follows it last until five o'clock: the prisoners then return to the workshops.

Art. 27. At seven o'clock in the summer, at eight in winter, work stops; bread is distributed for the last time in the workshops. For a quarter of an hour one of the prisoners or supervisors reads a passage from some instructive or uplifting work. This is followed by evening prayer.

Art. 28. At half-past seven in summer, half-past eight in winter, the prisoners must be back in their cells after the washing of hands and the inspection of clothes in the courtyard; at the first drum-roll, they must undress, and at the second get into bed. The cell doors are closed and the supervisors go the rounds in the corridors, to ensure order and silence (Faucher, 274–82).

We have, then, a public execution and a timetable. They do not punish the same crimes or the same type of delinquent. But they each define a certain penal style. Less than a century separates them. It was a time when, in Europe and in the United States, the entire economy of punishment was redistributed. It was a time of great "scandals" for traditional justice, a time of innumerable projects for reform. It saw a new theory of law and crime, a new moral or political justification of the right to punish; old laws were abolished, old customs died out. "Modern" codes were planned or drawn up: Russia, 1769; Prussia, 1780; Pennsylvania and Tuscany, 1786; Austria, 1788; France, 1791, Year IV, 1808 and 1810. It was a new age for penal justice.

Among so many changes, I shall consider one: the disappearance of torture as a public spectacle. Today we are rather inclined to ignore it; perhaps, in its time, it gave rise to too much inflated rhetoric; perhaps it has been attributed too readily and too emphatically to a process of "humanization," thus dispensing with the need for further analysis. And, in any case, how important is such a change, when compared with the great institutional transformations, the formulation of explicit, general codes and unified rules of procedure; with the almost universal adoption of the jury system, the definition of the essentially corrective character of the penalty and the tendency which has become increasingly marked since the nineteenth century, to adapt punishment to the individual offender? Punishment of a less immediately physical kind, a certain discretion in the art of inflicting pain, a combination of more subtle, more subdued sufferings, deprived of their visible display, should not all this be treated as a special case, an incidental effect of deeper changes? And yet the fact remains that a few decades saw the disappearance of the tortured, dismembered, amputated body, symbolically branded on face or shoulder, exposed alive or dead to public view. The body as the major target of penal repression disappeared.

By the end of the eighteenth and the beginning of the nineteenth century, the gloomy festival of punishment was dying out, though here and there it flickered momentarily into life. In this transformation, two processes were at work. They did not have quite the same chronology or the same raison d'être. The first was the disappearance of punishment as a spectacle. The ceremonial of punishment tended to decline; it survived only as a new legal or administrative practice. . . . The use of prisoners in public works, cleaning city streets or repairing the highways, was practised in Austria, Switzerland, and certain of the United States, such as Pennsylvania. These convicts, distinguished by their "infamous dress" and shaven heads, "were brought before the public. The sport of the idle and the vicious, they often become incensed, and naturally took violent revenge upon the aggressors. To prevent them from returning injuries which might be inflicted on them, they were encumbered with iron collars and chains to which bombshells were attached, to be dragged along while they performed their degrading service, under the eyes of keepers armed with swords, blunderbusses and other weapons of destruction" (Roberts Vaux, *Notices*, 21, quoted in Teeters, 1937, p. 24). This practice was abolished practically everywhere at the end of the eighteenth or the beginning of the nineteenth century. . . .

Punishment, then, will tend to become the most hidden part of the penal process. This has several consequences: it leaves the domain of more or less everyday perception and enters that of abstract consciousness; its effectiveness is seen as resulting from its inevitability, not from its visible intensity; it is the certainty of being punished and not the horrifying spectacle of public punishment that must discourage crime; the exemplary mechanics of punishment changes its mechanisms. . . .

The disappearance of public executions marks therefore the decline of the spectacle; but it also marks a slackening of the hold on the body. . . . One no longer touched the body, or at least as little as possible, and then only to reach something other than the body itself. It might be objected that imprisonment, confinement, forced labour, penal servitude, prohibition from entering certain areas, deportation—which have occupied so important a place in modern penal systems—are "physical" penalties: unlike fines, for example, they directly affect the body. But the punishment–body relation is not the same as it was in the torture during public executions. The body now serves as an instrument or intermediary: if one intervenes upon it to imprison it, or to make it work, it is in order to deprive the individual of a liberty that is regarded both as a right and as property. The body, according to this penalty, is caught up in a system of constraints and privations, obligations and prohibitions. Physical pain, the pain of the body itself, is no longer the constituent element of the penalty. . . . As a result of this new restraint, a whole army of technicians took over from the executioner, the immediate anatomist of pain: warders, doctors, chaplains, psychiatrists, psychologists, educationalists; by their very presence near the prisoner, they sing the praises that the law needs: they reassure it that the body and pain are not the ultimate objects of its punitive action....

The modern rituals of execution attest to this double process: the disappearance of the spectacle and the elimination of pain....

... But a punishment like forced labour or even imprisonment—mere loss of liberty—has never functioned without a certain additional element of punishment that certainly concerns the body itself: rationing of food, sexual deprivation, corporal punishment, solitary confinement. Are these the unintentional, but inevitable, consequence of imprisonment? In fact, in its most explicit practices, imprisonment has always involved a certain degree of physical pain. The criticism that was often levelled at the penitentiary system in the early nineteenth century (imprisonment is not a sufficient punishment: prisoners are less hungry, less cold, less deprived in general than many poor people or even workers) suggests a postulate that was never explicitly denied: it is just that a condemned man should suffer physically more than other men. It is difficult to dissociate punishment from additional physical pain. What would a non-corporal punishment be?...

The reduction in penal severity in the last 200 years is a phenomenon with which legal historians are well acquainted. But, for a long time, it has been regarded in an overall way as a quantitative phenomenon: less cruelty, less pain, more kindness, more respect, more "humanity." In fact, these changes are accompanied by a displacement in the very object of the punitive operation. Is there a diminution of intensity? Perhaps. There is certainly a change of objective.

If the penalty in its most severe forms no longer addresses itself to the body, on what does it lay hold?... It seems to be contained in the question itself: since it is no longer the body, it must be the soul. The expiation that once rained down upon the body must be replaced by a punishment that acts in depth on the heart, the thoughts, the will, the inclinations....

... They are punished by means of a punishment that has the function of making the offender "not only desirous, but also capable, of living within the law and of providing for his own needs"; they are punished by the internal economy of a penalty which, while intended to punish the crime, may be altered (shortened or, in certain cases, extended) according to changes in the prisoner's behaviour; and they are punished by the "security measures" that accompany the penalty (prohibition of entering certain areas, probation, obligatory medical treatment), and which are intended not to punish the offence, but to supervise the individual, to neutralize his dangerous state of mind, to alter his criminal tendencies, and to continue even when this change has been achieved.... During the 150 or 200 years that Europe has been setting up its new penal systems, the judges have gradually, by means of a process that goes back very far indeed, taken to judging something other than crimes, namely, the "soul" of the criminal....

... A corpus of knowledge, techniques, "scientific" discourses is formed and becomes entangled with the practice of the power to punish....

CRITICAL READING QUESTIONS

1. How did punishment change over time, according to Foucault? How are these changes related to evolving ideas of punishing the body versus punishing the soul?
2. What is the public's role in punishment, and how has it changed?
3. What is the purpose of punishment? How did the purpose change from the eighteenth to the nineteenth century?
4. Who decides and enacts punishment in Foucault's analysis? How is this person/institution related to ideas about why people commit crimes, the function of the criminal justice system, and the reasons for punishment?

REFERENCES

Faucher, L. *De la réforme des prisons*, 1838.

Pièces originales et procédures du procès fait à Robert-François Damiens, III, 1757.

Teeters, N.K., *They Were in Prison*, 1937.

Vaux, Roberts, *Notices*, 1768.

Małgorzata Paulina Pakula/Dreamstime

PHOTO 3.8 Are these people vandalizing a building or creating art? What would make this act a crime, and what would make it an artistic impression? Why does such categorization matter?

Summary

This chapter discussed the different kinds of deviance and crime that exist in society and how these categories are socially constructed. Explanations for these acts can be made at the individual level, by looking at a person's biology or personality, or at the social level, by focusing on a person's social environment. Most sociological work in this area focuses on social explanations. We also examined labelling theory and Rosenhan's experiment regarding the powerful impact of labelling someone a deviant. This chapter explored crime rates in Canada and around the world, including how these numbers are calculated. We ended by considering punishment's different functions in society and Foucault's famous discussion of changes in punishment.

Key Terms

consensus crimes 63
control theory 69
Crime Severity Index (CSI) 78
deterrence 90
deviance 62
general deterrence 90
labelling theory 69
learning theory 68
lesser crimes 62

normality of crime 65
parole 91
primary deviance 69
probation 91
punishment 90
recidivism rate 91
rehabilitation 90
restoration 91
retribution 90

For Further Reading

Anderson, Elijah. 1999. *Code of the Street*. New York: Norton.

Becker, Howard. 1963. *Outsiders: Studies in the Sociology of Deviance*. New York: Free Press.

Downes, David, Paul Rock, and Chris McCormick. 2013. *Understanding Deviance: A Guide to the Sociology of Deviance and Rule Breaking*, 2nd Canadian edn. Don Mills, ON: Oxford University Press.

Foucault, Michel. 1995. *Discipline and Punish: The Birth of the Prison*. New York: Vintage.

Goffman, Erving. 1986. *Stigma: Notes on the Management of Spoiled Identity*. New York: Simon and Schuster.

References

Anderson, Elijah. 1999. *Code of the Street*. New York: Norton

Aronson, Joshua, and Elliot Aronson, eds. 2011. *Readings about the Social Animal*. New York: Worth Publishers.

Becker, Howard. 1963. *Outsiders: Studies in the Sociology of Deviance*. New York: Free Press.

Berger, Peter. 1963. *Invitation to Sociology*. Garden City, NY: Doubleday.

—— and Thomas Luckmann. 1966. *The Social Construction of Reality: A Treatise in the Sociology of Knowledge*. New York: Anchor Books.

Brennan, Shannon. 2013. "Police-Reported Crime Statistics in Canada, 2011." Ottawa: Statistics Canada. http://www.statcan.gc.ca/pub/85-002-x/2012001/article/11692-eng.htm.

Canadian Correctional Services. 2017. "The Federal Offender Population, 2015." http://www.csc-scc.gc.ca/publications/005007-3033-eng.shtml.

Cohen, Stanley. 2011. *Folk Devils and Moral Panic*. New York: Routledge.

Collins, Randall. 1992. *Sociological Insight: An Introduction to Non-obvious Sociology*, 2nd edn. New York: Oxford University Press.

Doolittle, Robyn. 2017. "Why Police Dismiss 1 in 5 Sexual Assault Claims as Baseless." *The Globe and Mail*. https://www.theglobeandmail.com/news/investigations/unfounded-sexual-assault-canada-main/article33891309.

Durkheim, Émile. 1982. *The Rules of the Sociological Method*, edited by Steven Lukes, translated by W.D. Halls. New York: Free Press.

Furdyk, Brent. 2017. "The 50 Most-Watched Network TV Shows of the 2016–17 Season." ET Canada. http://etcanada.com/news/228113/the-50-most-watched-network-tv-shows-of-the-2016-2017-season.

Hirschi, Travis. 2004. "Self-Control and Crime." In R.F. Baumeister and K.D. Vohs, eds, *The Handbook of Self-Regulation Research, Theory, and Application*, 537–52. New York: Guilford.

HRSDC (Human Resources and Skills Development Canada. 2013. *Indicators of Well-Being in Canada—Security*. Ottawa: HRSDC.

Langan, Patrick A., and David J. Levin. 2002 (June). "Recidivism of Prisoners Released in 1994." Bureau of Justice Statistics Special Report. http://www.aci-adc.com/images/Recidivism/RecidivismofPrisonersReleased1994.pdf.

Latimer, J., and L. Foss. 2004. *Havens in a Heartless World*. New York: Basic Books.

—— 2005. "The Sentencing of Aboriginal and Non-Aboriginal Youth under the YOA: A Multivariate Analysis." *Canadian Journal of Criminology and Criminal Justice* 47(3): 481–500.

Merton, Robert K. 1957. *Social Theory and Social Structure*, rev. edn. New York: Free Press.

Milgram, S. 1963. "Behavioral Study of Obedience." *Journal of Abnormal and Social Psychology* 67: 371–8.

Newton, Paula, Julia Jones, and Holly Yan. 2017. "Quebec Mosque Shooting: 'Lone Wolf' Kills 6, Officials Say." CNN. http://www.cnn.com/2017/01/30/americas/quebec-mosque-shooting/index.html.

Paternoster, Ray. 2007. "Capital Punishment." In George Ritzer, ed., *The Blackwell Encyclopedia of Sociology*, vol. 2, 385–8. Malden, MA: Blackwell.

Pay Equity Commission. 2012. "Gender Wage Gap." http://www.payequity.gov.on.ca/en/about/pubs/genderwage/wagegap.php.

Pittman, Tyler, Candace Nykiforuk, Javier Mignone, Piush Mandhane, Allan Becker, and Anita Kozyrskyj. 2012. "The Association between Community Stressors and Asthma Prevalence of School Children in Winnipeg, Canada." *International Journal of Environmental Research and Public Health* 9(2): 579–95.

Rogers, Simon, and Mona Chalabi. 2013. "Death Penalty Statistics, Country by Country." *The Guardian* 13 December. http://www.theguardian.com/news/datablog/2011/mar/29/death-penalty-countries-world.

Statistics Canada. 2017. "Study: Women in Canada: Women in the Criminal Justice System." http://www.statcan.gc.ca/pub/85-002-x/2016001/article/14309-eng.htm.

Sutherland, Edwin H. 1947. *Criminology*, 4th edn. Philadelphia: Lippincott.

Zimbardo, P.G., C. Maslach, and C. Haney. 1999. *Reflections on the Stanford Prison Experiment: Genesis, Transformations, Consequences*. http://www.prisonexp.org/pdf/blass.pdf.

PART II

Social Inequality

Photo credit: artur maia de carvalho/Shutterstock

4 Social Inequality and Social Class

Chapter Outline

Photo credit: Khuroshvili Ilya/Shutterstock

Introduction

Do you think of yourself as working-class, middle-class, upper-class, or some other group? If you are like most Canadians, you see yourself as middle-class. In fact, 70 per cent of Canadians consider themselves to be middle-class (*Maclean's* 2017). Considering that most Canadians see themselves as within this group, what does it mean to be middle-class in Canadian society? Why do people choose to describe themselves as members of this class?

In this chapter, we will explore what two of the founders of sociology—Karl Marx and Max Weber—thought about social class. We will also examine the significance of social status and social mobility in Canada. Social class and social status are important because they shape our opportunities, from the neighbourhoods we grow up in to the schools we attend and the types of jobs we get. While most Canadians do not think much about the matter of social class, it has important implications for the kind of life we lead.

Karl Marx and Social Class

Karl Marx (1818–83) is one of the most important figures in the development of sociology and, as mentioned in Chapter 2, is the founder of conflict theory. He is also a significant figure outside sociology; his ideas shaped many historical events and are still debated today. Governments espousing Marxist ideology came to power in the Union of Soviet Socialist Republics (USSR or Soviet Union) in 1922 and the People's Republic of China in 1949. Marx's writings also inspired the rise of many of the world's labour unions and workers' parties, which advocate for workers' rights and safer working conditions.

It may surprise some that Marx's parents were middle-class and relatively wealthy. Marx studied at the University of Bonn and the University of Berlin. In 1843, he moved to Paris, where he met Friedrich Engels. He and Engels collaborated on their work throughout their lives. In 1849, Marx was exiled and moved to London with his family. His work was important as an academic theory and a way of understanding the world. It was also very political and focused on trying to change the world outside academia. For example, he campaigned for socialism and in workers' groups, such as the International Workingmen's Association.

Marx argued that the core struggle in all societies is **class struggle**. In our modern capitalist society, that is the conflict between those who own the means of production (capitalists, also called the bourgeoisie) and those who simply own their own labour power (workers, also called the proletariat). He called capitalism, the economic system in which businesses are privately owned and goods are sold on the market for profit, the "dictatorship of the **bourgeoisie**." For Marx, capitalism is controlled and run by a small group of wealthy business-owners. He argued that, like all previous economic systems, it is founded on internal tensions that make it unsustainable. He predicted that capitalism would eventually be replaced by socialism, an alternative economic system featuring collective ownership of the means of production. In socialism, power is held by the working class. Marx referred to this system as the "dictatorship of the **proletariat**" or a "workers' democracy." He also theorized that socialism would be replaced by communism, a completely classless society (Marx and Engels 1848).

Private Collection / Bridgeman Images

PHOTO 4.1 Karl Marx's work encourages us to think critically about how social class shapes our lives and society as a whole.

HIGHLIGHT

Getting to Know Karl Marx

- While he was a student at the University of Bonn, Marx was a member of the Poets' Club and a co-president of the Trier Tavern Club drinking society.
- In university, Marx was in a duel with another student.
- Marx married Jenny von Westphalen, a Prussian baroness, in 1843. Their relationship was controversial because of their different social classes and ethnic origins. They had seven children and, by all accounts, a very happy marriage.
- In 1837, Marx wrote a short novel, a play, and a series of love poems to his wife. All remain unpublished.

Marx actively fought for the implementation of socialism, arguing that academics should play an important part in toppling capitalism and causing revolutionary social change. In fact, in the final line of his *Theses on Feuerbach*, a work first published in 1888 and co-edited with Engels, Marx (2004; emphasis added) says that "the philosophers have only *interpreted* the world, in various ways. The point, however, is to *change* it." Marx sought to be part of that change by promoting the development of a socialist economic system.

Marx's view of the world emphasizes the economy's role in social life. He argued that historical periods are distinguished by the mode of production of goods and services that dominates the time. The mode of production is the way that we make things in our society. For example, in early feudalism (i.e., between the ninth and fifteenth centuries) the nobility owned land, including farms, homes, and villages, and peasants worked the land, mainly using human and animal energy. The mode of production creates the distinctions and relationships between classes in a society. The feudal system led to certain relationships between the nobility and the peasantry. Peasants were tied to their landlords, who gave them a place to live and protection in exchange for their labour.

Classes, for Marx, are groups of people who play different roles in the productive system. Capitalism has two main classes: the bourgeoisie (capitalist) and the proletariat (workers). The bourgeoisie are the people who own the means of production and **property**, which is any resource that can be used to produce things of value and to generate wealth. Land is an important type of property because it allows the owner to grow food or raise animals that can be sold. Other types of property include businesses or factories in which an owner can produce goods such as shoes, clothing, or other products to sell. Essentially, the bourgeoisie owns the means of producing more wealth.

The proletariat does not own the means of production. Members of the proletariat own only their capacity to labour (either physically or mentally), which they must sell to the capitalist. Thus, the proletariat must work in the capitalists' factories or on their farms to make a wage (a fraction of the profits from the bourgeoisie's sales, set by the bourgeoisie) to survive.

Marx argued that classes are relational and defined by their relationship to both the means of production and to each other. Capitalists cannot exist without workers to labour in their factories; at the same time, workers must have somewhere to sell their labour to make money to survive. However, the relationship between these two groups is coercive by nature. Workers are beholden to the capitalist, who can pay them low wages and give them poor working conditions. Marx argued that capitalism functions and continues to exist through this perpetual exploitation of the workers' labour and subsequent oppression.

Class Struggles

Despite the power differentiation between the bourgeoisie and proletariat, the two classes clearly depend on one another. The capitalist cannot have a functioning factory or farm without workers. And the worker needs the capitalist to make a wage in order to live. But the relationship between the two is by nature unequal, which inevitably leads to class struggles. As Marx (Marx and Engels 1848, 57) describes,

> The history of all hitherto existing society is the history of class struggles. Freeman and slave, patrician and plebian, lord and serf, guildmaster and journeyman, in a word, oppressor and oppressed, stood in constant opposition to one another, carried on an uninterrupted, now hidden, now open fight, a fight that each time ended, either in a revolutionary reconstitution of society at large, or in the common ruin of the contending classes.

According to Marx, class struggles exist because the classes want different things and have different interests. For example, capitalists want to make as much money as they can from their factories or farms. The capitalist must pay wages so that workers will be able to live and come back to work over time. However, they want to extract the most **surplus value**—the excess value that workers produce beyond the cost of their labour—from the workers that they can. Surplus value is the amount of money that capitalists get to keep after paying their workers' wages. It is not surprising that capitalists want as much of this surplus as possible, which means keeping wages low, having workers work quickly, and setting long work hours. As Marx (1867/2000, 218) said, "the rate of surplus value is . . . an exact expression of the degree of exploitation of labour power by capital, or of the labourer by the capitalist."

Workers and capitalists want very different things. Workers want to make a good wage that allows them to live and support their families. They want to work under safe conditions and for a reasonable number of hours. These desires can conflict with the capitalist's attempt to make large profits, which could include creating more cost-effective yet more dangerous workplaces.

Marx wrote many academic books about the problems created by capitalism and about a possible socialist future. As discussed earlier, he was also interested in helping to overthrow capitalism. He worked to help encourage a worker's revolution by explaining the perils of capitalism and the benefits of socialist and communist systems to a wider audience. In 1848, the Communist League commissioned Marx and Engels to write a short pamphlet outlining capitalism's main issues. The following is an excerpt from the result, *The Communist Manifesto (1848)*.

Manifesto of the Communist Party

Karl Marx and Friedrich Engels

I. Bourgeois and Proletarians[1]

. . . In the earlier epochs of history, we find almost everywhere a complicated arrangement of society into various orders, a manifold gradation of social rank. In ancient Rome we have patricians, knights, plebeians, slaves; in the Middle Ages, feudal lords, vassals, guild-masters, journeymen, apprentices, serfs; in almost all of these classes, again, subordinate gradations.

Marx, Karl, and Friedrich Engels. 1978. "Manifesto of the Communist Party." Exerpt from Robert Tucker, ed., *The Marx-Engels Reader*, 2nd edn, 473–83. New York; London, W.W. Norton & Company.

READING

The modern bourgeois society that has sprouted from the ruins of feudal society has not done away with class antagonisms. It has but established new classes, new conditions of oppression, new forms of struggle in place of the old ones.

Our epoch, the epoch of the bourgeoisie, possesses, however, this distinctive feature: it has simplified the class antagonisms: Society as a whole is more and more splitting up into two great hostile camps, into two great classes directly facing each other: Bourgeoisie and Proletariat.

From the serfs of the Middle Ages sprang the chartered burghers of the earliest towns. From these burgesses the first elements of the bourgeoisie were developed.

The discovery of America, the rounding of the Cape, opened up fresh ground for the rising bourgeoisie. The East-Indian and Chinese markets, the colonization of America, trade with the colonies, the increase in the means of exchange and in commodities generally, gave to commerce, to navigation, to industry, an impulse never before known, and thereby, to the revolutionary element in the tottering feudal society, a rapid development.

The feudal system of industry, under which industrial production was monopolized by closed guilds, now no longer sufficed for the growing wants of the new markets. The manufacturing system took its place. The guild-masters were pushed on one side by the manufacturing middle class; division of labour between the different corporate guilds vanished in the face of division of labour in each single workshop.

Meantime the markets kept ever growing, the demand ever rising. Even manufacture no longer sufficed. Thereupon, steam and machinery revolutionized industrial production. The place of manufacture was taken by the giant, Modern Industry, the place of the industrial middle class, by industrial millionaires, the leaders of whole industrial armies, the modern bourgeois.

Modern Industry has established the world market, for which the discovery of America paved the way. This market has given an immense development to commerce, to navigation, to communication by land. This development has, in its turn, reacted on the extension of industry; and in proportion as industry, commerce, navigation, railways extended, in the same proportion the bourgeoisie developed, increased its capital, and pushed into the background every class handed down from the Middle Ages.

We see, therefore, how the modern bourgeoisie is itself the product of a long course of development, of a series of revolutions in the modes of production and of exchange.

Each step in the development of the bourgeoisie was accompanied by a corresponding political advance of that class. An oppressed class under the sway of the feudal nobility, an armed and self-governing association in the medieval commune;[2] here independent urban republic (as in Italy and Germany), there taxable "third estate" of the monarchy (as in France), afterwards, in the period of manufacture proper, serving either the semi-feudal or the absolute monarchy as a counterpoise against the nobility, and, in fact, cornerstone of the great monarchies in general, the bourgeoisie has at last, since the establishment of Modern Industry and of the world market, conquered for itself, in the modern representative State, exclusive political sway. The executive of the modern State is but a committee for managing the common affairs of the whole bourgeoisie.

The bourgeoisie, historically, has played a most revolutionary part.

The bourgeoisie, wherever it has got the upper hand, has put an end to all feudal, patriarchal, idyllic relations. It has pitilessly torn asunder the motley feudal ties that bound man to his "natural superiors," and has left remaining no other nexus between man and man than naked self-interest, than callous "cash payment." It has drowned the most heavenly ecstasies of religious fervour, of chivalrous enthusiasm, of philistine sentimentalism, in the icy water of egotistical calculation. It has resolved personal worth into exchange value, and in place of the numberless indefeasible chartered freedoms, has set up that single, unconscionable freedom—Free Trade. In one word, for exploitation, veiled by religious and political illusions, it has substituted naked, shameless, direct, brutal exploitation.

The bourgeoisie has stripped of its halo every occupation hitherto honoured and looked up to with reverent awe. It has converted the physician, the lawyer, the priest, the poet, the man of science, into its paid wage-labourers.

The bourgeoisie has torn away from the family its sentimental veil, and has reduced the family relation to a mere money relation. . . .

The bourgeoisie cannot exist without constantly revolutionizing the instruments of production, and thereby the relations of production, and with them the whole relations of society. Conservation of the old modes of production in unaltered form, was, on the contrary, the first condition of existence for all earlier industrial classes. Constant revolutionizing of production, uninterrupted disturbance of all social conditions, everlasting uncertainty and agitation distinguish the bourgeois epoch from all earlier ones. All fixed, fast-frozen relations, with their train of ancient and venerable prejudices and opinions, are swept away, all new-formed ones become antiquated before they can ossify. All that is solid melts into air, all that is holy is profaned, and man is at last compelled to face with sober senses, his real conditions of life, and his relations with his kind.

The need of a constantly expanding market for its products chases the bourgeoisie over the whole surface of the globe. It must nestle everywhere, settle everywhere, establish connections everywhere. . . .

The bourgeoisie, by the rapid improvement of all instruments of production, by the immensely facilitated means of communication, draws all, even the most barbarian, nations into civilization. The cheap prices of its commodities are the heavy artillery with which it batters down all Chinese walls, with which it forces the barbarians' intensely obstinate hatred of foreigners to capitulate. It compels all nations, on pain of extinction, to adopt the bourgeois mode of production; it compels them to introduce what it calls civilization into their midst, i.e., to become bourgeois themselves. In one word, it creates a world after its own image.

The bourgeoisie has subjected the country to the rule of the towns. It has created enormous cities, has greatly increased the urban population as compared with the rural, and has thus rescued a considerable part of the population from the idiocy of rural life. Just as it has made the country dependent on the towns, so it has made barbarian and semi-barbarian countries dependent on the civilized ones, nations of peasants on nations of bourgeois, the East on the West.

The bourgeoisie keeps more and more doing away with the scattered state of the population, of the means of production, and of property. It has agglomerated population, centralized means of production, and has concentrated property in a few hands. The necessary consequence of this was political centralization. Independent, or but loosely connected provinces, with separate interests, laws, governments, and systems of taxation, became lumped together into one nation, with one government, one code of laws, one national class-interest, one frontier, and one customs-tariff.

The bourgeoisie, during its rule of scarce 100 years, has created more massive and more colossal productive forces than have all preceding generations together. Subjection of Nature's forces to man, machinery, application of chemistry to industry and agriculture, steam navigation, railways, electric telegraphs, clearing of whole continents for cultivation, canalization of rivers, whole populations conjured out of the ground—what earlier century had even a presentiment that such productive forces slumbered in the lap of social labour?

We see then: the means of production and of exchange, on whose foundation the bourgeoisie built itself up, were generated in feudal society. At a certain stage in the development of these means of production and of exchange, the conditions under which feudal society produced and exchanged, the feudal organization of agriculture and manufacturing industry, in one word, the feudal relations of property became no longer compatible with the already developed productive forces; they became so many fetters. They had to be burst asunder; they were burst asunder.

Into their place stepped free competition, accompanied by a social and political constitution adapted to it, and by the economical and political sway of the bourgeois class. . . .

The weapons with which the bourgeoisie felled feudalism to the ground are now turned against the bourgeoisie itself.

But not only has the bourgeoisie forged the weapons that bring death to itself; it has also called into existence the men who are to wield those weapons—the modern working class—the proletarians.

In proportion as the bourgeoisie, i.e., capital, is developed, in the same proportion is the proletariat, the modern working class, developed—a class of labourers, who live only so long as they find work, and who find work only so long as their labour increases capital. These labourers, who must sell themselves piecemeal, are a commodity, like every other article of commerce, and are consequently exposed to all the vicissitudes of competition, to all the fluctuations of the market.

Owing to the extensive use of machinery and to division of labour, the work of the proletarians has lost all individual character, and consequently, all charm for the workman. He becomes an appendage of the machine, and it is only the most simple, most monotonous, and most easily acquired knack, that is required of him. Hence, the cost of production of a workman is restricted, almost entirely, to the means of subsistence that he requires for his maintenance, and for the propagation of his race. But the price of a commodity, and therefore also of labour,[3] is equal to its cost of production. In proportion, therefore, as the repulsiveness of the work increases, the wage decreases. Nay more, in proportion as the use of machinery and division of labour increases, in the same proportion the burden of toil also increases, whether by prolongation of the working hours, by increase of the work exacted in a given time or by increased speed of the machinery, etc.

Modern industry has converted the little workshop of the patriarchal master into the great factory of the industrial capitalist. Masses of labourers, crowded into the factory, are organized like soldiers. As privates of the industrial army they are placed under the command of a perfect hierarchy of officers and sergeants. Not only are they slaves of the bourgeois class, and of the bourgeois State; they are daily and hourly enslaved by the machine, by the overlooker, and, above all, by the individual bourgeois manufacturer himself. The more openly this despotism proclaims gain to be its end and aim, the more petty, the more hateful and the more embittering it is.

The less the skill and exertion of strength implied in manual labour, in other words, the more modern industry becomes developed, the more is the labour of men superseded by that of women. Differences of age and sex have no longer any distinctive social validity for the working class. All are instruments of labour, more or less expensive to use, according to their age and sex.

No sooner is the exploitation of the labourer by the manufacturer, so far, at an end, that he receives his wages in cash, than he is set upon by the other portions of the bourgeoisie, the landlord, the shopkeeper, the pawnbroker, etc.

The lower strata of the middle class—the small tradespeople, shopkeepers, and retired tradesmen generally, the handicraftsmen and peasants—all these sink gradually into the proletariat, partly because their diminutive capital does not suffice for the scale on which Modern Industry is carried on, and is swamped in the competition with the large capitalists, partly because their specialized skill is rendered worthless by new methods of production. Thus the proletariat is recruited from all classes of the population. . . .

But with the development of industry the proletariat not only increases in number; it becomes concentrated in greater masses, its strength grows, and it feels that strength more. The various interests and conditions of life within the ranks of the proletariat are more and more equalized, in proportion as machinery obliterates all distinctions of labour, and nearly everywhere reduces wages to the same low level. The growing competition among the bourgeois, and the resulting commercial crises, make the wages of the workers ever more fluctuating. The unceasing improvement of machinery, ever more rapidly developing, makes their livelihood more and more precarious; the collisions between individual workmen and individual bourgeois take more and more the character of collisions between two classes. Thereupon the workers begin to form combinations (Trades Unions) against the bourgeois; they club together in order to keep up the rate of wages; they found permanent associations in order to make provision beforehand for these occasional revolts. Here and there the contest breaks out into riots.

Now and then the workers are victorious, but only for a time. The real fruit of their battles lies, not in the immediate result, but in the ever-expanding union of the workers. This union is helped on by the improved means of communication that are created by modern industry and that place the workers of different localities in contact with one another. It was just this contact that was needed to centralize the numerous local struggles, all of the same character, into one national struggle between classes. But every class struggle is a political struggle. And that union, to attain which the burghers of the Middle Ages, with their miserable highways, required centuries, the modern proletarians, thanks to railways, achieve in a few years.

This organization of the proletarians into a class, and consequently into a political party, is continually being upset again by the competition between the workers themselves. But it ever rises up again, stronger, firmer, mightier. It compels legislative recognition of particular interests of the workers, by taking advantage of the divisions among the bourgeoisie itself. Thus the ten-hours' bill in England was carried. . . .

The lower-middle class, the small manufacturer, the shopkeeper, the artisan, the peasant, all these fight against the bourgeoisie, to save from extinction their existence as fractions of the middle class. They are therefore not revolutionary, but conservative. Nay more, they are reactionary, for they try to roll back the wheel of history. If by chance they are revolutionary, they are so only in view of their impending transfer into the proletariat, they thus defend not their present, but their future interests, they desert their own standpoint to place themselves at that of the proletariat. . . .

Hitherto, every form of society has been based, as we have already seen, on the antagonism of oppressing and oppressed classes. But in order to oppress a class, certain conditions must be assured to it under which it can, at least, continue its slavish existence. The serf, in the period of serfdom, raised himself to membership in the commune, just as the petty bourgeois, under the yoke of feudal absolutism, managed to develop into a bourgeois. The modern labourer, on the contrary, instead of rising with the progress of industry, sinks deeper and deeper below the conditions of existence of his own class. He becomes a pauper, and pauperism develops more rapidly than population and wealth. And here it becomes evident, that the bourgeoisie is unfit any longer to be the ruling class in society, and to impose its conditions of existence upon society as an overriding law. It is unfit to rule because it is incompetent to assure an existence to its slave within his slavery, because it cannot help letting him sink into such a state, that it has to feed him, instead of being fed by him. Society can no longer live under this bourgeoisie, in other words, its existence is no longer compatible with society.

The essential condition for the existence, and for the sway of the bourgeois class, is the formation and augmentation of capital; the condition for capital is wage-labour. Wage-labour rests exclusively on competition between the labourers. The advance of industry, whose involuntary promoter is the bourgeoisie, replaces the isolation of the labourers, due to competition, by their revolutionary combination, due to association. The development of Modern Industry, therefore, cuts from under its feet the very foundation on which the bourgeoisie produces and appropriates products. What the bourgeoisie, therefore, produces, above all, is its own gravediggers. Its fall and the victory of the proletariat are equally inevitable.

CRITICAL READING QUESTIONS

1. What significant changes occurred with the rise of the bourgeoisie class?
2. Do you agree that class is the most important dimension of inequality? Why or why not?
3. The final stage proposed by Marx and Engels was a communist society without classes. Do you think a society or group of people could ever exist without some form of class hierarchy? Why or why not?
4. Is social class still relevant? Why or why not?

NOTES

1.   By bourgeoisie is meant the class of modern Capitalists, owners of the means of social production and employers of wage-labour. By proletariat, the class of modern wage-labourers who, having no means of production of their own, are reduced to selling their labour-power in order to live. [Engels, English Edition of 1888]

2.   "Commune" was the name taken, in France, by the nascent towns even before they had conquered from their feudal lords and masters local self-government and political rights as the "Third Estate." Generally speaking, for the economic development of the bourgeoisie, England is here taken as the typical country; for its political development, France. [*Engels, English Edition of 1888*]

This was the name given their urban communities by the townsmen of Italy and France, after they had purchased or wrested their initial rights of self-government from their feudal lords. [*Engels, German Edition of 1890*]

3.   Subsequently Marx pointed out that the worker sells not his labour but his labour power.

It seems clear from Marx's discussion that capitalism can create many problems for workers and that the inequality between those who own the means of production and those who own only their labour power can be severe. However, it is also clear that there are many more workers than there are capitalists. Why don't the workers simply rise up and ask for better wages, working conditions, and other benefits? Why don't they start the revolution Marx dreamed about? Marx outlined a number of reasons for the lack of such an uprising and for the difficulties in uniting to fight oppression.

One of the main reasons that workers do not join together is the role of ideology. **Ideologies** are sets of conscious and unconscious ideas or beliefs that govern and guide people's lives. Marx (2004, 64) said that the dominant ideologies in any historical epoch are those of the dominant class in that period: "The ideas of the ruling class are in every epoch the ruling ideas, i.e., the class which is the ruling material force of society, is at the same time its ruling intellectual force."

Most of us were raised within capitalist societies and therefore cannot see the many ideologies and assumptions upon which this system is based. Ideologies such as meritocracy, individualism, progress, evolution, expansion, and development are fundamentally intertwined with our economic system, yet they often seem so natural and invisible that they end up being accepted by those within the society.

For example, Canadian society has a strong belief in **meritocracy**, the idea that people will achieve based on their own merit. This ideology supports the idea that wealthy people earned their money from working hard and that those with less money must have not worked as hard or were less deserving. From a Marxist perspective, we can see that this ideology benefits the bourgeoisie by legitimizing the fact that they have money, highlighting the hard work and intelligence it took to get that money, and making it seem that anyone could achieve this status with effort and perseverance. It helps encourage the proletariat (the rest of us) to buy into the system of capitalism because it promotes the belief that we too can become rich and successful if we work hard enough. However, this ideology ignores the many other factors that determine one's social position. An individual's social class, which shapes his educational opportunities and social connections, also plays an important role in determining financial and other types of success. Marx would argue that

Kathy Hutchins/iStockphoto

PHOTO 4.2 Meritocracy is a very important ideology in Canadian society. We tend to believe that smart and hard-working people will make more money and be more successful than other people. To what extent is this true about people like the Kardashian family? How hard did they work to attain their success?

other ideologies, such as individualism and progress, also benefit the dominant class and legitimize the economic and social system as it is.

Marx claimed that workers in capitalism develop a **false consciousness**, a willingness to believe in ideologies that support the ruling class but are actually disadvantageous to working-class interests. Ideologies such as individualism and meritocracy all support and serve the interests of the dominant class. They blunt the working class's desire to unite and call upon capitalists and governments to be more responsive to their needs. Social institutions, such as the education system, mass media, and the family, teach us these ideologies and help to perpetuate them.

For Marx, even the government is simply a tool of capitalism because capitalists use the state to further their own interests. In fact, Marx (1975) argued that the state is used to sustain the class system that benefits the ruling class. Consequently, he argues that the state does not reflect the interest of the vast majority of people, the workers. This situation is complicated in a democracy by the fact that the workers have the right to vote. The small group of capitalists has to persuade the larger group of workers to accept the concentration of power in the former's hands. This is done, in part, by the capitalist control of ideas through avenues such as the media and school curricula. Through these mechanisms, the capitalist tries to persuade the workers that the current system is the optimal way of running society and is simply the "natural" way for things to be organized. However, Marx argued that when these softer ways of convincing people about the benefits of capitalism fail, the ruling class uses more coercive methods, such as the police, military, or the judicial system, to defend this system.

Marx and Engels demonstrated that, far from being inevitable, the current organization of the economy is socially constructed and can be changed. The means of production—in our case, capitalism—determines the resulting social systems, relations, class struggles, and ideologies in society. In essence, Marx and Engels argued that all aspects of society, from overarching power structures (i.e., the way the government is run) to daily individual experiences with exploitation (i.e., workers in factories), form as a result of the economic system or means of production.

Marx's ideas have formed how many sociologists and others think about social class. However, these ideas have not gone without criticism. Many people argue that there are no longer simply two classes, and they criticize him for seeing the economic world as such a sharp distinction between capitalists and workers. In some ways, this criticism is unfair. Marx (1907) identified two smaller and, in his opinion, less important class groupings: the petite bourgeoisie and the lumpenproletariat. The **petite bourgeoisie** ("little bourgeoisie") are small-scale capitalists, such as shopkeepers and managers. People in this group do not necessarily sell their labour like proletarians but neither do they buy the labour of others like the capitalists (Marx and Engels 1848). They often work alongside the labour they buy from others, unlike large-scale capitalists who do not work with labourers. For example, a petite bourgeoisie who owns a small coffee shop might, like his employees, make coffee. However, the owner of Starbucks, a large bourgeoisie, would not. Because the petite bourgeoisie work alongside their employees, they may know their workers better and be more sympathetic to their concerns. If the coffee shop is too hot or the espresso machine is unsafe to use, this may be more quickly noticed and of concern to an owner who also has to work in the store and make coffee than it would be to an owner of a large coffee company who rarely goes into the cafes. However, Marx said that the petite bourgeoisie would disappear over time, mostly because they would eventually fall into the proletariat class. The **lumpenproletariat** (translated roughly as "slum workers") is the lowest layer of the working class and includes beggars, prostitutes, petty criminals, and the chronically unemployed (Marx 1907). Marx largely dismissed this group, feeling that its members were highly unlikely to join what he hoped would be a workers' revolution.

Keeping Marx's classes in mind, where would a group such as physicians fit? This occupational group makes a relatively high salary yet does not own the means of production. Under Marx's conceptual framework, they would be considered proletarians. However, some theorists argue that workers such as physicians are not in the same fundamentally exploitative relationship with capitalists as the proletariat class that Marx discussed.

Economic systems have changed since Marx's time. He wrote in an era of industrial capitalism, when most individuals working in the formal labour market were employed in manufacturing. Today, however, most people work in other industries. In 2016, 79 per cent of Canadians had service jobs (e.g., retail, health, and education), with only 22 per cent working in the manufacturing sector (Statistics Canada 2016). As you can see, changes in the structure of the economic system complicate Marx's theories of class stratification.

HIGHLIGHT

Ideology and Positive Thinking

The Secret is a best-selling 2006 self-help book by Rhonda Byrne. Based on "the law of attraction," the book claims that positive thinking can create life-changing results, such as increased wealth, health, and happiness. The book has sold almost 20 million copies in 46 languages. Here are a few examples of Byrne's advice.

> Money is magnetic energy. You are a magnet attracting to you all things, via the signal you are emitting through your thoughts and feelings. To become a powerful money magnet:
> - Be clear about the amount of money you want to receive. State it and intend it! Don't think about how much money you earn, but how much you want to receive.
> - Visualize and imagine yourself spending all the money you want, as though you already have it.
> - Speak, act, and think from the mindset of being wealthy now. Eliminate thoughts and words of lack such as "I can't afford it," "It is too expensive."
> - Do whatever it takes for you to feel wealthy.
> - Do whatever it takes to feel good. The emotions of joy and happiness are powerful money magnets. Be happy now! (thesecret.tv/teachings-summary.html)

It is hard to argue that positive thinking is a bad thing—everyone likes a person with a positive attitude! But is there a danger in these kinds of teachings? Consider the advice in this book and answer the following questions:

1. How does the ideology of *The Secret* help perpetuate capitalism?
2. Who does this ideology benefit?
3. Why would people believe in these ideologies?
4. What risks can these ideologies pose for individuals, social groups, and society as a whole?

Class Consciousness

Class consciousness is a term used in Marxist theory to refer to people's beliefs regarding their social class and class interests. Marx (Marx and Engels 1848) distinguished between a "class in itself," a category of people with a common relation to the means of production (such as the worker or proletariat), and a "class for itself," a group organized in active pursuit of its own interests (such as unionized workers pushing for better working conditions). Class consciousness is an awareness of what is in the best interests of one's class and is an important precondition for organizing into a "class for itself" to advocate for class interests.

Marx wanted the working class to develop a class consciousness so that they could fight for socialism. Class consciousness has also been important in many capitalist societies, such as Canada, in leading to the rise of unions. Unions are organizations of employees who work together to negotiate a variety of common matters, including pay, benefits, hiring and firing practices, and working conditions. Unions bargain with the employer on behalf of workers and negotiate labour contracts (collective bargaining). These actions are a result of a group of people working as a class for itself, with the unions advocating for workers' rights.

Trade union density is the percentage of wage earners in a population who are part of a union. Table 4.1 shows this density across time and countries. We can see a wide range in union membership across countries. For example, 86 per cent of workers in Iceland are in a union while only one-tenth of workers in the United States are union members. Canada falls somewhere in the mid- to high range.

We can also see that, in general, union density is on the decline. Each country in the sample has seen a drop in union density over the 15-year period. In Canada, the decline has been relatively small, only 1.6 per cent. However, the decline in Sweden has been steep (13.3 per cent).

TABLE 4.1 | Trade union density, selected countries, 1999–2014 (per cent)

	1999	2005	2011	2014
Turkey	10.6	8.2	5.4	6.3*
Korea	11.7	9.9	9.9	10.1*
United States	13.4	12.0	11.3	10.7
Mexico	15.8	16.9	14.5	13.5
Japan	22.2	18.8	19.0	17.6
Australia	25.4	22.3	18.5	15.5
Canada	28.0	27.7	27.1	26.4
Ireland	38.7	34.0	32.6	27.4
Sweden	80.6	76.5	67.5	67.3
Iceland	87.4	84.0	85.2	86.4
Average of OECD[1] countries	20.8	18.8	17.5	16.7

[1]The OECD (Organisation for Economic Co-operation and Development) comprises 34 countries.
*The number reported for Turkey is from 2013, and the number reported for Korea is from 2012.

Source: Data from OECD, 2015, "Trade Union Density," OECD Stat (database), https://stats.oecd.org/Index.aspx?DataSetCode=TUD

REUTERS/Chris Helgren

PHOTO 4.3 Unions have fought for many different benefits for their members and for workers in general. At this strike, striking members of the auto workers union Unifor wave to passing vehicles outside the General Motors assembly plan in Ingersoll, Ontario.

Why are unionization rates declining? Comparing rates in Canada and the United States sheds some light on this question. These two countries had similar rates of union membership from 1920 to 1960. However, as you can see from Figure 4.1, the rates have diverged dramatically since this time.

There are many potential reasons for the decrease in American unionization rates. Some people argue that globalization and technological advances have undermined unions. Others claim that the decline in manufacturing has led to fewer union jobs. However, these factors have affected both the United States and Canada, but the latter maintains a relatively high rate of unionization. How can we explain this difference?

In general, Canadian labour laws and public policies have been more supportive of unions than have American laws and policies. Canadian law has simply been more union-friendly. For example, several Canadian provinces ban temporary or permanent strike replacements (people who work in place of striking employees, sometimes called scab workers). These laws do not exist in the United States. Also, 24 US states have "right to work" laws, which restrict a union's ability to require individual members to pay union dues. These laws make it more difficult for unions to fund their work. Furthermore, the process of creating a union is much quicker in Canada. It usually takes only five to 10 days, once the employees have signed a petition. This process can take months or years in the United States.

These examples clearly illustrate how public policies and laws can shape larger social structures in society, such as unionization rates (Warner 2013). Creating a union is one way for the working class to organize into a class for itself. However, these organizations face challenges, such as ideological barriers presented by the ruling classes and structural impediments enacted by them, such as laws.

Class struggle between workers and capitalists can be overt. When workers strike, create a union, or lead a revolution, they are open and clear about their unhappiness

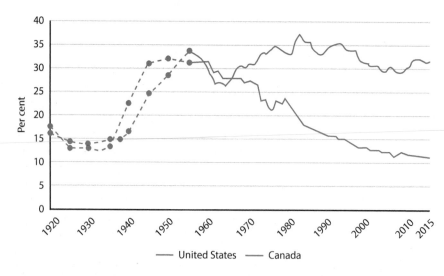

FIGURE 4.1   Unionization rate in the United States and Canada, 1920–2016

Sources: Based on Kris Warner, 2013, "The Real Reason for the Decline of American Unions," *Bloomberg View*, 23 January, www.bloomberg.com/view/echoes/8. Used with permission of Bloomberg L.P. Copyright © 2015. All rights reserved. Numbers after 2011 in Canada are from Government of Canada Appendix I at https://www.canada.ca/en/employment-social-development/services/collective-bargaining-data.html. Numbers after 2011 in the United States are from Bureau of Labor Statistics, 2018, "Union Members Summary," *Economic News Release*, 19 January, https://www.bls.gov/news.release/union2.nr0.htm.

with the power inequality between themselves and capitalists. Marx advocated for overt struggles against the capitalist system. However, workers can also engage in more covert actions to undermine capitalism, capitalists, and their workplaces. As Hollander and Einwohner (2004, 545) explain:

> overt resistance is behaviour that is visible and readily recognized by both targets and observers as resistance and, further, is intended to be recognized as such. This category includes collective acts such as social movements . . . as well as individual acts of refusal. . . . We use the term covert resistance to refer to acts that are intentional yet go unnoticed (and, therefore, unpunished) by their targets, although they are recognized as resistance by other, culturally aware observers.

Imagine that you think your boss or company is treating you badly. Perhaps you are paid a low wage, have to work a lot of unpaid overtime, have to adjust to changing schedules at the last minute, are forced to work in unsafe conditions, or are harassed at work. You have the option of overt resistance, such as forming a union or complaining to your boss's boss, but you fear losing your job or being punished. Instead, you show your unhappiness by engaging in more covert actions. Perhaps you work a little more slowly than you have to or waste time at work. You spend a few extra minutes checking your email or texting people. Perhaps you undermine your boss by talking about her with other co-workers or you don't quite follow the rules—you give customers free refills or you don't wear the proper uniform. You might push this covert resistance so far that you actually steal from your work by taking extra food or other things from the workplace. You justify this action by telling yourself that you're just levelling the playing field. This sort of resistance aims at regaining dignity from organizations that violate workers' interests and undermine their autonomy. Have you engaged in any of these activities at work? Are they ever justified? If so, in what context?

Max Weber and Social Status

Though highly influenced by Marx, Max Weber (1864–1920) took a slightly different approach to conceptualizing inequality. Born in Prussia, Weber became a faculty member at the University of Berlin and wrote a series of ground-breaking sociological works. His *The Protestant Ethic and the Spirit of Capitalism* (1905) was translated into English in 1930 by Talcott Parsons (one of the most famous structural functionalists, about whom we learned in the previous chapter). At the time of Weber's death, he was working on *Economy and Society*, which was completed by his wife, Marianne Weber, and published in 1922. *From Max Weber: Essays in Sociology* (1991), edited and translated by H.H. Gerth and C. Wright Mills, remains the most comprehensive collection of Weber's works. (You will remember C. Wright Mills from his theory of the sociological imagination.) As Gerth and Mills write in their introduction, "the prestige of Max Weber among European social scientists would be difficult to over-estimate. He is widely considered the greatest of German sociologists and . . . has become a leading influence in European and American thought" (in Shimer 1946, 374).

Weber began his theory of social inequality by looking at the distribution of power in society. In *Economy and Society*, he defines **power** in the following way:

> In general, we understand by "power" the chance of a man or of a number of men to realize their own will in a communal action even against the resistance of others who are participating in the same action (in Gerth and Mills 2009, 180).

HIGHLIGHT

Getting to Know Max Weber

- Max Weber's full name is Karl Emil Maximillian Weber. With these two additional names, is it any surprise that he, Karl Marx, and Emile Durkheim became the three founding fathers of sociology?
- For Christmas 1876, Weber gave his parents two historical essays that he had written: "About the Course of German History, with Special Reference to the Positions of the Emperor and the Pope" and "About the Roman Imperial Period from Constantine to the Migration of Nations." Quite a present from a 12-year-old!
- During his first years as a student at the University of Berlin, Weber spent much of his time "drinking and fencing"—a dangerous combination.
- Weber suffered from depression and insomnia and spent the summer and fall of 1900 in a sanatorium. He described his ongoing ordeal in his autobiography, which was later destroyed by his wife because she feared that public knowledge of his mental illness would tarnish his legacy.

While he agreed with Marx that economic power is very important, Weber argued that many other, non-economic factors are significant parts of who has power in society and who does not. Ideas and interests that emerge from politics, religion, and other institutions also shape who has power in society. Contrary to Marx, Weber contended that these other types of power are not simply secondary to the economy. He posited that there are three primary bases of power in society: economic class (income, wealth), social status (prestige, honour), and party (political power). For Weber, classes are about power in the economic order, status groups are about power in the social order, and parties are about power oriented toward influencing communal action.

Both Weber and Marx defined class based on an individual's relationship to the economy. Classes, for Weber, are groups of people who share a similar position with respect to the ownership of property or goods. They are economic categories developing out of human interaction in a market, a system of competitive exchange whereby people buy and sell things of value in pursuit of profit. According to Weber, a class is a group of people sharing a common situation in this market and, therefore, having common interests. The main division for Weber was between the classes with property and those without. So far, this description sounds very similar to Marx's theory of class, discussed earlier in the chapter. The difference between Marx and Weber lies in the finer details of their ideas about class and the divisions they saw. Weber said that class can be differentiated into the kinds of property and services that an individual can offer in a market. Whereas Marx described two main groups, Weber claimed that there were four classes: large capitalists, small capitalists, specialists, and the working class.

Large capitalists own large factories, farms, or other businesses that employ large numbers of workers; small capitalists (what Marx called the petite bourgeoisie) own smaller businesses with fewer employees. Specialists, such as doctors, lawyers, and professors, have marketable skills and training that they sell to the capitalist through their labour. The working class, which is similar to Marx's proletariat, are manual labourers. They do not have specialized education or training; therefore, they have less power and freedom in the labour market than specialists do.

Weber's second main basis of power is status. **Status groups** have a "style of life" based on social honour and prestige that is expressed in their interactions with each other. This kind of recognition can be formal—such as when we refer to a person with a special title or give them a degree to mark their status. The title "doctor" or "lawyer" denotes a

PHOTO 4.4 Working conditions in sweatshops, such as this one, can be quite dangerous and unsafe. Why are we more likely to find these types of sweatshops in developing countries?

particular type of education and occupation and cannot simply be given to anyone. However, status can also be informal, such as when we respect older people even if they have no specific title or position of authority. Social honour may be either positive or negative in that an individual may be given a high level of social esteem or honour or may be disrespected because she is seen to fall into an undesirable social category.

In general, people of high social class tend to have high status. For example, a CEO of a large company is from the capitalist class and also has a lot of status. She is likely to have a lifestyle that involves a large house, designer clothing, and luxury goods. Such people are accorded respect and esteem by others. Conversely, those with low social class tend to have low social status. People who work in fast-food restaurants, for example, have a low social class and receive little status or respect in society.

It is important to note, however, that social class and social status do not always correspond. For example, priests and rabbis have extremely high social status. They are accorded much distinction and esteem and are deferred to in a variety of social settings. Yet they are not necessarily of the upper social class. They are not capitalists who own the means of production; in fact, many of them make very little money. At the other end of the spectrum, plumbers or electricians might make a good salary and be self-employed (making them petite

Social Status Markers

Let's examine Weber's concept of "style of life" by looking at wealthy people as a status group. Go to this book's companion website, and watch two videos "How to Marry the Rich" and "I Tried to Be Instagram Famous," and then answer the following questions:

1. What social status markers are discussed in the videos? How do the videos suggest that you display an upper-class life?
2. Which markers are purely financial? What other types of markers are not based on money alone? Can all these markers be bought?
3. How have the markers of social status changed between the times that these videos were made? How have they remained the same? If you displayed all the markers suggested in the first video, would you be seen as cool by the people who made the second video? Why or why not?
4. How are markers of social status different across groups of people? Give some examples of the distinct social markers in your group of friends and in others your age. How do people your age mark social status?

ACTIVITY

bourgeoisie or bourgeoisie). However, people in these jobs are not generally accorded the respect or status given to a priest or rabbi. Weber's ideas encourage us to think about how social class and social status are distinct constructs and how power in society is multi-dimensional.

Status groups can be formed from a variety of dimensions. For example, men and women form different status groups. They have distinct "styles of life" and are accorded different levels of esteem. Sexual orientations, education levels, ethnicities, religions, and neighbourhood affiliations could also be status groups. Hence, individuals can be a part of many different status groups but are in only one social class.

Weber's last main dimension of power is party. **Parties** are organizations that attempt to influence social action and that focus on achieving some goal in the sphere of power. Parties are not simply political parties, such as the Liberals, NDP, Greens, Conservatives, or Bloc Québécois. Parties also include groups aimed at improving specific social problems (e.g., a block watch or a parent–teacher group), environmental groups (e.g., Greenpeace, World Wildlife Fund), or even sporting and recreation organizations.

As the preceding discussion shows, the theories of Marx and Weber have certain similarities and differences. Are their theories compatible? Which is more useful in helping to understand modern Canadian society?

Income Inequality in Canada

Many sociologists examine income inequality in Canada by using the concept of **socio-economic** status (SES). SES is a measure of an individual's or family's social and economic position relative to others. It is a composite scale that includes measures of income, educational attainment, and occupational prestige. Income refers to any wages, salaries, profits, rents, dividends, or pensions a person receives per year. Educational attainment is the highest level (grade or degree) a person has completed. Occupational prestige is measured by the educational attainment required, the income earned, and the associated skills of one's job. SES is typically divided into three categories—high, middle, and low.

You can see that SES incorporates ideas about social class and social status, as discussed by Marx and Weber. The concept also makes it possible to deal with some of the disjunctions that sometimes occur between class and status. Recall the earlier example of a plumber. SES can reconcile the apparent contradiction between a plumber's high wages and low occupational status.

One way to think about income inequality in Canada is to look at it over time. Much of the information on this topic (and much of the data presented in this book) comes from Statistics Canada, a government body that collects information about Canadian citizens and immigrants. This information is essential in helping us to understand the population and its various groups in areas such as health, income, and educational opportunities. Figure 4.2 shows Statistics Canada data (compiled by *The Globe and Mail*) that illustrates how much money you are likely to make as an adult based on how much money your parents make. If your parents are in the bottom 1 per cent of income, the data predict that you will make $36,500 per year. If your parents are in the top 1 per cent of earners, they predict that you will make $109,000 per year.

This figure clearly shows income inequality in Canada. How concerned should we be about this issue? If there is a lot of **social mobility** (movement on a stratification system, such as the class system) in Canada, income inequality is less of a problem. If the rich are getting richer because they are working harder and people can move from one class to another through hard work, the gap between the rich and the poor is less concerning.

This idea is an example of an **achievement-based stratification system**. In this system, people's rank depends on their accomplishments; those who work hard and are diligent achieve high social status or class. Conversely, an **ascription-based stratification system** determines an individual's rank by her ascribed characteristics (i.e., the features she is born with). If people of certain ethnicities, religions, or sexes hold certain ranks in society

RESEARCH METHOD
SURVEY

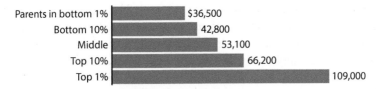

FIGURE 4.2 **How much a Canadian child would earn in adulthood, on average, based on their parents' position on the income ladder, 2016**

Source: Doug Saunders and Tom Cardoso, 2017, "A Tale of Two Canadas: Where You Grew up Affects Your Income in Adulthood," *The Globe and Mail* 23 June, https://www.theglobeandmail.com/news/national/a-tale-of-two-canadas-where-you-grow-up-affects-your-adult-income/article35444594. The Globe and Mail, source: Statscan, 2016 Census.

simply because of who they are (not what they have done), they live in an ascription-based system. Apartheid in South Africa was such a system. The minority white population ran the country, while the black majority was oppressed because of their skin colour.

We are all born with an SES determined by our parents' income, occupational status, and education. But the extent to which a society is achievement- or ascriptive-based depends on its level of social mobility. There are two types of social mobility—intergenerational and intragenerational. Intergenerational mobility occurs between generations. Your parents or grandparents might be working-class, but you are middle- or upper-class. Intragenerational mobility occurs within a single generation. Perhaps your parents were born into the working class but became middle-class during their lifetime.

Many studies compare social mobility across countries. Some measure **intergenerational income elasticity**—the statistical relationship between a parent's and child's economic standings. The higher the number, the less social mobility a society has and the greater the role of parents features in predicting a child's economic standing. Lower numbers indicate that children's economic standing is the result of their individual talents and capabilities. Of the 11 countries displayed in Figure 4.3, we can see that the UK and the

RESEARCH METHOD
SURVEY

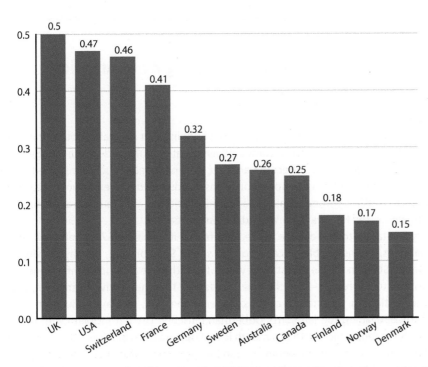

FIGURE 4.3 **Intergenerational income elasticities for eleven developed countries, 2015**

Source: Michael M. Brady, 2015, "Opportunity of Social Mobility Great in Scandinavia," *The Norwegian American* 20 August, http://www.norwegianamerican.com/opinion/opportunity-of-social-mobility-great-in-scandinavia. Courtesy of Michael A. Rogers.

US have very low mobility (with high numbers) while Norway and Denmark have very high mobility (and low numbers). In fact, intergenerational mobility is three times as likely in Norway or Denmark as it is in the UK or US. Canada has relatively high intergenerational social mobility, about twice the rate of the UK.

In his article on social mobility, Barrie McKenna (2012) explains a series of new studies that "turns conventional wisdom on its head" by showing that Americans enjoy less economic mobility than do Canadians. The United States is the richer country, but it is less equal and has less social mobility. McKenna suggests that in the United States, "inequality is inherited, much like hair and eye colour." A recent *MacLean's* magazine article makes this point when it argues that the "American Dream Is Moving to Canada" (Gilmore 2017).

Canadian public policy and tax systems account for Canadians being as much as three times more economically mobile than Americans. McKenna explains that "what distinguishes the two countries is what's happening at the tails . . . Rich kids grow up to be rich adults and poor kids stay poor. In Canada, that's not so much the case. . . . even the poorest of Canadian children have access to good schools, quality health care and decent homes" (McKenna 2012). While social mobility is higher in Canada, people still have difficulty moving up the social stratification system, and great inequality continues to exist.

As previously stated, each of us grows up in a particular class. The people we know also tend to be in the same class because we live in the same neighbourhoods, go to the same schools, or have similar circles of friends. For this reason, it is sometimes hard to truly understand how other people experience social class and inequality. To highlight these issues, Barbara Ehrenreich, a journalist and *New York Times* best-selling author, lived the life of the working poor in North America. Her account of this life first appeared as an article in *Harper's* and was subsequently published in book form. The following pages describe one of her experiences as a minimum-wage worker.

RESEARCH METHOD
PARTICIPANT
OBSERVATION

READING

Nickel-and-Dimed: On (Not) Getting by in America

Barbara Ehrenreich

At the beginning of June 1998 I leave behind everything that normally soothes the ego and sustains the body—home, career, companion, reputation, ATM card—for a plunge into the low-wage workforce. There, I become another, occupationally much diminished "Barbara Ehrenreich"—depicted on job-application forms as a divorced homemaker whose sole work experience consists of housekeeping in a few private homes. I am terrified, at the beginning, of being unmasked for what I am: a middle-class journalist . . .

My first task is to find a place to live. I figure that if I can earn $7 an hour—which, from the want ads, seems doable—I can afford to spend $500 on rent, or maybe, with severe economies, $600. In the Key West area, where I live, this pretty much confines me to flophouses and trailer homes—like the one, a pleasing 15-minute drive from town, that has no air-conditioning, no screens, no fans, no television, and, by way of diversion, only the challenge of evading the landlord's Doberman pinscher. The big problem with this place, though, is the rent, which at $675 a month is well beyond my reach. . . .

So I decide to make the common trade-off between affordability and convenience, and go for a $500-a-month efficiency 30 miles up a 2-lane highway from the employment

Barbara Ehrenreich. 1999. "Nickel-and-Dimed: On (Not) Getting by in America." *Harper's Magazine* January; 298, 174. Research Library Core: 37–52.

opportunities of Key West, meaning 45 minutes if there's no road construction and I don't get caught behind some sun-dazed Canadian tourists. . . .

But is it really possible to make a living on the kinds of jobs currently available to unskilled people? . . .

It may seem excessive to put this proposition to an experimental test. As certain family members keep unhelpfully reminding me, the viability of low-wage work could be tested, after a fashion, without ever leaving my study. I could just pay myself $7 an hour for 8 hours a day, charge myself for room and board, and total up the numbers after a month. Why leave the people and work that I love? But I am an experimental scientist by training. In that business, you don't just sit at a desk and theorize; you plunge into the everyday chaos of nature, where surprises lurk in the most mundane measurements. Maybe, when I got into it, I would discover some hidden economies in the world of the low-wage worker. After all, if 30 per cent of the workforce toils for less than $8 an hour, according to the EPI [Economic Policy Institute], they may have found some tricks as yet unknown to me. Maybe—who knows? . . .

On the morning of my first full day of job searching, I take a red pen to the want ads, which are auspiciously numerous. Everyone in Key West's booming "hospitality industry" seems to be looking for someone like me—trainable, flexible, and with suitably humble expectations as to pay. I know I possess certain traits that might be advantageous—I'm white and, I like to think, well-spoken and poised—but I decide on two rules: One, I cannot use any skills derived from my education or usual work—not that there are a lot of want ads for satirical essayists anyway. Two, I have to take the best-paid job that is offered me and of course do my best to hold it; no Marxist rants or sneaking off to read novels in the ladies' room. . . .

So I put on what I take to be a respectful-looking outfit of ironed Bermuda shorts and scooped-neck T-shirt and set out for a tour of the local hotels and supermarkets. Best Western, Econo Lodge, and HoJo's all let me fill out application forms, and these are, to my relief, interested in little more than whether I am a legal resident of the United States and have committed any felonies. . . .

At "The Palms," let's call it, a bouncy manager actually takes me around to see the rooms and meet the existing housekeepers, who, I note with satisfaction, look pretty much like me . . . Mostly, though, no one speaks to me or even looks at me except to proffer an application form. At my last stop, a palatial B&B, I wait 20 minutes to meet "Max," only to be told that there are no jobs now but there should be one soon, since "nobody lasts more than a couple weeks." (Because none of the people I talked to knew I was a reporter, I have changed their names to protect their privacy and in some cases perhaps, their jobs.)

Three days go by like this, and, to my chagrin, no one out of the approximately 20 places I've applied calls me for an interview. I had been vain enough to worry about coming across as too educated for the jobs I sought, but no one even seems interested in finding out how overqualified I am. . . . At one of the big discount hotel chains, . . . I go, as usual, for housekeeping and am sent, instead, to try out as a waitress at the attached "family restaurant," a dismal spot with a counter and about 30 tables that looks out on a parking garage and features such tempting fare as "Pollish [sic] sausage and BBQ sauce" on 95-degree days. Phillip, the dapper young West Indian who introduces himself as the manager, interviews me with about as much enthusiasm as if he were a clerk processing me for Medicare, the principal questions being what shifts can I work and when can I start. I mutter something about being woefully out of practice as a waitress, but he's already on to the uniform: I'm to show up tomorrow wearing black slacks and black shoes; he'll provide the rust-colored polo shirt with HEARTHSIDE embroidered on it, though I might want to wear my own shirt to get to work, ha ha. At the word tomorrow, something between fear and indignation rises in my chest. I want to say, "Thank you for your time, sir, but this is just an experiment, you know, not my actual life."

So begins my career at the Hearthside, I shall call it, one small profit centre within a global discount hotel chain, where for two weeks I work from 2:00 till 10:00 p.m. for $2.43 an hour plus tips. . . . For the next eight hours, I run after the agile Gail, absorbing bits of instruction along with fragments of personal tragedy. . . .

At least Gail puts to rest any fears I had of appearing overqualified. From the first day on, I find that of all the things I have left behind, such as home and identity, what I miss the most is competence. Not that I have ever felt utterly competent in the writing business, in which one day's success augurs nothing at all for the next. But in my writing life, I at least have some notion of procedure: do the research, make the outline, rough out a draft, etc. As a server, though, I am beset by requests like bees: more iced tea here, ketchup over there, a to-go box for table 14, and where are the high chairs, anyway? Of the 27 tables, up to 6 are usually mine at any time, though on slow afternoons or if Gail is off, I sometimes have the whole place to myself. There is the touch-screen computer-ordering system to master, which is, I suppose, meant to minimize server–cook contact, but in practice requires constant verbal fine-tuning: "That's gravy on the mashed, okay? None on the meatloaf," and so forth—while the cook scowls as if I were inventing these refinements just to torment him. Plus, something I had forgotten in the years since I was 18: about a third of a server's job is "side work" that's invisible to customers—sweeping, scrubbing, slicing, refilling, and restocking. If it isn't all done, every little bit of it, you're going to face the 6:00 p.m. dinner rush defenceless and probably go down in flames. I screw up dozens of times at the beginning, sustained in my shame entirely by Gail's support—"It's okay, baby, everyone does that sometime"—because, to my total surprise and despite the scientific detachment I am doing my best to maintain, I care. . . .

Ten days into it, this is beginning to look like a livable lifestyle. I like Gail, who is "looking at 50" but moves so fast she can alight in one place and then another without apparently being anywhere between them. I clown around with Lionel, the teenage Haitian busboy, and catch a few fragments of conversation with Joan, the svelte fortyish hostess and militant feminist who is the only one of us who dares to tell Jack [the cook] to shut the fuck up. I even warm up to Jack when, on a slow night and to make up for a particularly unwarranted attack on my abilities, or so I imagine, he tells me about his glory days as a young man at "coronary school"—or do you say "culinary"?—in Brooklyn, where he dated a knock-out Puerto Rican chick and learned everything there is to know about food. I finish up at 10:00 or 10:30, depending on how much side work I've been able to get done during the shift, and cruise home to the tapes I snatched up at random when I left my real home . . . Midnight snack is Wheat Thins and Monterey Jack, accompanied by cheap white wine on ice and whatever AMC has to offer. To bed by 1:30 or 2:00, up at 9:00 or 10:00, read for an hour while my uniform whirls around in the landlord's washing machine, and then it's another eight hours spent following Mao's central instruction, as laid out in the Little Red Book, which was: Serve the people.

I could drift along like this, in some dreamy proletarian idyll, except for two things. One is management. If I have kept this subject on the margins thus far it is because I still flinch to think that I spent all those weeks under the surveillance of men (and later women) whose job it was to monitor my behaviour for signs of sloth, theft, drug abuse, or worse. Not that managers and especially "assistant managers" in low-wage settings like this are exactly the class enemy. In the restaurant business, they are mostly former cooks or servers, still capable of pinch-hitting in the kitchen or on the floor, just as in hotels they are likely to be former clerks, and paid a salary of only about $400 a week. But everyone knows they have crossed over to the other side, which is, crudely put, corporate as opposed to human. Cooks want to prepare tasty meals; servers want to serve them graciously; but managers are there for only one reason—to make sure that money is made for some theoretical entity that exists far away in Chicago or New York, if a corporation can be said to have a physical existence at all. . . .

Managers can sit—for hours at a time if they want—but it's their job to see that no one else ever does, even when there's nothing to do, and this is why, for servers, slow times can be as exhausting as rushes. You start dragging out each little chore, because if the manager on duty catches you in an idle moment, he will give you something far nastier to do. So I wipe, I clean, I consolidate ketchup bottles and recheck the cheesecake supply, even tour the tables to make sure the customer evaluation forms are all standing perkily in their places—wondering all the time how many calories I burn in these strictly theatrical exercises. . . .

The other problem, in addition to the less-than-nurturing management style, is that this job shows no sign of being financially viable. You might imagine, from a comfortable distance, that people who live, year in and year out, on $6 to $10 an hour have discovered some survival stratagems unknown to the middle class. But no. It's not hard to get my co-workers to talk about their living situations, because housing, in almost every case, is the principal source of disruption in their lives, the first thing they fill you in on when they arrive for their shifts. After a week, I have compiled the following survey:

- Gail is sharing a room in a well-known downtown flophouse for which she and a roommate pay about $250 a week. Her roommate, a male friend, has begun hitting on her, driving her nuts, but the rent would be impossible alone.
- Claude, the Haitian cook, is desperate to get out of the two-room apartment he shares with his girlfriend and two other, unrelated, people. As far as I can determine, the other Haitian men (most of whom only speak Creole) live in similarly crowded situations.
- Annette, a 20-year-old server who is 6 months pregnant and has been abandoned by her boyfriend, lives with her mother, a postal clerk.
- Marianne and her boyfriend are paying $170 a week for a one-person trailer.
- Jack, who is, at $10 an hour, the wealthiest of us, lives in the trailer he owns, paying only the $400-a-month lot fee. . . .
- Tina and her husband are paying $60 a night for a double room in a Days Inn. This is because they have no car and the Days Inn is within walking distance of the Hearthside. When Marianne, one of the breakfast servers, is tossed out of her trailer for subletting (which is against the trailer-park rules), she leaves her boyfriend and moves in with Tina and her husband.
- Joan, who had fooled me with her numerous and tasteful outfits (hostesses wear their own clothes), lives in a van she parks behind a shopping centre at night and showers in Tina's motel room. The clothes are from thrift shops.

It strikes me, in my middle-class solipsism, that there is gross improvidence in some of these arrangements. When Gail and I are wrapping silverware in napkins—the only task for which we are permitted to sit—she tells me she is thinking of escaping from her roommate by moving into the Days Inn herself. I am astounded: How can she even think of paying between $40 and $60 a day? But if I was afraid of sounding like a social worker, I come out just sounding like a fool. She squints at me in disbelief, "And where am I supposed to get a month's rent and a month's deposit for an apartment?" I'd been feeling pretty smug about my $500 efficiency, but of course it was made possible only by the $1,300 I had allotted myself for start-up costs when I began my low-wage life: $1,000 for the first month's rent and deposit, $100 for initial groceries and cash in my pocket, $200 stuffed away for emergencies. In poverty, as in certain propositions in physics, starting conditions are everything.

There are no secret economies that nourish the poor; on the contrary, there are a host of special costs. If you can't put up the two months' rent you need to secure an apartment, you end up paying through the nose for a room by the week. If you have only a room, with a hot plate at best, you can't save by cooking up huge lentil stews that can be frozen for the week ahead. You eat fast food, or the hot dogs and Styrofoam cups of soup that can be microwaved in a convenience store. . . .

So unless I want to start using my car as a residence, I have to find a second, or alternative, job. I call all the hotels where I filled out housekeeping applications weeks ago—the Hyatt, Holiday Inn, Econo Lodge, HoJo's, Best Western, plus a half dozen or so locally run guesthouses. Nothing. Then I start making the rounds again, wasting whole mornings waiting for some assistant manager to show up, even dipping into places so creepy that the front-desk clerk greets you from behind bulletproof glass and sells pints of liquor over the counter. But either someone has exposed my real-life housekeeping habits—which are, shall we say, mellow—or I am at the wrong end of some infallible ethnic equation: most, but by no means all, of the working housekeepers I see on my job searches are African Americans, Spanish-speaking, or immigrants from the Central European post-Communist world, whereas servers are almost invariably white and monolingually English-speaking. When I finally get a positive response, I have been identified once again as server material. Jerry's, which is part of a well-known national family restaurant chain and physically attached here to another budget hotel chain, is ready to use me at once. The prospect is both exciting and terrifying, because, with about the same number of tables and counter seats, Jerry's attracts three or four times the volume of customers as the gloomy old Hearthside. . . .

I start out with the beautiful, heroic idea of handling the two jobs at once, and for two days I almost do it: the breakfast/lunch shift at Jerry's, which goes till 2:00, arriving at the Hearthside at 2:10, and attempting to hold out until 10:00. In the 10 minutes between jobs, I pick up a spicy chicken sandwich at the Wendy's drive-through window, gobble it down in the car, and change from khaki slacks to black, from Hawaiian to rust polo. There is a problem, though. When during the 3:00 to 4:00 p.m. dead time I finally sit down to wrap silver, my flesh seems to bond to the seat. I try to refuel with a purloined cup of soup, as I've seen Gail and Joan do dozens of times, but a manager catches me and hisses "No eating!" though there's not a customer around to be offended by the sight of food making contact with a server's lips. So I tell Gail I'm going to quit, and she hugs me and says she might just follow me to Jerry's herself.

But the chances of this are minuscule. She has left the flophouse and her annoying roommate and is back to living in her beat-up old truck. But guess what? she reports to me excitedly later that evening: Phillip has given her permission to park overnight in the hotel parking lot, as long as she keeps out of sight, and the parking lot should be totally safe, since it's patrolled by a hotel security guard! With the Hearthside offering benefits like that, how could anyone think of leaving? . . .

I make the decision to move closer to Key West. First, because of the drive. Second and third, also because of the drive: gas is eating up $4 to $5 a day, and although Jerry's is as high-volume as you can get, the tips average only 10 per cent, and not just for a newbie like me. Between the base pay of $2.15 an hour and the obligation to share tips with the busboys and dishwashers, we're averaging only about $7.50 an hour. Then there is the $30 I had to spend on the regulation tan slacks worn by Jerry's servers—a setback it could take weeks to absorb. (I had combed the town's two downscale department stores hoping for something cheaper but decided in the end that these marked-down Dockers, originally $49, were more likely to survive a daily washing.) Of my fellow servers, everyone who lacks a working husband or boyfriend seems to have a second job . . . Without the 45-minute commute, I can picture myself working 2 jobs and having the time to shower between them.

So I take the $500 deposit I have coming from my landlord, the $400 I have earned toward the next month's rent, plus the $200 reserved for emergencies, and use the $1,100 to pay the rent and deposit on trailer number 46 in the Overseas Trailer Park, a mile from the cluster of budget hotels that constitute Key West's version of an industrial park. Number 46 is about 8 feet in width and shaped like a barbell inside, with a narrow region—because of the sink and the stove—separating the bedroom from what might optimistically be called the "living" area, with its two-person table and half-sized couch. . . .

When my month-long plunge into poverty is almost over, I finally land my dream job—housekeeping. I do this by walking into the personnel office of the only place I figure I might have some credibility, the hotel attached to Jerry's, and confiding urgently that I have to have a second job if I am to pay my rent and, no, it couldn't be front-desk clerk. "All right," the personnel lady fairly spits, "So it's housekeeping," and she marches me back to meet Maria, the housekeeping manager, a tiny, frenetic Hispanic woman who greets me as "babe" and hands me a pamphlet emphasizing the need for a positive attitude. The hours are nine in the morning till whenever, the pay is $6.10 an hour, and there's one week of vacation a year. I don't have to ask about health insurance once I meet Carlotta, the middle-aged African-American woman who will be training me. Carla, as she tells me to call her, is missing all of her top front teeth.

On that first day of housekeeping and last day of my entire project—although I don't yet know it's the last—Carla is in a foul mood. We have been given 19 rooms to clean, most of them "checkouts," as opposed to "stay-overs," that require the whole enchilada of bed-stripping, vacuuming, and bathroom-scrubbing. When one of the rooms that had been listed as a stay-over turns out to be a checkout, Carla calls Maria to complain, but of course to no avail. "So make up the motherfucker," Carla orders me, and I do the beds while she sloshes around the bathroom. For four hours without a break I strip and remake beds, taking about four and a half minutes per queen-sized bed, which I could get down to three if there were any reason to. We try to avoid vacuuming by picking up the larger specks by hand, but often there is nothing to do but drag the monstrous vacuum cleaner—it weighs about 30 pounds—off our cart and try to wrestle it around the floor. Sometimes Carla hands me the squirt bottle of "BAM" (an acronym for something that begins, ominously, with "butyric"; the rest has been worn off the label) and lets me do the bathrooms. No service ethic challenges me here to new heights of performance. I just concentrate on removing the pubic hairs from the bathtubs, or at least the dark ones that I can see. . . .

I can do this two-job thing, is my theory, if I can drink enough caffeine . . . At eight, Ellen [a co-worker at Jerry's] and I grab a snack together standing at the mephitic end of the kitchen counter, but I can only manage two or three mozzarella sticks and lunch had been a mere handful of McNuggets. I am not tired at all, I assure myself, though it may be that there is simply no more "I" left to do the tiredness monitoring. What I would see, if I were more alert to the situation, is that the forces of destruction are already massing against me. There is only one cook on duty, a young man named Jesus ("Hay-Sue," that is) and he is new to the job. And there is Joy, who shows up to take over in the middle of the shift, wearing high heels and a long, clingy white dress and fuming as if she'd just been stood up in some cocktail bar.

Then it comes, the perfect storm. Four of my tables fill up at once. Four tables is nothing for me now, but only so long as they are obligingly staggered. As I bev table 27, tables 25, 28, and 24 are watching enviously. As I bev 25, 24 glowers because their bevs haven't even been ordered. Twenty-eight is four yuppyish types, meaning everything on the side and agonizing instructions as to the chicken Caesars. Twenty-five is a middle-aged black couple, who complain, with some justice, that the iced tea isn't fresh and the tabletop is sticky. But table 24 is the meteorological event of the century: 10 British tourists who seem to have made the decision to absorb the American experience entirely by mouth. Here everyone has at least two drinks—iced tea and milk shake, Michelob and water (with lemon slice, please)—and a huge promiscuous orgy of breakfast specials, mozz sticks, chicken strips, quesadillas, burgers with cheese and without, sides of hash browns with cheddar, with onions, with gravy, seasoned fries, plain fries, banana splits. Poor Jesus! Poor me . . .

Much of what happened next is lost in the fog of war. Jesus starts going under. The little printer on the counter in front of him is spewing out orders faster than he can rip them off, much less produce the meals. Even the invincible Ellen is ashen from stress. I bring table 24 their reheated main courses, which they immediately reject as either too cold or fossilized by the microwave. When I return to the kitchen with their trays (three trays in three trips), Joy confronts me with arms akimbo: "What is this?" She means the food—the plates of rejected pancakes, hash browns in assorted flavours, toasts, burgers, sausages, eggs. "Uh, scrambled with cheddar," I try, "and that's . . . " "NO," she screams in my face. "Is it a traditional, a super-scramble, an eye-opener?" I pretend to study my cheque for a clue, but entropy has been up to its tricks, not only on the plates but in my head, and I have to admit that the original order is beyond reconstruction. "You don't know an eye-opener from a traditional?" she demands in outrage. All I know, in fact, is that my legs have lost interest in the current venture and have announced their intention to fold. I am saved by a yuppie (mercifully not one of mine) who chooses this moment to charge into the kitchen to bellow that his food is 25 minutes late. Joy screams at him to get the hell out of her kitchen, please, and then turns on Jesus in a fury, hurling an empty tray across the room for emphasis.

I leave. I don't walk out, I just leave. I don't finish my side work or pick up my credit-card tips, if any, at the cash register or, of course, ask Joy's permission to go. And the surprising thing is that you can walk out without permission, that the door opens, that the thick tropical night air pans to let me pass, that my car is still parked where I left it. There is no vindication in this exit, just an overwhelming, dank sense of failure pressing down on me and the entire parking lot. I had gone into this venture in the spirit of science, to test a mathematical proposition, but somewhere along the line, in the tunnel vision imposed by long shifts and relentless concentration, it became a test of myself, and clearly I have failed. . . .

When I moved out of the trailer park, I gave the key to number 46 to Gail and arranged for my deposit to be transferred to her. She told me that Joan is still living in her van and that Stu had been fired from the Hearthside. . . .

In one month, I had earned approximately $1,040 and spent $517 on food, gas, toiletries, laundry, phone, and utilities. If I had remained in my $500 efficiency, I would have been able to pay the rent and have $22 left over (which is $78 less than the cash I had in my pocket at the start of the month). During this time I bought no clothing except for the required slacks and no prescription drugs or medical care (I did finally buy some vitamin B to compensate for the lack of vegetables in my diet). Perhaps I could have saved a little on food if I had gotten to a supermarket more often, instead of convenience stores, but it should be noted that I lost almost four pounds in four weeks, on a diet weighted heavily toward burgers and fries. . . .

CRITICAL READING QUESTIONS

1. What are the challenges of living on minimum wage? Is working for minimum wage sustainable? Why or why not?
2. What physical, psychological, and emotional problems come with the work Ehrenreich performed?
3. In her book, Ehrenreich writes that her experiences as a white woman were different from the experiences of men, visible minorities, and others. How do you think race, ethnicity, and gender affected Ehrenreich's experience of low-wage labour?
4. Ehrenreich often notes that her experiences were different from those of "real" minimum-wage workers. What advantages did Ehrenreich have that other minimum-wage workers might not?
5. This article was published in 1999 and is based on experiences in the United States. How would this situation be different in Canada? How have things changed?
6. How does this reading help us to understand the problems with living on minimum wage? What does it tell us about the issue that other means, such as a survey or interview, would not reveal?

Poverty

Poverty—a state in which resources (material or cultural) are lacking—is a serious social problem in the world. We can think about this issue in terms of relative poverty, the deprivation of one individual in comparison to another, or absolute poverty, the life-threatening deprivation of an individual. Approximately a billion people, or 20 per cent of the global population, live in absolute poverty. Both absolute and relative poverty are important concerns in Canada. People who are homeless or who are unable to buy food, clothing, and other necessities live in absolute poverty. Many more people in Canada live in a state of precarious housing and employment that is not necessarily life-threatening but places them in relative deprivation.

ACTIVITY

Creating Low-Income Cut-Offs (LICOs)

Defining poverty is a challenge because there are different thresholds (such as absolute and relative poverty) and because it is context-dependent. Statistics Canada (2006) created **low-income cut-offs (LICOs)** to indicate the point at which a family spends a greater proportion of its income on food, shelter, and clothing than an average family. These levels vary by family and community size; the LICOs in the following table represent the amount of money a person has to earn to be above the low-income threshold in Canada.

Low-income cut-offs (LICOs) before tax, Canada, 2015, by community size

Family Size	Rural	<30,000	30,000–99,999	100,000–499,999	500,000+
1 person	13,335	15,261	17,025	17,240	20,386
2 people	16,230	18,576	20,722	20,982	34,811
3 people	20,211	23,129	25,802	26,128	30,895
4 people	25,213	28,856	32,191	32,596	38,544
5 people	28,711	32,859	36,657	37,118	43,890
6 people	31,841	36,441	40,654	41,165	48,675
7+ people	34,972	40,024	44,649	45,211	53,460

Source: Statistics Canada, 2018, *Low Income Cut-Offs (LICOs) before and after Tax by Community and Family Size in 2016 Constant Dollars*, Catalogue no. 11-10-0195-01, Ottawa: Statistics Canada, http://www5.statcan.gc.ca/cansim/a05?lang=eng&id=2060092

1. Select a community size and a household size. For example, you could use your current living situation or the one you plan to have in the future. Using the table, determine the amount of money you need to live above the corresponding LICO. How much money would you have to make per hour (based on a 40-hour week) to pass that threshold?
2. The table below lists the minimum wage for each Canadian province and territory.
    a. Will working full-year, full-time at minimum wage allow you to live above the LICO? Could you take a vacation or time off if you or your family are ill? How much flexibility will you have in your work? Do you have health benefits for yourself and your family (i.e., dental, sick leave, prescriptions)?
    b. Look up the rent for an apartment or house in your community. Could you afford this rent, along with food and clothing, on the amount of money indicated in the LICO? Is the LICO a reasonable measure of what you would need to survive in your community? Why or why not?
    c. The LICO is based on the amount of money needed to pay for shelter, food, and clothing. What other expenses are not included? How much do they cost? Are the costs likely to differ depending on your age, gender, and family situation? Why or why not?

Minimum wage by province and territory, 2018

Province	Minimum Wage (in dollars)
Alberta	15.00
British Columbia	12.65 (11.40 for liquor servers)
Manitoba	11.35
New Brunswick	11.25
Newfoundland and Labrador	11.15
Northwest Territories	13.46
Nova Scotia	11.00 (10.50 for inexperienced workers)
Nunavut	13.00
Ontario	15.00 (13.05 for liquor servers; 14.10 for students under 18)
Prince Edward Island	11.55
Quebec	12.00 (9.80 if tips)
Saskatchewan	11.06
Yukon	11.51

Source: Statistics Canada, 2018, *Current and Forthcoming Minimum Hourly Wage Rates for Experienced Adult Workers in Canada*, Statistics Canada Minimum Wage Database, Ottawa: Statistics Canada, http://srv116.services.gc.ca/dimt-wid/sm-mw/rpt1.aspx

Better Beginnings Sudbury

PHOTO 4.5 Breakfast programs for school children are one way to address the symptoms of poverty (in this case, hunger) among at-risk groups (in this case, children). What other kinds of social programs try to minimize poverty's effects?

HIGHLIGHT

Creating a Basic Income in Canada?

It is clear that working full-time, full-year at minimum wage is still not enough to push someone over the poverty line in Canada. When I teach about this in my classes, I often have a student raise their hand and ask, "why don't they create the minimum wage by dividing the poverty line by the number of hours a full-time employee works?" This would mean that a person working full-time, full-year would be able to make enough to live out of poverty. This is a great question!

Advocates of a basic income are also concerned with how we can increase the income of the poorest working Canadians to help them reach the poverty line. A basic income is a guaranteed annual income that aims to reduce inequality and eliminate poverty among the working poor. If an individual earns below the poverty line, they would receive a tax credit to push their net income above the poverty line. A 2013 Environics poll found that a majority of Canadians across the political spectrum support a basic income. Ontario recently tested a basic income in three cities to see how the program would influence the health, education, and employment of recipients (Tencer 2017), but it was cancelled in 2018. Critics of these programs argue that they are too expensive and may not alleviate poverty because they are not targeted to the very poor and, instead, are spread across all individuals below the poverty line. Advocates emphasize the need to address poverty and see this as an important first step in helping all Canadians to live above the poverty line, particularly in a time of precarious work and difficulty for many in moving into employment. What do you think of the idea of a basic income?

Ehrenreich's article and the LICO activity demonstrate that living on minimum wage is a real struggle. In addition, many people are unable to find work or are unable to work because of health or other problems. These, and many other factors, lead to poverty. Almost one in seven Canadians lives in poverty, but one's propensity to live in this condition is not equally distributed. Table 4.2 compares the poverty rate among different groups of Canadians.

The table shows that the average poverty rate in the country increased from 1981 to 2015, although it was at its highest level in 1996. Women are more likely than men to live in poverty, but the discrepancy between these two groups has decreased. People who live within families are much less likely to live in poverty than those who are single. This last finding is not surprising when you consider that individuals living within families can share expenses (such as rent and car costs) and can rely on one another in times of resource scarcity (such as when one person loses a job or falls ill).

Poverty among the elderly is an interesting example of how social policies affect the lived experiences of individuals. As shown in Figure 4.4, poverty among this group was very high in the early and mid-1900s. To deal with this extremely important social issue, the Government of Canada instituted the **Canada Pension Plan (CPP)** in 1966. The first group to benefit from this plan turned 65 in 1976 and began to take the CPP at that time. We all pay a CPP premium on each of our paycheques throughout our working lives (you've probably noticed these deductions). When you reach the normal retirement age of 65, the CPP will provide you with regular pension benefit payments. Everyone in Canada will get this benefit when they retire at 65.

This program vastly reduced poverty among the elderly from around 33 per cent before the program was instituted (eligible citizens began collecting the pension in 1976)

TABLE 4.2 | **Poverty rate by group, Canada, 1981–2015**

Persons in Low Income	1981	1996	2007	2015
Sex				
Male	9.9	14.2	9.0	13.7
Female	13.3	16.2	9.3	14.7
Marital Status				
In Families	8.8	12.0	6.0	11.3
Unattached Individuals	35.5	36.1	27.6	29.8
Age				
Under 18	12.6	9.5	9.0	15.2
18–64	9.8	15.0	9.9	13.9
Over 65	21.0	9.7	4.8	14.3
National Average	11.6	15.2	9.1	14.2

Sources: Adapted from Citizens for Public Justice, 2012, *Poverty Trends Scorecard*, 5, http://www.cpj.ca/files/docs/poverty-trends-scorecard.pdf; AMSSA, 2013, *The Intersection of Poverty and Immigration in BC and Canada*, http://www.amssa.org/files/Info_Sheet; Statistics Canada, 2016, *Low Income Statistics by Age, Sex and Economic Family Type*, Catalogue no. 11-10-0136-01, Ottawa: Statistics Canada, http://www5.statcan.gc.ca/cansim/a05?lang=eng&id=2060041; and Statistics Canada, 2016, *Low Income Statistics by Economic Family Type*, Catalogue no. 11-10-0136-01, Ottawa: Statistics Canada, http://www5.statcan.gc.ca/cansim/a05?lang=eng&id=2060042

to 4 per cent in 1994, although poverty in this group is rising again (see Figure 4.4). These numbers illustrate that the CPP is very successful. Think about what programs we could institute to reduce poverty among other at-risk groups, such as children, women, new immigrants, Indigenous people, or single-parent families.

The **cycle of poverty** refers to how poverty tends to perpetuate itself and is therefore likely to continue for an individual or group unless there is some outside intervention. This cycle is perpetuated by such factors as low (or no) income, little education, lack of sufficient housing and other material resources, insufficient social connections, and/or poor health. All these disadvantages compound to create a cycle that is very difficult to break and makes it extremely challenging for individuals to escape poverty.

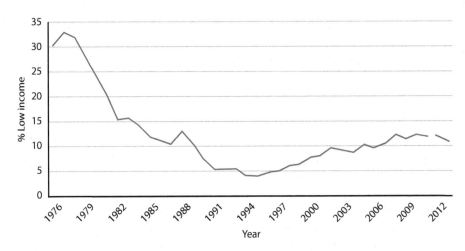

FIGURE 4.4 **Canada's elderly poverty rate (per cent), 1976–2013**

Source: Richard Shillington, 2016, *An Analysis of the Economic Circumstances of Canadian Seniors*, The Broadbent Institute, https://d3n8a8pro7vhmx.cloudfront.net/broadbent/pages/4904/attachments/original/1455216659/An_Analysis_of_the_Economic_Circumstances_of_Canadian_Seniors.pdf?1455216659

For example, if you are poor and living on the street, you might be looking for a job. However, a job search is difficult when you do not have an address to put on your resumé, a computer to print a resumé, or clean clothes to wear to an interview. Children who come from poor families might find it hard to get out of this situation because it is difficult for them to do well in school without proper food, clothing, or supplies. In these ways, poverty can be a self-perpetuating cycle.

In her article, Ehrenreich notes that living in poverty is very inefficient and expensive. If you do not have enough money to pay monthly rent upfront, you might have to pay daily rates at a hotel or motel, which is considerably more expensive. If you cannot afford a car, you might not be able to get to supermarkets. As a result, you would have to buy groceries in small quantities at a corner store or eat out, which is less efficient and more expensive than cooking at home.

Ehrenreich also outlines some of the serious consequences of living in poverty. Perhaps the most obvious is that individuals living in poverty tend to have inadequate housing—housing that is unsafe, in poor repair, too small, or temporary. This housing tends to be in neighbourhoods with high crime rates, high levels of traffic, few public spaces (such as parks), and poor social services (such as schools, libraries, or community centres). Moreover, poverty is associated with inadequate nutrition, poor health care, poor physical and mental health, increased stress, and shorter lifespans. Patrick DeLuca and Pavlos Kanaroglou compared the life expectancy of the 130 neighbourhoods in Hamilton, Ontario, and found that there was a 21-year difference in life expectancy between the poorest and the richest neighbourhoods (DeLuca and Kanaroglou 2015). This is a remarkable difference, given the fact that we have universal health care in Canada that is intended to provide the same level of care across the income spectrum.

Summary

This chapter explored the importance of social class, social status, and inequality in Canadian society. Karl Marx understood social class as being based on an individual's relationship to the means of production—you are either a capitalist who owns the means of production or a worker who owns only your labour power. Max Weber added the importance of social status (the honour and prestige accorded to various groups) to Marx's ideas. Modern Canadian society tends to use socio-economic status to talk about social inequality. Based on income, education, and occupational prestige, this concept considers issues of class and status. The chapter also discussed issues of social mobility in Canada, comparing mobility across countries. Finally, we examined the important social issue of poverty in Canada. The activity on LICOs showed how we define poverty and how various groups are more or less likely to live in poverty.

Key Terms

achievement-based stratification
    system 116
ascription-based stratification system 116
bourgeoisie (capitalist) 101
Canada Pension Plan (CPP) 126
class consciousness 111
classes 102
class struggle 101
cycle of poverty 127

false consciousness 109
ideology 108
intergenerational income elasticity 117
low-income cut-offs (LICOs) 124
lumpenproletariat 109
meritocracy 108
party 116
petite bourgeoisie 109
poverty 124

For Further Reading

Ehrenreich, Barbara. 2001. *Nickel and Dimed: On (Not) Getting by in America.* New York: Metropolitan Books.

Gerth, H.H., and C. Wright Mills, eds. 2009. *From Max Weber: Essays in Sociology.* New York: Routledge.

Giddens, Anthony. 1981. *The Class Structure of Advanced Societies.* London: Unwin Hynman.

Marx, Karl, and Frederick Engels. 1848. "Manifesto of the Communist Party." In *Marx/Engels Selected Works, Volume One,* 98–137. Moscow: Progress Publishers.

Tilly, Charles. 1999. *Durable Inequality.* Berkeley: University of California Press.

References

DeLuca, Patrick F., and Pavlos S. Kanaroglou. 2015. "Code Red: Explaining Average Age of Death in the City of Hamilton." *AIMS Public Health* 2(4): 730–45.

Gilmore, Scott. 2017. "The American Dream Has Moved to Canada". *Maclean's* 28 February. http://www.macleans.ca/news/canada/the-american-dream-moved-to-canada.

Hollander, Jocelyn A., and Rachel L. Einwohner. 2004. "Conceptualizing Resistance." *Sociological Forum* 19(4): 533–54.

McKenna, Barrie. 2012. "In Canada, Unlike the U.S., the American Dream Lives On." *The Globe and Mail* 15 January.

Maclean's Canada Project. 2017. "Why Everyone Feels Like They're in the Middle Class." 16 June. http://www.macleans.ca/economy/why-everyone-feels-like-theyre-in-the-middle-class.

Marx, Karl. 1867/2000. *Das Kapital.* Washington, DC: Regenery Publishing.

—— 1907. *The Eighteenth Brumaire of Louis Bonaparte.* Chicago: Charles H. Kerr.

—— 1975. "Critique of Hegel's Doctrine of State." In *Karl Marx: Early Writings,* translated by Rodney Livingstone and Gregor Benton. New York: Vintage.

—— 2004. *The German Ideology.* New York: International Publishers.

—— and Friedrich Engels. 1848. "Manifesto of the Communist Party." In *Marx/Engels Selected Works, Volume One,* 98–137. Moscow: Progress Publishers.

—— 1964. *The Communist Manifesto.* New York: Modern Reader Paperbacks.

Organisation for Economic Co-operation and Development (OECD). 2015. "Income Distribution and Poverty." http://www.oecd.org/social/income-distribution-database.htm.

—— n.d. "Bridging the Digital Divide." http://www.oecd.org/site/schoolingfortomorrowknowledgebase/themes/ict/bridgingthedigitaldivide.htm.

Shimer, William Allison. 1946. "Review of *From Max Weber.*" *The American Scholar* 15.

Statistics Canada. 2006. "Low-Income Cutoffs for 2005 and Low-Income Measures for 2004." *The Daily* 6 April. http://www.statcan.gc.ca/daily-quotidien/060406/dq060406d-eng.htm.

—— 2016. "Employment by Industry." CANSIM, table 282-0008. http://www.statcan.gc.ca/tables-tableaux/sum-som/l01/cst01/econ40-eng.htm.

Tencer, Daniel. 2017. "Basic Income Would Cost Canada $15 Billion Annually: Report." The Huffington Post Canada 6 June. http://www.huffingtonpost.ca/2017/06/06/basic-income-canada_n_16971060.html.

Tucker, Robert C., ed. 1978. *The Marx–Engels Reader.* London: Norton.

Warner, Kris. 2013. "The Real Reason for the Decline of American Unions." BloombergView *23 January.* http://www.bloombergview.com/articles/2013-01-23/the-real-reason-for-the-decline-of-american-unions.

Weber, Max 1958. *The Protestant Ethic and the Spirit of Capitalism.* New York: Scribner.

5 Race, Ethnicity, and Indigenous Peoples

Chapter Outline

Photo credit: Alex Wong/Getty Images

Introduction

Canada is one of the few countries that have actively embraced the idea of multicultur- alism. Prime Minister Justin Trudeau's comments on Canadian Multiculturalism Day in 2016 highlight multiculturalism's place in Canadian society:

> I join Canadians across the country today to celebrate multiculturalism, and our long and proud tradition of inclusion and diversity. As the first country in the world to adopt a policy of multiculturalism 45 years ago, Canada has shown time and time again that a country can be stronger not in spite of its differences, but because of them. As Canadians, we appreciate the immense freedom we have to show pride in our individual identities and ancestries. No matter our religion, where we were born, what colour our skin, or what language we speak, we are equal members of this great country . . . Multiculturalism is our strength, as synonymous with Canada as the Maple Leaf. (Trudeau 2016)

Despite this position, questions about the sustainability and value of multiculturalism are ever-present. While many people favour the policy, others challenge it and question how a multicultural country can manage the diversity of groups and values that it contains. For example, Parti Québécois member Louise Beaudoin argues that "multiculturalism is not a Quebec value. It may be a Canadian one, but it is not a Quebec one" (Kay 2011). These debates are present around the world, with German Chancellor Angela Merkel famously stating that Germany's attempts to create a multicultural society have "utterly failed" (Noack 2015). Do you think multiculturalism is a good policy and one that can be sustained?

Multiculturalism brings together diverse peoples, but it is not a complete solution to issues of inequality. As we have seen in our discussion of class and status inequality, these disparities can divide the people within a society. In this chapter, we will examine another important issue that can give rise to inequality—racial and ethnic differences. We begin by examining the importance of race and ethnicity in our society. We will then introduce the theory of social construction, which can help us to understand the concepts of race and ethnicity and is used throughout this book. We will also examine a variety of social processes that can be related to race and ethnicity, such as prejudice and discrimination, immigration, and multiculturalism.

Race and Ethnicity

The words *race* and *ethnicity* are often used interchangeably, but there are key distinctions between them. **Race** is a social distinction based on perceived physical or biological characteristics. For example, we often look at hair texture, eye colour, nose shape, or other physical traits to determine a person's racial group. **Ethnicity** is rooted in cultural differ- ences such as language, religion, and the shared history among people in a group. For example, the ethnic group of Italian Canadians may share a language, a cuisine, the Catholic religion, and a common hist- ory in Italy and in the migration to Canada.

Traditionally, we thought of race and ethnicity as natural and permanent. This view, known as **essentialism**, argues that some "essen- tial" or inherent element makes a person part of a specific race or ethnic group. From this perspective, each racial or ethnic group contains traits that have been carried from the past to the present with little or no change. As a result, ethnic groups and nationalities exist because they

PHOTO 5.1 According to research, a biracial couple expecting twins have about a 1 in 500 chance that their twins will have different skin colours like these twins do. These two girls have the same racial heritage—but how will they be seen differently because of their physical appearance? How does this challenge our ideas of the biological bases of race?

robh/iStockphoto

HIGHLIGHT

Police and Race in Canada

According to a 2017 article, the probability of being stopped by the police in Halifax is highly dependent on your race. Reporters Angela MacIvor and Phlis McGregor (2017) examined Halifax Regional Policy data and found that black people are three times more likely to be stopped than white people in "street checks." Jim Rankin and Patty Winsa (2012) found similar trends in Toronto where, between 2008 and 2011, the number of black males aged 15 to 24 stopped was greater than the actual number of black male youth in the city's population. In fact, each young black man was stopped an average of 3.5 times in one year. "Brown" young men (as identified in the study) were about twice as likely as their population size to be stopped, while young white men were stopped approximately as much as their population size (i.e., roughly once a year). Black men were also more likely to be stopped and documented by the police in each of the city's 72 patrol zones. Their likelihood of being stopped increased in predominately white areas.

There are several possible explanations for why the police stop young men of various races at such different rates. Some may argue that young black men are more likely to frequent areas of high crime (where most of the stopping by police happens) or that they are more likely to be involved in certain activities that attract police attention. Sociologists, however, would suggest that there are probably larger and more structural explanations. For example, stereotypes about black youth lead officers to stop, question, and document this group much more often than youth of other races.

High documenting levels that result from racial profiling are important for a number of reasons. Being stopped by the police multiple times per year could reasonably lead to increased fear and animosity toward police officers. It could also reduce trust in the police. Racial stereotypes and prejudice are important factors to consider when explaining these different policing outcomes for youth in Toronto.

Community groups and activists have challenged the use of carding practices and have been quite successful in these challenges. Ontario banned carding by police in certain

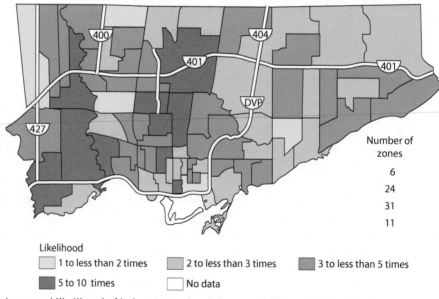

Number of zones

6

24

31

11

Likelihood

☐ 1 to less than 2 times   ☐ 2 to less than 3 times   ■ 3 to less than 5 times

■ 5 to 10 times   ☐ No data

Increased likelihood of being stopped and documented by police if you're black, compared to white (2009–10), Toronto

Source: Adapted from Jim Rankin, Fri Mar 09 2012. "Known to police: Toronto police stop and document black and brown people far more than whites." TheStar.com

situations beginning in January 2017. Following this ban, police can no longer card someone arbitrarily, based on a person's race, or because they are in a high-crime neighborhood. Many police officers support this ban and say that it will improve overall safety by fostering a better relationship between the community and law enforcement. Some activists, however, feel the ban does not go far enough. While the police can no longer stop a person "arbitrarily," the police can always stop a person if they say they are investigating a crime. And these carding rules do not apply when a person is stopped for other reasons, such as at a traffic stop (Draaisma 2017). Activists have called for carding to be banned in all situations. What might the implications of an overall ban of carding be for the police, the community, and individuals who have been targeted?

Black Lives Matter Vancouver

These women are members of the Vancouver chapter of Black Lives Matter. These activists work to bring awareness to a wide range of issues, including police surveillance of the black community, racism and exclusion in Canada's immigration policies, and the lack of black voices in the Canadian media.

are based on biological factors (such as similar appearance, skin colour, or eye colour) and in a territorial location (a region or country). This argument relies on kinship: members of an ethnic or racial group feel they share characteristics, origins, or sometimes even a blood relationship.

One of the criticisms of essentialism is that it sees race and ethnicity as fixed and permanent. Thus, it cannot account for the ways our ideas of different ethnic groups or races have changed. For example, our idea of who falls under the category of "white" has changed. In the early settlement of Canada and the United States, people who came from Greece and eastern Europe were not considered white, although they are often categorized in this way now. Finnish immigrants in North America were labelled as Asian, something that has also changed. If race is fixed and essential, how is it possible that our labels of racial groups differ over time and across countries? Most sociologists would argue that these changing definitions occur because race and ethnicity are both socially constructed categories.

Race and Ethnicity as Social Constructions

Our ideas of race and ethnicity are socially constructed. Berger and Luckmann (in Heibling 2008, 55) argue that

> all knowledge, including the most basic, taken-for-granted common sense knowledge of everyday life, is derived from and maintained by social interactions. When people interact, they do so with the understanding that their respective perceptions of reality are related to one another. And, when we are interacting together, our common knowledge of reality becomes reinforced. Through these processes, our ideas of deviance are socially constructed.

Social constructionists argue that racial and ethnic categories are not "natural" but are created within society. For example, many societies categorize people based on their skin colour. This choice is rooted in historical contexts (e.g., slavery, colonialism). However, we could just as easily use eye colour or height to divide people into groups. Such arbitrary focus on a certain feature highlights how the different physical characteristics perceived to be significant between racial categories hold no intrinsic value and are not rooted in biological differences between groups.

The role of biology in distinguishing between racial and ethnic groups is seriously undermined by the fact that all humanity is 99.9 per cent genetically similar. As the work of Spencer Wells makes clear, genetic testing cannot reveal a person's race. Wells (2002) examined the Y chromosome (the pieces of DNA carried by males) and found that all humans alive today share a common male ancestor who lived in eastern or southern Africa about 60,000 years ago. In other words, all humans trace their ancestors back to this one man, and apparent differences between people are simply "skin deep." In essence, all humanity is separated by only 2000 generations.

Another reason that the biological basis of race is questionable is that within-group variation is much larger than between-group variation. For example, a person might be categorized as "black" but have lighter skin than another person categorized as "white."

Definitions of races have also changed over time and across cultures. We already discussed that Canadians and Americans tend to define race primarily by unchanging physical characteristics and that groups such as Greeks and eastern Europeans were not considered white in the past but are today. However, in some parts of the world, race is not simply a matter of permanent physical features but is seen to be changeable. For example, in Brazil a person's race can change and is intimately connected with his or her class and social status. Roy (2001, 16) explains, "A disproportionate number of dark people are poor, but if a person becomes wealthier, he or she is understood by others to become whiter." In addition, rich non-white and interracial parents in Brazil are more likely than poorer people to call their children white. This system of racial and ethnic divisions challenges our usual understanding of these categories as being fixed and impossible to change; it supports the theory that race and ethnicity are shaped by the social context and are socially constructed.

RESEARCH METHOD
SURVEY

ACTIVITY

Defining and Calculating Racial Groups

Governments around the world conduct **censuses** to systematically collect and record data about the people living within their borders. The earliest censuses were collected in Egypt in about 3340 BCE. The Canadian government has conducted a census every five years since 1871. The census provides important demographic data about individuals living in Canada. This information is used to plan social services, including health care, education, and transportation. It also enables the government to track population changes and trends.

Censuses in Canada and other countries collect information about racial and ethnic groups. Questions about race and ethnicity are posed in different ways across countries and periods. Read the sections of the Canadian, American, and Irish censuses below, and compare them. Think about how you would identify yourself in each one.

CANADA

Source: Statistics Canada, 2015, 2016 *Census of Population Questions, Long Form (National Household Survey, Ottawa: Statistics Canada, http://www12.statcan.gc.ca/nhs-enm/2016/ref/questionnaires/questions-eng.cfm*

This question collects information on the ancestral origins of the population and provides information about the composition of Canada's diverse population.

1. **What were the ethnic or cultural origins of this person's ancestors?**

    An ancestor is usually more distant than a grandparent.

    For example, Canadian, English, Chinese, French, East Indian, Italian, German, Scottish, Cree, Mi'kmaq, Salish, Métis, Inuit, Filipino, Irish, Dutch, Ukrainian, Polish, Portuguese, Vietnamese, Korean, Jamaican, Greek, Iranian, Lebanese, Mexican, Somali, Colombian, etc.

    Specify as many origins as applicable using capital letters. ↗

2. **Is this person an Aboriginal person, that is, First Nations (North American Indian), Métis or Inuk (Inuit)?**

    Note: First Nations (North American Indian) includes Status and Non-Status Indians.

    If "Yes", mark the circle(s) that best describe(s) this person now.

    ☐ No, not an Aboriginal person. Continue with the next question.
    ☐ Yes, First Nations (North American Indian). Go to question 4.
    ☐ Yes, Métis. Go to question 4.
    ☐ Yes, Inuk (Inuit). Go to question 4.

This question collects information in accordance with the *Employment Equity Act* and its Regulations and Guidelines to support programs that promote equal opportunity for everyone to share in the social, cultural, and economic life of Canada

3. **Is this person:**

    Mark more than one circle or specify, if applicable.

    ☐ White   ☐ South Asian (*e.g., East Indian, Pakistani, Sri Lankan, etc.*)
    ☐ Chinese   ☐ Black   ☐ Filipino
    ☐ Latin American   ☐ Arab   ☐ Southeast Asian
    ☐ West Asian (*e.g., Iranian, Afghan, etc.*)   ☐ Korean   (*e.g., Vietnamese, Cambodian, Laotian, Thai, etc.*)
    ☐ Japanese   ☐ Other—Specify ↗

4. **Is this person a Status Indian (Registered or Treaty Indian as defined by the *Indian Act* of Canada)?**

    ☐ No   ☐ Yes, Status Indian (Registered or Treaty)

5. **Is this person a member of a First Nation/Indian band?**

    If "Yes ", which First Nation/Indian band?

    For example, Musqueam Indian Band, Sturgeon Lake First Nation, Atikamekw of Manawan.

    ☐ No   ☐ Yes, member of a First Nation/Indian band. (Specify name of First Nation/Indian band.)

1. What do these questions tell us about how Canada, the United States, and Ireland (see also page 136) think about race and ethnicity? Do these categories make sense? Why are some categories countries, some "racial" or ethnic groups, and others regions?
2. You will note that the current censuses allow respondents to define their ethnicity as within two different categories and to combine categories. Why is this option useful? Are there any problems with it?
3. Find a census from a different country online. How does it compare to these three censuses?

The question about race and ethnicity listed above is used in the Canadian census.

Continued

1. Is Person 1 of Hispanic, Latino, or Spanish origin?

☐ No, not of Hispanic, Latino, or Spanish origin
☐ Yes, Mexican, Mexican Am., Chicano
☐ Yes, Puerto Rican
☐ Yes, Cuban
☐ Yes, another Hispanic, Latino, or Spanish origin—*Print origin, for example Argentinean, Colombia, Dominican, Nicaraguan, Salvadoran, Spaniard, and so on.* ⟍

2. What is Person 1's race? Mark ☒ in one or more boxes.

☐ White
☐ Black, Africa Am., or Negro
☐ American Indian or Alaska Native—*Print name of enrolled or principal tribe.*
☐ Asian Indian
☐ Chinese
☐ Filipino
☐ Japanese
☐ Korean
☐ Vietnamese
☐ Other Asian—*Print race, for example, Hmong, Laotian, Thai, Pakistani, Cambodian, and so on.*

_____

☐ Native Hawaiian
☐ Guamanian or Chamorro
☐ Samoan
☐ Other Pacific Islander—*Print race, for example, Fijian, Tongan, and so on.*

_____

☐ Some other race—*Print race.*

_____ ⟍

UNITED STATES

Source: The United States Census Bureau. http://www.census.gov/history/pdf/ 2010questionnaire.pdf

What is your ethnic or cultural background?

(Choose ONE section for A to D, then ⊟ the appropriate box)

A. White

1 ☐ Irish
2 ☐ Irish Traveler
3 ☐ Any other White background

B. Black or Black Irish

4 ☐ African
5 ☐ Any other Black background

C. Asian or Asian Irish

6 ☐ Chinese
7 ☐ Any other Asian background

D. Other, including mixed race background

8 ☐ Other, write in description

IRELAND

Source: Central Statistics Office (Ireland). http://www.cso.ie/en/media/csoie/census/census2016/2016censusforms/65995_English_Household_2016_New_Version_Do_Not_Complete.pdf

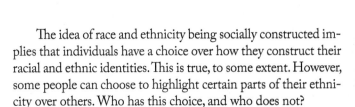

1. Why would some people argue that we should no longer collect information about race and ethnicity in Canada?

2. Why is it useful (or not useful) to collect information about race and ethnicity? How could we use this information to plan government programs (such as health care, education, pensions, policing), communities, or other things?

The idea of race and ethnicity being socially constructed implies that individuals have a choice over how they construct their racial and ethnic identities. This is true, to some extent. However, some people can choose to highlight certain parts of their ethnicity over others. Who has this choice, and who does not?

In the following article, American sociologist Mary C. Waters discusses what she labels optional ethnicities. She argues that white people in the United States have the ability to select the ethnic label they would like to claim or to claim no ethnic label at all. These white Americans can choose to be seen as a "hyphenated American" (e.g., German-American, Italian-American, Polish-American) or to simply be categorized as "American." For them, claiming an ethnicity is often symbolic. According to Waters, **symbolic ethnicity** is an individualistic label that has little cost for the individual. In this way, white people can celebrate Oktoberfest or Cinco de Mayo but ignore other ethnic holidays and traditions. Visible minorities, however, do not have this same freedom. They often have no control over the ethnic labels that others assign to them. As you read the article, think about whether (and, if so, how) Waters's argument applies in Canada. Does it need to be adapted for the Canadian context?

fivelakes-photos/Thinkstock

PHOTO 5.2 How does understanding this Oktoberfest parade through the lens of optional ethnicities change the way you see this event and others like it? What, if any, problems exist with these displays?

Optional Ethnicities: For Whites Only?

Mary C. Waters

. . .

Ethnic Identities for Whites in the 1990s

What does it mean to talk about ethnicity as an option for an individual? To argue that an individual has some degree of choice in their ethnic identity flies in the face of the common sense notion of ethnicity many of us believe in—that one's ethnic identity is a fixed characteristic, reflective of blood ties and given at birth. However, social scientists who study ethnicity have long concluded that while ethnicity is based in a *belief* in a common ancestry, ethnicity is primarily a *social* phenomenon, not a biological one (Alba 1985, 1990; Barth 1969; Weber [1921] 1968, p. 389). The belief that members of an ethnic group have that they share

Waters, Mary C. 1996. "Optional Ethnicities: For Whites Only?" In Silvia Pedraza and Ruben Rumbaut, eds, *Origins and Destinies*, 1st edn, 444–54. © 1996 South-Western, a part of Cengage, Inc. Reproduced with permission. www.cengage.com/permissions.

READING

a common ancestry may not be a fact. There is a great deal of change in ethnic identities across generations through intermarriage, changing allegiances, and changing social categories. There is also a much larger amount of change in the identities of individuals over their life than is commonly believed. While most people are aware of the phenomena known as "passing"—people raised as one race who change at some point and claim a different race as their identity—there are similar life-course changes in ethnicity that happen all the time and are not given the same degree of attention as "racial passing."

White Americans of European ancestry can be described as having a great deal of choice in terms of their ethnic identities. The two major types of options white Americans can exercise are (1) the option of whether to claim any specific ancestry, or to just be "white" or American, [Lieberson (1985) called these people "unhyphenated whites"] and (2) the choice of which of their European ancestries to choose to include in their description of their own identities. In both cases, the option of choosing how to present yourself on surveys and in everyday social interactions exists for whites because of social changes and societal conditions that have created a great deal of social mobility, immigrant assimilation, and political and economic power for whites in the United States. Specifically, the option of being able to not claim any ethnic identity exists for whites of European background in the United States because they are the majority group—in terms of holding political and social power, as well as being a numerical majority. The option of choosing among different ethnicities in their family backgrounds exists because the degree of discrimination and social distance attached to specific European backgrounds has diminished over time. . . .

Symbolic Ethnicities for White Americans

What do these ethnic identities mean to people and why do they cling to them rather than just abandoning the tie and calling themselves American? My own field research with suburban whites in California and Pennsylvania found that later-generation descendants of European origin maintain what are called "symbolic ethnicities." Symbolic ethnicity is a term coined by Herbert Gans (1979) to refer to ethnicity that is individualistic in nature and without real social cost for the individual. These symbolic identifications are essentially leisure time activities, rooted in nuclear family traditions and reinforced by the voluntary enjoyable aspects of being ethnic (Waters 1990). Richard Alba (1990) also found later-generation whites . . . who chose to keep a tie with an ethnic identity because of the enjoyable and voluntary aspects to those identities, along with the feelings of specialness they entailed. An example of symbolic ethnicity is individuals who identify as Irish, for example, on occasions such as Saint Patrick's Day, on family holidays, or for vacations. They do not usually belong to Irish-American organizations, live in Irish neighbourhoods, work in Irish jobs, or marry other Irish people. The symbolic meaning of being Irish American can be constructed by individuals from mass media images, family traditions, or other intermittent social activities. In other words, for later-generation white ethnics, ethnicity is not something that influences their lives unless they want it to. In the world of work and school and neighbourhood, individuals do not have to admit to being ethnic unless they choose to. And for an increasing number of European-origin individuals whose parents and grandparents have intermarried, the ethnicity they claim is largely a matter of personal choice as they sort through all of the possible combinations of groups in their genealogies. . . .

Race Relations and Symbolic Ethnicity

However much symbolic ethnicity is without cost for the individual, there is a cost associated with symbolic ethnicity for the society. That is because symbolic ethnicities of the type described here are confined to white Americans of European origin. Black Americans, Hispanic Americans, Asian Americans, and American Indians do not have the option of a symbolic ethnicity at present in the United States. For all of the ways in which ethnicity does not matter for white Americans, it does matter for non-whites. Who your ancestors are does affect your choice of spouse, where you live, what job you have, who your friends are, and what your chances are for success in American society, if those ancestors happen not to be from Europe. The reality is that white ethnics have a lot more choice and room for manoeuvre than they themselves think they do. The situation is very different for members of racial minorities, whose lives are strongly influenced by their race or national origin regardless of how much they may choose not to identify themselves in terms of their ancestries. . . .

One important implication of these identities is that they tend to be very individualistic. There is a tendency to view valuing diversity in a pluralist environment as equating all groups. The symbolic ethnic tends to think that all groups are equal; everyone has a background that is their right to celebrate and pass on to their children. This leads to the conclusion that all identities are equal and all identities in some sense are interchangeable—"I'm Italian American, you're Polish American. I'm Irish American, you're African American." The important thing is to treat people as individuals and all equally. However, this assumption ignores the very big difference between an individualistic symbolic ethnic identity and a socially enforced and imposed racial identity.

My favorite example of how this type of thinking can lead to some severe misunderstandings between people of different backgrounds is from the Dear Abby advice column. A few years back a person wrote in who had asked an acquaintance of Asian background where his family was from. His acquaintance answered that this was a rude question and he would not reply. The bewildered white asked Abby why it was rude, since he thought it was a sign of respect to wonder where people were from, and he certainly would not mind anyone asking HIM about where his family was from. Abby asked her readers to write in to say whether it was rude to ask about a person's ethnic background. She reported that she got a large response, that most non-whites thought it was a sign of disrespect, and whites thought it was flattering:

> Dear Abby,
> I am 100 per cent American and because I am of Asian ancestry I am often asked "What are you?" It's not the personal nature of this question that bothers me, it's the question itself. This query seems to question my very humanity. "What am I? Why I am a person like everyone else!"
> Signed, A REAL AMERICAN

> Dear Abby,
> Why do people resent being asked what they are? The Irish are so proud of being Irish, they tell you before you even ask. Tip O'Neill has never tried to hide his Irish ancestry.
> Signed, JIMMY.

In this exchange JIMMY cannot understand why Asians are not as happy to be asked about their ethnicity as he is, because he understands his ethnicity and theirs to be separate but equal. Everyone has to come from somewhere—his family from Ireland, another's family from Asia—each has a history and each should be proud of it. But the reason he cannot understand the perspective of the Asian American is that all ethnicities are not equal; all are not symbolic, costless, and voluntary. When white Americans equate their own symbolic ethnicities with the socially enforced identities of non-white Americans, they obscure the fact that the experiences of whites and non-whites have been qualitatively different in the United States and that the current identities of individuals partly reflect that unequal history.

In the next section I describe how relations between black and white students on college campuses reflect some of these asymmetries in the understanding of what a racial or ethnic identity means. While I focus on black and white students in the following discussion, you should be aware that the myriad other groups in the United States—Mexican Americans, American Indians, Japanese Americans—all have some degree of social and individual influences on their identities, which reflect the group's social and economic history and present circumstance.

Relations on College Campuses

Both black and white students face the task of developing their race and ethnic identities. Sociologists and psychologists note that at the time people leave home and begin to live independently from their parents, often ages 18 to 22, they report a heightened sense of racial and ethnic identity as they sort through how much of their beliefs and behaviors are idiosyncratic to their families and how much are shared with other people. It is not until one comes in close contact with many people who are different from oneself that individuals realize the ways in which their backgrounds may influence their individual personality. This involves coming into contact with people who are different in terms of their ethnicity, class, religion, region, and race. For white students, the ethnicity they claim is more often than not a symbolic one—with all of the voluntary, enjoyable, and intermittent characteristics I have described above.

Black students at the university are also developing identities through interactions with others who are different from them. Their identity development is more complicated than that of whites because of the added element of racial discrimination and racism, along with the "ethnic" developments of finding others who share their background. Thus black students have the positive attraction of being around other black students who share some cultural elements, as well as the need to band together with other students in a reactive and oppositional way in the face of racist incidents on campus. . . .

Many black students experience racism personally for the first time on campus. The upper-middle-class students from white suburbs were often isolated enough that their presence was not threatening to racists in their high schools. Also, their class background was known by their residence and this may have prevented attacks being directed at them. Often black students at the university who begin talking with other students and recognizing racial slights will remember incidents that happened to them earlier that they might not have thought were related to race. . . .

An example of the kinds of misunderstandings that can arise because of different understandings of the meanings and implications of symbolic versus oppositional identities concerns questions students ask one another in the dorms about personal appearances and customs. A very common type of interaction in the dorm concerns questions whites ask blacks about their hair. Because whites tend to know little about blacks, and blacks know a lot about whites, there is a general asymmetry in the level of curiosity people have about one another. Whites, as the numerical majority, have had little contact with black culture; blacks, especially those who are in college, have had to develop bicultural skills—knowledge about the social worlds of both whites and blacks. Miscommunication and hurt feelings about white students' questions about black students' hair illustrate this point. One of the things that happens freshman year is that white students are around black students as they fix their hair. White students are generally quite curious about black students' hair—they have basic questions such as how often blacks wash their hair, how they get it straightened or curled, what products they use on their hair, how they comb it, etc. Whites often wonder to themselves whether they should ask these questions. One thought experiment whites perform is to ask themselves whether a particular question would upset them. Adopting the "do unto others" rule, they ask themselves, "If a black person was curious about my hair would I get upset?" The answer usually is "No, I would be happy to tell them." Another example is an Italian American student wondering to herself, "Would I be upset if someone asked me about calamari?" The answer is no, so she asks her black roommate about collard greens, and the roommate explodes with an angry response such as, "Do you think all black people eat watermelon too?" Note that if this Italian American knew her friend was Trinidadian American and asked about peas and rice the situation would be more similar and would not necessarily ignite underlying tensions.

Like the debate in *Dear Abby*, these innocent questions are likely to lead to resentment. The issue of stereotypes about black Americans and the assumption that all blacks are alike and have the same stereotypical cultural traits has more power to hurt or offend a black person than vice versa. The innocent questions about black hair also bring up a number of asymmetries between the black and white experience. Because blacks tend to have more knowledge about whites than vice versa, there is not an even exchange going on; the black freshman is likely to have fewer basic questions about his white roommate than his white roommate has about him. Because of the differences historically in the group experiences of blacks and whites there are some connotations to black hair that don't exist about white hair. (For instance, is straightening your hair a form of assimilation, do some people distinguish between women having "good hair" and "bad hair" in terms of beauty and how is that related to looking "white"?). Finally, even a black freshman who cheerfully disregards or is unaware that there are these asymmetries will soon slam into another asymmetry if she willingly answers every innocent question asked of her. In a situation where blacks make up only 10 per cent of the student body, if every non-black needs to be educated about hair, she will have to explain it to nine other students. As one black student explained to me, after you've been asked a couple of times about something so personal you begin to feel like you are an attraction in a zoo, that you are at the university for the education of the white students. . . .

The implications of symbolic ethnicities for thinking about race relations are subtle but consequential. If your understanding of your own ethnicity and its relationship to society and politics is one of individual choice, it becomes harder to understand the need for programs like affirmative action, which recognize the ongoing need for group struggle and group recognition, in order to bring about social change. It also is hard for a white college student to understand the need that minority students feel to band together against discrimination. It also is easy, on the individual level, to expect everyone else to be able to turn their ethnicity on and off at will, the way you are able to, without understanding that ongoing discrimination and societal attention to minority status makes that impossible for individuals from minority groups to do. The paradox of symbolic ethnicity is that it depends upon the ultimate goal of a pluralist society, and at the same time makes it more difficult to achieve that ultimate goal. It is dependent upon the concept that all ethnicities mean the same thing, that enjoying the traditions of one's heritage is an option available to a group or an individual, but that such a heritage should not have any social costs associated with it.

As the Asian Americans who wrote to *Dear Abby* make clear, there are many societal issues and involuntary ascriptions associated with non-white identities. The developments necessary for this to change are not individual but societal in nature. Social mobility and declining racial and ethnic sensitivity are closely associated. The legacy and the present reality of discrimination on the basis of race or ethnicity must be overcome before the ideal of a pluralist society, where all heritages are treated equally and are equally available for individuals to choose or discard at will, is realized.

CRITICAL READING QUESTIONS

1. To what extent does Waters argue that we have a degree of choice over our ethnicity? Who has this choice, and who does not? Why?
2. What is a symbolic ethnicity? Who has this type of identity?
3. What is the potential conflict between people who have symbolic ethnicities and those who do not?

REFERENCES

Alba, Richard D. 1985. *Italian Americans: Into the Twilight of Ethnicity*. Englewood Cliffs, NJ: Prentice-Hall.

——— 1990. *Ethnic Identity: The Transformation of White America*. New Haven: Yale University Press.

Barth, Frederick. 1969. *Ethnic Groups and Boundaries*. Boston: Little, Brown.

Gans, Herbert. 1979. "Symbolic Ethnicity: The Future of Ethnic Groups and Cultures in America." *Ethnic and Racial Studies* 2: 1–20.

Lieberson, Stanley. 1985. *Making It Count: The Improvement of Social Research and Theory*. Berkeley: University of California Press.

Waters, Mary C. 1990. *Ethnic Options: Choosing Identities in America*. Berkeley: University of California Press.

Weber, Max. [1921]/1968. *Economy and Society: An Outline of Interpretive Sociology*. Eds. Guenther Roth and Claus Wittich, trans. Ephraim Fischoff. New York: Bedminster Press.

The Consequences of Social Constructions

The theory of **social construction** highlights the ways that the social categories we consider natural and unchanging, such as race and ethnicity, are in fact socially created. It helps us to understand how the norms, rules, and categories of our society come to be and how they can change. Although social constructionists argue that race is not a "real" thing—that there is no biological basis for racial categories and they change over time—our social construction of race has real consequences for individuals in society. Being defined as one race or another can shape the type of neighbourhood you live in, the job that you are likely to get, and the perceptions that others may have of you.

The idea that social constructions have real consequences is called the **Thomas principle**. According to W.I. Thomas and D.S. Thomas (a husband and wife team of sociologists), "If [people] define situations as real, then they are real in their consequences" (1928, 52). For example, ghosts are not real. But when a little boy cannot sleep at night because he is worried that there are ghosts under his bed, they have real consequences. It does not matter that when you look under the bed, there are no ghosts. Not being able to sleep is a real consequence of a social construction.

A humorous example of how our perceptions can be more real than reality is the famous toilet paper crisis of 1973. At that time, there was a lot of anxiety over oil shortages. When people heard of possible shortages, they would often stock up on gas or other commodities. On an episode of *The Tonight Show*, host Johnny Carson started his monologue by saying, "You know what's disappearing from the supermarket shelves? Toilet paper. There's an acute shortage of toilet paper in the United States." After the show aired, 20 million people immediately went to the grocery store and bought large quantities of the product (Crockett 2014). By the next day, most stores were out of toilet paper. The situation was so dire that Carson was forced to explain that the story was a joke. This clarification did little to help; once shoppers saw the empty shelves, they felt compelled to buy more. Even though there was no "real" shortage, seeing the low quantities of toilet paper at the store made people anxious and want to stock up. The perception that the story was real was more important than the fact that toilet paper was in abundant supply. The "shortage" lasted three weeks until the shelves could be resupplied.

Far more important, racism is a real consequence of our socially constructed ideas about race. It does not matter that race is not based in biology, our racial categories have important social consequences. **Racism** is an "organized system of race-based group privilege that operates at every level of society and is held together by a sophisticated ideology of /color/'race' supremacy" (Cazenave and Maddern 1999, 42). Racism leads to both privileges and sanctions. Privileges include the white privilege discussed in the box on page 144. Sanctions include restrictions and limitations on people in certain racial categories. For example, in 1885 the Canadian government imposed a head tax on Chinese immigrants. In 1923, the Chinese Immigration Act went further, stopping all immigration from China except for special groups such as clergy and business people. This act specifically targeted Chinese immigrants to Canada because of their race and country of origin. It was not repealed until 1947, and race-based selection criteria for immigration was not officially removed from Canadian immigration policy until 1967.

Another example of racism is Islamophobia. Islamophobia is the intense fear or hatred of Islam or Muslims. Islamphobia has become an increasingly important issue in Canada as a result of rising rates of hate crimes against Muslims in the country. These crimes against Muslims increased by 253 per cent in the period between 2012 and 2015 (from 45 crimes to 159 crimes per year) (Paradkar 2017). This very concerning increase led Iqra Khalid, the MP from Mississauga–Erin Mills, to try to find information to study these rising rates and realized that this information was not available. She put forward a motion in Parliament to condemn Islamophobia and to call on the government to begin a systematic study of how racism and racial discrimination can be reduced and how data can be collected on these issues. This motion, M-103, was passed by a vote of 201–91 in March 2017. As a result of this motion, the government has begun a large-scale study of racial discrimination and systemic racism in Canada. Discovering the root causes behind hate crimes and systemic racism is challenging, and collecting data on these issues can be an important first step in addressing this complex issues.

To understand the racial and ethnic inequality that occurs in Canada, we can examine how groups vary in terms of education and income. Table 5.1 compares income and education for several ethnic groups (that people self-identified with on the census). We can see that Japanese Canadians have the highest incomes, followed by white Canadians. First Nations people have the lowest incomes, making an average of $12,000 less than white Canadians per year.

Most people believe that Canada is a meritocracy and, as a result, expect that ethnic groups with high levels of education should have relatively high incomes. This correla-tion is certainly true for some groups in the table. Japanese Canadians, for example, have both the highest incomes and highest high-school graduation rate. However, white Canadians make very high incomes (the second highest in the table) but are among the lowest levels of high-school and university graduate rates. Filipino Canadians and Korean Canadians have very high graduation rates yet make very low incomes compared with other groups.

PHOTO 5.3 Protesters in Montreal show support for M-103, a parliamentary motion condemning islamophobia. The motion passed in 2017.

TABLE 5.1 | Income and education by ethnic group, Canada, 2016

Ethnic Group	Average Income ($)	Bachelor's or Higher Education (percentage)
Non-visible Minority	48,966	20
Japanese	48,276	37
Chinese	45,208	40
South Asian	41,585	38
South East Asian	37,059	20
Filipino	37,603	36
Arab	37,987	38
Latin American	37,522	25
West Asian	36,960	41
Korean	36,808	46
Black	35,580	21
Métis	42,067	11
First Nations	33,324	7
Inuit	36,374	4

Source: Adapted from Statistics Canada, 2008, *2006 Census*, Catalogue no. 97-564-XCB2006009.666, 97-564-XCB2006009-111111, Ottawa: Statistics Canada; Statistics Canada, 2016, *Census of Population*, Catalogue no. 98-400-X2016264, Ottawa: Statistics Canada; and Statistics Canada, 2016, *Census of Population*, Catalogue no. 98-400-X201689, Ottawa: Statistics Canada

There are a variety of explanations for this discrepancy. We could point to racism and discrimination, which is certainly an important part of the picture (and something we will be discussing later in the chapter). Another explanation is the Canadian immigration system, which attracts immigrants with high levels of education but often limits their ability to perform the jobs for which they were trained. We will discuss these important issues at the end of this chapter when we talk about immigration and multiculturalism in Canada.

Indigenous People in Canada

Indigenous people include First Nations, Inuit, and Métis people. **First Nations** is a Canadian term of ethnicity that refers to the Indigenous people who are neither Inuit nor Métis (indigenousfoundations.arts.ubc.ca). The use of the term *First* is important because it highlights that First Nations people were the original residents of what is now Canada. *Nations* recognizes that the bands residing across Canada have institutions, governments, and cultural practices like all nations (such as the Canadian nation). The pluralization denotes the vast diversity of this country's 663 First Nations groups, including their various languages, cultural practices, and traditions. First Nations, Inuit, and Métis people make up 4.3 per cent of the total population of Canada (Statistics Canada 2013). (*Inuit* is a general term for Aboriginal people living in the Artic; *Métis* people have both First Nations and European ancestors.)

Early encounters between Europeans and First Nations were trading relationships. The Royal Proclamation of 1763 recognized what it referred to as "Indian" nations or tribes and claimed sovereignty over Indian people. This proclamation instructed colonial governments to respect Indian land and resulted in many treaties between First Nations people and, following Confederation, the Canadian government. There were relatively few treaties in British Columbia, however, which resulted in land claim disputes that continue to this day.

The Indian Act of 1876 outlined whom the Government of Canada deemed to be "Indian" people and allowed it to regulate many aspects of their lives. The government worked actively in this period to attempt to assimilate Indigenous people by restricting their cultural practices. For example, from 1876 to 1996, 150,000 Indigenous children were forced to leave their homes and attend residential schools, which tried to resocialize them and destroy their culture (Truth and Reconciliation Commission of Canada 2015). There was also rampant physical, sexual, and psychological abuse at these schools.

HIGHLIGHT

White Privilege

One of the interesting challenges in studying inequality—be it racial, ethnic, class, gender, or other—is that it requires us to examine the disadvantages of various groups in society. This task is difficult because it goes against our society's dominant ideology that we live in a meritocracy where the smartest and hardest-working people are the ones who get ahead. How do we reconcile this view with the reality that, based on characteristics they do not control (social class, race, gender), some groups have more advantages than others?

Another reason that it is challenging to think about inequality is that it forces us to consider not only the disadvantages that some groups face but also the advantages that accrue to other groups. For example, we cannot think about the disadvantages to the poor without thinking of the advantages our society gives to the rich, the disadvantages to visible minorities without thinking of the advantages given to whites, or the disadvantages given to gays and lesbians without thinking of the advantages given to heterosexuals.

Peggy McIntosh (1988) wrote an interesting article in which she challenged herself to not only think about the disadvantages that visible minorities face but also to enumerate the advantages that she, as a white American, experiences in her daily life. She talks about these advantages of white privilege as an **invisible knapsack**—"an invisible package of unearned assets that I can count on cashing in each day, but about which I was 'meant' to remain oblivious. White privilege is like an invisible weightless knapsack of special provisions, maps, passports, codebooks, visas, clothes, tools, and blank checks" (1). Here are some examples of the privileges she experiences:

- I can if I wish arrange to be in the company of people of my race most of the time.
- I can be pretty sure that my neighbours will be neutral or pleasant to me.
- I can turn on the TV or open a paper and see people of my race widely represented.
- When I am told about our national heritage or about "civilization," I am shown that people of my colour made it what it is.
- I can go to a shop and find the music of my race, into a supermarket and find my staple foods, into a salon and find someone who can cut my hair.
- I can do well in a challenging situation without being called a credit to my race.
- I am never asked to speak for all people of my race.
- I can easily buy posters, postcards, picture books, cards, dolls, and toys featuring people of my race.
- I can take a job with an affirmative action employer without having co-workers suspect I got it because of my race.
- I can choose blemish cover or bandages in "flesh tone" and have them more or less match my skin (2–3).

With this list in mind, what are the potential problems of ignoring white privilege? How is white privilege similar to male privilege, heterosexual privilege, or middle-class privilege? How is it different?

According to the UN's Convention on the Prevention and Punishment of the Crime of Genocide (1948), forcibly moving children of one group to another is an act of genocide.

The residential schools also restricted the use of Indigenous languages. Children in the schools were not allowed to speak their native language but were forced to speak English or French. This rule is partly responsible for Indigenous languages being in danger of dying out. All but three of the original 65 languages are currently considered at risk of extinction. While 87 per cent of Indigenous people had a native language as their mother tongue in 1951, only 20 per cent do today (Norris 2014). Language is a critical part of cultural transmission, especially in groups that primarily pass culture from one generation to the next orally. We will discuss the important role of language further in Chapter 8.

The Canadian government also limited First Nations political rights. First Nations people did not have the right to vote in federal elections in Canada until 1960 and in provincial elections in Quebec until 1969, far later than any other racial or ethnic group in the country (see the box on p. 147). Working on land claims and participating in potlatches, an important cultural and economic practice in many First Nations communities, were illegal until 1951.

The consequences of these injustices are evident in the long-term inequality experienced by First Nations people in Canada. Along with Métis and Inuit people, First Nations individuals and families make roughly 73 per cent of the average income in

Canada (see Figure 5.1), up from 56 per cent in 1996. This is a significant gap. Poverty rates in Indigenous communities are also staggeringly high. In 2010, the poverty rate of 15.2 per cent among First Nations people was well above the national average of 9.0 per cent (Statistics Canada 2011). However, the child poverty rate reveals the starkest inequality between First Nations people and other Canadians. Poverty rates are two to three times higher for First Nations children than they are for other children. This is particularly stark for non-Status First Nations people. "Status" is about being registered under the Indian Act and makes a person eligible for benefits, rights, programs, and services. If one is not registered in this way, one does not have the same access to these benefits and programs. In Manitoba and Saskatchewan, more than two in three Status First Nations children live below the poverty line (see Figure 5.2).

While these statistics are alarming and should be cause for considerable concern, a number of possible solutions or policy alternatives have attempted to address the harsh inequalities between First Nations people and other Canadians (see Menzies 2009). First, education and recognition of First Nations issues are important. Most of today's students learn about residential schools and Indigenous culture in elementary or high school; this was certainly not the case 30 years ago. Second, movements and campaigns to attempt to redress and compensate for abuse and forced enrolment in residential schools have met with considerable success in Canada—leading to a commission, payment to victims, and apologies by government officials through the Truth and Reconciliation Commission and its final report (see Chapter 13).

Third, organizations such as the Assembly of First Nations, created in 1968, work to lobby government on behalf of First Nations people. First Nations people have also organized protest campaigns to respond to the various inequalities they experience. The Idle No More social movement, which has been ongoing since December 2012, is most

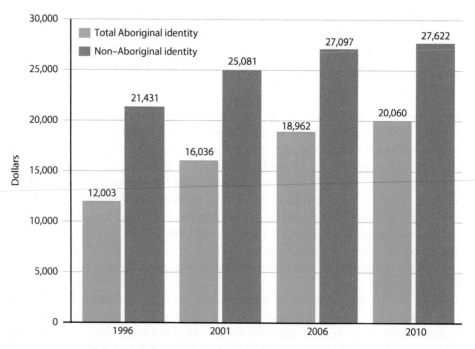

FIGURE 5.1   Median income for Aboriginal people and non-Aboriginal people, Canada, 1996–2010

Source: Adapted from Daniel Wilson and David Macdonald, 2010 (April), "The Income Gap between Aboriginal Peoples and the Rest of Canada," 8, GrowingGap.ca, http://www.policyalternatives.ca/sites/default/files/uploads/publications/reports/docs/Aboriginal%20Income%20Gap.pdf; and Statistics Canada, 2011, National Household Survey, http://www.statcan.gc.ca/pub/89-645-x/2015001/income-revenu-eng.htm

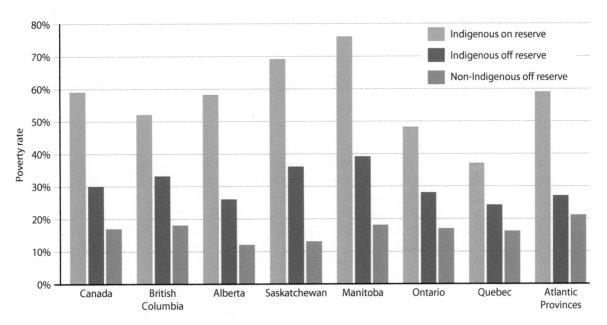

FIGURE 5.2 **Child poverty by First Nations status, provinces of Canada**

Source: David Macdonald and Daniel Wilson, 2016, *Shameful Neglect: Indigenous Child Poverty in Canada*, Canadian Centre for Policy Alternatives, https://www.policyalternatives.ca/sites/default/files/uploads/publications/National%20Office/2016/05/Indigenous_Child%20_Poverty.pdf

famous for the hunger strike by one of its leaders, Attawapiskat Chief Theresa Spence. However, Idle No More also engages in a variety of campaigns in the hope of achieving several goals, such as incorporating First Nations people more fully into policy-making, resolving land claims, and halting resource exploitation by the government. Social movements and protest as a method of countering inequality are discussed in the final chapter of this book.

Fourth, Indigenous groups, the Canadian government, and provincial governments have created a variety of social programs to help facilitate the health, education, and employment of Indigenous people. For example, programs facilitating university enrolment among Indigenous youth have been extremely successful in raising the university attendance rate in these communities. Finally, land claim legislation has helped to compensate Indigenous people for land that was illegally appropriated by the Canadian government. While these issues are extremely complicated and not easily solved, programs, policies, and political activism have helped to address some of them.

Jeff Corntassel is a Tsalagi (Cherokee Nation) scholar, writer, and activist. He is an associate professor at the University of Victoria, where his research focuses on Indigenous political movements, community resurgence, and sustainable self-determination. In the following reading, Corntassel challenges us to consider what peoplehood means for Indigenous communities, how it has been challenged over time, and what resurgence would mean in this context. When reading this article, consider how both Indigenous and non-Indigenous people can foster and support resurgence among diverse Indigenous communities.

PHOTO 5.4 In solidarity with the Idle No More movement, Indigenous and non-Indigenous people in Montreal participate in a teach-in, an informal educational forum used to educate the public about a social issue.

Photo by Corey Pool

READING

From "Re-envisioning Resurgence: Indigenous Pathways to Decolonization and Sustainable Self-Determination"

Jeff Corntassel

Introduction

In April 2010, three Mohawks from Kahnawake used their Haudenosaunee passports to travel from Canada to Bolivia as part of a Mohawk delegation to the World People's Conference on Climate Change. Haudenosaunee passports have been used extensively since the 1920's, beginning with Deskaheh, Cayuga Chief and Speaker of the Six Nations Council, who traveled to Geneva, Switzerland, to assert Haudenosaunee self-determination at the League of Nations. International recognition of the Haudenosaunee passport has been contentious at times, as the United States, Canada, and the United Kingdom refuse to recognize it as a viable form of identification for travel, and Kanen'tokon Hemlock, Tyler Hemlock, and Kahnawiio Dione's 2010 journey was no different; their planned 10-day trip turned into a 29-day struggle to get back to their homeland (Horn, 2010).

While the international journey of the Mohawk delegates was tumultuous at best, the questions posed by the Indigenous participants at the Bolivian conference challenged the three Mohawk travelers to the very core of their identities:

> "They asked us, 'So you're from that region of the world, are you still connected to nature? Is your community and your people still in tuned with the natural world?'" Hemlock said. "We had to honestly tell them, not really, to a degree but not really. So they asked us, 'What makes you Indigenous?'"
>
> Hemlock said that they explained where Kahnawake was situated and what surrounds us and the close proximity of Montreal. He stated that because of Kahnawake's location that, as a people, we too are struggling to try to maintain our identity and live in a sustainable way.
>
> "So they said, 'So how do you do it? What's the example that your community is giving to all the surrounding communities about how to live sustainably with the environment, what are you showing them?'" Hemlock recounted. "Again we had to say, we're doing our best in a lot of areas, but as a community we really have to ask ourselves that question of what are we doing? When we look at our community and seeing so much land being clear-cut; so many of the swamp and marshlands being land-filled; so many dump-sites. There's all these things within our own little community and we're supposed to be the Indigenous examples of living healthy and sustainably with the environment. (Horn, 2010)

While the three Mohawk delegates eventually made it home after a long, hard-fought battle to assert their self-determining authority, the above questions posed to them at the Bolivian conference remained discomforting. When asked about living sustainably today, Indigenous peoples inevitably confront the ongoing legacies of colonialism that have disrupted their individual and community relationships with the natural world. For example, what happens when the medicines, waters, and traditional foods that Indigenous peoples have relied on for millennia to sustain their communities become contaminated with toxins? What recourse do we have against those destructive forces and entities that have disconnected us from our longstanding relationships to our homelands, cultures, and communities? By addressing the legacies of ongoing, contemporary colonialism, this article explores possible Indigenous pathways to decolonization and resurgence, with an emphasis on identifying some examples of applied decolonizing practices occurring within communities today.

Jeff Corntassel, from "Re-envisioning Resurgence: Indigenous Pathways to Decolonization and Sustainable Self-Determination." (2012). Originally published in *Decolonization: Indigeneity, Education & Society, 1*(1), 86–101.

By asking "How will your ancestors and future generations recognize you as Indigenous?" I offer a challenge for us to begin re-envisioning and practicing everyday acts of resurgence.

...

Despite Prime Minister Harper's assertions, that "we" in Canada "have no history of colonialism" (Ljunggren, 2009), contemporary colonialism continues to disrupt Indigenous relationships with their homelands, cultures and communities. One of our biggest enemies is compartmentalization, as shape-shifting colonial entities attempt to sever our relationships to the natural world and define the terrain of struggle. For example, policymakers who frame new government initiatives as "economic development" miss the larger connections embedded within Indigenous economies linking homelands, cultures, and communities. By focusing on "everyday" acts of resurgence, one disrupts the colonial physical, social, and political boundaries designed to impede our actions to restore our nationhood. In order to live in a responsible way as self-determining nations, Indigenous peoples must confront existing colonial institutions, structures, and policies that attempt to displace us from our homelands and relationships, which impact the health and well-being of present generations of Indigenous youth and families. Indigenous resurgence means having the courage and imagination to envision life beyond the state.

Everyday renewal and community resurgence

Despite yonega (White settler) encroachment onto Indigenous homelands and waterways, our cultures and peoplehood (community) persist (Corntassel & Holm, forthcoming; Holm, Pearson, & Chavis, 2003; Corntassel, 2003). A peoplehood model provides a useful way of thinking about the nature of everyday resurgence practices both personally and collectively. If one thinks of peoplehood as the interlocking features of language, homeland, ceremonial cycles, and sacred living histories, a disruption to any one of these practices threatens all aspects of everyday life. The complex spiritual, political, and social relationships that hold peoplehood together are continuously renewed. These daily acts of renewal, whether through prayer, speaking your language, honoring your ancestors, etc., are the foundations of resurgence. It is through this renewal process that commitments are made to reclaim and restore cultural practices that have been neglected and/or disrupted. As Blackfeet scholar, Leroy Little Bear (2005), states: "A consequence of the idea of renewal is a large number of renewal ceremonies in Native American life-ways. It may be said that Native American history is not a temporal history but a history contained in stories that are told and re-told, in songs that are sung and re-sung, in ceremonies that are performed and re-performed through the seasonal rounds" (p. 10).

Our ceremonies are cyclical, as our stories need to be re-told and acted upon as part of our process of remembering and maintaining balance within our communities. It is the stories that sustain us and ensure our continuity as peoples. The Cherokee story of the first man and woman, Selu and Kanati (Corn Woman and the Hunter), provides important insights into how we should conduct ourselves as Cherokees, including our roles and responsibilities. It is about living in a state of to'hi, which are peaceful, healthy relationships. By extension, one practices Cherokee governance through gadugi, which is a spirit of community comaraderie where no one person is left alone to climb out of a life endeavour.

Putting gadugi and to'hi into everyday practice brings us back to a key question from the Indigenous peoples in Bolivia, "What's the example that your community is giving to all the surrounding communities about how to live sustainably with the environment, what are you showing them?" One example of renewal and resurgence relates to honoring our responsibilities to atsi'la (fire). Kitoowhagi or Kituwah mound has always been the spiritual and political center for Cherokees. It was the place where the atsi'la galunkw'ti'yu ("the honored or sacred fire") perpetually burned and served as the heart of the nation. Located near the junction of the Oconaluftee and Tuckasegee Rivers in North Carolina, Kituwah was continuously inhabited by Cherokees for over 11,000 years. Each year, Cherokees traveled great distances to Kituwah, bringing ashes from their clan town to add to the mound while taking ashes from Kituwah's sacred fire back to their villages. However, the Cherokee relationship with Kituwah was temporarily disrupted in 1761.

Under orders from General Jeffrey Amherst during the French and Indian War (1754–1763), Colonel James Grant and 2,000 British, Chickasaw, and Catawba soldiers were dispatched to South Carolina in 1761 to "punish" the Cherokees, despite their desire for peaceful relations with the British government. Cherokee Chief Ada-gal'kala had requested peace talks but Grant refused. Within twenty days, Grant and his soldiers destroyed 15 middle towns, burned over 1,000 acres of crops, and forced approximately 5,000 Cherokees to flee into the mountains. During these attacks on Cherokee clan towns, Kituwah mound was razed by Grant's troops. As keeper of the sacred fire, A-ga-yv-la ("Ancient one" or "Old Man of Kituwah") held his ground and attempted to defend Kituwah from British encroachment. In the end, however, A-ga-yv-la was killed; his bravery and love for the land are remembered to this day.

By the time Cherokees had reclaimed Kituwah, they were forcibly removed by the US government in the 1820's. Over time, the destruction of Kituwah continued and Cherokees no longer held the land. By the 1990's, the mound had been reduced to 170 feet in diameter and stood only 5 feet tall in the middle of a field once used as an airstrip. In 1996, at the urging of Cherokee activists, such as Tom Belt, the Eastern Band of Cherokees purchased the 309 acres containing Kituwah mound for $3.5 million. Despite yonega encroachment since 1761, Cherokees have maintained their relationship with Kituwah over the years by bringing ashes, dirt, and rocks from their own fireplaces and homes to build it up again. These are the everyday practices of resurgence that don't show up on the news or get much attention and yet they are vital to the sustainability of Indigenous nations. According to Cherokee Elder Benny Smith, "If we follow the teachings of Kituwah, there will be a return to it."

In 2009, Duke Energy began bulldozing a mountain directly overlooking Kituwah, and was planning to build a large power sub-station in the area, which was viewed by Cherokees as a desecration of this sacred place. The leadership of the Eastern Band of Cherokees, along with support from the Cherokee Nation and United Keetoowah Band of Cherokee Indians, strongly opposed the Duke Energy project and joined an alliance with other area residents to form "Citizens to Protect Kituwah Valley." With the resulting press uncovering Duke Energy's failure to follow proper procedures in the construction of the sub-station along with the threat of a lawsuit, Duke Energy ceased all construction near Kituwah mound in autumn 2010 (Thornton, 2011). These actions have mobilized Cherokees to honor their responsibilities to protect Kituwah and it has also led to daily acts of resurgence around this sacred place, whether by bringing ash and rocks to build up the mound again, or by practicing ceremonies on it again. To paraphrase Benny Smith, there has been a return to Kituwah through everyday acts of resurgence. These everyday acts of renewal are needed to combat the main barriers to resurgence: intimidation, cooptation, and the politics of distraction, which will be discussed in the following section.

Operationalizing the politics of distraction

The 'politics of distraction' (Hingagaroa, 2000) diverts our energy and attention away from community resurgence and "frames community relationships in state-centric terms" (Alfred & Corntassel, 2005, p. 600). These are the tools of shape-shifting colonial entities to separate us from our homelands, cultures, and communities. Nuu-chah-nulth scholar, Umeek (E. Richard Atleo), discusses how his nation counters the politics of distraction through ceremony:

> A central ceremony of hahuulism involves periodically, publicly, and reverently acknowledging that humans are characterized by short-term memory. Humans have a tendency to forget; they are easily distracted. Humans have a tendency to prefer the "quick fix."…The ancient Nuu-chah-nulth guarded against falling into such times with a periodic remembrance ceremony called a uuk*aana, which means 'we remember reality.' (2011, p. 164)

Within a colonial context, acts of remembrance are resurgence. As I see it, there are three main themes that are commonly invoked by colonial entities to divert attention away from deep decolonizing movements and push us towards a state agenda of co-optation and assimilation. The politics of distraction are manifested in three distinct ways:

- Rights;
- Reconciliation; and
- Resources.

I will examine each of these themes and their responses in order to uncover some deeper strategies for overcoming the politics of distraction. For example, rather than focus on the rights discourse, our energies should be directed where the real power lies: our inherent responsibilities. Additionally, processes of reconciliation are merely reinscribing the status quo; counter to reconciliation, resurgence takes the emphasis away from state frameworks of "forgive and forget" back to re-localized, community-centered actions premised on reconnecting with land, culture and community. Finally, the word resource is a way of commodifying and marketizing Indigenous homelands; in contrast, Indigenous peoples view their homelands and communities as a complex web of relationships.

...

From rights to responsibilities

When addressing contemporary shape-shifting colonialism, the rights discourse can only take struggles for Indigenous decolonization and resurgence so far. Indigenous mobilization strategies that invoke existing human rights norms, which are premised on state recognition of Indigenous self-determination, will not lead to a sustainable self-determination process that restores and regenerates Indigenous nations. According to Dene political theorist Glen Coulthard (2007), "the politics of recognition in its contemporary form promises to reproduce the very configurations of colonial power that Indigenous peoples' demands for recognition have historically sought to transcend" (p. 437). By embedding themselves within the state-centric rights discourse, "Indigenous nations run the risk of seeking political and/or economic solutions to contemporary challenges that require sustainable, spiritual foundations" (Corntassel, 2008, p. 115–16).

...

From reconciliation to resurgence

Reconciliation without meaningful restitution merely reinscribes the status quo without holding anyone accountable for ongoing injustices. At its core, reconciliation has a religious connotation premised on restoring one's relationship with God. In fact, most Indigenous nations don't have words for reconciliation in their languages, which is the truest test of its lack of relevance to communities. When put into practice, whether through a truth and reconciliation commission or another forum (in Canada, for example, the BC Treaty Process as well as the proposed "New Relationship" legislation utilize this terminology), reconciliation in practice tends "...to relegate all committed injustices to the past while attempting to legitimate the status quo" (Corntassel, et al, 2009, p. 145). As Taiaiake Alfred (2005) points out, "The logic of reconciliation as justice is clear: without massive restitution, including land, financial transfers, and other forms of assistance to compensate for past harms and continuing injustices committed against our peoples, reconciliation would permanently enshrine colonial injustices and is itself a further injustice" (p. 152). The permanence of these injustices becomes more apparent as the language of reconciliation is used to promote "certainty" of land title, which in turn attracts more foreign direct investment opportunities. Given an overwhelming desire to secure a stable land base to promote more corporate investment, the Government of Canada, as well as certain provinces, including British Columbia, have begun to use the language of reconciliation in negotiations with Indigenous peoples (for example, the BC Treaty Process) to establish the "certainty" of a land claim in such a way as to facilitate the extinguishment of original Indigenous title to the land (Alfred, 2005; Blackburn, 2005).

An alternative to state-centered processes that prioritize the legitimization of settler occupation of Indigenous homelands is community-centered resurgence. As Taiaiake Alfred (2005) points out, "resurgence and regeneration constitute a way to power-surge against the empire with integrity" (p. 24). This is how we move beyond political awareness to on-the-ground actions to defend our homelands. An example of community resurgence in action is the "Water Walkers" movement in Wikiwemikong Unceded First Nation in Ontario, Canada. The Water Walkers began in the winter of 2002 in response to increasing threats of environmental pollution to their community lakes and traditional waters. According to one of the leaders of this movement, Josephine Mandamin, they asked themselves, "What can we do to bring out, to tell people of our responsibilities as women, as keepers of life and the water, to respect our bodies as Nishnaabe-kwewag, as women?" (Bédard, 2008, p. 103). They decided as a group to undertake a spiritual walk around the entire perimeter of Lake Superior with buckets of water to raise awareness of the need to protect water. According to Josephine, "This journey with the pail of water that we carry is our way of Walking the Talk… Our great grandchildren and the next generation will be able to say, yes, our grandmothers and grandfathers kept this water for us!!" (Bédard, 2008, p. 104). Our commitment to our relationships means engaging in continuous cycles of renewal that are transmitted to future generations. These are the new stories of resistance and resurgence that compel us to remember our spiritual and political principles and values and act on them. By renewing our roles and responsibilities everyday, future generations will recognize us as Indigenous defenders of our lands, cultures, and communities.

Everyday decolonization and resurgence practices

If colonization is a disconnecting force, then resurgence is about reconnecting with homelands, cultures, and communities. Both decolonization and resurgence facilitate a renewal of our roles and responsibilities as Indigenous peoples to the sustainable praxis of Indigenous livelihoods, food security, community governance, and relationships to the natural world and ceremonial life that enables the transmission of these cultural practices to future generations (Corntassel, 2008). It is basically the implementation of digadadtsele'i as communities mobilize for a spiritual revolution. According to Alfred (2009), a process of Indigenous regeneration includes collective community efforts to achieve the following five objectives:

1. The restoration of indigenous presence(s) on the land and the revitalization of land-based practices;
2. An increased reliance on traditional diet(s) among Indigenous people;
3. The transmission of indigenous culture, spiritual teachings and knowledge of the land between Elders and youth;
4. The strengthening of familial activities and re-emergence of indigenous cultural and social institutions as governing authorities within First Nations; and,
5. Short-term and long-term initiatives and improvements in sustainable land-based economies as the primary economies of reserve based First Nations communities and as supplemental economies for urban indigenous communities. (p. 56)

While the above-listed indicators of cultural regeneration offer several promising pathways to community resurgence, the adequacy of these measures will vary from community to community. As Nishnaabekwe scholar Leanne Simpson points out, "Indigenous Knowledge is critical for resurgence" (Simpson, 2009, p. 75). She outlines a four-part strategy designed to transcend the politics of distraction and keep the focus on the revitalization of Indigenous communities:

1. Confront "funding" mentality—It is time to admit that colonizing governments and private corporations are not going to fund our decolonization;
2. Confronting linguistic genocide—There is little recognition or glory attached to it, but without it, we will lose ourselves;
3. Visioning resurgence—The importance of visioning and dreaming a better future based on our own Indigenous traditions cannot be underestimated;
4. The need to awaken ancient treaty and diplomatic mechanisms—Renewing our precolonial treaty relationships with contemporary neighbouring Indigenous Nations promotes decolonization and peaceful co-existence, and it builds solidarity among Indigenous Nations. (Simpson, 2008, pp. 77–84)

As Simpson's work highlights, everyday acts of resurgence aren't glamorous or expedient. It might involve a personal vow to only eat food that has been hunted, fished, or grown by Indigenous peoples, and/or speaking one's language to family members or in social media groups, or even growing traditional foods in your own backyard. For example, I recently requested seeds from the Cherokee Nation Heirloom Seed Project, including rare types of corn and centuries-old strains of tobacco, in order to revitalize ceremonies and traditional foods, while also producing more seeds for future Cherokees. This is small-scale, initial effort that might work toward re-generating the old trade networks between Indigenous communities as well as building healthy relationships by increasing food security and family well-being. Overall, one sees that grass-roots efforts like the ones referenced above don't rely heavily on rights as much as community responsibilities to protect traditional homelands and food systems. By resisting colonial author-ity and demarcating their homelands via place naming and traditional management practices, these everyday acts of resurgence have promoted the regeneration of sustainable food systems in community and are transmitting these teachings and values to future generations.

CRITICAL READING QUESTIONS

1. What is the peoplehood model? Where does it come from and how can it be renewed over time?
2. What are the politics of distraction? How can they be countered through ceremony?
3. What is the difference between reconciliation and resurgence? What does Corntassel think Indigenous people should focus on?
4. How can Indigenous and non-Indigenous people be involved in resurgence?

Prejudice and Discrimination

One of the important consequences of racial and ethnic distinctions is the rise of prejudice and discrimination. **Prejudice** is a negative attitude toward someone based solely on his membership in a group. If I do not like a person because I think he has an irritating personal-ity, that is not prejudice. However, if I dislike someone because she is Chinese, female, or poor, that is prejudice. Prejudice can lead to **discrimination**, the negative or positive treatment of someone as a result of his belonging (or being perceived as belonging) in a particular group.

Academic interest in prejudice increased after the atrocities of World War II against various populations, such as Jewish people, people with physical disabilities, and homosex-uals. The extreme implications of anti-Semitism in particular made people around the world ask themselves, "How do people develop prejudice?" and "Who is most likely to develop

HIGHLIGHT

Race and Voting in Canada

1867	Confederation; Only white men with property can vote in federal or provincial elections.
1885	"Indians" west of Ontario are prohibited from voting; "Indian" males in the east can vote if they own land apart from a reserve and have made at least $150 of improve-ments to this land; People of Chinese descent are denied the federal vote.
1898	White males without property receive the federal and provincial vote; "Indian" males east of Manitoba are denied the federal vote regardless of property.
1907	South Asians are denied the federal vote.
1917	People born in "enemy countries" are denied the vote.
1947	Chinese and South Asians are granted the federal vote.
1948	Japanese Canadians are granted the federal vote.
1960	"Indians" are granted the federal vote.
1969	"Indians" are granted the provincial vote in Quebec, the last province to do so.

prejudicial attitudes?" Theodore W. Adorno and his colleagues (1950) wrote some of the earliest research on prejudice. They argued that individuals with a certain personality type, called an **authoritarian personality**, are more likely to develop prejudicial attitudes. People with this personality tend to use strict or oppressive behaviour toward subordinates. They tend to see the world in terms of good and evil and strictly follow rules and orders. Such behaviour existed in the concentration camps, where many Nazi officers treated prisoners horrifically. When asked how they could do such barbaric things, many stated that they were simply following orders and adhering to the Nazi party's rules. Adorno and his colleagues claim that the authoritarian personality was simply more prevalent among the German population than others, such as the French or Belgian, and this is why the Holocaust occurred in Germany.

The idea that someone's personality makes her more or less likely to be prejudiced is very appealing. But most sociologists would question how some countries happen to have more or less of a certain personality type and how the number of people with this personality can rise and fall over time. The World Values Survey is a large international survey that asks citizens of various countries about their lives, values, and political participation. This information allows us to compare the attitudes and behaviours of citizens around the world. Table 5.2 lists, by country, people's responses to one question in the survey: How would you feel about having someone of a different race as a neighbour? Of the countries surveyed, South Koreans would be the most unhappy in this situation; Canadians would be the least unhappy.

If prejudice comes from personality, is it simply that nearly 14 times as many South Koreans as Canadians have this trait? Or does something in South Korean society that does not exist in Canada's lead to the development of prejudice? Most sociologists would argue that prejudice, and other attitudes, arise from our social context and socialization.

Lawrence Bobo (1983) was one of the first social scientists to examine how social context shapes people's attitudes, particularly prejudice. He argues that prejudice stems from social groups' competition for valued resources or opportunities. This **realistic conflict theory** (RCT) makes intuitive sense—when groups want access to the same things,

RESEARCH METHOD
SURVEY

TABLE 5.2 | Prejudice by country, 2010–2014

Country	Per cent Who Would "not like having someone of a different race as a neighbour"
Canada[1]	2.5
Sweden	2.8
Australia	5.0
Chile	5.6
United States	5.6
Netherlands	8.2
Mexico	10.2
China	10.5
Germany	14.8
Russia	17.2
Ghana	19.9
Japan	22.3
South Korea	34.1

[1] Canadian data is from the 2006 wave because information on Canadians was not collected in the 2010–14 wave.

Source: Data compiled from World Values Survey data analysis tool, 2010–14 wave, http://www.worldvaluessurvey.org/ WVSOnline.jsp

they compete with one another and can come to have increasingly negative attitudes toward one another. For example, if there are a limited number of good jobs, spaces in universities, or safe neighbourhoods, many groups will compete for access to them. Over time, these groups in competition come to see the "others" who are vying for similar resources in increasingly negative terms, see more clear boundaries between their own group and the other groups, and view their own group as superior.

To test these ideas, Muzafer Sherif and colleagues (1961) conducted the Robbers Cave experiment, which involved sending 22 11- to 12-year-old boys to summer camp for three weeks. The boys were very similar—they were all healthy, socially well-adjusted, intelligent, white, Protestant, and middle-class. One would expect these boys to get along well because their similarities meant that there was no obvious basis for prejudicial attitudes.

In the first week of camp, the boys were randomly divided into two groups—the Rattlers and the Eagles. The groups lived in far-apart cabins and did not interact with each other. Each group lived and played together for the week and did regular, fun camp activities; the boys swam and hiked and generally enjoyed their camp experience. Just like any summer camp, the kids in each group formed friendships with one another and developed a group identity.

RESEARCH METHOD
EXPERIMENT

The next week, the Rattlers and Eagles were introduced to one another. The boys from each group were set to participate in a series of competitions, including tug-of-war and capture the flag, to receive a trophy and strongly desired prizes. These competitions led to severe tensions between the groups. First, the groups exchanged verbal taunts (calling boys in the other group "stinkers" and "braggers"—some pretty serious taunts for 1961!). Then the boys became more aggressive. The Eagles ransacked the Rattlers' cabin; the Rattlers responded by burning the Eagles' flag. The boys developed increasingly negative attitudes toward those in the other group. Within one week, two groups of boys who were essentially the same on most dimensions—gender, race, class—and who had never previously met had developed intense animosity and prejudice toward one another. Just as Bobo had predicted, competing over resources led them to develop this prejudice.

After Sherif had created these tensions, he wanted to see how prejudice could be reduced. One popular theory at the time was **contact theory** (Allport 1954). This theory predicts that increasing contact between antagonistic groups will lead to a growing recognition of similarities and alter stereotypes about the other group, thereby reducing prejudice. To test this theory, Sherif created situations in which both groups would have to encounter one another. For example, the Rattlers and the Eagles started eating in the cafeteria at the same time. However, instead of leading to more positive attitudes between the groups, this change was just an opportunity to express dislike for the other group. The groups sat separately (think of cliques in your high-school cafeteria) and started a food fight. More contact between the groups was obviously not enough to reduce the conflict.

Sherif then tried to encourage cooperation between the groups. He created situations in which the two groups would have to work together for what he called superordinate goals, things that both groups desired but neither could accomplish alone. For example, the boys all wanted a movie night but had to pool their money in order to pay for the movie. Sherif also broke the water pipe that pumped water into the camp, and all the boys had to cooperate in order to fix it. It was only when the boys worked together to achieve these shared goals that their conflict and prejudice diminished. Look at Figures 5.3 and 5.4 to see how cooperation created more positive attitudes and ties between the groups.

What does this experiment tell us about how prejudice arises between groups and how we can reduce it? How can we apply these lessons to the real world? First, we see that the social context is very important for creating and reducing prejudice. It was not simply that some boys were more likely to be prejudiced than others but that all boys were more likely to develop prejudicial attitudes in situations of conflict and to reduce those attitudes in situations that required cooperation. This finding sheds light on prejudice in the real world—it can be increased or reduced by changing elements of the social context.

Second, this study lends some support to realistic conflict theory. When the boys were competing for something that both groups wanted, there was more conflict and prejudicial

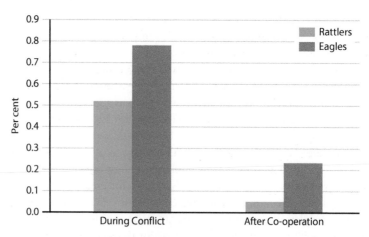

FIGURE 5.3   **Per cent of boys who had negative perceptions of all members of the other group**

Source: M. Sherif, O.J. Harvey, B.J. White, W. Hood, and C.W. Sherif, 1961, *Intergroup Conflict and Cooperation: The Robbers Cave Experiment*, Norman, OK: University Book Exchange

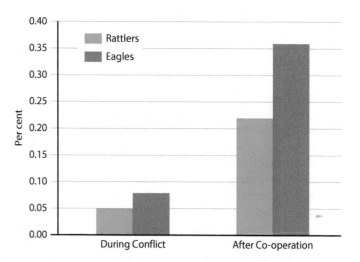

FIGURE 5.4   **Per cent of boys who listed a boy in the other cabin as their best friend**

Source: M. Sherif, O.J. Harvey, B.J. White, W. Hood, and C.W. Sherif, 1961, *Intergroup Conflict and Cooperation: The Robbers Cave Experiment*, Norman, OK: University Book Exchange

attitudes between the groups. This situation is similar to the real world, where ethnic, religious, gender, or other groups often compete for jobs, access to education, or other benefits.

Third, contact between groups is often not enough to reduce conflict or prejudice. Later research indicates that contact between groups reduces prejudice only when the groups are roughly equal in status, the contact is informal, and the contact permits the disconfirmation of stereotypes. It is also important that the contact involve cooperation, which is the final lesson of this study. Cooperating for the achievement of superordinate goals can lead to increased tolerance and positive attitudes among different groups in society. Think about how these lessons could apply to real-world conflicts between groups such as the Israelis and Palestinians. Can we use experiments such as Sherif's to understand, and potentially alleviate, conflict between groups? If so, how?

Immigration

The movement of people around the world is central to the process of globalization (see Chapter 12). While such movement has occurred throughout history, long-distance human migration for permanent settlement has become increasingly common over the past century. The result is a growing intermingling of the world's people, although not all countries receive or welcome migrants to the same degree.

Canada has one of the highest per capita **immigration** rates in the world, which makes our population very ethnically and culturally diverse. Nearly 22 per cent of Canada's population, or 6.8 million people, were born outside Canada in 2015 (see Figure 5.5). In contrast, some countries (e.g., Japan) have extremely low foreign-born populations (around 1.6 per cent of the population).

Canada has three broad categories of immigrants: economic, family class, and refugees. Most economic immigrants are skilled workers. Investors and entrepreneurs, who come under the Business Immigration Program, are also in this group. They can have less education and skills than other economic immigrants as long as they have at least $800,000 to invest in the Canadian economy. In 2014, economic immigrants made up 63.4 per cent of the total immigration to Canada, an increase from 38 per cent in 1991 (see Figure 5.6).

The Canadian government uses a point system to decide on which skilled workers to accept. An applicant can receive up to 25 points for education, 24 points for proficiency in English and/or French, 21 points for work experience, 10 points for age, 10 points for having arranged employment in Canada, and 10 points for indications of being adaptable to Canadian society. Those with more than 67 points are eligible to come to Canada.

Canadian citizens and permanent residents can sponsor their family members' immigration. Spouses, children, and parents who receive this sponsorship are family class immigrants. As Figure 5.6 shows, only 25.1 per cent of immigrants were from this category in 2014, a decline from a high of about 45 per cent in 1993.

The final group of immigrants is refugees, persons within or outside Canada who fear persecution in their country of origin based on a variety of reasons such as political beliefs or ethnic identity. Canada accepts thousands of refugees each year. However, the number of immigrants in this group has declined recently, from a high of 23 per cent in 1991 to only 11.4 per cent in 2014.

Canada's high immigration rate has changed the country's ethnic landscape considerably over the past 50 years. Figure 5.7 shows regions of immigrants' birth. Before 1971, most immigrants were from Europe. Since 1981, most have been from Asia. The number of immigrants from the Caribbean, Central and South America, and Africa have also increased over this period.

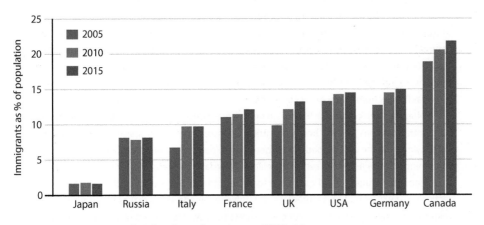

FIGURE 5.5   Per cent foreign-born by country, 2005–15

Source: Ashley Kirk, "Mapped: Which Country Has the Most Immigrants," *The Telegraph* 21 January, http://www .telegraph.co.uk/news/worldnews/middleeast/12111108/Mapped-Which-country-has-the-most-immigrants.html

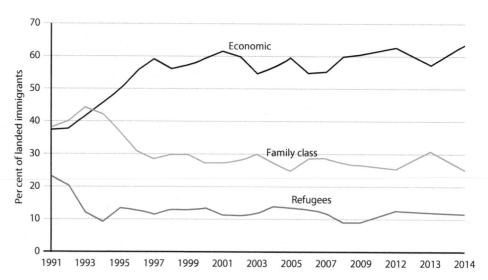

FIGURE 5.6   Immigrants to Canada by category of admission (percentage of landed immigrants)

Source: Adapted from Statistics Canada, 2012, *Ethnic Diversity and Immigration*, Catalogue no. 91-209-X, Ottawa: Statistics Canada, http://www.statcan.gc.ca/pub/11-402-x/2012000/chap/imm/imm-eng.htm?fpv=30000; and Statistics Canada, 2015, *Table 2: Number and Percentage Distribution of Immigrants by Region of Destination and Class, Canada, Provinces and Territories, 2012–2014*. Catalogue no. 91-209-X, Ottawa: Statistics Canada, http://www.statcan.gc.ca/pub/91-209-x/2016001/article/14615/tbl/tbl-02-eng.htm

HIGHLIGHT

The Canadian Syrian Refugee Program

The Syrian civil war, which has been ongoing since 2011, is a massive humanitarian crisis. The United Nations estimates that over half of the population in the country, 13.5 million Syrians, require humanitarian assistance. More than 6 million are internally displaced within Syria, and around 5 million are refugees outside of Syria (World Vision 2018). By 2017, most of the refugees had fled to Turkey, while almost 1 million refugees were in Europe.

Resettling refugees has a long history in Canada. Many Canadians, and the Canadian government, have struggled with how we can help this vast population of people who need humanitarian aid. In response to this, the Canadian government promised to take in 25,000 Syrian refugees in 2015 and had taken in 40,081 Syrians by 2017.

The government sponsors most refugees to Canada and other countries. However, the Canadian program of Syrian refugee resettlement was a bit different. Almost half of the refugees who came to Canada were privately sponsored by groups of average Canadian citizens called "Groups of Five." These groups are five or more Canadian citizens or permanent residents who live in the expected community of settlement and have collectively arranged to sponsor a refugee. This program has been important both for Syrian refugees in Canada and for refugees from many other countries.

Refugees often come with little or no money or possessions because they are fleeing very dangerous situations in their home countries. Sponsors commit to assisting these refugees with paying rent, the cost of food, and other living expenses as well as clothing, furniture, and other things they will need to set up their life in Canada. However, it is clear that money alone is not enough. Refugees need assistance to settle into the community and make social connections that will help them to integrate and thrive in Canada. What makes the Groups of Five unique is that they agree to help refugees integrate socially. This involves helping them to find a family doctor, apply for health care coverage, enroll their children in school, make friends in the

Continued

community, and find a job. These social connections are vital to new immigrants to Canada generally and refugees in particular, who are much less likely to have friends or family in the country.

This novel program whereby Canadian citizens sponsor refugees has been very successful in helping refugees settle in Canada. It has also been a generally positive experience for the sponsors, who have often developed strong bonds with the refugees they sponsor. However, challenges still arise. For example, the majority of the refugees did not speak English or French when they came to Canada, making finding a job, attending school, or making social connections difficult (Friesen 2016).

Research shows that, after a period of initial settlement, refugees are valuable contributors to Canadian society. In fact, 91 per cent of refugees graduate high school, and 29 per cent earn a university degree, much higher than the national average. According to Sharry Aiken, a professor of refugee law at Queen's University, "refugees that are actually employed, their incomes were on a par with economic immigrants, very much contradicting this notion that refugees are coming and acting as a drain for taxpayers and a drain on the Canadian economy" (Canadian Council for Refugees 2017).

Multiculturalism

As mentioned at the beginning of this chapter, Canada has embraced the principle of **multiculturalism**. Vince Wilson (1993) defines this term as a doctrine that provides a political framework for the official promotion of cultural differences as an integral component of society. Multiculturalism is based on the idea of pluralism, the belief that conflict is a central feature of societies and that ethnicity is an essential aspect of individual identity and group behaviour. Thus, individuals are encouraged to display and celebrate their ethnicity and distinctness.

Canada has been a pioneer in multiculturalism. It was the first country to make the concept official policy, passing the Canadian Multiculturalism Act in 1988. This act concerns the management, not the elimination, of racial and ethnic conflict. It pledges federal assistance in "bringing about equal access and participation for all Canadians in the economic, social, cultural and political life of the nation." Canada is one of a handful of countries to adopt such a policy. (Only Australia has officially embraced multiculturalism as robustly.)

Because of its support of multiculturalism and the accompanying belief that immigrants should retain ties to their countries and cultures of origin, Canada is often called a cultural "mosaic." This description directly contrasts with the American "melting pot" in which immigrants are often encouraged to shed their past connections. Instead, they are supposed to assimilate to the "American way of life" by adopting the language, values, norms, and world view of their new culture.

Canadian sociologist John Porter used the term *vertical mosaic* to describe Canadian society and, particularly, to highlight two of its important parts. First, as we have just discussed, Canada is a mosaic of different ethnicities, languages, regions of residence, and religions. Second, these groupings are unequal in both status and power. In *The Vertical Mosaic: An Analysis of Social Class and Power in Canada*, Porter (1965) described how the policy of multiculturalism is not benign but benefits certain groups at the expense of others. He argued that some groups, particularly those of British or French origins, have more status and power in Canada and, as a result, enjoy higher incomes and levels of education than other ethnic groups. He called the British and French in Canada charter groups, the original ethnic groups to settle a previously unoccupied or newly conquered region. These groups have more power than later immigrants and, in fact, get to decide which other groups can enter the territory and under what conditions. This situation leads to great inequality between charter groups and later immigrants. In addition, ethnic differences in a country reproduce class differences and can limit certain groups' social mobility.

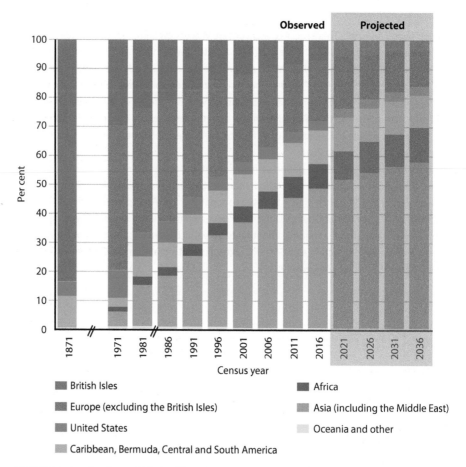

FIGURE 5.7   Region of birth of immigrants by period of immigration, Canada, 1871–2036 (projected)

Source: Statistics Canada, 2017, *Distribution of Foreign-Born Population, by Region of Birth, Canada, 1871 to 2036*, Ottawa: Statistics Canada, http://www.statcan.gc.ca//www.statcan.gc.ca/eng/dai/btd/othervisuals/other009

PHOTO 5.5 Arun Daniel, 11, from Sri Lanka learns how to curl in Toronto. Arun and his mother came to Canada as refugees. This curling lesson is a part of the "Together Project," a volunteer-run group that teaches new Canadians to curl. How might activities like this ease the transition to a new country?

Since 1965, several studies have shown that Porter's theory of great inequality within the mosaic continues. Small changes have occurred, including a slight reduction in income inequality based on ethnicity. However, in general, the economic elite is still mostly made up of individuals with British ethnic origins.

A **nation** is a group of people who are united by a common fate and who have a shared national character. This is often based on a shared language, ethnicity, and history (Bauer 1907, in Davis 1967, 150). A **nation-state** is a group of people who share a physical territory and government, although they may not share an ethnicity, language, or history. Canada is a nation-state. It has a common territory made up of a diverse set of peoples from a variety of language, cultural, and ethnic groups. In fact, this multicultural diversity is, for many people, what defines Canada. Benedict Anderson argues that nations are based on **imagined communities** because "the members of even the smallest nation will never know most of their fellow members, meet them, or even hear of them, yet in the minds of each lives the image of their communion" (Anderson 1983, 49). This idea highlights the socially constructed aspect of nations.

Canadian Citizenship Test

One of the last steps to becoming a Canadian citizen is taking the citizenship test, which Citizenship and Immigration Canada says, "shows what you know about Canada" (www.cic.gc.ca/english/citizenship/cit-test.asp). Applicants are instructed to prepare for the test by reading the department's study guide, *Discover Canada: The Rights and Responsibilities of Citizenship*. Go to this book's companion website, take the practice citizenship test, and answer the following questions:

1. How did you do on the test? Where did you learn the information covered?
2. What kinds of questions and topics are included in the test? How do they emphasize certain ways that we "imagine" Canada? What, if any, questions would you remove from the test?
3. What other types of questions might you add to the test if you were creating it? What other things should people know before becoming a Canadian citizen?

RESPONSES TO "How important are each of the following as a source of personal or collective pride in Canada?" 2013

	Very important	Somewhat important	TOTAL	Quebec only	All provinces other than Quebec	Difference between Quebec and all other provinces
Universal health care	74	20	94	92	95	3
Our country's reputation in the world	64	29	93	93	94	1
The Canadian Charter of Rights and Freedoms	60	30	90	89	90	1
Canada's economic performance	57	35	92	90	93	3
The Canadian passport	53	31	84	84	84	0
Our history	52	40	92	89	92	3
The national anthem	44	34	78	58	85	27
The Armed Forces	38	38	76	61	81	20
The federal system of governance	37	42	79	63	84	21
The 1867 Confederation agreements	33	42	75	62	79	17
Multiculturalism	30	38	68	62	70	8
The policy of official languages and bilingualism	26	35	61	82	55	−27
The War of 1812	23	38	61	33	70	37
The 1982 patriation of the Constitution	23	38	61	50	65	15
The monarchy	10	29	39	16	45	29

Source: Association for Canadian Studies, 2013, "Tim Horton Beats the Queen According to Youngest Canadians When Asked about Contribution to Nation Building," http://www.acs-aec.ca/pdf/polls/Tim%20Horton%20vs%20the%20 Queen%20and%20building%20Canada.docx

Now let's look at the symbols and institutions that represent Canada. In a 2012 poll, the Association for Canadian Studies (2013) asked Canadians, "How important are each of the following as a source of personal or collective pride in Canada? Are they very important, somewhat important, not very important or not important at all?"

Continued

ACTIVITY

- universal health care
- Canada's reputation in the world
- Canadian Charter of Rights and Freedoms
- Canada's economic performance
- the Canadian passport
- our history
- the national anthem
- the Armed Forces
- the federal system of governance
- the 1867 Confederation agreements
- multiculturalism
- the policy of official languages and bilingualism
- the War of 1812
- the 1982 patriation of the Constitution
- the monarchy

1. Answer the poll questions by ranking the items in the list very important, somewhat important, not very important, or not important at all.
2. Some of the survey's results are shown in the following table. What are Canadians most and least proud of? How do your results compare? How do people in Quebec agree and disagree with other Canadians?
3. How might different groups of Canadians answer these questions? For example, would you expect men and women to answer differently? How might new immigrants think differently about these institutions? Why?

HIGHLIGHT

How Well Does Canada Integrate Immigrants?

Coming to a new country is challenging. Individuals need to find jobs or enter school, make friends and social connections, learn about how to participate in the political system and how to access social services. The Migrant Integration Policy Index brings together data from countries around the world and measures how well they are doing at integrating newcomers along eight dimensions: labour market mobility, family reunion, education, health, political participation, access to permanent residency, access to citizenship, and protection from discrimination. Canada does fairly well on this index, raking sixth out of the 38 countries measured (see Figure 5.8). Sweden, Portugal, and Finland all outperform Canada on this Index (Migrant Integration Policy Index 2015).

There are some dimensions on which Canada is very successful at integrating newcomers. For example, Canada ranks first among all countries in our anti-discrimination protections for immigrants. Our Charter of Rights and Freedoms in Canada protects individuals from discrimination based on their national origin. This is a very important way that we, as a country, protect new Canadians from discrimination. However, we rank quite low on our access to health care for immigrants (18 out of 38). One of the reasons for this is the large variation in access across provinces and territories and the relatively long three-month waiting period to access health care. We also score relatively poorly on political participation among migrants (20th out of 38). This is, in part, because we do not allow even long-time permanent residents any rights to vote. In many European countries, long-time permanent residents can vote at least in local or city elections, giving them more access to the political system.

Immigrants are a vital and important part of Canadian society. These types of indices highlight the challenges that immigrants face and the many ways that countries can assist immigrants in integrating into a new country.

Continued

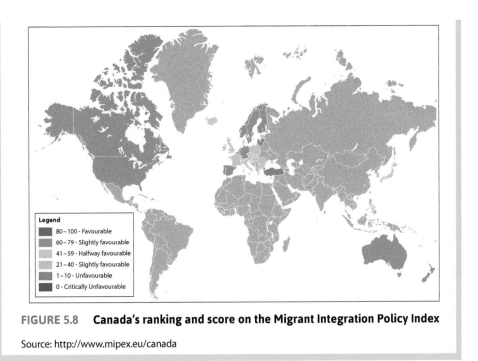

FIGURE 5.8   Canada's ranking and score on the Migrant Integration Policy Index

Source: http://www.mipex.eu/canada

Summary

We began this chapter by examining the differences between race and ethnicity. While race is based on perceived physical traits, ethnicity is based on cultural differences between people. The theory of social construction, introduced by Berger and Luckmann, can help us to understand how we create racial and ethnic categories in our society. The Thomas principle shows how these categories, despite being socially constructed, can have real consequences for individuals. Both theories can be applied to many concepts—such as gender, social class, and sexuality—that we will learn throughout this book. Through Sherif's experiment, we examined how prejudice and discrimination arise in society and how they can be reduced. We also talked about immigration and multiculturalism in Canada and concluded by examining the idea of Canada as an imagined community.

Key Terms

authoritarian personality 154
census 134
contact theory 155
discrimination 153
essentialism 131
ethnicity 131
First Nations 144
imagined communities 160
immigration 157
invisible knapsack 145
multiculturalism 159

nation 160
nation-state 160
prejudice 153
race 131
racism 142
realistic conflict theory 154
social construction 142
symbolic ethnicity 137
Thomas principle 142
vertical mosaic 159

For Further Reading

Anderson, Benedict. 1983. *Imagined Communities: Reflections on the Origin and Spread of Nationalism*. New York: Verso Books.

Berger, Peter L., and Thomas Luckmann. 1966. *The Social Construction of Reality: A Treatise in the Sociology of Knowledge*. New York: Anchor Books.

Koopmans, Ruud. 2013. "Multiculturalism and Immigration: A Contested Field in Cross-National Comparison." *Annual Review of Sociology* 39: 147–69.

Porter, John. 1965. *The Vertical Mosaic: An Analysis of Social Class and Power in Canada*. Toronto: University of Toronto Press.

Waters, Mary C. 1990. *Ethnic Options: Choosing Identities in America*. Berkeley: University of California Press.

References

Adorno, T.W., E. Frenkel-Brunswik, D.J. Levinson, and R.N. Sanford. 1950. *The Authoritarian Personality*. New York: Norton.

Allport, G.W. 1954. *The Nature of Prejudice*. Cambridge, MA: Perseus.

Anderson, Benedict. 1983. *Imagined Communities: Reflections on the Origin and Spread of Nationalism*. London: Verso.

Association for Canadian Studies. 2013. "Tim Horton Beats the Queen According to Youngest Canadians When Asked about Contribution to Nation Building." http://www.acs-aec.ca/pdf/polls/Tim%20Horton%20vs%20the%20Queen%20and%20building%20Canada.docx.

Berger, Peter, and Thomas Luckmann. 1966. *The Social Construction of Reality: A Treatise in the Sociology of Knowledge*. New York: Anchor Books.

Bobo, Lawrence. 1983. "Whites' Opposition to Busing: Symbolic Racism or Realistic Group Conflict?" *Journal of Personality and Social Psychology* 45(6): 1196–210.

Canadian Council for Refugees. 2017. "Refugees' Contributions in Canada." http://ccrweb.ca/en/refugees-contributions-canada.

Cazenave, Noel A., and Darlene Alvarez Maddern. 1999. "Defending the White Race: White Male Faculty Opposition to a White Racism Course." *Race and Society* 2: 25–50.

Crockett, Zachary. 2014. "The Great Toilet Paper Scare of 1973." *priceonomics* (blog) 9 July. http://priceonomics.com/the-great-toilet-paper-scare-of-1973.

Davis, Horace B. 1967. *Nationalism and Socialism: Marxist and Labor Theories of Nationalism to 1917*. New York: Monthly Review Press.

Draaisma, Muriel. 2017. "New Ontario Rule Banning Carding by Police Takes Effect." 1 January. http://www.cbc.ca/news/canada/toronto/carding-ontario-police-government-ban-1.3918134.

Friesen, Joe. 2016. "Syrian Exodus to Canada: One Year Later, a Look at Who the Refugees Are and Where They Went." *The Globe and Mail* 1 December. https://beta.theglobeandmail.com/news/national/syrian-refugees-in-canada-by-the-numbers/article33120934/?ref=http://www.theglobeandmail.com&.

Heibling, Marc. 2008. *Practising Citizenship and Heterogeneous Nationhood*. Amsterdam: Amsterdam University Press.

Kay, Barbara. 2011. "Barbara Kay: Multiculturalism 'Is Not a Quebec Value.'" *National Post* 19 January. http://news.nationalpost.com/full-comment/barbara-kay-multiculturalism-is-not-a-quebec-value.

McIntosh, Peggy. 1988. "White Privilege and Male Privilege: A Personal Account of Coming to See Correspondences through Work in Women's Studies." Wellesley College Center for Research on Women, Working Paper 189: 2-3. Wellesley, MA: Wellesley College.

MacIvor, Angela, and Phlis McGregor. 2017. "Black People 3 Times More Likely to Be Street Checked in Halifax, Police Say." 9 January. http://www.cbc.ca/news/canada/nova-scotia/halifax-black-street-checks-police-race-profiling-1.3925251.

Menzies, Charles R. 2009. "First Nations, Inequality, and the Legacy of Colonialism." In Edward Grabb and Neil Guppy, eds, *Social Inequality in Canada*, 5th edn, 295–304. Toronto: Pearson.

Migrant Integration Policy Index. 2015. http://www.mipex.eu.

Noack, Rick. 2015. "Multiculturalism Is a Sham, Says Angela Merkel." *The Washington Post* 14 December. https://www.washingtonpost.com/news/worldviews/wp/2015/12/14/angela-merkel-multiculturalism-is-a-sham/?utm_term=.4620ab31117e.

Norris, Mary Jane. 2014. "Aboriginal Languages in Canada: Emerging Trends and Perspectives on Second Language Acquisition." Ottawa: Statistics Canada. http://www.statcan.gc.ca/pub/11-008-x/2007001/9628-eng.htm.

Paradkar, Shree. 2017. "M-103 Study Should Explore How Islamophobia Is a Form of Racism." *Toronto Star* 19 September. https://www.thestar.com/news/gta/2017/09/19/islamophobia-is-not-colour-blind-paradkar.html.

Porter, John. 1965. *The Vertical Mosaic: An Analysis of Social Class and Power in Canada*. Toronto: University of Toronto Press.

Rankin, Jim, and Patty Winsa. 2012. "Known to Police: Toronto Police Stop and Document Black and Brown People Far More Than Whites." *Toronto Star* 9 March.

Roy, William G. 2001. *Making Societies*. Boston: Pine Forge Press.

Sherif, M., O.J. Harvey, B.J. White, W. Hood, and C.W. Sherif. 1961. *Intergroup Conflict and Cooperation: The Robbers Cave Experiment*. Norman, OK: University Book Exchange.

Statistics Canada. 2011. *National Household Survey*. Catalogue no. 99-010-X2011032. Ottawa: Statistics Canada. https://www12.statcan.gc.ca/nhs-enm/2011/dp-pd/dt-td/Index-eng.cfm

———. 2013. "Aboriginal Peoples in Canada: First Nations People, Métis and Inuit." Ottawa: Statistics Canada. http://www12.statcan.gc.ca/nhs-enm/2011/as-sa/99-011-x/99-011-x2011001-eng.pdf.

———. 2015. CANSIM. http://www5.statcan.gc.ca/cansim/home-accueil?lang=eng.

Thomas, W.I., and D.S. Thomas. 1928. *The Child in America*. New York: Knopf.

Trudeau, Justin. 2016. "Statement by the Prime Minister of Canada on Multiculturalism Day." 27 June. http://pm.gc.ca/eng/news/2016/06/27/statement-prime-minister-canada-multiculturalism-day.

Truth and Reconciliation Commission of Canada. 2015. "Honouring the Truth, Reconciling for the Future: Summary of the Final Report of the Truth and Reconciliation Commission of Canada." http://www.myrobust.com/websites/trcinstitution/File/Reports/Executive_Summary_English_Web.pdf.

Wells, Spencer. 2002. *The Journey of Man: A Genetic Odyssey*. Princeton, NJ: Princeton University Press.

Wilson, Vince Seymour. 1993. "The Tapestry Vision of Canadian Multiculturalism." *Canadian Journal of Political Science* 26(4): 657.

World Vision. 2018. "Syrian Refugee Crisis: Facts, FAQ and How to Help." https://www.worldvision.org/refugees-news-stories/syrian-refugee-crisis-facts.

Chapter Outline

Photo credit: EYESITE / Stockimo / Alamy Stock Photo

Introduction

How can we tell someone's sex? The International Olympics Committee (IOC), which governs the Olympics, has been struggling with this question. Up until the 1960s, female competitors had to parade, nude, in front of an all-female panel in order to have their sex "verified." These physical checks were replaced by tests of chromosome levels at the 1968 Olympics. However, these types of checks are both humiliating and not very effective. There is simply not such a clear line between "female" and "male" in either anatomy or chromosomes (Aschwanden 2016).

Take Maria Jose Martinez-Patino, a hurdler from Spain. After the chromosomal tests, she was told that she has a 46,XY karyotype—she was genetically male. However, she was also born with insensitivity to testosterone, so she developed as a female. She had no "advantage" as a result of the testosterone because her body was unable to use it. After this test, Maria's sports scholarship was revoked, and her records were erased. Maria has classically female anatomy—a vagina and breasts—and has always identified as female. As she says, she always "knew [she] was a woman." This case led to the ending of the chromosome tests in the 2000 Olympics; however, female athletes who are considered "suspicious" can still be tested and examined (Aschwanden 2016). What do these tests tell us about what it means to be a man or woman—is it simply a matter of anatomy or chromosomes, or is it something more?

Transgender athletes also challenge the Olympic Committees norms around sex-based competition categories. In November 2016, the IOC issued new guidelines that allow athletes who have transitioned their gender to compete without sex reassignment surgery. These new rules make it possible for athletes who had previously identified as female to compete in the male category without restriction. However, women who had previously identified as male were still subject to a set of criteria: they must declare a female identity for at least four years, and they must show that their testosterone levels have remained below a certain level for one year before competing and through the competition (Aschwanden 2016). Some applaud these new guidelines for being focused on both biological traits as well as gender identification and for not forcing individuals to undergo physical surgery in order to classify. Others wonder at the somewhat arbitrary lengths of time one must identify and the basis for the levels of testosterone that are deemed "female." In addition, these rules are still subject to criticism from those who feel that they have gone too far in allowing athletes to compete in categories into which they were not born. These rules and the complications they bring highlight the blurry lines of sex and gender.

Sex and Gender

In the previous chapters, we learned the importance of social class, social status, race, and ethnicity as dimensions of inequality. Another major type of inequality that exists in our society is based on the categories of sex and gender. **Sex** is a biological identity and can be divided into the main categories of male and female. **Gender** is a social concept referring to the entire array of social patterns we associate with men and women in society. Gender exists along the continuum of masculinity and femininity. In many ways, the difference between sex and gender mirrors the difference between race and ethnicity. While sex and race are based on perceived biological differences, gender and ethnicity are rooted in social and cultural constructions and distinctions.

There are certainly biological differences between men and women. For example, men are, on average, taller than women, and men and women have different reproductive organs. However, neither of these two distinctions is as clear-cut as it seems. Some women are very tall; some men are very short. Some people are born with the sexual organs of both sexes. Despite these issues, sex is based on perceived physical differences. It is important to note, though, that such differences do not explain gender-based social disparities. In effect, the way we expect men to act (what we deem "masculine" behaviour) and women to act (what we deem "feminine" behaviour) is socially constructed. As with ethnicity (see Chapter 5), our ideas of what is acceptable and laudable behaviour for men and women are socially created. The clear division between men/women and masculinity/ femininity is, at least partly, an illusion.

Thinking of sex as a dichotomy is problematic in a number of ways, as illustrated in the discussion of athletes at the Olympics. In addition, the existence of middle-sex categories challenges the male/female binary. Some Indigenous groups refer to "Two-Spirited" people who have both a masculine and feminine spirit. Other societies have three genders—men, women, and a third group that is variously named. This group is composed of biological males who are allowed to perform the social role of women in their society. They are not women or men but, as a rough translation, "male women." Some African and American-Indian societies have a group of individuals who are "manly hearted women." This group is made up of biological females who perform the social role of men in their society; they have the social responsibilities and privileges usually bestowed on only husbands and fathers. Having the wealth to buy a "wife" bestows the social status of male on these women (Lorber 1994).

Intersex people, those born with the sexual organs of both sexes, also present difficulties for our binary ideas of gender. Approximately 1 per cent of live births in North America are sexually ambiguous based on their anatomy (Fausto-Sterling 2000). Between 0.1 and 0.2 per cent of all births are so sexually ambiguous that specialists medically assign a sex to the child. Today, fewer people with ambiguous genitalia are forced to have this surgery—at least until they are old enough to select for themselves—than people were decades ago.

Individuals who are transgender also test our conceptions of sex and gender. There are a variety of different groups of people within this larger community, such as transgender, gender fluid, and agender people. Advocates for individuals within these groups have coined the term ***transgender (or trans) umbrella*** to encompass the variety of different sexual expressions in modern society. The struggles and triumphs of individuals within this community have attracted increased attention recently because of the prominence of transgender characters on shows such as *Orange Is the New Black* and *Glee* and the story of Caitlyn Jenner, who transitioned to living as a woman in 2015 and received an award from ESPY (a sports association) to honour her courage in this process. Figure 6.1 illustrates the term and the groups it encompasses.

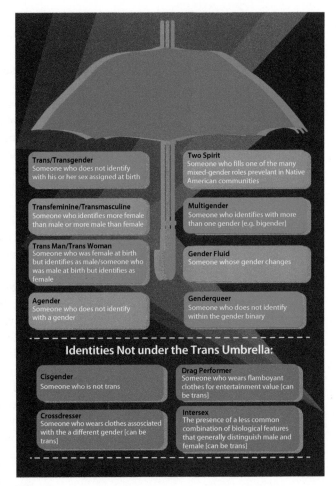

FIGURE 6.1   The trans umbrella

Source: Adapted from Trans Student Educational Resources, http://www.transstudent.org/graphics

Gender as a Social Construction

Recall that social construction is a two-step process. First, we classify experiences and act on the basis of these categories. Second, we forget that we have created these divisions and come to see them as natural and unchangeable. When we meet people, one of the first things we do is try to place them into previously learned categories. Are they

Photo by Dani Brubaker/Contour RA/Getty Images

PHOTO 6.1 Androgynous gender presentation is one way of challenging the gender binary. How does androgyny affect how you think about gender?

male or female? Old or young? Rich or poor? Doing so helps us to understand how we should interact with them. Not knowing how to categorize an individual can make your interactions uncomfortable because the societal norms are unclear.

Although it can cause potential struggles with social interactions, some people choose not to identify with a particular sex or not to raise their children with such an identity. In 2017, Kori Doty, a person who identifies as non-binary transgender, registered their child without listing sex. For the first time in Canada, a baby was issued a health card that does not specify their sex. Instead, the health card simply lists "U" (for unspecified or undetermined) in the space where sex is usually listed. As the child's parent explains, "I'm raising [my child] in such a way that until they have the sense of self and command of vocabulary to tell me who they are, I'm recognising them as a baby and trying to give them all the love and support to be the most whole person that they can be outside of the restrictions that come with the boy box and the girl box" (Millward 2017).

There are only a few examples of androgynous characters on television or in film because audiences cannot classify them as male or female and therefore generally find these characters difficult to understand. Androgynous simply refers to sexual ambiguity—a situation in which it is difficult to tell if a person is male or female. To find an example, we must look back to the early 1990s when Julia Sweeney performed her character Pat on "*Saturday Night Live*." Pat is intentionally androgynous. The humour came from other people's inability to tell Pat's sex and the resulting difficulty in their interactions, which constantly led to awkward situations.

Learning, understanding, and viewing one another as male and female are social processes. Our parents hold certain ideas about gender-appropriate behaviour, which they teach us. We later learn to perform our gender through socialization in schools. Expected behaviour is further reinforced within same-sex social circles during a period when boys tend to play with only other boys and girls with only other girls (Kimmel 2011). The media also inform our sense of gender-appropriate behaviour. This process continues into the workplace and our familial roles. Furthermore, social institutions support and perpetuate gender appropriate behaviour.

In Chapter 2, we talked about social roles, the sets of connected behaviours, beliefs, and norms that individuals perform in a social situation. **Gender roles** are one set of roles that we perform in society. Gender is not a thing that one is born with, but it is situationally constructed through individuals' performances. Goffman's (1959) dramaturgical perspective helped us to see how individuals perform roles in our day-to-day lives. We are actors on the stage of life, performing our gender through our clothes, mannerisms, and behaviours. Remember that the "front stage" is where individuals perform for others, whereas the "back stage" is where individuals do not need to perform. For many individuals, their front stage is living up to the expected gender norms, but their back stage reveals a different set of gender displays.

In her influential book *Gender Trouble*, the feminist scholar Judith Butler (1990) argues that all gender is created and sustained through performances. **Performativity** is "not a singular act, but a repetition and a ritual." What we take to be an "internal essence of gender is manufactured through a sustained set of acts, posited through the gendered stylization of the body"; what we take to be an "internal feature of ourselves is one that we anticipate and produce through certain bodily acts" (xv–xvi). While it appears that our gender is just a natural part of who we are, Butler argues that we create gender through our actions and interactions.

Performing Gender in Music

The media are an important avenue for learning about gender norms—how we should act as men and women and what is feminine and masculine behaviour. Music, in particular, is part of how we come to understand the role of men and women in society. However, as we listen to music, we rarely think critically about the messages it contains. In this activity, we will investigate examples of music that support a narrow understanding of masculinity and femininity as well as music that challenges our ideas of men's and women's roles in society.

Find the lyrics and videos to some songs that talk about gender, and answer the following questions. (You can get lyrics to many songs at www.azlyrics.com and find videos on YouTube.)

1. Find a song that you think reproduces gender stereotypes. How do the lyrics or video for this song reproduce these ideas?
2. Find a song that challenges our ideas of gender. How do the lyrics or the video for this song challenge these conceptions?
3. What types of music genres or artists are more likely to challenge gender roles, and which are less likely to do so?
4. Why do you think that musicians, record labels, or music sites release gender stereotypical or challenging music?

ACTIVITY

Butler (1990) argues that labelling a person as male or female is overly restrictive. A person defined as male, for example, is supposed to possess masculine and heterosexual traits (e.g., be sexually active, aggressive, attracted to females). These characteristics are exhibited as a "performance" but are not necessarily voluntary. Some men might naturally want to behave this way, but others might find that these behaviours do not reflect their sense of self. In this way, gender does not automatically stem from inherent personality characteristics but is the result of cultural norms and practices that are subsequently reinforced. The concepts of masculine and feminine, therefore, appear to be just as natural as the sex that they are attached to. And deviations, such as homosexuality or the display of the opposite gendered characteristics, are marginalized as being outside "normality."

Butler also claims that the accepted and "natural" binary composition of two sexes (leaving only the option of male or female) encourages us to see other dichotomies in categorizing people. For example, seeing only two sexes leads to an illusion of only two distinct and opposite genders (masculine or feminine) and two distinct and opposite sexualities (heterosexual or homosexual). Instead, she pushes us to think about gender and sexuality as continuums. While there are certainly men who are very masculine and women who are very feminine, there are also men who are more feminine and women who are more masculine.

Michael Messner (1997) notes that there are many social costs to displaying gender in ways that our society deems inappropriate. Messner particularly focuses on what he calls the **costs of masculinity**. While we often concentrate on the costs of being female (such as lower pay, discrimination, violence, and other factors—discussed in more detail later in this chapter), our society also has a very restrictive idea of what it means to be a man. Messner outlines the rules to masculinity. For example, men must avoid anything feminine. Those who like romantic comedies, music written and/or performed by women, or ballet cannot share these interests with others for fear of seeming less masculine. Masculinity is also defined by external success (money, fast cars, prestigious jobs). And men are expected to show little emotion and to be aggressive.

These rules for behaviour are very limiting for men. Furthermore, men are sanctioned for stepping outside these norms. Men who perform jobs that are considered feminine,

HIGHLIGHT

Pointlessly Gendered Products

It seems that almost anything can be gendered in our society. In Chapter 2, we looked at how toys and personal products reflect and reinforce our ideas of gender. Despite the fact that all shampoo has the same basic ingredients, it is marketed to women very differently from the way it is to men. Ads show men standing stoically in black-and-white industrial settings while women shampoo in vibrant colour in a rain forest.

These two brands of earplugs are essentially the same product. However, Sleep Pretty in Pink Women's Ear Plugs are targeted to female buyers while Skull Screws Ear Plugs are aimed at men. Why do companies advertise and package this product differently for men from the way they do for women? How do such products reinforce our ideas of gender?

such as nurse or daycare provider, have to deal with their masculinity being questioned. Men who break the rules might be degraded and lessened to the status of women. A man who fails to live up to gender norms might be called sissy, girlie, or gay, insinuating that he is like a woman or is homosexual and therefore inferior.

Gender and Institutions

Our ideas of sex and gender are socially constructed and created through interacting with agents of socialization (family, friends, peers), who encourage us to present our gender in particular ways. Gender and gender relations are also constantly reinforced through various institutions. Parents give different amounts of attention, reward different behaviours, and teach different skills to boys and girls. In this section, we will look at how the institutions of sport, work, and politics reinforce gender distinctions in society.

Gender and Sports

Sports are a social institution. They allow people with a common interest to unite across racial, ethnic, and class distinctions. They also reinforce social norms and values such as hard work, teamwork, and obedience to authority. As Messner (1992, 8) writes, sport is "not an expression of some biological human need, it is a social institution. Like other institutions, such as the economy, politics, and the family, the structure and values of sport emerge and change historically, largely as a result of struggles for power between groups of people."

Sports are an influential institution in many societies. Billions of people play and watch sports worldwide. Almost half of the globe's population, 3.2 billion people, watched at least a minute of the 2010 World Cup in South Africa (FIFA 2010). The 2017 Super Bowl was watched by 113.3 million people (Pallotta 2017). Needless to say, many people are exposed to professional sports. The content of sports, however, includes more than simply the activity.

As with other institutions in society, sports are highly gendered. On the micro level, language used in sports is gendered, such as when we refer to defence*men*. Females and femininity can hold negative connotations in sports, such as when someone comments on a man's lack of athletic ability by saying that "he runs (or throws) like a girl." On the macro level, sports are also gender-unequal. None of the top 50 paid athletes in world are women. Serena Williams is the first and only woman to appear on Forbes list of the top 100 paid athletes in the world at the 51st spot (Forbes 2017). The highest paid athlete in the NBA, LeBron James, made almost $31 million during the 2016–17 season, before endorsements (espn.go.com/nba/salaries). By contrast, Nneka Ogwumike, the highest paid athlete in

PHOTO 6.2 Nneka Ogwumike is the highest-paid player in the WNBA. In the 2016–17 wnba season, the maximum salary (before endorsements) for an individual player was US$109,000. In comparison, the 2017 minimum salary (before endorsements) for a player in the nba was $562,493.

HIGHLIGHT

Gentlemen Prefer Stout

What do men and women tend to drink at parties? Who would you expect to drink Hey Y'alls or Palm Bay coolers? What about beer? Jessica Streeter (2012) argues that even what we drink reinforces ideas of gender. She is particularly interested in the craft beer scene. Craft beer, which comes from small-scale producers, is becoming increasingly popular as drinkers look for options beyond the large-scale breweries such as Molson or Labatt.

Streeter claims that in the craft beer scene, women and new drinkers are encouraged to try fruit beers, blonde ales, and wheat beers, but men are offered dark India pale ales (IPAs), aged stouts, and a variety of high-alcohol beers. In other words, women and novices are offered light styles of beer. Bolder flavours, such as beers that are hoppy, bitter, or thick, are marketed to men, who are encouraged to advance beyond "girlier offerings."

You can see from this argument that even what we select to eat and drink is, in some ways, a gendered performance. When a woman says that she prefers fruit beers and a man says that he favours stouts, they are reporting their preferences. But their social environments shape these preferences, which reinforce dominant notions of masculinity and femininity. How and why do advertisers and producers reinforce these norms?

IvanMiladinovic/iStockphoto

© JMS Drinks Ltd.

PHOTO 6.3 These energy drinks are clearly marketed differently to men and women. The men's drinks feature words like "khaos," "jolt," and "monster" while the women's drinks are labelled "all natural," "organic," and "low calorie." Why are these similar products marketed so differently to men and women?

the WNBA, makes US$109,000 per year, before endorsements (Barker 2016). Despite a boom in female athletic participation, sports media are still dominated by coverage of male sports. Women's sports only received 3.2 per cent of the network sports news coverage, a decline from a high of 8 per cent in 1999 (Bianco 2015).

Gender and Work

Another major institution of society that reinforces our conceptions of gender and gender inequality is the workforce. Over the past 30 years, women's labour force participation has dramatically increased. In 1979, only 50 per cent of women worked outside the home for pay, while 94 per cent of men did. Thirty years later, the numbers were 81 per cent and 91 per cent, respectively. By 2014, women accounted for 47 per cent of the labour force (Statistics Canada 2017b). This rise in the number of women joining the workforce is the result of changing norms about the role of women in society, a greater need for dual-income households, and increased rates of women obtaining higher education. Despite there currently being more women in the workforce than ever before, there remains a great deal of inequality between what men and women earn, the types of jobs they have, and the household tasks they do in addition to their paid labour.

The gap between the income of men and women has fluctuated over time. As Figure 6.2 indicates, this difference has generally narrowed since 1976, but there has not been a steady decline. In fact, inequality between men's and women's earnings have stayed relatively stagnant since the early 1990s. In 2015, Canadian women made, on average, 87 per cent of what men made per hour.

One reason for this discrepancy is that men and women tend to perform different kinds of jobs. In fact, both groups are disproportionately concentrated in a small number of occupations. The industries in Canada with the greatest share of women (relative to men) are teaching, nursing, social work, clerical services, and sales. Fifty-six per cent of women work in one of these jobs, compared with only 17 per cent of men. Men are concentrated in a very different set of industries: management, natural sciences, construction, resource extraction, and trades. However, only 18 per cent of men were represented in these industries, meaning that women are much more concentrated in sex-typed industries than are men (Statistics Canada 2017b).

Some jobs that men and women perform require less education, such as sales and construction. However, the types of low-education jobs that men perform are usually better paid than those performed by women. This difference is, in part, explained by the higher rate of unionization in construction jobs than in sales work.

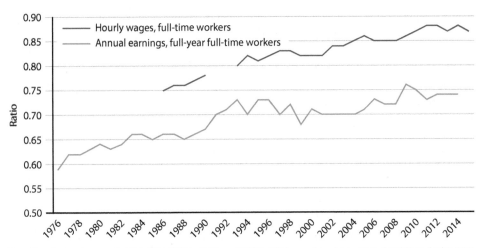

Note: Data for hourly wages in 1981, 1984, 1986 to 1990, and 1993 to 1996 came from Baker, Michael and Marie Drolet. 2010. "A new view of the male/female pay gap." *Canadian Public Policy* 36(4): 429–464.

FIGURE 6.2   Gender pay ratio of workers aged 25 to 54, Canada, 1976 to 2015

Source: Melissa Moyser, 2017, *Women and Paid Work*, Catalogue no. 89-503=X, Ottawa: Statistics Canada, https://www150.statcan.gc.ca/n1/pub/89-503-x/2015001/article/14694-eng.htm

There are two main ways that work is gendered. First, there is gender concentration among the people employed in certain kinds of work or among students in particular programs. We saw this occur in certain occupations such as sales or construction, which are female- and male-dominant, respectively. Second, work can also be imbued with gendered meaning and defined in gendered terms. For example, "caring" or "nurturing" professions tend to be seen as more feminine and appropriate for women. Take the difference between doctors and nurses. Nurses are expected to be more caring, whereas doctors (particularly specialists) are expected to focus on the science of medicine. Teaching is another good example. Elementary school teaching is associated with more nurturing; university-level teaching is often seen as a less "caring" job and is more focused on specific area–related expertise. Think about how many of your elementary school teachers were male and how many were female. Then do the same for your professors. You likely had more female teachers in elementary school and more male professors in university or college. Because university professors make more money and have a higher status than elementary school teachers, this inequality could be problematic.

The **feminization** of an occupational sphere occurs when a particular job, profession, or industry becomes dominated by or predominantly associated with women. Such feminized jobs are referred to as "pink collar." Examples of jobs that were previously mostly done by men but have been feminized include bank tellers, secretaries, teachers, and family doctors. The important thing to note is that a feminized occupation tends to lose prestige, wages, required skill levels, and opportunities for promotion. In 1891, only 14.3 per cent of Canada's clerical workers were women. This number has risen steadily; in 2009, 75.5 per cent were women. Meanwhile, the wages and possibilities for promotion in this job have steadily declined.

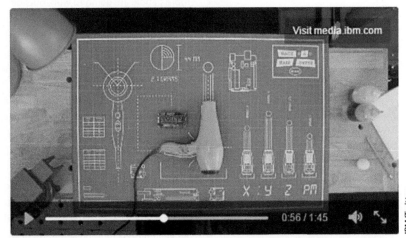

PHOTO 6.4 This campaign by IBM, whereby women are encouraged to try to "hack a hairdryer" in order to get them interested in science, was widely criticized for reinforcing gender stereotypes. Some posts from women scientists upon seeing the ad: "I leave hairdryer fixing to the men, I'm too busy making nanotech and treating cancer" and "That's ok IBM, I'd rather build satellites instead, but good luck with that whole hairdryer thing."

You might be surprised to learn that clerical work was traditionally a man's job. The male bookkeeper's duties included accounting, note-taking, and organizing tasks. As companies grew, there was an increasingly large amount of clerical work to be done, and businesses moved toward more efficient systems of managing such tasks. Instead of having one bookkeeper who would do a variety of challenging tasks, companies were hiring many more clerical staff to do smaller parts of the larger job, such as only typing or only answering the phone. This sort of assembly-line office work created very few opportunities for advancement—if all you did was answer the phone all day, how could you move up to other tasks?

In the early 1900s, when this change was happening, the prevalent ideas regarding women's capabilities led to a growing belief that women were ideally suited for this type of narrow and repetitive work. The expectation was that women would work only until they married, and if they continued past that point, their jobs would be secondary to their primary roles as mothers and wives. As William Leffingwell (1925, 116) explains:

> A woman is to be preferred for the secretarial position for she is not averse to doing minor tasks, work involving the handling of petty details, which would irk and irritate ambitious men, who usually feel that the work they are doing is of no importance if it can be performed by some person with a lower salary.

HIGHLIGHT

Gender Inequality at Work Will Take 30 to 180 Years to Eliminate!

Gender inequality in the workforce is not only unfair, it is also costly. A new report shows that Canada could add $150 billion to its overall economy by 2026 if it takes steps to combat gender inequality and could add $420 billion if we eliminate the gender pay gap altogether (Shakeri 2017). How would this happen?

The authors of the report from McKinsey Global Institute (MGI) argue that most of the growth in the economy as a whole comes from the increase in labour force participation—more people are going to work outside the home. In order to increase this participation further, more women need to enter the workforce, move from part-time to full-time work, and shift to more productive and higher-paying industries.

Canada is one of the world's leaders in women's equality, ranking in the top 10 of all countries in 2015 in MGI's report. However, Canada's progress in increasing gender equality has stalled over the past 20 years. Wage differences between women and men are no longer shrinking. If we continue to progress at this slower rate, the gender gap in Canadian society will take between 30 and 180 years to eliminate! The World Economic Forum, which also has a ranking of gender equality, also shows our overall declining progress in addressing gender equality. We were ranked first in 1995, but by 2016 we had fallen to 35th place in gender equality.

The report provides a series of recommendations for reducing gender inequality, particularly in the workforce. They suggest that companies should commit to diversity and emphasize its importance for the overall company and its profits. Companies should also set clear targets for representation of women and ethnic minorities and track their progress in reaching this equality. Workplaces should also have programs to mentor and promote women and minorities. And companies should raise awareness about subconscious biases and actively try to make the workplace more inclusive.

Most such men are also anxious to get ahead and to be promoted from position to position, and consequently if there is much work of a detail character to be done, and they are expected to perform it, they will not remain satisfied and will probably seek a position elsewhere.

Another concern when talking about the differential incomes and occupations of men and women is the **double shift** that women often perform. This term refers to individuals working outside the home for money and inside the home on unpaid, domestic tasks. Arlie Hochschild (Hochschild and Machung 1990) calls this situation the **second shift**. She finds that, in dual-earner heterosexual couples, women still tend to spend more hours per week on domestic labour (e.g., cleaning, cooking, and caring for children) than do men. This imbalance, she argues, is caused by our traditional understanding of gender roles whereby we expect women to do domestic work regardless of their labour outside the home.

As illustrated in Figure 6.3, women tend to work fewer hours outside the home than men. However, this disparity is shrinking. From 1986 to 2015, the amount of time women spent working outside the home increased from 3.3 to 7.5 hours per day. Now there is less than an hour's difference in the average amount women and men work per day for pay. The figure also shows that men are doing more housework and other unpaid work than they used to, although they still spend less time on such tasks than women do. If we look at both housework and other unpaid work, women do seven hours of this type of labour per day, on average, while men only do 5.5 hours. Most of this discrepancy comes in the form of child care, with fathers doing an average of 1.9 hours of child care per day while mothers do an average of 2.6 hours per day (Statistics Canada 2017a).

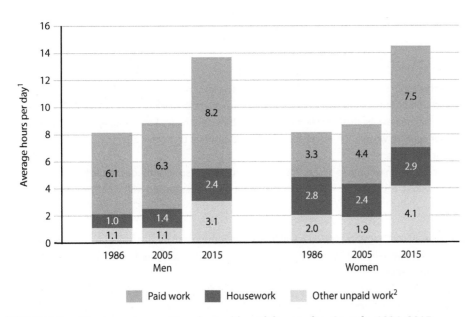

FIGURE 6.3   Time spent on paid and unpaid work by gender, Canada, 1986–2015

1. Numbers may not add up due to rounding.
2. Primary child care and shopping for goods and services.

Source: Adapted from Katherine Marshall, 2006, "Converging Gender Roles," *Perspectives,* 7(7) July, https://www.statcan.gc.ca/pub/75-001-x/10706/9268-eng.htm; and Statistics Canada, 2017, *Daily Average Time Spent in Hours on Various Activities by Age Group and Sex, 15 years and over, Canada and Provinces,* Catalogue no. 45-10-0014-01, Ottawa: Statistics Canada, https://www150.statcan.gc.ca/t1/tbl1/en/tv.action?pid=4510001401

Gender and Politics

The institution of politics is also affected by and affects gender. While there has been much improvement in women's representation in government, women still make up only 26.3 per cent of elected officials in the government of Canada (Anderssen 2015). While this is the biggest percentage ever for female representation in Parliament, it will take 100 years before we reach gender parity at this rate (Anderssen 2015). This number is not particularly impressive when compared with other countries; Canada ranks 62nd in the world, behind most of Europe and many developing countries. For example, Rwanda (61 per cent), Bolivia (53 per cent), and Cuba (49 per cent) all have considerably higher percentages of women in their parliaments (Inter-Parliamentary Union 2017). See Table 6.1 for the percentage of women who hold elected office in the world's regions.

Why are fewer women elected to political office? Many of the possible answers centre around the organization of politics in Canada and the world. For example, if political parties do not nominate women to be candidates in elections, people will not even have the option to vote for them. Because women are often excluded from informal party networks and do not have the connections to help them get nominated, they are less likely to be put on the ballot. They are also often unable to afford the expense of running for office. As previously discussed, women make less money than men do; they also frequently lack a network of people who could financially support their campaigns. Finally, political office requires considerable travel time, evening and weekend meetings, and other demands that might conflict with family obligations. Although both men and women have these responsibilities, we learned in the preceding section that women tend to spend more hours a day doing household and child care tasks. Becoming involved in a political campaign and holding office could, therefore, create an additional burden for women (Kunovich, Paxton, and Hughes 2007).

ACTIVITY

Gender Associations

Many people feel that they embrace gender equality. Yet years of socialization emphasizing different roles and expectations for men and women may have a lasting (and unconscious) effect. Banaji and Greenwald (2013) created an interesting test to examine how we make implicit associations between things. For example, even if we think that we support gender equality, we might harbour some stereotypical ideas that could affect how we act toward men and women in our daily lives.

Go to this book's companion website to access Project Implicit's test on social attitudes to see how you associate women and men with science and the liberal arts. You might be quite surprised with what you discover—I certainly was!

1. To what extent do you associate science with men and liberal arts with women (or vice versa)? Are you surprised with your results on the test? Why or why not? Discuss how they fit or counter your feelings about women in liberal arts and men in science.
2. Banaji and Greenwald found that across every country that they investigated, people usually associated men with science. Countries with the largest sex gap (where people are much more likely to associate science with males) also had the biggest difference between boys' and girls' performances in ninth-grade science. Why do you think this relationship exists?
3. How might we go about changing the associations people have between women and men and science? If they are unconscious ideas, how can we change them?

TABLE 6.1 | Historical comparisons of the percentage of women in parliaments across regions, 1955–2017

	1955	1965	1975	1985	1995	2005	2017[1]
Scandinavia	10.4	9.3	16.1	27.5	34.4	38.2	41.7
Western Industrial	3.6	4.0	5.5	8.6	12.8	22.7	25.2[2]
Eastern Europe	17.0	18.4	24.7	27.0	8.4	15.7	
Latin America	2.8	2.7	5.2	8.1	10.0	17.1	28.2[3]
Africa	1.0	3.2	5.3	8.0	9.8	16.3	23.8
Asia	5.2	5.3	2.8	5.6	8.8	15.3	19.7
Middle East	1.2	1.2	2.9	3.5	3.9	8.1	18.2

1. 2017 data from the Inter-Parliamentary Union, http://www.ipu.org/wmn-e/world.htm.
2. All European countries combined.
3. Includes all of the Americas.

Source: Compiled from Sheri Kunovich, Pamela Paxton, and Melanie M. Hughes, 2007, "Gender in Politics," *Annual Review of Sociology* 33: 263–84. Data for 2017 taken from the Inter-Parliamentary Union, 2017, *Women in National Parliaments*, http://www.ipu.org/wmn-e/world.htm

READING

The Rise and Stall of Canada's Gender-Equity Revolution

Neil Guppy and Nicole Luongo

Gender Equity Policies

Women's greater and more diverse participation within the public sphere clearly signals a major transformation in the social fabric of modern Canada. A second indicator of this revolutionary change is marked by public policies beneficial to gender equity. These policies, often legislated in reaction to, and not as causes of, the changes noted above, are also important in pinpointing where change might be required to complete the revolution.

In this section we quickly review policies that bear directly on women's public-sphere participation, taking our lead from the Gender Gap Report (Hausmann et al. 2014). We also examine, although briefly, the degree to which the types of recommendations being advanced to promote greater gender equity have changed since the 1970 Royal Commission on the Status of Women, a bellwether call for policy action in Canada.

Parental Leave Provisions

Women's labor force participation has risen significantly (see figure), with currently about 70 per cent of married women with children under three employed (CANSIM 282-0210; a fraction virtually unchanged for the past decade but that was just over 30 per cent in 1976). The establishment of stronger family-leave provisions for childcare seems essential (Marshall 2008; Pulkingham and van der Gaag 2004). Since 1971, Canada has had a tripartite structure of family-leave provisions, including job protection, employer-provided benefits, and paid leave via employment insurance (with some provincial variation). Protected employment leave covers up to 52 to 54 weeks in most provinces, and up to 70 weeks in Quebec. With few exceptions, most employers do not top up basic provisions: A paid leave of 50 weeks typically includes only a portion of insurable earnings (up to 55 per cent with a cap of $485

Guppy, Neil, and Nicole Luongo. 2015. "The Rise and Stall of Canada's Gender-Equity Revolution." *Canadian Review of Sociology* 52(2): 241–63.

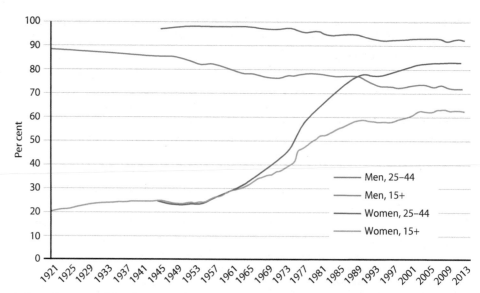

Labour force participation rates for women and men, by age, 1921–2013

Sources: CANSIM 282—0002; *Historical Statistics of Canada*, Statistics Canada, Editions 1 and 2.

per week, although for low-income families the cap can rise to 80 per cent; rates in Quebec are higher). Importantly, although leave provisions might significantly affect child development, increased leave provisions have not had a positive, lingering impact on women's (or men's) labor-force participation (Milligan 2014).

Paid paternity leave, which offers employed men the option to spend more time with newborn children, is underutilized (McKay, Marshall, and Doucet [2012] estimate that only 33 per cent of eligible men took paternity leave in 2008). Further evidence of men's reluctance to take on greater childcare responsibilities is the stalled take-up rates for days missed from work for personal or family responsibilities when there are preschool children at home— 1.8 days in 1997 rose to only 1.9 days in 2014, whereas corresponding numbers for women were 4.1 and 3.9 days (CANSIM 279-0033; *Work Absence Rates*). These gender differences indicate that there is significant room for men to contribute more to childcare, a contribution that would do much to promote gender equity.

Childcare

Although for the majority of Canadian families, whether married or common law, dual earning is the norm, social policy to optimize an appropriate work–family balance has not been forthcoming. Unlike many European nations, Canada lacks any semblance of a national daycare program. While a substantial amount of state funding does flow to families who have children, the use of that funding is dependent on how the family chooses to spend it. The money flows mainly as a Universal Child Care Benefit for children under six ($1,200 annually), and as a child tax benefit (replacing the older family allowance model) that targets funding to lower income families.

Quebec recently changed its baby bonus financial incentive scheme into a state-supported childcare program. No other province has such a scheme and, in general, Canada puts more resources into middle and late childhood (school-aged) programs than it does into early childhood programming (aged 1–5; see Beaujot, Du, and Ravanera 2013; Thévenon 2011). The utility of having a universal as opposed to a targeted program has been questioned, although the idea that some form of childcare program is necessary has been widely supported (see Baker 2011a). Stalker and Ornstein (2013) show that the Quebec program has assisted labor force participation by women and, simultaneously, has enhanced gender equity in the household division of labor. The continuing debate, and therefore lack of action, regarding a greater investment in early childhood speaks to the stalling of policy that would support gender equity progress (for an alternative interpretation see

Hallgrimsdottir, Benoit, and Phillips 2013). Furthermore, the need to take time off work to care for elderly parents is a growing issue for Canadian families, again stressing the need for better work–family arrangements.

Employment Policy

Legislation prohibiting sex discrimination (e.g., Charter of Rights and Freedoms) and promoting equal rights (e.g., equal pay for work of equal value, employment equity) were initiated largely in response to the feminist movement and women's heightened labor-force participation. Further, while these laws have cultural significance as signals of a new rhetoric of equality, evidence demonstrating that they have effectively promoted gender equity is scarce (although certain court cases have been beneficial, such as the Supreme Court ruling on the Canadian International Airlines proceedings that defined comparable cases for pay equity; see Bernstein, Dupuis, and Vallee 2009). In general, while legislation to promote gender equity has "had a definite positive effect," (Bernstein et al. 2009:495), most commentators point to a series of problems with these policies (Newman and Waite 2012:225–27).

Perhaps most significantly, labor laws often cater to the typical experience of male workers while ignoring the precarious, temporary nature of a significant portion of women's paid work (Vosko and Thomas 2014). A second problem is "rights without remedies," where workers bear rights but have limited opportunity for seeking redress. Complaints-based systems require workers to prove injustice, which can be difficult or impossible especially when a worker is not unionized (Vosko 2013). Third, the voluntary nature of some anti-discrimination laws places little onus on employers to confront gender-based inequities in practices that differentially impact low-wage workers, a sector that is heavily populated by females (e.g., employment-equity law).

New Family Forms

A major shift in household income has come in the transition from an era of the male breadwinner to the modern phase of dual earning couples. This has necessitated alterations in family policy, several of which we noted earlier as important stimuli for the growth in women's employment. These include legislation to ban marriage bars, and increased public access to safe abortions and family-planning technology.

The growth in the public acceptance of new family forms, as well as policy support for these forms, has been critical to expanding women's autonomy. Certainly, legal support for same-sex marriage has provided one important alternative to the traditional family. And the gradual legal acceptance of common-law relationships as equivalent to marriage has provided additional options while also affording greater recognition of property divisions should such relationships dissolve. Furthermore, more women and men are choosing child-lessness as an option. Among women over 50, childlessness increased from 14.1 per cent in 1990 to 20.4 per cent in 2011 (General Social Survey, special tabulation; see also Ravanera and Beaujot 2014). Although there is ongoing resistance to some of these changes, in par-ticular to abortion and same-sex marriage, it is clear that the variety of options for living arrangements has expanded over the last century.

The unevenness of change in gender equity can also been seen here. The feminization of poverty, once a major concern, has largely been eradicated in Canada (based on the 2011 figures for after-tax income, 8.7 per cent of men and 8.9 per cent of women fell below the Statistics Canada low-income line that year; CANSIM 202-0802). For women and men who are lone parents, however, the income gap differs significantly. Not only is the proportion of women living in poverty as lone parents double that of men (21.2 vs 12.4 per cent, re-spectively), but the number of poor families headed by a single woman as opposed to a single man is over eight times greater (341,000 vs 42,000, respectively; CANSIM 202-0804), even though male lone parent families are increasing faster (CANSIM 111-0011). Of course, women and men in other vulnerable groups suffer disproportionately from poverty, includ-ing the disabled, recent immigrants, and Aboriginal peoples, but in these subgroups the gender gaps are not as pronounced.

The Stalled Revolution

Is the gender-equity revolution merely incomplete or unfinished, or has it stalled? Certainly the turn to neoliberal policies documented above has been toxic for the feminist movement, a key agent of earlier change. While the effects of new policy directions have only begun to bite, the evidence we have presented, in figures and in research citations, includes a slowing in female labor force participation, a sag in pay equity, a slowing of domestic labor convergence, and formal political participation for women ranking Canada 61st in the world. We interpret this, and the rest of our evidence, as indicators of stalling. And we stress too that change has been uneven, with some women and some family types benefiting far less than others from greater gender equity (e.g., single parent women, Aboriginal and recent immigrant women, and working class women).

Identifying the exact reasons why the revolution has stalled and been uneven is our next focus. Part of the explanation lies in what England (2006:253–58) identifies as gender's "tenacity" as an organizing principle in the modern world. Highly related to this is men's reluctance to engage in traditional women's domains (e.g., child rearing, nursing). Men are thought to have less to gain from supposedly stooping to engage in feminized behaviors, where their efforts would typically bring less pay, not to mention ridicule and shame from other men and from some women. The benefactors of privilege—men—fail to see themselves as gendered beings.

The sociological literature is replete with cultural explanations for enduring gender difference. Chief among these are evaluations of worth biased in favor of men, plus people's staunch adherence to strong cultural definitions of femininity and masculinity. Decades of research demonstrate that performance evaluations and judgments of quality favor men, not only when others evaluate but when many people evaluate themselves (Ridgeway 2011, 2014). Furthermore, many people internalize standards of appropriate male and female behavior and feel accountable to these standards which, in turn, lead them to penalize or stigmatize others who violate the standards (Ridgeway 2011). In other words, these are deep cultural beliefs. For this reason, change is difficult, since cultural belief systems are obdurate despite ongoing changes in economic, educational, political, and domestic realms. Cultural beliefs are powerful independent forces, slow to adapt, and for this reason change in the family might be slower than in other institutional arenas where more public forces (e.g., markets and movements) are more influential.

Cultural change will indeed come, slowly following the altered practices charted above, but the final chapters may be the hardest struggle. Popular advice frequently enjoins young people today to "follow your passions," "realize your true self," and "study what you love." In the context of highly gendered scripts about femininity and masculinity, however, such slogans act to reinforce existing patterns of gender segregation. Gender is a fundamental axis of identity. Self-expression, therefore, tends to replicate traditional gender stereotypes about what constitutes appropriate female or male activity. This, in essence, is the conservative underside of popular culture in the modern world. While new explorations of sexuality are encouraging, and serve to shake up gendered conventions, people in power continue to repress significant gender equity progress. Meanwhile, violence against women, cyber misogyny, and fundamentalist religious revivals continue.

All of this speaks to the salience of gendered norms as powerful organizing forces, but it explains less about policy changes where surely the rise of neoliberal forms of governance are also an important explanatory factor in accounting for the stalled and uneven revolution. Neoliberalism favors the primacy of the individual over the collectivity. It also promotes a selective clawing back of the state with the consequent erosion of welfare state supports (Luxton 2010). These changes have been harder on women than men. The fiscalization of social policy (Brodie and Bakker 2008) is a consequence of neoliberalism, in which the state's role is increasingly defined as making capitalism work as opposed to a broader mandate of optimizing societal outcomes for all. Simultaneously, elite men press to make all areas of life open to profit making, so as to enhance their vested interests of power, prestige, and lifestyle (often to the detriment of women, especially Aboriginal, immigrant, and visible-minority women).

But popular culture plays into the mix as well, complicating easy paths of explanation. The ability to try on new roles and to play with identities is reflected in mainstream media and challenges hegemonic assumptions about sex and gender (see Budgeon 2014). Expressions of sexuality are more diverse while unconventional family forms have gained visibility and are gradually being normalized. Less encouraging, however, is that political alliances have also crumbled, particularly among feminists themselves who were so instrumental to former gains. More choices for some women have contributed to exclusion and fragmentation, both of which undermine the collective activism that was crucial for initiating earlier change. The unevenness we have alluded to, where different subpopulations have experienced less movement toward gender equity, is also apparent within feminism. Not only has the fight for gender equity taken a more individualized direction, but many women have felt silenced by the movement and bereft of its victories (Mohanty 1988; see also Clark Mane 2012).

More positively, the increased earning power of women has been consequential for their ability to gain autonomy. This has made it easier at least for some women to actively choose living alone or to have more power within marriage. In important ways, this reflects back on the idea of the "masculinization of women's roles" and suggests that, while such comparison is useful for charting change, it misrepresents new moments where the patterns of women's and men's lives are diverging.

CRITICAL READING QUESTIONS

1. What are the different parental leave benefits we have in Canada? Why are they important generally, and how do they affect gender inequality? Why might men be less likely to use these benefits?
2. How are other policies, such as child care, sex discrimination, and new family forms, related to gender inequality?
3. The article argues that progress toward gender equality has slowed. Why might this be? How might norms be related to the enduring nature of gender inequality?

Is it a problem that there are few women in Canada's Parliament? Research shows that having more women in government can be important both for the types of policies put forward and for the general perceptions of women's role in society. While it is certainly true that both male and female political leaders can be concerned with issues of gender equality, women are much more likely to prioritize those issues and to put them on the political agenda (Kunovich, Paxton, and Hughes 2007). For example, policies related to child care, violence prevention, and pay equity are more likely to be raised by women in political debates. This tendency does not mean that men do not care about these issues, only that they do not tend to be their top legislative priorities. It is important to note that women politicians certainly do not agree on solutions to these issues simply because they are women, but they are more likely to bring these issues into the debate.

Having women as elected officials has also been shown to change the public's perceptions of women's roles and abilities as leaders. Female politicians also provide role models for young women. In places where there are many women in politics, young girls have higher self-esteem and a greater knowledge of and interest in politics than do girls in other places (Kunovich, Paxton, and Hughes 2007).

HIGHLIGHT

Women and Political Rights in Canada

1867	Only white men with property can vote in federal and provincial elections.
1916	Women in Manitoba, Saskatchewan, and Alberta get the provincial vote.
1917	World War I nurses and female relatives of soldiers get the right to vote.
1918	Canadian women receive the federal vote.
1918	Mary Ellen Smith (British Columbia) becomes the first woman provincial cabinet minister.
1921	Mary Ellen Smith becomes the first woman federal cabinet minister.
1930	Cairine Wilson is named the first woman senator.
1940	Quebec, the last province to do so, gives women the right to vote provincially.
1951	Charlotte Whitten becomes mayor of Ottawa and the first woman mayor in Canada.
1991	Rita Johnson becomes the first woman premier (British Columbia).
1993	Kim Campbell becomes the first woman prime minister (non-elected).
2008	One province/territory (Nunavut) has a woman premier.
2011	The number of women premiers in Canada rises to four (Nunavut, Newfoundland and Labrador, British Columbia, and Alberta).
2015	There are three women premiers in Canada (British Columbia, Alberta, and Ontario).

Feminism and Feminist Theory

Feminism is concerned with equality between women and men. It focuses on attaining that equality in politics, in the economic system, and through social and cultural change. Feminism exists as a set of ideologies and as groups of people who support these ideologies. These groups seek equality of opportunity for women in multiple areas, including education, the workplace, and the family. Both men and women with these interests can be feminists.

Feminist theory focuses on how gender inequality comes about in society and how men and women's gender roles are created and recreated in society. This theory has been influential in many social sciences and humanities disciplines, including sociology, anthropology, political science, history, philosophy, English literature, and women's studies. In addition, it is rooted in the feminist movement and political action. Many scholars of this movement talk about feminist activism as happening in three distinct periods, or waves.

First-wave feminism began in the nineteenth century and was mostly centred in countries such as Canada, the United States, and the United Kingdom. This wave was focused on *de jure* inequalities, inequalities that are part of the legal and political system. For example, women's rights to vote and to hold property were of primary interest to first-wave feminists.

Second-wave feminism began in the United States in the early 1960s and spread throughout Europe and Canada. Second-wave feminists broadened the movement beyond political and legal rights and sought social change on a wide range of issues, including equality in the workplace and reproductive rights. During this period, women made widespread social gains and moved into a

United Nations/HeForShe

PHOTO 6.5   He for She is a campaign that brings women and men together to address gender inequality. They argue that gender inequality is bad for everyone—regardless of your gender. What do you think about this campaign? What is the role of men in supporting feminism?

new variety of professions and other areas of society traditionally dominated by males, such as the media, sports, and the military. This wave was also concerned with violence against women, including sexual violence and spousal abuse. The women's movement was quite successful at making these issues mainstream, getting marital rape laws passed, and establishing rape crisis centres and shelters for women who had been victims of abuse.

Third-wave feminism began in the early 1990s and continues to the present. This wave, which is a more diverse group of women's movements, arose as a critique of the previous wave. Many activists felt that the second wave was controlled by a small group of white middle-class women and that it did not represent the diverse experiences of women from different racial, ethnic, religious, class, and sexual groups (Staggenborg 2011). Third-wave feminism challenges what it sees as the essentialist nature of second-wave's definition of what it means to be a woman. This third wave also moved away from the focus on social and political rights. Instead, it tends to work in cultural arenas—for example, challenging gender depictions in the media, sexist language, and gendered norms around sexuality.

Intersectionality

The concept of **intersectionality**—the study of how various dimensions of inequality can combine—is one product of feminism's third wave. Kimberlé Williams Crenshaw coined the term in 1989 and explains it with the following metaphor:

> Discrimination, like traffic through an intersection, may flow in one direction, and it may flow in another. If an accident happens in an intersection, it can be caused by cars traveling from any number of directions and, sometimes, from all of them. Similarly, if a Black woman is harmed because she is in an intersection, her injury could result from sex discrimination or race discrimination. But it is not always easy to reconstruct an accident. Sometimes the skid marks and the injuries simply indicate that they occurred simultaneously, frustrating efforts to determine which driver caused the harm. (149)

Photo by Jason LaVeris/FilmMagic/Getty Images

PHOTO 6.6 At the 2014 MTV Video Music Awards, Beyoncé performed in front of a large sign that said "Feminist." Some praised her performance as a political statement and argued that it raised feminism's profile among young women. Others were more critical of the word being used by a performer who often uses her sexuality to sell her music. Do you think that Beyoncé is a feminist? How does this performance fit into (or challenge) our ideas of what a feminist is?

The theory came out of Crenshaw's research on work and discrimination in the 1980s. Crenshaw (1989) studied a group of black women in the United States who had filed a workplace discrimination lawsuit. A round of layoffs at their workplace had resulted in all the black women being fired. The trial judge ruled against these women—he said that there was no gender discrimination because white women were not fired and there was no racial discrimination because black men were not fired. As the law saw only two types of discrimination (discrimination against women based on their sex or discrimination against racial minorities based on their race), there was no discrimination in this case.

These black women and Crenshaw understood that the former's experience was rendered invisible by intersectionality. The fact that they were both black and women made the discrimination invisible. The theory of intersectionality highlights how various dimensions of inequality can intersect with one another. For example, we have very different stereotypes about young people who are in wheelchairs from those we do about older people in wheelchairs. Perhaps we assume that young people were injured in a sports or car accident and that older people are in poor health. We also have different expectations regarding gay men and lesbian women because of their gender. Seeing the complicated ways that inequalities intersect is a prime feature of third-wave feminist theory.

Figure 6.4 shows child poverty rates among Indigenous and non-Indigenous people in Canada by residence. It is clear that Indigenous children are more likely than non-Indigenous children to live in poverty. It is also clear that gender, immigration status, racial identity, and living on or off a reserve are also related to one's likelihood to live in poverty. However, what we miss by just seeing those direct relationships is the complicated way that all these factors work together to shape the outcomes for different kinds of people.

The figure is a good example of intersectionality because you can see how the various statuses interact with each other to create different outcomes. For example, non-Indigenous

HIGHLIGHT

Marx on Gender

Along with most other classical theorists, Karl Marx has been criticized as being "gender blind"—ignoring the role of gender in creating and perpetuating inequality in society. It is not surprising that none of the classical scholars (such as Marx, Durkheim, and Weber) talked much about gender; we are all a product of our historical period, and these men lived in the late 1800s to early 1900s when gender equality was not a popular topic. At the same time, we can certainly use their theories to understand issues of gender. For example, Marx's theory generally posits that all inequality stems from the capitalist system and the struggle between workers and capitalists. From this perspective, working-class men and women are both equally victimized by capitalists and the capitalist system that exploits their labour.

Feminist scholars have noted that this understanding of women and men as being equally exploited by capitalism misses the unique gender relations that occur within families. They argue that women are exploited not only by the capitalist when working outside the home (just as men are) but also by their spouses when working in the home without pay. Women's unpaid domestic labour benefits the capitalist because it makes it possible for men to return to work the next day, ready to labour for the capitalist. Families are the best and cheapest way to raise new workers. Women (as mothers and wives) keep all family earners (men) and earners-to-be (children) healthy and cared for. They do so at no cost to the capitalist, who later benefits from the surplus value the workers produce.

Marx's theory can be understood, at the broadest level, as a theory that sees the world in terms of those who have power and those who do not. While Marx was primarily concerned with the power of the capitalist over the worker, it is not difficult to see how we could extend this power dichotomy to the inequality that exists between men and women in society. What would other classical theorists, such as Émile Durkheim and Max Weber, say about the role of gender in society?

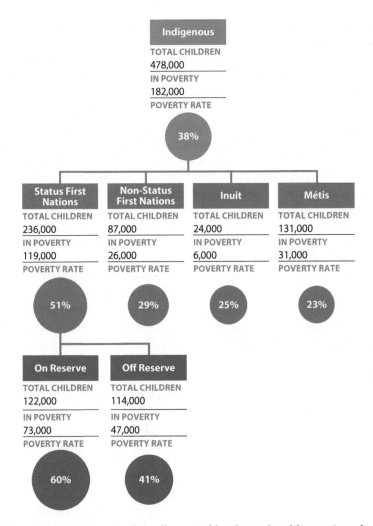

FIGURE 6.4   Child poverty rates by Indigenous identity and residence, Canada

Source: David McDonald, and Daniel Wilson, 2016, *Shameful Neglect: Indigenous Child Poverty in Canada,"* Canadian Centre for Policy Alternatives, https://www.policyalternatives.ca/sites/default/files/uploads/publications/National%20Office/2016/05/Indigenous_Child%20_Poverty.pdf

children are much less likely to live in poverty (17 per cent vs 38 per cent). However, children who are Métis or Inuit are much less likely than Indigenous people who are Status First Nations to live in poverty. And of those who are Status First Nations, those who live on-reserve are 1.5 times more likely than those who live off-reserve to live in poverty. These numbers indicate that it is not simply your Indigenous identity, residence, or immigrant status that predict your chances of living in poverty but that these different characteristics can interact and intersect to create more complicated inequalities.

Sexuality

Sexuality is feelings of sexual attraction and behaviours related to them. One important element of sexuality is **sexual orientation**, which involves whom you desire, with whom you want to have sexual relations, and with whom you have a sense of connectedness (Scott and Schwartz 2008). Our ideas about sexuality have changed considerably over the past 100 years. In general, there is an increasing openness to diverse sexual behaviours and attitudes, which has led to changing norms surrounding sexuality. For example, people today tend to have sex younger and with more partners and are more likely to

RESEARCH METHOD
INTERVIEW

engage in sexual activity outside of marriage than they were in the past. There is also an increasing acceptance of same-sex relationships.

The first systematic study of sex and sexuality was conducted by Alfred Kinsey in the 1940s. Kinsey's initial study interviewed 18,000 adults about their sexual behaviours, interests, and thoughts. Previously, we did not know much about these topics because no one had thought it appropriate (or interesting) to ask these questions. You can imagine how revolutionary (and shocking) this study was at the time!

Kinsey published *Sexual Behavior in the Human Male* in 1948 and *Sexual Behavior in the Human Female* in 1953, which together are known as the **Kinsey Reports**. The reports were highly controversial, but they became bestsellers and made Kinsey a celebrity. His work created a precedent for a legitimate study of human sexuality and laid the groundwork for a body of sexuality research in the social and biological sciences. His research showed that there was much more diversity in sexual desire and behaviour than was previously thought. After seeing this huge diversity, Kinsey argued that people should not think of sexuality as either normal or abnormal. We should define what is normal by looking at what people are doing, not by ideas of morality. For example, if most people have sexual relations before marriage, that is normal, regardless of society's moral ideals about premarital sex.

Perhaps Kinsey's most famous contribution to the study of sexuality is his **Heterosexual–Homosexual Rating Scale**, a seven-point scale of sexual inclinations (see Figure 6.5). After thousands of interviews with men and women, Kinsey argued that people are not simply gay or straight; therefore, we should not categorize people in this way. Instead, we should see that individuals have life histories that express different desires at different times. People can have more or less homosexual or heterosexual desires and experiences, but these things are not always related.

Kinsey's work highlighted the importance of social context in shaping sexual desire and behaviours. For example, Kinsey (Kinsey, Pomeroy, and Martin 1948) found that men's sexual behaviours differed by their social class—men of higher social class tended to be more experimental than those of lower social class. Women's behaviour differed by their age and their view of gender equality—those who were older and who had a more liberal view of women's role in society were much more likely to experiment sexually and have more partners (Kinsey 1953). In essence, Kinsey showed that what people do sexually is, at least in part, shaped by their characteristics, such as social class and age.

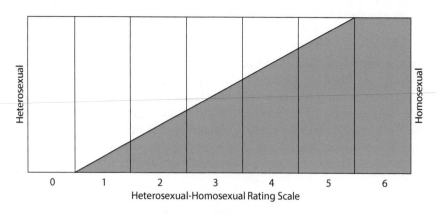

FIGURE 6.5   Kinsey's Heterosexual–Homosexual Rating Scale

0   Exclusively heterosexual with no homosexual tendencies
1   Predominantly heterosexual, only incidentally homosexual
2   Predominantly heterosexual, but more than incidentally homosexual
3   Equally heterosexual and homosexual
4   Predominantly homosexual, but more than incidentally heterosexual
5   Predominantly homosexual, only incidentally heterosexual
6   Exclusively homosexual with no heterosexual tendencies

Source: Courtesy of the Kinsey Institute for Research in Sex, Gender, and Reproduction

In the 1990s, further research on sexual attitudes and behaviours found that North Americans are fairly sexually conservative. Most people favour monogamy in sexual relationships both in principle and in practice. According to surveys, 93.7 per cent of married persons had been monogamous over the year before the study compared with only 38 per cent of single people. However, about 20–25 per cent of men and 10–15 per cent of women had had at least one extramarital affair during their marriage (Laumann et al. 1994). Surprisingly, this number seems to be declining—by 2000 only about 11 per cent of men and women had had an extramarital affair (Treas and Gieden 2000). If anything, this change shows a more traditional view of sexuality over time.

At the same time, there has been an increase in the percentage of people who identify as gay or lesbian. In the 1990s, 9.1 per cent of men and 4.3 per cent of women said they had had a same-sex sexual experience since puberty, but only 1.4 per cent of men and 2.8 per cent of women reported that they identified as homosexual. By 2010, 7 per cent of men and 7 per cent of women identified as gay, lesbian, or bisexual (NSSHB 2010). The larger number of people identifying as gay, lesbian, or bisexual is, at least in part, a result of declining rates of homophobia in society. **Homophobia** is a set of negative attitudes and beliefs about individuals who are **lesbian, gay, bisexual, transgender, or queer/questioning (LGBTQ)** that can lead to negative behaviours, prejudice, or discrimination. Sometimes these negative attitudes can manifest into behaviours such as hate crimes. According to Dowden and Brennan (2012), 16 per cent of hate crimes are based on sexual orientation, with 65 per cent being violent in nature.

Table 6.2 shows the percentage of people in various countries who say they would not like to live next to someone who is gay. Rates are lower in Canada than in other countries such as Turkey, Iraq, South Korea, and Ghana. These negative attitudes have declined in Canada, from 29.7 per cent in 1990 to 15.7 per cent in 2006 (the number is presumably still decreasing). Countries that we might expect to have tolerant attitudes, such as Germany and the United States, have a much larger number of people who hold negative attitudes toward homosexuals. However, some countries are much more tolerant than Canada, such as Spain, Sweden, and the Netherlands.

Herek (2002) examines the factors that predict homophobic attitudes and finds that the most important predictor of more tolerant attitudes toward lesbian, gay, bisexual, transgender, and queer/questioning people is simply knowing someone who is in one of these groups. Having a personal connection with a person who is LGBTQ makes you significantly more likely to have a positive attitude toward individuals in these groups. In addition, people who have more education and higher incomes and live in an urban setting are less likely to be homophobic. Finally, people with higher self-esteem tend to be more tolerant than those with lower self-esteem.

Despite the fact that attitudes toward LGBTQ people are becoming more positive, we still live in a **heteronormative** society; our social institutions, practices, and norms support an automatic assumption that other people are or should be heterosexual. For example, the poster shown in Photo 6.7 simply reminds you to be careful on the road. At the same time, it reinforces the idea that a family includes a woman, a man, and children. You might notice that when you meet a person, he or she might assume that you are heterosexual. For example, if you purchase a bouquet of flowers, the florist might assume that it is for someone of the opposite sex.

TABLE 6.2	Percentage of people who responded that they would not like to live next to a person who is homosexual, 2010–14
Sweden	4.2
Spain	5.1
Netherlands	6.9
Australia	13.4
Canada[1]	15.7
United States	20.4
Germany	22.4
Mexico	23.2
Chile	25.7
Philippines	27.9
China	52.7
Russia	66.2
Ghana	79.7
South Korea	79.8
Iraq	80.3
Turkey	85.4

1. Canadian data is from the 2006 wave because data were not collected in the later survey wave.

Source: World Values Survey, 2010–2014 wave, http://www.worldvaluessurvey.org/WVSOnline.jsp

Photo by Lisa Wade

PHOTO 6.7 Ads such as this one, however unintentional, present a hetero-normative idea of the family. What heteronormative images have you seen lately?

RESEARCH METHOD
SURVEY

Karin A. Martin (2009) conducted a study of how mothers help to perpetuate heteronormative ideals. She surveyed 600 mothers of children between the ages of three and six and found that the vast majority assumed that their children were heterosexual and interpreted their children's behaviours in ways that reinforced this idea. For example, mothers described the relationship between very young boys and girls as girlfriend–boyfriend, even when the children were too young to understand the relationships in this way.

When Martin asked the mothers to consider the possibility that their child might be gay, she found that two-thirds would "wait to see" what happened or prepare for the possibility by, for example, exposing her to children's books that featured gay characters. However, one-third of the mothers actively tried to prevent their child from developing or expressing a gay identity. As Martin describes, this group said they were parenting in a way that would prevent their child from being gay and therefore did not have to "worry" about it. One respondent said:

We model a heterosexual healthy marriage life in our family so I believe our daughter sees a correct woman's modeling as do our boys with their dad. Because I believe that it is a sin. . . . I believe that I can teach my children that this is a sin and model a good relationship for them, and this will never be an issue. Because I think if you raise them with good stability and the right surroundings, things like that do not appear to be normal to him so he would realize in his mind that a same-sex marriage just isn't normal nor is it a part of his lifestyle. (Martin 2009, 203)

These heteronormative sentiments could easily create a situation that makes homophobic attitudes more likely. Heteronormativity persists in our society, but there are also examples of increased tolerance and acceptance for a diversity of lifestyles. For example, American retailer JC Penney released an ad showing a family with two male parents (though the ad did spark some controversy). To avoid assumptions regarding sexual orientation, many individuals use the term *partner* to describe the person with whom they have an intimate relationship. These trends illustrate how our society is moving away from an automatic heteronormative assumption.

Just as gender is socially constructed, so is sexuality. Our ideas about what is normal sexuality, how many groups of sexual orientations there are, and how to delineate sexual preferences is created and reinforced in our society as we interact with one another. These ideas are also historically contingent—they have not always been as they are now. In "The Invention of Heterosexuality," Jonathan Ned Katz outlines how our modern ideas about heterosexuality and homosexuality are socially constructed and how they have changed. We think that heterosexuality is unchanging and universal; however, we create the categories of sexuality and then forget that we made them and see them as unchanging. Moreover, changes in these norms are tied to larger social, historical, economic, and political processes. In fact, heterosexuality is a modern invention and simply one way of perceiving and categorizing the social relations between the sexes.

The Invention of Heterosexuality

Johnathan Ned Katz

Heterosexuality is old as procreation, ancient as the lust of Eve and Adam. That first lady and gentleman, we assume, perceived themselves, behaved, and felt just like today's heterosexuals. We suppose that heterosexuality is unchanging, universal, essential: ahistorical.

Contrary to that common sense conjecture, the concept of heterosexuality is only one particular historical way of perceiving, categorizing, and imagining the social relations of the sexes. Not ancient at all, the idea of heterosexuality is a modern invention, dating to the late nineteenth century. The heterosexual belief, with its metaphysical claim to eternity, has a particular, pivotal place in the social universe of the late nineteenth and twentieth centuries that it did not inhabit earlier. This essay traces the historical process by which the heterosexual idea was created as ahistorical and taken-for-granted. . . .

Contrary to our usual assumption, past Americans and other peoples named, perceived, and socially organized the bodies, lusts, and intercourse of the sexes in ways radically different from the way we do. If we care to understand this vast past sexual diversity, we need to stop promiscuously projecting our own hetero and homo arrangement. Though lip service is often paid to the distorting, ethnocentric effect of such conceptual imperialism, the category heterosexuality continues to be applied uncritically as a universal analytical tool. Recognizing the time-bound and culturally specific character of the heterosexual category can help us begin to work toward a thoroughly historical view of sex. . . .

Before Heterosexuality: Early Victorian True Love, 1820–1860

In the early nineteenth-century United States, from about 1820 to 1860, the heterosexual did not exist. Middle-class white Americans idealized a True Womanhood, True Manhood, and True Love, all characterized by "purity"—the freedom from sensuality.[1] Presented mainly in literary and religious texts, this True Love was a fine romance with no lascivious kisses. This ideal contrasts strikingly with late nineteenth- and twentieth-century American incitements to a hetero sex.[2] . . .

The actors in this sexual economy were identified as manly men and womanly women and as procreators, not specifically as erotic beings or heterosexuals. Eros did not constitute the core of a heterosexual identity that inhered, democratically, in both men and women. True Women were defined by their distance from lust. True Men, though thought to live closer to carnality, and in less control of it, aspired to the same freedom from concupiscence.

Legitimate natural desire was for procreation and a proper manhood or womanhood; no heteroerotic desire was thought to be directed exclusively and naturally toward the other sex; lust in men was roving. The human body was thought of as a means toward procreation and production; penis and vagina were instruments of reproduction, not of pleasure. Human energy, thought of as a closed and severely limited system, was to be used in producing children and in work, not wasted in libidinous pleasures. . . .

Late Victorian Sex-Love: 1860–1892

. . . In the late nineteenth-century United States, several social factors converged to cause the eroticizing of consciousness, behaviour, emotion, and identity that became typical of the twentieth-century Western middle class. The transformation of the family from producer to consumer unit resulted in a change in family members' relation to their own

Katz, Jonathan Ned. 2009. Abridged version of "The Invention of Heterosexuality." *Socialist Review* 20(January–March): 7–34.

bodies; from being an instrument primarily of work, the human body was integrated into a new economy, and began more commonly to be perceived as a means of consumption and pleasure. . . .

In the late nineteenth century, the erotic became the raw material for a new consumer culture. Newspapers, books, plays, and films touching on sex, "normal" and "abnormal," became available for a price. Restaurants, bars, and baths opened, catering to sexual consumers with cash. Late Victorian entrepreneurs of desire incited the proliferation of a new eroticism, a commoditized culture of pleasure.

In these same years, the rise in power and prestige of medical doctors allowed these upwardly mobile professionals to prescribe a healthy new sexuality. Medical men, in the name of science, defined a new ideal of male–female relationships that included, in women as well as men, an essential, necessary, normal eroticism. Doctors, who had earlier named and judged the sex-enjoying woman a "nymphomaniac," now began to label women's *lack* of sexual pleasure a mental disturbance, speaking critically, for example, of female "frigidity" and "anesthesia."[3]

By the 1880s, the rise of doctors as a professional group fostered the rise of a new medical model of Normal Love, replete with sexuality. The new Normal Woman and Man were endowed with a healthy libido. . . .

Heterosexuality: The First Years, 1892–1900

In the periodization of heterosexual American history suggested here, the years 1892 to 1900 represent "The First Years" of the heterosexual epoch, eight key years in which the idea of the heterosexual and homosexual were initially and tentatively formulated by US doctors. The earliest-known American use of the word *heterosexual* occurs in a medical journal article by Dr James G. Kiernan of Chicago, read before the city's medical society on 7 March 1892 and published that May—portentous dates in sexual history.[4] But Dr Kiernan's heterosexuals were definitely not exemplars of normality. Heterosexuals, said Kiernan, were defined by a mental condition, "psychical hermaphroditism." Its symptoms were "inclinations to both sexes." These heterodox sexuals also betrayed inclinations "to abnormal methods of gratification," that is, techniques to insure pleasure without procreation. . . .

Though Kiernan used the new words *heterosexual* and *homosexual*, an old procreative standard and a new gender norm coexisted uneasily in his thought. His word *heterosexual* defined a mixed person and compound urge, abnormal because they wantonly included procreative and non-procreative objectives, as well as same-sex and different-sex attractions.

. . . The idea of heterosexuality as the master sex from which all others deviated was (like the idea of the master race) deeply authoritarian. The doctors' normalization of a sex that was hetero proclaimed a new heterosexual separatism—an erotic apartheid that forcefully segregated the sex normals from the sex perverts. . . . In 1901, in the comprehensive *Oxford English Dictionary*, *heterosexual* and *homosexual* had not yet made it.

The Distribution of the Heterosexual Mystique: 1900–1930

. . . In its earliest version, the twentieth-century heterosexual imperative usually continued to associate heterosexuality with a supposed human "need," "drive," or "instinct" for propagation, a procreant urge linked inexorably with carnal lust as it had not been earlier. In the early twentieth century, the falling birth rate, rising divorce rate, and "war of the sexes" of the middle class were matters of increasing public concern. Giving vent to heteroerotic emotions was thus praised as enhancing baby-making capacity, marital intimacy, and family stability. . . .

The first part of the new sex norm—hetero—referred to a basic gender divergence. The "oppositeness" of the sexes was alleged to be the basis for a universal, normal, erotic attraction between males and females. The stress on the sexes' "oppositeness," which harked back to the early nineteenth century, by no means simply registered biological differences of females and males. The early twentieth-century focus on physiological and gender dimorphism reflected the deep anxieties of men about the shifting work, social roles, and power of men over women, and about the ideals of womanhood and manhood. . . . The stress on gender difference was a conservative response to the changing social-sexual division of activity and feeling which gave rise to the independent "New Woman" of the 1880s and eroticized "Flapper" of the 1920s. . . .

The Heterosexual Steps Out: 1930–1945

In 1930, in *The New York Times*, heterosexuality first became a love that dared to speak its name. On 20 April of that year, the word *heterosexual* is first known to have appeared in *The New York Times Book Review*. There, a critic described the subject of André Gide's *The Immoralist* proceeding "from a heterosexual liaison to a homosexual one." The ability to slip between sexual categories was referred to casually as a rather unremarkable aspect of human possibility. . . .

In September the second reference to the hetero/homo dyad appeared in *The New York Times Book Review*, in a comment on Floyd Dell's *Love in the Machine Age*. This work revealed a prominent antipuritan of the 1930s using the dire threat of homosexuality as his rationale for greater heterosexual freedom. . . . Young people, Dell said, should be "permitted to develop normally to heterosexual adulthood." . . .

Heterosexual Hegemony: 1945–1965

The "cult of domesticity" following World War II—the reassociation of women with the home, motherhood, and childcare; men with fatherhood and wage work outside the home—was a period in which the predominance of the hetero norm went almost unchallenged, an era of heterosexual hegemony. This was an age in which conservative mental-health professionals reasserted the old link between heterosexuality and procreation. In contrast, sex-liberals of the day strove, ultimately with success, to expand the heterosexual ideal to include within the boundaries of normality a wider-than-ever range of non-procreative, premarital, and extramarital behaviours. But sex-liberal reform actually helped to extend and secure the dominance of the heterosexual idea, as we shall see when we get to Kinsey. . . .

The idea of the feminine female and masculine male as prolific breeders was also reflected in the stress, specific to the late 1940s, on the homosexual as sad symbol of "sterility"—that particular loaded term appears incessantly in comments on homosex dating to the fecund forties.

In 1948, in *The New York Times Book Review*, sex liberalism was in ascendancy. Dr Howard A. Rusk declared that Alfred Kinsey's just published report on *Sexual Behavior in the Human Male* had found "wide variations in sex concepts and behavior." This raised the question: "What is 'normal' and 'abnormal'?" In particular, the report had found that "homosexual experience is much more common than previously thought," and "there is often a mixture of both homo and hetero experience."[5] . . .

Kinsey also explicitly contested the idea of an absolute, either/or antithesis between hetero and homo persons. He denied that human beings "represent two discrete populations, heterosexual and homosexual." The world, he ordered, "is not to be divided into sheep and goats." The hetero/homo division was not nature's doing: "Only the human mind invents categories and tries to force facts into separated pigeon-holes. The living world is a continuum."[6]

With a wave of the taxonomist's hand, Kinsey dismissed the social and historical division of people into heteros and homos. His denial of heterosexual and homosexual personhood rejected the social reality and profound subjective force of a historically constructed tradition which, since 1892 in the United States, had cut the sexual population in two and helped to establish the social reality of a heterosexual and homosexual identity. . . .

Heterosexual History: Out of the Shadows

. . . Because much stress has been placed here on heterosexuality as word and concept, it seems important to affirm that heterosexuality (and homosexuality) came into existence before it was named and thought about. The formulation of the heterosexual idea did not create a heterosexual experience or behaviour; to suggest otherwise would be to ascribe determining power to labels and concepts. But the titling and envisioning of heterosexuality did play an important role in consolidating the construction of the heterosexual's social existence. Before the wide use of the word *heterosexual*, I suggest, women and men did not mutually lust with the same profound, sure sense of normalcy that followed the distribution of "heterosexual" as universal sanctifier.

According to this proposal, women and men make their own sexual histories. But they do not produce their sex lives just as they please. They make their sexualities within a particular mode of organization given by the past and altered by their changing desire, their present power and activity, and their vision of a better world. That hypothesis suggests a number of good reasons for the immediate inauguration of research on a historically specific heterosexuality. . . .

CRITICAL READING QUESTIONS

1.   What are the major periods in the development of the concept of heterosexuality?
2.   How did social, historical, economic, and political changes shape the development of our current ideas of heterosexuality? For example, what role did doctors, wars, economic changes, and women's rights play?
3.   The time period covered in this article ends at 1965. List three main ways that our ideas about heterosexuality and homosexuality have changed since then.

NOTES

1.   Barbara Welter, "The Cult of True Womanhood: 1820–1860," *American Quarterly*, vol. 18 (Summer 1966); Welter's analysis is extended here to include True Men and True Love.
2.   Some historians have recently told us to revise our idea of sexless Victorians: their experience and even their ideology, it is said, were more erotic than we previously thought. Despite the revisionists, I argue that "purity" was indeed the dominant, early Victorian, white middle-class standard. For the debate on Victorian sexuality see John D'Emilio and Estelle Freedman, *Intimate Matters: A History of Sexuality in America* (New York: Harper & Row, 1988), p. xii.
3.   This reference to females reminds us that the invention of heterosexuality had vastly different impacts on the histories of women and men. It also differed in its impact on lesbians and heterosexual women, homosexual and heterosexual men, the middle class and working class, and on different religious, racial, national, and geographic groups.
4.   Dr James G. Kiernan, "Responsibility in Sexual Perversion," *Chicago Medical Recorder*, vol. 3 (May 1892), pp. 185–210.
5.   Dr Howard A. Rusk, *New York Times Book Review*, 4 January 1948, p. 3.
6.   Alfred Kinsey, Wardell B. Pomeroy, Clyde E. Martin, *Sexual Behavior in the Human Male* (Philadelphia, W. B. Saunders, 1948), pp. 637, 639.

Summary

In this chapter, we examined the concepts of sex and gender. Sex is based on perceived biological and physical characteristics and is categorized into the main groups of male and female. Gender is based in cultural and social distinctions and exists along a continuum from masculine to feminine. Both gender and sex are socially constructed and created (and recreated) through performing gender roles in our daily lives. The example of gender in music was used to illustrate how the media and other institutions socialize us to perform our gender roles in particular ways. We discussed three major institutions of society that help to create and perpetuate gender distinctions and inequality in society—sports, the workplace, and politics. Feminist theory and the concept of intersectionality were introduced as ways to understand the importance of gender in our society. We ended this chapter by examining the changing ideas of sexuality in society. The LGBTQ movement has been important in fighting for political, cultural, and social acceptance of the diversity of sexual orientations in modern society. Homophobia has declined, but the generally heteronormative nature of our society as a whole remains.

Key Terms

costs of masculinity 169
double shift (second shift) 175
feminism 182
feminization 173
gender 166
gender roles 168
heteronormative 187
Heterosexual–Homosexual
    Rating Scale 186
homophobia 187

intersectionality 183
intersex 167
Kinsey Reports 186
LGBTQ (lesbian, gay, bisexual, trans-
    gender, or queer/questioning) 187
performativity 168
sex 166
sexual orientation 185
sexuality 185
transgender (or trans) umbrella 167

For Further Reading

Butler, Judith. 1990. *Gender Trouble: Feminism and the Subversion of Identity*. New York: Routledge.
Collins, Patricia H. 2005. *Black Sexual Politics*. New York: Routledge.
Foucault, Michel. 1976/1998. *The History of Sexuality Vol. 1: The Will to Knowledge*. London: Penguin.
Hochschild, Arlie, and Anne Machung. 1990. *The Second Shift*. New York: Avon Books.
Kimmel, Michael. 2011. *The Gendered Society*, 5th edn. New York: Oxford University Press.
Messner, M.A. 1997. *Politics of Masculinities: Men in Movements*. Lanham, MD: Alta Mira Press.
Smith, Dorothy E. 1987. *The Everyday World as Problematic*. Boston: Northeastern University Press.

References

Anderssen, Erin. 2015. "We Have a Record Number of Female MPs, but Hold the Applause." *The Globe and Mail* 20 October. https://www.theglobeandmail.com/life/we-have-a-record-number-of-female-mps-but-hold-the-applause/article26887164.
Aschwanden, Christie. 2016. The Olympics Are Still Struggling to Define Gender. 28 June. Fivethirtyeight.com.
Banaji, Mahzarin R., and Anthony G. Greenwald. 2013. *Blind Spot: Hidden Biases of Good People*. New York: Delacorte.
Barker, Barbara. 2016. "For WNBA Players, the Real Money is Overseas." *Newsday* 19 November. http://www.newsday.com/sports/columnists/barbara-barker/wnba-players-are-underpaid-shouldn-t-have-to-play-overseas-1.12639553.
Bianco, Marci. 2015. "There Is Less Women's Sports Coverage on TV News Today Than There Was in 1989." *Quartz* 16 June. https://qz.com/428680/there-is-less-womens-sports-coverage-on-tv-today-than-there-was-in-1989.
Blumer, Herbert. 1969. *Symbolic Interactionism: Perspective and Method*. Englewood Cliffs, NJ: Prentice-Hall.

Butler, Judith. 1990. *Gender Trouble: Feminism and the Subversion of Identity*. New York: Routledge.
Crenshaw, Kimberlé W. 1989. "Demarginalizing the Intersection of Race and Sex: A Black Feminist Critique of Antidiscrimination Doctrine, Feminist Theory and Antiracist Politics, 1989." *University of Chicago Legal Forum* 139–67.
Dowden, Cara, and Shannon Brennan. 2012. "Police-Reported Hate Crime in Canada, 2010." *Juristat* 12 April. http://www.statcan.gc.ca/pub/85-002-x/2012001/article/11635-eng.pdf.
Fausto-Sterling, Anne. 2000. *Sexing the Body: Gender Politics and the Construction of Sexuality*. New York: Basic Books.
FIFA. 2010. "2010 FIFA World Cup South Africa: Television Audience Report." http://www.fifa.com/mm/document/affederation/tv/01/47/32/73/2010fifaworldcupsouthafricatvaudiencereport.pdf.
Forbes. 2017. "The World's Highest Paid Athletes." https://www.forbes.com/athletes/#14b5f63f55ae.
Goffman, Erving. 1959. *The Presentation of Self in Everyday Life*. New York: Anchor Books.

Government of Canada. 1995. *Employment Equity Act*. http://laws-lois . justice.gc.ca/eng/acts/E-5.401.

Herek, G.M. 2002. "Heterosexuals' Attitudes toward Bisexual Men and Women in the United States." *Journal of Sex Research* 39(4): 264–74.

Hochschild, Arlie, and Anne Machung. 1990. *The Second Shift*. New York: Avon Books.

Inter-Parliamentary Union. 2017. "Women in National Parliaments." http://www.ipu.org/wmn-e/classif.htm.

Kimmel, Michael. 2011. *The Gendered Society*. New York: Oxford University Press.

Kinsey, Alfred C. 1953. *Sexual Behavior in the Human Female*. Philadelphia: WB Saunders.

——— Wardell B. Pomeroy, and Clyde E. Martin. 1948. *Sexual Behavior in the Human Male*. Philadelphia: WB Saunders.

Kunovich, Sheri, Pamela Paxton, and Melanie M. Hughes. 2007. "Gender in Politics." *Annual Review of Sociology* 33: 263–84.

Laumann, Edward O., John H. Gagnon, Robert T. Michael, and Stuart Michaels. 1994. *The Social Organization of Sexuality*. Chicago: University of Chicago Press.

Leffingwell, William. 1925. *Office Management: Principles and Practice*. Chicago: A.W. Shaw.

Lorber, Judith. 1994. *Paradoxes of Gender*. New Haven, CT: Yale University Press.

McAdam, D. 1986. "Recruitment to High-Risk Activism—The Case of Freedom Summer." *American Journal of Sociology* 92: 64–90.

Martin, Karin A. 2009. "Normalizing Heterosexuality: Mothers' Assumptions, Talk, and Strategies with Young Children." *American Sociological Review* 74(2): 190–207.

Messner, Michael A. 1992. *Power at Play: Sports and the Problem of Masculinity*. Boston: Beacon Press.

——— 1997. *Politics of Masculinities: Men in Movements*. Lanham, MD: AltaMira Press.

Millward, David. 2017. "Canadian Baby Register 'Gender Unspecified' in Possible World First." *The Telegraph* 3 July. https://www.telegraph.co.uk/news/2017/07/03/canadian-baby-registered-gender-unspecified-possible-world-first.

NSSHB (National Survey of Sexual Health and Behavior). 2010. Special Issue: *"Findings from the National Survey of Sexual Health and Behavior, Centre for Sexual Health Promotion, Indiana University."* *Journal of Sexual Medicine* 7(5): 243–373

Pallotta, Frank. 2017. "More Than 111 Million People Watched Super Bowl LI." CNN Media. https://money.cnn.com/2017/02/06/media/super-bowl-ratings-patriots-falcons.

Scott, BarBara Marliene, and Mary Ann A. Schwartz. 2008. *Sociology: Making Sense of the Social World*. Boston: Allyn and Bacon.

Shakeri, Sima. 2017. "Reducing Canada's Workplace Gender Gap Would Add $150 Billion to GDP." *Huffington Post*. https://www.huffingtonpost.ca/2017/06/29/reducing-canadas-workplace-gender-gap-would-add-150-billion-to_a_23008616.

Staggenborg, Suzanne. 2011. *Social Movements*, 2nd edn. Toronto: Oxford University Press.

Statistics Canada. 2017a. *Daily Average Time Spent in Hours on Various Activities by Age Group and Sex, 15 years and over, Canada and Provinces*. Catalogue no. 45-10-0014-01. Ottawa: Statistics Canada. https://www150.statcan.gc.ca/t1/tbl1/en/tv.action?pid=4510001401.

——— 2017b. "The surge of women in the workforce." 3 March. http://www.statcan.gc.ca/pub/11-630-x/11-630-x2015009-eng.htm.

Streeter, Jessica. 2012. "Gentlemen Prefer Stouts." *Contexts* (Summer): 5.

Treas, J., and D. Gieden. 2000. "Sexual Infidelity among Married and Cohabiting Americans." *Journal of Marriage and the Family* 62(1): 48–60.

PART III

The Role of Institutions

Photo credit: Tobias Fischer/Unsplash

7 The Media

Chapter Outline

Photo credit: Orhan Tsolak / Alamy Stock Photo

Introduction

Sociology is centrally concerned with the role of institutions in our society—such as the family, the education system, and the government. We focus on the important ways that these institutions can shape us as individuals and alter society as a whole. However, we tend to see the institution of the media in a different way. When studying the media, the focus is on how individuals consume it and the messages that they relay. We are less likely to think of the important implications the media, and our exposure to it, have on society as a whole. This chapter examines the role of the media in society. We assess how the mass media have developed and how changes in the media have fundamentally shaped society as a whole. We also consider how the ownership of the media and differential access to the media can shape what we see and the implications this has for our understandings of the world around us.

Language

The media are fundamentally related to language. Language is constantly evolving to represent changes in culture. Each year, dictionaries add a list of new words to reflect these changes. In 2016, the "word of the year," according to Oxford Dictionaries, was post-truth—defined as "relating to or denoting circumstances in which objective facts are less influential in shaping public opinion than appeals to emotion and personal belief" (Oxford Dictionaries 2017). The *Oxford English Dictionary* added the following words in 2017: *squadgoals, chest bump, Kodak moment, shoestring fries, climate refugees, and climate deniers*. Do you know what all these words mean? Do you think your parents would? Are you surprised by any of these additions? Are there any words on this list that you thought were already in the dictionary? The world is filled with language; there are roughly 7000 languages spoken around the world today. Sociologists have long been interested in this area because, as Durkheim (in Traugott 1978, 102) argued, every language "represents a certain articulation of thought." Languages differ significantly, not just in words but also in ways of making sense of the social world. The difficulties of trying to learn a new language as an adult make these differences clear. Similarly, attempting to translate poetry or humour from one language to another is often problematic, and meanings can be "lost in translation." It is not enough to simply translate the words—you have to understand how the language and culture work in order to make the joke or poem make sense.

Durkheim's understanding of the connection between language and thought was partly stimulated by the work of anthropologists who studied languages in North America. One such anthropologist, Edward Sapir (1884–1939), compared Indigenous languages with the European languages with which he was familiar. He thought that these languages are so dissimilar because they are based in cultures that understand the world in very different ways. Based on this idea, Sapir and Benjamin Whorf developed the **Sapir–Whorf hypothesis**, which argues that language influences thought. Whorf (1956, 212–14) describes this relationship in the following way:

> We dissect nature along lines laid down by our native language. The categories and types that we isolate from the world of phenomena we do not find there because they stare every observer in the face; on

PHOTO 7.1 The term *squadgoals*—a person or thing seen as a model to aspire to or emulate, especially with one's friends (often as a hashtag in social media)—was added to the *Oxford English Dictionary* in 2017.

WENN Rights Ltd / Alamy Stock Photo

the contrary, the world is presented in a kaleidoscope flux of impressions which has to be organized by our minds—and this means largely by the linguistic systems of our minds. We cut nature up, organize it into concepts, and ascribe significances as we do, largely because we are parties to an agreement to organize it in this way—an agreement that holds throughout our speech community and is codified in the patterns of our language . . . all observers are not led by the same physical evidence to the same picture of the universe, unless their linguistic backgrounds are similar, or can in some way be calibrated.

An example of the connection between language and thought is the use of **honorifics** (a linguistic means of conveying respect to a person). Honorifics are not often used in English. When you address another person—no matter if he is your best friend, grandparent, teacher, or the prime minister—you use the word you. The French language, however, has two levels of formality. When you initially meet someone or speak to someone older or to whom you owe respect, you use *vous* (the plural for "you"). For your friends, family members, and others with whom you have a more informal relationship, you use the singular *tu*. Many people who learn French later in life find it hard to understand when they should use each term and, especially, when they can move from *vous* to *tu*. When does your relationship transition into a more informal one? This question is not simply a linguistic issue; it is also related to a cultural understanding of whom you should respect and how relationships change.

Korean has seven levels of respect, which are used to mark the formality of the conversation as well as elements of the speaker and listener's relationship. For example, you can use particular noun or verb endings to indicate clearly if your conversation partner has a higher or lower status than you. In other words, you would speak to an older relative, your boss, or your teacher differently from the way you would to a younger person or an employee. These rules of speech are quite complicated but are very important. If you refer to someone too casually (or too impersonally), you could cause offence.

Sapir and Whorf would argue that these differences in the use of honorifics illustrate something about these cultures as a whole. Because North American or English culture (where English is spoken) tends to pride itself on individualism and equality, there is less need to differentiate people in language based on their status. In cultures that value the role of the collective, respect for authority, and hierarchy (such as Korea), the need to distinguish speakers based on their status and to defer to authorities is a cultural element that is built into the language.

Robert B. Moore illustrates the relationship among language, thought, and culture in the following article. Moore argues that "language not only *expresses* ideas and concepts but actually *shapes* thought." His article highlights the use of racist terms and expressions in English and the ways this language reflects an underlying racism in our culture.

Racism in the English Language

Robert B. Moore

...

Language and Culture

An integral part of any culture is its language. Language not only develops in conjunction with a society's historical, economic, and political evolution; it also reflects that society's attitudes and thinking. Language not only *expresses* ideas and concepts but actually

Moore, Robert B. 1976. "Racism in the English Language," excerpts. New York: Council on Interracial Books for Children.

shapes thought.[1] If one accepts that our dominant white culture is racist, then one would expect our language—an indispensable transmitter of culture—to be racist as well. Whites, as the dominant group, are not subjected to the same abusive characterization by our language that people of colour receive. Aspects of racism in the English language that will be discussed in this essay include terminology, symbolism, politics, ethnocentrism, and context. . . .

Depending on one's culture, one interacts with time in a very distinct fashion. One example which gives some cross-cultural insights into the concept of time is language. In Spanish, a watch is said to "walk." In English, the watch "runs." In German, the watch "functions." And in French, the watch "marches." In the Indian culture of the Southwest, people do not refer to time in this way. The value of the watch is displaced with the value of "what time it's getting to be." Viewing these five cultural perspectives on time, one can see some definite emphasis and values that each culture places on time. For example, a cultural perspective may provide a clue to why the negative stereotype of the slow and lazy Mexican who lives in the "Land of Manana" exists in the Anglo value system, where time "flies," the watch "runs," and "time is money."

A Short Play on "Black" and "White" Words

Some may blackly (angrily) accuse me of trying to blacken (defame) the English language, to give it a black eye (a mark of shame) by writing such black words (hostile). They may denigrate (to cast aspersions; to darken) me by accusing me of being blackhearted (malevolent), of having a black outlook (pessimistic, dismal) on life, of being a blackguard (scoundrel)—which would certainly be a black mark (detrimental fact) against me. Some may black-brow (scowl at) me and hope that a black cat crosses in front of me because of this black deed. I may become a black sheep (one who causes shame or embarrassment because of deviation from the accepted standards), who will be blackballed (ostracized) by being placed on a blacklist (list of undesirables) in an attempt to blackmail (to force or coerce into a particular action) me to retract my words. But attempts to blackjack (to compel by threat) me will have a Chinaman's chance of success, for I am not a yellow-bellied Indian-giver of words, who will whitewash (cover up or gloss over vices or crimes) a black lie (harmful, inexcusable). I challenge the purity and innocence (white) of the English language. I don't see things in black and white (entirely bad or entirely good) terms, for I am a white man (marked by upright firmness) if there ever was one. However, it would be a black day when I would not "call a spade a spade," even though some will suggest a white man calling the English language racist is like the pot calling the kettle black. While many may be niggardly (grudging, scanty) in their support, others will be honest and decent—and to them I say, that's very white of you (honest, decent).

The preceding is of course a white lie (not intended to cause harm), meant only to illustrate some examples of racist terminology in the English language. . . .

Colour Symbolism

The symbolism of white as positive and black as negative is pervasive in our culture, with the black/white words used in the beginning of this essay only one of many aspects. "Good guys" wear white hats and ride white horses, "bad guys" wear black hats and ride black horses. Angels are white, and devils are black. The definition of *black* includes "without any moral light or goodness, evil, wicked, indicating disgrace, sinful," while that of *white* includes "morally pure, spotless, innocent, free from evil intent." . . .

Three of the dictionary definitions of white are "fairness of complexion, purity, innocence." These definitions affect the standards of beauty in our culture, in which whiteness represents the norm. "Blondes have more fun" and "Wouldn't you really rather be a blonde?" are sexist in their attitudes toward women generally, but are racist white standards when applied to Third World women. . . .

Passive Voice

Another means by which language shapes our perspective has been noted by Thomas Greenfield,[2] who writes that the achievements of black people—and black people themselves—have been hidden in . . .

> . . . the linguistic ghetto of the passive voice, the subordinate clause, and the "understood" subject. The seemingly innocuous distinction (between active/ passive voice) holds enormous implications for writers and speakers. When it is effectively applied, the rhetorical impact of the passive voice—the art of making the creator or instigator of action totally disappear from a reader's perception—can be devastating.

For instance, some history texts will discuss how European immigrants came to the United States seeking a better life and expanded opportunities, but will note that "slaves were *brought* to America." Not only does this omit the destruction of African societies and families, but it ignores the role of northern merchants and southern slaveholders in the profitable trade in human beings. Other books will state that "the continental railroad *was built*," conveniently omitting information about the Chinese labourers who built much of it or the oppression they suffered.

Politics and Terminology

"Culturally deprived," "economically disadvantaged," and "underdeveloped" are other terms which mislead and distort our awareness of reality. The application of the term "culturally deprived" to Third World children in this society reflects a value judgment. It assumes that the dominant whites are cultured and all others are without culture. In fact, Third World children generally are bicultural, and many are bilingual, having grown up in their own culture as well as absorbing the dominant culture. In many ways, they are equipped with skills and experiences which white youth have been deprived of, since most white youth develop in a monocultural, monolingual environment. Burgest[3] suggests that the term "culturally deprived" be replaced by "culturally dispossessed," and that the term "economically disadvantaged" be replaced by "economically exploited." Both these terms present a perspective and implication that provide an entirely different frame of reference as to the reality of the Third World experience in US society.

Similarly, many nations of the Third World are described as "underdeveloped." These less wealthy nations are generally those that suffered under colonialism and neo-colonialism. The "developed" nations are those that exploited their resources and wealth. Therefore, rather than referring to these countries as "underdeveloped," a more appropriate and meaningful designation might be "over exploited." . . . Transpose this term next time you read about "underdeveloped nations" and note the different meaning that results.

Terms such as "culturally deprived," "economically disadvantaged," and "underdeveloped" place the responsibility for their own conditions on those being so described. This is known as "Blaming the Victim."[4] It places responsibility for poverty in the victims of poverty. It removes the blame from those in power who benefit from, and continue to permit, poverty.

Still another example involves the use of "non-white," "minority," or "Third World." While people of colour are a minority in the US, they are part of the vast majority of the world's population, in which white people are a distinct minority. Thus, by utilizing the term minority to describe people of colour in the US, we can lose sight of the global majority/minority reality—a fact of some importance in the increasing and interconnected struggles of people of colour inside and outside the US.

"Loaded" Words and Native Americans

Many words lead to a demeaning characterization of groups of people. For instance, Columbus, it is said, "discovered" America. The word *discover* is defined as "to gain sight or knowledge of something previously unseen or unknown; to discover may be to find some existent thing that was previously unknown." Thus, a continent inhabited by millions of human beings cannot be "discovered." For history books to continue this usage represents a Eurocentric (white European) perspective on world history and ignores the existence of, and the perspective of, Native Americans. "Discovery," as used in the Euro-American context, implies the right to take what one finds, ignoring the rights of those who already inhabit or own the "discovered" thing.

Eurocentrism is also apparent in the usage of "victory" and "massacre" to describe the battles between Native Americans and whites. *Victory* is defined in the dictionary as "a success or triumph over an enemy in battle or war; the decisive defeat of an opponent." *Conquest* denotes the "taking over of control by the victor, and the obedience of the conquered." *Massacre* is defined as "the unnecessary, indiscriminate killing of a number of human beings, as in barbarous warfare or persecution, or for revenge or plunder." *Defend* is described as "to ward off attack from; guard against assault or injury; to strive to keep safe by resisting attack."

Eurocentrism turns these definitions around to serve the purpose of distorting history and justifying Euro-American conquest of the Native American homelands. Euro-Americans are not described in history books as invading Native American lands, but rather as defending *their* homes against "Indian" attacks. Since European communities were constantly encroaching on land already occupied, then a more honest interpretation would state that it was the Native Americans who were "warding off," "guarding," and "defending" their homelands.

Native American victories are invariably defined as "massacres," while the indiscriminate killing, extermination, and plunder of Native American nations by Euro-Americans is defined as "victory." Distortion of history by the choice of "loaded" words used to describe historical events is a common racist practice. Rather than portraying Native Americans as human beings in highly defined and complex societies, cultures, and civilizations, history books use such adjectives as "savages," "beasts," "primitive," and "backward." Native people are referred to as "squaw," "brave," or "papoose" instead of "woman," "man," or "baby.". . .

Wrap-Up

A *Saturday Review* editorial[5] on "The Environment of Language" stated that language . . .

> . . . has as much to do with the philosophical and political conditioning of a society as geography or climate . . . People in Western cultures do not realize the extent to which their racial attitudes have been conditioned since early childhood by the power of words to ennoble or condemn, argue or detract, glorify or demean. Negative language infects the subconscious of most Western people from the time they first learn to speak. Prejudice is not merely imparted or superimposed. It is metabolized in the bloodstream of society. What is needed is not so much a change in language as an awareness of the power of words to condition attitudes. If we can at least recognize the underpinnings of prejudice, we may be in a position to deal with the effects.

To recognize the racism in language is an important first step. Consciousness of the influence of language on our perceptions can help to negate much of that influence. But it is not enough to simply become aware of the effects of racism in conditioning attitudes. While we may not be able to change the language, we can definitely change our usage of the language. We can avoid using words that degrade people. We can make a conscious effort to use terminology that reflects a progressive perspective, as opposed to a distorting perspective. It is important for educators to provide students with opportunities to explore racism in language and to increase their awareness of it, as well as learning terminology that is positive and does not perpetuate negative human values.

CRITICAL READING QUESTIONS

1. According to Moore, what is the relationship between language and culture?

2. How does Moore explain the relationship between language and culture with reference to the use of black/white terms, "Native Americans," and terms about Africa and developing countries?

3. How could this argument be extended to terms about gender? How are gendered terms used in the English language? How do these terms perpetuate sexist ideas?

4. To what extent and where have you heard these terms before? How much has changed in our use of racist, sexist, and other types of discriminatory language?

NOTES

1. Podiat, S. (1967, March). How bigotry builds through language. *Negro Digest*.
2. Greenfield, T. (1975, April). Race and passive voice at Monticello. *Crisis*.
3. Burgest, D.R. (1973, July). Racism in everyday speech and social work jargon. *Social Work*.
4. Ryan, W. (1971). *Blaming the victim*. Pantheon Books.
5. The environment of language. (1967, April 8). *Saturday Review*.

Media

Media, the plural of the Latin word *medius* ("middle"), refer to the technological processes that facilitate communication between a sender and a receiver. **Mass media** send a message from one source to many people. Modern society has many kinds of mass media, including radio, television, books, the Internet, movies, music, and magazines. Using a telephone or writing a letter is not normally understood to be mass media because the contents involve private communication between two people and are not intended for a large audience.

Media are important socializing agents in our society; they teach us about the norms and expectations for different people and situations. The significance of the media is, in part, a result of our very high level of exposure to it. According to a recent study, the average Canadian adult watches 26 hours of television a week (Jackson 2017). Canadians spend an average of about 16 hours per week online, twice the global average (Jackson 2017). In addition, Canadians spend considerable amounts of time listening to the radio and reading newspapers and magazines. In this section, we examine changes in the media and the important role the media play in our society.

One of the most important scholars of media was Marshall McLuhan (1911–80), a Canadian academic who worked at the University of Toronto and founded the Centre for Culture and Technology. McLuhan (1964) is most famous for the statement the **"medium is the message."** He argued that the content of the medium, such as the words on an Internet news site, is not as important as the physical or psychological effects of that medium. Different media have different effects because of the form of their messages. These various forms alter how we experience the world, how we interact with others, and how we process and communicate information. For example, in print media, our visual sense rules; in radio, our aural; in television, both. In essence, McLuhan argued that the medium's properties (not just the messages' content) affect us as individuals and our social world as a whole. The media can shape and change us; as we develop new technologies, we are changed as a result.

The development of the printing press illustrates how changing mediums can affect individuals and society. The printing press was invented in China in 1041, but the version developed by Gutenberg in 1450 in Europe was particularly efficient and easy to use. This new press led to the production of the first mass-produced Bible in 1455. Previously, monks copied Bibles by hand, which took a long time. Not surprisingly, copies were scarce and very expensive.

The invention of the European printing press had significant (and, in some cases, unintended) effects on society. A major consequence was the challenge to the elite's ability to hoard information and knowledge. Before the printing press, only very rich and well-connected individuals had books. The press made it possible for more people to purchase them. It increased the number of books available because they could be mass-produced relatively quickly. When only monks transcribed books, it was easy for the powerful to control what was printed. The printing press effectively opened a massive communication channel, allowing many groups and interests to promote their messages. One of the first things printed on the printing press in Europe was Martin Luther's *The 95 Theses*—a list of complaints about the Catholic Church that led to the creation of Protestantism. This work certainly challenged the status quo!

The printing press also led to the rise of individualism. Individuals became less reliant on others (especially elites) for information. People gained more access to books, pamphlets, and newsletters on a wide variety of subjects. This shift effectively helped to democratize access to information on, for example, how to cure illnesses, build machines, or start a political movement. Moreover, literacy rates among different groups of people, including the poor, women, and children, improved.

The invention of the printing press was not simply a change in media; it fundamentally changed the nature of society as a whole. Centuries later, the rise of the Internet did the same. The Internet further democratizes access to information and content. Anyone can now read an almost unlimited number of books, magazines, and newspapers online as well as watch videos, movies, and TV shows. However, as we will discuss later in this chapter, there is still inequality regarding who has access to and knowledge about using computers and the Internet.

PHOTO 7.2 How has technology changed during your life? Did you have access to any computer devices—such as a tablet or smartphone—when you were a child? How would you have grown up differently if you had or hadn't had access to these devices?

Corporate Concentration and the Media

One key concern with modern mass media is the extent to which they are controlled by a limited number of people. Recent decades have seen an increase in the **corporate concentration** of media ownership. In other words, the media are increasingly owned and controlled by fewer huge media corporations and conglomerates. Canada has the most concentrated media ownership of any G8 country. The "Big 10" Canadian media companies controlled 83.4 per cent of all mass media in the country in 2014 (see Figure 7.1 for media concentration in the top 1, 4, and 10 companies). This number is a substantial increase from the 70 per cent controlled by these companies in the 1990s.

Such concentration could lead to fewer viewpoints being expressed in the media. And this concentration is much higher in Canada than it is in other countries (see Figure 7.2). Certainly, Canada's situation is not the same as having a single state-run

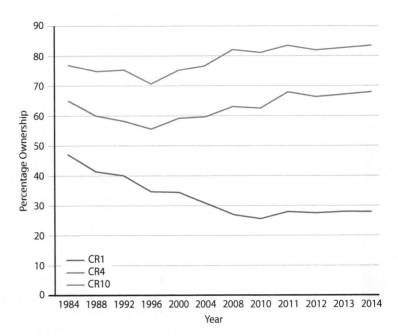

FIGURE 7.1   **Percentage of Canadian media concentrated in the largest 1, 4, and 10 companies**

Source: Canadian Media Concentration Research Project. http://www.cmcrp.org/
Axes: Year and Percentage Ownership

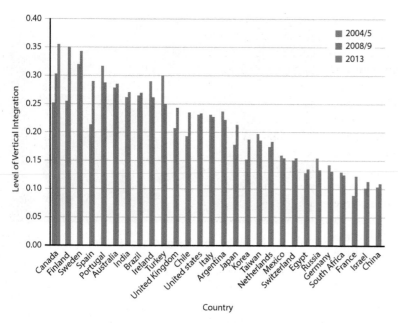

FIGURE 7.2   Vertical integration and cross-media ownership—Canada in a global context, 2004–2013

Source: Canadian Media Concentration Research Project. http://www.cmcrp.org/
Axes: Country, Level of Vertical Integration

newspaper, but how much competition is enough to ensure a free and independent press?

This pattern of media control has long historical roots. The town newspaper was once a family-owned business, as were the dairy, hardware store, and grocery store. Today, provision of these basic items is controlled by large firms—CanWest (newspaper), Saputo (dairy), Home Depot (hardware), and Safeway (groceries). Family-owned businesses have not disappeared, but they are now far less powerful and face continual threat (whether from Walmart, Amazon, or other big-box stores or online retailers). It may not be significant that we all get our milk or our light bulbs from the same store. However, we may be more concerned that our news and, as a consequence, our information about the world is filtered by a smaller and smaller group.

This issue is at the core of C. Wright Mills's *The Power Elite* (1956). In this book, Mills argues that the **power elite**, a group of leaders in the military, corporate, and political spheres of society, have interwoven and complementary interests. He also found an interchangeability of top positions within these three institutions, and, as a result, the most powerful people in each develop a class consciousness and a similar set of interests.

READING

From *The Power Elite*

C. Wright Mills

. . .

The Nature of the Power Elite

We study history, it has been said, to rid ourselves of it, and the history of the power elite is a clear case for which this maxim is correct. Like the tempo of American life in general, the long-term trends of the power structure have been greatly speeded up since World War II, and certain newer trends within and between the dominant institutions have also set the shape of the power elite. . . .

I. In so far as the structural clue to the power elite today lies in the political order, that clue is the decline of politics as genuine and public debate of alternative decisions—with nationally responsible and policy-coherent parties and with autonomous organizations connecting the lower and middle levels of power with the top levels of decision. America is now in considerable part more a formal political democracy than a democratic social structure, and even the formal political mechanics are weak.

The long-time tendency of business and government to become more intricately and deeply involved with each other has, in the fifth epoch, reached a new point of explicitness. The two cannot now be seen clearly as two distinct worlds. It is in terms of the

Mills, C. Wright. 1956. *The Power Elite*, pp. 269–97. Oxford: Oxford University Press, Inc..

executive agencies of the state that the rapprochement has proceeded most decisively. The growth of the executive branch of the government, with its agencies that patrol the complex economy, does not mean merely the "enlargement of government" as some sort of autonomous bureaucracy: it has meant the ascendancy of the corporation's man as a political eminence. . . .

III. In so far as the structural clue to the power elite today lies in the economic order, that clue is the fact that the economy is at once a permanent-war economy and a private-corporation economy. American capitalism is now in considerable part a military capitalism, and the most important relation of the big corporation to the state rests on the coincidence of interests between military and corporate needs, as defined by warlords and corporate rich. Within the elite as a whole, this coincidence of interest between the high military and the corporate chieftains strengthens both of them and further subordinates the role of the merely political men. Not politicians, but corporate executives, sit with the military and plan the organization of war effort. . . .

The power elite is composed of political, economic, and military men, but this instituted elite is frequently in some tension: it comes together only on certain coinciding points and only on certain occasions of "crisis": In the long peace of the nineteenth century, the military were not in the high councils of state, not of the political directorate, and neither were the economic men—they made raids upon the state but they did not join its directorate. During the thirties, the political man was ascendant. Now the military and the corporate men are in top positions.

Of the three types of circle that compose the power elite today, it is the military that has benefited the most in its enhanced power although the corporate circles have also become more explicitly entrenched in the more public decision-making circles. It is the professional politician that has lost the most, so much that in examining the events and decisions, one is tempted to speak of a political vacuum in which the corporate rich and the high warlord, in their coinciding interests, rule.

It should not be said that the three "take turns" in carrying the initiative, for the mechanics of the power elite are not often as deliberate as that would imply. At times, of course, it is—as when political men, thinking they can borrow the prestige of generals, find that they must pay for it, or, as when during big slumps, economic men feel the need of a politician at once safe and possessing vote appeal. Today all three are involved in virtually all widely ramifying decisions. Which of the three types seems to lead depends upon "the tasks of the period" as they, the elite, define them. Just now, these tasks centre upon "defence" and international affairs. Accordingly, as we have seen, the military are ascendant in two senses: as personnel and as justifying ideology. That is why, just now, we can most easily specify the unity and the shape of the power elite in terms of the military ascendancy. . . .

Neither the idea of a "ruling class" nor of a simple monolithic rise of "bureaucratic politicians" nor of a "military clique" is adequate. The power elite today involves the often uneasy coincidence of economic, military, and political power.

The Composition of the Power Elite

Despite their social similarity and psychological affinities, the members of the power elite do not constitute a club having a permanent membership with fixed and formal boundaries. It is of the nature of the power elite that within it there is a good deal of shifting about, and that it thus does not consist of one small set of the same men in the same positions in the same hierarchies. Because men know each other personally does not mean that among them there is a unity of policy; and because they do not know each other personally does not mean that among them there is a disunity. The conception of the power elite does not rest, as I have repeatedly said, primarily upon personal friendship.

As the requirements of the top places in each of the major hierarchies become similar, the types of men occupying these roles at the top—by selection and by training in the jobs—become similar. This is no mere deduction from structure to personnel. That it is a fact is revealed by the heavy traffic that has been going on between the three structures, often in very intricate patterns. The chief executives, the warlords, and selected politicians came into contact with one another in an intimate, working way during World War II; after that war ended, they continued their associations, out of common beliefs, social congeniality, and coinciding interests. Noticeable proportions of top men from the military, the economic, and the political worlds have during the last 15 years occupied positions in one or both of the other worlds: between these higher circles there is an interchangeability of position, based formally upon the supposed transferability of "executive ability," based in substance upon the co-optation by cliques of insiders. As members of a power elite, many of those busy in this traffic have come to look upon "the government" as an umbrella under whose authority they do their work. . . .

Given the formal similarity of the three hierarchies in which the several members of the elite spend their working lives, given the ramifications of the decisions made in each upon the others, given the coincidence of interest that prevails among them at many points, and given the administrative vacuum of the American civilian state along with its enlargement of tasks—given these trends of structure, and adding to them the psychological affinities we have noted—we should indeed be surprised were we to find that men said to be skilled in administrative contacts and full of organizing ability would fail to do more than get in touch with one another. They have, of course, done much more than that: increasingly, they assume positions in one another's domains. . . .

These men are not necessarily familiar with every major arena of power. We refer to one man who moves in and between perhaps two circles—say the industrial and the military—and to another man who moves in the military and the political, and to a third who moves in the political as well as among opinion-makers. These in-between types most closely display our image of the power elite's structure and operation, even of behind-the-scenes operations. To the extent that there is any "invisible elite," these advisory and liaison types are its core. Even if—as I believe to be very likely—many of them are, at least in the first part of their careers, "agents" of the various elites rather than themselves elite, it is they who are most active in organizing the several top milieux into a structure of power and maintaining it. . . .

The Interests of the Power Elite

The conception of the power elite and of its unity rests upon the corresponding developments and the coincidence of interests among economic, political, and military organizations. It also rests upon the similarity of origin and outlook, and the social and personal intermingling of the top circles from each of these dominant hierarchies. This conjunction of institutional and psychological forces, in turn, is revealed by the heavy personnel traffic within and between the big three institutional orders, as well as by the rise of go-betweens as in the high-level lobbying. The conception of the power elite, accordingly, does *not* rest upon the assumption that American history since the origins of World War II must be understood as a secret plot, or as a great and coordinated conspiracy of the members of this elite. The conception rests upon quite impersonal grounds.

There is, however, little doubt that the American power elite—which contains, we are told, some of the greatest organizers in the world—has also planned and has plotted. The rise of the elite, as we have already made clear, was not and could not have been caused by a plot; and the tenability of the conception does not rest upon the existence of any secret or any publicly known organization. But, once the conjunction of structural trend and of the personal will to utilize it gave rise to the power elite, then plans and programs did occur to its members and indeed it is not possible to interpret many events and official policies of the fifth epoch without reference to the power elite. "There is a great difference," Richard Hofstadter has remarked, "between locating conspiracies in history and saying that history is, in effect, a conspiracy. . ."

So far as explicit organization—conspiratorial or not—is concerned, the power elite, by its very nature, is more likely to use existing organizations, working within and between them, than to set up explicit organizations whose membership is strictly limited to its own members. But if there is no machinery in existence to ensure, for example, that military and political factors will be balanced in decisions made, they will invent such machinery and use it, as with the

National Security Council. Moreover, in a formally democratic polity, the aims and the powers of the various elements of this elite are further supported by an aspect of the permanent war economy: the assumption that the security of the nation supposedly rests upon great secrecy of plan and intent. Many higher events that would reveal the working of the power elite can be withheld from public knowledge under the guise of secrecy. With the wide secrecy covering their operations and decisions, the power elite can mask their intentions, operations, and further consolidation. Any secrecy that is imposed upon those in positions to observe high decision-makers clearly works for and not against the operations of the power elite.

There is accordingly reason to suspect—but by the nature of the case, no proof—that the power elite is not altogether "surfaced." There is nothing hidden about it, although its activities are not publicized. As an elite, it is not organized, although its members often know one another, seem quite naturally to work together, and share many organizations in common. There is nothing conspiratorial about it, although its decisions are often publicly unknown and its mode of operation manipulative rather than explicit.

Conclusion

The idea of the power elite rests upon and enables us to make sense of (1) the decisive institutional trends that characterize the structure of our epoch, in particular, the military ascendancy in a privately incorporated economy, and more broadly, the several coincidences of objective interests between economic, military, and political institutions; (2) the social similarities and the psychological affinities of the men who occupy the command posts of these structures, in particular the increased interchangeability of the top positions in each of them and the increased traffic between these orders in the careers of men of power; (3) the ramifications, to the point of virtual totality, of the kind of decisions that are made at the top, and the rise to power of a set of men who, by training and bent, are professional organizers of considerable force and who are unrestrained by democratic party training. . . .

As a result, the political directorate, the corporate rich, and the ascendant military have come together as the power elite, and the expanded and centralized hierarchies which they head have encroached upon the old balances and have now relegated them to the middle levels of power. Now the balancing society is a conception that pertains accurately to the middle levels, and on that level the balance has become more often an affair of entrenched provincial and nationally irresponsible forces and demands than a centre of power and national decision.

CRITICAL READING QUESTIONS

1. Who are the power elite? What are the three types of institutions that make up the power elite?
2. How do the interests of these three groups coincide, and how do they conflict? How do they come to share these commonalities?
3. Does Mills think that the power elite has control because of a conspiracy? How do they continue to exist?

Effects of Media Concentration

As mentioned in the previous section, corporate concentration in the media and other areas can limit the free exchange of ideas and the diversity of content we receive as media consumers. The two main types of media diversity that can be affected are idea diversity and demographic diversity.

Idea diversity refers to the range of viewpoints expressed in the media marketplace of ideas. Media conglomerates have the power to censor information according to their

PHOTO 7.3 *Orange Is the New Black* attempts to show demographic diversity both in front of and behind the camera. Is it important to depict diversity in television shows? Can this lead to more inclusiveness in society as a whole?

interests. In *Manufacturing Consent: The Political Economy of the Mass Media*, Noam Chomsky and Edward S. Herman (2002) argue that wealthy and powerful people control the mass media. Because the mass media are one of the primary means of socialization and persuasion in our society, elites are able to create news that reflects their own interests. Herman and Chomsky also argue that elites can use this media control to legitimize the class system and other inequalities in our society.

Demographic diversity refers to how the media represents and addresses the interests of a diversity of people from a variety of races, ethnicities, genders, sexual orientations, and classes. One might argue that a way to ensure demographically diverse content is to support demographically diverse ownership (Gamson and Latteier 2004). In the United States, where more data are collected on this issue, less than 5 per cent of the media is owned by women or ethnic minorities (Byerly 2006). This lack of diversity in ownership could limit the variety of characters and shows presented. However, it is possible that a homogeneous group of media owners could be showing a range of characters.

A recent study of the top 100 films of the year found that only 31.4 per cent of the speaking roles in movies were female in 2015. Characters who were LGBTQ amounted to less than 1 per cent of the speaking roles. And in the top 100 films, there were no transgender people with speaking roles (Smith, Choueiti, and Pieper 2016). A GLAAD study of diversity on US television found that while ethnic minorities make up 28 per cent of the country's population, they account for only 23 per cent of characters on American television (Elber 2013). And only 1 per cent of the characters on television are people with disabilities (Mitovich 2015).

This lack of diversity has many serious implications for viewers. For example, it can have negative effects on the self-esteem of various groups. Martins and Harrison (2012) surveyed 396 black and white preteens in the United States to examine television's effect on children's self-esteem. They found that television exposure led to decreased self-esteem for white and black girls and black boys. However, it was associated with increased self-esteem among white boys.

In the following article, Canadian sociologists Shyon Baumann and Loretta Ho investigate how meanings are attached to different racial identities in Canadian television advertising. They focus on food advertising, but consider how these ideas might extend to racial stereotypes in other types of media or in everyday life.

READING

Cultural Schemas for Racial Identity in Canadian Television Advertising

Shyon Baumann and Loretta Ho

What meanings are attached to race in advertising? This paper addresses this question through an analysis of racial representation in Canadian prime-time television commercials. Sociological work on media content is founded on the premise that the nature of media content reflects and reproduces important dimensions of culture, of which schemas for

Baumann, Shyon, and Loretta Ho. 2014. "Cultural Schemas for Racial Identity in Canadian Television Advertising." *Canadian Review of Sociology* 52(2): 152–69.

racial identity are one salient case. Through investigating schemas for racial identities in advertising, we can uncover understandings of race in Canadian society that are otherwise difficult to measure.

We take the empirical case of food and dining commercials on prime-time Canadian television to address two core research questions. First, how do representations of race vary across different categories of foods? We pose this question to understand the patterns in which different racial groups are presented. Second, what clusterings of contexts, relationships, and character traits are members of different racial groups associated with, and what can these clusterings tell us about how race functions symbolically within commercials? We answer these questions by first examining quantitative data on the distribution of racial representation across different categories of food commercials and comparing these results with data on the distribution of product categories by race. Then, to gain a deeper understanding of the symbolic functions of race, and to address our second question, we conduct a qualitative reading of the predominant cultural schemas for racial identity emerging from our sample. Cultural schemas are broader than stereotypes (associations between a group and a trait) insofar as they define group boundaries, and provide scripts for understanding categories (e.g., categories of people) and for guiding behaviors in social settings (see Blair-Loy 2001; Brubaker, Loveman, and Stamatov 2004; DiMaggio 1997). For example, Baumann and de Laat (2012) provide evidence of a cultural schema for gender and age identity that understands older men as "society's bosses." Rather than just an association between a group and a trait, the cultural schema of society's bosses encompasses an association, as well as suggestions for how to interact with this group, and how to value and understand this group's place in society. Similarly, Roth (**2012**) argues that a "Hispanicized" schema for race constructs Latino as a racial category (as opposed to an ethnicity), and also suggests how to understand their place and value in society, with attendant scripts for interactions and expectations about Latino identity. Cultural schemas are socially constructed through circulating knowledge, beliefs, and values. Individuals both encounter and reproduce cultural schemas through daily social interactions. In addition to learning about cultural schemas through face-to-face interactions, we follow others in arguing that the media are another source for cultural schemas (see, e.g., DiMaggio 1997:280).

Based on our quantitative and qualitative findings, we identify six cultural schemas for racial identity: *White nostalgia, White natural, White highbrow, White nuclear family, Black blue collar,* and *Asian technocrat.* Some of our findings confirm previous research on representation of race and ethnicity in the media, but we also describe cultural schemas about White racial representation that were not found in earlier work.

Scholars have argued that depictions of visible minorities in Canadian media arise from a dominant racial discourse that demeans, demonizes, and stereotypes these groups (Henry and Tator 2003; Jiwani 2009a; Mahtani 2009). We build on this prior literature by examining race in Canadian advertising, in contrast to past studies' predominant examination of news coverage. Advertising is particularly susceptible to stereotypical depictions of social groups, including racial groups, that are shaped by dominant cultural schemas of identity. The media in general, and advertising in particular, play a role in reproducing cultural schemas by using existing cultural schemas to produce content. Constraints on time and space for content mean that advertising often presents extreme versions of schemas that are widely available and culturally predominant in order to efficiently and effectively communicate with broad audiences (Goffman 1979; Schudson 1984). Advertising therefore provides an excellent empirical site for learning about cultural schemas. In systematically studying television commercials, this paper documents portrayals that differ from prior research on race in other forms of Canadian media.

Data and Methods

This paper is part of a larger project analyzing Canadian television advertising. The project includes content analysis of a sample of prime-time (8–11 PM) commercials on three Canadian networks—CBC, CTV, and Global. Despite the growth of Internet entertainment options, television commercials remain the largest advertising medium reaching the broadest audience. The sample was constructed from recordings of broadcasts for 21 evenings, comprised of Sunday through Saturday for each network. In order to diversify the time of year represented in the sample, recordings were spaced over an 18-month period, from July 2008 to December 2009.

Moreover, in order to develop a qualitative analysis of cultural schemas, we limit our study to the product category of food and dining, and only for visually present human characters (not voice-overs or animated characters). We specifically consider food and dining commercials for a number of reasons. First, as the largest product category of commercials in our sample, racial representation is relatively diverse here. Second, food and dining are an enormous market, so these types of ads have a broad target audience and important implications for a diverse general public. Third, food is a cultural object embedded with rich and multiple meanings. Across all races, the production and consumption of food play an important and symbolic role in everyday experiences, family and cultural traditions, and holidays. Following in a tradition of examining patterns in advertising to uncover cultural schemas (Goffman 1979), we expect broadly resonant messages about race in food ads.

Our sample for this analysis includes 244 commercials featuring 1,063 characters (primary and secondary combined). We proceed first by breaking down the food and dining commercials to subtypes of this product category. Because particular kinds of food have particular cultural meanings, status, and market locations, we hope to uncover patterns in racial group associations with particular food types that reveal something about the cultural schemas for these groups. These quantitative findings give us a snapshot of racial representation, allowing us to make preliminary comparisons between stereotypes found in previous literature and those that seem to be in operation in our sample.

Race and Connections to Food and Dining Subtypes

How does race correlate with food and dining subtypes? Taking cues from both the scientific and social scientific fields of food studies, we reviewed our food commercials and developed a typology of categories that are mutually exclusive and that allow us to describe the majority of ads (see Table 7.1).

TABLE 7.1 | Distribution of Characters in Food/Dining Commercials across Racial Categories

Food/dining category	Per cent White	Per cent Black	Per cent East/Southeast Asian	Total (N)
Whole foods	97	2	1	100% (235)
Fast food restaurants	80	14	6	100% (206)
Table service restaurants	87	11	2	100% (195)
Health foods	82	14	5	100% (180)
Processed foods	98	1	1	100% (172)
Other	85	8	7	100% (75)
Number of commercials	227	23	9	

Note:
Row totals may not add up to 100% due to rounding. SCAP SAMPLE
$X^2 = 64.011$, 10 df, $p < .001$.

Source: Shyon Baumann and Loretta Ho, "Cultural Schemas for Racial Identity in Canadian Television Advertising." *Canadian Review of Sociology* 51.2 (2014), 152-69

We present our data first percentaged across rows in Table 7. 1, to show the racial distribution of characters within each food/dining category. Before looking at each category, note that Whites are overrepresented overall in food advertisements compared to their Black and East/Southeast Asian counterparts; their representation in all categories of food ads combined (87 per cent) is higher than their representation in the general sample of commercials (79 per cent) and than their proportion of the Canadian population (80 per cent).

There are several notable relationships in Table 7. 1. The whole foods category is almost exclusively White, while fast food commercials are more dispersed across racial groups, with Blacks and East/Southeast Asians overrepresented relative to their proportion in food commercials generally. Health food commercials are very similar to fast food restaurants in the breakdown of the race of characters, with representation from all three groups. Processed food commercials closely resemble the racial distribution of characters in commercials for whole foods, almost exclusively White.

The overall picture provided by these results is that whereas Whites are strongly associated with whole foods, Blacks and East/Southeast Asians are most often linked to fast food. These predominant linkages coexist with other secondary associations, namely Whites with processed foods, and Blacks with health foods. A chi-square analysis confirms that the differences between the racial groups are significant at the $p < .001$ level. While predominant associations conform to racial stereotypes, such as those found in the literature review, secondary associations are less prevalent, and less easily explained. In order to illuminate these associations and develop a better understanding of them, we conduct a qualitative reading of the ads.

Tradition, Status, Naturalness, and Family

This in-depth qualitative analysis illuminates how observed associations in advertising inform cultural schemas for racial identity. What social characteristics of each of these racial groups tend to be emphasized, or downplayed, to produce the particular associations we find? To connect our theoretical understanding of race and representation with our empirical analysis of food advertising, we identify six schemas. We are not suggesting that these are an exhaustive list of the dominant schemas for racial identity in our culture; rather, these are the schemas that emerge in our data.

Four schemas pertain to Whites, one to Blacks, and one to East/Southeast Asians. The small number of schemas in these food commercials for Black and East/Southeast Asian characters is related to the small number of primary characters of these races in food ads. We first review these six schemas, and then discuss their cultural significance and possible relationships between them.

"White Nostalgia" Schema

This schema is represented in 58 ads in our sample. Two variations of this schema exist, one that is more closely related to food production, and the other to food consumption. These variations of the "Nostalgia" schema establish the idea that Whites have a long history of producing and consuming quality foods that have an enduring presence in the marketplace. For example, in the production variation, a commercial for Oka cheese depicts a production process circa mid-1800s, while a voice-over informs viewers that White monks have been "crafting" this product for generations. The use of the word "craft" suggests that production is not a mechanical process to mass-produce food; rather, it is an art that skillful monks engaged in to create legacy artisanal cheeses now enjoyed at important social gatherings. We also saw the authority and expertise of traditional food production associated with Whites in ads featuring historical production of bread (Dempster's) and jam (Smucker's). In the other variation, an ad for Ritz crackers romanticizes the consumption of food. A simple scene of a boy laying down crackers for a girl to follow, reminiscent of the children's tale Hansel and Gretel, coupled with the song of uncomplicated friendship and love for an angelic girl, attempts to transport us to a childhood when Ritz crackers were frequently enjoyed. Visual images, shot in a glowing soft light, trigger warm memories of consuming the snack. These nostalgic food commercials link Whites with brands that have an established status, and our sample of ads features only Whites as the bearers of tradition in food.

"White Natural" Schema

In this second schema, appearing in 18 ads, Whites are symbolically linked to nature and the wholesome foods it has to offer. A clear example of this imagery can be found in a relatively upmarket supermarket brand line of foods (President's Choice), where the CEO of the company is shown joining White male farmers from different provinces in their fields, presumably chatting to them about their produce. The CEO's voice-over, heard during the frames featuring farmers, justifies his company's choice to buy local—to support the Canadian farmer and the economy, and for "plain great eating." This ad illustrates the "White Natural" schema in several ways. Only White men are shown, in both producer and consumer roles. Five White farmers symbolize "the Canadian farmer," the ultimate producer of "plain great eating." This schema is noteworthy for the extent to which it diverges from social reality. In farmers' fields across the country, a great deal of agricultural work in Canada is done by racialized minorities, both Canadian and temporary foreign workers. This exclusion of minority farmworkers in ads reinforces the notion that Whites are especially in tune with, and are authorities on the natural world and are responsible for wholesome and natural food production.

"White Highbrow" Schema

It is important to note that not many high-end or luxury food products are advertised on television. However, the "White Highbrow" schema, used in seven ads, was still applicable to advertisements of food products that were not high-end per se, but relied on cues of high cultural and economic capital as selling points. For example, although Europe's Best Frozen Fruits is an affordable food product, the advertisement portrays a family with high cultural and economic capital. Cues include Baroque background music and an elegant dining table and room, with proper settings (including a napkin ring) prepared even for dessert. High economic capital is suggested through the modern and very large kitchen with expensive-looking appliances and kitchen utensils. That both parents are wearing business casual clothes implies that they hold well-paying white collar jobs. In our sample, highbrow status, as expressed through traditional symbols of high cultural and economic capital, is associated only with White characters.

"White Nuclear Family" Schema

The "White Nuclear Family" schema is the most common in our study. Represented by 50 ads, it cuts across advertisements for all our food and dining subtypes. In many of these ads, the White nuclear family is depicted at the dinner table, with one parent at the head, leading conversation as the family enjoys their food (e.g., Mr. Sub, Maple Leaf Prime, Dan Active). Although all ads in this category feature the typical configuration of mother, father, and children, some ads also explicitly depict the mother having the primary responsibility of preparing and serving food to her husband and children. This schema variously features additional elements of idealized family dynamics, such as the mother serving as the guardian of family health (Beagan et al. 2008), or the father as breadwinner. Moreover, the White nuclear family is shown to be both socially and physically healthy. Despite the social reality of a vast reduction in family meals and indeed in nuclear families themselves, the White nuclear family schema suggests that social stability and healthy eating alike are associated with Whiteness.

"Black Blue Collar" Schema

Because White characters so vastly outnumber non-White characters in commercials, the depictions of racial minorities in commercials are relatively powerful insofar as a relatively small number of them represent the schemas for racial minorities. From our sample, only one clear schema for Black characters emerged, which we label the "Black blue collar" schema, appearing in 11 ads. It is communicated through showing Blacks in a variety of blue collar work settings, most prominently in factories and auto body shops. For example, an ad for "Honey Bunches of Oats" begins with a female voice-over asking "What's our favorite part of Honey Bunches of Oats?" A White food scientist examining a single flake under a microscope responds, "The crispy flakes." The camera then pans to the factory, where among other workers, we are shown two Black men in front of a packaging machine. The first simply smiles while holding a box of cereal, while the other performs a little dance.

The predominant subtext of this schema is one of safe inclusivity. On the one hand, commercials with Black characters provide diversity in advertising. It is recognition of both the racial diversity of the target market for the advertising and of society as a whole. Furthermore, the schema is not inherently negative, insofar as it does not play into traditional negative stereotypes of Blacks. On the other hand, this schema positions Blacks within a relatively *narrow* relationship to food—as working-class producers. This schema avoids the more negative connotations of associations with underclass membership, which at any rate would not make sense from a marketing point of view. Furthermore, because Black characters comprise so few of the total number of characters in our sample of ads, there is no other clear characterization of this racial group to nuance or to compete with this frame. The contrast between a White scientist and a dancing blue collar Black character reifies the Whiteness of the food scientist in this commercial and, implicitly, scientists in general, in contrast to the racial diversity of the category of manufacturing workers.

"Asian Technocrat" Schema

Unlike any of the other schemas we identify in the commercials in our sample, the schema of the "Asian technocrat" is quite negative. It is used in various forms in ads featuring Asians. In this schema, noted in six ads, Asians are portrayed as unemotional overachievers who respond to any and all situations in a robotic way. Again, as with Black characters, Asian characters are represented by a relatively small number of characters, and so only one schema emerged from our reading of the ads. This schema is illustrated by an ad for Baskin Robbins Ice Cream. An Asian grandfather sits in a rocking chair in the family room when the granddaughter approaches, appearing downtrodden. Grandpa asks, "What's the matter?" The granddaughter shows Grandpa a math test with a red F at the top and bemoans, "Mom said if I got an A we can get Reese shakes at Baskin Robbins." Grandpa uses his blue pen to change the F to an A, and states, "See you in the car." He vanishes, leaving his granddaughter to stare at her test with a complete lack of expression on her face.

The characteristics of the Asian technocrat, achievement-oriented, and robotic are communicated through the granddaughter. Immediately, viewers will recognize the Asian student who expects to perform well in math, or in all academic subjects, for that matter (Louie 2004). Though she fails to achieve an A, which contradicts the model minority stereotype, her reaction conforms to the overused robotic trope (Wang 2010). Moreover, the failing grade for the Asian student is a (supposedly) comedic inversion of the well-worn schema of Asian academic achievement, and retains the link between Asian identity and a focus on academics. Upon receiving a failing grade, her emotions are simplistic and one-dimensional; she is sad. Even after her grandfather decides to take her out for an ice cream anyway, she is unable to demonstrate the basic and antilogous emotion of happiness, let alone more complex emotions that may arise in this situation: surprise, relief, or even guilt. In fact, she stands with her corrected test, face completely blank. It is hard to tell whether or not she was feeling *any* emotion at the offer of ice cream, which she previously lamented over not being able to have, given her bad grade. The grandfather, too, is portrayed as a technocrat. He approaches his granddaughter's emotions as a problem to be solved. She is sad, so change her mark and take her out to ice cream. He is frugal with his words, uttered in a matter-of-fact and monotonous way. Making no attempt to emotionally console the granddaughter, he instantly disappears, to solve her problem in a practical way, through buying ice cream. The robotic mannerisms portrayed by Grandpa and his granddaughter achieve the marketer's manifest goal of providing comedic relief. A latent result is that these types of images reinforce the stereotype that Asians are industrious but emotionless individuals interested only in climbing up the social ladder through academic excellence.

Discussion and Conclusion

Despite the often-touted differences between Canada and the United States when it comes to issues of race, we find strong similarities between rates and modes of racial representation in advertising. We find underrepresentation of many visible minority groups, but an overrepresentation of Black characters relative to their proportion in the Canadian population, at a rate that resembles their representation in American media. This fact points to an overlap between American and Canadian racial representations in advertising, rather than a divergence. Moreover, as has been found in American research, the representations of Whites in advertising are more diversified and positive than the representations of other races.

Our paper is strongly aligned with Henry and Tator's (2009) claims that "[m]edia discourse plays a large role in reproducing the collective belief system of the dominant White society and the core values of this society" (p. 711) and that the "dominant discourses and representations . . . reinforce the construct of whiteness as the normative universe" (p. 712). Our argument supports the main claims of prior scholars of Canadian media insofar as we find highly unequal racialized media content. However, we arrive at our argument through the identification of six schemas for racial identity that have not been identified before in Canadian media.

Our examination of how Whites, Blacks, and East/Southeast Asians are represented in Canadian prime-time food and dining commercials identified significant variations between these three groups. In terms of food subtypes, Whites were most often associated with whole foods, while Blacks' and East/Southeast Asians' appearances were most strongly concentrated in fast food commercials. This finding about fast food supports Henderson and Baldasty's (2003) research on U.S. commercials, and we agree with their interpretation that the association suggests a symbolic connection between race and class.

The cultural schemas we identify provide information about the symbolism attached to race in this sample of mainstream Canadian media content. We interpret the messages we see in these commercials as reflections of some of the dominant cultural schemas for these groups, and at the same time as agents for the reproduction of those dominant cultural schemas. The messages that come through are not only that Whites are associated with whole foods, highbrow food, and natural food, but that Whites *are* wholesome, highbrow, and in tune with the natural. Whiteness comes to symbolize all of these abstract ideas, assigning a type of visual "tangibility" through concrete examples. Furthermore, these schemas contribute to the construction of a script of what it means to be White, including the normalcy (however inaccurate) of the nuclear family, and associations with legitimate or highbrow culture and with authority and tradition. Our qualitative analysis helps to explain the initially surprising association between Whites and processed foods (to the near complete exclusion of other groups). In these commercials we see Whites associated with nostalgia and tradition, ideas on which these generally long-standing and well-known brands are trading. Although it is mostly true that Whites were the group that consumed these brands many decades ago, the continuation of this association may perpetuate a symbolic connection between Whites (but not other groups) and an idealized present and future.

In contrast to the various White schemas, these commercials provide just one schema each for Blacks and East/Southeast Asians. The narrowness of the representations is significant, because they present just one way to be a member of each of these groups. While the schema for Blacks is not overtly negative, it is nonetheless problematic. As the only clear schema in our sample for Blacks, it constrains this group to a relatively disadvantaged socioeconomic position. There is a poignant contrast here with the White Highbrow schema for the difference in status accorded to each group. Our quantitative findings show that Blacks are disproportionately associated with fast food commercials. This association exists within a social context where fast food is connected to lower levels of cultural capital (Johnston and Baumann 2010), and it is much less frequently consumed by people from higher socioeconomic status groups (Kim and Leigh 2011). Regarding health food commercials, this finding corroborates some of the more specific findings regarding stereotypical corporeality of African Americans in earlier content analysis work (Burton and Klemm 2011; Millard and Grant 2006; Plous and Neptune 1997). Bristol et al. (1995) observe an emphasis on Black bodies in advertising and interpret this emphasis as part of a schematic White/brains versus Black/brawn dichotomy in popular culture. Health food's connection to the body and bodily appearance can thus illuminate the association we find with Blacks.

The schema for East/Southeast Asians is narrow and negative. As the only schema for this group in our sample, it effectively Others them through implicit suggestions of their robotic, emotionless nature. It corroborates other earlier content analysis findings on Asian Americans (Pake and Shah 2003; Wang 2010). There is another poignant contrast, in this case with the White Nuclear Family schema, for the difference in warmth and emotionality accorded to each group.

Our findings point to a problem with the underrepresentation and misrepresentation of visible minorities in the media. Underrepresentation is a problem because it reinforces narrow cultural schemas for what it means to be a member of these groups, including dominant societal expectations (and self-expectations) about the identities and behaviors of group members. The rich, broad, multidimensional, and positive cultural schemas for Whiteness set up a contrast to other groups where Whiteness is implicitly preferable. Whiteness appears in commercials as a balance between production/consumption, labor/leisure, discipline/emotion, mind/body, with Blackness appearing as too bodily or Asianness as too robotic. We interpret the minority cultural schemas as both dependent on, and helping to constitute, the White cultural schemas. It is in contrast to one another that they appear as broad or narrow, and through which their significance is constructed.

In our view, advertisers utilize (rather than invent) dominant cultural schemas (of which race is just one kind), and the organizational constraints (on both time and the need to resonate with broad audiences) that apply to marketing make those schemas especially salient, and therefore ripe for analysis. Although food and dining advertising is a culturally rich source for identifying racial cultural schemas, this empirical choice has influenced which of the particular schemas we identify. We would strongly suggest, however, that these schemas are broader than the realm of food and dining, and encourage future researchers to systematically examine other forms of advertising and other media in Canada.

CRITICAL READING QUESTIONS

1. What are cultural schemas? How are they related to racial identities?
2. This article is based on food advertisements. Do you think that the findings would be different if they examined other kinds of advertisements, such as ads for cars, shoes, or beauty products? What if they studied television programs instead?
3. In this article, the authors compare racial schemas and depictions in the US and Canada. How are they different, and why might this be?
4. How might social class be related to these racial depictions?

RESEARCH METHOD
SURVEY

The study shows that children from certain groups (females and ethnic minorities) suffer lower self-esteem when they are not exposed to TV role models who look like them. When individuals who share their racial and gender characteristics are shown, they are engaging in negative behaviours, which can also cause the viewer's feelings of self-worth to drop. The study authors found that white male characters are mostly portrayed as powerful, strong, rational, and central to the storyline. Female characters are more likely to appear emotional, sensitive, and as a sidekick or love interest. Black male characters are shown as threatening or unruly; black female characters are exotic and sexually available (Martins and Harrison 2012). As a result, young white boys had a better set of positive media representation than the children in the other groups.

A UCLA study found that there are benefits to having more diversity in the media. Hunt (in Lee 2013) analyzed more than 1000 television shows across 67 networks. Shows with a more diverse cast tended to have higher ratings than other shows—in fact, shows with casts that were between 31 per cent and 40 per cent minority did the best in ratings measures. Shows with very low levels of diversity (10 per cent or less) tended to have lower ratings. Clearly, diversity is not only important for audiences, but it also benefits media corporations.

HIGHLIGHT

Oscars So White

In 2016, when the list of Oscar nominees was released, there was a pronounced backlash. For the second year in a row, all 10 of the nominees in the four top acting categories were white actors. There was no racial or ethnic diversity in the best actress, best actor, best supporting actress, or best supporting actor categories. The reaction led to the campaign Oscars So White. Many actors and directors refused to attend the ceremony, and articles appeared in the media criticizing the Academy for their lack of diversity.

One explanation for the lack of diversity in nominations is simply that there were no good performances from non-white actors in this year. However, what seems much more likely is that the way that actors, and others, get nominated, structures the types of people who will get selected for awards. In order to vote for the winner of the Academy awards, you need to be a member of the Academy. But how do you become a member? Two people who are already members must sponsor you, which is then approved by the Board of Governors (Oscars.org, 2017). Given that only 7 per cent of the members of the Academy were non-white in 2016, it is not surprising that there was so little diversity in the actors nominated. We can also imagine that a group that is 93 per cent white is also more likely to nominate other white people to join the Academy, perpetuating the inequality over time.

The Academy has responded to the Oscars So White campaign and has committed to doubling the number of ethnic minorities in the Academy by 2020. If they were to meet this ambitious target, there would still only be 14 per cent ethnic minorities in the Academy, far below their representation in the population as a whole (which is 38 per cent in the US) (Cox 2017).

Despite not yet reaching their targets or the diversity that exists in the population as a whole, the drive toward equality has already yielded results. The 2018 Oscars nominated black actors Daniel Kaluuya (for his lead role in *Get Out*), Denzel Washington (for his lead role in *Roman J. Israel, Esq.*), Octavia Spencer (for her supporting role in *The Shape of Water*), and Mary J. Blige (for her supporting role in *Mudbound* and for her original song in the film). *Get Out* also received nominations for best picture, best director, and best original screenplay for Jordan Peele. This is certainly progress. However, activists were quick to note that while there was a larger group of black actors and directors nominated, there were no Latino or Asian people nominated. While it is important to note the achievements of the movement #Oscarssowhite, we want to remain critical of the general lack of diversity in these types of awards and the ways that institutions perpetuate this inequality over time.

New Media and Social Media

The media environment has undergone widespread change over the past 20 to 30 years with the rise in new media. **New media** are accessible on demand, is digital, and is interactive, encouraging user comments and feedback. Some examples of new media are the Internet, websites, video games, CDs, and DVDs. Wikipedia combines a number of features of new media: it is digitally based, incorporates images and video links, and allows interactive and creative participation among users.

Social media, a type of new media, allow the creation and online sharing of information in communities and networks. According to Kaplan and Haenlein (2010), social media technologies can be classified into six types: collaborative projects (Wikipedia), blogs and microblogs (Twitter), content communities (YouTube), social networking sites (Facebook), virtual game worlds (*Clash of Clans*), and virtual social worlds (*Minecraft* or *Second Life*). However, the boundaries between the different types are increasingly blurred.

Social media are used mainly for social interaction. The high usage rates of these technologies indicate that they are filling important social functions for many people. In fact, many argue that technology is transforming how we engage with others and how we spend our time. More and more people are willing to make social connections and seek companionship through social media such as Tinder or Grindr. The Internet is also an effective way for users to connect with people across great distances, such as through Skype. Moreover, our expectations and norms about love, friendship, and identity are strongly informed by our use of social media. What it means to "friend" someone, for example, is very different in the Facebook era than it was 50 years ago.

With the largest concentration of Internet users in the world, state investment in technological infrastructure, and high use of technology, South Korea is often seen as the first digital democracy. Many commentators have credited the strong role of the Internet and television for changing Korean social norms. For example, previous taboos, including divorce, extramarital affairs, and cohabitation, are changing. In the just 10 years, South Korea's divorce rate increased by 250 per cent (Onishi 2003). Koreans' changing attitudes about these issues are reflected in television programs, many of which are centred on the lives of women. *The Woman Next Door* focuses on the marriages and affairs of three women in their thirties and challenges traditional norms in Korean society whereby men were allowed to engage in affairs and wives were expected to remain faithful.

We can also see that social media have created many large-scale changes in Canada. The biggest change is in the scale of our social networks—we can interact with many more people than was possible in the past. Traditionally, our social networks were limited by our geography, but physical presence is no longer a precondition for establishing a friendship or tie. Think about how you show friends your vacation photos. Twenty years ago, you would have had to meet in person, flip through hard copies of the photos, and explain them. Doing this with all your Facebook or Instagram friends would take a long time. Now you can simply upload all your photos to Facebook and add descriptions; your friends can view the photos at their leisure, increasing this interaction of photo-sharing. Although you can certainly share your photos with a larger group of people, the quality of the interaction is possibly lower. Not all your Facebook friends will commit the half hour they might have spent looking at your photos in the past.

HIGHLIGHT

The Ice Bucket Challenge and Social Change

In the summer of 2014, the "Ice Bucket Challenge" became a viral charity campaign. This campaign aimed to raise awareness about ALS (amyotrophic lateral sclerosis), also known as Lou Gehrig's disease. People filmed themselves dumping a bucket of ice water on their head and challenged their friends to do the same within 24 hours or donate to the ALS cause. Many celebrities participated, including Chris Pratt, Oprah, LeBron James, Amy Schumer, David Beckham, Macklemore, Lady Gaga, Selena Gomez, and Kerry Washington. Some dismissed the campaign as sensational and not leading to real social change. For example, some noted that many of the celebrities did not mention ALS in their videos. Was this simply a trend in which people got involved just to participate in the "latest thing"?

The campaign did have some very real effects. According to the ALS Association, the campaign raised more than $100 million dollars in a 30-day period! This money fully funded a number of research projects. One of these projects, Project MinE, has identified a new gene associated with the disease, which experts say could lead to new treatments (Woolf 2016). The ALS Society of Canada is trying to keep this momentum going. They initiated a new campaign for Ice Bucket Challenge 2017 with the hashtag #EveryAugustUntilACure. What can we learn from this campaign that could be applied to other social causes?

Twocoms/Shutterstock

Justin Timberlake, Jimmy Fallon, and Mark Zuckerberg all dumped a bucket filled with ice water over their heads in order to raise awareness of ALS. How can celebrity engagement in this type of campaign help to increase awareness and lead to social change?

Social media also place fewer restrictions on your communication. Previously, the only way to get your message to a large group of people was to talk with them face to face (perhaps in a speech to a large crowd); otherwise, you could be censored. For example, if you write a letter to the editor, the publication has the power to select (or not select) your letter for printing. If you wanted to air your advertisement on TV, the station could refuse your ad or make you change its content. But with social media, you can distribute your message to a virtually unlimited number of people with very little censorship (at least in Canada). If you're upset with something the prime minister does, you can post your feelings on a blog, Twitter, or Facebook, where all your friends and followers can read it.

There are obvious benefits to social media. However, we must not overestimate the diversity of social media networks. While it might seem that we can have contact and communication with virtually anyone, we know that individuals tend to create online communities of similar people who share their opinions. It is not surprising that, just as in face-to-face friendships, we tend to seek out others like us online. As a result, we are exposed to a limited number of views. People who hold very different beliefs or perspectives than we do are unlikely to be in our online circle of friends. Perhaps you are part of a political or religious group online. These groups will likely only have other members who share your political or religious ideology, which could simply reinforce the opinions you already have instead of exposing you to new ideas and information.

The ability to spread information about ourselves and others so easily has created a lack of privacy, which can be a particular problem for young people. One in five Internet users between the ages of 15 and 29 has been cyberbullied or cyberstalked (Statistics Canada 2016). **Cyberbullying** involves the use of the Internet and related technologies to repeatedly intimidate or harass others (Statistics Canada 2016). This is particularly prevalent for LGBTQ young people. In fact, one in three LGBTQ young people reports being cyberbullied or cyberstalked (Statistics Canada 2016). High-profile incidents of cyberbullying in Canada led to the tragic death of Amanda Todd, a 15-year old girl from BC who died from suicide after being cyberbullied. In response to this serious issue, the Canadian government introduced legislation to deal with cyberbullying. Bill C-13 works to fight online harassment by making it illegal to distribute intimate images of a person without their consent (Puzic 2015).

The percentage of Canadians who use the Internet has increased over time. In 2013, 87 per cent were connected to the Internet, making us the sixteenth most connected country in the world. This is an increase from 80 per cent only seven years earlier. (CIRA 2014). However, use of the Internet and other communication technologies is not equally distributed across all groups. The **digital divide** is the inequality between groups with regard to their access to information and communication technologies (ICTs) and to their use of such technologies. The divide within one country occurs between individuals, households, and geographic areas at different socio-economic levels. The divide between countries, referred to as the global digital divide, measures the gap between the digital access and use of technologies across countries.

Age is a major dimension of the digital divide in Canada. As of 2013, young people 16 to 24 were the most likely to go online, with 84.2 per cent of this group going online while only 8.7 per cent of those over 65 and over had Internet service (Geist 2013).

Women and men are roughly equal in terms of Internet use, at 79.7 and 81.0 per cent, respectively (Statistics Canada 2012). However, their usage patterns are very different. Women are more likely to frequent social networking websites, with 37 per cent using such sites daily compared with only 24 per cent of men, according to a 2012 poll (Ipsos Reid 2012).

A strong urban/rural digital divide also exists. This is, in part, because of the lack of Internet services in rural communities. While 100 per cent of the urban centres in Canada have broadband Internet services, only 85 per cent of rural communities did as of 2014. And this is particularly problematic in remote areas, such as Nunavut, where only 27 per cent of communities had Internet access (CIRA 2014).

Finally, and perhaps most significantly, there is a large digital divide between the richest and poorest Canadians. While 95 per cent of Canadians in the highest income quartile (top 25 per cent of earners) had access to the Internet in 2014, just 62 per cent in the lowest income quartile (the bottom 25 per cent of earners) had access (CIRA 2014).

As illustrated in Figure 7.3, the digital divide is much more extreme across countries. While Canada, Europe, and Australia have nearly universal access to computers and

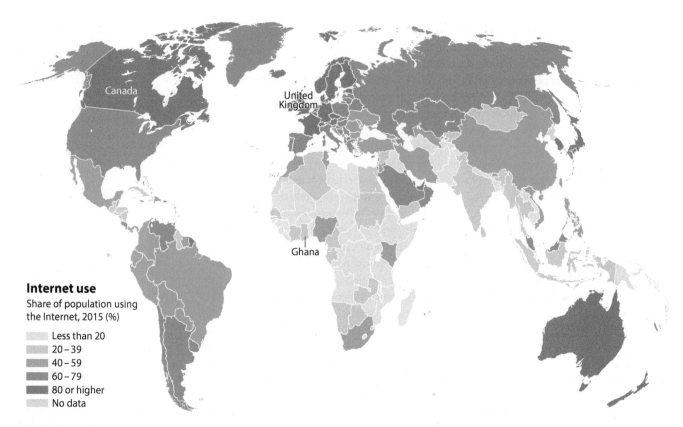

Internet use

Share of population using
the Internet, 2015 (%)

	Less than 20
	20 – 39
	40 – 59
	60 – 79
	80 or higher
	No data

FIGURE 7.3   Share of the population using the Internet, 2015

Source: The World Bank. http://www.worldbank.org/en/about/contacts

Internet technology (from 80 to 100 per cent of all citizens), many areas of Africa and Asia have levels lower than 20 per cent. The situation in Ghana, where the Internet is delivered through phone connections, illustrates the challenges of the global digital divide. The country has only 240,000 phones for its 20 million people, and the phone lines are spread across a nation the size of Great Britain. A business phone line costs about $1000, as much as office rent would cost for a year. Even if a person has access to a phone, about half of all calls do not go through because of system failures. Cellphones are available (300,000 in total), but they are very costly (about 10 times the cost of one in Canada) and also frequently drop calls because of the relatively few cellphone towers. This situation makes it clear that we cannot simply eliminate the digital divide in a country such as Ghana by sending computers. Even if there were staff who knew how to use them, computers are next to useless without an Internet connection or stable power supply (Oppong-Tawiah and Boateng 2011; Zachary 2002).

The digital divide has important consequences, both within Canada and around the world. First, it creates unequal access to information. For example, in countries with limited access, schools must rely on expensive books that quickly become outdated instead of using Internet resources that are cheaper and more current. Access to the Internet and computers can also allow people to learn computer skills that are useful for employment and job training. Second, Internet access is important for commerce. Businesses that are able to get online can sell their products to a larger group of people. Consumers with Internet access can purchase a larger variety of products, usually for less money, than those who can access only local businesses. Third, the Internet can be an important social outlet for people. For certain groups of Canadians, such as the elderly, rural people, and those who have lower incomes, the lack of access can reduce feelings of social connection with others. Finally, the Internet can provide important means of political organizing.

ACTIVITY

The Reality of Reality TV

Another major change in the media over the past 20 years is the rise of reality programming. The first reality television show was *Cops*, which has run since 1989. This show uses actual video footage of police officers in their daily work and shows arrests, car chases, and investigations as they happen.

Technological advancements helped to make reality TV possible. The availability of less expensive and smaller cameras allowed crew members to follow the action as it happened. In the case of *Cops*, cameras could be mounted on police cars to catch police work in real time. This programming was very appealing to television stations and production studios because it was relatively inexpensive. There was no need to pay writers, actors, or costume designers. TV crews could simply film real people on the ground, in the course of their daily lives.

As other reality shows followed, people began to wonder how "real" these shows were. In many ways, *Cops* is real. The people are not actors; they are real police officers and real suspects. The show is based on real situations (e.g., actual arrests) that are not scripted. There is minimal narration and no host. In fact, it was originally seen by some as educational programming about the police and their work. However, its content and narratives are edited to fit into a 30-minute time slot (including commercial breaks). The editors use storytelling devices, such as featuring heroes and villains without ambiguity. They also select the most interesting and dramatic police work—there is no episode of officers giving out parking tickets!

These manipulated aspects of the show have important consequences. They exaggerate the rate and severity of certain types of crimes in the public's mind. There is much more coverage, for example, of assault and other violent crimes than of white-collar crimes such as tax evasion. To keep viewership, the show also focuses on crimes that are committed by strangers and that are particularly dramatic, even though these crimes are relatively rare. *Cops* also distorts reality by depicting those who are arrested for crimes as violent, stupid, poor, and visible minorities. While some criminals fall into these stereotypes, many are non-violent, smart, rich, and white. Police officers are depicted as heroes who are always doing the right thing, which ignores the reality of police brutality and excessive force. (Chapter 3 discusses these issues in more detail.)

In this activity, we will look at other types of reality programming, including shows based on survival (*Survivor*, *The Amazing Race*), biography (*Keeping up with the Kardashians*, *The Real Housewives* franchise), competition (*Dancing with the Stars*, *America's Next Top Model*), and love (*The Bachelor*, *The Millionaire Matchmaker*). With these shows in mind, answer the following questions.

1. Go to this book's companion website to access an interview with Troy DeVolld, a producer of *The Osbournes*, *The Surreal Life*, *The Bachelor*, and *Dancing with the Stars and the following article:* www.rd.com/culture/13-secrets-reality-tv-show-producers-wont-tell-you. Based on these articles, how "real" are reality shows? How are they cast and scripted? What is a Frankenbite, and how could it distort the reality of these shows?

2. To what extent does it matter that reality shows are scripted? How do they distort our image of reality?

3. What types of values and behaviours do reality shows display? Should we be concerned about these shows purporting to represent reality? Why or why not?

In countries with non-democratic political regimes, the Internet can provide access to information that the government might censor. It can also provide a way of organizing people into activism, such as in the Arab Spring.

How do we address these significant inequalities? Close the Gap is an international non-profit organization that "aims to bridge the digital divide by offering high-quality, pre-owned computers donated by European companies to educational, medical, and social projects in developing and emerging countries" (http://close-the-gap.org/discover-us/mission). The organization also works with local groups to bring software and training to recipients.

Friedrich Stark / Alamy Stock Photo

PHOTO 7.4 Internet cafes like this one often provide people's only link to the Internet. What are the implications of having such limited access to the Internet? How does accessing the Internet through a cafe, instead of at home, change the types of activities one can engage in online and the benefits of Internet access?

David J. Green - Lifestyle / Alamy Stock Photo

PHOTO 7.5 Should we be concerned about children playing violent video games? Are they just entertainment, or are they also teaching lessons about how to interact with others?

Violence in the Media

The prevalence of violence in modern media is a major concern. It seems intuitive that violence in the media would have a negative effect on viewers. However, how could we test the impact of violent media on individuals?

In general, research has consistently shown that violent content can have serious consequences. This is particularly true for young children who watch violent media content because it can lead them to become less sensitive to the pain and suffering of others, increase their fear of the world around them, and make them more likely to engage in violent or aggressive ways toward others (APA 2013). These effects can be long-lasting. For example, Huesmann and Eron followed children over time and found that kids who watched a high level of violent television when they were eight years old were more likely to be aggressive as teenagers and more likely to be arrested and prosecuted for criminal acts as adults (APA 2013). Research on violent video games in particular shows that playing these games can have a desensitization effect, lowering concern for others in need. In one study, researchers looked at 780 young adults (average age 19.6 years old) from four American universities. They found that those who played violent video games had lower levels of concern for others and were less likely to help strangers in need (Fraser et al. 2012).

Most research finds that viewing violence in the media can have serious implications for viewers' attitudes and behaviours (Murray 2008). Viewing violence is associated with more aggressive behaviour and a more tolerant attitude toward the use of violence to solve problems. As we have just seen, being exposed to high levels of media violence may lead individuals to become desensitized to violence. Finally, exposure to media violence may lead viewers to overestimate their risk of victimization and be more fearful of crime. In light of the increased prevalence of media violence and its serious effects for individuals and society, these issues are of concern to the public and policy-makers.

Media Literacy

In light of the serious implications of the media in the socialization process, many critics have argued that we should increase **media literacy** in an effort to regain control over our media consumption. Media literacy is an educational tool that helps individuals analyze and evaluate the messages they receive from the media. It works to empower people to examine and think more critically about the media messages they receive.

ACTIVITY

Using Media Literacy with Alcohol and Tobacco Ads

Advertising is all around us, and our exposure to it is increasing. The market research firm Yankelovich estimates that a person living in New York City was exposed to about 2000 advertisements a day 30 years ago. Today, a New Yorker sees an average of 5000 ads a day (Schroeder 2016). Clearly, one of the primary purposes of these ads is to sell products; however, they also communicate other messages and rely on certain techniques. Look at these ads and answering the following questions.

char abumansoor / Alamy Stock Photo

Canadian Club - owned by Beam Suntory

Jeff Morgan 09 / Alamy Stock Photo

Agencja Fotograficzna Caro / Alamy Stock Photo

1. What techniques are used in these ads? Do they focus on the quality of the products or on other things?
2. Do all these ads show the product that they are selling? How prominent is the product in the ad? Why would you show (or not show) a product in an ad?
3. What message are these ads trying to send about the products? What type of person uses each product? What would the advertisers like you to associate their product with?

Continued

4. Research has shown that cigarette ads, in particular, tend to exploit people's desire for freedom and/or adventure. Can you see the use of these concepts in the ads presented here? What other types of products focus on freedom or adventure?

5. The Dos Equis advertisements, the Dove "Real Beauty" campaign, and others either make fun of or challenge our conventional ideas of how advertising should be done. To what extent do you think these ads are effective? Why do you think advertisers would use such ads?

6. *Adbusters* creates "spoof ads" that challenge advertising messages. Visit www.adbusters.org/spoofs-ads (or access the direct link available on this book's companion website) to see some of these ads. What do you think of them? Are they effective at pointing out some of the problematic messages in advertising? How could they be more effective?

**RESEARCH METHOD
EXPERIMENT**

Media literacy programs can take place in schools, online, or at community centres. Even a parent who watches television with his or her child and talks critically about what they are seeing engages in media literacy training. There are three main stages in media literacy education. First, one must become aware of one's media "diet"—the media that one consumes. It is obvious to think about the television shows that you watch, the radio that you listen to, or the Internet news you read. However, it is also important to consider all the more incidental media to which you are exposed—billboards on the highway, advertisements on Google, or radio in the background at a store.

The second stage is to learn specific skills of critical viewing, which requires you to analyze both what is shown on television and what is left out. Perhaps you notice that the TV shows you watch feature a lot of upper-class characters and that very few poor or homeless characters are depicted. Or perhaps you notice a lot of white lead characters but not many visible minority lead characters in the movies you see.

Finally, media literacy pushes you to question what is behind the media and why certain messages are relayed while others are not. For example, TV shows might focus on upper-class characters because producers think that audience members will find them more interesting and compelling. But seeing so many upper-class characters also distorts our idea of how much money most people in society have, what regular jobs and careers are, and what we should aspire to be. Seeing so many extremely thin women or muscular men on television might distort our idea of beauty and a "regular" body shape. This can have severe implications for individual self-esteem and lead to eating disorders and other health issues. By thinking critically about who produces the media for what purpose and who benefits from media images, we can better understand what we see. This comprehension can help individuals to be more critical about the media messages they receive.

Alternative Media

As we have discussed in this chapter, one major concern with media concentration is a potential decline in the diversity of perspectives available to consumers. One way to address this issue is **alternative media**, which provide "alternative information to the mainstream media in a given context, whether the mainstream media are commercial, publicly supported, or government-owned" (Atton 2002). Blogs, websites such as Indymedia, community- or student-run newspapers, public broadcasting radio and television stations, and pirate stations are examples of alternative media.

Alternative media are defined by four main characteristics. The message is not corporately controlled and is not based on a profit motive, since alternative media are non-profit. The messages' content tends to be anti-establishment, subversive, and change-centred. Alternative media are usually distributed in a creative way, focusing on being visually appealing and interesting. Finally, the relationship between the producer and consumer is fundamentally different. Traditional or corporate media are unidirectional—as a consumer you simply receive the message, but you do not have the opportunity to shape it. Alternative media have a two-way relationship; consumers can comment on and shape the media they consume. Alternative media, then, provide an interesting way to exert power and control over the media messages and content you receive.

Summary

Language is everywhere—without it you would not even be able to read this book! We began this chapter by examining the importance of language and how language shapes thought and is shaped by culture. These connections were illustrated by examining racist terms in the English language. The chapter then discussed the mass media's role as a mode of communication. We looked at the evolution of the media, using Marshall McLuhan's famous idea that "the medium is the message," and discussed the rise in corporate concentration and its effects on the diversity of ideas available. C. Wright Mills's concept of the power elite illuminated how an increasingly small group of people holds power in the major political, military, and corporate institutions of society. This chapter also examined the rising importance of new media and social media, the digital divide, violence in the media, the need for media literacy, and alternative media.

Key Terms

alternative media 224
corporate concentration 203
cyberbullying 219
demographic diversity 208
digital divide 219
honorifics 198
idea diversity 207
mass media 202

media 202
media literacy 222
"medium is the message" 202
new media 217
power elite 204
Sapir–Whorf hypothesis 197
social media 217

For Further Reading

Chomsky, Noam, and Edward S. Herman. 2002. *Manufacturing Consent: The Political Economy of the Mass Media.* New York: Pantheon Books.

McLuhan, Marshall. 1964. *Understanding Media: The Extensions of Man.* New York: McGraw Hill.

Mills, C. Wright. 1956. *The Power Elite.* New York: Oxford University Press.

Whorf, Benjamin. 1956. *Language, Thought, and Reality: Selected Writings of Benjamin Lee Whorf.* Cambridge, MA: MIT Press.

References

APA (American Psychological Association). 2013. "Violence in the Media: Psychologists Study Potential Harmful Effects." November. http://www.apa.org/action/resources/research-in-action/protect.aspx.

Atton, Chris. 2002. *Alternative Media.* Thousand Oaks, CA: Sage.

Byerly, Carolyn. 2006. "Gender and Race in Media Ownership." *WIMN'S Voices* (blog) 28 October. http://www.wimnonline.org/WIMNSVoicesBlog/?p=302.

Chomsky, Noam, and Edward S. Herman. 2002. *Manufacturing Consent: The Political Economy of the Mass Media.* New York: Pantheon Books.

CIRA. 2014. "The Canadian Internet." https://cira.ca/factbook/2014/the-canadian-internet.html.

Cox, David. 2017. "Did #OscarsSoWhite Work? Looking beyond Hollywood's Diversity Drought," *The Guardian* 25 February. https://www.theguardian.com/film/2017/feb/25/did-oscars-so-white-work-looking-beyond-the-diversity-drought-in-hollywood.

Elber, Lynn. 2013. "GLAAD Study Finds Fewer Gay Characters on Network TV This Season." CTV News 11 October. http://www.ctvnews.ca/entertainment/glaad-study-finds-fewer-gay-characters-on-network-tv-this-season-1.1493495.

Fraser, Ashley M., Laura M. Padilla-Walker, Sarah M. Coyne, Larry J. Nelson, and Laura A. Stockdale. 2012. "Associations between Violent Video Gaming, Empathetic Concern, and Prosocial Behavior towards Strangers, Friends, and Family Members." *Journal of Youth and Adolescence* May: 636–49.

Gamson, Joshua, and Pearl Latteier. 2004. "Do Media Monsters Devour Diversity?" *Contexts* 3(3): 26–31.

Geist, Michael. 2013. "Statscan Data Points to Canada's Growing Digital Divide: Geist." *Toronto Star* 1 November. https://www.thestar.com/business/tech_news/2013/11/01/statscan_data_points_to_canadas_growing_digital_divide_geist.html.

Ipsos Reid. 2012. "The IpsosCanadian inter@ctive Reid Report: 2012 Fact Guide." http://www.ipsos.ca/common/dl/pdf/Ipsos_InteractiveReidReport_FactGuide_2012.pdf.

Jackson, Emily. 2017. "Canadians Still Spend a Day a Week (26 hours) Watching TV Even with Streaming Surge." *Financial Post* 8 November. https://business.financialpost.com/telecom/more-canadians-go-online-for-tv-music-as-traditional-broadcasting-dips-crtc.

Kaplan, Andreas M., and Michael Haenlein. 2010. "Users of the World, Unite! The Challenges and Opportunities of Social Media." *Business Horizons* 53(1): 61.

Lee, Cynthia. 2013. "Study Finds TV Shows with Ethnically Diverse Casts, Writers Have Higher Ratings." UCLA Newsroom 8 October. http://newsroom.ucla.edu/releases/study-finds-that-tv-shows-with -248757.

McLuhan, Marshall. 1964. *Understanding Media: The Extensions of Man*. New York: McGraw-Hill.

Martins, Nicole, and Kristen Harrison. 2012. "Racial Differences in the Relationship between Children's Television Use and Self-Esteem: A Longitudinal Panel Study." *Communication Research* 39(3): 338–57.

Mills, C. Wright. 1956. *The Power Elite*. New York: Oxford University Press.

Mitovich, Matt Webb. 2015. "GLAAD Report: LGBT Representation on TV Is up, but Still Very White." *TVLine* 27 October. http://tvline.com/2015/10/27/glaad-study-lgbt-representation-on-tv.

Murray, John P. 2008. "Media Violence: The Effects Are Both Real and Strong." *American Behavioral Scientist* 51(8): 1212–30.

Onishi, Norimitsu. 2003. "Divorce in South Korea: Striking a New Attitude." *The New York Times* 21 September. http://www.nytimes.com/2003/09/21/world/divorce-in-south-korea-striking-a-new-attitude.html.

Oppong-Tawiah, D., and Boateng, R. 2011. "ICT and Bridging the Digital Divide in Ghana: A Culture, Policy & Technology Approach." Paper presented at Africa Digital Week, Accra, Ghana, 25–29 July.

Oscars.org. 2017. "Academy Membership." http://www.oscars.org/about/join-academy.

Oxford Dictionaries. 2017. "Word of the Year." https://en.oxforddictionaries.com/word-of-the-year/word-of-the-year-2016.

Puzic, Sonja. 2015. "Anti-cyberbullying Law, Bill C-13, Now in Effect." CTV News 9 March. https://www.ctvnews.ca/politics/anti-cyberbullying-law-bill-c-13-now-in-effect-1.2270460.

Schroeder, Jules. 2016. "Will the App Disrupt the $160 Billion Ad Industry by Replacing Ads with Positive Messages?" *Forbes* 2 June. https://www.forbes.com/sites/julesschroeder/2016/06/02/will-this-app-disrupt-the-160-billion-ad-industry-by-replacing-ads-with-positive-messages/#5b3fbde64e5e.

Smith, Stacy L., Marc Choueti, and Katherine Pieper. 2016. "Inclusion or Invisibility? Comprehensive Annenberg Report on Diversity in Entertainment." USC Annenberg. http://annenberg.usc.edu/pages/~/media/MDSCI/CARDReport%20FINAL%2022216.ashx.

Statistics Canada. 2012. "Internet Use by Individuals, by Selected Characteristics." Ottawa: Statistics Canada. http://www.statcan.gc.ca/tables-tableaux/sum-som/l01/cst01/comm35a-eng.htm.

———. 2016. "Study: Cyberbullying and Cyberstalking among Internet Users Aged 15 to 29 in Canada." Ottawa: Statistics Canada. http://www.statcan.gc.ca/daily-quotidien/161219/dq161219a-eng.htm.

Traugott, Mark, ed. 1978. *Émile Durkheim: On Institutional Analysis*. Chicago: University of Chicago Press.

Whorf, Benjamin. 1956. *Language, Thought, and Reality: Selected Writings of Benjamin Lee Whorf*. Cambridge, MA: MIT Press.

Woolf, Nicky. 2016. "Remember the Ice Bucket Challenge? It Just Funded an ALS Breakthrough." *The Guardian* 27 July. https://www.theguardian.com/society/2016/jul/26/ice-bucket-challenge-als-charity-gene-discovery.

Zachary, G. Pascale. 2002. "Ghana's Digital Dilemma." MIT *Technology Review* 1 July. http://www.technologyreview.com/featuredstory/401607/ghanas-digital-dilemma.

8 The Family and Intimate Relationships

Chapter Outline

Photo credit: Gemma Evans

Introduction

One challenge that sociologists face is trying to make sense of things with which we are very familiar but might not have examined critically. As quoted in Chapter 1, Peter Berger (1963) argued that sociology helps us to see "the general in the particular" and the "strange in the familiar." Each of us has a lifetime of experiences in society, including experiences of a particular family context. From all these experiences, we come to generalize about how families function. However, sometimes this familiarity can be a challenge; it can be quite hard to study an institution such as the family because it is all around us. We also all have a very particular experience of family life—your family surely shares some features with your friends' families, but it is probably different as well. If you compare your family with others you see on television, in the news, or in the larger community, you probably notice even starker differences.

In this chapter, we will examine the family in a larger comparative perspective. We will also examine the intimate relationships that often form the foundation of families. How do we come to find and select mates, and how might this be changing over time? We will also assess the major changes are happening to the family and the functions of the family in society. By taking a step back from our own particular experiences, we can come to understand the role of intimate relationships and the family in society as a whole.

What Is the Family?

Families are groups of people related by birth, affinity, or cohabitation. Families clearly differ radically from one another, and what people think of as a family has changed. In general, we think of an individual's **family household** as a group of people who share a relationship by blood, marriage, or legal adoption living together. **Marriage** is the legal union of two people, allowing them to live together and to have children. A **nuclear family** consists of two adults living with one or more children. An **extended family** moves beyond the nuclear, or immediate, family and consists of more than two generations who share the same residence.

Barbara Davatz, As Time Goes By 1982 1988 1997 2014, Edition Patrick Frey, 2015

PHOTO 8.1 Photographer Barbara Davatz took pictures of families over 24 years. The image here shows Carole and Serge in 1982, 1988, and 2014. Besides their wonderful style, how else has this couple changed over time?

Comedy and the TV Family

Society has many stereotypes about men's and women's roles in romantic relationships and parenting. Think of the jokes you have heard about husbands and wives. Here are a few examples (from www.funnigurl.com):

> How many men does it take to change a roll of toilet paper?
> *Who knows? It hasn't happened yet!!*

> What do you instantly know about a well-dressed man?
> *His wife is good at picking out clothes.*

> I married Miss Right.
> *I just didn't know her first name was "Always."*

> I haven't spoken to my wife for 18 months:
> *I don't like to interrupt her.*

The general themes of these and similar jokes—that husbands and fathers are lazy and unable to do anything for themselves and that wives are bossy and nagging—are part of the overarching repertoire of how we understand men's and women's roles in relationships and families. You don't typically hear, for example, a joke about wives being lazy or men nagging.

Think about television shows such as *Leave It to Beaver, The Brady Bunch, The Cosby Show, Roseanne, Gilmore Girls, Malcolm in the Middle, Parenthood,* and *Modern Family*. (If you have not seen some of these shows, watch some clips on YouTube or read about the show on Wikipedia.) As you answer the following questions, keep in mind how jokes may be used to perpetuate and exaggerate stereotypes of gendered roles in the family.

1. How have depictions of the family changed? How did the earliest show on our list (*Leave It to Beaver*) depict the role of husbands and wives and their relationship with their children? How does this show portray the functions of the family and the role of the family in society? How does this depiction relate to the larger social context in which this show existed?
2. How did later shows (*The Brady Bunch, The Cosby Show*, and *Roseanne*) challenge some earlier depictions of the family? How are these challenges related to our changing ideas of gender norms and family relationships in society?
3. How do the most recent shows (*Gilmore Girls, Malcolm in the Middle, Parenthood,* and *Modern Family*) further expand or change our perception of the role of spouses and parents in society? How do these shows reflect the times in which they were made? Are these positive reflections of the family today?
4. What shows do you watch that depict a positive view of the family and spousal relationships? What shows have negative depictions? What are the larger social implications of television shows presenting families in these ways?

The Canadian family is undergoing some widespread changes, as illustrated in Figure 8.1. These trends reflect a changing set of norms and expectations surrounding the family, particularly marriage and children, in modern Canadian society. Note the decline in the traditional nuclear family and the growth in the number of unmarried couples living together.

Andrew Cherlin (2004) argues that modern society is characterized by the "**deinstitutionalization of marriage.**" Our understanding of the norms and rules surrounding marriage has changed, and people are increasingly questioning the role of marriage in their lives and in society as a whole. There are five main ways that marriage is becoming deinstitutionalized. First, fewer people are getting married because they are choosing to remain single or to **cohabitate** (i.e., same-sex or opposite-sex couples who live together without being legally married). Cohabitation gained popularity in the 1970s, and the rate accelerated into the twenty-first century. Many cohabitating couples in Canada become common-law, a relationship that Canadian law treats as analogous to marriage.

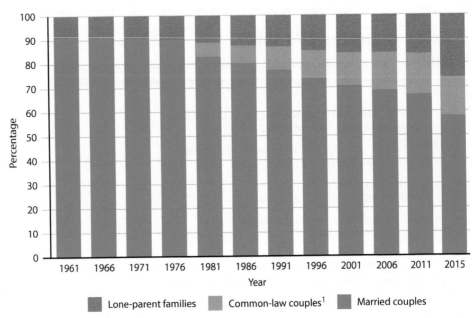

FIGURE 8.1   **Distribution (in percentage) of census families by family structure, Canada, 1961–2015**

Notes: Historical comparisons for census families, particularly lone-parent families, must be interpreted with
caution due to conceptual changes in 2001. For more information, see "Concepts and Definitions" in *Family
Portrait: Continuity and Change in Canadian Families and Households in 2006, 2006 Census.*

1. Data on common-law couples are not available prior to the 1981 census.

2. Data for 2015 is from Statistics Canada, 2016. *Census Population.* Catalogue no. 98-400-X2016128. Ottawa:
Statistics Canada.

Source: Adapted from Statistics Canada, 2012, "Fifty Years of Families in Canada: 1961 to 2011," *Census
in Brief*, Catalogue no. 98-312-X2011003, Ottawa: Statistics Canada, http://www12.statcan.gc.ca/census-
recensement/2011/ as-sa/98-312-x/98-312-x2011003_1-eng.pdf

These unions are especially popular in Quebec, where almost twice as many people
live common-law as in the rest of the country. The number is also higher than that of
many other countries (see Table 8.1). Many attribute the high rate of common-law marriage in Quebec to the province's Quiet Revolution in the 1960s–1970s, a period of
significant social and cultural upheaval. In particular, there was a widespread rejection
of the Catholic Church and a questioning of this institution's extremely powerful role
in Quebec society at that time. Others argue that factors such as greater access to con-
traception, the strength of the women's movement, and the comparatively high rate of
women's participation in the paid labour force might account for the higher rates of
common-law couples in Quebec. In addition, Quebec law has more liberal divorce laws
and common-law legislation, making cohabitation a more attractive choice for couples
(Milan, Vézina, and Wells 2007).

Second, the roles of individuals in couples (married or not) have become increasingly questioned in modern society. As women enter the labour force in larger numbers, the division of labour in the home can be challenged. We no longer simply assume
that women will be homemakers and men breadwinners. Since there are more women
working outside the home and more men staying home to raise children, the traditional
gender roles in marriage are questioned. Our basic understanding of what men and
women "do" in a relationship is eroding, leading to a lack of clarity about how marriages
and the family work in modern society. Chapter 6 discussed the large-scale changes to
gender roles in society; this increased flexibility of gender roles in marriages can lead to
a greater diversity of family arrangements, including the rise of lone-parent families and
same-sex marriages.

TABLE 8.1 | Common-law couples, Canada and selected countries, by year

	Percentage of All Couples	Reference Year
Canada	16.7	2011
Quebec	37.8	2011
Other provinces and territories	14.5	2011
Sweden	18.3	2011
Finland	21.8	2011
United Kingdom	17.4	2016

Sources: Adapted from, https://www.imfcanada.org/archive/34/cohabitation; Sweden: http://ec.europa.eu/eurostat/statistics-explained/index.php/Marriages_and_births_in_Sweden; Finland: http://www.stat.fi/til/perh/2011/02/perh_2011_02_2012-11-09_kat_001_en.html; UK: https://www.ons.gov.uk/peoplepopulationandcommunity/birthsdeathsandmarriages/families/bulletins/familiesandhouseholds/2016

Third, norms about having children have also changed. In the past, it was socially acceptable only to have children in a marital relationship. Today, many people are single parents, and many unmarried couples have children. Furthermore, more people choose to remain childless.

Fourth, divorce rates rose steeply between 1970 and 1990, although they have stabilized since that time. These heightened divorce rates challenge the idea that individuals should remain married "till death do us part"—even if they are unhappy or the relationship is abusive. It is also associated with a declining stigma associated with divorce and a waning of religious influences that traditionally prohibited this act.

HIGHLIGHT

Mixed Couples on the Rise

Mixed couples, where either one partner is a visible minority and the other is not or the two partners are from different visible minority groups, are on the rise in Canada. The percentage of mixed couples almost doubled in the 20 years between 1991 and 2011. This change to the family highlights how the family is, in many ways, a mirror of larger processes in society. As a society we are becoming more diverse, and so is the family. A recent newspaper article highlights the ways that relationships between people from different ethnic and racial backgrounds can foster greater cultural understanding.

For example, Dylan Rudder, who is Trinidadian, met his Salvadorian girlfriend, Gabriela Trujillo, when they were both students at Humber College in Toronto. They began sharing their cultures as soon as they started dating. After a somewhat awkward first date in which he tried to make her guacamole (with not very successful results!), they fast became a couple. The seven couples interviewed for the article all highlight that the beauty of being in a mixed relationship is getting to learn about someone else's culture and perspective while getting to celebrate your own culture (Khoo 2017). These couples also highlight the discrimination and stereotypes that they have encountered as part of mixed-race couples. However, they argue that their relationships can work to open up conversations about race, stereotypes, and culture.

Finally, there is a rising diversity in the forms of marriages in modern society. With the rise of marriages between couples from different ethnic, racial, religious, and class backgrounds, couples are becoming more diverse than ever before. Mixed unions in Canada, where either one partner is a visible minority and the other is not or when the two partners are from different visible minority groups, have risen in Canada over time. In 1991, only 2.6 per cent of couples were in mixed unions whereas by 2011 this number had increased to 4.6 per cent (Maheux 2016). This is still a relatively small number, but it is almost double the rate over 20 years. The legalization of gay marriage in Canada and other countries further adds to the diversity of marriage as an institution in modern society.

The first four trends have challenged the traditional idea of marriage in a way that many argue undermine it as an institution. However, many claim that the fifth change supports and reinforces traditional ideas of marriage as new groups of people opt into and support the institution.

Larger Social Changes That Affect the Family

Changes in marriage and the family can be tied to many larger social changes. As we have already seen, the rise of women's rights is a major change in Canadian society. This movement accounts for rising rates of university enrolment and graduation among women and an increased number of women in the paid workforce. These changes, in turn, are associated with lower levels of marriage, later age at the birth of a first child, and a higher divorce rate. Divorce, for example, is much more likely among women who make money independently from the family unit.

Our society is also becoming increasingly tolerant of diversity. This development partly explains the rise of marriages between people from different racial, ethnic, or religious backgrounds. This more inclusive ideology in modern society is also a factor in the mobilization for legalizing same-sex marriage.

RESEARCH METHOD
INTERVIEW

Another major change that has affected the family is the declining levels of religiosity in Canada and other Western nations. Religions are generally strong supporters of a traditional view of marriage and child-rearing. With the decline of religiosity in a society, we tend to see higher rates of cohabitation without marriage, more children raised by unmarried parents, and a rise in divorce rates.

Finally, modern society is characterized by a rising tide of individualism. In essence, we are more concerned with individual happiness and fulfillment than we were in the past. In Canada, most people pick jobs and romantic partners based on their own interests and preferences. Young people usually resist the idea that they are simply expected to perform the same job as their parents or that their parents will select their mate for them. This surge in individualism occurred at the same time that religion's power over individuals was waning; both trends have radically altered our ideas about the nature of marriage.

Originally, marriage was seen as a way to bind larger families and communities. **Institutional marriages** have a collective focus; that is, they focus on how a marriage will solidify ties between families and communities and benefit society as a whole. Think about how spouses were selected historically in royal weddings. No one cared whether a prince and princess from different countries liked one another or would fall in love. All that mattered was that the marriage would lead to a coalition between their countries. Institutional marriages are about the needs of society, not the individuals' need to be happy and fulfilled (Wilcox and Nock 2006).

Over time, people began to think that marriages should be based on bonds of sentiment, friendship, and sexual ties. **Companionate marriages** make a clear

HIGHLIGHT

Arranged Marriages

In an **arranged marriage**, a third party selects the bride and groom. Parents or others might make the match without consulting the children. However, the children usually have some level of control over choosing among partners deemed appropriate by their parents. This type of marriage was common worldwide until the eighteenth century and remains prevalent in many areas, including parts of Asia, Africa, the Middle East, and Latin America. Arranged marriages also occur in Canada, particularly among certain ethnic minorities.

Our modern ideas about marriage, and the role of romantic love within it, seem inconsistent with arranged marriage. But research shows that these marriages might be more likely to develop into lasting love than previously thought (Bentley 2011). According to research conducted by Robert Epstein (in Bentley 2011), individuals in arranged marriages tend to feel more in love over time while individuals in non-arranged marriages (most people in North America) tend to feel less in love. Epstein interviewed 30 individuals in 22 marriages and found that within 10 years, the self-rated satisfaction among individuals in arranged marriages was twice as high as it was for those in non-arranged marriages. There are many possible reasons for this. Arranged marriages are carefully planned and considered by families and communities, while non-arranged marriages can be spontaneous and may be less thought out. As a result, individuals in arranged marriages may be more likely to remain married, even if times are difficult, because they have the interests of their extended families to consider. Those in non-arranged marriages tend to be more focused on romantic love and can often overlook other critical compatibility issues. It is also possible, however, that those in arranged marriages might be more likely to report being in love because of different expectations. These different levels of reporting may not reflect true differences in feelings.

Epstein's research shows that the more parents are involved in the selection process, the more successful the resulting marriage tends to be. Parents can help weed out potential mates with "deal breaker" features—perhaps an incompatibility on values, the number of children they want, or where they want to live. Parents are also important because their support can help to solidify the marriage. This support can come in the form of financial help for the wedding, for one or both spouses to attend school, for a home, or for help with children. Along with emotional support, this assistance can provide the resources needed to help single people transition into being married and, perhaps, being parents.

division of labour between breadwinner (usually the husband) and the homemaker (usually the wife). Consequently, husbands and wives are expected to be one another's companions. They are friends and confidants who need and rely on one another to perform the role that they cannot. In companionate marriages, romantic love is very important (Wilcox and Nock 2006). These relationships are based on the satisfaction of the couple, the family as a whole, and the roles the couple plays within the family.

Lauer and Yodanis (2011) argue that we now live in a time of **individualized marriages**. These marriages are focused on each spouse's satisfaction, ability to develop and express his or her sense of self, happiness, and fulfillment. Individualized marriages tend to be more flexible than the other types described because they attempt to meet the varied needs of individual spouses. Despite these challenges to traditional ideas of marriage and the rise of individualized marriages, the vast majority of people still get married at some point in their lives, even if these marriages don't last as long as past unions.

In the following reading from Yodanis and Lauer, we unpack why people marry in modern society and how our explanations for marriage are very individualistic. How are larger social structures and changes shaping our very personal decisions about intimate relationships and marriage?

READING

Getting Married: The Public Nature of our Private Relationships

Carrie Yodanis and Sean Lauer

What about Love?

The social constraints encouraging us to marry are hard to see. We rarely think about them. Instead, we continue to think about marriage as a personal and private relationship. When people are asked why they got married, love is the number one reason given, with over 90 per cent of married people saying that love is a very important reason for marriage.[1] But, as we will argue here, even love is not personal and private. Rather, it is the socially acceptable motive to give for marriage. It is part of the rules, expectations, and taken-for-granted assumptions of marriage.

Sociologists have argued that the motives people give for what they do are shaped by external expectations and constraints. And like behaviors themselves, certain motives are considered socially acceptable and expected. Only some motives are defined as legitimate for given situations and at certain points in time. Others are not. We use the acceptable motives to explain and justify our behaviors, regardless of our actual reasons for behavior, because when we do, our behavior is accepted.[2]

Today, individualized motives are socially acceptable in the United States.[3] Americans cherish the ability to act on their own as individuals—to succeed or fail on their own terms. Americans believe in individual choice and individual responsibility for the choices they make. Americans, as compared to people from other cultures, are more likely to believe that they have choice and control over their situations, even to the point of believing they have more choice than they actually have.[4] Researchers asked American and Japanese students to list all of the choices they made the day before. The American students reported that they made 50 per cent more choices than the Japanese students reported, although their days were actually quite similar. During another study, Eastern European participants were asked to choose between seven sodas. The Eastern European participants responded that they had no choice—they were all soda. In comparison, Americans saw choice in objectively similar options. In products such as bottled water and makeup, we believe we have choice. In the end, however, "though we may feel steeped in variety, we actually have far fewer qualitatively different options than we realize."[5] Yet it is important for us to believe that we have choice in order to believe that we are acting as free individuals. As one author wrote in a book on sexual relationships,

Yodanis, Carrie, and Sean Lauer. 2016. *Getting Married: The Public Nature of Our Private Relationships*, pp. 28–32 and 67–71. New York, Routledge.

Of all the convictions that govern sexual conduct in the secular West, perhaps the most important is that there *are* no longer any rules. To suggest otherwise is to challenge the very fabric of how we perceive ourselves: as free, self-actualized individuals carving out our destinies from a sea of limitless options.[6]

Love is the primary socially acceptable motive for marriage. It is a motive that emphasizes personal choice and freedom. People say they are marrying because they want to, because they are in love. But love is not merely a personal feeling. It is part of the rules and expectations of marriage. When people say that they are marrying because they are in love and are soul mates, the decision to marry and the quality of the marriage are accepted and unchallenged. Other motivations, particular those related to constraints, lead to questions and concerns. For example, these were the vows imagined by Dev, Aziz Ansari's character in his show, *Master of None*:

> *Rachel, I'm . . . not 100% sure about this. Are you the one person that I'm supposed to be with forever? I don't f*cking know. And what's the other option? We break up? That seems shitty too. And I love you. I do . . . I don't know, I guess . . . getting married just is a safer bet at this point. [sighs] Sorry, I was just thinking about other paths my life could have taken.*
>
> *Dev, you're a great guy. You really are. But you're right. Are we supposed to be together forever? [inhales sharply] I don't know . . . And I've basically invested two of my prime years with you, so I should just go all in. That's just math. So let's do this. Quickly.*
>
> *Do you, Dev, take Rachel to be your partner in a possibly outdated institution in order to have a "normal" life? Are you ready to give up an idealistic search for a soul mate and try to make it work with Rachel so you can move forward with your life?*
>
> *I do.*
>
> *And do you, Rachel, promise to make a crazy eternal bond with this gentleman who you happen to be dating at this stage in your life when people normally get married?*
>
> *I do.*
>
> *I now pronounce you two people who might realize they've made an unfortunate mistake in about three years.*[7]

Imagine if these were real vows at a wedding. The celebratory atmosphere of the wedding would quickly turn sour, and guests may regret giving gifts to the now perceived-to-be unhappy couple. In fact, it can even be considered fraud to marry without love. For example, it is illegal to marry someone for the purpose of immigrating to the country, so immigration officers search for proof of love between partners before approving the visa of an immigrating spouse.[8]

When we use love as a motive for marriage and an explanation for when and whom we marry, we downplay or dismiss the constraints, rules, and expectations that shape our behavior. Instead, we emphasize individual choice. We marry because we are in love, we explain, not because marriage is required by the government and the church, or because of social pressure from your grandmother, or because of the risk and uncertainty of ending up 40 and not married. Instead, we claim it is all about love. Yet the rules, expectations, pressures, and constraints are still there, shaping and guiding what we do—even the motive we give for getting married.

In the book *Talk of Love*, a sociologist studied how couples talk about love. She found that people hold onto and discuss romantic notions of love despite the fact that they see these ideas as largely myths and unrealistic to their own marriages. The romantic love persists, the author concluded, because it helps us to act within the constraints of marriage, "recasting them as matters of individual volition."[9]

The mythic, romantic love, common in popular culture, is based on the idea that love is obvious and sure. It involves the idea that love can happen "at first sight," that there is "one true love" for everyone, that love can "conquer anything," and that love lasts and a couple can "live happily ever after." The concept of the "soul mate" is rooted in these ideas of romantic love.[10]

These ideas of romantic love persist, the author argued, because they parallel the rules and expectations of marriage and help us to make the otherwise overwhelming decision to marry. Marriage is a daunting thing to do. Think about it for a minute. You are supposed to select, from all of the people out there, only one person to marry. You are supposed to be married to this person for the rest of your life. Yet nearly everyone makes the decision to get married and about whom to marry in a relatively short period of their lives. People use cultural ideas of romantic love to make the decision and action of getting married easier. We tell ourselves that we know that we have successfully found our soul mate—our one true love. Our love will endure and will help us overcome challenges that come along, and we will be happy together for the rest of our lives. Telling ourselves these things, based on the notion of romantic love, helps us to enter marriage, with its requirements, in what would otherwise be an overwhelming act:

> The love myth answers that question, "What do I need to feel about someone in order to marry [commit myself to] him or her?" . . . In order to marry, individuals must develop certain cultural, psychological, and even cognitive equipment. They must be prepared to feel, or at least convince others that they feel, that one other person is the uniquely right "one."[11]

By this point, you may be thinking that sociologists aren't a romantic group of folks. We wouldn't say that, overall. Like everyone, sociologists feel and express love with intimate partners. They just also critically examine the context in which this love is felt and expressed. It may be best to describe sociologists as analytically romantic, which adds a whole new interesting dimension to love!

NOTES

1.   Pew Research Center 2010.
2.   Mills 1959.
3.   Bellah, Madsen, Sullivan, Swidler, and Tiption 1985; Cherlin 2009; Wuthnow 1991.
4.   Iyengar 2010.
5.   Iyengar 2010, p. 156.
6.   Hills 2015, p. 57.
7.   *Master of None* 2015.
8.   Satzewich 2014.
9.   Swidler 2001, p. 118.
10. Swidler 2001.
11. Swidler 2001, pp. 130–1.

Thinking about Change

In 1972, Jessie Bernard, a sociologist, predicted that the future of marriage would be a range of possible marriages. Anything would be possible, she wrote. Traditional marriages would continue, but they would exist alongside marriages, which included:

- No children
- More than two spouses
- Open sexual relationships
- A "free-wheeling" emphasis on spouses' individuality and independence, including partial commitment, maintaining separate households, and having "weekend marriages"
- "Temporary permanent" relationships, in which couples would outline how long the marriage would last and opt for an extension if desired

In other words, Bernard predicted there would not be an established way to be married. Rather, people would be free to develop their relationships as they see fit and "tailor them to their circumstances and preferences."[1]

Social scientists, in a range of fields, have argued that essentially this future has arrived. For example, a psychologist wrote an interesting book, *The Paradox of Choice*, about the problems of having too much choice. His basic argument is that when people are faced with too many choices, they end up being dissatisfied with any choice they make or become unable to make a choice at all. He used a wide list of examples, including choice in salad dressing, phone plans, health care, and jam. He also highlighted relationships as an example of increasing choice. He wrote,

> In the past, the "default" options were so powerful, and dominant that few perceived themselves to be making choices . . . The anomalous few who departed from the pattern were seen as social renegades, subjects of gossip and speculation. These days, it's hard to figure out what kind of romantic choice would warrant such attention. Wherever we look, we see almost every imaginable arrangement of intimate relations . . . Today, all romantic possibilities are on the table; all choices are real.[2]

In other words, he concluded that there are no longer established ideas about how relationships "should" be and so people need to constantly make choices about what kind of relationship they want.

Even some sociologists have argued that people are free from social constraints in the modern world because social rules and expectations have weakened.[3] As a result, individuals can and indeed must figure out for themselves how best to organize their love lives and relationships. Now is the era of "do-it-yourself" biographies, they say. Anything is possible. Everything is acceptable. Again, the choices are unlimited. As one author noted,

> Of all the dreams today's young Westerners are sold about what our lives could look like, the biggest is that we have limitless opportunities, that we are free to pursue whatever work, relationships, and ways of being we like.[4]

Other sociologists have been critical of this idea.[5] Indeed, at its core, sociology focuses on how individuals can't and don't act completely independently of social forces. The sociological imagination involves understanding that an individual's experiences are shaped by the time and place within which their experiences occur. Put another way, there is a connection between private or individual troubles and public or social issues.[6] Take the example of marital problems and divorce rates. When a couple is constantly arguing, they experience that as a private problem. If divorce rates are high, however, that is a public issue. The marital problems of the couple and the divorce rate are linked. A couple who is constantly arguing may divorce, but only if they live in a time and place in which the social rules make divorce a possible and likely outcome of marital problems. Historically, there have been significant jumps in divorce rates right after laws were changed to make it easier to get a divorce. This does not mean that all of a sudden, once divorce laws changed, couples no longer got along. Rather, prior to changes in divorce laws, couples could argue all the time but could not divorce because getting a divorce was hard to do. External social forces shape what people do in their most private relationships. As we saw in this book, this holds true not just for marital troubles but for all kinds of marital behaviors, including selecting a partner, getting engaged, and having children.

We are not the first to make this point. Many others have made this same argument for a long time.[7] However, this point often gets lost in the emphasis on individual choice and freedom. As one author described it, the "shell" of marriage may have changed giving us, in theory, the potential to be more creative in our lives and relationships, yet the soul of marriage—its dreams, conscience, ethics, and rules—hasn't necessarily evolved to keep up.

Instead we follow viscerally many of the same premises and orthodoxies as our parents, as if marriage is a Procrustean structure to which we must conform ourselves, rather than the other way around.[8]

People do decide how to act. But these decisions and actions never happen in isolation. Every person is surrounded by other people within a society, and people together create the social forces, processes, structures, rules, and expectations that are the contexts within which each individual person acts. Individuals have agency to act, but any action does not emerge purely from within an individual. Rather action is an outcome of the individual's interaction with the social world, including the rules, opportunities, and constraints that are built into a society. Individual action is never wholly determined by social structures, but at the same time, the individual, necessarily a part of society, can never act completely free of their social context. We are all actors acting within social contexts, which guide, shape, and limit our behaviors. Even when an individual goes against the social rules, breaks down social barriers, or leads a social movement to dramatic change, social rules still shape how they behave, including the need to react against the rules and expectations.

There are people who forge their own paths and are exceptions to the general patterns. This is certainly true today and has always been in the past. The book *Uncommon Arrangements*, for example, documents the creative living and loving arrangements of some couples between 1910 and 1939. These couples had open sexual relationships and same- and opposite-sex partners, welcomed friends and lovers into their families and households, had children with lovers, and lived oceans apart, often maintaining caring and loving relationships with each other all the while.[9]

Another book *Spinster* discusses two terms that described women who didn't marry more than 100 years ago. In 1895, the term "bachelor girl," discussed in a *Vogue* column of the same name, referred to a woman who lived alone and supported herself by getting an education and having a career. Around the same time, the term "new woman" also referred to independent, self-sufficient, and sexual women who were pursuing careers. As one man described in a letter to his mother in 1898,

> There is a girl in N.Y. who has been much more to me than any other girl I ever knew. We are not engaged and it is practically sure that we never shall be. She is a "new woman," ambitious and energetic, a hard worker . . . she has no idea of getting married, at any rate to me.[10]

There have always been people who have done things differently. Nonetheless, doing something different can require managing ongoing disapproval from family, neighbors, friends, coworkers, and strangers. And even if some individuals do not follow the social rules and expectations, the rules and expectations are likely to persist—constraining and shaping the behaviors of others—despite the actions of these individuals.

Social rules, expectations, and assumptions do change and evolve over time. Individuals create the rules and so they can change them. Marriage is not exactly the same as it was 100 years ago or 50 years ago. This is because the rules and expectations for how to have relationships shifted, as did patterns in marital behaviors.

Yet as the rules and expectations change, this does not mean that rules and expectations completely disappear. Instead, new rules and expectations replace old ones. Change does not mean anything goes. It means that something else goes.

We can think about our relationships following trends.[11] There are trends in nearly all parts of relationships. Dating trends change over time, including the order in which couples go to dinner and have sex. Even what a couple does on a date is shaped by trends. The age when people marry follows trends. And there are trends regarding how couples act in marriage. Having separate bedrooms, a practice that was recently called a new trend, is not new at all, but was practiced in the past. When we are living in a particular moment and place, with particular rules, we tend to follow these rules and be on trend. In another time or place, with different rules, we would follow those trends and behave differently.

It is often easy to get caught up in and fixate on the change, missing the larger picture. The story of change is exciting. Change can appear to be quite large and dramatic. It elicits shock and surprise, exciting news headlines, and juicy gossip.

But the story of change has two parts. The first part asks, what do people do differently? The second part asks, what do most people continue to do? As we discussed earlier, people are marrying later today and are less likely to marry today than in the past, but the vast majority of people still marry at some point in their lives.[12] Interracial marriages are more common now than in past decades, but the vast majority of marriages are still between couples of the same racial background.[13] Cohabitation has increased dramatically since the 1970s, but the vast majority of couples in the United States are still married rather than cohabiting.[14] There is unquestionably change in marriage. Yet the majority of people continue to do things the same way.

PHOTO 8.2 In modern society, some intimate partner relationships still include a strong division of labour. As individualism in relationships has increased, the variety of partnership options has also risen, with individuals being more able to negotiate their roles within their partnerships.

Also, change over time is not always in a clear direction. Whether looking at the age of first marriage, the proportion of people who marry, or childlessness, change ebbs and flows over time. Behaviors increase and decrease, rates go up and down, practices go back and forth rather than going in a straight line toward a clear direction.[15] For example, women and men were *older* when they married in 1890 than they were in 1950.[16] *More* women and men *never* married in 1920 than in 1980.[17] Women born in 1910 were *more likely* to be childless than women born in 1960.[18]

Marriage is changing today, but marriage has always changed. For example, in what year do you think this statement was made? "A woman may now refuse to marry at all, and earn her own living in singleness." Answer: 1891.[19] In other words, more than 100 years ago, there was talk of change in the institution of marriage—change that actually seems a lot like the change we talk about now. In 100 years from now, what will we think of the quotes made about marriage today?

CRITICAL READING QUESTIONS

1. What is the role of romantic love in modern relationships? How is this related to our perceptions of individualism and individual choice in Canadian society?

2. What sorts of constraints exist on our ability to form any kind of marriage or intimate relationship that we would like? Are there rules, expectations, or norms that limit our freedoms in these relationships?

3. How have the constraints on marriage and other intimate relationships changed over time, and how do they differ across countries? What are the positive and negative implications of these changes?

4. How can we see problems within marriage (such as divorce, abuse, or other issues) as personal troubles or public issues? How does this change how we might want to deal with these issues?

NOTES

1. Bernard 1972, p. 302.
2. Schwartz 2004, pp. 38–9.
3. Beck and Beck-Gernsheim 2002; Cherlin 2004; Giddens 1992.
4. Hills 2015, p. 49.
5. Gross 2005; Jamieson 1999; Lauer and Yodanis 2010; Smart and Shipman 2004.
6. Mills 1959.
7. Baker 2014; Eekelaar 2007; Heaphy, Smart, and Einarsdottir 2013; Kingston 2004; Manfield and Collard 1988; Smith 1993; among many others, included those cited throughout this book.

8.   Haag 2011, p. 100.
9.   Roiphe 2007.
10. Bolick 2015, p. 100.
11. Aspers and Godart 2013.
12. Goldstein and Kenny 2001; Manning, Brown, and Payne 2014.
13. Rosenfeld 2007; Taylor, Wang, Parker, Passel, Patter, and Motel 2012.
14. U.S. Census Bureau 2014.
15. Yodanis and Lauer 2014.
16. Elliott, Krivickas, Brault, and Kreider 2012; Fitch and Ruggles 2000.
17. Elliott et al. 2012; Fitch and Ruggles 2000.
18. Kirmeyer and Hamilton 2011.
19. Campbell 1891; Smock 2004.

To this point, we have been discussing marriage as a **monogamous** relationship. However, certain cultures practise **polygamy** (having one or more spouse at the same time). Canada's most famous case of polygamy is in Bountiful, British Columbia. Based on the Fundamentalist Church of Jesus Christ of Latter Day Saints, an offshoot of the Mormon Church, this polygamous commune has been criticized for what some argue are forced marriages of underage women and the abuse of women and children. Polygamy is illegal in Canada, but this law had not been implemented in Bountiful. In 2017, the government attempted to prosecute Winston Blackmore and James Oler for polygamy. Blackmore has had 24 wives over a 25-year period and has produced 145 children. Oler is on trial for marrying four women between 1993 and 2009 (Brend 2017). The case went to the BC Supreme Court, which had to adjudicate between two contradicting principles—the right of individuals to practise their religion and the illegality of polygamy.

A woman from Bountiful, who shares a husband with her sister and has nine children, testified about her experience:

> I did not know him well, I knew he was in good standing in the church. . . .
> He [my father] told me, "You do not have to marry him if you don't want to."
> I felt good about him, and I married him. My sister wife and I have lived at
> times in the same home, we've lived in different homes. I feel that we are both
> very committed in having a good relationship with each other. . . . I feel that
> my husband really supported me through my years of education and he really
> has been a life-long friend to me, as well as watched my children when I went
> to school. . . . I believe that there's so many people in mainstream society that
> make so many assumptions about us that we are treated with bias and prejudice,
> and that affects my everyday life. If I wanted to go anywhere and get any sort of
> counselling in mainstream society, I feel like I would not be accepted. . . . My
> beliefs are that living in plural marriage isn't for everyone (Canadian Press 2011).

In an earlier 2011 case, the courts found in favour of the government and ruled that the polygamous marriages could not continue. The community members' religious freedom was seen as less important than the necessity of protecting women and children from abuse.

A 2011 University of British Columbia study demonstrated that a link exists between polygamous relationships (typically men with many female partners) and other social problems. The study found that this intra-sexual competition between men to find multiple female partners and the resources to support these multiple partners and children leads to greater gender inequality, poverty, and crime (including sexual assault and murder) than occurred in societies that practise solely monogamous relationships. This situation illustrates support for the court's decision that polygamous relationships harm society (Henrich, Boyd, and Richerson 2012). What do you think of polygamous marriages and families? Do they have to be associated with abuse of women and children? How do they challenge our ideas about marriage and the family?

ACTIVITY

Increasing or Decreasing Fertility in Quebec and China

We often hear about the low **fertility rates**, the average number of children per woman over her lifetime, in many Western countries. These countries (including Canada and the United States) are below the replacement rate of fertility, meaning that people are not having enough children to replace the population. Other countries worry that their fertility rates are too high and face the difficult social problem of overpopulation. In certain cases, such as Quebec and China, the government has implemented policies to affect fertility rates.

Go to this book's companion website, read the Population Change and Lifecourse Strategic Cluster's policy brief, and answer the following questions:

1. Why would the Quebec government, or any government, want to increase the fertility rate? What are the benefits of higher fertility rates?
2. What specific policies have been enacted in Quebec to try to increase the fertility rate? Why might policy-makers think that these measures would increase fertility?
3. How successful have these policies been at increasing fertility in Quebec? What are the other implications of these policies?

Now go to this book's companion website to read a BBC article about recent changes to China's **one-child policy**. After you read the article, answer these questions:

1. Why would China want to reduce its fertility rate? How can high fertility be a problem?
2. What specific policies have been enacted by the Chinese government to try to limit fertility? Are there exceptions to these policies? If so, why might they have been created?
3. What consequences have arisen from this policy? What are the unintended consequences?

Theorizing the Family

Our ideas about the family depend, to a large extent, on the theoretical perspective we use to understand it. Two theoretical traditions used to explain the family's role in society are structural functionalism and conflict theory, which are discussed throughout this book. Each approach paints a very different picture of the family's role and impact in modern society.

Structural functionalists focus on the functions of the family and the ways families can help to create stability and order in society as a whole. From a structural functionalist perspective, the family performs a wide variety of important roles that fall into four main categories: reproduction, socialization, support, and regulation. In terms of reproduction, families help to maintain the population by having and raising children. The family also cares for children's physical and emotional needs. The essential process of socializing children into the larger culture and teaching them the norms and rules of society begins in the family. Families are also important because they can share resources. Parents support children when they are young (and sometimes later in life); children often support parents in their old age. Families work to regulate behaviour as well. For example, the family traditionally helps to control sexual behaviour. This function might be declining as more people engage in sexual activity before and outside marriage.

Talcott Parsons was instrumental in developing structural functionalist theory in the 1950s and 1960s (Parsons and Bales 1955). He argued that the nuclear family was very important (particularly for American society, where his research was based) because its structure frees individuals from the obligations of an extended family. It gives individuals in family units the mobility needed in industrial society, where people often have to move

SolStock/iStockphoto

PHOTO 8.3 How do same-sex marriages fit into traditional theoretical understandings of the family? Do we have to tailor these theories in order to understand same-sex marriages, or can they be easily applied? Why or why not?

from place to place for work. Without the same close ties to extended families and the need to consider them in one's life plans, it is easier to move nuclear families. Parsons also argued that the nuclear family system works well to distinguish clearly between the "expressive" roles of women and the "instrumental" roles of men (Kimmel 2011).

The structural functionalist perspective of the family has great appeal. It makes sense to think about the important functions the family performs for individuals and society. All societies are based on family units that provide important resources, support, and socialization for children. However, many argue that this theory overemphasizes the family's harmonious elements and tends to ignore the disharmony—such as the discord between parents and children, between siblings, and between spouses. Clearly, not everyone enjoys the functionality and stability of the family setting! This approach also focuses on the positive nature of the family, which promotes and rationalizes the family as it is. However, many social problems arise, such as abuse and mistreatment, that might be ignored by looking at only the functions of families.

Conflict theory offers a different lens on the family and its role in society. At its root, this approach is always concerned with the unequal distribution of resources between those with and without power. Not surprisingly, conflict theorists do not see the family as the harmonious institution that structural functionalists do. Instead, they see the family as an arena for a wide variety of conflicts. For example, women and men have differing levels of power within the family, as do older and younger family members. Such conflicts are related to power within the family, who has it, and how it is used.

HIGHLIGHT

Renting Families in Japan

Family members are an important part of our lives—they provide care and company, as well as help to mark important events such as holidays, weddings, and religious ceremonies. But what if you don't have a family? How can these functions be fulfilled when the number of people living alone, getting divorced, or migrating to other parts of the world is rising? In Japan, companies are stepping in to help people deal with these new circumstances.

In the early 1990s, Japan Efficiency Corporation was "doing the booming business [of] renting families to the lonely," especially the elderly (Kubota 2009). With the declining number of children per couple and the higher propensity of children to live far away from their aging parents, the elderly had fewer people to care for their physical and emotional needs. Office Agents, a Tokyo firm, offers friends and family for rent as event guests. They have about a thousand "fakes" available for occasions such as weddings and funerals. The company reports that many brides and grooms do not even know which of their guests are real and which ones are rented.

Perhaps most interestingly, the Hagemashi Tai agency rents temporary "husbands" to single mothers. Having a husband can be socially useful in many situations—for example, in daycare or elementary school admission interviews. Single mothers can even rent a "dad" to help children with homework, resolve issues with neighbours, or take children to events (Kubota 2009).

At a purely rational level, the idea of renting family members to serve particular social purposes makes sense because it may be the most efficient way to fulfill the short-term goal of appearing to have family or friends. However, to many Canadians, renting a family might seem odd and perhaps even offensive because it challenges our fundamental ideas about the nature of the relationship between family members. Do you see this trend catching on in Canada? Why or why not? How is it similar to, or different from, renting an escort to attend an event? What does it say about our emphasis on idealized notions of the nuclear family and the pressure to conform?

Arguing from a conflict and feminist perspective, Collins (1975) states that the family is an arena for gender conflict in which males have historically been more powerful. This causes discord among opposite-sex partners, who struggle with their different roles in the relationship and the division of power and labour in the family unit. For example, many couples argue about who will do housework or control the finances.

Age-based conflict is also prevalent in the family. Parents have more power in the family than children do because of their greater access to resources. As children try to influence their parents' decisions or become autonomous, conflicts can arise. Although they can be benign, such as when children want to eat dessert and parents say no, they

HIGHLIGHT

Family Violence

Conflict theorists posit that a dire consequence of family power struggles is **family violence**, defined by the Canadian government as "any form of abuse, mistreatment, or neglect that

These photographs are from a campaign against family violence by the YWCA. How do these images highlight the diverse types of family violence and the role of bystanders in preventing this violence?

a child or adult experiences from a family member, or from someone with whom they have an intimate relationship" (Department of Justice 2013). Family violence can take the form of physical, sexual, emotional, and financial abuse of a spouse, child, or elder. Honour killings and forced marriage are also included in this term.

Government of Alberta

Family violence is a widespread problem around the world. According to the Uniform Crime Reporting and Homicide Surveys (Statistics Canada 2017), 26 per cent of police-reported crime involves family violence, half of which is spousal abuse and half child abuse. Just under 9 million, or about one in three, Canadians report experiencing abuse before the age of 15 (Statistics Canada 2017). Most researchers assume that family violence is much more widespread than even these alarming numbers suggest, given that as few as 25 per cent of victims of spousal abuse report the incident to the police.

can be much more serious, such as when parents abuse their children physically, emotionally, or sexually. This abuse is possible only because of the differential levels of power and resources in the family.

Conflict theorists agree with structural functionalists that the family works to socialize young people. However, the conflict theorists argue that this socialization is problematic because it reproduces existing inequalities, particularly class inequalities. Melvin Kohn (1959) was particularly interested in how parents socialize their children differently depending on their social class and how these various emphases in socialization help to reproduce social class distinctions. He compared 200 white, working-class American families who had children in the fifth grade with 200 white middle-class families. He showed the parents a list of characteristics that most parents would want to foster in their children: honest, happy, considerate, obedient, dependable, good manners, self-control, popular, good student, neat, curious, ambitious, able to defend self, affectionate, liked by adults, able to play by self, and act in a serious way. He asked them to rank the ones that they considered most important for their child's age. He also asked which traits the parents thought were most important for girls of that age and for boys of that age.

RESEARCH METHOD
INTERVIEW

In general, Kohn (1959) found that most mothers from both groups wanted their children to display these traits. However, when choosing the most important characteristics, middle- and working-class mothers differed. Middle-class mothers were more likely to say that internal factors and an ability to be self-directed were important. For example, they were more likely to rank happiness, self-control, and curiosity as important characteristics for children. Working-class mothers were more likely to value obedience and neatness.

Such differences could have serious implications for the children's educational and career prospects. High-status and well-paying jobs tend to emphasize curiosity and self-control. For example, lawyers, doctors, and CEOs must be curious and self-directed. However, lower-status jobs tend to be more focused on obedience to authority and superiors. People who work in a factory are expected to follow orders, not to think outside the box. If a lawyer, business leader, or doctor just followed orders, she might be fired.

Kohn also found that middle-class mothers tended to value the same things in boys and girls. However, working-class mothers valued different things for each sex. They rated school performance and ambition as more important for boys but neatness and good manners as more important for girls. Think about how encouraging these different values in boys and girls reproduces a gendered division of labour and directs women and men into different types of occupations. This study highlights both how the family socializes children and how this socialization can work to reproduce societal inequalities.

The process of mate selection and dating creates the conditions for marriage, cohabitation, and family. Research shows that men and women tend to look for different features in spouses. This is, in part, because of gender stereotypes about how men and women should act and what role they should play in a relationship. These differences are also related to how we understand the marital (or spousal) relationship. Is it one in which partners engage in very different roles, with one partner (often the woman) staying at home to raise children and the other partner (often the man) working? Or is it one of equal partners?

Dating has changed a lot in the modern world. Aziz Ansari, comedian and creator of the show *Master of None*, teamed up with NYU sociologist Erik Klinenberg to explore how technology has created the perception that there is increased choice in dating. This has led to some positive and some negative consequences for the modern dater. The following excerpt from the book *Modern Romance* explores some of these possibilities and pitfalls.

Modern Romance

Aziz Ansari and Erik Klinenberg

My parents had an arranged marriage. This always fascinated me. I am perpetually indecisive on even the most mundane decisions, and I couldn't imagine leaving such an important choice to other people. I asked my dad to describe his experience to me.

This was his process.

He told his parents he was ready to get married, so his family arranged meetings with three neighboring families. The first girl, he said, was a "little too tall," and the second girl was a "little too short." Then he met my mom. After he quickly deduced that she was the appropriate height (finally!), they talked for about thirty minutes. They decided it would work. A week later, they were married.

And they still are, thirty-five years later. Happily so—and probably more so than most older white people I know who had nonarranged marriages.

So that's how my dad decided on whom he was going to spend the rest of his life with. Meeting a few people, analyzing their height, and deciding on one after talking to her for thirty minutes.

It was like he went on that MTV dating show *Next* and married my mom.

Let's look at how I do things, maybe with a slightly less important decision. How about the time I had to pick where to eat dinner in Seattle when I was on tour in the spring of 2014?

First I texted four friends who travel and eat out a lot and whose judgment on food I really trust. While I waited for recommendations from them, I checked the website Eater for its "Heat Map," which includes new, tasty restaurants in the city. I also checked the "Eater 38," which is the site's list of the thirty-eight essential Seattle restaurants and standbys. Then I checked reviews on Yelp to see what the consensus was on there. I also checked an online guide to Seattle in *GQ* magazine. I narrowed down my search after consulting all these recommendations and then went on the restaurant websites to check out the menus.

At this point I filtered all these options down by tastiness, distance, and what my tumtum told me it wanted to eat.

Finally, after much deliberation, I made my selection: Il Corvo. A delicious Italian place that sounded amazing. Fresh-made pasta. They only did three different types a day. I was very excited.

Unfortunately, it was closed. It only served lunch.

By now I had run out of time because I had a show to do, so I ended up making a peanut-butter-and-banana sandwich on the bus.

This kind of rigor goes into a lot of my decision making. Whether it's where I'm eating, where I'm traveling, or, god forbid, something I'm buying, I feel compelled to do a lot of research to make sure I'm getting *the best*.

At certain times, though, this "I need the best" mentality can be debilitating. I wish I could just eat somewhere that looks good and be happy with my choice. But I can't. The problem is that I know somewhere there is a perfect meal for me and I have to do however much research I can to find it.

That's the thing about the Internet: It doesn't simply help us find the best thing out there; it has helped produce the idea that there *is* a best thing and, if we search hard enough,

Ansari, Aziz, and Erik Klinenberg. 2015. "Choice and Options" from *Modern Romance*, ch. 4. Copyright © 2015 by Modern Romance Corporation. Used by permission of Penguin Press, an imprint of Penguin Publishing Group, a division of Penguin Random House LLC. All rights reserved.

we can find it. And in turn there are a whole bunch of inferior things that we'd be foolish to choose.

Here's a quick list of things I can think of that I've spent at least five to ten minutes researching:

- Electric citrus juicer (Waiting on this one to arrive in the mail. Hope I didn't fuck it up. Don't want too much pulp in my juice!)
- Taxidermy (I started off looking for a deer or a bear, but I ended up finding a beautiful penguin in Paris. His name is Winston.)
- Which prestigious TV drama to binge-watch next (*The Americans*, *House of Cards*, or *Orphan Black*? The answer: I watched all of them while telling my publisher I was writing this book.)
- Bag for my laptop
- Protective case for my laptop
- Internet-blocking program so I can stop using my laptop so much
- Museums (Gotta peep the exhibits online before I commit to driving all the way out there, right?)
- Coasters (If you dig deep, you can find some dope coasters with dinosaurs on them!)
- Vanilla ice cream (Had to step it up from Breyers, and there's a *lot* of debate in the ice cream fan community—there are fierce debates on those message boards.)

It's not just me, though. I may take things to extremes sometimes, but we live in a culture that tells us we want and deserve the best, and now we have the technology to get it. Think about the overwhelming popularity of websites that are dedicated to our pursuit of the best things available. Yelp for restaurants. TripAdvisor for travel. Rotten Tomatoes and Metacritic for movies.

A few decades ago, if I wanted to research vanilla ice cream, what would I have even done? Cold-approach chubby guys and then slowly steer the convo toward ice cream to get their take? No thanks.

Nowadays the Internet is my chubby friend. It is the whole world's chubby friend.

The "Best" Romantic Partner?

If this mentality has so pervaded our decision making, then it stands to reason that it is also affecting our search for a romantic partner, especially if it's going to be long-term. In a sense, it already has. Remember: We are no longer the generation of the "good enough" marriage. We are now looking for our soul mates. And even after we find our soul mates, if we start feeling unhappy, we get divorced.

If you are looking for your soul mate, now is the time to do it. Consider the rich social infrastructure of bars, nightclubs, and restaurants in cities. Add to that the massive online dating industry. Then throw in the fact that people now get married later in life than ever before and spend their twenties in "early adulthood," which is basically dedicated to exploring romantic options and having experiences that previous generations couldn't have imagined.

College, finding our careers, moving out on our own to different cities and parts of the world—in early adulthood we are constantly being introduced to new and exciting pools of romantic options.

Even the advances in the past few years are pretty absurd. You can stand in line at the grocery store and swipe sixty people's faces on Tinder while you wait to buy hamburger buns. That's twenty times more people than my dad met on his marriage journey. (Note: For those wondering, the *best* hamburger buns are Martin's Potato Rolls. Trust me!)

When you think about all this, you have to acknowledge something profound about the current situation: In the history of our species, no group has ever had as many romantic options as we have now.

So, in theory, this should be a great thing. More options is better, right?

Well. It's not that easy.

Barry Schwartz is a professor of psychology at Swarthmore College who has spent much of his career studying the annoying problems that come from having an abundance of options.

Schwartz's research, and a considerable amount of scholarship from other social scientists too, shows that when we have more options, we are actually less satisfied and sometimes even have a harder time making a choice at all.

When I thought back to that sad peanut-butter-and-banana sandwich I had in Seattle, this idea resonated with me.

Schwartz's way of thinking about choice grew popular when he published his book *The Paradox of Choice*. But for decades most people presumed the opposite: The more choices we had, the more likely we would be able to maximize our happiness.

In the 1950s the pioneering scholar Herbert Simon paved the way for people like Schwarz by showing that most of the time people are not all that interested in getting the best possible option. Generally, Simon argued, people and organizations lack the time, knowledge, and inclination to seek out "the best" and are surprisingly content with a suboptimal outcome. Maximizing is just too difficult, so we wind up being "satisficers" (a term that combines "satisfy" and "suffice"). We may fantasize about having the best of something, but usually we are happy to have something that's "good enough."

According to Simon, people can be maximizers and satisficers in different contexts. For example, when it comes to, let's say, tacos, I'm a maximizer. I'll do a rigorous amount of research to make sure I'm getting the best taco I can find, because for me there is a huge difference in the taco experience. A satisficer will just get tacos wherever they see a decent taco stand and call it a day. I hate getting tacos with these people. Enjoy your nasty tacos, losers.

If I'm picking gasoline for my car, though, I'm more of a satisficer. I drive into whatever gas station is close, load the cheapest shit I can to fill my tank, and get the fuck out of there. It sounds pretty mean to my car, but I really don't give a shit and notice no difference in performance for the quality of gas. Sorry, Prius.

Now, I understand that there is a certain kind of "car guy" out there who would find my choice of gasoline as horrifying as I find the choice of suboptimal tacos. To that I say: Stop caring so much about gasoline, you ding-dong! Spend that money on good tacos like a nice, normal person.

What Schwartz suggests, however, is that cultural, economic, and technological changes since the time that Simon wrote have changed the choice-making context. Because of smartphones and the Internet, our options are no longer limited to what's in the physical store where we are standing. We can choose from what's in *every* store, everywhere. We have far more opportunities to become maximizers than we would have had just a few decades ago. And that new context is changing who we are and how we live.

I noticed this in myself with Christmas ornaments. Why would I be anything but a satisficer with Christmas ornaments? It's pretty standard. The balls, the string of lights, etc. Well, do some Internet searching and you find some amazing ornaments. A *Back to the Future* DeLorean, little dinosaurs (!), a funny dude on a motorcycle. I ordered them all!

These types of ornaments wouldn't have even entered my mind before the Internet allowed me to see these other options. Now my standards for Christmas ornaments have gone up, and I wanted the best. Sadly, due to shipping delays, most of the ornaments I ordered arrived in late January, but my tree was extra dope in February.

Besides gasoline, it's damn near impossible for me to think of anything where I won't put in time to find the best. I'm a maximizer in nearly everything. Bottled water? Yup. You buy one of the bozo brands and you get bottled water that's just tap water in a bottle. Potato chips? Ruffles? No, thank you. Pass the Sweet Onion Kettle Chips. Candles? If you only knew how good the candles in my house smell.

It's so easy to find and get the best, so why not?

What happens to people who look for and find the best? Well, it's bad news again. Schwartz, along with two business school professors, did a study of college seniors preparing to enter the workforce.[1] For six months the researchers followed the seniors as they applied for and started new jobs. They then classified the students into maximizers (students who were looking for the best job) and satisficers (students who were looking for a job that met certain minimum requirements and was "good enough").

Here's what they found: On average, the maximizers put much more time and effort into their job search. They did more research, asked more friends for advice, and went on more interviews. In return, the maximizers in the study got better jobs. They received, on average, a 20 per cent higher starting salary than the satisficers.

After they started their jobs, though, Schwartz and his colleagues asked the participants how satisfied they were. What they found was amazing. Even though the maximizers had better jobs than the satisficers, by every psychological measure they felt *worse* about them. Overall, maximizers had less job satisfaction and were less certain they'd selected the right job at all. The satisficers, by contrast, were generally more positive about their jobs, the search process, and their lives in general.

The satisficers had jobs that paid less money, but they somehow felt better about them.

Searching for a job when you're in college is hardly a typical situation, so I asked Schwartz if perhaps this study was just capturing something unique. It wasn't.

Schwartz is an encyclopedia of psychological research on choice problems. If asked to give a quote about him for the back of a book cover, I would say, "This motherfucker knows choice."

As he explained it, the maximizers in the job-search experiment were doing what maximizers generally do: Rather than compare actual jobs, with their various pros and cons, in their minds they wound up selecting the features of each particular job and creating a "fantasy job," an ideal that neither they nor, probably, anyone else would ever get.

Johnny Satisficer is sitting around at his dum-dum job, eating his disgusting subpar taco and thinking about hanging his generic Christmas ornaments later on. But he's totally happy about that.

Meanwhile, I've just found out the taco place I researched for hours is closed on Sundays, and even though this year I have my dope Christmas ornaments, I'm worried there's a better Christmas ornament out there that I don't know about yet and am spending my holidays with the Internet instead of my family.

The Paradox of Choice in Relationships

When applied to modern romance, the implications of these ideas on choice are slightly terrifying.

If we are the generation with the greatest set of options, what happens to our decision making? By Schwartz's logic, we are probably looking for "the best" and, in fact, we are looking for our soul mates too. Is this possible to find? "How many people do you need to see before you know you've found the best?" Schwartz asked. "The answer is every damn person there is. How else do you know it's the best? If you're looking for the best, this is a recipe for complete misery."

Complete misery! (Read in a scary Aziz whisper voice.)*

If you are in a big city or on an online dating site, you are flooded with options. Seeing all these options, like the people in the job example, are we now comparing our potential partners not to other potential partners but rather to an idealized person whom no one could measure up to?

And what if you're not looking for your soul mate yet but just want to date someone and commit to a girlfriend or boyfriend? How does our increase in options affect our ability to commit? To be honest, even picking lunch in Seattle was pretty tough.

If we, like the people in the job study, are creating a "fantasy" person full of all our desired qualities, doesn't the vast potential of the Internet and all our other romantic pools give us the illusion that this fantasy person does, in fact, exist? Why settle for anything less?

When we brought these ideas up in focus groups, people responded to these notions immediately. In the city with arguably the most options, New York City, people discussed how it was hard to settle down because every corner you turned revealed more potential opportunities.

I've felt it myself. For much of the past few years, I split my time between New York and L.A. When I first started dating my current girlfriend, when I was in New York, I'd see people everywhere and feel like, *Shit, should I ever take myself out of the single world? There's so many people!* Then I got back to L.A., where instead of walking in streets and subway stations full of potential options, I would be alone in my Prius filled with shitty gasoline, listening to a dumb podcast. I couldn't wait to get home and hold my girlfriend.

*NOTE: If you listen to the audiobook version of this, I'm not going to say, "Read in a scary Aziz whisper voice," or this note, because I'm just going to do the actual voice, and I think it should be pretty terrifying.

CRITICAL READING QUESTIONS

1. How has the process of selecting a mate changed in modern Canadian and American society? What factors have created this different dating landscape? Consider the role of technology in these changes.
2. How satisfied do you think most people are with the new dating landscape? Compare this with how Ansari describes the experience of his parents or the experience of older people in your life.
3. How are these changes related to our modern focus on individualism? Does this relate to the rise of individualistic marriages, as described by Yodanis and Lauer?
4. How can we apply these findings to other areas of life, such as careers?

Summary

This chapter critically examined the role of intimate relationships and the family in society. We began by talking about major changes in the family, including Andrew Cherlin's argument regarding the deinstitutionalization of marriage. These changes are related to larger social processes, such as the rise of women's rights and individualism and the decline of religiosity. We also discussed how different theoretical perspectives, such as structural functionalism and conflict theory, understand the family's role in society. We also assessed dating and intimate relationships, which often provide the foundation for families. The reading from Yodanis and Lauer examined the role of romantic love in marriages and how our ideas of the importance of love have changed over time. We ended by examining the larger patterns of dating and selecting mates and how these are changing in modern times, with serious implications for the family.

Key Terms

arranged marriage 233
cohabitation 229
companionate marriage 232
deinstitutionalization of marriage 229
extended family 228
family 228
family household 228
family violence 243

fertility rate 241
individualized marriage 233
institutional marriage 232
marriage 228
monogamy 240
nuclear family 228
one-child policy 241
polygamy 240

For Further Reading

Cherlin, Andrew J. 2004. "The Deinstitutionalization of Marriage in America." *Journal of Marriage and the Family* 66: 848–61.

Engels, Friedrich. 1894/1946. *The Origin of the Family, Private Property and the State.* New York: International Publishers.

Kimmel, Michael. 2012. *The Gendered Society*, 5th edn. New York: Oxford University Press.

Lauer, Sean, and Carrie Yodanis. 2011. "Individualized Marriage and the Integration of Resources." *Journal of Marriage and the Family* 73: 669–83.

Parsons, Talcott, and Robert F. Bales. 1955. *Family Socialization and Interaction Process.* Glencoe, IL: Free Press.

References

Bentley, Paul. 2011. "Why an Arranged Marriage 'Is More Likely to Develop into Lasting Love.'" *Daily Mail* 4 March. http://www.dailymail.co.uk/news/article-1363176/Why-arranged-marriage-likely-develop-lasting-love.html.

Berger, Peter. 1963. *Invitation to Sociology.* Garden City, NY: Doubleday.

Brend, Yvette. 2017. "Accused Polygamists Plead Not Guilty in Trial Testing the Limits of Religious Freedom in Canada." CBC News 18 April. http://www.cbc.ca/news/canada/british-columbia/bountiful-polygamist-trial-winston-blackmore-oler-mormon-sect-1.4073950.

Canadian Press. 2011. "Plural Wife Describes Life in Bountiful Commune." 27 January. http://www.ctvnews.ca/plural-wife-describes-life-in-bountiful-commune-1.600642.

Cherlin, Andrew J. 2004. "The Deinstitutionalization of Marriage in America." *Journal of Marriage and the Family* 66: 848–61.

Collins, Randall. 1975. *Conflict Society: Towards an Explanatory Science.* New York: Academic Press.

Department of Justice. 2013. "Family Violence." http://www.justice.gc.ca/eng/cj-jp/fv-vf.

Henrich, Joseph, Robert Boyd, and Peter J. Richerson. 2012. "The Puzzle of Monogamous Marriage." *Philosophical Transactions of The Royal Society of Biological Sciences* 367: 657–69.

Khoo, Isabelle. 2017. "Mixed Couples Share What They've Learned about Each Other's Cultures." *Huffington Post Canada* 19 April. https://www.huffingtonpost.ca/2017/04/19/mixed-couples-culture_n_16089958.html.

Kimmel, Michael. 2011. *The Gendered Society*, 5th edn. New York: Oxford University Press.

Kohn, Melvin L. 1959. "Social Class and Parental Values." *American Journal of Sociology* 64(4): 337–51.

Kubota, Yoko. 2009. "Tokyo Firm Rents Fake Family, Friends for Weddings." *Reuters* 8 June. http://www.reuters.com/article/2009/06/08/us-japan-weddings-isUSTRE55771IY20090608.

Lauer, Sean, and Carrie Yodanis. 2011. "Individualized Marriage and the Integration of Resources." *Journal of Marriage and the Family* 73: 669–83.

Maheux, Helene. 2016. "Mixed Unions in Canada." Ottawa: Statistics Canada. http://www12.statcan.gc.ca/nhs-enm/2011/as-sa/99-010-x/99-010-x2011003_3-eng.cfm.

Milan, Anne, Mireille Vézina, and Carrie Wells. 2007. *2006 Census: Family Portrait: Continuity and Change in Canadian Families and Households in 2006: Findings.* Ottawa: Statistics Canada. http://www12.statcan.ca/census-recensement/2006/as-sa/97-553/index-eng.cfm.

Parsons, Talcott, and Robert F. Bales. 1955. *Family Socialization and Interaction Process.* Glencoe, IL: Free Press.

Statistics Canada. 2017. "Section 2: Police-Reported Family Violence in Canada—An Overview." Ottawa: Statistics Canada. http://www.statcan.gc.ca/pub/85-002-x/2017001/article/14698/02-eng.htm.

Wilcox, W. Bradford, and Steven L. Nock. 2006. "What's Love Got to Do with It? Equality, Equity, Commitment and Women's Marital Quality." *Social Forces* 84(3): 1321–45.

Chapter Outline

Photo credit: Rawpixel.com/Shutterstock

Introduction

You are probably very familiar with the institution of education. The average Canadian youth spends 30 per cent of each weekday in schooling. (The only other activity in which they spend this much time is sleeping!) If you are the typical undergraduate student, you have been in this system almost your whole life. Perhaps you started in pre-school when you were three or four years old, moved through elementary and high school, and now are in a university or college. You might have also attended other classes outside school—perhaps piano, tennis, or Japanese lessons. Unless you took some time off between high school and post-secondary education, you probably cannot even remember when the majority of your waking hours were spent somewhere other than in school. And you are currently gaining even more schooling. Why did you make the decision to continue your education? What is the role of the education system in society as a whole?

The Schooled Society

Schooling and the education system have fundamentally changed in modern society. Scott Davies and Neil Guppy (2018) argue that we live in a **"schooled society."** There are three main reasons for this. First, there is a growth in modern schooling. Today, there is mass post-secondary enrolment in Canada, with more than half of graduating high-school seniors attending college or university (Davies and Guppy 2018). These rates are growing over time. We can also see that this trend is similar around the world. Figure 9.1 compares the percentage of the population in the 25–34-year-old cohort and the 55–64-year-old cohort with post-secondary education. We can see that in all

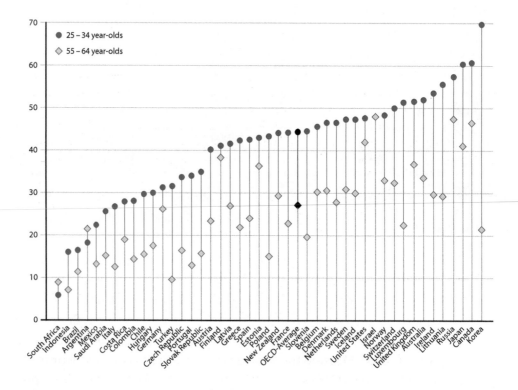

FIGURE 9.1   Completion of post-secondary education, comparison of 25–34-year-olds and 55–64-year-olds, countries and OECD average, 2017 or latest available

Source: OECD, 2018, "Population with Tertiary Education (Indicator)," OECD Data, https://data.oecd.org/eduatt/population-with-tertiary-education.htm

countries, the percentage of the population that has attended post-secondary education has increased over time.

Second, schooling has become increasingly integral to modern life. Individuals with a post-secondary degree earn higher incomes, on average, and are less likely to experience unemployment (Davies and Guppy 2018). (We will discuss these important implications later in this chapter.) Governments have become more interested in education's role in improving national productivity and have called for a focus on the development of highly educated "knowledge workers." Many countries, including Canada, previously emphasized manual labour and resource extraction. These changes can be linked to the decline in the primary sector (where jobs did not usually require much education). Today, the government tries to encourage the growth of jobs that require higher education in part because they often are more stable and have better pay. The evolution of working conditions and employment sectors in Canada is discussed in more detail in Chapter 10.

Finally, the forms and functions of education are increasing and diversifying in our modern schooled society. Historically, schools focused on reading, writing, and basic math. The current system is expected to teach these skills as well as a host of additional subjects, such as physical education, media literacy, drug and alcohol awareness, environmental responsibility, and sex education. Modern schools are seen as ways to solve a myriad of social problems. For example, French immersion programs were established across Canada in the 1970s as a means of dealing with issues of national integration and supporting new policies of bilingualism. These programs worked to foster national solidarity and entrench bilingualism. French immersion has been highly successful, enrolling approximately 300,000 students across Canada (or 7 per cent of eligible students; Davies and Guppy 2018). Mandarin immersion programs have been established in Alberta and British Columbia to further the national policy of multiculturalism.

The Functions of Education

The education system has several functions. The obvious and intended ones, such as teaching students basic knowledge and skills, are known as **manifest functions**. While learning to read, write, and do math are certainly part of education, sociologists have also focused on the **latent functions** of education, which are unintended. These functions fall into three broad categories: **socialization** of young people, **selection** of people into employment, and **legitimation** of certain types of knowledge and divisions in society. Durkheim, Marx, and Weber were all interested in these functions of education and saw them as integral to modern society. Let's explore how each of these sociologists understood education's role in society.

Socialization

Durkheim focused on the socializing role of the education system. The common theme in Durkheim's work is a fundamental concern with the functioning of society and what accounts for its solidarity and cohesion. This is the basis for structural functionalist theory generally and is the core of his interest in the education system.

Durkheim (1956) argued that universal education serves the needs of society in a number of ways. Tasked with providing individuals with training for life in broader society, schools convey basic knowledge and skills that will be useful for members of society. In addition, individuals need specialized training for the specific roles that they will occupy in life, such as an occupation. Durkheim argued that in the complex division of labour that characterizes modern society, education should be aligned with one's future occupational aspirations; that is, teachers should learn how to teach, and lawyers should learn how to practise the law.

HIGHLIGHT

Pressure to Perform in University

The importance placed on obtaining a post-secondary education can cause stress in many students. According to Bradshaw (2013), more and more students in Canadian universities deal with this pressure by using illegal prescription drugs. "Study drugs" are increasingly being sold, particularly in times of anxiety (such as exams). These medications are usually for patients with attention deficit hyperactivity disorder (ADHD); however, according to the Center on Young Adult Health and Development, nearly one-third of post-secondary students have misused stimulant prescription drugs at least once while attending university or college (Brennan 2015).

These drugs can have serious health risks if not taken properly under medical guidance. Stimulants such as methylphenidate, amphetamine, and dextroamphetamine—commonly known as Ritalin, Adderall, or Concerta—have after-effects. For example, the "come down" from these drugs can cause sleeping problems. Use of these drugs can also cause loss of appetite and dehydration. Besides health risks, possessing these drugs without a prescription is a violation of the Controlled Drugs and Substances Act, an offence that carries a maximum prison sentence of seven years (http://laws-lois.justice.gc.ca/eng/acts/C-38.8).

Duke University made the non-prescription use of these types of study drugs an offence under its rules on academic dishonesty. Yet most students interviewed for Bradshaw's (2013) article disagreed with this decision. One second-year University of British Columbia student argues that "it's still your work, . . . because you're still studying, you're just doing it with an increased mental capacity."

Why do you think study drugs are becoming increasingly popular? Are they a legitimate way of dealing with the increased stress of university life or a way of cheating?

Education also socializes children into the mainstream. Each society has unique needs; schools can provide the guidelines that help us fit into society. Education acts as the social "glue" that helps a highly differentiated society remain normatively coherent by offering a "moral education" whereby young people learn the norms and values of their society and the importance of following these rules of behaviour. Moral education is "the means by which society perpetually re-creates the conditions of its very existence," and schooling is about the "systematic socialization of the young generation" (Durkheim 1956, 123, 124). Socialization occurs when children are given grades and gold stars for following the rules. This practice helps to bring together children of different backgrounds by tying them into the cohesive whole of society.

You will see in Chapter 12 that Durkheim argued that there are two types of societies, those based on mechanical solidarity (everyone is similar) and those based on organic solidarity (people are dissimilar but interdependent). From a structural functionalist perspective, Durkheim saw religion as a source of moral guidance in societies based on mechanical solidarity. However, with the cultural diversity in modern society and waning of religion's influence on our daily lives, Durkheim claimed that education is the new way to morally integrate people into our modern society, which is based on organic solidarity.

Durkheim focused on the education system's part in training young people to fit into society and play the many roles expected of them. As a result, he saw the education system as an important part of how society reproduces itself. He explained that education "is only the image and reflection of society . . . it does not create it" (Durkheim 1897/1951, 371). For Durkheim and others who focus on the socializing role of the education system, education plays a fundamental role in promoting social order and in creating stability in society.

Selection

A second major function of the education system is to select individuals by awarding badges of ability through "sorting, differentially rewarding, and certifying graduates of elementary, secondary, and post-secondary schools" (Davies and Guppy 2018). Focusing on this element of the education system, Weber argued that schools are based on bureaucracies and work to confer status and prestige.

Weber was interested in the rise of rationalization in society, particularly the development of bureaucracies in a number of different areas. (We will discuss this topic in more detail in the next chapter.) The education system—including your university or college—is filled with bureaucracies. There are many positive aspects of the bureaucratization of the education system. For example, universities are very efficient systems for producing degrees. It is clear what classes and grades are needed to graduate, and most students earn degrees in four years. These educational bureaucracies also strive to be fair. Student numbers, not names, are often used on exams so that the professor or teaching assistant grades the tests without regard to his or her personal opinion of the student.

Just as they are efficient at producing degrees, universities and colleges can be frustrating in the amount of red tape students have to go through to fulfill all the requirements. They can limit your choice of classes—you need certain courses in a certain order to get your degree, regardless of your interests or abilities. They can also be very depersonalizing. The use of those student numbers, which is efficient and perhaps fairer, might make you feel as though you are not being treated as a unique individual.

PHOTO 9.1 Think about how you felt when you received your report card at school. Why are reports cards used, and what are the potential problems with this form of evaluation? Some schools are suggesting moving away from giving letter grades to students. Why might this be a good or bad idea?

John Howard/Thinkstock

A consequence of the rise of bureaucracies in society as a whole, including in the education system, is a growing need for individuals to have specialized certifications linked to specific occupations. Instead of providing a general education to all young people, modern society requires individuals to be trained in particular tasks, such as medicine, engineering, or social work. Weber highlighted how this specialization leads to an increasingly complicated set of certifications and degrees that can prevent certain people from entering a trade or profession. While it makes sense for certain professionals to earn a specialized degree, the practice also allows these individuals to gain significant control over entrance to their respective fields and to monopolize access to the elite positions and status.

Randall Collins (1979) called Weber's observation **credentialing**, the attestation of a qualification or competence issued to an individual by a party with authority to do so, such as a university. In this process, high-status groups maintain their social position by acquiring more education and educational credentials and keeping others out of these routes to upward mobility. Occupational groups have an obvious interest in making it difficult to enter their occupations (making it so that you need a BSc before entering medical school or a bachelor's degree before entering teaching college). By limiting the number of people who may practise in their area, they can reduce competition and keep their pay and job security high.

Legitimation

The third major function of the education system is to legitimate certain kinds of knowledge and divisions in society. In 1846, Canadian educational reformer Egerton Ryerson (after whom Ryerson University is named) began promoting the idea of a free and compulsory universal school system. He argued that this system would help to produce order, facilitate social control, and avert potential conflict arising from a new wave of immigrants to Canada at the time. Ryerson warned that new Irish labourers entering Canada were dangerous: "the physical disease and death which have accompanied their influx among us may be the precursor of the worst pestilence of social insubordination and disorder" (in Schecter 1977, 373). He claimed that education could assimilate these "alien" labourers into the dominant Protestant culture.

Karl Marx (Marx and Engels 1964) noted the general tendency of dominant groups to attempt to subdue the masses. He argued that the education system is a part of this process by maintaining social inequality and preserving the power of capitalists who are already in control of society. This position is consistent with Marx's overall theory that society's dominant institutions (including schools, religions, and the state) support and reproduce the capitalist system. In essence, Marx argued that schools work to systematically reproduce class relations and the capitalist order with each new generation of students.

As we have learned from Marx earlier in this book, "the ruling ideas of each age have ever been the ideas of its ruling class" (Marx and Engels 1964, 125). The ruling class diffuses its ideas throughout society in several ways, such as by setting the school curriculum. In formal education, a **curriculum** is the planned interaction of pupils with instructional content, materials, resources, and processes for evaluating the attainment of educational objectives (Adams and Adams 2003). Marx claimed that ideas are disseminated through both the official and what he called the **hidden curriculum**, the lessons that are not normally considered part of the academic program but that schools unintentionally or secondarily provide. He argued that along with teaching social studies, English, and science, schools teach students to be submissive, docile, punctual, and hard-working—all the traits that make for "good" workers in the capitalist system. In this way, education dulls the lower classes into obedient workers. Individual traits, such as punctuality, perseverance, and obedience, are rewarded with high grades and praise in school. For example, students are told to be quiet when the teacher is talking and to raise their hand when they would like to speak. The education system encourages and fosters this conformity to authority, which benefits the overarching interests of the society's powerful.

How Can We Measure the "College or University Experience"?

Universities and colleges are increasingly interested in comparing post-secondary institutions and students' on-campus experiences. How do we judge the "best" university, professor, or campus? How you answer this question depends on who you are within the institution (a university president, professor, or student) and what you think the role of a university is in society at large.

Looking at online resources that attempt to quantify and compare universities and professors pushes us to think critically about what we value in a university education and how to best assess how well your school or professors provide your education. Go to this book's companion website to access three measures of the university experience: *Maclean's* system of ranking Canadian universities and colleges, Rate My Professors' criteria, and *Playboy's* selection of the top party schools in North America. After you've examined these sites, answer the following questions:

1. How do these organizations judge a "good" school? What criteria do they use? How do their criteria differ?
2. Based on the criteria of each measure, what are the most important things about universities and the role of universities in society as a whole?
3. Who makes each of these lists? On whose interests does each of these rankings focus?
4. Which ranking do you think is best? Which is worst? What would you include in the perfect ranking?
5. How could you use these rankings? What problems or unintended consequences could arise from measuring post-secondary education in these ways?

In "A Matter of Degrees," William Beaver examines the various theories that sociologists use to explain education's role in modern society. When reading this article, try to connect the theories Beaver discusses with the ideas of Durkheim, Weber, and Marx.

A Matter of Degrees

William Beaver

Americans value few things more than college degrees. Right now, 29 per cent of adults over age 25 have a bachelor's or higher. That figure has more than doubled since the 1970s, and many within the educational establishment argue it will have to increase significantly for the United States to remain globally competitive.

The number of graduate degrees also continues to rise—masters' have doubled since 1980 and record numbers are enrolled in master's programs, a recent article in *The New York Times* reported.

In many ways these numbers aren't surprising. Early on, students learn that a college degree is the starting point to making it in American society. . . .

Media reports periodically reinforce such beliefs, reminding us that degree-holders have important income advantages. A recent news story in *The Washington Post* reported that in tough economic times, those with college degrees are much more likely to avoid lay-offs and maintain their incomes than those with high-school diplomas or less.

But what exactly do degrees do for people? The conventional wisdom holds that college graduates acquire skills that better prepare them for the world of work, which makes them more attractive to employers. Thus, students and parents are willing to pay the continually rising costs of higher education, assuming the pay-off will be worth it.

Beaver, William. 2009. "A Matter of Degrees?" *Contexts* 8(2): 22–6.

Although college graduates do have higher incomes, the reasons why, and our ever-increasing need to acquire educational credentials, are tied to larger social forces that sociologists have explored—forces that will continue to impact all those trying to climb the ladder of success.

The most popular view on the purpose of a college degree is known as the human capital model, which argues students attend college to acquire the knowledge and skills modern societies require, and that this allows them to obtain meaningful employment.

It's the model most students seem to accept, too. For example, surveys conducted by UCLA's Higher Education Research Institute found that 72 per cent of college freshman cite "to get a better job" as the major reason for going to college.

However, if the human capital model is correct, it must be assumed students acquire skills in the classroom that are directly transferable to the job. One can certainly argue certain majors like accounting and computer science offer more skill-training than others, and research indicates that with these types of majors, employers do tend to hire on the basis of perceived skills.

The fact of the matter is, though, most college students don't major in areas that teach job skills. Some 22 per cent of students currently major in business, but even within the business curriculum not all areas of study focus on acquiring specific skills. Moreover, many students continue to major in the social sciences and liberal arts, where there is little or no skill-training.

Along these lines, it would be logical to assume those possessing the necessary job skills, as indicated by their college major, would be more productive. Yet, the research that does exist on this idea suggests job productivity isn't significantly related to major. . . .

Why We Credential

Max Weber is credited with being the first sociologist to closely examine the function of degrees. He concluded educational credentials had much less to do with acquiring job skills than providing occupational and professional groups with a way of excluding certain individuals. The ability to exclude not only gives these groups power but helps to ensure that those hired will be loyal to the organization.

Weber's basic insights provided the foundation for modern credentialing theory, the most important work about which remains Randall Collins's *The Credentialed Society*. His detailed historical and social analysis supported Weber's contention that degrees allow certain occupational groups to exclude individuals, and that even business degrees seldom provide actual job training but do serve as indicators that a potential employee possesses the correct values that make compliance with organizational standards more likely.

There are always uncertainties about how new hires will adjust. The last thing most employers want is for them to "rock the boat," which could threaten stability within the organization. It's assumed individuals with the appropriate college degree will be more likely to fit in, but why? Part of the answer is self-selection. That is, students choose a college major that appeals to them, hoping to land a job and the start of a career, and hence are more than willing to conform. On the other hand, it's also likely that being exposed to a curriculum socializes students to acquire values associated with a profession. For years sociologists have investigated this so-called hidden curriculum.

For example, prospective managers are taught that their interests and the interests of workers are often in conflict and that their loyalties should be tied to management. Credentialing theorists have also suggested possessing the appropriate values is particularly important in higher-level positions, where individuals are often given more autonomy and are less likely to be closely monitored. So perhaps it isn't surprising that business researchers Nasrollah Ahadiat and Kenneth Smith discovered employers considered "professional conduct" the most important attribute when hiring accounting graduates.

Besides conformity and control, credentialing theory emphasizes that degrees also confer status on those who hold them. Along these lines, sociologist David K. Brown traced the development of the credentialing system to the late nineteenth century and the rise of large-scale bureaucratic organizations where individuals with management skills were needed.

It was assumed college graduates possessed the cognitive and verbal abilities good managers needed, which also reduced the uncertainty associated with hiring. Interestingly, studies do show college tends to increase cognitive abilities, so in many cases these assumptions weren't unfounded. Nonetheless, degrees provided a claim of competence or status that came to be taken for granted.

Thus credentials, as David Labaree points out in his book *How to Succeed in College without Really Learning*, have exchange value because they allow students to obtain employment based largely on the status a degree confers. However, much less use value is apparent because the connection between degrees and actual job performance is questionable.

The Pay Gap

Many students pursue a degree to position themselves to earn a higher income, and it has been well established that college graduates earn more. In fact, four-year degree holders earn nearly 45 per cent more per year than high-school graduates, according to the U.S. Census Bureau.

Indeed, the pay gap is one of the strongest arguments for the conventional wisdom of the human capital model, because it seems to demonstrate that employers are willing to pay for the skills college graduates possess. On the other hand, it's difficult to know exactly how much degrees are really worth because the most capable students go to college. As a result, there's no control group of equally capable, non-degree students available for comparison.

Nonetheless, credentialing theorists would agree that income and degrees are clearly related. Research by Ross Boylan found the largest gains in income occur soon after obtaining a degree. In this regard, reports from the Bureau of Labor Statistics show income gains for students are small unless they obtain a credential, even though students could certainly acquire job skills without earning a degree.

Consider that the median weekly income of individuals with some college but no degree in 2004 was $574, compared to $916 for those with a bachelor's. This suggests degrees do serve as status indicators. Just as important, Boylan found income gains experienced by degree holders are often relative. That is, as the number of people with degrees increase, degree holders take jobs formerly held by high-school graduates. Hence, the relative value of a degree actually increases because non-degree holders are forced into even lower-paying jobs.

One result, according to D.W. Livingstone in his book *The Education–Jobs Gap*, is that workers are often underemployed, because employers have increased the educational requirements for jobs whose basic content hasn't changed. Research by Stephen Vaisey discovered that nearly 55 per cent of workers are overqualified, which has produced increasing levels of job dissatisfaction, to say nothing of the fact that workers are forced to pursue even higher, increasingly expensive credentials (which is particularly burdensome to lower income groups) if they want a chance to be hired.

This phenomenon has been termed "defensive credentialing," where students attend college to keep from losing ground to degree holders. As one student recently put it, "I don't like college much, but what kind of job can I get without a degree?" Similarly, as the number of bachelor's degrees climbs, more have pursued graduate degrees, hoping to gain some advantage. This also helps explain the increase in the number of master's degrees.

Credentialing and Higher Education

The role of higher education in a credentialing system seems obvious—to grant degrees to those who earn them. But there's still more involved. Although higher education certainly responds to the demands of industry and students for credentials, colleges haven't just been passive participants waiting for students to enroll. They've used the credentialing system to their advantage, having relied on demographic changes.

By the late 1970s, higher education faced a troubling reality. The education of the baby boom generation that had produced the so-called golden years of higher education, when enrolments tripled, was coming to an end. The last of the boomers would be graduating in a few years and the future looked grim. The Carnegie Council warned enrolments could decline by as much as 50 per cent, while others predicted 30 per cent of colleges might have to close or merge. To survive, they would have to recruit more students from a dwindling pool.

Hence, colleges began to enroll a more academically diverse group of students and recruit more women and minorities, many of whom represented first-generation college students. To a lesser extent, the situation was helped by the fact that more students were completing high school. According to the U.S. Department of Education, between 1972 and 1985 high-school completion rates increased by roughly 2.6 per cent, and then climbed by about 3 per cent by 1999.

Moreover, the curriculum, particularly at less prestigious institutions, was expanded and further vocationalized. In fact, W. Norton Grubb and Marvin Lazerson in their book *The Education Gospel and the Economic Power of Schooling* maintain that expansion in higher education has only occurred when more occupational majors have been added to the curriculum.

In the early 1970s, 58 per cent of majors were considered occupational and by the late 1980s that figure had climbed to 65 per cent. These types of degrees can be particularly appealing to first-generation college students, who often come from working- and lower-class backgrounds and want a degree that seems to improve their chances for employment and justifies the considerable investment.

New degree programs were often in subject areas that in the past hadn't required a bachelor's degree for employment. For example, females who might have needed a certificate or an associate degree to secure work as a secretary could now earn a four-year degree in office management. Such was also true for other areas, ranging from various medical technologies to the performing arts, which reinforced the credentialing system in two significant ways. First, a more diverse group of students earned degrees, many of whom might not have obtained them in the past. Second, by creating new majors, credentialing was expanded into vocational areas not traditionally associated with a four-year degree, while at the same time reinforcing the notion that a college degree imparts job skills. . . .

CRITICAL READING QUESTIONS

1. What evidence does Beaver use to support the **human capital model**? Does he find this theory convincing? Which classical theory (Durkheim's, Weber's, or Marx's) does this theory most closely resemble?
2. What classical theory discussed in this book is related to the screening and sorting theory? What evidence supports this theory, and how accurate does Beaver think this theory is?
3. What is **defensive credentialing**?
4. Why has there been an expansion in the number and types of degrees?

Education and Social Inequality

Canadians pride themselves on living in a meritocracy, a society in which individuals achieve based on their personal merit. While Canada has many features of a meritocracy, not all individuals are equally likely to succeed in our society. In the previous chapters, we learned the importance of social class, race, ethnicity, and gender in shaping people's opportunities. Despite the significance of these individual characteristics in shaping our lives, we are not simply passive agents who are doomed to certain kinds of lives. Many individuals who come from disadvantaged backgrounds achieve great things, and many people who come from positions of advantage do not have high-paying jobs or high-status degrees.

The education system is a centrally important institution in a meritocracy because it has the potential to level the playing field and provide equal opportunities for individuals to work hard and move up the social hierarchy. Yet all Western countries have a clear pattern of inequality that suggests that the educational system is not meritocratic. For example, children from lower-class families tend to do worse in the education system than those from higher-class backgrounds.

It is important to note that not all dimensions of inequality work in relation to educational outcomes as we might expect. For example, when it comes to gender inequality, one would guess that men would be advantaged in the education system. However, women tend to perform better than men in schools and are more likely to earn degrees. In addition, some visible minority groups perform better than the majority white population, although this trend varies across racial and ethnic groups.

Education and Social Class

The largest and most persistent inequality in educational outcomes is based on social class. The relationship between these two factors is persistent over time, robust across measures, and exists across country contexts. According to Statistics Canada (See Figure 9.2), high-income Canadians are much more likely to earn degrees than those from low-income backgrounds. In fact, 79 per cent of the top 20 per cent of income earners attended post-secondary education. Among the lowest 20 per cent of income earners, this number was only 47 per cent. This is a large gap between the top and bottom earners. However, the gap between the attendance of the richest and poorest group has declined somewhat over time. In 2001, the richest 20 per cent were 35 per cent more likely to have attended post-secondary education. By 2014, the gap had declined to 32 per cent (See Figure 9.2).

There are a variety of reasons that individuals from low-income backgrounds are less likely to perform well in schools and achieve degrees. Lower-class families might have **different expectations** and values from those of upper-class families. A second reason could be **differential association**; that is, children from lower-class backgrounds

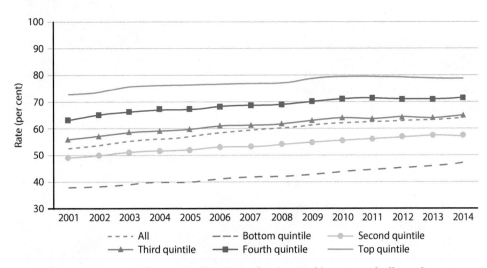

FIGURE 9.2   **Post-secondary attendance rate by parental income quintile and year, Canada**

Source: Marc Frenette, 2017, *Postsecondary Enrolment by Parental Income: Recent National and Provincial Trends. Economic Insights*, 10 April, Catalogue no. 11-626-X, Ottawa: Statistics Canada, http://www.statcan.gc.ca/pub/11-626-x/11-626-x2017070-eng.htm

are less likely to have role models who were high achievers in school or who attended university or college. As a result, these children lack the knowledge of how to work within the educational system (e.g., how to apply to university, what classes to take in high school to get into university). **Differential preparation** is another possible explanation. Children from families with more money are more likely to have private tutors, go on educational trips, have educational toys, and have books and newspapers around the home. These resources help to prepare them for school and to succeed in the educational system.

Social class is also important because it can help to determine your position within the organization of a school. **Streaming**, also sometimes called **tracking**, is the practice of placing students with comparable skills or needs together. Streaming includes putting students in specific schools for high or low achievement or in specific classes such as enriched/advanced or applied/basic or giving students harder or easier work within one class.

Streaming students into groups with similar skill levels has many advantages. It allows students to advance according to their ability, thus helping to preserve their interest and incentive to perform. Because bright students are not bored by the slower participation of others, they also are more likely to continue to engage in the class. Moreover, teachers can adapt their teaching styles and materials to the type of students in their classes and the abilities of these students. This approach can be beneficial to students because they will have material targeted to their ability level.

These purported advantages explain why streaming remains popular in schools in Canada and around the world. However, streaming also has some noteworthy disadvantages. The stigma attached to being assigned to the lower-ability group might discourage

ESB Professional/Shutterstock

PHOTO 9.2 When students are streamed into higher performing classes, teachers can offer a more tailored educational experience for their students and can further increase the performance of already high-acheiving students over time. How might streaming impact lower performing students?

the learning of children labelled in this way. This situation can create a **self-fulfilling prophecy**. Robert K. Merton (1968, 477) coined this term in *Social Theory and Social Structure* and defined it in the following way:

> The self-fulfilling prophecy is, in the beginning, a *false* definition of the situation evoking a new behaviour which makes the original false conception come "true." This specious validity of the self-fulfilling prophecy perpetuates a reign of error. For the prophet will cite the actual course of events as proof that he was right from the very beginning. (emphasis in original)

In other words, a strongly held belief thought to be true (even if it is false) may have such an influence on a person that his or her actions ultimately realize the belief (Merton 1949). This idea might remind you of the Thomas principle (see Chapter 5). Both stress the importance of our perceptions of a situation and how (even if they are not based in reality) these perceptions can change our "real" experiences.

A famous experiment showing the self-fulfilling prophecy's effect in the education system involved students in a San Francisco elementary school (Wineburg 1987). The researchers selected 60 children at random and told their teachers that, based on IQ tests, they were "expected to bloom." The researchers returned a year later to conduct new IQ tests. The 60 children who were selected enjoyed significant gains, far above the students who had not been labelled as particularly intelligent or with high potential. Remember that the two groups were the same—the label was unrelated to actual performance on the test. However, the teachers' belief that certain students were smarter *made* these students smarter (or at least perform better on the second IQ test).

How do students who are expected to do better end up performing better, even when their ability is no greater than others'? Barr and Dreeben (1983) looked at first-grade classes in which students were grouped by their reading ability at the beginning of the year. Students in higher-ability groups learned more new words and improved their reading skills more rapidly than students in the low-ability groups. Better readers were placed in high-ability groups at the beginning of the year, and they received more instructional time, were exposed to more new words, and experienced a faster pace of instruction than students in the low-ability groups. In short, higher-performing students received more learning opportunities than lower-performing students; consequently, the gap between high- and low-achieving students grew larger over the course of the year.

These experiments show the powerful effect of positive expectations. Many researchers and observers have generalized these findings to argue that there must be powerful negative effects of negative expectations. However, running an experiment with negative expectations would be unethical. Suppose you told teachers that certain students are slow learners. They might hold the pupils back or spend less time instructing them. Because we cannot test this directly, it is important to question whether the effect of the positive expectation experiments would hold true of students expected to perform poorly. Would it really hold students back in the same way that positive expectations can benefit students?

If all students were equally likely to make it into the high- and low-ability streams and student placement was based solely on their ability, streaming would not reproduce inequalities. However, when students with the same test scores and grades are compared, students from higher socio-economic status (SES) families are still more likely than low SES students to be enrolled in high-track classes (Gamoran and Mare 1989). Thus, the former are advantaged regardless of their ability and test scores; they are not only more likely to be prepared for school, but they are also more likely to be placed in the high-ability stream, with all its benefits.

Annette Lareau's (2003) *Unequal Childhoods: Class, Race, and Family Life* addresses this issue. Through interviews and observations of 10 families, Lareau examined the factors that lead to different educational outcomes across SES groups. First, parents who went to university are more knowledgeable regarding which classes are the "best" and most likely to prepare children for higher education. Parents with higher SES have the means to send their children to enrichment schools and to enrol them in extracurricular activities. Second, university-educated parents are better integrated into school networks—through Parent Teacher Associations and volunteering—which gives them more information about classes and teachers. Finally, these parents influence their children's class selection by encouraging them to challenge themselves and to think about the long-term consequences of their choices, such as which classes best prepare them for university.

Streaming seems to have serious benefits for some students at the cost of others. Students in the advanced classes do better, in part because they tend to be taught by more experienced teachers (Kelly 2004). In fact, research shows that similar students will perform quite differently if they are placed into a high or a low stream. Being put into a low stream will reduce their learning, while being in a high stream will increase it, even if these students have similar abilities at the beginning. Streaming also has long-term implications. For example, high-streamed students are more likely to attend university. Streaming can create what is referred to as a cumulative disadvantage; the most advanced individuals are awarded the best opportunities, which increases inequality (DiPrete et al. 2006).

RESEARCH METHOD
INTERVIEW

Education and Gender

When we discuss inequality, we are sometimes tempted to think that certain groups are always disadvantaged. For example, we know that women tend to make less money than men and are more likely to live in poverty. It therefore seems logical to assume that women, and other groups who are similarly disadvantaged, are disadvantaged in all realms of society, including education. Yet, as previously mentioned, Canadian women currently tend to do better, on average, than men in the educational system (see Figure 9.3). For example, since 1990 women have earned more degrees (both undergraduate and advanced) than men in Canada.

How can we understand this **gender reversal in educational outcomes**? Since the 1960s, the women's movement has had many important implications for society in Canada, the United States, and western Europe. The movement was instrumental in gaining women more opportunities to enter higher education. Furthermore, women in this period were entering the workforce at higher rates than ever before and were becoming involved in more professionalized occupations, which required more education.

The declining influence of religion, something we talked about in Chapter 1, changed our expectations about the need for men and women to marry and the timing and number of children couples had. With delayed marriages, a rise in the number of people choosing to remain single, and a decline in the number of children per couple, women had more time and ability to pursue higher education. The invention of modern birth control

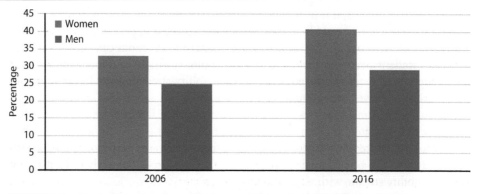

FIGURE 9.3   **Post-secondary attendance rate by sex, Canada, 2006 and 2016**

Source: Statistics Canada, 2017, "Education in Canada: Key Results from the 2016 Census," *The Daily* 29 November, Catalogue no. 11-001-X, Ottawa: Statistics Canada, https://www150.statcan.gc.ca/n1/daily-quotidien/171129/dq171129a-eng.htm

methods, particularly the birth control pill, was also very important. The pill, first approved for contraceptive use in the United States in 1960 and in Canada a few years later, is currently used by more than 100 million women worldwide (Shader and Zonderman 2006). The pill's invention and availability was a major development in women's engagement in the education system. Now that women could control when and how many children they had (at least to some extent), they could remain in education longer and pursue degrees with fewer interruptions.

While women have made large gains in terms of attendance and completion of university degrees, women still make less than men once they have completed school. In fact, women earn about 15 per cent less than men early in their careers (Blau 1998). These early income inequalities are important because they tend to grow over time (Marini 1989). One of the main reasons given for women earning less than men even though they are more likely to earn a degree is the different majors that women and men select. Men are overrepresented in majors such as engineering, which are more likely to lead to high-paying jobs. In addition, women are not able to translate their degrees into earnings the same way that men do.

Educational attainment also varies widely by race and ethnic group. As we learned in Chapter 5, racial and ethnic groups have very different rates of high-school and university graduation. However, as with gender, these inequalities do not always follow the general trends of discrimination that we observe in society as a whole. Ann Mullen discusses how men's and women's performances in higher education differ by social class and ethnicity. As you read Mullen's article, keep in mind the concept of intersectionality (introduced in Chapter 6).

PHOTO 9.3 Despite the gender reversal of education outcomes, the wage gap between men and women continues. Based on what you have learned in this chapter, how do you explain this situation?

Lighthaunter/Thinkstock

READING

The Not-So-Pink Ivory Tower

Ann Mullen

Since 1982, women in the United States have been graduating from college at higher rates than men; they currently earn 57 per cent of all bachelor's degrees. Some view this trend as a triumphant indicator of gender egalitarianism, while others sound the alarm about the supposed "male crisis" in higher education and the problem of increasingly "feminized" universities. . . .

Who's Getting Degrees

During the past 40 years, the gender distribution of bachelor's degrees reversed. In 1970, men earned 57 per cent of all degrees; today, women do. This trend leads some to conclude that women are squeezing men out of higher education, and that women's success has led to men's decline. In fact, this zero-sum scenario is incorrect: the college-going rates for both men and

Mullen, Ann. 2012. "The Not-So-Pink Ivory Tower." *Contexts* 11(4): 34–8.

women have increased substantially. Both genders are far more likely to graduate from college now than at any previous point in time. Women's increasing graduation rate isn't due to a decrease in the number of graduating male students, but to the fact that women's increases occurred faster than men's. Particularly between 1970 and 1990, as employment opportunities for women expanded, their college graduation rates grew more rapidly than did those of men.

The rates of growth for men and women have now equalized. Over the past decade, the number of degrees earned by both men and women actually increased by the identical rate of 38 per cent. The U.S. Department of Education predicts that over the course of the next decade women's share of bachelor's degrees will rise by only one percentage point, to 58 per cent of all degrees. In looking at these figures, we see that women's successes did not come at the expense of men, and that the gender gap is not growing uncontrollably. It has in fact stabilized, and has held steady for more than 10 years.

To fully assess the gender distribution of bachelor's degrees, we also need to look at what kinds of men and women graduate from college, and whether men and women of different racial, ethnic, and class backgrounds have the same chances of graduating. Among 25- to 29-year-olds, across all racial and ethnic groups, more women than men hold bachelor's degrees. The gap is just over 7 per cent among whites and Hispanics, 6 per cent among blacks, and about 10 per cent for Asians.

But in terms of race and ethnicity, the gaps in college completion far exceed that of gender: 56 per cent of Asians between 25 and 29 years old hold bachelor's degrees, compared to only 39 per cent of whites, 20 per cent of blacks, and nearly 13 per cent of Hispanics. Both white and Asian men are far more likely than black or Hispanic students of either gender to earn a bachelor's degree. These racial gaps are actually larger now than they were in the 1960s: while students from all backgrounds are now more likely to graduate from college, the rates have increased more quickly for whites and Asians.

Social class continues to be the strongest predictor of who will attend and graduate from college—one that far outweighs the effects of either gender, or race and ethnicity. Surveys by the U.S. Department of Education show that 70 per cent of high-school students from wealthy families will enter four-year colleges, compared to only 21 per cent of their peers from low-income families. Gender differences also vary by social class background. According to education policy analyst Jackie King, for the wealthiest students, the gender gap actually favours men. (For families in the highest income quartile, men comprise 52 per cent of college students, compared to 44 per cent in the lowest income quartile, and 47 per cent in the middle two quartiles.) Age also plays a role: among adults 25 years and older, women are far more likely than men to return to college for a bachelor's degree. But among those 24 and under, women make up only 55 per cent of all students, and the gender difference among enrolment rates for recent high-school graduates is small (41 per cent of men and 44 per cent of women).

In other words, women's overall advantage in earning college degrees is not shared equally among all women. White women, Asian women, and wealthy women outpace women from other backgrounds. Gender differences are largest among students 25 years and up, Asians, and low-income students. But differences in relation to class, race, and ethnicity greatly overshadow gender gaps in degree attainment.

Not at Caltech

In assessing gender equity in higher education, it's also necessary to take into account where men and women earn their degrees. While more women than men tend to graduate from college, women are disproportionately represented in less competitive institutions. Sociologist Jayne Baker and I found that women earned more than 60 per cent of degrees in the least selective institutions, but only slightly more than half in the most selective institutions. Women's gains have been greatest at institutions with lower standardized test scores and higher acceptance rates, while men and women are roughly on par with each other at elite institutions. Women are also underrepresented at the top science and engineering institutions, like Caltech and MIT. So, while women may be in the majority overall, their integration into higher education has been uneven, and they are more likely to attend lower-status institutions.

Perhaps the most striking disparities are in the choice of college majors. In spite of their overall minority status, men still earn 83 per cent of all degrees in engineering, 82 per cent in computer and information sciences, 70 per cent in philosophy, and 69 per cent in economics. Women, on the other hand, continue to earn the lion's share of degrees in traditionally female-dominated fields: 77 per cent in psychology, 80 per cent in education, and 85 per cent in nursing and other health professions. About a third of all men (or women) would have to change majors in order to achieve gender parity across majors today. This hasn't changed much in the last 25 years. (Through the 1970s and early 1980s, fields moved steadily toward becoming more integrated, but in the mid-1980s, this trend slowed and then stalled, shifting very little since then.)

Sociologists Paula England and Su Li found that most of the decrease in segregation came from the growth of gender-integrated fields, like business, and from the flow of women into previously male-dominated fields. Men are much less likely to move into female-dominated fields. They also found that women's entrance into predominantly male fields discourages later cohorts of men from choosing those fields. Women gain status and pay by entering predominantly male fields, while men lose out when they enter devalued, predominantly female fields of study.

Women and men are ostensibly free to select any field they wish, and they no longer face the blatant kinds of barriers to entry that have historically existed. But, other factors influence students' choices subtly, but powerfully. Sociologist Shelly Correll has done innovative experiments with undergraduate students that demonstrate how cultural beliefs about gender shape individuals' career aspirations. When exposed to the idea that men are better at certain tasks, male participants in the study rated their own abilities higher than the women, even though they were all given the same scores. These subjective assessments of their own competencies then influenced students' interest in related careers. Correll argues that widely shared cultural beliefs about gender and different kinds of competencies (like math and science) bias men's and women's perceptions of their own abilities, and their interest in pursuing these fields. She finds that men assess their own capabilities in math more generously than do women, which then encourages them to go into math and science fields. . . .

After College

Paradoxically, women's success in closing the gender gap in higher education has not closed the gender gaps in the labour market. Men and women still generally work in different kinds of jobs, and women still earn considerably less than men (even with the same levels of education). Occupational segregation remains high and the trend toward narrowing the gender gap in pay has slowed. Currently, young, college-educated, full-time working women can expect to earn only 80 per cent of the salaries of men ($40,000 annually compared to $49,800), a ratio identical to that of 1995. In fact, women with bachelor's degrees earn the same as men with associate degrees. Some of this pay gap can be attributed to students' undergraduate fields of study. Engineering graduates, for example, earn about $55,000 annually in their first year after graduation, while education majors bring home only $30,500. However, even after taking into account fields of study, women still earn less than men.

These pay disparities suggest an economic rationale for women's vigorous pursuit of higher education. Not only do women need to acquire more education in order to earn the same salaries as men, they also receive higher returns on their educational investments. Education scholar Laura Perna has found that even though women's salaries are lower than men's, women enjoy a greater pay-off in graduating from college than men do. In the early years after graduating, a woman with a college degree will earn 55 per cent more than a woman with a high-school degree. For men, that difference is only 17 per cent. What's more, men with only a high-school education earn a third more than women do, and are more likely to find work in traditionally male blue-collar jobs that offer healthcare and other benefits—which are not available in the sales and service jobs typically held by women.

Though men with high-school educations enjoy higher salaries and better benefits than do women, they are also more vulnerable to unemployment. In general, the rates of unemployment are twice as high for high-school graduates as they are for college graduates. They are also slightly higher for men than for women at all educational levels below the bachelor's degree. According to data from a 2010 U.S. Census survey, the unemployment rate for high-school graduates was 11.3 per cent for men versus 9 per cent for women (compared to 4.8 per cent and 4.7 per cent, respectively, for those with at least a bachelor's degree), due in part to the effects of the recent recession on the manufacturing sector.

Along with offering access to better jobs, higher salaries, and less risk of unemployment, going to college offers a host of other advantages. College graduates live longer, healthier lives. They are less likely to smoke, drink too much, or suffer from anxiety, depression, obesity, and a variety of illnesses. They are more likely to vote, to volunteer, and to be civically engaged. Because of this broad array of social and economic benefits, we should be concerned about patterns of underrepresentation for any group.

Incomplete Integration

To some, the fact that women earn 57 per cent of all degrees to men's 43 per cent suggests the gender pendulum has swung too far. They claim that if the ratio still favored men, there would be widespread protest. But such claims fail to see the full picture: though women earn more degrees than men, the gender integration of higher education is far from complete. Men and women still diverge in the fields of study they choose, their experiences during college, and the kinds of jobs they get after graduating.

In the early 1970s, when men earned 57 per cent of college degrees, women faced exclusion and discrimination in the labor market and earned less than two-thirds of what men earned. Many professions, and most positions of power and authority, were almost completely closed to women. While the ratio of college graduates now favours women, women are not benefiting from more education in ways that men did 40 years ago. In terms of the economic rewards of completing college, women are far from matching men, let alone outpacing them.

By paying exclusive attention to the gender ratio, we tend to overlook much more serious and enduring disparities of social class, race, and ethnicity. This lessens our ability to understand how gender advantages vary across groups. If there is a crisis of access to higher education, it is not so much a gender crisis, as one of race and class. Young black and Hispanic men and men from low-income families are among the most disadvantaged, but women from these groups also lag behind their white, Asian, and middle-class counterparts. Addressing the formidable racial and economic gaps in college access will improve low-income and minority men's chances far more than closing the gender gap would.

The higher proportion of degrees earned by women does not mean that higher education is feminizing, or that men are getting crowded out. It seems that if women hold an advantage in any area, even a relatively slim one, we jump to the conclusion that it indicates a catastrophe for men. In the case of access to college degrees, that's simply not true.

CRITICAL READING QUESTIONS

1. How has the percentage of women and men earning degrees changed? What would you expect the situation to be in 10 years?
2. What is the role of race and ethnicity in the relationship between gender and degrees? Do all ethnic groups have the same gap between men and women in terms of the number of degrees earned?
3. What is the role of social class in the relationship between gender and degrees?
4. Why is it important to assess men's and women's majors when talking about inequality in education? How is this factor related to the types of jobs that men and women perform?

RECOMMENDED RESOURCES

1. England, Paula, and Su Li. "Desegregation Stalled: The Changing Gender Composition of College Majors, 1971–2002." *Gender & Society* (2006), 20: 657–677. Reviews trends in the gender segregation of fields of study and the reasons behind shifts toward integration as well as the stalling of desegregation.
2. Sax, Linda J. *The Gender Gap in College: Maximizing the Developmental Potential of Women and Men* (Jossey-Bass, 2008). Examines the impact of college experiences, peer groups, and faculty on a comprehensive array of student outcomes.
3. U.S. Department of Education, National Center for Education Statistics, Institute of Education Sciences. (Washington DC, various years). *Digest of Education Statistics and The Condition of Education.* Comprehensive compendiums of education statistics, including a wide range of gender, race, ethnicity, and class indicators.

ACTIVITY

Critically Analyzing School Curriculum

Every province and territory in Canada outlines a specific curriculum for each grade in order to standardize what is taught to students across all the schools in the area. These curricula, along with the teaching resources on which they rely, are given to teachers at all levels to help them plan their classes. As we have learned in this chapter, the decisions of what will and will not be taught shape what students learn and their world view. Consequently, a curriculum is not neutral in its effect on students.

In this activity, we will explore the Grade 9/10 curriculum in Ontario. Go to this book's companion website to access this curriculum, or search online for your preferred province and grade. Then answer the following questions:

1. What topics and materials are covered that might not have been 50 or 100 years ago?
2. What topics and materials might have been dropped from earlier curricula? What does this difference tell us about the changing ideas of education's role in modern society?
3. How does this curriculum tackle issues of social inequality? Looking at the specific subject areas and the additional resources on the web page, how do the curriculum designers address gender, ethnic, and class inequality?
4. How does this curriculum address the value of multiculturalism in Canadian society? Where are ideas about multiculturalism and diversity included in this curriculum?
5. How does this curriculum deal with other social issues, such as concerns with the environment or the changing importance of technology in society? Where do these concerns appear in the curriculum?
6. How does this curriculum reflect larger changes in society?

Education, Cultural Capital, and Social Capital

One reason that education can perpetuate social inequality, or lead to social mobility, is its relationship to different forms of capital. When we think about capital, we tend to think about economic capital, things that have a monetary or exchange value (see Chapter 4). However, there are other kinds, such as social and cultural capital; these resources can be acquired through the education system and affect one's chance of future success.

Cultural capital is the non-economic social assets that promote social mobility. For example, we can earn degrees, learn a more refined style of speech, or adopt elite social tastes, which can make us appear to belong to a higher social class than the one into which we were born. To Pierre Bourdieu, who developed the concept, cultural capital is essentially the cultural knowledge that we learn over the course of our lives that confers power and status (Bourdieu and Passeron 1973). Cultural capital is comprised of the behaviours, knowledge, and values that indicate your social class. For example, liking the theatre and classical music is considered more sophisticated than liking action movies and heavy metal. Some individuals or families are more likely to possess sophisticated tastes and styles. In addition, this cultural capital is taught and institutionalized in the education system.

Social capital is the collective value of all of one's social networks. Essentially, it is about whom you know and the "norms of reciprocity" that develop between people who know one another. Social capital is important because it can provide a wide variety of benefits. For example, having wide social networks can help to foster trust among people, provide resources and information, and lead to cooperation. Both cultural and social capital can be acquired through the education system (Bourdieu and Passeron 1990).

An example of social capital in education is the Greek system. Rushing in a fraternity or sorority is a very common social activity in American, and in some Canadian, schools. The networks afforded through membership in these communities help individuals to expand their social capital and gain access to social circles, which can influence their future success in work and other realms. For example, 85 per cent of Fortune 500 CEOs have been in the Greek system, and the majority of US presidents were in fraternities (University of Missouri 2013).

According to Marx and other conflict theorists, the education system reflects the interests and experiences of the dominant class in society. Children from the dominant class in a society tend to do better in this system because they enter it already having certain types of cultural and social skills that facilitate their progress. Children from the working class, however, must learn these skills in schools, which can slow down their progress in other areas of the curriculum. Marx also argued that, even if children from the working class can learn the social and cultural skills that upper-class children naturally possess, these skills will never be natural for them. Teachers, principals, employers, and other children detect who innately possesses these social and cultural skills and tend to reward those students, perhaps by streaming them into advance placement classes or other special educational opportunities.

The Consequences of Degrees

A person's level of education has many serious and important consequences. We have already indicated two of the most important effects: earning more money and being less likely to fall into unemployment. According to the *US News and World Report*, individuals with bachelor's degrees earn about $2.27 million over the course of their lifetime (Burnsed 2011). This amount is considerably more than that of individuals with some college education ($1.55 million) or a high-school diploma ($1.30 million). People who earn master's, doctoral, or professional degrees earn, on average, $2.67 million, $3.25 million, and $3.65 million, respectively (see Figure 9.4).

The report showed, however, that the benefit of earning a degree is not equally distributed across groups. For example, whites earn more than any other ethnic group. The only exception is that Asian Americans with master's, doctoral, or professional degrees are able to out-earn white workers with degrees of the same level. Latinos and African Americans need to earn a master's degree in order to make the same amount of money over the course of their lives as a white worker with a bachelor's degree (i.e., complete two more years of post-secondary education) (Burnsed 2011).

Women are also less likely to reap the rewards of degrees, just as Mullen described in her article earlier in this chapter. The *US News and World Report* finds that, on average, women have to earn a PhD to make more money over their lifetimes ($2.86 million) than men with only a bachelor's degree ($2.60 million; Burnsed 2011). In summary, while university and college degrees clearly increase the lifetime earnings of all groups, not all individuals are equally able to turn their degrees into earnings.

Another benefit of education is that it can protect individuals from unemployment. Figure 9.5 shows the unemployment rate for 25–64-year-olds in OECD countries based

(A)

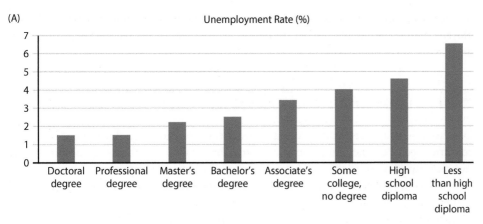

(B)

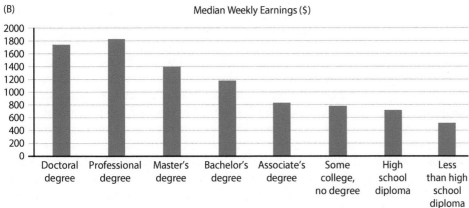

FIGURE 9.4   **Earnings and unemployment rates by education attainment, United States**

Source: Data from Bureau of Labour Statistics, 2015, *Employment Projections*, 2 April, http://www.bls.gov/emp/ep_chart_001.htm

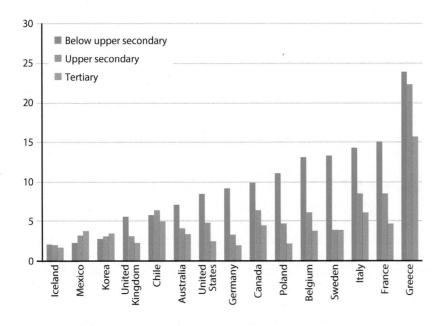

FIGURE 9.5   **Percentage of 25- to 64-year-olds who are unemployed, by education level, OECD average, 2015**

Source: Data from OECD, 2018, "Unemployment rates by education level (indicator)," OECD, Stat (database), https://data.oecd.org/unemp/unemployment-rates-by-education-level.htm

on their education level. In general, those with less education are more likely to be unemployed. Their unemployment rate is more than twice that of people with a post-secondary degree.

Education around the World

Education is an important institution in every country. However, the amount of money countries spend on the education system and the results from these expenditures differ significantly. Countries that spend a lot on education hope that this money will lead to better educational outcomes, such as higher achievement on international tests and higher graduation rates.

Figure 9.6 shows the relationship between the amounts of money a government spends on tertiary education (education after high school) and the percentage of the population ages 25–34 with a post-secondary degree. You can see that, in general, the more money a government spends on education, the higher its degree attainment rate. For example, Sweden and Norway spend more than Mexico and Italy on education, and more of their young people have degrees. However, this relationship is not universal. At $29,328 per student, the United States spends the most of all countries but has a rate of completion similar that of to Chile, which spends only about $7,836 per student.

Another exception is Korea, a remarkable success story in educational attainment. The country spends relatively little per student but has one of the highest rates of education completion in the world: 69 per cent of Koreans between the ages of 25 and 34 have a university or college degree (OECD 2016). The Korean government spent 6.3 per cent of its 2013 GDP on education, a much higher level of spending than the OECD average (OECD 2016). Yet student expenditures are quite low because the Korean education system serves a very sizeable population.

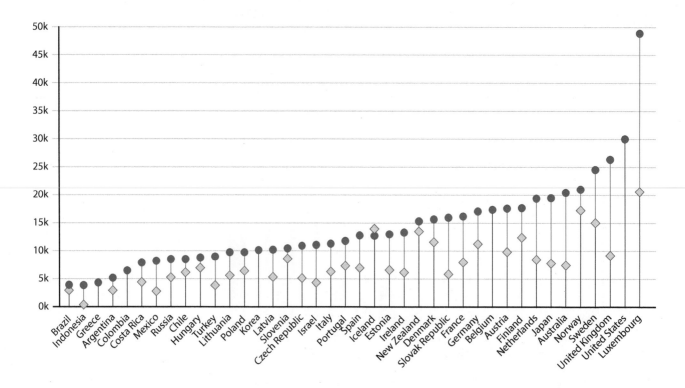

FIGURE 9.6   **Education spending, by country, 2014**

Source: OECD, 2018, "Education Spending (indicator)," OECD, Stat (database), https://data.oecd.org/eduresource/education-spending.htm

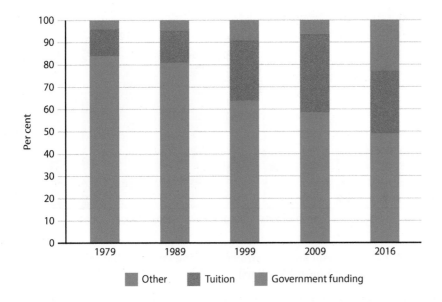

FIGURE 9.7 University operating revenue by source, Canada

Source: Adapted from Iglika Ivanova, 2012, "Seven Reasons Why You Should Support a Move to Low Tuition Fees for Higher Education," *Policy Note* 29 May, http:/www.policynote.ca/seven-reasons-why-you-should-support-a-move -to-low-tuition-fees-for-higher-education; and Statistics Canada, 2017, "Expenditures of Universities and Degree-Granting Colleges (x 1,000)," *The Daily* 13 July, https://www.caubo.ca/latest-news/financial-information-of-universities-and-degree-granting-colleges-20152016

Most universities in Canada are publicly funded and operated. The federal government is the majority funder, but its share is decreasing. As shown in Figure 9.7, government funding accounted for 84 per cent of universities' operating budget in 1979. Today, that amount has declined to about 49 per cent. To return to the funding levels of the early 1980s, the government would have to invest an additional $4 billion in post-secondary education.

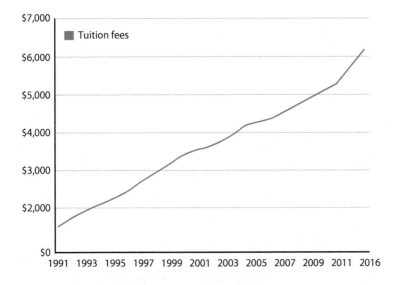

FIGURE 9.8 Undergraduate tuition fees, Canada, 1991–2016

Source: Data from CNW, 2011, "Tuition Fees Increase in Most Provinces: Students Call for Federal Leadership on Education," *Cision* 16 September, http://www.newswire.ca/en/story/842221/tuition-fees-increase-in-most-provinces-students-call-for-federal-leadership-on-education; and Statistics Canada, 2015, "University Tuition Fees, 2015/2016," *The Daily* 9 September, Catalogue no. 11-001-X, Ottawa: Statistics Canada, http://www.statcan.gc.ca/daily-quotidien/150909/dq150909b-eng.htm

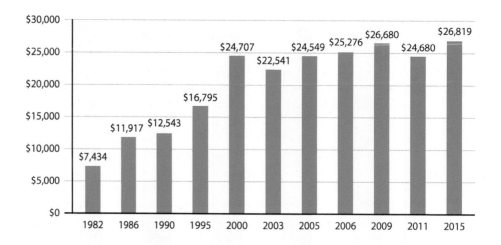

FIGURE 9.9   **Average debt among borrowers at graduation for bachelor's degree gradu-ates, Canada, 1982–2015 (in 2011 dollars)**

Source: 1982–2011 data from Statistics Canada's National Graduate Surveys, Canadian University Survey Consortium Graduating Student Surveys, http://higheredstrategy.com/a-closer-look-at-student-debt-part-1; 2015 data from Prairie Research Associates, 2015, "Canadian University Survey Consortium: 2015 Graduating University Student Survey," http://www.cusc-ccreu.ca/CUSC_2015_Graduating_Master%20Report_English.pdf

Most of the remaining money used to run post-secondary education in Canada comes from higher tuition fees. In 1979, about 10 per cent of university budgets came from tuition fees; the number is currently 28 per cent. The average tuition fee in Canada was about $1100 per year in 1991. Now, average tuition is $6191 a year (see Figure 9.8). As a result, students leaving university have larger debts than ever before. As shown in Figure 9.9, the average student debt has increased by 300 per cent between 1982 and 2015.

HIGHLIGHT

The Corporatization of Universities

With reduced government funding and the unpopularity of increasing tuition fees, creating corporate partnerships and running universities with business or management techniques have become more popular. This **corporatization** can take the form of naming campus buildings after major donors or corporate sponsors (e.g., the Clayton H. Riddell Faculty of Environment, Earth, and Resources at the University of Manitoba; the K.C. Irving Chemistry Centre at the University of Prince Edward Island; and the Wayne & William White Engineering Design Centre at the University of British Columbia). In many cases, these donations are from wealthy alumni or successful community members who simply want to support higher education. However, these relationships become controversial when donors seek to influence the research or teaching at the institution.

There has been an ongoing conflict over the relationship between the University of Calgary and the oil company Enbridge. Enbridge pledged $225,000 a year for 10 years to pay for a faculty position and scholarships for students. In return for this money, a building on campus would be named for the company. In addition, Enbridge would receive "customized opportunities" for their executives to meet with researchers at the university, and the university would agree to cooperate in a larger project focused on cleaning up a high-profile oil spill from one of Enbridge's pipelines (Bakx 2015). Many faculty members raised concerns about this deal and the implications it could have for the freedom of university researchers to do their work and for faculty to teach about environmental issues in their classes. The sponsorship deal was eventually changed, and Enbridge's name was removed from the building, although the corporation still contributes to the university as a whole.

Universities also make money by signing deals with companies that give the latter a monopoly on selling products on campus. For example, perhaps you can buy only Coca-Cola or Pepsi products at your school. It is not difficult to imagine why a company would want to sign such a deal with a university—it exposes its products to thousands of captive students who are making consumer choices that will continue throughout their lives. For example, if you become a Coke drinker early, you will probably remain one for life!

Exclusive deals between universities and companies gained popularity in the 1990s. Twenty-one Canadian and many American universities have signed such exclusive—and very lucrative—deals with the cola giants. In its 11-year contract with Coca-Cola, McGill University received a small fee every time a Coke product was sold on its campus. While the exact amount could not be revealed, the estimated revenue was more than $1.5 million, money that was used to renovate the student union building (Chester 1999). Other universities have earned even more. The University of Missouri received $16 million for its 10-year deal with Coke in 1995; the University of Minnesota was given $28 million in its 10-year contract with Coke the same year; and the University of Maryland received $58 million from Pepsi in a 15-year deal.

Have you noticed any of these arrangements at your university or college? What do you think of such agreements? What are the benefits and drawbacks to accepting money from large corporations?

CTV Atlantic

PHOTO 9.4 At this demonstration against tuition hikes in Nova Scotia in 2016, students call for lower tuition fees or free tuition. Have there been protests against tuition fee increases on your campus?

Rising tuition and debt is a problem in many countries. For example, student debt is quite high in the US. The US government drastically cut funding for public universities and colleges between 1988 and 1998. As a result, tuition fees are now 50 per cent of the average income of a middle-class family (Canadian Federation of Students 2013).

The history of tuition fees in Germany is quite different. Traditionally, university tuition was free in Germany. When the governments of seven out of Germany's 16 states began to charge fees, there was much opposition, including large protests held by students and unions. By 2012, all but two states had returned to the previous system of free higher education (Canadian Federation of Students 2013).

Canadian students concerned with rising tuition fees and student debt have followed this success and have started the Education Is a Right campaign. This campaign pushes for increased funding for education and reduced tuition fees. It involves a range of tactics, including an annual student protest in February. (For more information on this movement, see http://cfs-ns.ca/education-is-a-right.)

Summary

The education system is one of modern society's central institutions and permeates many aspects of our day-to-day lives. This system works to socialize, select, and legitimize knowledge in our society. It is clear that not all individuals have equal access to or perform equally well in the education system. In this chapter, we critically examined the role of this system in perpetuating, and potentially alleviating, social inequality, including the role of cultural and social capital in this relationship. We also discussed education around the world, comparing funding in various countries. The issues of rising tuition fees and the corporatization of the university illustrate the widespread changes occurring in education in Canada and around the world, changes that have important implications for educational outcomes across groups.

Key Terms

corporatization 274
credentialing 256
cultural capital 269
curriculum 256
defensive credentialing 260
different expectations 261
differential association 261
differential preparation 262
gender reversal in educational
    outcomes 264
hidden curriculum 256

human capital model 260
latent functions 253
legitimation 253
manifest functions 253
schooled society 252
selection 253
self-fulfilling prophecy 263
social capital 270
socialization (function of education) 253
streaming (tracking) 262

For Further Reading

Bourdieu, Pierre, and Jean Claude Passeron. 1990. *Reproduction in Education, Society and Culture*, 2nd edn. London: Sage.

Coleman, James. 1990. *Foundations of Social Theory*. Cambridge, MA: Harvard University Press.

Collins, Randall. 1979. *The Credential Society: An Historical Sociology of Education and Stratification*. New York: Academic Press.

Davies, Scott, and Neil Guppy. 2018. *The Schooled Society: An Introduction to the Sociology of Education*, 3rd edn. Don Mills, ON: Oxford University Press.

Durkheim, Émile. 1956. *Education and Sociology*. Glencoe, IL: Free Press.

References

Adams, Kathy L., and Dale E. Adams. 2003. *Urban Education: A Reference Handbook*. Santa Barbara, CA: ABC-CLIO.

Bakx, Kyle. 2015. "University of Calgary Needs to Take Hard Look at Corporate Sponsorships, Critics Say." CBC News 3 November. http://www.cbc.ca/news/canada/calgary/enbridge-university-calgary-inquiry-1.3289259.

Barr, Rebecca, and Robert Dreeben. 1983. *How Schools Work*. Chicago: University of Chicago Press.

Blau, Francine D. 1998. "Trends in the Well-Being of American Women, 1970–1995." *Journal of Economic Literature* 36: 112–65.

Bourdieu, Pierre, and Jean Claude Passeron. 1973. "Cultural Reproduction and Social Reproduction." In Richard K. Brown, ed., *Knowledge, Education and Cultural Change*, 71–112. London: Tavistock.

——— 1990. *Reproduction in Education, Society and Culture*, 2nd edn. London: Sage.

Bradshaw, James. 2013. "Students Reaching for ADHD Drugs to Deal with Academic Stress." *The Globe and Mail* 18 October.

Brennan, Colin. 2015. "Popping Pills: Examining the Use of Study Drugs during Finals." *USA Today College* 16 December. http://college.usatoday.com/2015/12/16/popping-pills-examining-the-use-of-study-drugs-during-finals.

Burnsed, Brian. 2011. "How Higher Education Affects Lifetime Salary: College Degrees Significantly Boost Earnings, but Women and Minorities Benefit Less." *US News and World Report* 5 August.

Canadian Federation of Students. 2013. "International Comparisons." http://cfs-fcee.ca/the-issues/tuition-fees-and-access-to-education/international-comparisons.

Chester, Bronwyn. 1999. "McGill and Coke Set to Ink Deal." *The McGill Reporter* 9 September. http://reporter-archive.mcgill.ca/Rep/r3201/coke.html.

Collins, Randal. 1979. *The Credential Society: An Historical Sociology of Education and Stratification*. New York: Academic Press.

Davies, Scott, and Neil Guppy. 2018. *The Schooled Society: An Introduction to the Sociology of Education*. Don Mills, ON: Oxford University Press.

DiPrete, Thomas A., Gregory M. Eirich, Karen S. Cook, and Douglas S. Massey. 2006. "Cumulative Advantage as a Mechanism for Inequality: A Review of Theoretical and Empirical Developments." *Annual Review of Sociology* 32: 271–97.

Durkheim, Émile. 1897/1951. *Suicide: A Study in Sociology*. Glencoe, IL: Free Press.

——— 1956. *Education and Sociology*. Glencoe, IL: Free Press.

Gamoran, A., and R. Mare. 1989. "Secondary School Tracking and Educational Inequality: Compensation, Reinforcement, or Neutrality?" *American Journal of Sociology* 94: 1146–83.

Kelly, William, ed. 2004. *Fanning the Flames: Fans and Consumer Culture in Contemporary Japan*. New York: SUNY.

Lareau, Annette. 2003. *Unequal Childhoods: Class, Race, and Family Life*. Berkeley: University of California Press.

Marini, Margaret Mooney. 1989. "Sex Differences in Earnings in the United States." *Annual Review of Sociology* 15: 343–80.

Marx, Karl, and Friedrich Engels. 1964. *The Communist Manifesto*. New York: Modern Reader Paperbacks.

Merton, Robert K. 1949. *Social Theory and Social Structure*. New York: Free Press.

——— 1968. *Social Theory and Social Structure*, enlarged edn. New York: Free Press.

OECD (Organisation for Economic Co-operation and Development). 2016. "Education at a Glance 2016: OECD Indicators." Paris: OECD Publishing. http://dx.doi.org/10.1787/eag-2016.en.

Schecter, Stephen. 1977. "Capitalism, Class, and Educational Reform in Canada." In L. Panitch, ed., *The Canadian State: Political Economy and Political Power*. Toronto: University of Toronto Press.

Shader, Laurel, and Jonathan Zonderman. 2006. *Birth Control Pills*. New York: Infobased Publishing.

Thomas, W.I., and D.S. Thomas. 1928. *The Child in America*. New York: Knopf.

University of Missouri. 2013. "Student Involvement: National Statistics." http://www.umkc.edu/getinvolved/fsa-national-statistics.asp.

Wineburg, Samuel. 1987. "The Self-Fulfillment of the Self-Fulfilling Prophecy." *Educational Researcher* 16: 28–44.

10 Work and Rationalization

Chapter Outline

Photo credit: Kichigin/Shutterstock

Introduction

Sociologists have long been interested in the changing nature of society. Max Weber, in particular, focused on the rise of rationality, the scientific understanding and processes oriented toward rational goals. He described how this new world contrasts with earlier faith-based societies in which the world seemed unknowable and mystical. This chapter will focus on the process of rationalization in society. It will also look at the role of work and occupations in society and how they are becoming increasingly rationalized. We will examine a number of key changes in the Canadian labour market, including the rise of scientific management, the rise in precarious employment, outsourcing and automation, and the prevalence of emotional labour.

The Rationalized World

Weber (1965) argued that prior to the Enlightenment (a period in Europe in the late seventeenth and eighteenth centuries), we lived in an enchanted world. People had very little understanding of why natural events occurred—at this time, they still believed that the sun rotated around the earth. They saw the world as magical and invested with other-worldly forces. They explained droughts and plagues by claiming that God was angry or Mother Nature was out of sync. The only way to "solve" these events was to appease God, such as by performing a ritual or sacrifice.

The Enlightenment, or "Age of Reason," was an exciting period in Europe—people came to embrace new ideas of science, logic, and reasoning, as well as the use of evidence to make sense of the world. This era came with new ways of understanding the natural and social worlds. For example, people used to think that things fall to the ground because it was simply in their nature to do so. Through experiments and logic, gravity was discovered.

The Age of Reason also marked a decline in religion's role in society. Instead of always looking to religious institutions and leaders to make sense of the world, people increasingly looked to science. For example, while the church tells us to have faith that humans were created in God's image because that is what the Bible says, Darwin demonstrated that humans have evolved over millennia through the process of natural selection. This new way of seeing the world—through science and the principles of rationality—weakened the influence of religious authorities. Weber called this process the **disenchantment of the world**.

Rationalization is a way of solving problems that is based on four main factors: predictability, calculability, efficiency, and control. Predictability means that things can be repeated with the expectation of the same results. When a scientist does an experiment, for example, she will replicate it many times to make sure that the findings are correct. Calculability focuses on things that can be counted and quantified. In modern society, we tend to like to measure things with numbers and to compare things numerically—we assess a runner's ability by comparing their race times and academic ability by comparing grades, even though there are other, less tangible ways to measure these things. Rationality is also based on efficiency, the best means to a given end. For instance, it would seem nonsensical to drive from Vancouver to Toronto through Mexico. The route might be more enjoyable, but it is not efficient because it would take longer and therefore does not fit with our modern principles of rationality. Finally, rationality is based on ideas of control and an enhanced certainty of outcomes, such as knowing exactly how long a trip will take by looking it up on Google maps, thus providing a basis for choosing how to undertake the task.

Rationalization has changed many aspects of society and permeates modern life. Living in such a world has many benefits. Most important, rational systems are very efficient. We can make many more products and run organizations more efficiently in a rationalized world. Rationalization and the rise of science also help us to solve certain problems. When we thought that the plague was caused by bad humours or evil natures, we were ill-equipped to stop it. When we realized that vermin living in the city caused the plague, we could address the problem by improving sanitation. The Age of Reason allowed us to make sense of the world and afforded us some control over it. In this rationalized world, we tend to live longer and healthier lives, partly because of our understanding of science.

Despite these benefits, rationalization is not without its downsides. Weber (1965) argued that the process of disenchantment is also a process of disillusionment. As the world becomes less enchanted and less magical, it also becomes less meaningful for people. Part of what makes us human is our ability to be creative, emotional, and spontaneous. None of these qualities makes sense in a rationalized world. Creativity is absent from mass-produced consumer goods, and the worker is unable to express individuality or make unique additions to the product. Spontaneity is taken away when we are always looking for the most efficient way to do things. In this way, the rise of rationality might be robbing us of our very humanity.

The prototype of rationalization in modern society is the **bureaucracy**. The word originated in 1789 and is based on the French root *bureau*, which means "office or desk," and the Greek root *kratia*, which means "power or rule." Bureaucracy, then, is the rule of the office or desk and is essentially a machine made of humans. Bureaucracies rose to prominence as an organizational form in the twentieth century. Examples in modern society include non-profit organizations (such as your university, the YMCA or YWCA, and the United Nations) and for-profit companies (such as Starbucks, Microsoft, or Apple).

According to Weber (1965), bureaucracies have six core features:

1. They are based on hierarchically organized "offices."
2. They have a vertical chain of command. Your university probably has professors who report to a chair who reports to the dean.

PHOTO 10.1 Universities are bureaucracies. How does this increase efficiency, predictability, calculability, and control? What are the potential positive and negative implications of this way of organizing higher education?

Maha Sultan/Trinity News

3. They have a clear, formal division of labour. In your university, there are people who teach classes (professors), those who run the library (librarians), and those who clean and maintain the buildings (janitors and maintenance staff). The university could not run without these and many other individuals. However, they do not switch from one task to the other—there is a clear separation of roles, with different people doing different tasks.

4. They are dominated by technical qualifications. Specific degrees and qualifications are needed to perform each job.

5. They have impersonal decision-making. All prospective students submit the same application that is judged without knowing the student's name or identifying features.

6. They are staffed by full-time, salaried employees.

A prototypical bureaucracy is McDonald's, which has more than 30,000 restaurants in 118 countries (James 2009). In the following article, George Ritzer applies Weber's ideas about the rise of rationality to the emergence of fast-food restaurants and discusses how these establishments have affected society (a process he calls **McDonaldization**).

The "McDonaldization" of Society

George Ritzer

A wide-ranging process of *rationalization* is occurring across American society and is having an increasingly powerful impact in many other parts of the world. It encompasses such disparate phenomena as fast-food restaurants, TV dinners, packaged tours, industrial robots, plea bargaining, and open-heart surgery on an assembly-line basis. As widespread and as important as these developments are, it is clear that we have barely begun a process that promises even more extraordinary changes (e.g. genetic engineering) in the years to come. We can think of rationalization as a historical process and rationality as the end result of that development. As an historical process, rationalization has distinctive roots in the Western world. Writing in the late nineteenth and early twentieth centuries, the great German sociologist Max Weber saw his society as the centre of the ongoing process of rationalization and the bureaucracy as its paradigm case. The model of rationalization, at least in contemporary America, is no longer the bureaucracy, but might be better thought of as the fast-food restaurant. As a result, our concern here is with what might be termed the "McDonaldization of Society." While the fast-food restaurant is not the ultimate expression of rationality, it is the current exemplar for future developments in rationalization.

A society characterized by rationality is one which emphasizes *efficiency*, *predictability*, *calculability*, *substitution of non-human for human technology*, and *control over uncertainty*. In discussing the various dimensions of rationalization, we will be little concerned with the gains already made, and yet to be realized, by greater rationalization. These advantages are widely discussed in schools and in the mass media. In fact, we are in danger of being seduced by the innumerable advantages already offered, and promised in the future, by rationalization. The glitter of these accomplishments and promises has served to distract most people from the grave dangers posed by progressive rationalization. In other words, we are ultimately concerned here with the irrational consequences that often flow from rational systems. Thus, the second major theme of this essay might be termed "the irrationality of rationality."

Ritzer, George. 1983. The "McDonaldization" of Society, *Journal of American Culture* 6(1): 100-7. Spring.

In spite of the emphasis here on the problems posed by rationalization, this will not be one of those pleas for a return to a less rationalized way of life. Although there is certainly room for less rationalized pockets in a rational society, in most cases we cannot, and should not, try to reverse the process of rationalization. In our rush to critique rationalization we cannot ignore its many advantages (McDonald's does offer a lot of tasty food at relatively low cost). Furthermore, we should not romanticize the "noble" life of the pre-rational society with its many problems and disadvantages. We would not, in most cases, want to recreate a life beset by these problems, even if it was possible to do so. Instead, what we need [to] do is gain a better understanding of the process of rationalization so that we can come to exercise more and better control over it. . . .

Efficiency

The process of rationalization leads to a society in which a great deal of emphasis is placed on finding the best or optimum means to any given end. Whatever a group of people define as an end, and everything they so define, is to be pursued by attempting to find the best means to achieve the end. . . .

The modern American family, often with two wage earners, has little time to prepare elaborate meals. For the relatively few who still cook such meals, there is likely to be great reliance on cookbooks that make cooking from scratch much more efficient. However, such cooking is relatively rare today. Most families take as their objective quickly and easily pre-pared meals. To this end, much use is made of pre-packaged meals and frozen TV dinners.

For many modern families, the TV dinner is no longer efficient enough. To many people, eating out, particularly in a fast-food restaurant, is a far more efficient way of obtaining their meals. Fast-food restaurants capitalize on this by being organized so that diners are fed as efficiently as possible. They offer a limited, simple menu that can be cooked and served in an assembly-line fashion. The latest development in fast-food restaurants, the addition of drive-through windows, constitutes an effort to increase still further the efficiency of the dining experience. The family now can simply drive through, pick up its order, and eat it while driving to the next, undoubtedly efficiently organized, activity. The success of the fast-food restaurant has come full circle with frozen-food manufacturers now touting products for the home modelled after those served in fast-food restaurants.

Increasingly, efficiently organized food production and distribution systems lie at the base of the ability of people to eat their food efficiently at home, in the fast-food restaurant, or in their cars. Farms, groves, ranches, slaughterhouses, warehouses, transportation sys-tems, and retailers are all oriented toward increasing efficiency. A notable example is chicken production where they are mass bred, force fed (often with many chemicals), slaughtered on an assembly line, iced or fast frozen and shipped to all parts of the country. Some may argue that such chickens do not taste as good as the fresh-killed, local variety, but their complaints are likely to be drowned in a flood of mass-produced chickens. . . .

The fast-food restaurant is certainly not the only place one can spend money. The centre of spending is now the modern shopping centre and the supermarket. These are organized in a highly efficient manner in order to aid business. Supermarkets have grown even more ef-ficient recently with the advent of computer scanning devices which expedite the checkout process and, at the same time, make the work of stockpeople more efficient by eliminating the need to stamp prices on the items.

When our shoppers return home (in efficiently produced cars and on efficiently built roads) they are likely to enter apartments or suburban tract houses which have been effi-ciently constructed. Among other things, this means there is little or nothing to distinguish one apartment or house from many others. In constructing such dwellings, esthetic elements like trees or hills are likely to be levelled if they stand in the way of efficient construction. . . .

If the family is unhappy with the efficiency that pervades virtually every facet of daily life, it might seek relief in leisure-time activities that it may assume to be immune from the process of rationalization. However, even in these areas, the principles of efficiency are omnipresent. International travel is affordable for many only through organized tours that efficiently transport large groups of tourists from one site to another. The modern amusement park is often little more than a vast, elaborate people-moving machine designed to transport people through the park and its various attractions as efficiently as possible. Campgrounds, trout farms, sporting events, and night clubs are other examples of entertainment that have grown increasingly efficient. . . .

Predictability

A second component of rationalization involves the effort to ensure predictability from one place to another. In a rational society, people want to know what to expect when they enter a given setting or acquire some sort of commodity. They neither want nor expect surprises. They want to know that if they journey to another locale, the setting they enter or the commodity they buy will be essentially the same as the setting they entered or product they purchased earlier. Furthermore, people want to be sure that what they encounter is much like what they encountered at earlier times. In order to ensure predictability over time and place a rational society must emphasize such things as discipline, order, systemization, formalization, routine, consistency, and methodical operation. . . .

Fast-food restaurants rank very high on the dimension of predictability. In order to help ensure consistency, the fast-food restaurant offers only a limited menu. Predictable end-products are made possible by the use of similar raw materials, technologies, and preparation and serving techniques. Not only the food is predictable; the physical structures, the logo, the "ambience," and even the personnel are as well.

The food that is shipped to our homes and our fast-food restaurants is itself affected by the process of increasing predictability. Thus our favourite white bread is indistinguishable from one place to another. In fact, food producers have made great efforts to ensure such predictability. . . .

Other leisure-time activities have grown similarly predictable. Camping in the wild is loaded with uncertainties—bugs, bears, rain, cold, and the like. To make camping more predictable, organized grounds have sprung up around the country. Gone are many of the elements of unpredictability replaced by RVs, paved over parking lots, sanitized campsites, fences, and enclosed camp centres that provide laundry and food services, recreational activities, television, and video games. Sporting events, too, have in a variety of ways been made more predictable. The use of artificial turf in baseball makes for a more predictable bounce of a ball. . . .

Calculability or Quantity Rather Than Quality

It could easily be argued that the emphasis on quantifiable measures, on things that can be counted, is *the* most defining characteristic of a rational society. Quality is notoriously difficult to evaluate. How do we assess the quality of a hamburger, or a physician, or a student? Instead of even trying, in an increasing number of cases, a rational society seeks to develop a series of quantifiable measures that it takes as surrogates for quality. . . .

. . . One of the most obvious examples in the university is the emphasis given to grades and cumulative grade point averages. With less and less contact between professor and student, there is little real effort to assess the quality of what students know, let alone the quality of their overall abilities. Instead, the sole measure of the quality of most college students is their grade in a given course and their grade point averages. Another blatant example is the emphasis on a variety of uniform exams such as SATs and GREs in which the essence of an applicant is reduced to a few simple scores and percentiles.

Within the educational institution, the importance of grades is well known, but somewhat less known is the way quantifiable factors have become an essential part of the process of evaluating college professors. For example, teaching ability is very hard to evaluate. Administrators have difficulty assessing teaching quality and thus substitute quantitative scores. Of course each score involves qualitative judgments, but this is conveniently ignored.

Student opinion polls are taken and the scores are summed, averaged, and compared. Those who score well are deemed good teachers while those who don't are seen as poor teachers. There are many problems involved in relying on these scores such as the fact that easy teachers in "gut" courses may well obtain high ratings while rigorous teachers of difficult courses are likely to score poorly. . . .

Politics offers a number of interesting examples of the substitution of quantitative for qualitative measures. Presidential candidates are obsessed by their ratings in the polls and often adjust what they say or do to what the pollsters tell them is likely to increase their ratings. Even sitting presidents (and other politicians) are highly attuned to the polls. The emphasis often seems to be on their impact on the polls of taking a specific political position rather than the qualities of that position. . . .

Substitution of Non-Human Technology

In spite of Herculean efforts, there are important limits to the ability to rationalize what human beings think and do. Seemingly no matter what one does, people still retain at least the ultimate capacity to think and act in a variety of unanticipated ways. Thus, in spite of great efforts to make human behaviour more efficient, more predictable, more calculable, people continue to act in unforeseen ways. People continue to make home cooked meals from scratch, to camp in tents in the wild, to eat in old-fashioned diners, and to sabotage the assembly lines. Because of these realities, there is great interest among those who foster increasing rationality in using rational technologies to limit individual independence and ultimately to replace human beings with machines and other technologies that lack the ability to think and act in unpredictable ways.

McDonald's does not yet have robots to serve us food, but it does have teenagers whose ability to act autonomously is almost completely eliminated by techniques, procedures, routines, and machines. There are numerous examples of this including rules which prescribe all the things a counterperson should do in dealing with a customer as well as a large variety of technologies which determine the actions of workers such as drink dispensers which shut themselves off when the cup is full; buzzers, lights, and bells which indicate when food (e.g. French fries) is done; and cash registers which have the prices of each item programmed in. One of the latest attempts to constrain individual action is Denny's use of pre-measured packages of dehydrated food that are "cooked" simply by putting them under the hot water tap. Because of such tools and machines, as well as the elaborate rules dictating worker behaviour, people often feel like they are dealing with human robots when they relate to the personnel of a fast-food restaurant. When human robots are found, mechanical robots cannot be far behind. Once people are reduced to a few robot-like actions, it is a relatively easy step to replace them with mechanical robots. Thus Burgerworld is reportedly opening a prototypical restaurant in which mechanical robots serve the food.

Much of the recent history of work, especially manual work, is a history of efforts to replace human technology with non-human technology. Scientific management was oriented to the development of an elaborate and rigid set of rules about how jobs were to be done. The workers were to blindly and obediently follow those rules and not to do the work the way they saw fit. The various skills needed to perform a task were carefully delineated and broken down into a series of routine steps that could be taught to all workers. The skills, in other words, were built into the routines rather than belonging to skilled craftspersons. Similar points can be made about the assembly line which is basically a set of non-human technologies that have the needed steps and skills built into them. The human worker is reduced to performing a limited number of simple, repetitive operations. However, the control of this technology over the individual worker is so great and omnipresent that individual workers have reacted negatively manifesting such things as tardiness, absenteeism, turnover, and even sabotage. We are now witnessing a new stage in this technological development with automated processes now totally replacing many workers with robots. With the coming of robots we have reached the ultimate stage in the replacement of human with non-human technology. . . .

Control

This leads us to the fifth major dimension of rationalization—control. Rational systems are oriented toward, and structured to expedite, control in a variety of senses. At the most general level, we can say that rational systems are set up to allow for greater control over the uncertainties of life—birth, death, food production and distribution, housing, religious salvation, and many, many others. More specifically, rational systems are oriented to gaining greater control over the major source of uncertainty in social life—other people. Among other things, this means control over subordinates by superiors and control of clients and customers by workers. . . .

At a more specific level, the rationalization of food preparation and serving at McDonald's gives it great control over its employees. The automobile assembly line has a similar impact. In fact, the vast majority of the structures of a rational society exert extraordinary control over the people who labour in them. But because of the limits that still exist on the degree of control that rational structures can exercise over individuals, many rationalizing employers are driven to seek to more fully rationalize their operations and totally eliminate the worker. The result is an automated, robot-like technology over which, barring some *2001* rebellion, there is almost total control.

In addition to control over employees, rational systems are also interested in controlling the customer/clients they serve. For example, the fast-food restaurant with its counter, the absence of waiters and waitresses, the limited seating, and the drive-through windows all tend to lead customers to do certain things and not to do others.

CRITICAL READING QUESTIONS

1. How do McDonald's and other fast-food restaurants embody the ideas of rationalization?
2. What are the benefits of McDonaldization?
3. What are the costs of McDonaldization?
4. Ritzer outlines many other examples of things that have become "McDonaldized" in modern society, including camping, education, work, politics, and television. Take one of these examples, and outline how it has become more efficient, predictable, calculable, and controlled.

Undoubtedly, the process of rationalization occurs in modern society. As Ritzer notes, we cannot and should not try to stop it. There are many important benefits to rationalization. It allows us to produce a wider range of goods and services and to make them available to a much larger portion of the population. These goods are convenient and cheaper alternatives to higher-priced customized goods. Rationalization also allows us to create goods of uniform quality and to provide a sense of familiarity and stability for the consumer.

Does this mean that everything in modern society is rationalized or McDonaldized? Ritzer (2011) argues that two main types of organizations are not. First, organizations that are traceable to an earlier "premodern" age, such as independent corner stores or garage sales, are not McDonaldized. Moreover, some businesses are in direct opposition to McDonaldized companies. People who do not want to stay at a Holiday Inn or other chain hotel can stay at a bed and breakfast, where they get personalized attention and a homemade breakfast from a friendly proprietor. If you do not want to go to the rationalized Tim Horton's or Starbucks, you can go to an independent coffee shop.

Despite the existence of some non-rationalized parts of society, the general trend is toward increasing rationalization. Ritzer highlights how this can create what Weber

viafilms/iStockphoto

PHOTO 10.2 Lemonade stand kits rationalize the process of making a lemonade stand. They give you a sales banner, price sign, sell it as a way to "gain life-long business skills," and tell you that you will "achieve your highest lemonade sales imaginable!" This is certainly more efficient than having a child make their own sign or organize their own table. However, how does it reduce the creativity and diversity in the stands?

referred to as the **irrationality of rationality**. On a general level, the irrationality of rationality is simply that rationalized systems can create negative outcomes. For example, the rationalized education system, in which you have a student number and are judged based on your grade point average, can be alienating and frustrating. While it may be "fairer" to give each student a standardized test, doing so ignores a student's individuality. It is also irrational to think that each student understands the material in the same way.

The irrationality of rationality can also be seen in the fact that rationalized systems are sometimes unreasonable, which leads to negative effects. As previously mentioned, bureaucracies involve a lot of red tape (an excessive adherence to formal rules that hinders the functioning of organizations). Anyone who has filled out student loan forms has had first-hand experience with this phenomenon. If you have ever worked on a committee, such as a student council, think of the issues (such as decorations for a dance) that were long debated and went through an unnecessarily tedious approval process that was disproportionate to its significance.

Returning to Ritzer's main example, it is easy to see that the rationalized system of McDonald's has negative consequences. For example, McDonald's (and other fast-food restaurants) produces huge amounts of waste, which is bad for the environment. It also produces food that, although cheap and plentiful, leads to obesity and other health problems.

The 2004 documentary *Super Size Me* focuses on the negative health effects of McDonald's. The film follows Morgan Spurlock as he eats only McDonald's food for 30 days and experiences drastic changes to his physical and psychological well-being. Spurlock, then 32 years old, consumed an average of 5000 calories a day. He gained 24.5 pounds, increased his body mass by 13 per cent, and experienced mood swings and sexual dysfunction. It took only 30 days to gain the weight but 14 months to lose it.

One of the goals of McDonaldization is to make consumers' lives easier, yet rationalized systems also get consumers to do more of the labour originally assigned to workers. This practice allows corporations to save money on labour. For example, as we discussed in Chapter 4, consumers now pump their own gas, check out their own groceries, and do online banking, all under the facade that it is more efficient to do so. However, this is also beneficial for the company, which no longer has to hire as many staff to work at their stores.

Another potential drawback of rationalization and McDonaldization is that it produces a focus on efficiency and calculability that spreads to all aspects of our lives. In a rationalized world, we are encouraged to see everything through the lens of rationalization. For example, we come to see things that previously were viewed as having no monetary value as having a price.

Commodities are products that have some monetary value, are standardized, and are mass-produced by many different producers. Consumer goods, such as clothing, cars, and food, are commodities. **Commodification** is the transformation of what is normally a non-commodity into a commodity—that is, the assigning of monetary value. Commodification refers to the process through which social relations are reduced to an exchange relation, or as Karl Marx (Marx and Engels 1964) called it, "callous 'cash payment.'" Marx focused on the commodification of the labour process in which the real, material activity of labour by individual workers was transformed into abstract labour, just another cost in the process of production. The cost of labour could be measured in terms of hours and dollars.

Modern society has many examples of commodification. When we bottle water, we take something that was not seen as a commodity (it was something everyone could get free) and make it into one (something that is bought and sold). There are even oxygen bars where you can buy air. Imagine trying to explain to your grandparents that even air has to be bought! Other things that were never thought of as having a cash value are also now commodified. For example, human organs are bought and sold around the world, and people can pay women to be a surrogate mother for them. In a rationalized world, more and more realms of life are controlled by and valued with money.

In modern society, culture can also be commodified. The process can reduce ideas, customs, and behaviours to items that can be bought and sold. When culture is commodified, it becomes mass-produced and removed from its original meaning and significance.

There are many examples of the commodification of culture. Katy Perry's 2013 American Music Awards performance involved the use of Japanese cultural symbols, such as the kimono, traditional fans, and parasols. This use, which was unrelated to the song Perry performed ("Unconditionally"), was widely criticized. Critics argued that she was using Japanese culture to sell her song while misrepresenting it (for example, she dressed as a geisha without representing the historic and cultural meaning and altered her kimono to show her legs and cleavage). That same year, Selena Gomez performed at the MTV Music Awards wearing an Indian-inspired costume and wearing a bindi on her forehead. A bindi is a traditional Hindu marking on the forehead that has cultural and religious significance. Critics questioned her use of this symbol without any cultural context or explanation. Another common and recognizable cultural commodification is the T-shirt featuring a picture of Che Guevara, a major figure in the Cuban Revolution who subsequently became a symbol of rebellion and counterculture.

Dennis MacDonald / Alamy Stock Photo

PHOTO 10.3 This Las Vegas oxygen bar offers flavoured oxygen. This is based on the belief that extra oxygen to the brain might increase your mental performance—which could be useful at the casino! What is the effect of selling something like oxygen? How does it change the way we feel about it as something everyone should have access to?

The Commodification of Love

According to a Pew Research study on men's and women's attitudes and behaviours, 93 per cent of married people and 84 per cent of unmarried people say love is a very important reason to get married (Cohn 2013). The survey also found that men and women were equally likely to report that love is a very important reason to get married. People are clearly looking for love, which can be time-consuming. In a world where we are trying to accomplish tasks in the most efficient way possible, even the search for love can be commodified and rationalized.

The American novelist Jonathan Franzen (2012) wrote:

You can all supply your own favorite, most nauseating examples of the commodification of love. Mine include the wedding industry, TV ads that feature cute young children or the giving of automobiles as Christmas presents, and the particularly grotesque equation of diamond jewellery with everlasting devotion. The message, in each case, is that if you love somebody you should buy stuff.

Visit these websites, and then answer the following questions:

- eHarmony (www.eharmony.ca)
- J-Date (www.jdate.com)
- Tinder (www.tinder.com)

Continued

ACTIVITY

- Gay Dating (www.gaydating.com)
- Ashley Madison (www.ashleymadison.com)
- Just Lunch (www.itsjustlunch.com)

1. What features do these websites emphasize in the matching process? (How should you be picking a partner?)
2. How do these sites emphasize the four major components of rationality and McDonaldization?
3. How do the sites commodify love and sexuality?
4. Think of four more examples of how love is commodified and rationalized in modern society.
5. What are the benefits of this process of commodification and rationalization of love?
6. What are the costs of this process?

Indigenous symbols have long been appropriated and commodified. For example, sports teams such as the Cleveland Indians and the Washington Redskins have been criticized for their racist and negative depictions of Indigenous people. The clothing company Urban Outfitters has also caused controversy through its use of Navajo tribe patterns in their clothing designs. Use of Indigenous symbols at the 2010 Vancouver Olympics, particularly the Inuksuk (used by Inuit people to mark paths), was also criticized. Do you think that this instance is cultural commodification? Is it a positive or negative use of the symbol? Is it similar to, or different from, Katy Perry's or Selena Gomez's appropriation of cultural symbols?

Sarah Stewart / Alamy Stock Photo

PHOTO 10.4 Kim Kardashian wears cornrows in her hair. Do you think that this is cultural appropriation? Should we be able to use cultural symbols that are borrowed in this way? Why or why not?

The Division of Labour in Society

The question of what holds society together has long intrigued sociologists and other social scientists. As a structural functionalist, Émile Durkheim (1960) was interested in examining how things come to function as they do. His work focused on how the glue that holds society together has changed. We have moved from a time characterized by mechanical solidarity to one characterized by organic solidarity. As you will learn in Chapter 12, in a society exhibiting the former, cohesion and integration come from the fact that individuals are all the same. Small-scale "traditional" societies are based on mechanical solidarity. Think of a small village society in 1500. Most people in that village would do similar sorts of jobs, would have the same level of education (which would probably be quite low), and would be from the same religious and ethnic group.

Modern and industrial societies, such as Canada, are characterized by organic solidarity. In these societies, we are not tied together because we are so similar but because we are so different. People in modern societies are very diverse—they have different religious beliefs, come from different cultural traditions, and have different interests and values. However, we need one another because we are so specialized that we cannot survive without others who do different tasks.

For Durkheim, one of the major differences between societies based on mechanical solidarity and those based on organic solidarity is the extent to which these societies have a complex **division of labour** (the specialization of labour into specific and distinct tasks). Societies based on mechanical solidarity have very little division of labour—most people perform a variety of tasks to navigate their daily life. Everyone grows their own food, sews their own clothes, and makes their own candles.

A society based on organic solidarity has a much more complex division of labour, which has both advantages and disadvantages. If tasks are split into smaller and simpler units, we can hire cheaper unskilled labour to perform them. For example, if you no longer need to hire a tailor to design, measure, and sew your clothes but can have one person who only designs, one who only cuts material, and one who only sews, you can have people with fewer skills doing each job. Moreover, one worker is no longer instrumental to a whole factory. If your tailor quits, you are left with no means to get clothes. However, if the fabric cutter in a factory leaves, you can easily find another unskilled worker to do the job, and the overall production is not seriously affected. It is also possible to use more machinery when the tasks are broken down—a machine can cut material, but it cannot do all the parts of production. A high degree of division of labour is therefore a very efficient and cheap way of making products.

Scientific Management

Frederick Taylor developed the principle of **scientific management** (also known as **Taylorism**) within the manufacturing industries of the 1880s and 1890s. This theory applies scientific principles and methods to labour management and involves creating divisions in the labour process. Its methods sought to rationalize work and make it more efficient by dividing it into smaller and smaller tasks. Henry Ford, the founder of the Ford Motor Company, helped to perfect these ideas of scientific management at the turn of the nineteenth century. Ford developed the modern method of mass production, in particular the assembly line. Although Ford's methods of scientific management were used to improve the speed and standardization of production in the automotive industry, his principles have been applied to many manufacturing processes and other workplaces (Bonanno 2012).

Ford practised two main principles of scientific management: the standardization of products and the use of specialized equipment. Using scientific management, products are not handmade or unique. Instead, they are made with machines using moulds and models without the need for skilled craftspeople. This system of production relies on the use of specific machines and tools designed so that workers do not need specialized skills to work on the assembly line. A worker can easily be trained to do a small repetitive task and can be replaced without much difficulty (Beyon and Nichol 2006).

Increased efficiency and productivity are the two main benefits of scientific management. However, the system also has many disadvantages. For example, Taylor (1947) found that the workers he studied often became dissatisfied with the work environment and angry at their treatment by management. This was partly because, under scientific management, the conception of work was separated from its execution. Managers—with the help of efficiency experts—conceived of how the work was to be done, while the workers were expected to do what they were told in an unthinking and uncreative manner. Because workers were asked to do only one or a few repetitive tasks, most of their skills and abilities (including the ability to think) were not used. In general, scientific management

PHOTO 10.5 The Ford Motor Company's assembly lines are a classic example of mass production. Such scientific management made it possible to create the Ford Model T, the first automobile that a wide range of consumers could afford.

Science History Images / Alamy Stock Photo

separates "head" work from "hand" work. Before Taylor and other innovators of scientific management, the skilled worker performed both head and hand work by exercising control and creativity at work—they decided how they worked as well as doing the physical tasks of the work themselves. Taylor took the time to understand the head work that skilled workers were doing and then divided it into simpler, repetitive tasks that anyone could easily learn. As a result, workers had to do only easy and monotonous hand work.

Scientific management practices have had many far-reaching implications for how we work today. These systems of work led to **automation** whereby control systems for operating equipment are run with minimal or reduced human activity. The benefit of automation is that it saves labour (and, as a result, money for business owners) and can help to improve the quality and precision of the labour process. However, it can also lead to a loss of jobs and changes the nature of the work for those who remain on the assembly line—who now are just working with machines instead of fellow employees. **Outsourcing** is another major implication of scientific management. Because labour is divided into smaller and smaller components, companies can separate the production processes. And this often involves moving their manufacturing division, telephone call centre, or their entire business to another country in an attempt to save money.

HIGHLIGHT

Will Robots Replace Us All?

Imagine you walk into a grocery store, and there are no workers. Instead, a computer with facial recognition software welcomes you by name and directs you to the items that you are looking for. You select those items from a small area because there are only samples in the store. You scan them yourself with your phone and then leave (with nothing in your bag). Robots in the back of the store put the items you have selected into a box and a driverless car delivers them to your home that day. You never interact with another person.

This experience is an extreme example of automation, the process of replacing human labour with mechanical labour. About 46 per cent of the work done in Canada is at risk of being automated (Tencer 2017). This means that automation could replace the equivalent of 7.7 million Canadian jobs (Tencer 2017). Not all jobs are equally at risk. In fact, educational services, hospitals, and scientific jobs are the least likely to be automated, with only 30 per cent of the workforce in these areas at risk (see figure below).

Accommodation and food sales are the jobs most likely to be automated, with about 69 per cent of these jobs at risk of being replaced by machines. This is because half the time worked by salespeople and cashiers is spent on tasks that can be automated by technology that has already been invented. About one quarter of the salespeople's tasks could be automated this year, and 58 per cent could be automated by 2020 (Cain Miller 2017). You can see this when you go to a McDonald's and order from a computer or when you check out your groceries yourself at a grocery store.

Small regional economies specializing in manufacturing and resource extraction (such as mining, forestry, and fishing) are most susceptible to automation. For example, up to 48 per cent of the workers in Kitchener-Waterloo, 46 per cent of the workers in Hamilton, and 46 per cent of the workers in Calgary are at risk of automation (Tencer 2017)

Companies are embracing automation because it saves money, since they have fewer workers to pay. While the overall Canadian economy could benefit from these technological advances, we must also prepare for the job losses and greater income inequality that could come from automation. In order to deal with these problems, governments could spend money on education and skills training to help workers and businesses adjust to increased automation and job losses in certain industries (Blatchford 2017).

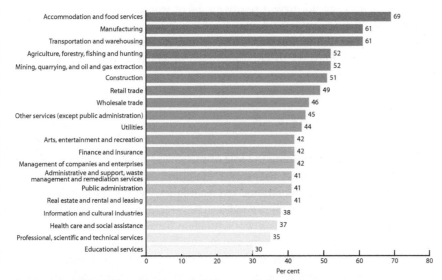

Per cent of work activities with the potential for automation, by industry

Source: McKinsey Global Institute, 2017, Brookfield Institute for Innovation + Entrepreneurship Analysis. This image was published in: "Mapping Automation." Brookfield Institute https://brookfieldinstitute.ca/commentary/mapping-automation/

This store relies on automated checkout counters where you scan and pay for your items without having to interact with a cashier. Businesses are moving toward automation to save money. What are the implications of this for the customers and the workers?

In scientific management, the worker is merely a cog in the machine. In fact, Taylor had a negative view of the worker. When describing the "average worker," he explains (Taylor 1947, 59):

Now one of the very first requirements for a man . . . is that he shall be so stupid and so phlegmatic that he more nearly resembles in his mental make-up the ox than any other type . . . He is so stupid that the word "percentage" has no meaning to him, and he must consequently be trained by a man more intelligent than himself into the habit of working in accordance with the laws of this science before he can be successful.

Henry Ford also did not have a positive view of workers. In his autobiography, he explains that "repetitive labor—the doing of one thing over and over again and always in the same way—is a terrifying prospect to a certain kind of man. It is terrifying to me . . . The average worker, I am sorry to say, wants a job in which he does not have to think" (Ford 1922, 103).

The Alienation of Labour

Marx, who spent his life examining the role of social class in society, feared the effect of these types of labour changes on the worker. He clearly noted that work in capitalism, using scientific management and rationalized techniques, was very productive (Marx and Engels 1964). Under capitalism, more goods can be created faster than ever before. However, Marx also noted that capitalism was a problem because it distorted the process of work, something that should be creative and enjoyable for the worker.

This distortion occurs in four main ways. First, capitalism transforms a naturally social and collective activity into a process that is about pursuing one's own interests. Workers compete with each other for jobs or promotions, while capitalists try to maximize profits by exploiting workers. Second, in capitalism, workers create wealth through their labour and the goods they produce, but they get only a small portion of this money. If a person works faster or more productively, the additional profit (surplus) does not go to him but to the capitalist.

Third, as the division of labour in jobs increases, more surplus is created for capitalists. However, this change reduces the natural enjoyment of labour. Before the rise of factories, workers could labour in their own small cottage industries. A cobbler making shoes in his own family business has creative control over the process and the enjoyment of creating the whole product. In modern factories or other work settings, workers all perform smaller portions of jobs that are less enjoyable. It is much less satisfying to add the sole to a hundred identical shoes a day in a factory than to make three beautiful unique pairs of shoes in your independent business.

Finally, according to Marx, capitalism distorts work because it separates workers from the product they make, the production process, other workers, and themselves. Workers are **alienated** from the product because they have no creative control over what they make. They are alienated from the production process because they have no control over how they work—they do not create the assembly lines or stores in which they labour or have any control over how they make their products. They are alienated from other workers because they are separated from others on the assembly line and are forced to compete with the other workers. They are alienated from themselves because the process of work has become routine and exploitative. These four types of alienation were, for Marx, the by-product of capitalism. The rise of scientific management, spearheaded by people such as Taylor and Ford, furthered these problems.

Changes in Work in Canada

The nature of work in the Canadian economy has changed significantly over the past 100 years. One major change is in the types of jobs that workers perform and the economic sector in which they work. The economy has three major sectors. The **primary**

sector extracts or harvests resources. Activities associated with the primary sector include mining, forestry, farming, and fishing. This sector has seen a sharp decline over the past 50 years. While 48 per cent of the 1951 workforce was engaged in this type of work (mostly in the extraction of natural resources), only 3.5 per cent was employed in the primary sector in 2016 (see Figure 10.1).

The **secondary sector** manufactures finished goods. This part of the economy includes automobile production, textile manufacturing, and construction. This sector has also declined, although not to the same extent as the primary sector. As Figure 10.1 shows, the amount of the population involved in this sector has dropped to approximately 18 per cent.

The **tertiary sector** of the economy is the service industry, including services to individuals and businesses. Retail sales, transportation and distribution, entertainment, the hospitality industry, tourism, banking, health care, and law are all part of this sector. The service sector is increasing rapidly in Canada—from 21 per cent of employees in 1951 to 78.5 per cent in 2016.

Service sector jobs tend to have lower wages than other occupations. Eight out of the 10 lowest-paying jobs in Canada are service sector jobs (Statistics Canada 2017). This includes bartenders, food service workers, hosts/hostesses, food counter attendants, gas station attendants, shoe repair persons, hairstylists, and cashiers. Canadians working in goods-producing industries such as manufacturing make, on average, $24.83 per hour compared with those working in accommodation and food services, who make on average $14.10 an hour. However, it is important to note that the service sector includes a great level of diversity in earnings. Some jobs, such as those in health care, teaching, and management, require high levels of education and training. These jobs tend to pay considerably more than those in manufacturing and other goods-producing jobs. Occupations within the service sector requiring less education, such as hospitality and retail services, tend to make very low wages (Statistics Canada 2017).

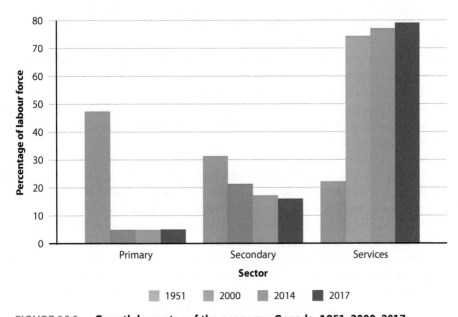

FIGURE 10.1   **Growth by sector of the economy, Canada, 1951, 2000, 2017**

Sources: Adapted from Chris O'Halloran, "Workers of Tomorrow: A Position Paper on the Promise and Problem of Young Workers and Unions," Service Sector Growth, https://d3n8a8pro7vhmx.cloudfront.net/afl/pages/2401/attachments/original/1257453539/pp-youth.pdf?1257453539; Statistics Canada, 2018, *Labour Force Characteristics by Industry, Annual (x 1,000)*, Catalogue no. 14-10-0023-01, Ottawa: Statistics Canada, http://www.statcan.gc.ca/tables-tableaux/sum-som/l01/cst01/labor10a-eng.htm

HIGHLIGHT

Even Kids Have a Wage Gap

The wage gap appears to begin in childhood. According to a 2009 University of Michigan survey, girls spend an average of two more hours per week on household chores than boys do. Another survey found that boys tend to make more money for completing chores than do girls. This is, in part, because boys tend to perform different types of chores from those that girls do and these chores earn better pay. For example, mowing the lawn or shoveling snow (chores that boys are more likely to perform) earns higher allowance wages than folding laundry or helping with cooking (chores associated with girls).

While it is clear that these divisions are not rigid, and many girls and boys perform each type of chore, this division perpetuates larger-scale inequalities in the labour force (Chemaly 2013).

Precarious Employment

Service sector jobs vary considerably not only in their wages but also in their stability and potential for promotion. Government jobs, teaching, and business are considered "good" service jobs because of their higher pay, job security, and possibility for advancement. Service jobs in retail sales and food services tend to lack these advantages. This second set of jobs, sometimes called McJobs, is **precarious employment**. Precarious work typically gives employers full control over their workers' labour process. Companies are able to hire and fire employees with ease and frequency, since the kind of work they typically do makes them readily replaceable. Precarious labour is characterized by the "three Ds"—dirty, dangerous, and demeaning.

RESEARCH METHOD
SURVEY

RESEARCH METHOD
INTERVIEW

A large study conducted at McMaster University in 2013 combined data from a survey of 3244 workers and 82 interviews (PEPSO, McMaster University, and United Way Toronto 2013). The study found that at least 20 per cent of Canadians work in precarious employment and that this area had grown by nearly 50 per cent in the previous 20 years. Research also shows that immigrants, visible minorities, and women tend to be overrepresented in these types of jobs.

Access Alliance Canada's (2013) report *Where Are the Good Jobs?* highlights the serious consequences of precarious employment (see also Shakya and Janczur 2013). This research shows how being stuck in these jobs causes harmful economic, social, and health effects. The researchers interviewed precariously employed individuals and found that despite working multiple jobs, most of them were living close to the poverty line. They reported that the precarious nature of their employment spilled into other areas of their lives, making decisions about things such as family, housing, and relationships difficult. The health impacts—workplace injuries, as well as depression, chronic pain, diabetes, and heart disease—are particularly concerning. These issues are even more difficult to deal with because most precariously employed individuals do not tend to have health benefits, including extended health coverage or sick leave.

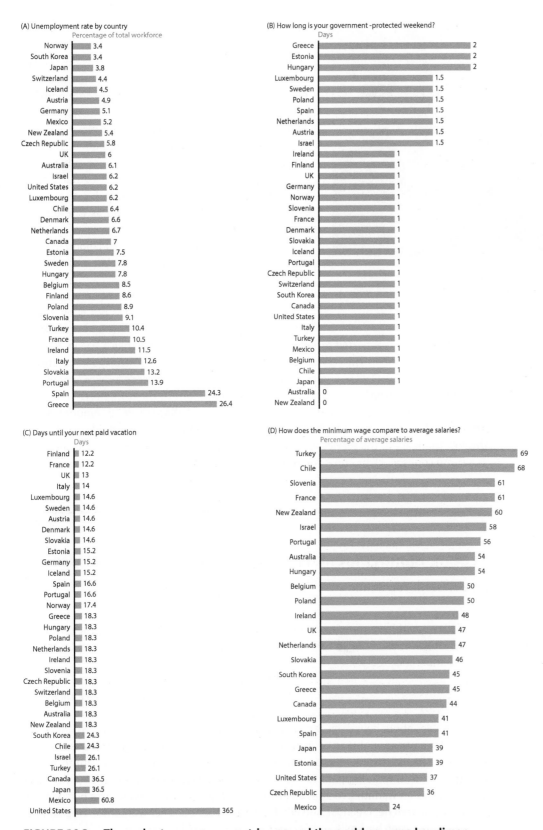

(A) Unemployment rate by country
Percentage of total workforce

Norway	3.4
South Korea	3.4
Japan	3.8
Switzerland	4.4
Iceland	4.5
Austria	4.9
Germany	5.1
Mexico	5.2
New Zealand	5.4
Czech Republic	5.8
UK	6
Australia	6.1
Israel	6.2
United States	6.2
Luxembourg	6.2
Chile	6.4
Denmark	6.6
Netherlands	6.7
Canada	7
Estonia	7.5
Sweden	7.8
Hungary	7.8
Belgium	8.5
Finland	8.6
Poland	8.9
Slovenia	9.1
Turkey	10.4
France	10.5
Ireland	11.5
Italy	12.6
Slovakia	13.2
Portugal	13.9
Spain	24.3
Greece	26.4

(B) How long is your government-protected weekend?
Days

Greece	2
Estonia	2
Hungary	2
Luxembourg	1.5
Sweden	1.5
Poland	1.5
Spain	1.5
Netherlands	1.5
Austria	1.5
Israel	1.5
Ireland	1
Finland	1
UK	1
Germany	1
Norway	1
Slovenia	1
France	1
Denmark	1
Slovakia	1
Iceland	1
Portugal	1
Czech Republic	1
Switzerland	1
South Korea	1
Canada	1
United States	1
Italy	1
Turkey	1
Mexico	1
Belgium	1
Chile	1
Japan	1
Australia	0
New Zealand	0

(C) Days until your next paid vacation
Days

Finland	12.2
France	12.2
UK	13
Italy	14
Luxembourg	14.6
Sweden	14.6
Austria	14.6
Denmark	14.6
Slovakia	14.6
Estonia	15.2
Germany	15.2
Iceland	15.2
Spain	16.6
Portugal	16.6
Norway	17.4
Greece	18.3
Hungary	18.3
Poland	18.3
Netherlands	18.3
Ireland	18.3
Slovenia	18.3
Czech Republic	18.3
Switzerland	18.3
Belgium	18.3
Australia	18.3
New Zealand	18.3
South Korea	24.3
Chile	24.3
Israel	26.1
Turkey	26.1
Canada	36.5
Japan	36.5
Mexico	60.8
United States	365

(D) How does the minimum wage compare to average salaries?
Percentage of average salaries

Turkey	69
Chile	68
Slovenia	61
France	61
New Zealand	60
Israel	58
Portugal	56
Australia	54
Hungary	54
Belgium	50
Poland	50
Ireland	48
UK	47
Netherlands	47
Slovakia	46
South Korea	45
Greece	45
Canada	44
Luxembourg	41
Spain	41
Japan	39
Estonia	39
United States	37
Czech Republic	36
Mexico	24

FIGURE 10.2 **These charts compare countries around the world on some key dimensions of working rights and conditions. Compare the unemployment rates, minimum wages, and regulations around weekend and vacation times across countries. Where would you want to live and work?**

Source: Richard Macauley, 2014, "The World's Most Worker-Friendly Countries, in Seven Charts," *Quartz* 30 December, https://qz.com/302264/the-best-places-in-the-world-to-work-in-7-charts

PHOTO 10.6 Along with customer service professionals and nurses, psychologists, counsellors, social workers, and therapists perform emotional labour as a major part of their daily responsibilities.

RESEARCH METHOD
INTERVIEW

Emotional Labour

Another challenge of service sector work is the need to engage in **emotional labour** (the emotional management done by workers and a process of commodifying emotional displays at work). Arlie Russell Hochschild (1983) defines the term as the result of work that involves direct contact with the public. Through this contact, the employee is expected not only to provide the public with a product or service but also to make the customer feel a certain way. Employees are trained to do this by employers, and as a result, the employer controls the emotional responses of employees. Through the process of emotional labour, workers must control their own feelings to achieve the desired effect in others.

Nurses, servers, and telemarketers, among others, must perform emotional labour. It is not enough that a nurse takes your blood; he must chat and smile while doing it. A server is expected to welcome you warmly and treat you like a friend, not just bring you your dinner. The service sector often requires workers to engage in emotional labour. Hochschild (1983) argues that this emotional labour leads service workers to become alienated from themselves and their own emotions in the workplace.

Hochschild (1983) looks at a variety of professions that engage in emotion work. One of the best examples is flight attendant. As you read about Hochschild's research on this job, think about the service work that you have done (in a restaurant, as a babysitter, as a camp counsellor) and how you might have engaged in emotional labour in this job.

READING

Feeling Management: From Private to Commercial Uses

Arlie Russell Hochschild

> If they could have turned every one of us into sweet quiet Southern belles with velvet voices like Rosalyn Carter, this is what they would want to stamp out on an assembly line.
>
> —Flight attendant, Delta Airlines

. . . When rules about how to feel and how to express feeling are set by management, when workers have weaker rights to courtesy than customers do, when deep and surface acting are forms of labour to be sold, and when private capacities for empathy and warmth are put to corporate uses, what happens to the way a person relates to her feelings or to her face? When worked-up warmth becomes an instrument of service work, what can a person learn about herself from her feelings? And when a worker abandons her work smile, what kind of tie remains between her smile and her self?

Hochschild, Arlie Russell. 2009. "Feeling Management: From Private to Commerial Uses," *The Managed Heart: Commercialization of Human Feeling*, 2nd edn, pp. 89–136. Berkeley: University of California Press.

Display is what is sold, but over the long run display comes to assume a certain relation to feeling. As enlightened management realizes, a separation of display and feeling is hard to keep up over long periods. A principle of *emotive dissonance*, analogous to the principle of cognitive dissonance, is at work. Maintaining a difference between feeling and feigning over the long run leads to strain. We try to reduce this strain by pulling the two closer together either by changing what we feel or by changing what we feign. When display is required by the job, it is usually feeling that has to change; and when conditions estrange us from our face, they sometimes estrange us from feeling as well.

Take the case of the flight attendant. Corporate logic in the airline industry creates a series of links between competition, market expansion, advertising, heightened passenger expectations about rights to display, and company demands for acting. When conditions allow this logic to work, the result is a successful transmutation of the private emotional system we have described. The old elements of emotional exchange—feeling rules, surface acting, and deep acting—are now arranged in a different way. Stanislavski's *if* moves from stage to airline cabin ("act as if the cabin were your own living room") as does the actor's use of emotion memory. Private use gives way to corporate use. . . .

Behind the Demand for Acting

"A market for emotional labour" is not a phrase that company employees use. Upper management talks about getting the best market share of the flying public. Advertising personnel talk about reaching that market. In-flight service supervisors talk about getting "positive attitude" and "professional service" from flight attendants, who in turn talk about "handling rates." Nevertheless, the efforts of these four groups, taken together, set up the sale of emotional labour. . . .

As competition grew from the 1930s through the early 1970s, the airlines expanded that visible role [with the customer]. Through the 1950s and 1960s the flight attendant became a main subject of airline advertising, the spearhead of market expansion.[1] The image they chose, among many possible ones, was that of a beautiful and smartly dressed Southern white woman, the supposed epitome of gracious manners and warm personal service.[2]

Because airline ads raise expectations, they subtly rewrite job descriptions and redefine roles. . . .

The ads promise service that is "human" and personal. The omnipresent smile suggests, first of all, that the flight attendant is friendly, helpful, and open to requests. But when words are added, the smile can be sexualized, as in "We really move our tails for you to make your every wish come true" (Continental), or "Fly me, you'll like it" (National). Such innuendos lend strength to the conventional fantasy that in the air, anything can happen. As one flight attendant put it: "You have married men with three kids getting on the plane and suddenly they feel anything goes. It's like they leave that reality on the ground, and you fit into their fantasy as some geisha girl. It happens over and over again." . . .

Behind the Supply of Acting: Selection

Even before an applicant for a flight attendant's job is interviewed, she is introduced to the rules of the game. Success will depend in part on whether she has a knack for perceiving the rules and taking them seriously. Applicants are urged to read a preinterview pamphlet before coming in. In the 1979–1980 *Airline Guide to Stewardess and Steward Careers*, there is a section called "The Interview." Under the subheading "Appearance," the manual suggests that facial expressions should be "sincere" and "unaffected." One should have a "modest but friendly smile" and be "generally alert, attentive, not overly aggressive, but not reticent either." Under "Mannerisms," subheading "Friendliness," it is suggested that a successful candidate must be "outgoing but not effusive," "enthusiastic with calm and poise," and "vivacious but not effervescent." As the manual continues: "Maintaining eye contact with the interviewer demonstrates sincerity and confidence, but don't overdo it. Avoid cold or continuous staring." Training, it seems, begins even before recruitment. . . .

Different companies favour different variations of the ideal type of sociability. Veteran employees talk about differences in company personality as matter-of-factly as they talk about differences in uniform or shoe style. United Airlines, the consensus has it, is "the girl-next-door," the neighbourhood babysitter grown up. Pan Am is upper class, sophisticated, and slightly reserved in its graciousness. PSA is brassy, fun-loving, and sexy. . . .

The trainees, it seemed to me, were also chosen for their ability to take stage directions about how to "project" an image. They were selected for being able to act well—that is, without showing the effort involved. They had to be able to appear at home on stage. . . .

Somewhat humbled and displaced, the worker was now prepared to identify with Delta. Delta was described as a brilliant financial success (which it is), an airline known for fine treatment of its personnel (also true, for the most part), a company with a history of the "personal touch." Orientation talks described the company's beginnings as a family enterprise in the 1920s, when the founder, Collett Woolman, personally pinned an orchid on each new flight attendant. It was the flight attendant's job to represent the company proudly, and actually identifying with the company would make that easier to do.

Training seemed to foster the sense that it was safe to feel dependent on the company. Temporarily rootless, the worker was encouraged to believe that this company of 36,000 employees operated as a "family." The head of the training centre, a gentle, wise, authoritative figure in her fifties, appeared each morning in the auditorium; she was "mommy," the real authority on day-to-day problems. Her company superior, a slightly younger man, seemed to be "daddy." Other supervisors were introduced as concerned extensions of these initial training parents. (The vast majority of trainees were between 19 and 22 years old.) As one speaker told the recruits: "Your supervisor is your friend. You can go to her and talk about anything, and I mean *anything*." The trainees were divided up into small groups; one class of 123 students (which included 3 males and 9 blacks) was divided into four sub-groups, each yielding the more intimate ties of solidarity that were to be the prototype of later bonds at work. . . .

Beyond this, there were actual appeals to modify feeling states. The deepest appeal in the Delta training program was to the trainee's capacity to act as if the airplane cabin (where she works) were her home (where she doesn't work). Trainees were asked to think of a passenger *as if* he were a "personal guest in your living room." The workers' emotional memories of offering personal hospitality were called up and put to use, as Stanislavski would recommend. As one recent graduate put it:

> You think how the new person resembles someone you know. *You see your sister's eyes in someone sitting at that seat.* That makes you want to put out for them. I like to think of the cabin as the living room of my own home. When someone drops in [at home], you may not know them, but you get something for them. You put that on a grand scale—thirty-six passengers per flight attendant—but *it's the same feeling.*

On the face of it, the analogy between home and airplane cabin unites different kinds of experiences and obscures what is different about them. It can unite the empathy of friend for friend with the empathy of worker for customer, because it assumes that empathy is the *same sort of feeling* in either case. Trainees wrote in their notebooks, "Adopt the passenger's point of view," and the understanding was that this could be done in the same way one adopts a friend's point of view. The analogy between home and cabin also joins the worker to her company; just as she naturally protects members of her own family, she will naturally defend the company. Impersonal relations are to be seen *as if* they were personal. Relations based on getting and giving money are to be seen *as if* they were relations free of money. The company brilliantly extends and uses its workers' basic human empathy, all the while maintaining that it is not interfering in their "personal" lives. . . .

Collective Emotional Labour

To thwart cynicism about the living room analogy, to catch it as it collapses in the face of other realizations, the company eye shifts to another field of emotion work—the field in which flight attendants interact with each other. This is a strategic point of entry for the company because if the company can influence how flight attendants deal with each other's feeling on the job, it can assure proper support for private emotion management.

As trainers well know, flight attendants typically work in teams of two and must work on fairly intimate terms with all others on the crew. In fact, workers commonly say the work simply cannot be done well unless they work well together. The reason for this is that the job is partly an "emotional tone" road show, and the proper tone is kept up in large part by friendly conversation, banter, and joking, as ice cubes, trays, and plastic cups are passed from aisle to aisle to the galley, down to the kitchen, and up again. Indeed, starting with the bus ride to the plane, by bantering back and forth the flight attendant does important relational work: she checks on people's moods, relaxes tension, and warms up ties so that each pair of individuals becomes a team. She also banters to keep herself in the right frame of mind. As one worker put it, "Oh, we banter a lot. It keeps you going. You last longer." . . .

Once established, team solidarity can have two effects. It can improve morale and thus improve service. But it can also become the basis for sharing grudges against the passengers or the company. Perhaps it is the second possibility that trainers meant to avoid when in Recurrent Training they offered examples of "bad" social emotion management. One teacher cautioned her students: "When you're angry with a passenger, don't head for the galley to blow off steam with another flight attendant." In the galley, the second flight attendant, instead of calming the angry worker down, may further rile her up; she may become an accomplice to the aggrieved worker. Then, as the instructor put it, "There'll be *two* of you hot to trot."

The message was, when you're angry, go to a teammate who will calm you down. Support for anger or a sense of grievance—regardless of what inspires it—is bad for service and bad for the company. Thus, the informal ways in which workers check on the legitimacy of a grievance or look for support in blowing off steam become points of entry for company "suggestions." . . .

Achieving the Transmutation

To the extent that emotion management actually works—so that Bloody Marys do not spill "by accident" on white pantsuits, and blowups occur in backstage offices instead of in airplane aisles—something like alchemy occurs. Civility and a general sense of well-being have been enhanced and emotional "pollution" controlled. Even when people are paid to be nice, it is hard for them to be nice at all times, and when their efforts succeed, it is a remarkable accomplishment.

What makes this accomplishment possible is a transmutation of three basic elements of emotional life: emotion work, feeling rules, and social exchange.

First, emotion work is no longer a private act but a public act, bought on the one hand and sold on the other. Those who direct emotion work are no longer the individuals themselves but are instead paid stage managers who select, train, and supervise others.

Second, feeling rules are no longer simply matters of personal discretion, negotiated with another person in private but are spelled out publicly—in the *Airline Guide to Stewardess and Steward Careers*, in the *World Airways Flight Manual*, in training programs, and in the discourse of supervisors at all levels.

Third, social exchange is forced into narrow channels; there may be hiding places along shore, but there is much less room for individual navigation of the emotional waters.

The whole system of emotional exchange in private life has as its ostensible purpose the welfare and pleasure of the people involved. When this emotional system is thrust into a commercial setting, it is transmuted. A profit motive is slipped in under acts of emotion management, under the rules that govern them, under the gift exchange. Who benefits now, and who pays? . . .

In relation to each issue, emotional labour poses a challenge to a person's sense of self. In each case, the problem was not one that would cause much concern among those who do not do emotional labour—the assembly line worker or the wallpaper machine operator, for example. In each case the issue of estrangement between what a person senses as her "true self" and her inner and outer acting becomes something to work out, to take a position on.

When a flight attendant feels that her smile is "not an indication of how she really feels," or when she feels that her deep or surface acting is not meaningful, it is a sign that she is straining to disguise the failure of a more general transmutation. It indicates that emotion work now performed on a commercial stage, with commercial directors and standardized props, is failing to involve the actors or convince the audience in a way that it once did.

When feelings are successfully commercialized, the worker does not feel phony or alien; she feels somehow satisfied in how personal her service actually was. Deep acting is a help in doing this, not a source of estrangement. But when commercialization of feeling as a general process collapses into its separate elements, display becomes hollow and emotional labour is withdrawn. The task becomes one of disguising the failed transmutation. In either case, whether proudly or resentfully, face and feelings have been used as instruments. An American Airlines worker said: "Do you know what they call us when we get sick? *Breakage*. How's that for a 'positive attitude'? Breakage is what they call people that go to the complaint service to cancel for illness." Or again, as a San Francisco base manager at United remarked ruefully: "And we call them bodies. Do we have enough 'bodies' for the flight?" Feeling can become an instrument, but whose instrument?

CRITICAL READING QUESTIONS

1. Why do organizations want workers to perform emotional labour? What function does it serve?
2. What are the costs of emotional labour for the employee? How can these problems be dealt with by the employee?
3. How does the performance of emotional labour relate to Goffman's dramaturgical perspective (see Chapter 2)?

NOTES

1. When an airline commands a market monopoly, as it is likely to do when it is owned by government, it does not need to compete for passengers by advertising friendly flight attendants. Many flight attendants told me that their counterparts on Lufthansa (the German national airline) and even more on El Al and Aeroflot (the Israeli and Russian national airlines) were notably lacking in assertive friendliness.
2. A black female flight attendant, who had been hired in the early 1970s when Delta faced an affirmative action suit, wondered aloud why blacks were not pictured in local Georgia advertising. She concluded: "They want that market, and that market doesn't include blacks. They go along with that." Although Delta's central offices are in Atlanta, which is predominantly black, few blacks worked for Delta in capacity.

ACTIVITY

Training Employees for Emotional Labour

Organizations in a variety of industries actively work to teach their employees to engage in emotional labour. Go to this book's companion website to watch two customer service training videos, and then answer the following questions:

1. What is the point of these videos? How do they relate to the concept of emotional labour?
2. In the longer version of the customer service training video, the narrator explains that customer service representatives should aim to show they care, show they understand, and make the customer feel that he can trust them to take care of the situation. How are each of these tasks related to emotional labour?

3. The videos often discuss the need to apologize. Why do the trainers feel that apologizing is important? How could apologizing cause problems for an employee?

The next set of questions relates to a University of Memphis study of how effective employees are at emotional labour. Go to this book's companion website to watch a video regarding this research, and then answer the following questions.

1. Do you think Julianne Pierce's test to assess an employee's ability to perform emotional labour is useful? What does this test measure well, and how could it be improved?
2. What is the difference between **surface acting** and **deep acting**? What are the costs of surface acting for the employee? How do these concepts relate to what you learned from Hochschild's article?
3. How does the video suggest that employees could be more satisfied at work? Do you think that this plan would work? Why or why not?
4. If you've had a service industry job, such as a restaurant server or salesperson, how did you feel about performing emotional labour? Did you have to represent a certain type of identity as a representative of your company?
5. How do employees sometimes resist companies' attempts to force them to engage in emotional labour? Are these techniques effective? Why or why not?

Summary

We began this chapter by learning about Weber's theory of rationalization in modern society and examining the rise of bureaucracies as a prototype of this process. George Ritzer built on Weber's theory by applying the idea of rationalization to the development of McDonald's and showing how much of modern society is becoming "McDonaldized." One of the by-products of this situation is the increasing commodification of many elements of our lives, from products and our labour to culture and love. We then turned to another major change in modern society, discussed by Durkheim—the increased division of labour over time. This division of labour is seen in processes of scientific management, developed by Taylor and Ford, and, according to Marx, can lead to feelings of alienation for workers. Finally, we discussed changes in work in Canada, including the rise of the service sector, precarious employment, and emotional labour.

Key Terms

alienation 292
automation 290
bureaucracy 280
commodification 286
commodity 286
deep acting 301
disenchantment of the world 279
division of labour 288
emotional labour 296
irrationality of rationality 286

McDonaldization 281
outsourcing 290
precarious employment 294
primary sector 292
rationalization 279
scientific management (Taylorism) 289
secondary sector 293
surface acting 301
tertiary (service) sector 293

For Further Reading

Hochschild, Arlie Russell. 1983. *The Managed Heart: Commercialization of Human Feeling*. Berkeley: University of California Press.

Marx, Karl, and Friedrich Engels. 1964. *The Communist Manifesto*. New York: Modern Reader Paperbacks.

Ritzer, George. 2011. *The McDonaldization of Society*, 6th edn. Los Angeles: Sage.

Weber, Max. 1965. *The Sociology of Religion*. London: Methuen.

——— 1968. *Economy and Society*, vol. 1, ch. 2–4. New York: Bedminster.

References

Access Alliance. 2013. *Where Are the Good Jobs? Ten Stories of "Working Rough, Living Poor."* Toronto: Access Alliance Multicultural Health and Community Services. http://accessalliance.ca/sites/accessalliance.files/Summary_Where%20are%20the%20Good%20Jobs%20Report% 202013.pdf.

Beyon, Huw, and Theo Nichol, eds. 2006. *The Fordism of Ford and Modern Management: Fordism and Post-Fordism*. Cheltenham, UK: Elgar.

Blatchford, Andy. 2017. "Bank of Canada Warns of Rising Inequality from Automation." *Huffington Post Business* 18 April. http://www.huffingtonpost.ca/2017/04/18/automation-canada-inequality-bank-of-canada_n_16084044.html.

Bonanno, Allessandro. 2012. "Fordism post Fordism." In George Ritzer, ed., *The Encyclopedia of Globalization*, 680–2. Malden, MA: Wiley-Blackwell.

Cain Miller, Claire. 2017. "Amazon's Move Signals End of Line for Many Cashiers." *The New York Times* 18 June. https://www.nytimes.com/2017/06/17/upshot/amazons-move-signals-end-of-line-for-many-cashiers.html.

Chemaly, Soroya. 2013. "Even Little Kids Have a Wage Gap." Salon.com 15 August. http://www.salon.com/2013/08/15/even_little_kids_have_a_wage_gap.

Cohn, D'Vera. 2013. "Love and Marriage." Pew Research Social and Demographic Trends. http://www.pewsocialtrends.org/2013/02/13/love-and-marriage.

Durkheim, Émile. 1960. *The Division of Labour in Society*. Glencoe, IL: Free Press.

Ford, Henry. 1922. *My Life and Work*. Garden City, NY: Doubleday.

Franzen, Jonathan. 2012. *Farther Away: Essays*. New York: Farrar, Straus, and Giroux.

Hochschild, Arlie Russell. 1983. *The Managed Heart: Commercialization of Human Feeling*. Berkeley: University of California Press.

James, Randy. 2009. "A Brief History of McDonalds Abroad." Times.com 28 October. http://content.time.com/time/world/article/0,8599,1932839,00.html.

Marx, Karl, and Friedrich Engels. 1964. *The Communist Manifesto*. New York: Modern Reader Paperbacks.

PEPSO (Poverty and Employment Precarity in Southern Ontario), McMaster University, and United Way Toronto. 2013. "It's More Than Poverty: Employment Precarity and Household Well-Being." Toronto: United Way.

Ritzer, George. 2011. *The McDonaldization of Society*, 6th edn. Los Angeles: Sage.

Shakya, Yogendra B., and Axelle Janczur. 2013. "Where Are the Good Jobs?" *Toronto Star* 30 July.

Statistics Canada. 2017. "The 10 Occupations with the Lowest Average Full Time Hourly Wage, 2016." CANSIM Table 285-0050. http://www.statcan.gc.ca/daily-quotidien/170615/t002a-eng.htm.

Taylor, Frederick W. 1947. *The Principles of Scientific Management*. New York: Harper & Row.

Tencer, Daniel. 2017. "Canadian Cities and Industries Most at Risk from Automation." *Huffington Post* 9 June. https://www.huffingtonpost.ca/2017/06/09/automation-forecast-canada_n_17017124.html.

Weber, Max. 1965. *The Sociology of Religion*. London: Methuen.

11 Health

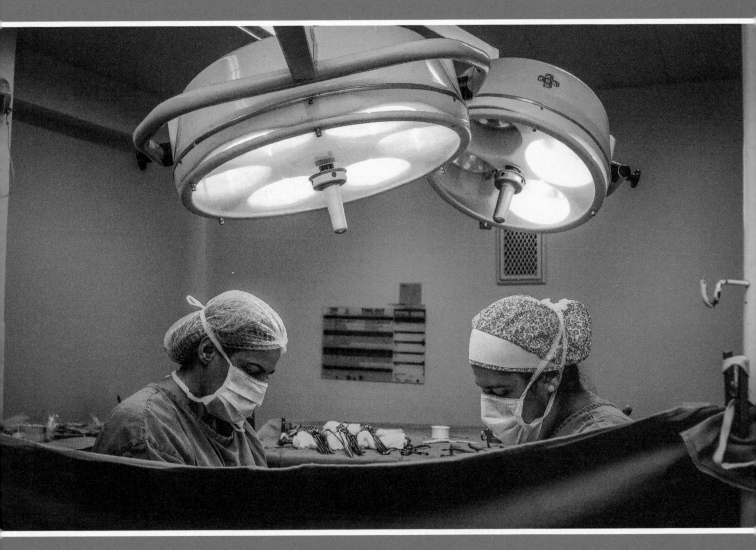

Chapter Outline

Photo Credit: Vidal Balielo Jr./Pexels

What Is Health?

We all want to be "healthy." But what does that mean? According to the World Health Organization, **health** is "a state of complete physical, mental and social well-being" (WHO 2017a). This definition of health encompasses more than simply not being physically ill. It also requires mental health and social connections with others. Let's consider each of these components of health.

Physical health is related to the functioning of the body. We can have physical illnesses that are short-term or prolonged. Short-term illnesses include having a cold or stomach distress, both of which last less than a week. Other physical health issues are more prolonged, such as arthritis. Physical illnesses can also be acute or chronic. Acute illnesses are severe and begin quickly, such as breaking an arm. Chronic illnesses are slow to develop and longer-term, such as asthma. When we think of health, we often focus on physical health because physical illnesses and injuries can be easier to see or diagnose.

Mental health is a state of "well-being in which every individual realizes his or her own potential, can cope with the normal stresses of life, can work productively and fruitfully, and is able to make a contribution to her or his community" (WHO 2017a). While mental health issues can be harder to see, they are also critical to our functioning in society and our ability to enjoy happy and fruitful lives. Both physical and mental health can differ across individuals. What is "normal" mental or physical health is not the same for everyone. Just as some people have higher or lower blood pressure as part of the normal functioning of their bodies, people's mental health differs. However, mental health issues are related to one's ability to cope with the regular problems and issues that come up in one's life.

The World Health Organization's definition of health also focuses on social health. This is something that we do not tend to consider when thinking about whether someone is "healthy" or "unhealthy." Sociologists who study health are very interested in the role of social connections in our health. Much research shows that the more integrated an individual is with others and with institutions in our society, the healthier they tend to be. Think back on Durkheim's early study of suicide. He argued that one of the main predictors of death by suicide was a lack of social integration. Even since the early days of our discipline, sociologists have recognized the critical importance of social integration to our health!

HIGHLIGHT

Mental Health on Campus

Mental health is an important issue on university and college campuses. A survey from the Center for Innovation in Campus Mental Health (2017) found that about one in five students at post-secondary institutions used mental health services on their campus each year. Most of these students were dealing with anxiety, depression, and relationship problems (AUCCCD 2014). Suicidal thoughts, self-injury, and alcohol abuse were also significant reasons that students accessed mental health services on their campuses.

Accessing mental health services can be very important for students. It helps students to deal with the stresses of university life and can have positive effects on their classes, relationships, and lives. In fact, 70 per cent of students who went to counselling services on their campuses said that going to these services helped with their academic performance (AUCCCD 2014).

However, not all students use counselling services when they experience stress and anxiety. While males make up 44 per cent of university students, they only account for 34 per cent of those who seek help at counselling centres (AUCCCD 2014). The relationship between gender and seeking mental health help highlights the importance of traditional conceptions of masculinity. Males often face pressure to keep their feelings inside and not to reach out for help when they feel stressed or depressed. These narrow conceptions of masculinity and expectations of men in our society can have profoundly negative implications for young men's mental health.

Counselling centres are critical for student mental health. However, there are other ways that we can address the issue of mental health on campus. Ji-Youn is the founder of a group called The Tipping Point. She was a student at the University of British Columbia and dropped out in 2016 in her third year because of mental health issues. She was experiencing clinical depression, post-traumatic stress disorder (PTSD), and suicidal ideation. On the night of her last exam, Ji-Youn wrote a blog post and shared it on Facebook. She talked about the anxiety she felt in school and the effect of social expectations on her mental health. After writing this blog post, she received many emails from other current and former students who experienced similar problems. She decided to start The Tipping Point, a website that brings together current and former students to ask "what would the ideal university environment that supports mental health look like?" The group is an advocacy movement that encourages post-secondary institutions to make systemic changes to better support student mental health. Essentially, Ji-Youn reconceptualized her personal trouble of depression as a larger social issue and created The Tipping Point to address the issue at a societal level.

Universities and colleges are very concerned with the mental health and well-being of students. This is why many universities have created mental health or counselling centres to help students deal with the stresses associated with university life. What are the services available on your university campus?

The Sociology of Health

It might surprise you to see a chapter on health in this sociology textbook. Some students might wonder what sociology has to say about health. Aren't medical doctors and health professionals usually the ones who do health research? Certainly, medical doctors are actively involved in researching health. However, their interests and perspectives on health are very different from the perspective of sociologists of health. In a similar way, sociologists of education may study and understand education in ways different from those of teachers in elementary or high school classes. Taken together, these perspectives can be complementary and can help us to understand the various ways that health affects individuals and societies.

Medical doctors tend to focus on the immediate causes of illness. For example, if you go to the doctor with the flu, she will ask if you have been in contact with others who are also sick. Then she will treat your flu with medicine or other treatments, such as prescription drugs or bed rest. Sociologists take a different approach to the study of health. They focus on the social causes of disease within a population rather than on the immediate causes of an individual's illness. Why, for example, are some people much more likely to get the flu than others? Could it be that people living in poor housing conditions, where the heating is not very good and there is not much insulation, are more likely to get the flu? If this is the case, protecting people from the flu may require us to deal with larger issues of safe housing. Health sociologists tend to look at larger social causes of health and illness and, as a result, look for larger social solutions to health problems.

Sociologists are interested in the larger social causes of health and health outcomes. They are also interested in how different groups of people come to have different health outcomes—for example, poorer people tend to have much worse health than richer people. Why might this be? In order to address the health of a population as a whole, sociologists would argue that we cannot simply give antibiotics to individuals (although these medications can be very important because they might cure the individual's illness), we must find larger social solutions to health problems within a population.

HIGHLIGHT

Classic Theory of Health and Illness—The Sick Role

Sociologists have long been interested in health and how illness affects individuals. Talcott Parsons, one of the earliest structural functionalists, wrote about health and illness in his book *The Social System* (1951). As a structural functionalist, he was interested in how illness can disrupt the usual social cohesion that characterizes society. Remember, structural functionalists argue that society usually functions smoothly. However, illness can disrupt the regular order of society. How does it do this? When a person is ill, they often cannot participate fully in society. Perhaps they cannot go to work, care for their children, or engage in other responsibilities. In this way, illness causes disruption to the normal patterns of social life.

Parsons was interested in how people who are ill work to minimize the disruptive impact of illness. He called this the "**sick role**." We learn how to play the sick role through socialization, and we enact this role in interaction with others when we are sick. Essentially, the sick role is a set of social expectations about how to act when we are sick. The role includes three main parts. First, the sick person is not held personally responsible for his or her poor health. We do not blame a person for being ill. Second, the sick person is entitled to certain rights and privileges, including a release from normal responsibilities. We allow and expect that a person who is ill will not go to work or write an exam. Third, the sick person is expected to take sensible steps to regain their health. We expect that a person who is ill will take medications that are prescribed to them and will rest until they are better. We would be surprised, and perhaps unhappy, if we found out that a person with an infectious disease was not taking their antibiotics and was going to work. This violates our expectation that the person who is ill is "trying" to get better.

This theory is a very useful way to think about how we expect a person to act when they are ill. However, there have been critiques of this theory. First, when is a person allowed to take on the sick role? It is easy to see that if someone breaks their leg or gets the flu, they are excused from work or school. However, with illnesses that are less visible and/or harder to diagnose, such as depression or chronic fatigue, society is not always willing to let a person take on the sick role with all its privileges. Second, we want to consider who has the power to deem who is sick and who is not. When you are ill and need to miss a test, for example, there is probably a group of people at your university who get to decide whether your illness justifies you missing the test and whether you should get a makeup exam. The power to decide who counts as ill and who does not needs to be taken into consideration. Finally, we want to consider how our definition of the sick role has changed over time and differs across cultures. What did we previously consider an illness that we no longer see in this way?

Social Determinants of Health

Sociologists focus on the larger social factors that shape our health. These are called the **social determinants of health**. In general, social determinants of health are the larger social factors that shape the kind of lives we lead and the health of those lives. They include the conditions in which we are born and are raised as well as where we live, work, and grow old. The factors are shaped by larger distributions of money and power at the local, national, and global levels. The social determinants of health are major factors in creating health disparities and unequal health conditions for people both within Canada and around the world.

Figure 11.1 illustrates the social determinants of health. If we begin at the centre of the circle, we see the most immediate factors affecting our health. Our age, sex, and other genetic factors shape our health. Older people, for example, tend to be less healthy than younger ones. The next set of factors that shape our health is individual lifestyle factors. For example, smoking can be very dangerous for your health. Research has shown that exercising and eating well can make you healthier and increase your life expectancy. The next circle includes social and community networks. Having close friends with whom you can discuss important issues and with whom you can relax and have fun is important for our mental well-being as well as our physical health.

The next set of factors includes a whole range of social determinants of health related to living and working conditions. For example, if you live in a community with a lot of air pollution, you may be more likely to have asthma. If you live in a country with good health care services and universal access to those services, you will, on average, be much healthier than if you lived in a country where those services were either not available or were not accessible by everyone. As seen in the figure, other factors include education and housing conditions.

The last set of factors is general socio-economic, cultural, and environmental conditions. Individuals who live in countries with a greater level of inequality between the rich and the poor tend to have poorer health (Pickett and Wilkinson 2011). It is not simply that the poor are better off in societies that are more equal. Interestingly, even

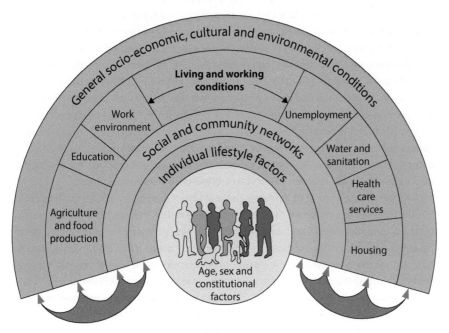

FIGURE 11.1   The social determinants of health

Source: Göran Dahlgren and Margaret Whitehead, 1991, *Policies and Strategies to Promote Social Equity in Health*, Stockholm: Institute for Future Studies

rich people are better off in equal societies. In more equal societies, general health and welfare is better than in societies with more inequality. There are many reasons for this. For example, in more equal societies, there is less crime and violence, which is good for all people, rich and poor. In addition, in more equal societies there is less risk of falling into poverty, which reduces stress and anxiety for all people in a society.

As you can see from Figure 11.1 and our discussion of the social determinants of health, only the first and perhaps the second circle are individual factors. A variety of larger social factors shape the health of the lives we lead.

HIGHLIGHT

The Social Determinants of Tuberculosis

Tuberculosis (TB) is a disease caused by bacteria attacking the lungs. It is spread from infected to healthy people through coughing. We often think of TB as a disease that has been eradicated. However, TB is still a very serious and important cause of death in many places around the world. In fact, TB is the world's most deadly infectious disease, causing more deaths annually than any other infectious disease, including HIV. TB leads to death in about 50 per cent of cases, if left untreated (CBC 2017).

India is the global epicentre of the TB epidemic (Mehra 2017). There were 423,000 deaths from TB in India in 2016. This is about one-third of all deaths from TB in that year around the world (1.4 million) (NPR 2017). TB is costly both in terms of human life and for the overall economy of India, costing India about $24 billion per year. This is because the disease affects mostly people between the ages of 15 and 55. This age group represents a majority of the workforce, thus decreasing productivity and increasing unemployment.

India has worked to lower the high rates of TB infections. The Indian government has a number of health programs that have been relatively effective, and TB rates in India decreased 12 per cent between 2015 and 2016 (NPR 2017). Despite the efficacy of these programs, they can be challenging for people to access. For example, many people have to travel long distances to access care for TB, which is expensive. It is also expensive for individuals to purchase the drugs that they need to deal with TB. Finally, there is a stigma to being diagnosed and labelled as a TB patient, which can negatively affect individuals and families who have the disease.

While it is important to treat individuals with TB, health sociologists argue that we also have to look at the social and economic factors that lead to the high rates of TB in certain areas, such as India. These researchers argue that "poverty sustains TB and TB ensures poverty" (Mehra 2017). This is because TB is much more likely to spread in poor housing conditions. For example, the disease spreads rapidly in housing that is crowded and poorly ventilated. In order to deal with high TB rates in India, we must address social and economic factors, such as poor housing conditions, access to medical care, and other larger social factors.

Ninety-five per cent of TB infections occur in low- and middle-income countries (WHO 2017b). However, it is important to note that the same factors that lead to high rates of TB in India are also critical factors in some areas of Canada. Saskatchewan, Manitoba, and Nunavut have very high rates of TB compared to other places in Canada (CBC 2017). And the rates of infection are much higher within Indigenous communities in these provinces and territories. In fact, two-thirds of all TB cases in Saskatchewan are in Indigenous communities. Poorly ventilated housing and overcrowded living conditions are key factors explaining the high rates of infection in these communities (CBC 2017).

In order to deal with infectious diseases like TB, we must consider not only the individual factors that lead to transmission but also the larger social factors that lead some groups to be more at risk than others. Only by addressing larger social factors, like housing, access to care, and economic conditions, can we address these types of health concerns across communities and countries.

The Freshman 15 and Binge Drinking: Health as a Personal Trouble or Public Issue

Sociology is focused on connecting personal troubles and public issues. In many ways, a focus on the social determinants of health is a call to look at health as a public issue. In this activity, consider two health-related issues that might affect students: the "Freshman 15" and binge drinking.

The "Freshman 15" is a slang term that describes how students often gain weight in their first year of college or university. Consider the issue of weight gain in first-year university as a personal trouble or public issue.

1. What are the individual decisions that students make that lead to weight gain in first-year university (how is it a personal trouble)? How are eating, exercising, and other habits related to potential weight gain?
2. How could the Freshman 15 be seen as a public issue? Consider how food availability, the organizations of dorms or other student housing, the schedule of university classes, and other factors shape the sorts of decisions students make regarding food and exercise.
3. If we consider this issue a personal trouble, how can we address it? If we see it as a public issue, what sorts of solutions might we propose?

Binge drinking is another major issue on many university campuses. Binge drinking is defined as men consuming five drinks within two hours and women consuming four drinks within two hours. This drinking will, on average, increase blood alcohol level to 0.08 (CDC 2017). Binge drinking can be dangerous to one's health. It can lead to increased risk of high blood pressure, stroke, heart disease, and liver failure. In addition, binge drinking is also associated with memory problems and alcohol dependence. Finally, binge drinking puts one at a higher risk of engaging in, or being the victim of, violence (CDC 2017). With these serious concerns in mind, how can we see binge drinking as a personal trouble or public issue?

1. How is binge drinking a personal trouble? What individual factors lead some people to engage in this behaviour?
2. How is binge drinking a public issue? Why might it be more common on university and college campuses than in other places? Why are some dorms, campuses, or areas more likely to encourage binge drinking? What social factors are related to this behaviour?
3. If binge drinking is a personal trouble, how can we deal with it? If binge drinking is a public issue, what sorts of solutions might we propose?

Health Inequality

Canadians are healthier today than ever before. Figure 11.2 shows life expectancy for Canadian men and women over time. For example, Canadians born in 1920 only lived 60 years, on average. Yet if you were born in 2007, you are expected to live to 81. This is a huge growth in life expectancy! There are many reasons for these longer lives. Many diseases that had high death rates have been eradicated, including polio, scarlet fever, and diphtheria. We also have a decrease in infant mortality, with many more children living past their first year of life. Better health technology and access to health care have also increased our lifespans.

However, not everyone is benefiting equally from this general improvement in health. This is what the study of health disparities is all about. **Health disparities** are the differences in health status across groups linked to social, economic, or environmental conditions. For example, a person's social class, education, gender, and location of residence are very important predictors of how healthy they will be and how long they will live.

In order to consider these health disparities, we have to decide how to measure health. There are a number of different measures of health. First, we can measure

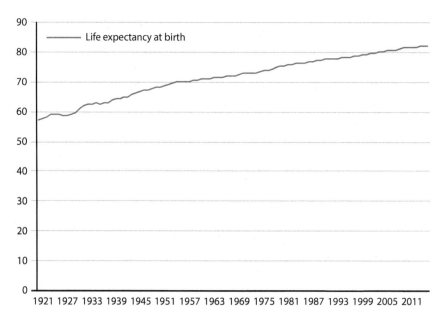

FIGURE 11.2   Life expectancy at birth, 1920–2016, Canada

Source: Adapted from Yves Decady and Lawson Greenberg, 2015, *Ninety Years of Change in Life Expectancy.* Catalogue no. 82-624-X. Otttawa: Statistics Canada, https://www150.statcan.gc.ca/n1/pub/82-624-x/2014001/article/14009/c-g/desc/desc-01-eng.htm; and World Bank, 2017, "Life Expectancy at Birth, Total (Years)," https://data.worldbank.org/indicator/SP.DYN.LE00.IN?cid=GPD_10

life expectancy, the average number of years a population at some age can expect to live. Second, we can measure **healthy life expectancy**. This is a measure of the average number of healthy years one can expect to live if current patterns of death and illness remain the same. For example, we could measure how many years a person is expected to live without limitation of activity or free from chronic diseases. A third measure of health is to assess the number of physically and mentally unhealthy days an individual or group has per month. Finally, we can measure health by assessing **chronic disease prevalence**. Essentially, this is a measure of how common chronic diseases, such as asthma, cancer, or diabetes, are across groups of people. With these different measures in mind, let us consider some of the most important types of health disparities.

Class

Social class is a very important predictor of health. This should not be surprising, given what we have learned about the importance of social class generally. Social class shapes our educational opportunities and outcomes, our jobs and work experiences, and (as far back as the second chapter of this book) even our personalities and the traits our parents encourage in us! Given the power of social class across such a wide range of areas, it is not surprising that it is a critical component in shaping the quality and length of the lives that we lead.

There are strong health inequalities related to social class in Canada. For example, smoking rates, mental health, and hospitalization for chronic respiratory illnesses are much higher among the bottom 20 per cent of earners than among the top 20 per cent of earners. Take smoking as an example. In general, rates of smoking are declining. Rates of smoking decreased for the population as a whole between 2003 and 2015 (Canadian Institute of Health Research 2015). However, there was no change in smoking rates for the bottom 20 per cent of earners. This is one of the biggest reasons why the bottom 20 per cent of earners are much more likely to go to the hospital for chronic respiratory disease (something that is strongly related to smoking rates). In fact, this group is three times more likely to go to the hospital for this disease than the top 20 per cent of earners. Finally, poorer Canadians rate their mental health worse than richer Canadians. The number of people who report their mental health to be "fair" or "poor" is increasing for all groups except the top 20 per cent of earners, who have the same rate of poor mental health over time (Canadian Institute for Health Information 2015).

While most health indicators are generally improving for all groups of Canadians, the poor are seeing less improvement than the rich. For example, there has been a reduction in the general rate of motor vehicle accidents across the whole population; however, poorer Canadians have seen less of a reduction than the rich. And there are lower rates of infant mortality for all Canadians; however, the poor are not experiencing the rate of improvement in infant mortality seen among the rich (Canadian Institute for Health Information 2015).

This class inequality in health is even more striking, since Canada has a universal system of health care. In theory, all Canadians should have access to health care, including doctors, hospitals, and other services, within the Canadian health care system. We will discuss the Canadian health care system in more detail in the section on Health Policy. With this universal system in mind, why are there still such stark inequalities in health care outcomes for the rich and poor in Canada?

One way to think through these issues is to consider how social class affects our health over the course of our lives. Social class has a particularly pronounced effect on the health of children. This is because parents with more money can provide an environment and resources that foster good health. For example, they are able to buy better quality food—perhaps organic fresh food instead of pre-packaged, less healthy food. They also tend to have more time to cook food for their children instead of having to rely on unhealthy fast food. Parents with more money are also more likely to live in neighbourhoods that have parks to play in and are safe for children to run around outside. Higher income is also associated with better housing conditions, such as living in a home with good insulation and heating and free from mould or pests. Parents with more money are also more likely to have access to better medical care. This may seem surprising given our universal health care system. However, this system does not provide for prescription drugs and preventative care, which can be very important. All of these factors contribute to the better health of children from richer families. And the effect of family income on the health of children increases over time (Case, Lubotsky, and Paxson 2002). For example, chronic conditions like asthma are less likely to occur in richer families. And when they do occur, they are more likely to be kept under control because of better housing conditions, access to medical care, and other factors.

Social class and area of residence are strongly connected. James Chesire, from the University College London, showed this in his analysis of life expectancy along the London subway line. As shown in Figure 11.3, where you are born even within one city has serious effects on your health. There is an 11-year gap in life expectancy between the richest areas of London, like Charing Cross, and the poorest areas of the city, like Stockwell Lane. In some areas, every two stations that you travel along the subway is associated with a shorter life expectancy of one full year. In fact, travelling 20 minutes on the Central subway line was equivalent to 12 years' difference in average life expectancy. This is the same difference in life expectancy as that between the UK as a whole and Guatemala. All within one city! This important study illustrates how social conditions within even a small area can shape our health.

Global Health Inequality

In the same way that social class and income affect health within a country, the wealth of a country also affects the health of its citizens more generally. Not surprisingly, wealthier countries tend to have healthier populations. You can see in Figure 11.4 that increasing the GDP of a country from $5000 to $20,000 is associated with a huge increase in the

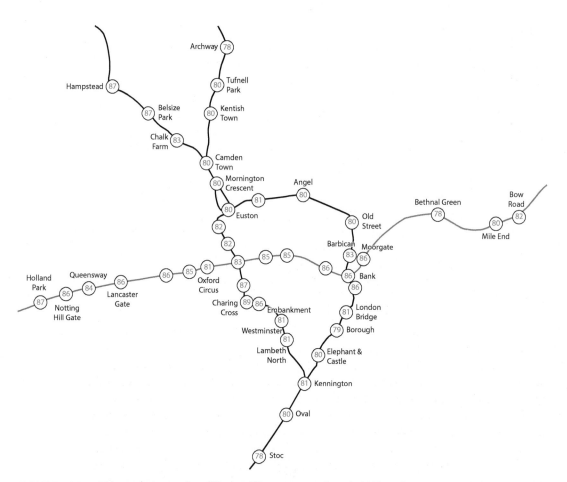

FIGURE 11.3   This map shows the different life expectancies of children born around each subway stop in London, UK. What larger factors explain how our neighbourhood can shape our health?

Source: Based on http://life.mappinglondon.co.uk

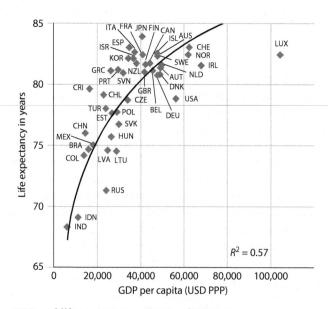

FIGURE 11.4   **GDP and life expectancy, 2015 or latest year**

Source: OECD, 2017, "Health at a Glance," OECD, Stat (database), https://www.oecd-ilibrary.org/social-issues-migration-health/health-at-a-glance-2017/life-expectancy-at-birth-and-health-spending-per-capita-2015-or-nearest-year_health_glance-2017-graph8-en

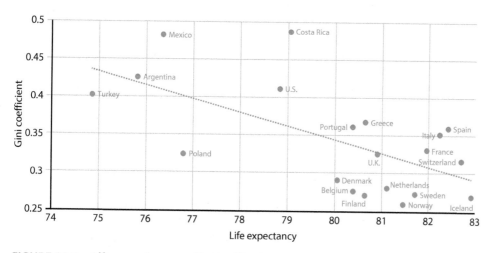

FIGURE 11.5   **Life expectancy and inequality, 2012**

Source: https://inequality.org/facts/inequality-and-health

country's life expectancy—almost five years. However, once your country is relatively wealthy, with a GDP of more than $25,000, there is very little effect of increased wealth on life expectancy. In fact, Israel, with a GDP under $30,000, has about the same life expectancy as Norway where the GDP is twice as high.

It is clear that wealth matters; however, being wealthy is not enough to lead to longer lives. It is also the case that countries that are more equal tend to have healthier populations. You can see from Figure 11.5 that countries with more equality (those with lower Gini coefficients) have citizens who live longer, on average. Take, for example, Iceland. It is the most equal country on this chart, and it also has the longest life expectancy. Turkey, Argentina, and Mexico are quite unequal, compared to the other countries on the chart. They all have much shorter life expectancies. It is important to note that the relationship between inequality and life expectancy plays a role even in rich countries. The US is the richest of all the countries on this chart; however, its life expectancy is only moderate. The fact is that the US is quite an unequal society, which accounts for the shorter lifespan in that country.

Education

Education is another important predictor of health. Clearly, social class and education are related. As we have learned, people with higher education tend to be in a higher social class and make more money. However, the importance of education is so strong that it matters even apart from its relationship with income and class

There are three main reasons that education is a key predictor of health. First, education is related to social class and income. And as we learned in the previous section, these factors are both very important predictors of good health. Second, education tends to improve our ability to understand health information. Information about healthy food is often complicated and ever-changing. Should we eat fewer carbs or more whole grain carbs? Should we have less fat or more of certain types of fat? Having more education makes it more likely that you will both understand this information and, as a result, change your behaviours in healthy ways. Third, education increases your feelings of efficacy, the belief that you can change things around you. People who feel efficacious are more likely to change their health behaviours when needed. For example, if you have a heart attack and your doctor tells you that you need to quit smoking, you have the choice of either trying to change your behaviour or giving up, feeling that it is impossible to change your fate. In this example, those who make an effort to change their behaviour, such as quitting smoking, will have better health outcomes overall.

Much research has shown the positive effects of education on health. For example, those with more education are more likely to engage in preventative health behaviours, such as doing aerobic exercise and eating healthier food. They are also less likely to engage in behaviours that are bad for their health like smoking (Kenkel, Lillard, and Mathios 2006) or being overweight (Himes and Reynolds 2005).

Race and Ethnicity

Race and ethnicity are also related to health outcomes in Canada. There are two core reasons for this. First, racism and discrimination affect the life experiences of visible minorities and Indigenous peoples in Canada. For example, racism and discrimination can shape your access to the health care system. Despite our universal system of health care, some racial and ethnic groups do not have the same access to this system because of racism. Second, the relationship between ethnicity and health outcomes is at least partly shaped by social class. We know that many racial and ethnic minorities tend to have lower earnings and wealth than white Canadians. For this reason, the relationship between ethnicity and health outcomes is at least partly the result of the lower earnings and social class, on average, of visible minorities and Indigenous peoples in Canada.

In Canada, health outcomes for Indigenous peoples are particularly unequal. Comparing life expectancies illustrates these disparities. Life expectancy for Canadians as a whole in 2017 was 79 years for men and 83 years for women. Métis and First Nations peoples both had significantly shorter lives, on average, with men in these groups living 73–4 years and women living 78–80 years. Inuit peoples have the shortest lifespans, with Inuit men living 64 years, on average, and Inuit women living 73 years, on average (Statistics Canada 2017b). There is a 15-year disparity between the life expectancy of Inuit men and the general male population in Canada.

There are many reasons for the shorter life expectancy in First Nations, Inuit, and Métis communities. It is important to begin with the two core explanations from above. First, racism and discrimination, which are the results of long-standing colonial legacies, are important factors explaining the shorter life expectancy and general health outcomes in these groups. Second, the relationship between Indigeneity and health is partly shaped by social class. Veenstra (2009) shows that socio-economic status, as measured by educational attainment and income, partly explained the association between Aboriginal identification (as per Statistics Canada labels) and health outcomes.

There are additional factors that can help to explain health outcomes in Indigenous communities. First, housing conditions, including crowding in housing and poor ventilation, are particularly prevalent in many Indigenous communities (University of Ottawa 2017). These conditions are often particularly problematic on reserves. Such conditions are related to respiratory health issues such as asthma. Second, access to safe and clean water is an important issue in many Indigenous communities, but it is not generally a concern in other Canadian cities or towns. Access to safe water is critical for overall health and for limiting the spread of illnesses. Third, the higher number of Indigenous peoples in rural communities limits access to health care. There are fewer doctors and hospitals in rural communities, in general, making access to preventative care and urgent care more difficult. Fourth, food prices and food insecurity are issues in many remote communities, including Indigenous communities, which have negative implications for health outcomes because people cannot easily access or afford fresh fruit, vegetables, and other food items (University of Ottawa 2017).

Gender

Gender is also strongly related to health. As most people know, women live longer than men. This has been true over time in Canada. There are a number of reasons why women live longer than men, on average, and these reasons start as early as birth and continue to play out throughout the life course. Girls are less likely to die right after birth than boys. Then, in childhood, we socialize girls and boys in different ways. Boys are encouraged to be more aggressive and tend to engage in more risk-taking behaviour. As a result, boys are three times more likely to die from accidents, four times more likely to die from suicide, and five times more likely to die from homicide (CDC 2014).

The difference in how we socialize girls and boys has long-term effects. For example, men are much more likely to die from heart disease than are women. Research has shown that one reason for this is our cultural definition of masculinity, which focuses on financial success, keeping emotions in, and aggressive behaviour. All of these behaviours are what medical doctors call "coronary prone behaviour," which increase your risk of having a heart attack (CDC 2014).

An interesting puzzle when considering the relationship between gender and health is that while women live longer than men, they tend to report poorer health. For example, women have higher rates of acute conditions and non-fatal chronic conditions, such as arthritis, osteoporosis, and depression. They spend 40 per cent more days in bed sick each year, and their activities are restricted because of health 25 per cent more than men's. They have more doctors' visits and twice the number of surgeries per year than men (National Center for Health Statistics 2003; Canadian Institute for Health Information 2015).

What can explain this puzzle? If women are in poorer health than men, why do they live longer? First, it is possible that the relationship is in the exact opposite direction. The fact that women live longer is a reason that they have poorer health. The longer you live, the more likely you are to make it to old age when most of our health problems happen. Because many more men die in childhood or early adulthood from things like accidents and violence, they are less likely to develop long-term chronic illnesses.

We should also consider how our ideas of traditional masculinity and femininity might be shaping how men and women use the medical system. For example, our ideas of masculinity encourage men to be tough and unemotional. This could be part of the reason that men are less likely to go to the doctor when they are ill or to take preventative measures to protect their health, such as going for annual check-ups (Springer and Mouzon 2011).

Obesity: Intersectionality in Health Inequalities

All of these dimensions of inequality work together to create different health outcomes across groups of people. We can see this when examining obesity. **Obesity** is a significant social problem in Canada and in many countries around the world. We measure whether a person is overweight or obese by using the Body Mass Index (BMI). A person can calculate their BMI by dividing their height by their weight squared. A healthy BMI is between 18.5 and 24.9. Individuals who have a BMI between 25 and 29.9 are categorized as overweight, and those with a BMI over 30 are labelled obese (Statistics Canada 2016). Obesity can be very serious for both children and adults. Being overweight as a child can have long-term effects throughout the life course. And, obesity in adults is linked with an increased risk of heart disease, high blood pressure, type 2 diabetes, and some cancers (NIH 2013).

Obesity has both individual and social causes. If it were simply a matter of biology, we would expect that rates of obesity would be similar across groups and countries and over time. However, the social problem of obesity is a relatively modern phenomenon that only happens in some countries. It is also stratified by social factors such as gender, age, social class, race, and ethnicity.

Let's begin by comparing across countries. A majority (54 per cent) of the Canadian population is either overweight or obese. This is much higher than the historic rates of obesity in Canada. The rate of obesity alone increased from 6 per cent in 1982 to 25 per cent by 2015 (Statistics Canada 2016). Obesity rates also differ widely across countries. Figure 11.6 shows obesity rates across a selection of countries. Canada's rates are in the

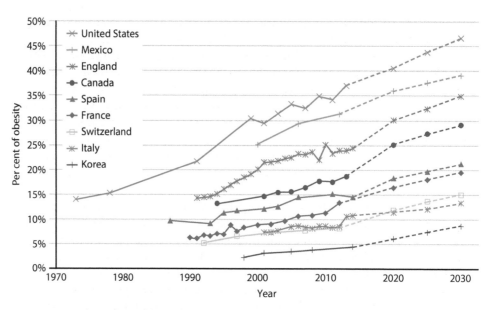

FIGURE 11.6   **Obesity rates, by country**

Source: OECD, 2017, "OECD Obesity Update 2017," *OECD Health Statistics* (database), http://www.oecd.org/health/obesity-update.htm

middle of the group shown in this figure. The United States has much higher rates of obesity, as do Mexico and England. Rates of obesity are quite low in countries such as South Korea, Italy, and France. It is important to note, however, that the rates of obesity are increasing in all the countries in this figure over time.

Obesity is also highly variant across social groups within Canada. For example, men are much more likely to be obese or overweight than are women in Canada. Almost two-thirds of men (62 per cent) are overweight or obese. However, less than half (46 per cent) of women fall into either of these categories (Statistics Canada 2016).

Obesity is also related to social class. It is now much more common for people with less money to be overweight than those with more money. For example, 20 per cent of women in the bottom 20 per cent of earners are obese whereas only 13 per cent of women in the top 20 per cent of earners fall into this category (Canadian Institute for Health Information 2015).

The relationship between obesity and social class has changed over time. It used to be that being thin was associated with poverty—not having enough money to buy food and having to work in manual labour made you thin. Richer people could afford more and fattier foods and did not have to work physically to make money. In this context, being heavier was associated with richness and luxury. Today, these relationships are the exact opposite. Cheaper food, like fast food, is much fattier than expensive food such as organic produce and lean meats. People with more money are also more likely to have the resources to buy gym memberships, purchase organic vegetables, and live in areas with parks for exercising. In this new context, having money is associated with thinness. These changes highlight the changing social construction of the "healthy" body and what type of body is desirable in a society.

Obesity is also related to age. Young people are much less likely to be overweight or obese. One-quarter of Canadians between the ages of 18 and 19 are overweight or obese. However, more than half of Canadians over 65 fall into these categories (Statistics Canada 2016). There are many reasons for this. Children often engage in much more physical activity than adults. For example, most schools have gym classes that are required for all students. Children also do not tend to have the sorts of chronic or long-term health conditions that lead to being overweight or obese. However, obesity in children in

Canada is on the rise and is of great concern because of the long-term consequences of obesity for health as children grow.

While individuals do make decisions about their eating habits and exercise, individual choices alone do not account for the rapid rise in obesity in Canada and around the world. There are many larger social reasons that account for the rising rates of obesity. For example, modern society tends to be very sedentary. Most people work in jobs that involve little physical activity. Professors, doctors, accountants, cashiers, and office workers are mostly sitting all day. Think about your life as a student and the hours you spend sitting in lecture halls or in front of the computer working on assignments. Second, the rise of technology, such as television, computers, and smartphones means that we spend more of our leisure time sitting. It also means that we can do a lot of things at home that used to involve a walk to the store because of online conveniences—such as ordering our groceries, making bank payments, and taking classes. Third, modern society is also characterized by a constant feeling of being rushed. Because of this, we have less time to cook and make food at home. As a result, we rely more on pre-prepared foods and fast foods, which are less healthy.

Once we see the problem of obesity as a social problem and not simply a personal issue, we can come to larger social solutions. For example, there are calls to bring more physical education into children's school day and take away unhealthy foods in school cafeterias to address obesity among children. Does your campus offer pop machines or water fountains? Many cities are creating more parks and other facilities where people

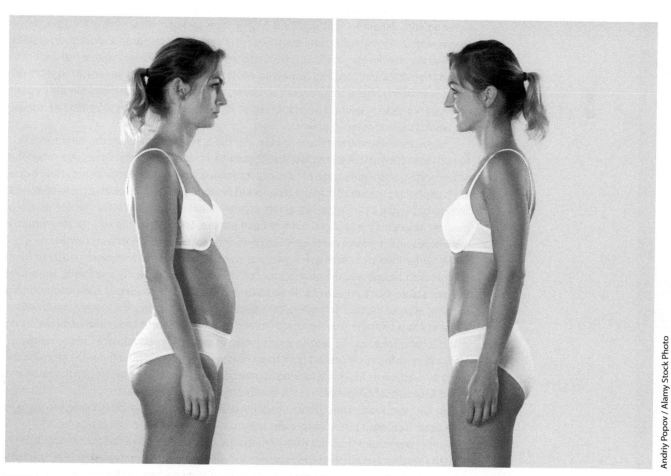

PHOTO 11.1 The photograph on the right was digitally altered. Images like these have led to the call to ban altering images in this way. A law was passed in France in 2017 to prevent advertisers from altering images without explicitly warning that the image was altered. How have these laws challenged what we see as the ideal and healthy body?

Andriy Popov / Alamy Stock Photo

READING

can exercise without paying for an expensive gym. And some areas are passing laws that fast-food restaurants have to list the calorie counts of their foods, cannot use trans fats, or have to pay a tax on unhealthy foods. These are all small parts of how we can, as a society, address the complex problem of rising obesity rates.

Michael Marmot is a health researcher and chair of the Commission on the Social Determinants of Health at the World Health Organization (WHO). He has spent more than 30 years studying health and how social conditions can lead to very important health inequalities among people. In the following excerpt from his book *The Health Gap*, Marmot discusses some of his most important studies. Think about how these studies can help us to understand the larger social determinants of health and how this is related to unequal health outcomes across social groups.

The Health Gap

Michael Marmot

Excerpt from the Introduction

As Japanese migrate across the Pacific, their rate of heart disease goes up and their rate of stroke goes down.[2] Would I like to work on this for my Berkeley PhD? Would I! It was a brilliant natural experiment. If you were trying to sort out genetic and environmental contributions to disease, here were people with, presumably, the same genetic endowment living in different environments. Japanese in Hawaii had higher rates of heart disease than those in Japan, Japanese in California higher rates than those in Hawaii, and white Americans higher rates still.

This was terrific. You couldn't have designed a better experiment to test the impact on health of 'environment', broadly conceived. Most likely, the changing rates of disease are telling us something about culture and way of life, linked to the environment. Simple hypothesis: Americanisation leads to heart disease, or Japanese culture protects from heart disease. But what does that mean in practice?

Conventional wisdom at the time was, and still is, that fatty diets are the culprit. Indeed, I have chaired committees saying just that.[3] Japanese-Americans had diets that were somewhat Americanised, with higher levels of fat than a traditional Japanese diet, and as a result had higher levels of plasma cholesterol than did Japanese in Japan.[4] Diet and high levels of cholesterol were likely to be playing a part in the higher rate of heart disease. What's more, the higher the level of plasma cholesterol, the higher the risk of heart disease. So much for the egg-package insert. It missed idea one. It grieves me to say it, but conventional wisdom is not *always* wrong.

Now for idea two. Japanese-Americans may be taller, fatter and more partial to hamburgers than Japanese in the old country, but their approach to family and friends resembles the more close-knit culture of Japan more than it does the more socially and geographically mobile culture of the US. That's interesting, but is it important for health? A Japanese-American social scientist with the very Japanese-American name of Scott Matsumoto had speculated that the cohesive nature of Japanese culture was a powerful mechanism for reducing stress.[5] Such a diminution could protect from heart disease. I particularly liked the idea of turning the study of stress on its head. Not looking at how being under pressure messes up the heart and blood vessels, but how people's social relationships were positive and supportive. We humans gossip and schmooze; apes groom. If, whether human or non-human primate, we support each other it changes hormonal profiles and may lower risk of heart attacks.

If this were true, I thought, then perhaps the Japanese in Hawaii had more opportunity to maintain their culture than the Japanese in California—hence the lower rate of heart disease in Hawaii. It seemed a reasonable speculation, but I had no test for it.

Marmot, Michael. 2015. *The Health Gap*, pp. 8–12 and 13–14. London: Bloomsbury Press.

I had the data to test the hypothesis much more directly among the California Japanese. Men who were more involved with Japanese culture and had cohesive social relations should have lower rates of heart disease than those who were more acculturated—had adopted more of the American way of life. That is what I found. And this research result, perhaps, is where the egg cartons got their 'news'. The apparent protection from heart disease among the California men who were more 'Japanese' culturally and socially could *not* be explained by dietary patterns, nor by smoking, nor by blood pressure levels, nor by obesity. The culture effect was not a proxy for the usual suspects of diet and smoking.[6]

Two ideas then: conventional wisdom is correct, smoking and diet are important causes of heart disease; and, while correct, conventional wisdom is also limited—other things are going on. In the case of Japanese-Americans, it was the protective effect of being culturally Japanese.

Everything I will show you in this book conforms to that simple proposition—conventional wisdom is correct, but limited, when it comes to causes of disease. In rich countries, for example, we understand a good deal about why one individual gets sick and another does not: their habits of smoking, diet, drinking alcohol, physical inactivity, in addition to genetic makeup—we could call that conventional wisdom. But being emotionally abused by your spouse, having family troubles, being unlucky in love, being marginal in society, can all increase risk of disease; just as living in supportive, cohesive social groups can be protective. If we want to understand why health and disease are distributed the way they are, we have to understand these social causes; all the more so if we want to do something about it.

The British Civil Service changed my life. Not very romantic, a bit like being inspired by a chartered accountant. The measured pace and careful rhythms of Her Majesty's loyal servants had a profound effect on everything I did subsequently. Well, not quite the conservatism of the actual practices of the civil service, but the drama of the patterns of health that we found there. Inequality is central.

The civil service seems the very antithesis of dramatic. Please bear with me. You have been, let's say, invited to a meeting with a top-grade civil servant. It is a trial by hierarchy. You arrive at the building and someone is watching the door—he is part of the office support grades, as is the person who checks your bag and lets you through the security gate. A clerical assistant checks your name and calls up to the office on the fifth floor. A higher-grade clerical person comes to escort you upstairs, where a low-grade executive officer greets you. Two technical people, a doctor and a statistician, who will be joining the meeting, are already waiting. Then the great man's, or woman's, high-flying junior administrator says that Richard, or Fiona, will be ready shortly. Finally you are ushered in to the real deal where studied informality is now the rule. In the last ten minutes you have completed a journey up the civil service ranking ladder—takes some people a lifetime: office support grades, through clerical assistants, clerical officers, executive grades, professionals, junior administrators to, at the pinnacle, senior administrators. So far so boring: little different from a private insurance company.

The striking thing about this procession up the bureaucratic ladder is that health maps on to it, remarkably closely. Those at the bottom, the men at the door, have the worst health, on average. And so it goes. Each person we meet has worse health, and shorter life expectancy, than the next one a little higher up the ladder, but better health than the one lower down. Health is correlated with seniority. In our first study, 1978–1984, of mortality of civil servants (the Whitehall Study), who were all men unfortunately, men at the bottom had a mortality rate four times higher than the men at the top—they were four times more likely to die in a specific period of time. In between top and bottom, health improved steadily with rank.[7] This linking of social position with health—higher rank, better health—I call the social gradient in health. Investigating the causes of the gradient, teasing out the policy implications of such health inequalities, and advocating for change, have been at the centre of my activities since.

I arrived at Whitehall through a slightly circuitous route, intellectual as well as geographic.

You couldn't be interested in public health, or even just interested, and not aware that people in poor countries have high rates of illness and die younger compared with those in rich countries. Poverty damages health. What about poverty in rich countries? It was a niche interest in the US of the 1970s. After all, the USA thought of itself as a classless society, so there could not be differences between social classes in rates of health disease, right? Wrong—a piece of conventional wisdom that was completely wrong. The actual truth was handed around almost like Samizdat literature in the former Soviet Union in the form of a small number of papers, one of which was written by Len Syme and my colleague Lisa Berkman, now at Harvard.[8] People with social disadvantage did suffer worse health in the USA. It was, though, far from a mainstream preoccupation. Race and ethnicity were dominant concerns. Class and health was not a serious subject for study. Inequality and health was completely off the agenda, bar a few trailblazers, writing about the evils of capitalism.[9]

If there was a country on the planet that was aware of social class distinctions and had a tradition of studying social class differences in health, it was the United Kingdom. And if there was a place in Britain that excelled at social stratification it was the British Civil Service, familiarly known as Whitehall. . . .

. . . Twice is a coincidence, three times a trend. In the 1970s I had done only two big studies, Japanese migrants and now Whitehall civil servants, and both had flown in the face of conventional wisdom. At the time, everyone 'knew' that people in top jobs had a high risk of heart attacks because of the stress they were under. Sir William Osler, great medical teacher from John Hopkins University and the University of Oxford, had, around 1920, described heart disease as being more common in men in high-status occupations. Osler fuelled the speculation that it was the stress of these jobs that was killing people.

We found the opposite. High-grade men had lower risk of dying from heart attacks, and most other causes of death, than everyone below them, and as I described earlier, it was a social gradient, progressively higher mortality going hand in hand with progressively lower grade of employment.

Further, conventional explanations did not work. True, smoking was more common as one descended the social ladder, but plasma cholesterol was marginally higher in the high grades, and the social gradient in obesity and high blood pressure was modest. Together, these conventional risk factors accounted for about a third of the social gradient in mortality.[10] Something else had to be going on. In that sense, it was similar to my studies of Japanese-Americans. The conventional risk factors mattered, but something else accounted for the different risks of disease between social groups. In the Japanese case we thought it was the stress-reducing effects of traditional Japanese culture.

You may think: stress in the civil service? Surely not! My colleagues Tores Theorell in Stockholm and Robert Karasek, the man who was eating eggs in Massachusetts, had elaborated a theory of work stress. It was not high demand that was stressful, but a combination of high demand and low control.[11] To describe it as a Eureka moment goes too far, but it did provide a potential explanation of the Whitehall findings. Whoever spread the rumour that it is more stressful at the top? People up there have more psychological demands, but they also have more control.

Control over your life loomed large as a hypothesis for why, in rich countries, people in higher social positions should have better health.

CRITICAL READING QUESTIONS

1. What is the Whitewall study? What does it tell us about the role of social status and health?
2. Explain Marmot's study of Japanese men in California and Japan. How does this study help us to understand the complex ways of how culture shapes health outcomes?
3. Why should we be concerned with issues of health inequality? How can understanding these larger issues of health inequality help us to improve health?

NOTES

2. Gordon, T. Further mortality experience among Japanese Americans. *Public Health Report*. 1967. 82: 973–84.

3. Committee on Medical Aspects of Food Policy. *Nutritional Aspects of Cardiovascular Disease*. London: HMSO. 1994. 1–186.

4. Nichaman, M..Z., H.B. Hamilton, A. Kagan, S. Sacks, T. Greer, S.L. Syme. Epidemiologic studies of coronary heart disease and stroke in Japanese men living in Japan, Hawaii, and California. *American Journal of Epidemiology*. 1975: 102: 491-501.

5. Matsumoto, Y.S. Social stress and coronary heart disease in Japan: a hypothesis. *Milbank MemFund Quarterly*. 1970: 48: 9-36.

6. Marmot, M.G., S.L. Myme. Acculturation and CHD in Japanese-Americans. *American Journal of Epidemiology*. 1976. 104: 225–47.

7. Marmot, M.G., M.J. Shipley, G. Rose. Inequalities in death—specific explanations of a general pattern? *Lancet*. 984. 1 (8384): 1003–6.

8. Syme, S.L., L.F. Berkman. Social class, susceptibility, and sickness. *American Journal of Epidemiology*. 1976. 104: 1–8

9. Navarro, V. *Medicine under Capitalism*. Croom Helm, 1976.

10. Van Rossum, C.T.M., M.J. Shipley, H. Van de Mheen, D.E. Grobbee, M.G. Marmot. Employment grade differences in cause specific mortality. A 25 year follow up of civil servants from the first Whitehall study. *Journal of Epidemiology and Community Health*. 2000: 54 (3): 178–84.

11. Karasek, R., T. Reorell. Healthy Work: Stress, Productivity, and the Reconstruction of Working Life. New York: Basic Books, 1990.

Health Care Systems around the World

Health care is delivered through health care systems. **Health care systems** are the organizations of people, resources, and institutions that provide and deliver health care to a population. Health care systems differ in the extent to which they are funded and controlled by governments. On one end of the spectrum are systems called "socialized" medicine. In socialized medicine, the government owns and operates most medical facilities and employs most doctors. Both Britain and Sweden have socialized health care systems. On the other end of the spectrum are systems in which individuals personally pay for their health care with no government assistance. In the middle ground are countries and systems in which the government pays some portion of the cost of medical care or the cost for some people. This third, mixed system exists in the US where veterans and seniors get free health care coverage from the government. Other people purchase health insurance from private companies or through their employers.

Canada also has one of the intermediary systems, although government plays a larger role in Canada than it does in the US. The Canadian system is "socialized insurance." In a socialized insurance system, the government pays doctors and hospitals for the services they provide according to a schedule of fees set annually by governments in consultation with professional medical associations. This differs from the socialized system in Britain and Sweden in that Canadian doctors are private practitioners paid on a fee per service basis. This is sometimes called a "single-payer" system because the government alone pays for health care (without the individual having to also pay a portion of their own care). The Canadian health care system has been a socialized insurance, single-payer system since 1972. The system provides access to universal comprehensive coverage for hospital and outpatient services that are deemed necessary by a doctor.

The Canadian health care system is a national system, and the federal government sets standards for health care under the 1984 Canada Health Act. This is important because, while it is a national system, it is, in fact, the provincial governments who actually deliver and administer health care within their provinces. Because of this, it is important

HIGHLIGHT

Causes of Death over Time

1921–25	2012
1. Heart disease;	1. Cancer;
2. Influenza, bronchitis, pneumonia;	2. Heart Disease;
3. Diseases of early infancy;	3. Stroke;
4. Tuberculosis; and	4. Chronic Lower Respiratory Disease; and
5. Cancer.	5. Accident.

Sources: (1921–25) Katherine Arnup, 2015, "Death, Dying, and Canadian Families," *The Vanier Institute of the Family*, p. 6; (2012) Statistics Canada, CANSIM Table 102-0561, https://www.statcan.gc.ca/pub/82-625-x/2017001/article/14776-eng.htm

that the federal government sets out the rules to ensure that health care is of the same quality across the country.

There are five main **standards for health care in Canada** as set by the Canada Health Act: universality, accessibility, portability, comprehensive coverage, and public administration. First, the system is universal in that it covers all Canadians. Second, the system is accessible. It must provide reasonable access for everyone and must be unimpeded by financial or other barriers so that no can be discriminated against on the basis of age, income, or health status. Third, the system is comprehensive. This means that it must cover all medically necessary services. Fourth, health care must be portable. Because it is a national system, Canadians must be able to access coverage in any province and take their medical coverage with them if they move to another province. Finally, the system is publicly administered. A public body operates the system on a not-for-profit basis (Government of Canada 2003).

There are important criticisms of the Canadian health care system. These criticisms often focus on the ways that the system does not fully live up to the five standards that it sets. For example, some people argue that the system is not comprehensive enough. It does not cover, for example, regular dental care, drugs, ambulance transport, or private hospital beds. Instead, these services are often paid for through employee benefits or by the individual. This means that not all Canadians are getting the same level of health care, and it is part of the reason that health disparities still occur in a country like Canada where health care is supposed to be universal.

Health Policy

All health care systems are based on a set of health policies. **Health policies** are the decisions and actions that are undertaken to achieve specific health care goals within a health care system. These policies are much more specific than the overall health care system. For example, governments in many countries are attempting to tackle health problems such as drug use, addressing rising obesity rates, lowering smoking rates, and encouraging people to get vaccinations. These specific policies are aimed at improving the health of the population as a whole.

One health care policy that has garnered much attention across countries is the social problem of drug use and abuse, particularly opioid use. Opioids are drugs that include prescription pain relievers, heroin, and fentanyl. These drugs are very addictive and can lead to substance abuse problems, overdose, and even death. There has been a large increase in the number of overdoses and deaths in the past five years from opioids in Canada.

Fentanyl is a synthetic opiate pain reliever. It is legally prescribed to patients, often after surgery or to deal with severe pain or injury. It is a very effective drug because it is so potent. In fact, it is much more potent than heroin and about 100 times more potent than morphine. It is also very addictive. Fentanyl is responsible for a majority of all overdose deaths in Canada, and its share of overdose deaths is increasing over time. In fact, 74 per cent of apparent opioid-related deaths in Canada involved fentanyl in 2017 compared to 53 per cent in 2016 (Government of Canada 2017). Figure 11.7 shows the massive increase in overdose deaths between 2007 and 2016 and the critical role fentanyl played in this increase.

Dealing with complex health issues such as drug addiction and overdoses is challenging. There are a variety of ways that health policy can try to address these issues. For example, many cities have created safe injection sites to supervise the injection of illegal drugs and reduce overdoses. Drug treatment programs or education programs to discourage drug use are also important parts of reducing drug-related deaths. In the next reading, sociologist Lindsey Richardson describes her research with an interdisciplinary research team. This work is an innovative way of addressing the opioid crisis. Read the following discussion of their research and plans to tackle these complicated issues.

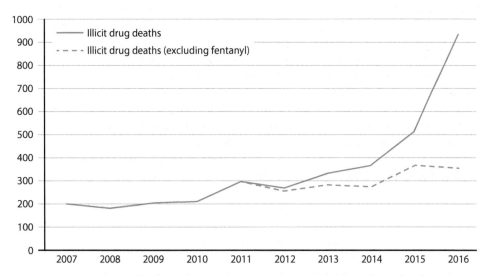

FIGURE 11.7   Illicit drug overdose deaths including and excluding fentanyl, 2007–16

Source: United Nations Office on Drugs and Crime, 2017, *August 2017—Canada: Fentanyl Use for Increase in Drug Overdose Deaths in British Columbia*, UNODC Laboratory and Scientific Section Portals, https://www.unodc.org/LSS/Announcement/Details/2689e611-db92-4a8a-868f-ad6c6685cd0e. Copyright © Province of British Columbia. All rights reserved. Reproduced with permission of the Province of British Columbia.

READING

The Downsides and Dangers of "Cheque Day"

Lindsey Richardson

On Thursday, Aug. 25, the day after provincial income-assistance recipients received their support payments, the sirens started: Ambulance, police and fire engines throughout Vancouver were responding to a spike in accidental drug overdoses. Although media reports on overdoses have rightfully focused on the toll caused by fentanyl, a new and more powerful opioid, that particular Thursday is not unique.

Sirens are heard throughout Vancouver every month on the days after "cheque day," and are part of a long-standing monthly ritual that locals also refer to as "Welfare Wednesday" or "Mardi Gras." Drug dealers collect outstanding debts. The hashtag #WelfareWednesday is used to advertise drink specials. Community workers hand out fruit to people standing in line at the bank. Thanks to quick action by first responders, family members and health providers, almost all overdoses do not result in death. Some, devastatingly, do.

Amidst what has now been declared an overdose epidemic and public-health emergency, recent research conducted at the B.C. Centre for Disease Control documented a 40-per-cent increase in fatal overdoses on the days following assistance payments. Insite's subsequent decision to open its doors 24 hours a day around cheque day—and its exceptional capacity to prevent accidental overdoses from becoming lethal—will hopefully do something to stem the tide of completely preventable deaths that occur at this time every month. No one has ever died of an overdose at Insite.

However, overdose increases around cheque day do not just occur in Vancouver. They have been documented across the province, across the country and around the world. Insite's commendable efforts will do little to help someone in Surrey, Prince George or Thunder Bay.

While fatal overdose is the worst of the drug-related harms that spike around cheque day, it is not the only one. A growing list of studies document increases in everything from people leaving hospital against the advice of their doctors and clients being unable to access services that are either closed or have lineups out the door, to police being called in to assist in the ER and street-level violence. These are things Insite cannot fix.

The rise in drug use and drug-related harm around cheque day is an example of a logical administrative decision that has unintended yet severe health, social and economic consequences. Yet most jurisdictions in Canada and the United States deliver social-assistance payments in the same way: once a month, on the same day for everyone.

Academics, health-care practitioners and others have been calling for the system to be changed. It seems like an intuitive next step. But is it really that simple? The existing system already demonstrates how what might seem like a straightforward approach might not be upon closer examination.

Our researchers at the B.C. Centre for Excellence in HIV/AIDS are trying to find out whether there may be a better way. In October, 2015, we initiated an experimental study in the Downtown Eastside testing whether not paying study volunteers at the same time each month can do anything to reduce drug use and drug-related harms. We are examining what happens when people get paid at a different time than everybody else. We are also looking at what happens when they are paid—like most people in regular jobs—twice a month instead of monthly.

Richardson, Lindsey. 2016. "The Downsides and Dangers of 'Cheque Day.'" *The Globe and Mail* 4 September.

And while there are already ways to vary payment frequency in the province (for example, "mid-month" split payments administered by the Ministry of Social Development and Social Innovation), such setups are often mandatory conditions resulting from some previous transgression. Further, their impacts have not been evaluated. There is a serious need for research evidence that examines potential health and social policy solutions, not just health and social problems.

It is clear there are alternatives to the "once a month, all at the same time" approach to income-assistance payments. When the study is over, we hope we will have some sense of whether a change at the policy level—and finding a way to give people some choice in the matter—can help quiet the monthly chorus of sirens and keep people alive.

CRITICAL READING QUESTIONS

1. How is drug use a personal trouble, and how is it a public issue?
2. How are welfare cheques distributed in BC? Why do these researchers think that the timing of welfare cheques could be a problem?
3. What kinds of solutions do they propose to the problems of "cheque day"?
4. There are many other social factors that lead to drug use and overdoses. What other factors might be important (other than the timing of welfare cheques)? What other solutions might we propose to deal with the social problem of drug use and overdoses?

Disability

A **disability** is a mental or physical condition that limits a person's daily activities and restricts what they can do (Statistics Canada 2012). When thinking about disabilities, many disability rights activists argue for a "**people first philosophy**," an approach that focuses on the individual and her abilities rather than her limitations. This would mean using language such as "people with disabilities" rather than people who are "disabled." It focuses on the person and not the disability. This can be very important because of the discrimination and stigma often faced by people with disabilities. **Ableism** is the term for discrimination against people who have a cognitive or physical disability on the basis of stereotypes about their limitations.

The study of disabilities is important to health sociology for a number of reasons. First, disabilities can be related to health inequalities. Disability can shape your access to the health care system and the kind of care that you receive. Second, countries have very different policies for addressing the various concerns of groups that experience disabilities. These policies can help individuals who have disabilities participate fully in society.

One of the most important advances in disability rights in Canada was the constitutional recognition of the rights of people with disabilities in the Canadian Charter of Rights and Freedoms in 1981. This was one of the first important policy gains of the disability rights community in Canada. Because of this, it is illegal to discriminate against people with disabilities in Canada.

Internationally, most countries in the world have signed the **United Nations Convention on the Rights of Persons with Disabilities (CRPD).** The convention sets out a list of rights that people with disabilities have and how the state should work to protect these rights. In all, 168 countries (87 per cent of United Nations members) have

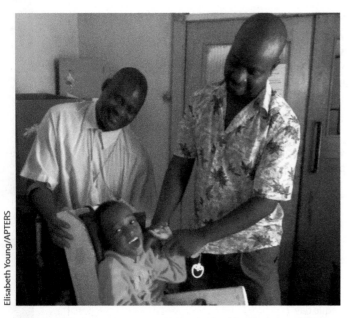

PHOTO 11.2 Apters is an organization in Zambia that uses recycled paper to make papier mâché chairs and walking aids for people with disabilities. What other innovations can we develop to help foster the integration of people with disabilities?

signed on to this convention, agreeing to enact its principles. Canada signed the convention and ratified it in 2010 (United Nations 2016).

The CRPD has many components that work to lay out the rights of persons with disabilities. Countries that join in the convention promise to develop and carry out policies that help to protect the rights of people with disabilities and eliminate discrimination (Article 4). They also agree to fight stereotypes and prejudices and promote awareness of the capabilities of persons with disabilities (Article 8). Part of this is related to creating legal recognition that persons are equal before the law, to prohibiting discrimination on the basis of disability, and to guaranteeing equal legal protection (Article 5). The convention requires countries to eliminate barriers and ensure that persons with disabilities can access their environment, transportation, and public services (Article 9). Countries also agree to ensure equal access to education (Article 24), equal rights to work and employment (Article 27), and equal participation in political life, including the right to vote (Article 29) (United Nations 2016).

ACTIVITY

Accessibility in Everyday Life

Almost 14 per cent of all Canadians report having a disability that limits their daily activity (Statistics Canada 2017a). There is a wide diversity of types of disabilities that individuals can have. Figure 11.8 shows the prevalence of different types of disabilities among people in Canada. The majority of disabilities are physical, including those that are related to pain, flexibility, mobility, dexterity, seeing, and hearing. Learning, memory, and mental health disabilities are also prevalent in the Canadian population.

Canada has committed to the CRPD, which requires us to provide a society free from discrimination against people with disabilities and facilitate the working, studying, and general integration of people with disabilities. Consider the different types of disabilities, physical, cognitive, and developmental. How effectively are we creating an inclusive environment for people with these different types of disabilities?

Begin by watching these videos in which two young women talk about their experiences with disability and ableism.

www.youtube.com/watch?v=g8zR2HJYb2g
www.youtube.com/watch?v=X1xnyVCBYNQ

Consider the experiences discussed in these videos, and answer the following questions:

1. What sorts of activities were discussed in these videos that might provide different types of challenges to people with disabilities?
2. How is the idea of ableism related to the stories of these two women?
3. How can social support, such as groups on campus, friends, and family, help to make our community more accepting and accessible for people with diverse abilities?

Now consider your day and the different activities in which you engage—from waking up in the morning, taking the bus to school, attending classes, socializing with your friends, or working at a part-time job.

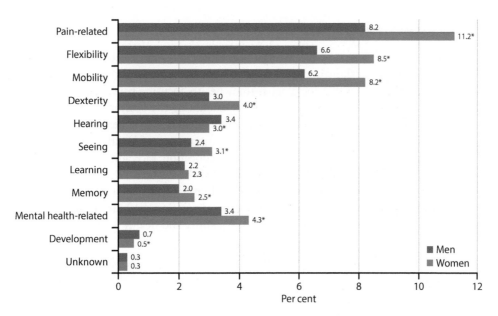

FIGURE 11.8 **Prevalence of disabilities, by type and sex, 15 years and older, Canada, 2012**

Source: Rubab Arim, 2015, "A Profile of Persons with Disabilities among Canadians Aged 15 Years or Older," *Canadian Survey on Disability, 2012*, Catalogue 89-654-X, Ottawa: Statistics Canada, https://www150.statcan.gc.ca/n1/pub/89-654-x/89-654-x2015001-eng.htm

1. How accessible are these activities for individuals who have a physical disability, such using a wheelchair or being sight-impaired? Would some of these activities be challenging for people with a physical disability? How accessible are these activities for individuals who have a cognitive disability? Would some of these activities be challenging for people with a cognitive disability?

2. What has been done to make these activities more accessible to those with a physical or cognitive disability? What more could be done? How could we alter the environment to make it easier to go to class, take notes or engage in class sessions, travel to school, or do other things?

3. What sort of resources are available on your campus to make it more inclusive for individuals with different sorts of disabilities? What other services do you think might be useful or important?

PHOTO 11.3 Justine Clarke, the first Miss World contestant to compete in a wheelchair, is fighting to make pageants more inclusive. How do individual acts like this work to challenge stereotypes about disability in society?

Summary

This chapter began by discussing the complex and multifaceted nature of health, which includes physical, mental, and social health. We examined the sociology of health and assessed the ways that sociologists study health, focusing particularly on the social determinants of health. Through the activity examining the Freshman 15 and binge drinking, we came to see how what appear to be individual health issues are often related to larger social contexts. We assessed the critical importance of health inequalities, particularly those based on social class, global health, education, race and ethnicity, and gender. The reading by Michael Marmot also highlighted these issues of health inequalities. We considered the role of health care systems and health policies for dealing with health issues within populations. The chapter ended by discussing disability in society and how disability can be related to both health inequalities and health policies.

Key Terms

ableism 325
chronic disease prevalence 310
disability 325
health 304
health care systems 321
health disparities 309
health policy 322
healthy life expectancy 310
life expectancy 310

mental health 304
obesity 315
people first philosophy 325
sick role 306
social determinants of health 307
standards for health care in Canada 322
UN Convention on the Rights of Persons with Disabilities (CRPD) 325

For Further Reading

Davidson, Alan. 2014. *Social Determinants of Health: A Comparative Approach*. Toronto: Oxford University Press.
Marmot, Michael. 2015. *The Health Gap*. New York: Bloomsbury.
Segal, Alexander, and Christopher Fries. 2011. *Pursuing Health and Wellness: Healthy Societies, Healthy People*. Toronto: Oxford University Press.

References

AUCCCD (Association for University and College Counselling Center Directors). 2014. "AUCCCD Annual Survey." http://campusmentalhealth .ca/resource/aucccd-annual-survey.

Canadian Institute of Health Research. 2015. "Smoking." https:// yourhealthsystem.cihi.ca/hsp/inbrief?lang=en#!/indicators/009/ smoking/;mapC1;mapLevel2.

———. 2015. "Trends in Income Related Inequalities in Canada." https://www.cihi.ca/en/summary_report_inequalities_2015_en.pdf.

Case, Anne, Darren Lubotsky, and Christina Paxson. 2002. "Economic Status and Health in Childhood: The Origins of the Gradient." *The American Economic Review* 92(5): 1308–34.

CBC (Canadian Broadcasting Corporation). 2017. "TB Is Still Here: Sask. Health Workers Talk Prevention, Treatment at Conference." 5 June. http://www.cbc.ca/news/canada/saskatoon/tuberculosis-sask-2017-symposium-kris-stewart-1.4146162.

CDC (Center for Disease Control). 2014. "Suicide and Self-Inflicted Injury." https://www.cdc.gov/nchs/fastats/suicide.htm.

———. 2017. "Fact Sheets: Binge Drinking." https://www.cdc.gov/ alcohol/fact-sheets/binge-drinking.htm.

Center for Innovation in Campus Mental Health. 2017. "Whitepaper of Post-secondary Student Mental Health." http://campusmentalhealth .ca/literature/white-paper-postsecondary-student-mental-health.

Government of Canada. 2003. "2003 First Ministers Health Accord." https://www.canada.ca/en/health-canada/services/health-care -system/health-care-system-delivery/federal-provincial-territorial -collaboration/2003-first-ministers-accord-health-care -renewal/2003-first-ministers-health-accord.html.

———2017. "National Report: Apparent Opioid Related Deaths in Canada." https://www.canada.ca/en/public-health/services/publications/ healthy-living/apparent-opioid-related-deaths-report-2016-2017 -december.html.

Himes, Christine L., and Sandra L. Reynolds. 2005. "The Changing Relationship between Obesity and Educational Status." *Gender Issues* 22(2): 45–57.

Kenkel, Donald S., Dean R. Lillard, and Alan D. Mathios. 2006. "The Roles of High School Completion and GED Receipt in Smoking and Obesity." National Bureau of Economic Research Working Paper 11990. Cambridge, MA: National Bureau of Economic Research.

Mehra, Chapal. 2017. "India Cannot Eliminate TB by 2017 without Also Tackling Poverty and Under Nutrition." 6 May. http://www .huffingtonpost.in/chapal-mehra/india-cannot-eliminate-tb-by -2025-without-also-tackling-poverty_a_22116851.

NIH (National Institute for Health). 2013. "Why Obesity Is a Health Problem?" https://www.nhlbi.nih.gov/health/educational/wecan/healthy-weight-basics/obesity.htm.

NPR (National Public Radio). 2017. "Why Does India Lead the World in Deaths from TB?" 9 November. https://www.npr.org /sections/goatsandsoda/2017/11/09/561834263/why-does-india-lead -the-world-in-deaths-from-tb.

Parsons, Talcott. 1991. *The Social System*. London: Routledge.

Pickett, Kate, and Richard Wilkinson. 2011. *The Spirit Level: Why Greater Equality Makes Societies Stronger*. New York: Bloomsbury.

Springer, Kristin, and Dawne Marie Mouzon. 2011. "'Macho Men' and Preventative Health Care: Implications for Older Men in Different Social Classes." *Journal of Health and Social Behavior* (June): 1–16.

Statistics Canada. 2012. "Disability in Canada." http://www.statcan .gc.ca/pub/89-654-x/89-654-x2013002-eng.htm.

———. 2015. CANSIM. http://www5.statcan.gc.ca/cansim/home-accueil?lang=eng.

———. 2016. CANSIM, Table 105-0501, and Catalogue no. 82-221-X." https://www.statcan.gc.ca/tables-tableaux/sum-som/l01/cst01 /health81b-eng.htm.

———. 2017a. "A Profile of Persons with Disabilities among Canadians Aged 15 and Older, 2012." http://www.statcan.gc.ca/pub/89-654 -x/89-654-x2015001-eng.htm.

———. 2017b. "Projected Life Expectancy at Birth by Sex, by Aboriginal Identity, 2017." Table 91-547-XIE. https://www.statcan.gc.ca /pub/89-645-x/2010001/c-g/c-g013-eng.htm.

United Nations. 2016. "Convention on the Rights of Persons with Disabilities." https://www.un.org/development/desa/disabilities /convention-on-the-rights-of-persons-with-disabilities.html.

University of Ottawa. 2017. "The Health of Indigenous People in Canada." http://www.med.uottawa.ca/SIM/data/Vul_Indigenous_e.htm.

Veenstra, Gerry. 2009. "Racialized Identity and Health in Canada: Results from a Nationally Representative Survey." *Social Science and Medicine* 69(4): 538–42.

WHO (World Health Organization). 2017a. "Constitution of WHO: Principles." http://www.who.int/about/mission/en.

———. 2017b. "Tuberculosis." http://www.who.int/mediacentre /factsheets/fs104/en.

12 Globalization and Global Inequality

Chapter Outline

Photo credit: Krizjohn Rosales/Pexels

Introduction

The world feels more interconnected than ever before. The process of globalization is all around us. Its implications are complicated, and whether we see it as promising or dangerous very much depends on the theoretical lens used to examine it. In this chapter, we will discuss three core theories of globalization (modernization, world systems, and world society). We will also look at global inequality and examine how we can measure it, how it has changed, and how we can help alleviate it. Let's begin by thinking about globalization.

What Is Globalization?

We have all heard that we live in a globalized world. But what does this mean? What is globalization, how does it happen, and what effects does it have on Canada and other countries? **Globalization** is a process of increasing interconnectedness of people, products, ideas, and places. Globalization has several causes; for example, improvements in transportation systems and in communication and information technologies are particularly important factors. These developments facilitate the easy movement of people, products, and ideas, which can lead to political, economic, social, and cultural integration.

Globalization increases interconnectedness in three main ways. First, material or physical connections increase. The movement of goods, people, and money across national borders is relatively fluid. These increased flows are facilitated by shared global infrastructure. For example, physical global infrastructure, such as international transportation and banking systems, are shared across countries and make increased interaction and the exchange of goods and money relatively easy. In addition, normative similarities such as trade agreements and friendly relations between countries develop from global infrastructure and make the movement of people and goods easier.

The importance of this physical interconnectedness is evident when we travel to different countries. Twenty years ago, people travelling from Canada to Europe had to take traveller's cheques or the currency of each country they would be visiting (e.g., British pounds, French francs, German marks, Italian lira). Now we can all simply use our bankcard at any bank in Europe or pay with our credit card at any store or restaurant. The international banking system has facilitated European travel, and the use of the euro, the common currency of many European countries, makes moving between nations easier than ever before. (No more converting currencies in our heads!)

Second, globalization entails a spatio-temporal element; places that once felt very far away now feel much closer. We can get on a plane and be halfway around the world in a few hours, or we can use technology such as Skype to talk to or email friends who live in other cities or countries. The impact of distant events also becomes more relevant to our day-to-day lives. Tsunamis or famines occurring in other lands seem more real to us because we can easily (and almost instantly) see pictures or videos of them. The 9/11 terrorist attacks occurred around 9:00 a.m., yet many people did not hear about them until that afternoon or evening. Social media such as Twitter informed people of the Las Vegas concert mass shooting minutes after it occurred in 2017.

This spatio-temporal convergence is the basis of theorist Marshall McLuhan's concept of the global village. The ease of international communication has allowed us to form an increasingly interconnected and unified global community where we can easily interact with and learn about faraway people and places. Through media such as the Internet, we can join Facebook groups, read blogs, or follow the Twitter feeds of people from other countries or continents and can easily connect with family and friends who live far away. We can learn about world events and share updates about our lives instantaneously. McLuhan believed that this increased shared interaction creates a greater global responsibility for social betterment through heightened awareness. (We learned about McLuhan

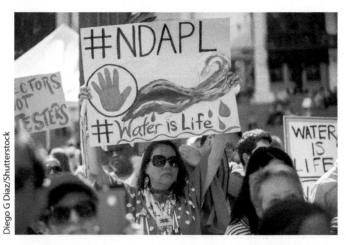

Diego G Diaz/Shutterstock

PHOTO 12.1 Oil pipeline construction can have important consequences for the Canadian and world economy, the environment, and domestic and international politics. These protesters at Standing Rock are resisting the building of a pipeline. How does this development illustrate the three main dimensions of globalization?

in Chapter 7 on the media.) For example, people from around the world re-tweeted BlackLivesMatter and were Facebook supporters of the protests at Standing Rock who were resisting the North Dakota pipeline (NoDAPL).

Another example of the spatio-temporal element of globalization is the impact that distant wars and conflicts can have on our daily lives. These effects can range from stricter airport security to higher gas prices. The latter helps to show the spatio-temporal element of globalization. Everyone has heard the complaint that the price of gas is rising. Oil companies, the news media, and other observers note that these prices are rising because of the conflicts in the Middle East, where much of the world's oil deposits exist. This relationship illustrates the globalized nature of world economies because an overseas conflict affects our daily activity of buying gas.

The world's oil supply is a globalized commodity market. Canada produces a lot of oil—in fact, Alberta has the world's third largest oil reserves (behind only Saudi Arabia and Venezuela). Canada has 170.2 billion barrels, or about 11 per cent of the global oil reserve, and uses about 860 million barrels of oil a year (Alberta Energy 2014). These figures indicate that we have enough oil to meet our current use. If Canadians got all their oil from Alberta, global conflicts should not affect the price of gas in Canada. In other words, it should not matter that there are tensions or wars in the Middle East if we ship oil from Alberta to the other provinces and territories. However, all of our oil, along with the oil from the Middle East and other regions, goes onto the global market, and we compete with other countries to purchase it. As a result, international conflicts outside our control cause prices in Canada to fluctuate, despite our access to our own oil supply.

Finally, globalization has a cognitive element that involves the dissemination of ideas and culture throughout the world. This diffusion creates a situation in which cultural models can become increasingly similar across countries. If you have ever been in a remote location in another country and heard a Taylor Swift song on the radio or seen a McDonald's, you have witnessed the global dispersion of culture.

One positive example of the dissemination of cultural ideals is the spread of the concept of human rights. Most people would agree that individuals have the right to not suffer intentional and unwanted physical harm (unless provoked or legally necessary), to choose how to spend their time (within reasonable constraints), to have access to clean water and other resources necessary for survival, and to practise the religion of their choice. The first major human rights legislation, the International Declaration of Human Rights, was passed by the United Nations General Assembly in 1948. At that time, 48 countries signed the declaration, supporting the idea of human rights internationally. More recently, the United Nations (UN) passed the Convention on the Rights of Persons with Disabilities, which was signed by 91 countries and ratified in 2008. These two conventions illustrate the increased international support for the idea of human rights and the global spread of this cultural norm.

However, sharing ideas and cultural models is not always positive. Hearing a Selena Gomez song or seeing a Starbucks abroad would be a happy surprise to some and a disappointment to others. Other cultural ideals, such as consumerism and materialism, also spread from country to country. Bennett and colleagues (2004) found that Western ideals of beauty have significant reach, affecting many women and girls in other parts of the world. They compared young Ghanaian women with a very low body mass index (BMI) with a friend who had a normal index. Each young woman completed a survey on her eating habits and self-image. The researchers found that the rise in eating disorders in Ghana was partly explained by the low-weight girls' desire to conform to Western beauty standards. Other studies also report an increase in eating disorders among ethnic Fijian girls following the introduction of Western television. In essence, weight concerns and anorexia became more common as exposure to Western media increased.

RESEARCH METHOD
SURVEY

Understanding Globalization

It is important to recognize that globalization does not occur in one direction—we are not simply becoming more globalized. In other words, globalization is not a process of linear evolution but one that involves advances and regressions. The world is generally becoming more interconnected, but there are still times when countries or individuals become more isolationist. For example, a country might raise taxes on imported goods, restrict the amount of foreign content on television, or increase the barriers to immigration. Globalization is also not always a harmonious process. Not all individuals agree that becoming more interconnected is a good idea or is beneficial for all. For some countries, increased globalization can lead to a waning of culture, increased unemployment, and loss of autonomy over national services and resources. Academics, politicians, and the public continue to debate globalization's potential advantages and disadvantages, and concerned citizens and social movements encourage, contest, and challenge this process.

Globalization is a complicated process that can greatly affect individuals, communities, countries, and the world. How we understand globalization depends on our theoretical perspective. There are three main theories of globalization and global inequality in sociology: modernization theory, world systems theory, and world society theory. The following sections examine these approaches and the ways these different theoretical lenses can help us to shed light on different aspects of globalization.

Modernization Theory

Modernization theory attempts to isolate the features that predict which societies will progress and develop. This theory argues that a society's internal features, including its economic, social, and cultural systems, can either help or hinder development. Modernization theory claims that countries are poor because they cling to traditional and inefficient attitudes, technologies, and institutions. In contrast, modern societies embrace industrial capitalism, advanced technologies, and modern institutions. With enough time and the help of "correct" behaviours, all societies can become modernized and develop like Western societies.

Modernization theory encourages all countries to strive to modernize in the same way that western Europe and North America did. This process requires that societies go through a set of established stages. W.W. Rostow (1991) describes these steps in his famous book *The Stages of Economic Growth: A Non-Communist Manifesto* (a play on the title of Marx and Engels's *Communist Manifesto*). Rostow argues that all societies start as traditional societies, which emphasize the importance of history and tradition. Traditional societies are static and rigid in that they have very little economic mobility and prioritize stability over change. They are based on subsistence agriculture (the growing of crops to feed the farmer's own livestock and family) or hunting and gathering. These societies, such as the feudal societies of medieval Europe, focus on spiritual richness but lack material abundance.

As the demand for raw materials increased, these traditional societies could not keep up. They were pushed to develop more productive, commercial agriculture and to create **cash crops** (crops to be sold instead of consumed by the producers). Widespread technological advances, including the development of irrigation systems and efficient transportation, led to increased productivity and the broader dissemination of goods. All these changes facilitated an increase in social mobility and put the previous social equilibrium, which had existed for centuries, in flux. This period is called the pre-conditions to takeoff (Rostow 1991).

The second period is economic takeoff, during which manufacturing becomes more efficient and increases in size and scale. Because of this mass productivity, societies are

HIGHLIGHT

Modernization Theory and Émile Durkheim

Modernization theory takes some of its ideas from Émile Durkheim (1960), who was interested in the social evolution of societies. He argued that like organisms, societies progress through several stages: they start simple and evolve into something that is more complex.

Sociologists often focus on social problems, but Durkheim was more interested in how society functions fairly effectively, even when people have conflicting interests. In particular, he was interested in explaining social solidarity, a feeling of unity among people in a society. How do we explain this harmony? How has the foundation of such solidarity changed as societies have altered?

Durkheim argued that early societies were based on **mechanical solidarity**. Each unit (such as a family) basically provided for its own production and consumption needs, and sub-units could survive in isolation from one another. A family might live on a small subsistence farm where it would grow its own crops and make its own clothes, candles, and soap. In these societies, each unit could survive on its own—a family did not need to rely on anyone else to make goods for it or provide it with services. However, these societies were held together by a shared sense of collective conscious, the shared beliefs and sentiments that created solidarity between people. For example, most people in a village or town were of the same religion and thus had a shared set of beliefs about appropriate behaviours and attitudes.

Modern societies tend to be comprised of people who are quite different from one another. There is no common adherence to a collective conscience—people are from different religions, cultural traditions, or philosophies, especially in a country as multicultural as Canada. As a result, individuals are guided by distinct norms and values that could weaken the overall collective conscience. However, modern societies also have an increased division of labour, with more people engaging in specialized tasks and activities. Some people are teachers, some farmers, others architects. Because different people perform different functions in society, no group can survive on its own. Farmers have food, but they probably cannot build their own houses or educate their children; they need architects and teachers, just as the architects and teachers need farmers to grow their food. These societies are based on organic solidarity: because people are dissimilar and specialized, they depend on one another to provide what they cannot supply for themselves.

In many ways, it is quite clear that we live in a society characterized by organic solidarity. However, the rise of technology could be undermining our dependency on one another (and the solidarity that this dependency can bring). In our daily lives, we encounter numerous scenarios in which we use machines to perform a function instead of relying on another human. We bank online or use an ATM rather than wait for a teller; we get our own soft drink at a fast-food restaurant rather than wait for a cashier to do it for us; we even check out our own groceries at the supermarket. Even more complex tasks are being replaced by technological media. For example, we self-diagnose our ailments on WebMD rather than consult a doctor or purchase Rosetta Stone to learn a language rather than take a course.

able to produce goods for both domestic consumption and export. Markets emerge as people produce goods to trade with others for profit. This phase is also a time of rising individualism, which is focused on individual material enrichment and can undermine family ties and time-honoured norms and values.

Next, societies move toward technological maturity. In this period, all sectors of society become involved in market production, and international trade rises. Economies become increasingly diversified, with many different goods and services produced and sold. This period is also associated with a great reduction in absolute poverty. Cities grow as people leave rural villages in search of jobs and economic opportunities in urban areas. The rise of individualism and an increased sense of efficacy generate social movements demanding greater political rights to, for example, provide universal basic education and increase the rights of various groups, such as women and minorities.

The final period of development is mass consumption. The mass production that occurred in the previous period stimulates this stage. People soon feel that they need the new diversity of products available and consume those goods accordingly. Because consumers now have more disposable income, they are able to consume more. Canadian society currently resides in this stage of mass consumption.

Modernization theorists argue that, for most of human history, the whole world was poor. In fact, countries began moving out of poverty only a few centuries ago. From this perspective, it is the current affluence in some modern countries that is historically unusual. How have some countries been able to move out of poverty? During the Middle Ages, a proliferation of exploration and trade brought wealth to a growing share of people in western Europe. The growth of capitalism and the rise of the Industrial Revolution also created vast new wealth. This affluence was initially concentrated in the hands of the few; however, the industrial system was so productive that its benefits soon expanded to include a growing number of people. Today, middle-income countries in Latin America and Asia are also industrializing and becoming wealthier as a result.

PHOTO 12.2 Black Friday, held the day after American Thanksgiving, is an extreme example of concentrated mass consumption. Retailers offer extreme sales and special deals to encourage the consumption of goods beyond basic needs. In 2016, US consumers spent more than $68 billion on this one day. Black Friday has come to Canadian stores, even though Canadians celebrate Thanksgiving more than a month earlier. How does Black Friday illustrate the mass consumption that occurs in modern society?

If industrialization has such potential to reduce poverty, why isn't the whole world moving in this direction? Modernization theory points to tradition as the greatest barrier to development. Traditional family values, gender roles, and cultural models can hinder the adoption of new technologies and procedures. For example, if a society believes that women should not work outside the home, there are fewer workers to produce goods. Not all societies seek new technology or embrace new methods of production; many people resist such advances because they see them as threats to their social and cultural systems and beliefs.

Modernization theorists argue that traditional societies should embrace modern technologies and production methods. A specific change that would help countries develop is to focus on cash crops of high-yield agricultural products. As mentioned earlier, traditional societies are based on subsistence farming, while more developed countries sell their crops for profit. Most farms in Canada and other developed countries currently practise **monocropping**, an economically efficient and profitable method of repeatedly growing one high-yield crop. Farmers using this technique can purchase specialized equipment and design their fields and irrigation systems for the specific crop. By adopting this method, they can use the profits to purchase consumer goods and other products that will improve their lives. In theory, the process would lead to more economic productivity and to Rostow's period of economic takeoff.

Monocropping could increase short-term food production and lead to prosperity. However, it has certain disadvantages. Relying on cash crops can be volatile and unsustainable. Prices for major cash crops are set on a global scale; therefore, nations, regions, or individual producers of these crops are at the market's mercy. (This situation is similar to Canadian oil being put on the global market and its price being affected by global production and conflict.) Monocropping is also controversial because it has long-term environmental disadvantages. It can damage the soil, lead to the growth of parasites, and increase crop vulnerability to opportunistic insects and plants.

Modernization theory as a whole has been criticized on a number of different fronts. Some argue that it fails to recognize that rich nations industrialized from a position of global strength, colonizing other countries and taking their resources. As a result, the countries that colonized early were able to accumulate wealth, while the colonized

ACTIVITY

The Ecological Footprint

We can get a sense of how much we affect the natural environment by calculating our **ecological footprint**—the amount of land and sea necessary to supply the resources a human population consumes and to process the waste it produces. We can use this information to estimate how much of the earth (or how many earths) it would take to support an individual or country if everybody followed a given way of life (www.footprintnetwork.org).

Go to this book's companion website to access a test that calculates your ecological footprint. When you have completed the test, answer the following questions:

1. How many earths would there have to be for everyone to live your lifestyle?
2. Where did most of your footprint come from—carbon, food, housing, or goods and services? Were you surprised at the areas where you had the largest and smallest footprints? If so, why?
3. How did your footprint compare with others from your country? Why is your footprint larger or smaller than the average Canadian's?
4. What advice does the test give for reducing your footprint? What other methods could you use to reduce it? Discuss which ways would be easiest and which would be hardest.

Now let's look at a bigger picture and compare ecological footprints in different parts of the world. The figure below shows the relationship between a country's footprint and its **Human Development Index (HDI)**, a number that combines a variety of measures regarding the health and quality of life in a country (e.g., life expectancy, education, and income). Examine the figure, and then answer the following questions:

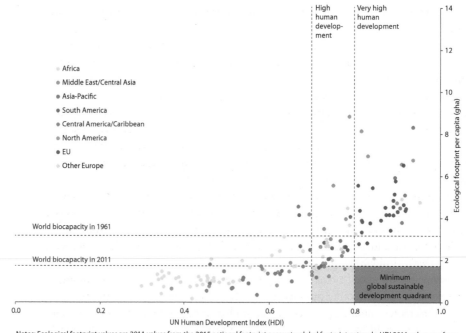

Notes: Ecological footprint values are 2011 values from the 2015 national footprint accounts, global footprint network; HDI 2011 values are from the 2014 human development report, UNDP

FIGURE 12.1   Human welfare and ecological footprints compared

Source: Ecological footprint values are 2011 values from the 2015 National Footprint Accounts, Global Footprint Network. http://www.footprintnetwork.org. HDI 2011 values are from the 2014 Human Development Report, United Nations Development Programme.

1. Which regions have the largest ecological footprints, and which have the smallest? How do the world's regions differ in their human development and in their ecological footprint?
2. How is a country's human development related to its ecological footprint? Why do you think this relationship exists?

countries were exploited and became poorer. In other words, the European takeoff period was fuelled by the resources (including natural resources and human resources in the form of forced slavery) taken from other countries. Colonization was hugely problematic at the time and is now an unrealistic (and undesirable) avenue for development. Furthermore, the idea that poor countries remain poor because of "backward" ways or a refusal to embrace technologies or progress suggests that all countries have the same resources and opportunities to develop, which is surely not the case.

Modernization theory is also criticized for being ethnocentric, or judging other cultures by the standards of one's own. Many question whether it is fair to measure other countries against Western standards or to assume that the Western mode of doing things is best. Western notions of development have led to many problems, such as environmental degradation and materialism. Is it, then, good to push other countries to become more like Western nations?

World Systems Theory

Developed by Immanuel Wallerstein (2011) as a critique of modernization theory, **world systems theory** highlights the inherent inequality that occurs through globalization and global development. World systems theory understands globalization in a way very different from the way that modernization theory does; it sees the world as a transnational division of labour between core, semi-periphery, and periphery countries.

Core countries are the most powerful nations in the world. Their power is based on their economic diversification, high level of industrialization, high-skill labour, and focus on the manufacturing of goods instead of simply extracting raw resources for export. These nations dominate new technologies and industries and can exert significant economic and military influence over other countries. Core countries have been traditionally found in the northwest of Europe; however, Canada, the United States, and Japan are now part of the core.

Periphery countries are the least powerful of the three types of countries. They are not economically diversified and are only minimally industrialized. These countries focus on extracting raw materials for export to core countries. Periphery nations, which are concentrated in Latin America and sub-Saharan Africa, are attractive to core countries' business interests because they tend to have lenient labour and environmental laws.

Semi-periphery countries, such as China, India, Brazil, and South Africa, combine characteristics of the core and periphery. They are often countries moving toward industrialization and economic diversification. Canada was once a semi-periphery country, when its economy was focused on resource extraction and it had very low levels of industrialization.

As the example of Canada's shift from the periphery to the core highlights, countries can gain power over time. They can also lose power. Many countries, such as the Netherlands and the United Kingdom, have had the distinction of being superpowers for a time. However, this status is hard to maintain.

World systems theory is based on Marxist principles. Think of the core countries as the capitalists. They benefit from the labour of the proletariat countries (the periphery) in a number of ways. First, companies in the core take the resources from the periphery countries, such as the United States extracting oil from the Middle East. Second, they use periphery countries' labour power and pay very low wages (which they cannot do in their own countries because of unions and labour laws). A classic example is companies such as Nike or Walmart, both American corporations, outsourcing their labour to countries such as Bangladesh or China. Third, core countries pollute periphery countries and deplete their resources. Companies from the core might clear forests to make space for factories, which decreases air quality. As with labour exploitation, environmental protection laws prohibit companies from engaging in these practices in their own countries. Finally, the capitalists in core countries sell the goods produced in the periphery to the workers in the periphery. These wealthy owners bring the resulting profits back to the core countries. In this way, poorer nations keep getting poorer and can never catch up economically.

According to world systems theorists, the unequal trade relations between the core and periphery countries create many problems for the periphery. Periphery countries are pressured to produce a small variety of cash crops that are oriented to export (as the modernization theorists encourage). For example, these countries might be encouraged to produce coffee beans for export instead of fruits and vegetables, which could feed the local population. In addition, periphery countries are urged to extract natural resources in their raw formats and export them to core countries, where they are processed (e.g., mined stones set in rings or furniture built out of raw lumber) to make a profit. This process destroys the local environment in peripheral countries. It also creates low-wage and low-skill work in the periphery while taking the higher wage and higher skill work to the core.

ACTIVITY

Commodity Chains and Global Inequality

Chances are that the clothing you wear, the computer you use, and the car or bus you take to school are made in countries other than Canada. Goods come to Canada through **commodity chains**, which gather resources, transform them into commodities, and distribute them to consumers. This process is a natural part of globalization.

Greg Linden, Kenneth Kraemer, and Jason Dedrick (2009) were interested in the commodity chains of an Apple iPod. They examined where the product originated and where its value went. They write: "An iPod is designed and marketed by a US company, assembled by Taiwanese manufacturers in China, and includes key parts from Japanese, Korean and US suppliers" (140). This list does not even scratch the surface regarding the places where the raw materials—silicon, copper, gold, aluminum—and chemicals come from; they could, for example, originate in the United States, Canada, Russia, Brazil, India, Zambia, or elsewhere. Most of the profit, however, goes to the United States, with very little remaining in the countries where the iPod is made (see the following table).

TABLE 12.1 | **The geography of the captured value in a single $299 iPod**

	Country of Final Sale	United States	Japan	Korea	Taiwan	Total
Distribution and Retail	75					75
Apple		80				80
Top 10 Components		7	27	1	5	40
TOTAL	75	87	27	1	5	195

Source: Greg Linden, Kenneth L. Kraemer, and Jason Dedrick, 2009, "Who Captures Value in a Global Innovation Network? The Case of Apple's iPod," *Communications of the ACM* 52(3): 140–4.

For this activity, choose a product (either a Starbucks coffee and cup or a Nike shoe), and look at its manufacturing and delivery routes. What stops (farms, factories, regions, countries) contribute to making the finished product? Use the Internet to research where your chosen product comes from and how it is made. Then check the CIA's *World Factbook* online (or access the direct link on this book's companion website) for information about the countries involved in making the product. Click on the economy, people, and government links to examine the conditions in these countries, including average life expectancy, infant mortality rate, unemployment rate, percentage of the population living below the poverty line, and inequality. With this information in mind, why do you think that your product was made in those countries? What is the implication of this process for global inequality?

Local industries in the periphery cannot compete with companies from the core. As a result, few local businesses develop in the periphery, and workers must buy their processed goods from the core countries at high cost, creating more debt. For example, periphery countries sell cheap resources and raw materials to the core. To do so, they must buy expensive fertilizers, pesticides, and mechanical equipment from the core. This downward cycle leads the periphery to become poorer as the core becomes richer. Just as in Marx's theory, poor and rich countries depend on one another, but the benefits of their relationship are skewed toward the rich core nations.

World systems theory argues that resources flow from the periphery to the core and ideas flow in the opposite direction. For example, the flow of news and entertainment media privileges the core's needs and interests. News about the core is reported everywhere in the periphery, while news about the periphery is rarely reported in the core. Thus, people in the periphery know a lot about processes and current events in core countries. Donald Trump's inauguration was reported all over the world; however, news from other parts of the world is rarely covered in core media outlets. For example, the Paris terrorist attacks that happened on 13 November 2015 killed 130 people and were widely covered in the media. Moments of silence for these victims were held around the world, and the flag was lowered on Parliament Hill in Ottawa. However, two suicide bombers in Lebanon the day before killed 37 and wounded 180 and were not mentioned in much of the same coverage. This highlights the Western bias of our news. This lack of dialogue with non-Western countries perpetuates exploitation and global inequality because those with the means to help create change (such as core country citizens) are usually unaware of events in the periphery.

Like all theories, world systems theory has been criticized. For example, many people note that foreign trade has assisted some countries. For example, trade with rich countries has helped the economies of Singapore, Hong Kong, and Japan. Others also argue that as modernization theory predicts, foreign investment stimulates growth, not economic decline. Furthermore, the ability of countries to move into the core counters the claim that globalization will lead to increased poverty in the periphery.

In this chapter's first reading, Daina Stukuls Eglitis asks why rich nations don't do more to reduce world poverty. This is a great question—most people in core countries believe that global poverty is a significant social issue. However, global poverty continues and may even be worsening. How do we explain this trend? Eglitis argues that people in rich countries benefit from global poverty. This argument is difficult to accept, especially for those who live in a rich country.

The Uses of Global Poverty: How Economic Inequality Benefits the West

Daina Stukuls Eglitis

Why don't rich nations do more to reduce the severe poverty that paralyzes much of the world? This selection argues that people in rich countries, including the United States, actually benefit from global poverty in a number of ways.

Eglitis, Daina Stukuls. 2009. "The Uses of Global Poverty: How Economic Inequality Benefits the West." In John Macionis, Nijole V. Benokraitis and Bruce Ravelli, eds, Seeing Ourselves: Classic, Contemporary, and Cross Cultural Readings in Sociology, 8th edn, 229–36. Toronto: Pearson Education Canada. By permission of the author.

READING

In the global village, there stand a wide variety of homes, from the stately mansion on the hill, to the modest abode blessed with electricity and running water, to the adequate but unheated (or uncooled) hut, to the flood-prone, tattered shanty cobbled together from gathered scrap. Those who live on the hill are aware of their neighbours, as their neighbours are aware of them. Most inhabitants of the global village recognize that wealth and the accompanying opportunities for education, healthcare, and consumption are not evenly divided and that a substantial gap exists between the more and less materially blessed populations. Not everyone agrees on why that is the case. . . .

What have been the responses of well-off states to this global class system with its extremes of wealth and poverty? Not surprisingly, perhaps, political rhetoric has consistently elevated the goal of spreading the prosperity enjoyed by the advanced industrial states of the West around the globe. . . .

If shared global prosperity was the goal, it seems safe to say that while there was some modest progress made in areas like Latin America, Eastern Europe, and parts of Asia, "we" did not really succeed, because the global wealth gap is still massive and growing. The rich countries remain rich, and the poor countries, for the most part, remain trapped in desperate, dire poverty. This has not changed. . . .

Western rhetoric, assistance programs, and advice seem to support the goal of global prosperity and its extension to the 1.3 billion who live on less than $1 per day and those millions or even billions more who eke out a sparse existence just above the threshold of absolute poverty. But the reality of prosperity has touched only a relative few countries, while the struggle to meet basic needs touches many more. Social indicators like the GNI PPP [gross national income purchasing power parity] highlight the differences we find in our village. But what explains them? Why does global poverty exist and persist? Why does a global class system with a thin layer of rich states and broad strata of poor countries exist and persist? What explains why some villagers inhabit houses on the mount while others squat in mud huts below? Possible answers are many. This article explores one way of understanding the yawning gap between the planet's wealthiest and poorest states.

In 1971, sociologist Herbert Gans published an article entitled "The Uses of Poverty: The Poor Pay All."[1] In the article, Gans utilized a conservative theoretical perspective in sociology, functionalism, to inquire about the persistence of poverty in America. The functionalist perspective takes as its starting point the position that essentially all institutions and social phenomena that exist in society contribute in some manner to that society— that is, they are functional for society. If they did not contribute to the social order, the functionalists maintain, they would disappear. Using this perspective, functionalists may inquire about, for instance, the functions, both obvious and hidden (or manifest and latent, to use sociologist Robert Merton's terms), of institutions like the education system or the family or social phenomena like punishment for deviance. These social theorists assume that institutions or phenomena exist because they are functional, and hence their guiding question is: What function do they serve?

Gans posed a similar question about poverty, asking: What are the uses of poverty? Clearly, the notion that poverty is functional for society as a whole is ludicrous: Who would suggest that it is functional for those who endure economic deprivation? So Gans offered a modified functionalist analysis: ". . . instead of identifying functions for an entire social system, I shall identify them for the interest groups, socio-economic classes, and other population aggregates with shared values that 'inhabit' a social system. I suspect that in a modern heterogeneous society, few phenomena are functional or dysfunctional for the society as a whole, and that most result in benefits to some groups and costs to others."

Gans sought to explain the existence and persistence of poverty in modern, wealthy America by highlighting the way that the existence of poverty has benefits for the nonpoor—not just "evil" individuals like the loan shark or the slumlord, but for "normal" members of nonpoor classes. He identified 13 "uses" of poverty, including the notions that the existence of a poor class "ensures that society's 'dirty work' will be done," that the poor "buy goods others do not want and thus prolong the economic usefulness of such goods," and "the poor can be identified and punished as alleged or real deviants in order to uphold the legitimacy of conventional norms." He was not arguing that poverty is good. He was suggesting that understanding poverty's existence and persistence means recognizing that the poor have positive social and economic functions for the nonpoor. Thus, one would conclude that the elimination of poverty, while elevated as a societal goal, would be, in practice, costly to the nonpoor.

While Gans's theoretically based inquiry into poverty was focused on America's poor, the same question might be asked about the existence of global poverty: What are the "uses" of global poverty for the better-off countries of the world economic system? The purpose of such an inquiry would be, as it was in Gans's inquiry, not to use a functionalist analysis to legitimate poverty or the highly skewed distribution of wealth in the global system, but to contribute to a deeper understanding of why it continues to exist by explaining how its persistence confers benefits on well-off states and their inhabitants.

The argument is not that advanced states are consciously conspiring to keep the poor states destitute: well-off countries have historically sought to offer help to less developed countries. In reality, however, there are limited incentives for the better-off states to support the full industrial and technological (and even democratic) development of all the states in the global system. To the degree that the existence of a class of poor states is positively functional for wealthy states, we can begin to imagine why development and assistance programs that help ensure survival, but not prosperity, for poor populations are quite characteristic of Western policy.

This article notes 11 "uses" of global poverty. Global poverty is not, from this perspective, functional for the global community as a whole. The notion that the poverty of billions who live in economically marginal states is globally "useful" would be absurd. But it is not absurd to ask how the existence of a class of poor states serves wealthy states. In fact, asking such a question might contribute to a better understanding of the dual phenomena of global poverty and the global "class" system.

Point 1: The existence of global poverty helps ensure the wealth of affordable goods for Western consumers.

The cornucopia of decently priced goods of reasonable quality enjoyed by Western consumers is underpinned by the low-wage work done in low-income countries. The labels on the clothing you are wearing right now likely contain the familiar words "Made in China" or perhaps "Made in Pakistan." Your clothing is probably of reasonable quality, and you likely paid a reasonable (but not necessarily cheap) price for it.

The Western consumer of textiles such as off-the-rack clothing is a beneficiary of a globalized manufacturing process that has seen the movement of manufacturing to low-wage areas located in poor states that provide ready pools of workers needy enough to labour for a pittance. In China, the average hourly wage of apparel workers is about 23 cents. This benefits the consumer of that apparel. The worker herself (workers in this industry are usually female) derives less benefit: the average hourly wage needed to meet basic needs in China, according to Women's Edge, an advocacy group, is 87 cents.[2] . . .

Stories about low-wage workers in developing countries have, in recent years, emerged in the Western press and provoked some expressions of outrage and the formation of groups like United Students Against Sweatshops. These expressions have been small and limited. Imagine, however, the outrage if popular sports shoes, already pricey, climbed another $50 in cost as a result of manufacturers opting for well-paid, unionized labour. Or imagine if the price of a head of iceberg lettuce, America's favourite vegetable, suddenly doubled in price to $3.00. Which outrage would be more potent?

Point 2: The existence of global poverty benefits Western companies and shareholders in the form of increased profit margins.

Labour costs typically constitute a high percentage of a company's expenditures. By reducing labour costs, companies can both keep prices reasonable (which benefits, as noted, the consumer) and raise profit margins. Not surprisingly, then, companies are not likely to locate in—and are more likely to leave—locations where wages are relatively high. The use of poor female workers in the Third World is, in this respect, especially "beneficial" to companies. Women comprise about 80 per cent of workers in Export Processing Zones and are often paid 20 per cent to 50 per cent less than male counterparts. The less costly the workforce, the greater the opportunity for profit. Not coincidentally, countries with an ample supply of poor workers willing to work for miserable wages are also countries with lax safety and environmental regulations, which also keeps down the costs to the Western employer and pushes up the profits. Hence, companies benefit directly from the existence of economically deprived would-be workers willing (or not in a position to be unwilling) to work for paltry wages in potentially hazardous, or at least very unpleasant, conditions.

Point 3: The existence of global poverty fosters access to resources in poor states that are needed in or desired by the West.
Poor states may sell raw goods at low prices to Western states, which can transform the resource into a more valuable finished product. The position of the poor states in the world economy makes it less likely that they can derive the full benefit of the resources they possess for the government and people. The case of oil in resource-rich but desperately poor Nigeria is an example. Seven major foreign oil companies operate in Nigeria, all representing interests in wealthy states. The vast majority of benefits from Nigeria's oil has accrued not to the country's people, but to the companies (and consumers) of the wealthy states. . . .

Point 4: The existence of global poverty helps support Western medical advances.
The poor provide a pool of guinea pigs for the testing of medicines developed for use primarily in the West. The beneficiaries are not the poor themselves but Western consumers of advanced medicine (60 per cent of profits are made in the United States, which leads the world in drug consumption) and the pharmaceutical companies, which stand astride a $350 billion (and growing) industry. A series of reports in *The Washington Post* in December 2000 documents the disturbing practice of conducting drug trials on ill inhabitants of poor states. For instance, an unapproved antibiotic was tested by a major pharmaceutical company on sick children during a meningitis epidemic in Nigeria. The country's lax regulatory oversight, the sense among some doctors that they could not object to experiment conditions for political or economic reasons, the dearth of alternative healthcare options, combined with the desire of the company to rapidly prepare for the market a potential "blockbuster" drug underpinned a situation in which disease victims were treated as test subjects rather than patients. This case highlights the way that nonpoor states actually benefit from the existence of poor states with struggling, sick populations. . . .

Point 5: The existence of global poverty contributes to the advancement of Western economies and societies with the human capital of poor states.
Poorer states like India have become intellectual feeders of well-educated and bright individuals whose skills cannot be fully rewarded in less developed states. The magnetic draw of a better life in economies that amply reward their human capital pulls the brightest minds from their countries of origin, a process referred to as "brain drain." Advanced economies such as the United States and England are beneficiaries of brain drain. The United States has moved to take advantage of the pool of highly educated workers from the developing world. . . .

Point 6: The existence of global poverty may contribute to the pacification of the Western proletariat, or "Workers of the World, A Blue Light Special!"
To some degree, the broad availability of good, inexpensive merchandise may help obscure class divisions in the West, at least in the arena of consumption. It is clear that those with

greater wealth can consume more high-quality goods, but low-end "designer" merchandise is accessible to the less well-off in cathedrals of consumption such as Wal-Mart. At K-Mart, for instance, Martha Stewart peddles her wares, intended to transform "homemaking chores . . . into what we like to call 'domestic art.'" Thanks in part to the low-wage workers in places like China, these goods are available to the unwashed masses (now washed by Martha's smart and cozy towels) as well as to better-situated homemakers. Consumption appears to be one of the great equalizers of modern society. (It is worth noting, though, that many members of the Western working class are also "victims" of global poverty, since many jobs have gone abroad to low-wage areas, leaving behind, for less educated workers, positions in the less remunerative and less secure service industry or leaving former industrial workers jobless.)

Point 7: Global poverty benefits the West because poor countries make optimal dumping grounds for goods that are dangerous, expired, or illegal.
Wealthy countries and their inhabitants may utilize poorer states as repositories for dangerous or unwanted material such as nuclear waste. The desperation of cash-strapped states benefits better-off countries, which might otherwise have difficulty ridding themselves of the dangerous by-products of their industrial and consumer economies. For instance, in December 2000, the Russian Parliament, in an initial vote on the issue, overwhelmingly supported the amendment of an environmental law to permit the importation of foreign nuclear waste. The alteration of the law was supported by the Atomic Ministry of the Russian Federation, which suggested that over the next decade, Russia might earn up to $21 billion from the importation of spent nuclear fuel from states like Japan, Germany, and South Korea. Likely repositories of the radioactive refuse are Mayak and Krasnoyarsk, already among the most contaminated sites on the planet. . . .

Point 8: The existence of global poverty provides jobs for specialists employed to assist, advise, and study the world's poor and to protect the "better-off" from them.
Within this group of specialists we find people in a variety of professions. There are those who are professional development workers, operating through organizations like the United States Agency for International Development (USAID) . . .

Academics in fields as diverse as economics, sociology, international affairs, political science, and anthropology study, write about, and "decipher" the lives of the poor and the condition of poor states. Texts on development, articles debating why poverty persists, and books from university presses are only some of the products of this research. Journalists and novelists can build careers around bringing colourful, compelling representations of the poor to the warm living rooms of literate, well-off consumers. Still others are charged with the task of protecting wealthy states from "invasions" of the poor: US border patrols, for instance, employ thousands to keep those seeking better fortunes out of US territory.

Point 9: Global poverty benefits inhabitants of wealthy countries, who can feel good about helping the global poor through charitable work and charitable giving.
From the celebrity-studded musical production "We are the World" to trick-or-treating for UNICEF, those who inhabit the wealthy corners of the world feel good about themselves for sharing their good fortune. The website of World Vision, a faith-based charity that offers the opportunity to sponsor poor children, features a speak-out area for contributors. On that site, a young Canadian sponsor wrote, "A few days ago I woke up early and turned the TV on . . . looking at those children made me realize I could help them. I thought if I have enough money to pay for the Internet, cellphone, and a couple of other things I didn't need, I said to myself, [then] why not give that money to people who need it instead of spending it all in [sic] luxury and things that are not really important. . . . I immediately picked up the phone and called to sponsor a child! I am happy. I can help someone who needs it!"[3]

Apparently, we need not feel guilt about consuming many times what the unfortunate inhabitants of the world's poor states do if only we are willing to give up a few of our luxuries to help them . . .

A related point is that the poor we see on television or hear about in news or music give those of us in wealthy countries the opportunity to feel good about ourselves, regardless of our position in the socio-economic structure of our own states. . . .

Point 10: The poverty of less developed states makes possible the massive flow of resources westward.

Imagine if large and largely poor countries like China, Nigeria, and India consumed at US rates. At present, Americans consume a tremendously disproportionate share of the world's resources. With their profligate use of all manner of resources, most notably fossil fuels, Americans are the greediest consumers of natural resources on the planet. On both an absolute and per capita basis, most world resources flow westward. Notably, a 4 October 2000 article in *The Seattle Times* reported that bicycles, long a characteristic and popular means of transport for Chinese commuters, are losing popularity: "Increasingly, young Chinese are not even bothering to learn to ride bikes, because growing wealth has unleashed a plethora of transportation choices, public and private."[4] The new transportation of choice is still largely public buses or private taxis: the Chinese have not yet graduated to mass private cars. But it is interesting to ponder whether there would be enough (affordable) oil for everyone if the Chinese, with their growing population and prosperity, became a country of two-vehicle families or developed a taste and market for gas-guzzling sports utility vehicles. In this case, the West likely benefits from the fact that few can afford (at least at present) to consume at the rate its people do.

Point 11: The poorer countries, which reproduce at rates higher than Western states, are useful scapegoats for real and potential global environmental threats.

What is the bigger environmental threat to our planet? Is it the rapid growth of the populations of developing states or the rapid consumption of resources by the much smaller populations of developed states? The overdevelopment of the West may well be the bigger threat, though the growth of populations in Third World countries, which is often linked to conditions of underdevelopment, such as a lack of birth control and the need to have "extra" children as a hedge against high child mortality rates, makes an attractive alternative explanation for those who would not wish to fault the SUV-driving, disposable-diaper using, BBQ-loving American consumer for threats to the global environment. While some Western policy-makers express concern about the environmental threats emerging from rapid population growth or the use of "dirty" technology in developing states, there is comparably little serious attention given to the global threat presented by the profligate consumption by Western states. The poor divert attention from the environmental problems caused by Western overconsumption.

I have talked about 11 ways that the continued existence of global poverty benefits those who reside in wealthy states. The argument I have offered to explain the persistence of a strata of poor states and the yawning global gap highlights the idea that while global poverty (and the status quo) is beneficial to the wealthy West, serious steps to alleviate it will not be taken.

It is surely the case that poverty does not have to exist. But while we in the West derive the benefits and bonuses of these economic inequalities, it seems likely that our efforts to support, advise, and assist the less developed states will remain at levels that are financially and politically convenient and feasible, and will target survival rather than true prosperity for those outside our gated, privileged, greedy Western neighbourhood. In Gans's words, "Phenomena like poverty can be eliminated only when they become dysfunctional for the affluent or powerful, or when the powerless can obtain enough power to change society."

CRITICAL READING QUESTIONS

1. How does this article use ideas from structural functionalism (see Chapter 2)?
2. The quote on page 108 claims that global poverty benefits (is "functional" for) only some people in the world. Who benefits from global poverty and how?
3. How does this article use ideas from conflict theory (see Chapter 2)?
4. Of the 11 functions of global poverty outlined in this article, which three do you think the most convincing or important? Which three are the least convincing or important? Give reasons to support your answers.

NOTES

1. *Social Policy*, July/August 1971.
2. Information on issues of trade and Chinese women is available at http://www.womensedge.org. The information cited is from the April 2000 web issue of *Notes from the Edge*.
3. The charity's website address is http//www.worldvision.org.
4. The article is cited at the website of the Competitive Enterprise Institute: http://www.cei.org/CHNReader.asp?ID=1227.

World Society Theory

The third theory of globalization that we will examine is **world society theory**. John W. Meyer and colleagues (1997) originated this theory, which focuses on the importance of global institutions and cultural models in shaping the behaviour of nations, organizations, and individuals. In contrast to world systems and modernization theory, the world society tradition explains global change as the consequence of emerging global institutions and a "world culture" since World War II.

World society theory argues that countries are becoming increasingly similar. They are coming to see things in a way that is consistent with Enlightenment ideals of progress, science, and human rights. As a result, both individuals and nation-states tend to adopt common cultural frames or perspectives, resulting in one world culture. While this theory emphasizes the positive elements of globalization, such as the spread of ideals of human rights, science, and tolerance, it is important to note that negative ideas, such as consumerism, materialism, and violence, can also become common cultural frames.

World society theory is rooted in comparative education research conducted in the 1970s. Researchers noted that education systems in sub-Saharan Africa were surprisingly similar to the education systems in western Europe and North America, despite the vast cultural, economic, and social differences in the societies as a whole. Theorists sought to explain these similarities by arguing that they resulted from some underlying dominant, legitimatized, or taken-for-granted views. In this way, education systems were based on cultural models that spread across countries and provided blueprints for what a good education system should be (Meyer et al. 1997). International organizations are a very important part of the institutionalization of these cultural models.

One cultural ideal that has spread in modernity is individualism and individual rights. At the end of World War II, individuals and societies began to change their focus from the rights of groups (corporatism) to the rights of individuals (individualism). This shift led to many social changes. For example, the rise and spread of capitalist ideologies are based on an individual worker's (or capitalist's) ability to make a wage (or profit). Democracy is based on the idea of one person, one vote.

The world society framework can help us to understand certain globalization processes. For example, Frank, Camp, and Boutcher (2010) examined the changing regulations of sex and sexuality (including laws about adultery, sodomy, child sexual abuse, and rape). They found that between 1945 and 2005, the criminal regulations concerning adultery and sodomy drastically diminished; those regarding rape and child sexual abuse expanded. During the period under study, 68 per cent of the laws about adultery and 81 per cent of those about sodomy lessened or eliminated state punishment for these acts. This change is in stark opposition to the laws about child sexual abuse and rape—85 per cent of the laws about child sexual abuse and 98 per cent of the laws about rape criminalized or increased the punishment for these two crimes.

Frank and colleagues (2010) suggest that we can understand these changes using world society theory. Early laws regulating sex and sexuality focused on the perceived needs of society as a whole, namely, the procreative functions of sex. Therefore, sexual activity that was procreative and could lead to "legitimate" heirs (e.g., heterosexual sex between husbands and wives) was protected. Under this type of social focus, sexual activity that was non-procreative (sodomy or homosexuality) or that undermined the family (adultery) was heavily regulated.

Today, laws about sexuality focus on protecting an individual's autonomy. As such, laws focused on an individual's right to consent to sexual activity prevail. Rape and child sexual abuse laws are much more common now. These laws are based on the ideas of individual rights and the need for individual consent, which is absent in instances of rape and abuse. Other sexual acts, such as adultery and sodomy, are less of a concern in many societies because they are seen to occur between consenting adults and to not violate a person's individual rights. Frank and colleagues (2010) argue that the rising regulation of rape and child sexual abuse (and the declining regulation of adultery and sodomy, both of which were previously illegal in most countries) indicates a widespread international change in norms about individualism.

Canadian laws on marital rape are a case in point. Before 1983, there was (legally) no such thing as marital rape in Canada. It was thought impossible for a man to rape his wife because rape was defined as an act that occurred outside marriage. A judge explained the situation in this way: "The intercourse which takes place between husband and wife is not by virtue of any special consent on her part, but is mere submission to an obligation imposed on her by law" (Frank et al. 2010, 872). Marital exemptions to rape laws basically focused on corporatist needs (the need of society to create babies) over the individual rights of women to consent to sexual activity. The law was eventually changed to prioritize women's right to give or deny consent.

Global Inequality

In Chapter 4, we learned about income inequality in Canada. It is clear that income is unevenly distributed in Canada and, over time, the richest Canadians earn an increasingly larger share of all income made in the country. Not only are there inequalities in income within countries, but there are also wide, and even starker, disparities between countries. Modernization, world systems, and world society theories have different perspectives on the promise and pitfalls of globalization, but they all see these vast inequalities.

Global inequality is increasing over time. In the period between 2010 and 2015, the richest 1 per cent of the global population increased their share of global wealth so much that they now make the same amount as the bottom 99 per cent of all earners. While there has always been great inequality between the top 1 per cent and the bottom 99 per cent, the richest 1 per cent only had 44 per cent of all wealth in 2010. Five years later, this had risen to almost 50 per cent (see Figure 12.2). These statistics present an extremely high level of income inequality between individuals and countries. Although some progress has been made, UNICEF estimates that at this rate of change, it would take more than 800 years for the bottom billion people to achieve 10 per cent of the world's income. This conclusion is particularly troublesome because approximately 50 per cent of children live below the $2-a-day international poverty line.

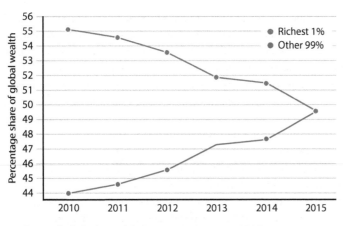

FIGURE 12.2   Share of global wealth for top 1 per cent, 2010–15

Source: Alex Gray, 2016, "3 Charts That Explain Global Inequality," *World Economic Forum* 20 January, https://www.weforum.org/agenda/2016/01/3-charts-that-explain-global-inequality. The material from "An Economy for the 1%, 18th January 2016" is reproduced with the permission of Oxfam, Oxfam House, John Smith Drive, Cowley, Oxford OX4 2JY, UK www.oxfam.org.uk. Oxfam does not necessarily endorse any text or activities that accompany the materials.

One way to compare income inequality across countries systematically is with the **Gini index**, developed by the Italian sociologist Corrado Gini. This index measures income inequality on a scale of 0 to 1; 0 represents perfect equality in a society (all individuals in the society make the same income), and 1 represents the maximum level of inequality in a society (one person receives all the society's income). In other words, the lower the Gini index, the more equal the country.

Figure 12.3 shows the Gini levels of most countries in the world. We can see that Canada is a relatively equal society, with a Gini of 0.313 (OECD 2015). The Scandinavian countries and many other nations in western and eastern Europe are just as equal (Iceland is the most equal society in the world; its Gini index is 0.246). Countries in Africa and South and Central America, as well as the United States, are the most unequal countries.

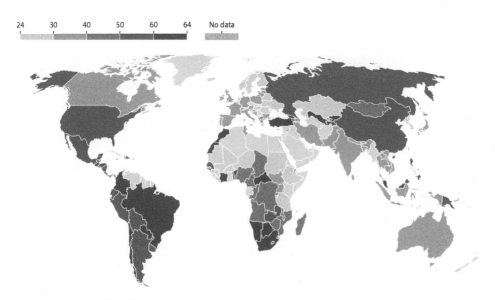

FIGURE 12.3   Gini index

Source: Caelainn Barr, 2017, "Inequality Index: Where Are the World's Most Unequal Countries?" *The Guardian* 26 April, https://www.theguardian.com/inequality/datablog/2017/apr/26/inequality-index-where-are-the-worlds-most-unequal-countries. Copyright Guardian News & Media Ltd 2019.

However, Africa has a huge amount of variability in terms of inequality—from the very high level in South Africa (the second most unequal place in the world, with a Gini of 0.63) to the very low level in Ethiopia (0.33 Gini index—almost as equal as Canada).

The Gini index measures inequality by comparing the incomes of the richest and the poorest in a society or across countries. However, we can also compare inequalities in health, education, employment, or a variety of other measures. Table 12.2 compares the wealth, inequality, health, and well-being outcomes, including **infant mortality rate**, for seven countries. These nations spend different amounts on health care and have different levels of inequality (as measured by their Gini indices).

People who live in countries with higher GDP (i.e., more wealth) generally have better health; they live longer lives, and fewer children die in their first year. In addition, governments in rich countries tend to spend more money on health care—Sweden, Canada, Japan, and the United States spend more than Mexico, South Africa, and India. However, more spending does not always buy better health. The United States spends more than 1.5 times as much per person on health care as Japan and Canada, yet it has a much shorter life expectancy than the other two countries.

One of the main reasons for this situation is that wealthy countries differ significantly in terms of their levels of equality. The Gini indices in Table 12.2 indicate that the gap between the rich and the poor is greater in the United States than it is in Canada, Japan, or Sweden. In general, research shows that the higher the level of inequality in a country, the less healthy its population. A country's health care system also influences this relationship. Sweden, Canada, and Japan all have universal health care systems administered by their respective governments. The United States has no such system; therefore, access is very different across groups of Americans.

Another interesting comparison is between India and South Africa. People living in India are doing much better in terms of general well-being. While South Africa has a GDP five times higher than India, South Africans live 11 years less on average, partly because of the extreme inequality in the country.

Inequality in a society can have serious and wide-reaching implications. Richard Wilkinson and Kate Pickett (2010) argue that more equal societies do better in a variety of ways than less equal ones. Furthermore, not only are equal societies simply better for those at the bottom of the social hierarchy, but the society as a whole functions better. The researchers compiled information from 20 sets of data collected by the UN, the World

TABLE 12.2 | GDP, health spending, and Gini by country (2014, 2015)

	Wealth and Inequality in Country			Health and Well-Being Outcomes	
	GDP per Capita (in thousands)	Health as per cent of GDP	Gini Index	Human Development	Life Expectancy
Sweden	53.25	11.9	24.9	0.913	82.3
Canada	44.77	10.4	32.1	0.920	82.2
United States	59.50	17.1	45.0	0.920	77.2
Japan	38.55	10.2	37.9	0.903	83.7
Mexico	9.25	6.3	48.2	0.762	77.0
South Africa	6.09	8.8	62.5	0.666	57.0
India	1.85	4.7	35.2	0.624	68.3

Source: Adapted from International Monetary Fund, 2017, GDP Per Capita, Current Prices, http://www.imf.org/external/datamapper/NGDPDPC@WEO/OEMDC/ADVEC/WEOWORLD; Central Intelligence Agency, 2014, The World Factbook, https://www.cia.gov/library/publications/the-world-factbook/rankorder/2172rank.html; and United Nations Development Programme, 2018, "Table 1. Human Development Index and Its Components," Human Development Reports, http://hdr.undp.org/en/composite/HDI

Micro-financing and Global Inequality

Global poverty is an extremely complex issue. How can we address such a large and seemingly insurmountable problem? One innovative solution is **micro-financing**, the provision of small loans to individuals and small businesses who lack access to banking and loans. For example, a farmer could ask for a small loan to buy a cart to sell their produce, or a group of women could ask for a small loan to buy a sewing machine to make clothing. These loans aim to help lift individuals, families, and communities out of poverty by providing small amounts of start-up capital for entrepreneurial projects. They are intended to help individuals generate income, build wealth, and exit poverty. In this activity, we will learn about micro-financing and how it works. Please go to the following website to learn about micro-financing programs: www.kiva.org.

1. How does this organization present micro-financing? What is the point of these programs?
2. What types of things can you support through micro-financing? What other areas should also be included? Which seem most important for dealing with global poverty?
3. How well have these programs worked in the past? What are the effects of these programs?
4. Look at the loans requested. What types of people, places, and projects are listed? Which do you find most compelling and why?
5. What kinds of problems might there be with micro-financing? What sorts of critiques have these programs received?

Bank, the World Health Organization, and the US Census. They found, for example, that crime rates are closely tied to inequality. In particular, violent crime tends to be much more prevalent in countries, regions, and cities with high levels of inequality.

Wilkinson and Pickett (2010) also maintain that everyone, not just the poor, is adversely affected by inequality. For example, Britain and the United States have relatively high levels of inequality and very high levels of mental health problems—25 per cent of Brits and more than 25 per cent of Americans report experiencing mental health problems in any given year. The relatively more equal countries of Japan, Germany, Sweden, and Italy have far fewer mental health problems, with less than 10 per cent of citizens per year reporting mental health issues. Inequality also leads to consumerism, isolation, and anxiety, experiences that are associated with mental illness. Thus, according to Wilkinson and Pickett, the structures of these unequal societies lead to higher levels of mental health problems for both the rich and the poor—problems that cannot be solved through individual mental health solutions because they are inextricably linked to the unequal nature of these societies as a whole.

Global inequality is a serious problem that many individuals, organizations, countries, and international bodies have tried to resolve. There are several ways to address global inequality. Three main strategies, which have been the focus of much international and domestic debate, are development assistance, debt relief, and micro-financing.

Development assistance is financial aid given by governments and some non-governmental charitable agencies to support a country's economic, social, and political development. One of this strategy's primary goals is to reduce global poverty. The UN has developed a set of eight Millennium Development Goals, including cutting extreme poverty in half, reducing the spread of diseases such as HIV/AIDS, and providing universal primary education. The UN's plan for tackling these problems centres on development assistance, a plan agreed to by all the world's countries and leading development institutions. This type of partnership has been relatively successful at dealing with some elements of global inequality.

The level of debt in some developing nations is a significant impediment to improving living conditions. Many developing countries and their citizens are burdened with insurmountable debts. In fact, developing countries now spend $13 on debt repayment

PHOTO 12.3 The UN is actively working to reduce global poverty. Its Millennium Development Goals are one way that individuals and countries can come together to deal with the challenging social problem of global inequality.

From Millennium Development Goals, United Nations © 2015 United Nations. Reprinted with the permission of the United Nations

for every dollar they receive in development assistance (Shah 2005). For example, Nigeria has borrowed $5 billion. Because of high interest rates, it still owes $28 billion, despite having already repaid $16 billion. A country's debt works just like a personal credit card debt. Once the balance reaches a certain point, the monthly payments go toward the interest, and it becomes impossible to pay off the principal.

With so much money going to debt repayment (particularly interest), developing countries have less money to spend on important social programs that would improve their citizens' lives, such as education, health care, and other government services. As well, increasing globalization and international privatization of resources force poorer countries to sell off their profitable national institutions to help pay off the debt, which creates higher unemployment and problems for their future GDP. In response to these problems, international campaigns have called on richer countries to forgive the debt of developing nations. For example, Jubilee 2000 brought together citizens from 40 countries to call for the cancellation of Third World debt by 2000. Make Poverty History has also been lobbying for debt relief for developing countries. In Chapter 13, we will learn more about how such social movements can help to create social change.

In many ways, global poverty seems almost insurmountable. One new, innovative way of dealing with the problem is **fair trade certification**. The following article explains this strategy, its benefits, and some concerns regarding its practice.

PHOTO 12.4 These women in Bangladesh attend a micro-finance training session. Micro-finance attempts to address global poverty and inequality. Why might microfinancing be more effective than traditional bank loans at reducing poverty?

The Problem with Fair Trade Coffee

Nicki Lisa Cole and Keith Brown

Byron Corrales is known for growing some of the best coffee in Central America. His family-owned farm sits next to a nature reserve in a cloud forest north of Matagalpa, Nicaragua. Byron speaks poetically about his coffee: each morning he wakes and listens to his trees, trying to understand their needs. On his organic farm, Byron takes great efforts to reduce his oil consumption, lower his carbon footprint, and pay his employees a fair wage. He views himself as a socially conscious farmer and even sells some of his beans to Paul and Joan Katzeff, owners of Thanksgiving Coffee Company, longtime champions of the fair trade movement.

Corrales and the Katzeffs represent the core values of the fair trade movement. Corrales works meticulously to care for the local ecosystem and pay his workers fairly. The Katzeffs educate their consumers about fair trade's benefits and pay a premium for Corrales' coffee. Yet they all refuse to certify their coffee as "fair trade" with the largest certifier in the United States. They are part of a growing faction of small farmers and U.S. buyers of fair trade coffee who find themselves increasingly frustrated with the fair trade certification process.

While there is some diversity of opinion about what fair trade means, certification is designed to provide economic premiums for social and environmental investments—important for farmers who have historically received inadequate compensation for their crops. Recently some members of the global fair trade movement have become angry with Fair Trade USA, the organization that sets certification policy and licenses products for distribution in the United States. In January 2012, Fair Trade USA unilaterally altered their coffee sourcing policy to include not just cooperatives of small producers, but also large scale plantations. Under the slogan "Fair Trade for All," this new policy has changed the meaning of certification, and may negatively impact the very small-scale farmers fair trade was originally meant to protect.

We have interviewed fair trade store owners, coffeehouse managers and baristas, importers and exporters, coffee industry consultants, cooperative and movement leaders, farmers, artisans, and consumers. We have also conducted content analysis of fair trade advertisements and story displays, attended conferences around the United States, and lived alongside farmers in Nicaragua. Through this research, we came to learn how important fair trade certification is to small producers. We also learned that farmers' displeasure with Fair Trade USA's new policy reflects a long-standing tension between the founding values of the fair trade movement and profit-driven ethos of the fair trade market.

A Brief History of Fair Trade

European and American imports of textiles and handcrafts from war-torn and poverty-stricken communities around the world provided the foundation for today's fair trade system. In the mid-1980s, the concept was forever changed when coffee was folded into the fair trade model. At this time, a range of progressive entrepreneurs, including Paul Katzeff, began importing coffee from Nicaragua as an expression of support for Sandinista farmers. These Nicaraguan farmers were suffering from malnutrition and even starvation during the U.S.-imposed boycott of their country's goods. Over time, these seemingly disparate efforts—importing handicrafts, coffee, and other goods—coalesced into fair trade certification.

What Is Fair Trade Certified Coffee?

Fair trade certification guarantees that coffee producers are paid a stable, minimum price per pound for their product. Historically, this protection has been offered to small producers who are members of democratically organized cooperatives. These cooperatives give producers entry into a global market that is dominated by large transnational buyers.

Cole, Nicki Lisa, and Keith Brown. 2014. "The Problem with Fair Trade Coffee." Contexts 13(1): 50–5.

The minimum price per pound is set by Fairtrade International, the umbrella organization that, until 2012, determined the global standards for fair trade criteria. The guaranteed minimum price creates economic stability for producers who would otherwise be at the whims of the volatile New York commodities market, which sets the international price for coffee. The New York "C" price can fluctuate widely, and was as low as 41 cents per pound in 2001. Depending on how the coffee is processed prior to export, the fair trade minimum price is either $1.35 or $1.40 per pound, which includes a 20-cent per pound premium earmarked for development in producing communities. Because Fairtrade International sets a minimum price, coffee that is certified can be—and often is—sold for more. Sometimes a buyer pays more based on quality, and, when the New York price exceeds the fair trade minimum, the fair trade price increases to best it by 10 cents.

The fair trade system also provides small loans to producer groups to facilitate improved infrastructure for farms and communities. In the past, these benefits were available only to small producers affiliated with democratically organized cooperatives, since the movement was conceived to both increase access to the global market and protection from manipulative and exploitative buyers. Until recently, this was an important hallmark of fair trade certified coffee, as most of the world's coffee is grown by small-scale producers in remote areas. (To learn more about the coffee beans you consume, ask your local coffee vendor where their coffee is purchased, and on what terms.)

Independent labeling organizations such as Max Havelaar in the Netherlands (established in 1988) and TransFair in the U.S. (now Fair Trade USA, established in 1998) set national standards for fair trade certification. Fairtrade International (formerly Fairtrade Labeling Organizations International) was formed in 1997 as an umbrella organization to coordinate the various definitions of fair trade across national borders. These groups' dogged efforts provided legitimacy to the fair trade label and helped grow the movement throughout the late 1990s and early 2000s.

The tremendous growth of the fair trade coffee market has been beneficial to the many small farmers around the world. U.S. importers alone have paid over $61 million in premiums to producer cooperatives since 1998. It's neither a perfect system nor a solution to global poverty, but many lives have been improved through farmer and buyer participation in fair trade programs. However, on January 1, 2012, the fair trade movement underwent a significant change: Fair Trade USA implemented a new policy that would fold coffee produced on large-scale plantations into its certification system. Calling the change the "Fair Trade for All" policy, the organization claimed that including more types of farms would vastly increase the number of people served by the movement. There is a long-standing tension between the founding values of the fair trade movement and the profit-driven ethos of the fair trade market.

This seemingly benevolent change stirred controversy within the specialty coffee industry. Many believe that it breaks with the founding goal of the movement—to empower small producers in the global market. To implement "Fair Trade for All," Fair Trade USA was forced to sever its ties with Fairtrade International. The global group felt the move to include large-scale, commercial farms was a betrayal of the core values of fair trade.

The Case for Fair Trade for All

In an open letter addressed to all fair trade supporters, Paul Rice, the founder and CEO of Fair Trade USA, cites three reasons for the change in his organization's policy. First, he claims that Fair Trade for All will reduce inconsistencies in the certification process. Some products, like bananas and tea grown on plantations, were already eligible for fair trade certification. By including coffee plantations, the certification process will be more consistent across products. Second, Rice wants to greatly increase consumer awareness about fair trade initiatives, further increasing the market for fair trade products. He believes consistency across all products will give consumers a clearer understanding of the overriding principles of fair trade.

Third, Rice argues that greater sales of fair trade products will help educate consumers about the plight of producers around the world. By his own estimate, a greater demand for fair trade will help an additional four million people gain access to fair trade benefits, including improved living conditions.

Rice believes that the new policy will extend benefits to not only farmers who own their land and are members of cooperatives, but also to tens of thousands of laborers who migrate seasonally to pick coffee. In Nicaragua, for instance, many coffee pickers are represented by the Association of Rural Workers, a large trade union that helps fight for better working conditions. Leaders of this organization told us that fair trade is just a "drop in the bucket" of the coffee market and that it offers no benefits to many coffee pickers who do not own their own land.

According to Fair Trade USA, laborers around the world would see improved wages and working conditions that currently only reach those farmers already fortunate enough to be landholders and cooperative members.

Backlash

At the Specialty Coffee Association of America's annual industry convention held in Portland, Oregon, in 2012, dissent was in the air. From baristas to buyers, roasters, coffee company owners, and producers, thousands assembled from around the world for the five-day meeting. As it followed so closely on the heels of Fair Trade USA's announcement of their new policy, the tension at the convention was palpable.

On the third morning, over a hundred people came together to discuss the future of fair trade in the United States. Through our own research, we've come to align ourselves with the critics present at this meeting. We find many flaws in "Fair Trade for All."

One of the most serious problems is that the supply for fair trade coffee currently outpaces demand. Today, only about 20 per cent of the global supply of fair trade certified coffee is actually sold at the fair trade minimum price. As a result, many farmers work hard to meet fair trade certification's standards, but sell their coffee at the lower prices set on the commodities market.

Samuel Kamau, Executive Director of the African Fine Coffees Association, described how this disparity affects small producers when he spoke with Nicki at the convention: ". . . [W]e got so efficient in fair trade production, fair trade [buyers are] no longer interested in us . . . we over-produced fair trade certified coffee." Kamau explained that despite being members of certified fair trade cooperatives, many small producers are forced to sell their coffee with no guaranteed minimum price. It remains unclear to many within the fair trade movement why Fair Trade USA wants to increase the supply of fair trade coffee by including large plantations when demand, while growing, is still insufficient.

Aside from the supply and demand issue, the Fair Trade for All campaign mistakenly assumes that plantations will provide the same health, safety, and economic benefits for farmers as do cooperatives. Anthropologists and sociologists have been looking at this issue for the last decade and have shown that workers on fair trade plantations for products like tea and bananas do not receive the same benefits as farmers working in cooperatives.

CRITICAL READING QUESTIONS

1. What is fair trade certification? Why do farmers, buyers and consumers look for this certification?
2. What institutions support fair trade? What institutions might undermine fair trade certification?
3. How does allowing large-scale producers of coffee to get fair trade certification change what it means to be fair trade? What are the positive and negative implications of this change to the certification process?
4. Do you consume fair trade products? Why or why not? What kinds of policies or campaigns could increase individual consumption of these types of products?

Summary

Sociologists are fundamentally concerned with inequality. In Chapter 4, we learned how social class and social status can create inequalities within a country. In this chapter, we extended our focus to examine how inequality can arise between countries. Understanding how our world is becoming increasingly globalized can help us to make sense of how global inequality has arisen and how we can work to reduce it. The three theoretical lenses we covered in this chapter (modernization theory, world systems theory, and world society theory) understand globalization differently, but they all note the inequality resulting from this process. We also discussed ways to measure and compare global inequality, such as the Gini and human development indices. We ended this chapter by exploring three ways to relieve global inequality: development assistance, debt relief, and micro-financing programs.

Key Terms

cash crops 333
commodity chain 338
core countries 337
ecological footprint 336
fair trade certification 350
Gini index 347
globalization 331
Human Development
    Index (HDI) 336

infant mortality rate 348
mechanical solidarity 334
micro-financing 349
modernization theory 333
monocropping 335
periphery countries 337
semi-periphery countries 337
world society theory 345
world systems theory 337

For Further Reading

Durkheim, Émile. 1960. *Division of Labour in Society*. Glencoe, IL: Free Press.

Krücken, Georg, and Gili S. Drori, eds. 2009. *World Society: The Writings of John W. Meyer*. Oxford: Oxford University Press.

Martell, Luke. 2017. *The Sociology of Globalization*, 2nd edn. Cambridge: Polity Press.

Sassen, Sasia. 2007. *A Sociology of Globalization*. New York: Norton.

Wallerstein, Immanuel. 2011. *The Modern World System*. Berkeley: University of California Press.

Wilkinson, Richard, and Kate Pickett. 2010. *The Spirit Level: Why More Equal Societies Almost Always Do Better*. New York: Bloomsbury.

References

Alberta Energy. 2014. "Facts and Statistics." http://www.energy.alberta.ca/oilsands/791.asp.

Bennett, Dinah, Michael Sharpe, Chris Freeman, and Alan Carson. 2004. "Anorexia Nervosa among Female Secondary Students in Ghana." *British Journal of Psychiatry* 185: 312–17.

Durkheim, Émile. 1960. *The Division of Labour in Society*. Glencoe, IL: Free Press.

Frank, David John, Bayliss J. Camp, and Steven A. Boutcher. 2010. "Worldwide Trends in the Criminal Regulation of Sex, 1945 to 2005." *American Sociological Review* 75(6): 867–93.

Linden, Greg, Kenneth L. Kraemer, and Jason Dedrick. 2009. "Who Captures Value in a Global Innovation Network? The Case of Apple's iPod." *Communications of the ACM* 52(3): 140–4.

McLuhan, Marshall. 1964. *Understanding Media: The Extensions of Man*. New York: McGraw-Hill.

Meyer, John W., John Boli, George M. Thomas, and Francisco O. Ramirez. 1997. "World Society and the Nation-State." *American Journal of Sociology* 103: 144–81.

OECD. 2015. OECD Income Distribution Database. http://www.oecd.org/social/income-distribution-database.htm.

Rostow, W.W. 1991. *The Stages of Economic Growth: A Non-Communist Manifesto*. Cambridge: Cambridge University Press.

Shah, Anup. 2005. "The Scale of the Debt Crisis." Global Issues.org. http://www.globalissues.org/article/30/the-scale-of-the-debt-crisis.

United Nations. 1948. *Convention on the Prevention and Punishment of the Crime of Genocide*. https://treaties.un.org/doc/Publication/UNTS/Volume%2078/volume-78-I-1021-English.pdf.

Wallerstein, Immanuel. 2011. *The Modern World System*. Berkeley: University of California Press.

Wilkinson, Richard, and Kate Pickett. 2010. *The Spirit Level: Why More Equal Societies Almost Always Do Better*. New York: Bloomsbury.

PART IV

Social Change

Photo Credit: Vlad Tchompalov/Unsplash

Chapter Outline

THE CANADIAN PRESS/Chris Young

Introduction

Throughout this book, we have learned about how our society operates. We began by examining how we learn to fit into society through socialization, the ways we differentiate people and how doing so can lead to inequality, and the major social institutions and their roles. The final core area of sociology is the study of social change. For many students, learning about the inequality that exists in our society and how societal institutions often help to perpetuate that inequality can be frustrating. They ask: How can we change our society and make it more equal and just? How can we alter institutions to address important social problems? In this chapter and the next, we will learn about the major routes to social change.

How Does Society Reproduce Itself?

We all want to change some things about society. Yet, for a variety of reasons, society generally stays the same. We are all socialized to follow the rules and norms of society and to fit in. Those who question or resist the social order are punished for their deviance. A child who will not listen to the teacher in class, who does not like to do the activities usually associated with her age group or gender, or who does not dress in a conventional way might be punished by being suspended, receiving poor grades, or being isolated or bullied by other children. Even later in life, we are rewarded for doing what we are "supposed to"—going to university, getting a "good" job, finding a partner, and raising a family. In general, we are taught not to question why things are as they are and to simply accept that the way our society is set up is the natural order. If formal laws and regulations are not enough to encourage us to conform, informal social sanctions such as exclusion and shaming ensure that we follow the rules.

Despite these disincentives, social change does happen. **Social change**, at a general level, is the transformation of culture and social institutions over time. Sometimes this change occurs quite quickly, such as in the invention of new computer technology that revolutionized how we interact with one another. At other times, things happen more slowly, such as shifting gender norms (see Chapter 6). Social change can be intentional—for example, when a new law is passed to legalize marijuana or gay marriage. However, social change is often unintentional. The printing press, discussed in Chapter 7, was not invented to create social change but still altered many facets of society and social interaction.

Finally, while we tend to think of many social changes as natural and inevitable, they were often quite contentious at the time. The women's suffrage movement required the dissolution of many informal norms about women's behaviour, such as the idea that it was natural for women to remain within the domestic sphere and that they did not belong in the public sphere. The removal of formal laws restricting women's roles in public life brought about gradual social change. Women's

PHOTO 13.1 In Ottawa in 1938, a plaque commemorating the Famous Five, whose work led to the Persons Case and women's right to hold public office in Canada, was unveiled. This change in law was part of the larger and longer transformation of gender roles in Canada. From left to right in the front row are Muir Edwards, daughter-in-law of Henrietta Muir Edwards; J.C. Kenwood, daughter of Judge Emily Murphy; Prime Minister Mackenzie King; and Nellie McClung. In the rear row, from left to right, are Senators Iva Campbell Fallis and Cairine Wilson.

Eugene M. Finn / National Film Board of Canada. Photothèque / Library and Archives Canada / C-054523

suffrage, the legalization of marriage between people of different races, and the abolition of slavery seem like things that everyone would have surely supported. However, these were very controversial proposals, and many people fought vigorously against them.

The Routes to Social Change

Social change can happen through institutional channels, particularly through the state. The state provides an important arena for creating social change through elections, laws, and social policy. Social change can also occur outside the state's institutions, through cultural change or the work of social movements. This chapter focuses on state-based social change; the next examines social change outside the state.

To consider the general routes to social change, let's think about the expansion of LGBTQ rights. If you are interested in these rights and are working within the state, you could elect political leaders who are also concerned with LGBTQ rights—perhaps those who advocate for the passing of same-sex marriage laws or anti-discrimination laws. You could also challenge the legality of discriminating against gays and lesbians. The latter is, in fact, how gay marriage became legal in Canada. Gay couples argued in court that not being allowed to marry simply because of their sexual orientation was discriminatory. The Supreme Court of Canada agreed, finding the law unconstitutional and instructing Parliament to change it. Another approach is to change the policies of government or government agencies. For example, it used to be harder for gay and lesbian people to adopt children than it was for people who were heterosexual. During this time, passing a policy in adoption agencies that excludes sexual orientation as a basis for determining who would be a good parent would have made the process easier.

The Rise of the State

The **state** is a set of institutions that includes four components: political decision-makers, who are either elected or appointed; administrative units or bureaucracies, such as a ministry of health or education; a judiciary or legal system; and security services (police within a country and armies outside). States are also attached to a geographic territory and maintain a monopoly and autonomy on rule-making, coercion, and violence within that territory. The state is, arguably, the most powerful institution in contemporary society. It is the only institution with the legal right to tax you; use violence on you through the police, military, and court systems; permit or force you to kill by sending you to war; legally hold you in prison; and, in some places, kill you via capital punishment (Stanbridge and Ramos 2012).

The state's right to use violence is considered justifiable because it works to maintain social order and to defend the nation's interests. As Max Weber famously said, the power of the state ultimately flows from its monopoly on the legitimate use of violence (in Gerth and Mills 1946). However, the state cannot wield these powers in any way it chooses. If people feel that it uses violence in an illegitimate way, they can resist through civil unrest. The state can also be subject to sanctions from the international community and, eventually, a decline in state power.

The state is also powerful because it can set policies and laws governing your behaviour—how you can buy or sell a car, rent a house, or become licensed to work as a teacher or doctor; whom you can marry, and many other facets of your daily life. We permit the state to do these things because they provide us with services such as schools, roads, and health care, ensure a safe and orderly society, and protect our national interests (Stanbridge and Ramos 2012).

States, like other institutions in society, change over time. The state emerged in its modern form between the twelfth and eighteenth centuries in western Europe. The three major explanations for this rise focus on the importance of the state for managing increasingly large territories, enacting war, and controlling the economy. Let's examine each function in turn.

From 1100 to 1600 in Europe, there was a rise of "political units persisting in time and fixed in space, the development of permanent, impersonal institutions, agreement on the need for an authority which can give final judgments, and the acceptance of the idea that this authority should receive the basic loyalty of its subjects" (Strayer 1970, 10). As territories grew in geographic size and population, the state was needed to better manage and control these larger areas and groups of people. This **managerial perspective** focuses on the evolving practices relating to the recruitment, training, and employment of administrators needed to manage these new bureaucracies. The individual bureaucrats who occupy these offices are important because they convince the population that a central state can fulfill the needs and interests of the people, who often have intense local loyalties. It makes sense that individuals of this time would be much more connected to their local communities, which were filled with people they knew personally and who tended to be similar to them, instead of a distant, impersonal state. However, communities came to accept the obligations created by the individual bureaucrats through centralized state government.

The state was also instituted to create a monopoly on the acceptable use of violence, particularly in relation to the ability to wage war. This **militaristic perspective** is related to Weber's earlier claim that the state is the only legitimate user of violence within a territory. Early European states developed through war, particularly through conquering neighbouring lands. The states with the better bureaucracies were more financially equipped to wage war because they were more efficient at taxation (they knew who lived where, the amount of property people owned, and what people were doing that could be taxed). In addition, knowing the population enabled these states to conscript soldiers more effectively.

From the beginning, the modern state was essentially intended for war-making and was centrally concerned with establishing and maintaining its military might. Wars and who won them created the national boundaries in Europe and the original context of the state system (Poggi 2004). As Charles Tilly (1985, 42) argues, "War made the state, and the state made war." His central claim is that the state is a "protection racket"—it trades security in exchange for revenues. Essentially, cooperation between people is difficult without a third party; citizens therefore cede to the state their rights to do whatever they want in return for a guarantee of protection.

As Tilly (1985, 172) explains:

> The pursuit of war involved them willy-nilly in extraction of resources for war-making from the populations over which they had control and in the promotion of capital accumulation by those who could help them borrow and buy. War-making, extraction, and capital accumulation interacted to shape European State making. Power holders did not undertake those three momentous tasks with the intention of creating national states—(centralized, differentiated, autonomous, extensive political organizations). Nor did they foresee that national states would emerge from war-making, extraction and capital accumulation . . . instead, they warred in order to check or overcome their competitors and thus to enjoy the advantages of power within a secure or expanding territory. To make more effective war, they attempted to locate more capital. In the short run, they might acquire that capital by conquest, by selling off their assets, or by coercing or dispossessing accumulators of capital. In the long run, the quest inevitably involved them in establishing regular access to capitalists who could supply and arrange credit and in imposing one form of regular taxation or another on the people and activities within their spheres of control.

To have military might, states must engage in four things: war-making (eliminating or neutralizing their rivals outside the territories), state-making (eliminating or neutralizing their rivals inside their territory), protection (eliminating or neutralizing their clients' enemies), and extraction (acquiring the means of carrying out the first three activities).

Finally, the state is the result of class struggle in capitalism and works to regulate economic relations. This perspective is related to Marx's theories and can be termed the **economic perspective**, which argues that the state is needed to regulate economic interests and the clashing of these interests between groups in a capitalist society. Marx argued that the state usually "resolves" these conflicts by siding with capitalists (Marx and Engels 1964). For Marx, the state—what he called "the executive committee of the bourgeoisie"—is just an extension of the dominant capitalist class.

From the economic perspective, the state manages economic relations to facilitate the work of capitalists. The formation of states allows for a power centre to have an increasing reach. The state is able to standardize and secure relations between many individuals across wide spaces. This capacity is important for capitalism because it makes both the production and exchange of goods easier and more calculable. The state also imposes rules of law about property, which helps in the exchange of goods and services between partners.

The Welfare State

To this point, our discussion of the state has highlighted its many important functions and its origins. However, this depiction emphasizes the negative things that the state can do (coerce you and make you pay taxes). Why do humans create states, and why do we, as individuals, give them power even when we know that doing so restricts our individual freedoms? One of the main reasons has already been mentioned: the state offers many important benefits, such as health care, education, and clean water, that we cannot enjoy as isolated individuals. Without people joining to create these services, we would not all have access to these important things.

These benefits are part of the **welfare state**, a particular type of state that performs three basic functions. It attempts to provide a minimum income for individuals; to reduce the potential economic insecurity that could come from events such as illness, old age, and unemployment; and to give the public a range of social services (Briggs 2000). In a welfare state, the government plays a primary role in the promotion of its citizens' economic and social well-being. Such states expand their bureaucracies in order to provide a variety of programs that reduce economic inequality in society (Peoples 2012).

The twentieth century saw the development of welfare states around the world. The expenditures of these states vary greatly (see Table 13.1). The countries of Europe, particularly Sweden, France, Germany, the Netherlands, Italy, and Greece, have the highest spending on welfare programs as a percentage of their overall GDP. Spending is much lower in the United States, Ireland, Mexico, and South Korea.

We might expect that countries with higher GDPs would spend more on welfare. Yet the group of countries that spend 24 per cent or more of their GDPs on welfare have GDPs from $26,526 to $49,508 per capita, whereas the countries that spend less than 20 per cent of their GDPs on welfare have GDPs from $35,751 to $71,405 per capita. There does not seem to be a direct relationship between a county's overall GDP and its welfare spending. Canada is a case in point. The Canadian welfare state is weak in comparison with those of European countries. Expenditures are only 17.2 per cent of our GDP even though we are a relatively wealthy country.

TABLE 13.1 | Welfare expenditures by country, 2016

Nation	Welfare Expenditure (% of GDP)	GDP per Capita (PPP US$)
France	31.5	41,466
Italy	28.9	38,345
Sweden	27.1	49,508
Greece	27.0	26,526
Germany	25.3	48,885
Spain	24.6	36,462
Netherlands	22.0	51,320
United Kingdom	21.5	43,081
Poland	20.2	27,923
United States	19.4	57,638
Australia	19.1	46,790
Canada	17.2*	44,025
Ireland	16.1	71,405
Iceland	16.1	51,399
South Korea	10.4	35,751

Sources: Adapted from OECD, 2016, "Welfare Expenditure," *OECD*, Statistics Extractor. Canadian Data from 2015. http://stats.oecd.org/Index.aspx?DataSetCode=SOCX_AGG#; and World Bank, 2013, "GDP Per Capita," https://data.worldbank.org/indicator/NY.GDP.PCAP.PP.CD?name_desc=false
*Numbers for Canada are from 2015.

The Welfare State in Canada

A hundred years ago, care for those in need, including health and welfare services, was provided at the local community level. Community groups and charities attempted to provide minimal social services. One of Canada's first government social programs was the Mothers' Pension Act, passed in Manitoba in 1916 to provide widowed, divorced, or deserted mothers with an income. During the Great Depression, the unemployment rate reached 30 per cent, and the federal government was under considerable pressure to become involved in dealing with this important social issue. This widespread unemployment and poverty created many social problems that touched a huge proportion of Canadians. For example, access to health care, which had long been seen as a problem for only the poor, became a concern for the majority of the population. When these problems were seen as public issues instead of personal troubles (as C. Wright Mills explained), the government responded in the form of social programs.

The rise of the welfare state in Canada occurred around the time of World War II when the federal government instituted a group of wide-reaching welfare

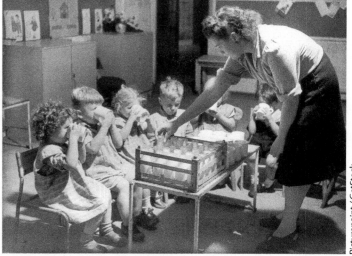

PHOTO 13.2 Canadian schoolchildren receive their milk ration in 1947. During World War II, adequate nutrition became a priority for the Canadian state. The country's first national nutrition education program arose as a result of the rise of the welfare state.

Picturepoint / GetStock

measures. By the beginning of the war, Canadians increasingly accepted the idea that the state had a responsibility to help provide economic and social security and expected these social programs to continue after the war. In the 1950s and early 1960s, permanent programs for the funding of hospitals, higher education, and vocational training were introduced or extended. In the 1960s, Liberal Prime Minister Lester B. Pearson introduced three major pieces of social legislation that have been pivotal to the Canadian welfare state: the Canada Pension Plan, the Canada Assistance Plan, and medicare. The last was based on a program created by Saskatchewan Premier Tommy Douglas, who later became the leader of the New Democratic Party.

In the 1970s, the number and type of social programs provided by the Canadian government grew. Consequently, the government began spending more money on social programs. These new investments improved income security, particularly for the elderly, persons with disabilities, single parents, and the unemployed. For example, the family allowance benefit provided income to parents, post-secondary education covered a wider section of the population, and health care became widely available for the first time. As unemployment grew in the 1970s, programs such as unemployment insurance and social assistance automatically expanded. The impact of this greater spending was particularly evident from the mid-1970s when the economy entered a period of decline after 10 years of growth. These conditions ushered in a call to decrease government spending, particularly for social programs.

Similar calls in the 1980s led the federal and provincial governments to make a number of changes. The governments changed eligibility and benefits, particularly for unemployment insurance and social assistance. They also privatized many provincial social programs by outsourcing responsibility for social services, attempted to raise revenues through medicare premiums and user fees, and moved to decrease social-program budgets and terminate some social programs, such as the aforementioned family allowance.

In many countries, including Canada, the welfare state has declined. Evidence includes less generous benefits and more rigorous eligibility tests (van den Berg et al. 2008). Many countries around the world, including in Europe, are retrenching their social welfare programs. Even countries with very strong and entrenched programs, such as Sweden, have decreased their social spending.

The Welfare State and Social Inequality

Social programs enacted through the welfare state are important for a variety of reasons. We have already mentioned that they are instrumental in dealing with and reducing inequality. A wide body of evidence shows the significant effects of welfare programs on inequality. For example, taxes and transfers considerably reduce poverty in most countries whose welfare spending constitutes at least a fifth of their GDP (Kenworthy 1999; Bradley et al. 2003).

Most welfare states have considerably lower poverty rates than they had before the implementation of welfare programs. Table 13.2 lists a selection of countries and the percentage of their populations that live under the absolute poverty line before and after welfare policies were enacted. Through the implementation of welfare policies, all the countries included cut their poverty rate by at least half. For example, Canada's poverty rate fell from 22.5 per cent to 6.5 per cent.

Social Policy: Universal and Means-Tested Programs

Social programs in the welfare state can be categorized as either universal or means-tested. **Universal programs** are available to all citizens, regardless of income or wealth. These programs tend to be very popular because everyone benefits equally. All people over 60 can receive the Canada Pension Plan (CPP), all children get access to public

TABLE 13.2 | Absolute poverty by country

Country	Absolute Poverty Rate (Threshold set at 40% of US median household income)	
	Pre-welfare	Post-welfare
Australia	23.3	11.9
Belgium	26.8	6.0
Canada	22.5	6.5
Denmark	26.4	5.9
Finland	11.9	3.7
France	36.1	9.8
Germany	15.2	4.3
Italy	30.7	14.3
Netherlands	22.1	7.3
Norway	9.2	1.7
Sweden	23.7	5.8
Switzerland	12.5	3.8
United Kingdom	16.8	8.7
United States	21.0	11.7

Sources: L. Kenworthy, 1999, "Do Social-Welfare Policies Reduce Poverty? A Cross-National Assessment," *Social Forces* 77(3): 1119–39; D. Bradley, E. Huber, S. Moller, F. Nielson, and J.D. Stephens, 2003, "Determinants of Relative Poverty in Advanced Capitalist Democracies," *American Sociological Review* 68(3): 22–51.

education, and all Canadians have access to health care. Because these programs are available to everyone, all citizens have a stake in seeing them continue and thrive. However, universal programs might not be the most efficient way to deal with issues such as poverty. If some of the money allocated to addressing poverty among the elderly goes to rich seniors who do not need the CPP payment, we have less money for seniors who are living at or near the poverty line. In other words, these misallocated payments create inefficiencies in the system by assisting people who are not at risk of living in poverty.

A **means-tested program** relies on a determination of whether an individual or family needs government assistance. In Canada, means tests are used for student finance (for post-secondary education), legal aid, and welfare (direct transfer payments to individuals to combat poverty). Compared to universal programs, means-tested programs are a more efficient way to address inequality. By simply giving more money to people who have less and giving no benefit to people who already have enough, you can reduce the gap between the rich and the poor.

Yet means-tested programs are often less popular than universal programs. The former tend to have less political support because they are seen to benefit only a small group of people. In contrast, universal programs are viewed as something that all citizens share. Some people also argue that means-tested programs carry a stigma. For example, many schools have free lunch programs for students from low-income homes. Children who participate in this program may be teased by other students. To combat this social stigma, many schools make it difficult to tell which students get lunch for free and which pay.

PHOTO 13.3 Despite the existence of social programs that address poverty, homelessness remains an often life-threatening state for many Canadians. This image highlights the serious consequences of homelessness within one city, Winnipeg.

Means-tested programs are also often criticized based on access issues. Means tests, particularly complicated ones, can make accessing social programs difficult. Sometimes individuals cannot easily decipher whether they qualify for different programs and under which conditions. The work required to verify that the tests are satisfied can increase administrative costs. Some argue that these costs can offset part of the savings from not giving the benefit universally.

Despite these drawbacks, means-tested programs such as the **Guaranteed Income Supplement (GIS)** can decrease inequality. Like the CPP, the GIS is a pension benefit for seniors, but it is for only those below a certain income level. In 1961, before the CPP and GIS were implemented, the incidence of poverty for families headed by individuals over 65 years of age was 43.9 per cent. Seniors between the ages of 65 and 69 who were living alone had a 64.1 per cent chance of being low-income, and those over the age of 70 had a 72.5 per cent chance. These figures are all substantially higher than the number for the overall Canadian population, which was 25.3 per cent at the time (Perry 1989, 701–9). After the CPP and GIS were instituted, poverty among seniors declined sharply, from approximately 30 to 5 per cent. These programs have been critical in decreasing poverty among seniors (Osberg 2001).

Another group of Canadians very likely to live in poverty is children. The national poverty rate is 13.4 per cent; however, 17 per cent of children live in poverty (Statistics Canada 2017). Children in single-parent households are particularly at risk of living in poverty, with 39 per cent of them living below the poverty line (Statistics Canada 2017). This pressing issue has serious long-term consequences, particularly for children who experience extended periods of poverty. These children are more likely to have health problems, delayed social and intellectual development, and behavioural problems. They also have lower levels of educational attainment, on average, than children who have not experienced poverty (Frenette 2007) and a higher chance of being poor as adults (Fleury 2008). As the OECD (2005, 1) notes, "Failure to tackle the poverty and exclusion facing millions of families and their children is not only socially reprehensible, but it will also weigh heavily on countries' capacity to sustain economic growth in years to come."

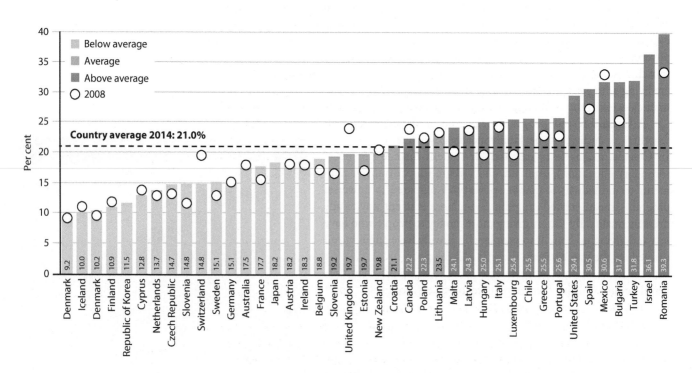

FIGURE 13.1   **Percentage of children aged 0–17 living in poverty, by country**

Source: Charlotte Edmond, 2017, "These Rich Countries Have High Levels of Child Poverty," *World Economic Forum* 28 June, https://www.weforum.org/agenda/2017/06/these-rich-countries-have-high-levels-of-child-poverty. Courtesy of UNICEF Innocenti.

Canada does quite poorly in cross-national comparisons of poverty rates among children. Out of 41 countries shown in Figure 13.1, Canada ranks almost right in the middle in terms of child poverty. Countries such as Denmark, Iceland, and Norway have child poverty rates less than half the rate in Canada (see Figure 13.1).

Reparation Programs

In Chapter 11, we learned about restorative justice, in which offenders restore order by compensating or fixing the injustice caused by their crime. One part of restorative justice can be the payment of reparations. **Reparation programs** are measures taken by the state to redress gross and systematic violations of human rights or humanitarian law through some form of compensation or restitution to the victims. They are examples of social policies that deal with inequality and injustice on a societal level. Reparations seriously consider and publicly recognize the suffering of victims through symbolic means, such as an apology, or material means, such as monetary payments.

HIGHLIGHT

Programs to Deal with Child Poverty in Canada

Canada has a number of social programs designed to assist families with children. Such programs include a child tax benefit (a monthly payment to help families pay for the extra costs associated with having children, about $120 per child per month to the age of 18) and the child fitness tax credit (for the payment of children's fitness activities such as hockey, soccer, or dance class). These are all universal benefits; thus, families with very high incomes get the same benefits as those with very low incomes. In fact, high-income families are more likely to benefit from the child fitness tax credit because they are more likely to be able to afford the cost of sports teams and dance lessons.

These programs tend to be very popular among the Canadian population because all individuals with children can benefit from them. However, Campaign 2000 argues that if the government eliminated these benefits, it could substantially reduce child poverty (Jones 2012). The group claims that an estimated 174,000 children would be lifted out of poverty if the government allocated the money spent on these benefits toward ones for families making less than $25,000 a year.

This result has obvious advantages for the people who would emerge from poverty. Reducing child poverty also has many social benefits. Sid Frankel, a member of Campaign 2000 and University of Manitoba social work professor, explains that it would be a boost to the economy because children living in poverty are less likely to obtain higher education, which makes them more likely to be unemployed later in life (Jones 2012). Children who grow up in poverty tend to have more health problems throughout their lives and, as a result, use the health care system more than children who grow up with higher incomes. In this way, reallocating money to those most in need assists both individuals and society.

There has been an attempt to alter some of the child care benefits to make them means-tested. The new child care benefit (CCB) calculates the amount of money that you receive based on the number of children in your care and your net income. The more money you make, the smaller the amount of the benefit you receive. Families that make less than $30,000 per year receive the most benefit. This way of allocating child care benefits is, in part, means-tested (Government of Canada 2017). While all people with children get a benefit, families with more need get more money from the government.

Reparations have been made to several groups, including Japanese Canadians and Japanese Americans after their forced internment in World War II, Jewish people after the Holocaust, black South Africans after apartheid, and, most recently, Indigenous people in Canada after the residential school system (see the activity on p. 375).

The Truth and Reconciliation Commission of Canada

Since the 1870s, there have been more than 130 residential schools located across Canada, the last of which closed in 1996. Paid for by the government and operated by churches, the intention of the schools was to eliminate parental involvement in the intellectual, cultural, and spiritual development of Indigenous children. More than 150,000 Indigenous children attended these schools, often against their own will and their parents' wishes. At these schools, the children were forbidden to speak their language or practise their own culture. Many were also subjected to physical, sexual, and psychological abuse. The significant impact of these schools goes beyond the students; it has also affected subsequent generations and contributed to a host of ongoing social problems.

It is difficult to imagine what could be done to address the intense and widespread injustice of the residential schools. With the assistance of the Assembly of First Nations and Inuit organizations, former students have sued the Canadian federal government and the churches responsible for the schools. These cases led to the Indian Residential Schools Settlement Agreement, the largest class-action settlement in Canadian history, in 2007. This agreement seeks to repair the harm caused by residential schools by compensating former students and calling for the establishment of the **Truth and Reconciliation Commission of Canada (TRC)**.

THE CANADIAN PRESS/Darryl Dyck

PHOTO 13.4 In September 2013, the Truth and Reconciliation Commission of Canada held a one-week national event in Vancouver that culminated in the Walk for Reconciliation. Tens of thousands of people participated in the walk.

The TRC worked for six years, collecting documents and more than 6000 accounts from those who funded the schools, officials of the institutions that operated the schools, survivors, their families, communities, and anyone else personally affected by the residential school experience. The TRC's final report, released on 2 June 2015, includes 94 recommendations, such as legislation for education, child welfare, and Aboriginal languages and the implementation of the UN's Declaration on the Rights of Indigenous Peoples (Watters 2015).

In the following reading, we will learn about the important work of the Truth and Reconciliation Commission in Canada. How is this commission an example of reparations, and how is it being implemented in Canada?

TRC Principles of Reconciliation and "The Canadian Reconciliation Landscape: Current Perspectives of Indigenous Peoples and Non-Indigenous Canadians"

The Truth and Reconciliation Commission of Canada
Principles of Reconciliation

The Truth and Reconciliation Commission of Canada believes that in order for Canada to flourish in the twenty-first century, reconciliation between Aboriginal and non-Aboriginal Canada must be based on the following principles.

1. The *United Nations Declaration on the Rights of Indigenous Peoples* is the framework for reconciliation at all levels and across all sectors of Canadian society.
2. First Nations, Inuit, and Métis peoples, as the original peoples of this country and as self-determining peoples, have Treaty, constitutional, and human rights that must be recognized and respected.
3. Reconciliation is a process of healing of relationships that requires public truth sharing, apology, and commemoration that acknowledge and redress past harms.
4. Reconciliation requires constructive action on addressing the ongoing legacies of colonialism that have had destructive impacts on Aboriginal peoples' education, culture and languages, health, child welfare, the administration of justice, and economic opportunities and prosperity.
5. Reconciliation must create a more equitable and inclusive society by closing the gaps in social, health, and economic outcomes that exist between Aboriginal and non-Aboriginal Canadians.
6. All Canadians, as Treaty peoples, share responsibility for establishing and maintaining mutually respectful relationships.
7. The perspectives and understandings of Aboriginal Elders and Traditional Knowledge Keepers of the ethics, concepts, and practices of reconciliation are vital to long-term reconciliation.
8. Supporting Aboriginal peoples' cultural revitalization and integrating Indigenous knowledge systems, oral histories, laws, protocols, and connections to the land into the reconciliation process are essential.

Truth and Reconciliation Commission of Canada. 2015. *What We Have Learned: Principles of Truth and Reconciliation, pp. 3–4. Reconciliation* Canada. The Canadian Reconciliation Landscape, 2017.

Reconciliation Canada. 2017. The Canadian Reconciliation Landscape. http://reconciliationcanada.ca/staging/wp-content/uploads/2017/05/NationalNarrativeReport-ReconciliationCanada-ReleasedMay2017_2.pdf.

9. Reconciliation requires political will, joint leadership, trust building accountability, and transparency, as well as a substantial investment of resources.

10. Reconciliation requires sustained public education and dialogue, including youth engagement, about the history and legacy of residential schools, Treaties, and Aboriginal rights, as well as the historical and contemporary contributions of Aboriginal peoples to Canadian society.

The Canadian Reconciliation Landscape

Current Perspectives of Indigenous Peoples and Non-Indigenous Canadians

Background

Over the past decade, we have witnessed growing momentum in the reconciliation movement in Canada. We have an opportunity now more than ever, to create a new way forward in our relationships with one another. The Truth and Reconciliation Commission in its final report placed much of the responsibility for this change on governments and Indigenous leaders, but it will also require meaningful engagement among Indigenous Peoples and other peoples in Canada.

This raises the question of what the collective perspective currently is among both populations with respect to reconciliation and the journey ahead. Do Indigenous Peoples and non-Indigenous Canadians share a similar or distinct view on reconciliation? Is there a basis for common ground upon which to build a path forward? What areas of divergence might exist that represent significant barriers requiring attention?

National survey of Indigenous Peoples and non-Indigenous Canadians

To answer these questions, Reconciliation Canada commissioned a national public opinion survey to measure the perspectives of Indigenous Peoples and non-Indigenous Canadians on key aspects of reconciliation, identifying areas of alignment and divergence with respect to the following themes:

- The need for reconciliation
- How reconciliation is perceived
- Barriers to reconciliation
- Support for reconciliation actions
- Responsibility for reconciliation

By developing an accurate understanding of the perspectives of both populations at this point in time, we can begin to identify areas of congruence and opportunity as well as current obstacles to progress. It is important to publicize the results broadly to dispel inaccurate assumptions and stereotypes about general attitudes toward Indigenous–non-Indigenous relations and reconciliation.

The research consisted of online surveys conducted with representative samples of Indigenous Peoples (N=521) and non-Indigenous Canadians (n=1,529) in September 2016. Detailed survey data available upon request.

Key Findings

The survey reveals that Indigenous Peoples and non-Indigenous Canadians share remarkably similar perspectives on most aspects of reconciliation. Indigenous Peoples tend to feel stronger and/or hold more definitive views in many cases, but this reflects a difference in the intensity of views held rather than a difference of opinion.

The need for reconciliation

There is general agreement among both populations that the current relationship between Indigenous Peoples and non-Indigenous Canadians is much more negative than positive. What underlies this belief are shared perceptions of discrimination and racism, negative

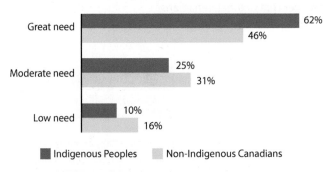

Percentage by group who say there is a "need for reconcilliation"

Sources: Kiersz, Andy. 2014 (November). "Here Are the Most Unequal Countries in the World." *Business Insider*. http://www.businessinsider.com/gini-index-income-inequality-world-map-2014-11.

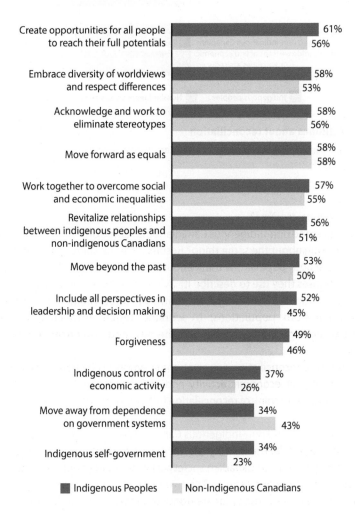

What does reconciliation mean to you?

Source. Reconciliation Canada. 2017. The Canadian Reconciliation Landscape, p. 2

stereotypes, social and economic disparities, an absence of dialogue, and a mutual sense of mistrust.

Both populations also further agree on the need for reconciliation between them, although Indigenous Peoples feel stronger about this (62 per cent say there is a great need, compared with 46 per cent of other Canadians).

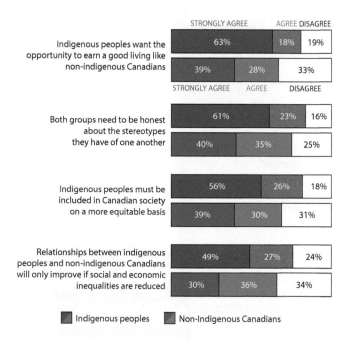

Attitudes about reconciliation

Source: Reconciliation Canada. 2017. The Canadian Reconciliation Landscape, p. 3

How is reconciliation perceived?

Indigenous Peoples and non-Indigenous Canadians may agree on the need for reconciliation, but are they thinking about the same thing? Results from the survey confirm the answer in broad terms is yes: Both populations think about reconciliation in a similar way in terms of the words and phrases they use to describe it.

Shared conceptions of reconciliation centre on three themes: a) creating greater equality between both populations; b) working together to create opportunities and reduce barriers; and c) moving beyond the past and away from a dependency on government.

A few aspects of reconciliation are given more emphasis by Indigenous Peoples (e.g., Indigenous control over economic activity and self-government), while non-Indigenous Canadians are more apt to think of reconciliation in terms of moving away from dependence on government systems.

Indigenous Peoples and non-Indigenous Canadians are also in agreement on a number of aspects about reconciliation, notably the value of acknowledging the unique contributions of Indigenous Peoples to Canadian society, as well as providing for greater opportunity and equality for Indigenous Peoples. The two populations are further aligned on taking steps towards the necessary institutional reform and individual changes required to move reconciliation forward.

At the same time, the two populations differ noticeably in the strength of opinions about reconciliation in terms of the necessity of addressing the past, and Indigenous perspectives on issues such as wealth sharing and decision-making.

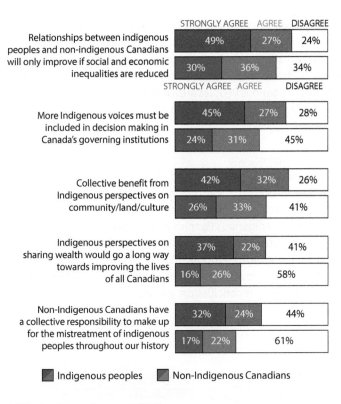

	STRONGLY AGREE	AGREE	DISAGREE
Relationships between indigenous peoples and non-indigenous Canadians will only improve if social and economic inequalities are reduced	49%	27%	24%
	30%	36%	34%

STRONGLY AGREE   AGREE   DISAGREE

More Indigenous voices must be included in decision making in Canada's governing institutions	45%	27%	28%
	24%	31%	45%

Collective benefit from Indigenous perspectives on community/land/culture	42%	32%	26%
	26%	33%	41%

Indigenous perspectives on sharing wealth would go a long way towards improving the lives of all Canadians	37%	22%	41%
	16%	26%	58%

Non-Indigenous Canadians have a collective responsibility to make up for the mistreatment of indigenous peoples throughout our history	32%	24%	44%
	17%	22%	61%

■ Indigenous peoples   ▨ Non-Indigenous Canadians

Attitudes towards reconciliation

Source: Reconciliation Canada. 2017. The Canadian Reconciliation Landscape, p. 3

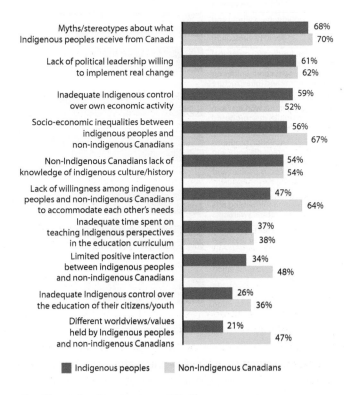

	Indigenous peoples	Non-Indigenous Canadians
Myths/stereotypes about what Indigenous peoples receive from Canada	68%	70%
Lack of political leadership willing to implement real change	61%	62%
Inadequate Indigenous control over own economic activity	59%	52%
Socio-economic inequalities between indigenous peoples and non-indigenous Canadians	56%	67%
Non-Indigenous Canadians lack of knowledge of indigenous culture/history	54%	54%
Lack of willingness among indigenous peoples and non-indigenous Canadians to accommodate each other's needs	47%	64%
Inadequate time spent on teaching Indigenous perspectives in the education curriculum	37%	38%
Limited positive interaction between indigenous peoples and non-indigenous Canadians	34%	48%
Inadequate Indigenous control over the education of their citizens/youth	26%	36%
Different worldviews/values held by Indigenous peoples and non-indigenous Canadians	21%	47%

■ Indigenous peoples   ▢ Non-Indigenous Canadians

Significant barriers to reconciliation

Source: Reconciliation Canada. 2017. The Canadian Reconciliation Landscape, p. 4

Barriers to reconciliation

Indigenous Peoples and non-Indigenous Canadians identify a similar set of major barriers to achieving reconciliation, principally regarding what is perceived as a dysfunctional relationship and mistrust of the other, socio-economic inequalities, and an absence of political leadership. Indigenous Peoples are more likely to consider barriers to be major ones, but the two populations generally agree on which represent the most significant barriers still to overcome.

Support for reconciliation actions

Indigenous Peoples and non-Indigenous Canadians voice support for a similar set of actions to move reconciliation forward. Clear majorities from both populations express strong or moderate support for each of 19 proposed reconciliation actions, although strong support levels are higher among Indigenous Peoples in most cases.

Across the list, the strongest support is expressed for increased funding in a number of areas, including Indigenous schools, living conditions on reserves, cultural awareness training for people providing services to Indigenous people, youth-focused reconciliation programs, and reconciliation programs that promote dialogue and build relationships.

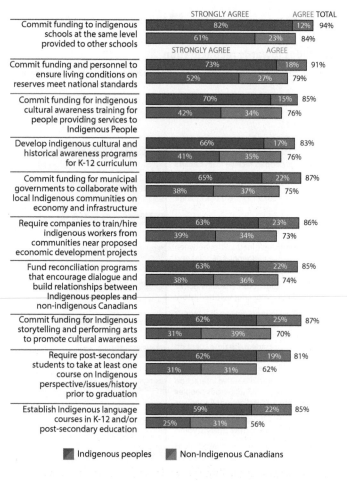

Support for actions to achieve reconciliation (top 10)

Source: Reconciliation Canada. 2017. The Canadian Reconciliation Landscape, p. 4

Strong majority support is also voiced by both populations for steps to support local economic development by requiring companies to train and/or hire Indigenous workers, and denying project development until affected Indigenous communities grant approval.

Responsibility for reconciliation

Indigenous Peoples and non-Indigenous Canadians alike identify governments as being most responsible for funding actions to bring about reconciliation. Of equal importance, a significant proportion of all respondents consider this the collective responsibility of both Indigenous and non-Indigenous people in Canada. Smaller percentages list Indigenous Peoples, specifically Indigenous-led organizations, followed by Canadian churches, non-Indigenous Canadians, and businesses in Canada as holding responsibility. The majority of individuals in both populations also say they would be prepared to take one or more specific actions to help bring about reconciliation, involving both active and passive steps. In all cases, Indigenous Peoples are more likely than non-Indigenous Canadians to indicate an intention to act.

Respondents from both samples say they would be most likely to commit their time to re-examine their individual perceptions and attitudes, participate in educational events (webinars, local seminars, storytelling events), and read relevant reconciliation material (UN Declaration, TRC 94 Calls to Action).

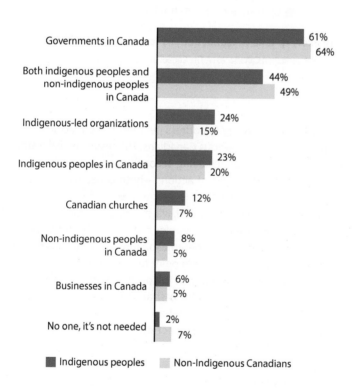

Who is most responsible for leadership in bringing about reconciliation?

Source: Reconciliation Canada. 2017. The Canadian Reconciliation Landscape, p. 5

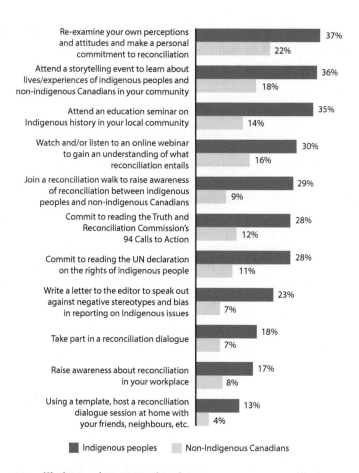

Very likely to take personal actions to support reconciliation

Source: Reconciliation Canada. 2017. The Canadian Reconciliation Landscape, p. 5

Conclusion

This study is the first national survey to address perspectives on reconciliation among both Indigenous Peoples and non-Indigenous Canadians. The results reveal a striking alignment of views about the importance of achieving reconciliation, how it is currently perceived, barriers to achieving it, and the types of actions—both collective and personal—that are required to make reconciliation a reality.

Opinions and attitudes, however hopeful, will not alone be sufficient to heal the historic and current divisions among Indigenous Peoples and non-Indigenous Canadians. But they matter greatly in reflecting commonly shared aspirations of both populations for a better collective and provide an important starting point for genuine progress.

While we have an incredible window of opportunity to create lasting change, maintaining the momentum will require a shared commitment by all peoples. This poses the question of what now are the barriers to achieving reconciliation? How can you, as a reader of this report, take action to contribute to the reconciliation movement?

About Reconciliation Canada

Born from the vision of Chief Dr. Robert Joseph, Gwawaenuk Elder, Reconciliation Canada is a charitable, nonpartisan, national organization that promotes reconciliation by engaging Canadians from every part of society in open and honest dialogue and transformative experiences that revitalize relationships among Indigenous peoples and all Canadians. Its initiatives include reconciliation dialogue workshops, reconciliation leadership learning experiences, economic reconciliation, and public awareness activities.

Reconciliation Canada thanks all who contributed to the production of this survey report, including Daniel Savas of Savas Consulting, Discourse Media and Keith Neuman of The Environics Institute.

*Please note an adjustment has been made to the terminology in the report, replacing 'Aboriginal', as it appeared in the original questionnaire, with 'Indigenous'. This reflects recent changes in the political and legal landscape both within Canada and the broader international community.

CRITICAL READING QUESTIONS

1. What are the principles of reconciliation? Why are these core principles important? What groups are part of reconciliation, according to these principles?
2. How do Indigenous and non-Indigenous people feel about reconciliation, according to the report? Why might different groups feel differently and focus on different elements of reconciliation?
3. What barriers might there be to reconciliation, and how might these barriers be overcome?

The Truth and Reconciliation Commission of Canada

Explore the TRC's website (www.trc.ca), and then answer the following questions. (A direct link to the commission's final report is available on this book's companion website.)

1. Why was the TRC established, and what did it hope to accomplish?
2. Who are the commissioners? How were they selected, and why is their selection important?
3. What is the truth and reconciliation part of the agreement (particularly the national public events, the "It Matters to Me" Twibbon Campaign, and the National Research Centre)? What is its purpose, and how was it achieved? What was the public's role in this process?
4. What types of reparations are being paid? What is the purpose of these reparations, and who receives them? What is the difference between the Common Experience Payment and the Independent Assessment Payment?
5. Go to this book's companion website to access apologies made to Indigenous people by Stephen Harper, the Anglican Church, and the United Church. What is the role of apologies in this process? Why are they important (or not important)?
6. Explore your campus, and consider how it has taken steps to implement the recommendations of the TRC. Some possible ways that campuses have done this is to: create new classes, majors, or institutes; include land acknowledgements in public events and courses; or create archives or other physical places on campus related to the TRC. How has your campus responded to the TRC?

ACTIVITY

How the State Involves the Public

One of the primary ways that the state engages the public is through regular **elections**, a formal decision-making process in which eligible citizens select individuals for public office. Elections are a critical part of representative democracies such as Canada. That said, the percentage of Canadians who vote in elections has declined significantly (see Figure 13.2). The 1950s and 1960s were a high point of voting in Canada, with almost 80 per cent of registered voters going to the polls during those years. The federal election of 2011 saw a voting rate of only 61.1 per cent of eligible voters; however, there was an increase in voting rates in the 2015 election to almost 70 per cent. This surprising rise in voting rates after decades of decline is heartening for citizens concerned about the health of our democracy.

Along with the overall decline in voting in Canada, it is important to note that the rates of voting differ by group. For example, young people are much less likely to vote than older

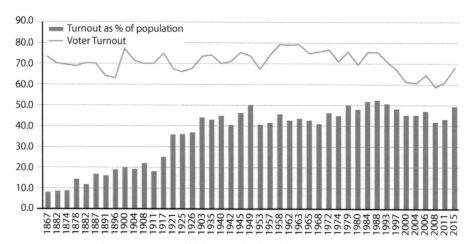

FIGURE 13.2   Voting in Canada, 1867–2015 (per cent)

Source: Andrew Heard. https://www.sfu.ca/~aheard/elections/historical-turnout.html

people: 57.1 per cent of people ages 18 to 24 vote, while about 78.8 per cent of people ages 65 to 74 do (see Figure 13.4). Voting rates decline again for those 75 years and over. The reasons for not voting are many, as illustrated in Table 13.3. Almost half of the people who report not voting say it is because they are too busy. An additional 40 per cent of non-voters report that they did not have sufficient information or interest in the elections. Together, this is the vast majority of people who do not participate in elections. Increasing interest and feelings of efficacy could dramatically increase the overall percentage of Canadians who vote.

Research on voter turnout indicates two main theories to explain changing voting patterns, the **life-cycle effect** and **generational replacement**. The life-cycle effect argues that fewer young people vote because of a variety of structural, social, and economic circumstances. As these young non-voters age, they become more likely to vote. A number of recent studies have pushed us to question this theory. For example, an Elections Canada

PHOTO 13.5 Highly visible and simple Elections Canada signage attempts to draw the eye and to reduce barriers to voting that depend on literacy or language skills. What other methods could increase voter turnout in Canada?

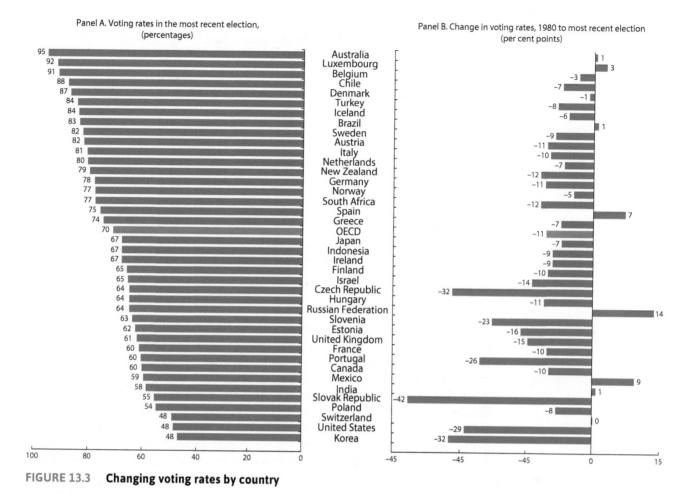

FIGURE 13.3   **Changing voting rates by country**

Source: OECD, 2011, "Society at a Glance: OECD Social Indicators," OECD, Stat (database), http://www.oecd-ilibrary.org/sites/soc_glance-2011-en/08/04/
g8_co4-01.html?contentType=&itemId=/content/chapter/soc_glance-2011-29-en&containerItemId=/content/serial/19991290&accessItemIds=/content/
book/soc_glance-2011-en&mimeType=text/html

study finds "not only are young people participating less than their elders, their willingness
to participate appears to be declining over time" (Barnes and Virgint 2013).

Generational replacement studies have grouped the electorate into approximate "generations" according to age and tracked their voting propensities. These studies find that voters
of the middle generations (born between 1945 and 1959) and those of the oldest generations

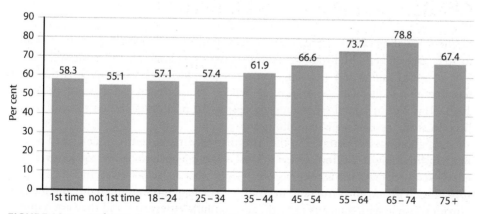

FIGURE 13.4   **Estimated voter turnout in Canada by age group, 2015 federal general
election (per cent)**

Source: Elections Canada, 2016, Estimation of Voter Turnout by Age Group and Gender at the 2015 General Election,
http://www.elections.ca/res/rec/part/estim/42ge/42_e.pdf.. Reproduced with permission of Elections Canada.

TABLE 13.3 | Reasons for not voting, Canada, 2015

Reasons for Not Voting	All Non-voters
Everyday life or health reasons (e.g. too busy, illness)	47.9
Political reasons (e.g. lack of interest or information)	39.5
Electoral process reasons (e.g. no id, hard to get to polls)	7.6
All other reasons	5.0

Source: Elections Canada, 2015, *Turnout and Reasons for Not Voting during the 42nd General Election: Results from the Labour Force Survey*, http://www.elections.ca/content.aspx?section=res&dir=rec/eval/pes2015/lfs&document=index&lang=e

RESEARCH METHOD
SURVEY

(born before 1945) have a high propensity to vote. These generations are being replaced by younger ones (born after 1960) that have a lower propensity to engage in this way. Some of the studies' authors have proposed that this generational replacement could account for the decrease in voter turnout (Barnes and Virgint 2013). If so, voting should continue to drop.

Following the 2011 general election, Blais and Loewen (2011) used census data to examine youth electoral engagement in Canada. They found that today's young people are better educated, earn less income, and are more likely to have been born in Canada than young people of previous generations. Education and being born in Canada are both very important predictors of one's propensity to vote. Comparing young people between the ages of 18 and 24 who are students with those who are not shows that the former are 9 per cent more likely to participate in politics. Young people in this age group who were born in Canada are 12 per cent more likely to vote than those not born in the country. Blais and Loewen argue that this difference is because "those who are born outside of Canada take slightly longer than their Canadian-born counterparts to come to socialize into Canadian politics." In addition to the importance of these socio-demographic factors, they found that interest in and information about politics have an even greater effect on youth voting behaviour. Why do you think that young people vote at a relatively low rate? What are the implications for society at large?

Challenges Facing the Modern State

Declines in voting rates in Canada and other countries challenge the government's ability to engage citizens. Many argue that these low voting levels are the result of the lower level of social capital and civic engagement in our society. Social capital is the social resources that individuals can draw on in making decisions and taking action (Coleman 1990). This type of capital is based on people's social relations and their sense of underlying trust and confidence in one another.

Social capital is illustrated in the "**rotating credit associations**" described by cultural anthropologist Clifford Geertz (1962). These associations are cooperative economic ventures practised among people in Southeast Asian societies. Individuals pool their resources and then rotate in drawing on the general fund of credit. The method provides people with a means to begin an economic enterprise, and they are required to pay back into the pool from their earnings. These rotating credit associations require trust and cooperation among people and would be impossible without social capital. You would never contribute to the pool if you did not trust that you could take out money later when you needed it. We can also find examples of social trust and cooperation in other groups, particularly families. These feelings, which are at the heart of social capital, provide an important resource on which individuals can draw.

Robert D. Putnam's (1993) influential study of regional government in Italy, *Making Democracy Work*, helped to illustrate the importance of social capital. In the early 1970s, Italy created a new system of 20 regional governments, which were all set up in the same way and had the same institutions. However, the citizens in some regions were more satisfied with their governments, and some governments were able to institute policies and function more effectively than others. The question was, "Why were some regional governments more effective than others?" Putnam and his colleagues worked to answer this query by comparing all 20 governments, using such sources as survey data of citizen engagement and participation. They found that wealth was not the most important predictor of regional success. Instead, governments tended to work more effectively and citizens were more satisfied and engaged in regions with strong civic traditions. Regions with more "**civicness**"—the fabric of values, norms, institutions, and associations—had higher levels of solidarity, mutual trust, and tolerance among citizens (Putnam 1993). This greater social capital, in turn, made for more effective governance.

RESEARCH METHOD
SURVEY

HIGHLIGHT

The Decline of Close Social Connections

We live in a time when people often feel very connected. Having a lot of Facebook friends or Twitter followers can make us feel integrated and tied to others. However, recent research has shown that we might, in fact, be *less* connected than ever before. The General Social Survey in the United States finds that Americans have, on average, one-third fewer confidants than they did 30 years ago. In general, they have also shifted away from ties formed in places such as churches, clubs, neighbourhood groups, and sports teams (see McPherson, Smith-Lovin, and Brashears 2008).

The survey also asked respondents how many "discussion partners" (people with whom they discuss important issues) they have. The number for the average person has decreased from 2.9 to 2.1 since 1985. Almost half the population reports that they discuss important matters with only one other person or with no one at all. People who are very well connected, who have more than four discussion partners, have decreased from one-third of the population to only one-fifth. And the number of people who have no one other than a spouse with whom to discuss their problems has increased by 50 per cent over the past 30 years (McPherson, Smith-Lovin, and Brashears 2008).

One interesting trend to note is that highly educated people tend to have more confidants than those with less education. As the following figure shows, each additional year of education increases the number of discussion partners. Highly educated people also have a smaller proportion of family in their networks than people with less education, which means that the former are more likely than others to be exposed to new perspectives by talking outside their family circle.

The decline in the number of confidants seems surprising in light of the highly interconnected nature of modern society, including the widespread use of social media on the Internet. But some researchers argue that Internet use might interfere with communication in the home and neighbourhood. While the Internet can help us to interact with people across larger geographical areas, these looser ties might be replacing the stronger ones to confidants that we had in the past. For instance, we might be connected to a lot of people on Facebook, but these contacts are what sociologists call weak ties—friends of friends or acquaintances. They might expose us to a greater range of information than close ties, but

Continued

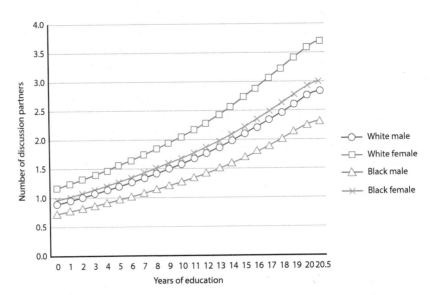

Projected number of discussion partners by sex, race, and level of education

Source: Matthew E. Brashears, 2011, "Small Networks and High Isolation? A Reexamination of American Discussion Networks," Social Networks 33(4): 331–41. Copyright © 2011 Elsevier B.V. All rights reserved.

they are less likely to provide emotional support because we cannot rely on most of them when we are in need or confide in them when we have a problem.

However, not everyone sees the creation of this wider net of weak ties as a negative thing. According to Veenhof et al. (2008), Internet users may be at least as socially engaged as non-users. Their study found that although Internet users have larger networks and more frequent interactions with friends and family, they tend to spend less in-person time and, of course, more time online. However, a large number of Internet users are civically and politically engaged, using the Internet for these types of activities.

In particular, the researchers examined how Internet use might be particularly important for certain groups of Canadians. They found, for example, that recent immigrants are especially likely to use the Internet to maintain ties with family and friends in their country of origin and to integrate into larger Canadian society.

PHOTO 13.A What are the differences between "friends" on Facebook and friends in real life? Why does it matter that we are replacing real-world friends with online friendships?

Putnam and others claim that voting rates are declining because of the decrease in social capital and civicness in modern society. Individuals are less likely to trust one another, less likely to participate together in social groups and organizations, and less likely to cooperate with one another. In the influential *Bowling Alone: The Collapse and Revival of American Community*, Putnam (2000) argues that American society has seen a decline in social capital and **civic engagement**, activities that address social issues. This change is particularly concerning because social capital and civic engagement are related to a number of positive social outcomes. For example, societies with high amounts of social capital tend to have lower levels of crime, healthier people, less poverty and unemployment, and many other benefits. Can we apply Putnam's arguments to the Canadian case? Keep this question in mind when reading the following excerpt.

Bowling Alone: America's Declining Social Capital

Robert D. Putnam

Many students of the new democracies that have emerged over the past decade and a half have emphasized the importance of a strong and active civil society to the consolidation of democracy. Especially with regard to the postcommunist countries, scholars and democratic activists alike have lamented the absence or obliteration of traditions of independent civic engagement and a widespread tendency toward passive reliance on the state. To those concerned with the weakness of civil societies in the developing or postcommunist world, the advanced Western democracies and above all the United States have typically been taken as models to be emulated. There is striking evidence, however, that the vibrancy of American civil society has notably declined over the past several decades. . . .

. . . Researchers in such fields as education, urban poverty, unemployment, the control of crime and drug abuse, and even health have discovered that successful outcomes are more likely in civically engaged communities. Similarly, research on the varying economic attainments of different ethnic groups in the United States has demonstrated the importance of social bonds within each group. These results are consistent with research in a wide range of settings that demonstrates the vital importance of social networks for job placement and many other economic outcomes . . .

The norms and networks of civic engagement also powerfully affect the performance of representative government. That, at least, was the central conclusion of my own 20-year, quasi-experimental study of subnational governments in different regions of Italy.[1] Although all these regional governments seemed identical on paper, their levels of effectiveness varied dramatically. Systematic inquiry showed that the quality of governance was determined by long-standing traditions of civic engagement (or its absence). Voter turnout, newspaper readership, membership in choral societies and football clubs—these were the hallmarks of a successful region. In fact, historical analysis suggested that these networks of organized reciprocity and civic solidarity, far from being an epiphenomenon of socio-economic modernization, were a precondition for it.

. . . Social scientists in several fields have recently suggested a common framework for understanding these phenomena, a framework that rests on the concept of social capital.[2] By analogy with notions of physical capital and human capital—tools and training that enhance

Putnam, Robert D. 1995. "Bowling Alone: The Collapse and Revival of American Community." Journal of Democracy 6(1): 65–78..

individual productivity—"social capital" refers to features of social organization such as networks, norms, and social trust that facilitate coordination and co-operation for mutual benefit.

For a variety of reasons, life is easier in a community blessed with a substantial stock of social capital. In the first place, networks of civic engagement foster sturdy norms of generalized reciprocity and encourage the emergence of social trust. Such networks facilitate coordination and communication, amplify reputations, and thus allow dilemmas of collective action to be resolved. When economic and political negotiation is embedded in dense networks of social interaction, incentives for opportunism are reduced. At the same time, networks of civic engagement embody past success at collaboration, which can serve as a cultural template for future collaboration. Finally, dense networks of interaction probably broaden the participants' sense of self, developing the "I" into the "we," or (in the language of rational-choice theorists) enhancing the participants' "taste" for collective benefits.

I do not intend here to survey (much less contribute to) the development of the theory of social capital. Instead, I use the central premise of that rapidly growing body of work—that social connections and civic engagement pervasively influence our public life, as well as our private prospects—as the starting point for an empirical survey of trends in social capital in contemporary America. I concentrate here entirely on the American case, although the developments I portray may in some measure characterize many contemporary societies.

Whatever Happened to Civic Engagement?

We begin with familiar evidence on changing patterns of political participation, not least because it is immediately relevant to issues of democracy in the narrow sense. Consider the well-known decline in turnout in national elections over the last three decades. From a relative high point in the early 1960s, voter turnout had by 1990 declined by nearly a quarter; tens of millions of Americans had forsaken their parents' habitual readiness to engage in the simplest act of citizenship. Broadly similar trends also characterize participation in state and local elections.

It is not just the voting booth that has been increasingly deserted by Americans. A series of identical questions posed by the Roper Organization to national samples 10 times each year over the last two decades reveals that since 1973 the number of Americans who report that "in the past year" they have "attended a public meeting on town or school affairs" has fallen by more than a third (from 22 per cent in 1973 to 13 per cent in 1993). Similar (or even greater) relative declines are evident in responses to questions about attending a political rally or speech, serving on a committee of some local organization, and working for a political party. By almost every measure, Americans' direct engagement in politics and government has fallen steadily and sharply over the last generation, despite the fact that average levels of education—the best individual-level predictor of political participation—have risen sharply throughout this period. Every year over the last decade or two, millions more have withdrawn from the affairs of their communities.

Not coincidentally, Americans have also disengaged psychologically from politics and government over this era. The proportion of Americans who reply that they "trust the government in Washington" only "some of the time" or "almost never" has risen steadily from 30 per cent in 1966 to 75 per cent in 1992 . . .

Religious affiliation is by far the most common associational membership among Americans. Indeed, by many measures America continues to be . . . an astonishingly "churched" society. For example, the United States has more houses of worship per capita than any other nation on earth. Yet religious sentiment in America seems to be becoming somewhat less tied to institutions and more self-defined.

How have these complex crosscurrents played out over the last three or four decades in terms of Americans' engagement with organized religion? The general pattern is clear: the 1960s witnessed a significant drop in reported weekly churchgoing—from roughly 48 per cent in the late 1950s to roughly 41 per cent in the early 1970s. Since then, it has stagnated or (according to some surveys) declined still further. . . .

For many years, labour unions provided one of the most common organizational affiliations among American workers. Yet union membership has been falling for nearly four decades, with the steepest decline occurring between 1975 and 1985. . . .

Next, we turn to evidence on membership in (and volunteering for) civic and fraternal organizations. These data show some striking patterns. . . .

. . . Evidence on "regular" (as opposed to occasional or "drop-by") volunteering is available from the Labor Department's Current Population Surveys of 1974 and 1989. These estimates suggest that serious volunteering declined by roughly one-sixth over these 15 years, from 24 per cent of adults in 1974 to 20 per cent in 1989. . . .

Fraternal organizations have also witnessed a substantial drop in membership during the 1980s and 1990s. Membership is down significantly in such groups as the Lions (off 12 per cent since 1983), the Elks (off 18 per cent since 1979), the Shriners (off 27 per cent since 1979), the Jaycees (off 44 per cent since 1979), and the Masons (down 39 per cent since 1959). In sum, after expanding steadily throughout most of this century, many major civic organizations have experienced a sudden, substantial, and nearly simultaneous decline in membership over the last decade or two.

The most whimsical yet discomfiting bit of evidence of social disengagement in contemporary America that I have discovered is this: more Americans are bowling today than ever before, but bowling in organized leagues has plummeted in the last decade or so. Between 1980 and 1993 the total number of bowlers in America increased by 10 per cent, while league bowling decreased by 40 per cent. (Lest this be thought a wholly trivial example, I should note that nearly 80 million Americans went bowling at least once during 1993, *nearly a third more than voted in the 1994 congressional elections* and roughly the same number as claim to attend church regularly. Even after the 1980s' plunge in league bowling, nearly 3 per cent of American adults regularly bowl in leagues.) . . . The broader social significance, however, lies in the social interaction and even occasionally civic conversations over beer and pizza that solo bowlers forgo. Whether or not bowling beats balloting in the eyes of most Americans, bowling teams illustrate yet another vanishing form of social capital.

Countertrends

At this point, however, we must confront a serious counterargument. Perhaps the traditional forms of civic organization whose decay we have been tracing have been replaced by vibrant new organizations. For example, national environmental organizations (like the Sierra Club) and feminist groups (like the National Organization for Women) grew rapidly during the 1970s and 1980s and now count hundreds of thousands of dues-paying members. An even more dramatic example is the American Association of Retired Persons (AARP), which grew exponentially from 400,000 card-carrying members in 1960 to 33 million in 1993, becoming (after the Catholic Church) the largest private organization in the world. The national administrators of these organizations are among the most feared lobbyists in Washington, in large part because of their massive mailing lists of presumably loyal members.

These new mass-membership organizations are plainly of great political importance. From the point of view of social connectedness, however, they are sufficiently different from classic "secondary associations" that we need to invent a new label—perhaps "tertiary associations." For the vast majority of their members, the only act of membership consists in writing a cheque for dues or perhaps occasionally reading a newsletter. Few ever attend any meetings of such organizations, and most are unlikely ever (knowingly) to encounter any other member. The bond between any two members of the Sierra Club is less like the bond between any two members of a gardening club and more like the bond between any two Red Sox fans (or perhaps any two devoted Honda owners): they root for the same team and they share some of the same interests, but they are unaware of each other's existence. Their ties, in short, are to common symbols, common leaders, and perhaps common ideals, but not to one another. The theory of social capital argues that associational membership should, for example, increase social trust, but this prediction is much less straightforward with regard to membership in tertiary associations. From the point of view of social connectedness, the Environmental Defense Fund and a bowling league are just not in the same category. . . .

Within all educational categories, total associational membership declined significantly between 1967 and 1993. Among the college-educated, the average number of group memberships per person fell from 2.8 to 2.0 (a 26-per-cent decline); among high-school graduates, the number fell from 1.8 to 1.2 (32 per cent); and among those with fewer than 12 years of education, the number fell from 1.4 to 1.1 (25 per cent). In other words, at *all* educational (and hence social) levels of American society, and counting *all* sorts of group memberships, *the average number of associational memberships has fallen by about a fourth over the last quarter-century.* . . .

Americans are also less trusting. The proportion of Americans saying that most people can be trusted fell by more than a third between 1960, when 58 per cent chose that alternative, and 1993, when only 37 per cent did. The same trend is apparent in all educational groups; indeed, because social trust is also correlated with education and because educational levels have risen sharply, the overall decrease in social trust is even more apparent if we control for education.

Our discussion of trends in social connectedness and civic engagement has tacitly assumed that all the forms of social capital that we have discussed are themselves coherently correlated across individuals. This is in fact true. Members of associations are much more likely than nonmembers to participate in politics, to spend time with neighbours, to express social trust, and so on.

The close correlation between social trust and associational membership is true not only across time and across individuals, but also across countries. Evidence from the 1991 World Values Survey demonstrates the following:[3]

. . . Across the 35 countries in this survey, social trust and civic engagement are strongly correlated; the greater the density of associational membership in a society, the more trusting its citizens. Trust and engagement are two facets of the same underlying factor—social capital. . . .

Why Is US Social Capital Eroding?

As we have seen, something has happened in America in the last two or three decades to diminish civic engagement and social connectedness. What could that "something" be? Here are several possible explanations, along with some initial evidence on each. . . .

Mobility: The "re-potting" hypothesis. Numerous studies of organizational involvement have shown that residential stability and such related phenomena as homeownership are clearly associated with greater civic engagement. Mobility, like frequent re-potting of plants, tends to disrupt root systems, and it takes time for an uprooted individual to put down new roots. It seems plausible that the automobile, suburbanization, and the movement to the Sun Belt have reduced the social rootedness of the average American, but one fundamental difficulty with this hypothesis is apparent: the best evidence shows that residential stability and homeownership in America have risen modestly since 1965, and are surely higher now than during the 1950s, when civic engagement and social connectedness by our measures was definitely higher.

Other demographic transformations. A range of additional changes have transformed the American family since the 1960s—fewer marriages, more divorces, fewer children, lower real wages, and so on. Each of these changes might account for some of the slackening of civic engagement, since married, middle-class parents are generally more socially involved than other people. Moreover, the changes in scale that have swept over the American economy in these years—illustrated by the replacement of the corner grocery by the supermarket and now perhaps of the supermarket by electronic shopping at home, or the replacement of community-based enterprises by outposts of distant multinational firms—may perhaps have undermined the material and even physical basis for civic engagement.

The technological transformation of leisure. There is reason to believe that deep-seated technological trends are radically "privatizing" or "individualizing" our use of leisure time and thus disrupting many opportunities for social-capital formation. The most obvious and probably the most powerful instrument of this revolution is television. Time-budget studies in the 1960s showed that the growth in time spent watching television dwarfed all other changes in the way Americans passed their days and nights. Television has made our communities (or, rather, what we experience as our communities) wider and shallower. In the language of economics, electronic technology enables individual tastes to be satisfied more fully, but at the cost of the positive social externalities associated with more primitive forms of entertainment. The same logic applies to the replacement of vaudeville by the movies and now of movies by the VCR. The new "virtual reality" helmets that we will soon don to be entertained in total isolation are merely the latest extension of this trend. Is technology thus driving a wedge between our individual interests and our collective interests? It is a question that seems worth exploring more systematically. . . .

NOTES

1. Robert D. Putnam, *Making Democracy Work: Civic Traditions in Modern Italy* (Princeton: Princeton University Press, 1993).

2. James S. Coleman deserves primary credit for developing the "social capital" theoretical framework. See his "Social Capital in the Creation of Human Capital," *American Journal of Sociology* (Supplement) 94 (1988): S95–S120, as well as his *The Foundations of Social Theory* (Cambridge: Harvard University Press, 1990), 300–21. See also Mark Granovetter, "Economic Action and Social Structure: The Problem of Embeddedness," *American Journal of Sociology* 91 (1985): 481–510; Glenn C. Loury, "Why Should We Care about Group Inequality?" *Social Philosophy and Policy* 5 (1987): 249–71; and Robert D. Putnam, "The Prosperous Community: Social Capital and Public Life," *American Prospect* 13 (1993): 35–42. To my knowledge, the first scholar to use the term *social capital* in its current sense was Jane Jacobs, in *The Death and Life of Great American Cities* (New York: Random House, 1961), 138.

3. I am grateful to Ronald Inglehart, who directs this unique cross-national project, for sharing these highly useful data with me. See his "The Impact of Culture on Economic Development: Theory, Hypotheses, and Some Empirical Tests" (unpublished manuscript, University of Michigan, 1994).

CRITICAL READING QUESTIONS

1. According to Putnam, what is social capital and why is it important?

2. How is bowling an example of declining civic engagement? What are some other pieces of evidence, aside from lower voting rates?

3. What are some of the arguments Putnam gives for the decreasing levels of social capital? What might he say about the rise of the Internet (e.g., social networking sites, online activism, etc.) for the development of social capital?

HIGHLIGHT

Are Canadians Bowling Alone? Civic Engagement in Canada

Robert Putnam argues that we are "bowling alone," meaning that we are no longer involved in the civic and community groups that once defined Canadian and American society. This is very concerning because these sorts of groups and the connections they foster create the foundation for a strong democracy, vibrant community, and trusting society. Recent data, however, suggest that this decline in social capital may not be happening in Canada. In fact, there has been an increase in the percentage of Canadians who are members of civic and other types of groups. But who is participating and in what types of ways?

The Canadian General Social Survey has asked about engagement in a variety of community groups since 2003. Because of this, we can see trends in participation in these groups over time and see that we are not, in fact, declining in our participation in civil society. Looking at the first figure, you can see that the number of people who are part of a group or association in Canada has increased from 61 per cent in 2003 to 65 per cent in 2013. This change is much larger for women, who have increased their participation by 6 per cent whereas men have only increased their participation by 3 per cent. Now women and men have roughly the same level of engagement in these groups.

Age is also importantly related to engagement in organizations in Canada. Young people participate more than any other age group, with 69 per cent of people between the ages of 15 and 24 engaging in organizations. Young people have also seen a particularly notable increase in their engagement over time, with all age groups between 15 and 44 increasing their engagement by 5 per cent over the past 10 years. The oldest groups are not participating at such a high rate, but the increase in their engagement has been stark. In fact, for those over the age of 75, there has been a 14 per cent increase in engagement in groups over the past 10 years!

We can see that the most popular group in which to engage is sports and other recreation groups (see the second figure). It seems we are in many bowling leagues (and soccer clubs, running groups, and hockey teams). This accounts for almost one-third of all group memberships. Canadians also participate frequently in unions, with about 30 per cent of Canadians being members of these organizations. About 20 per cent of Canadians participate in cultural, educational, or hobby groups. And, the neighborhood/school groups and religious groups that Putnam was particularly concerned about also are popular among Canadians, with between 15 and 20 per cent of Canadians engaging in these types of organizations.

Finally, income and education are both related to engagement in groups. As we can see from the final figure, the more money you make and the more education you have, the more likely you are to participate in these types of organizations. It is clear from much past work that engagement in organizations and groups is important for both individuals and the community as a whole. Why might Canadians be re-engaging in these types of organizations? Why are some groups of Canadians more likely to do this than others?

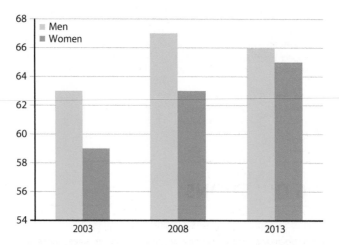

Percentage of Canadians who are a member of a group, by gender and age, 2003–13

Source: Statistics Canada, 2015, "Table 1: Participation in Groups, Organizations or Associations, 2003, 2008 and 2013," Spotlight on Canadians: Results from the General Social Survey, Catalogue no. 89-652-X, Ottawa: Statistics Canada, http://www.statcan.gc.ca/pub/89-652-x/2015006/t/tbl01-eng.htm

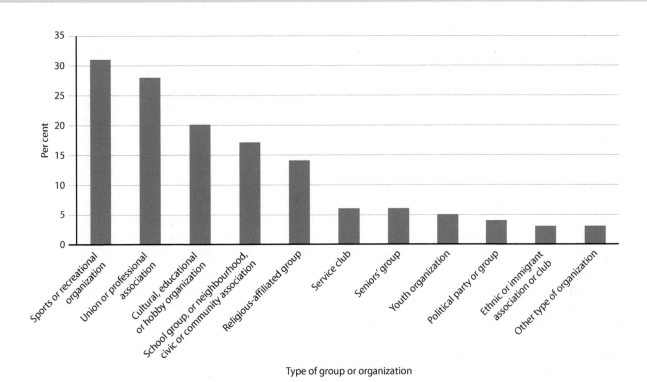

People who are members of groups, by type of group, 2013

Source: Martin Turcotte, 2013, "Civic Engagement and Political Participation in Canada," Statistics Canada. 2013. "Table 4: Participation in Groups, Organizations, or Associations, People between 25 and 64 Years, 2013." Spotlight on Canadians: Results from the General Social Survey. Statistics Canada Catalogue no. 89-652-X. Ottawa. https://www150.statcan.gc.ca/n1/pub/89-652-x/89-652-x2015006-eng.htm

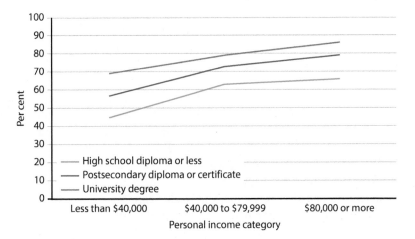

People who are members of groups, by education and income, 2013

Source: Martin Turcotte, 2013, "Civic Engagement and Political Participation in Canada," Statistics Canada. 2013. "Table 4: Participation in Groups, Organizations, or Associations, People between 25 and 64 Years, 2013." Spotlight on Canadians: Results from the General Social Survey. Statistics Canada Catalogue no. 89-652-X. Ottawa. https://www150.statcan.gc.ca/n1/pub/89-652-x/89-652-x2015006-eng.htm

ACTIVITY

Civil Society on Campus and among the Young

It is clear from the work of Coleman, Putnam, and others that social capital and civicness are very important. How actively involved are students on your campus in comparison with those on other Canadian campuses? Why do you think this is the case? What are the implications of having an active (or inactive) campus?

Look for measures of engagement at your college or university, including the number of students who voted in recent student elections, the existence of clubs on campus, social events on campus, student athletics, student newspapers, alumni associations, and other groups and activities.

1. Do you think that your university administration encourages this kind of social capital? If so, how? Why do you think they encourage it?
2. What are the implications of this engagement on your campus? Is civicness related to such things as your campus's score on student satisfaction, graduation rates, or student achievement? Why or why not?
3. What factors make your campus engaged or not? How does the size of the campus, its location, number of students living on campus, or diversity of students influence student engagement?

Now compare your school to another Canadian college or university. Select one that differs from yours in terms of size, location, student body, or some other factor, and find the measures listed above. Note the similarities and differences between the two campuses.

1. Why is one campus more or less active than the other? What features seem to lead to higher engagement?
2. What are the implications of these differences for student satisfaction and educational outcomes?
3. If you think that engagement on campus is a positive thing, how could you encourage more students to engage in campus life and activities?
4. How could colleges and universities support your efforts to increase civicness?

Summary

This chapter began by examining how society changes over time. Social change can happen either through the state, the focus of this chapter, or outside the state, the focus of the next chapter. Because of the state's significance in social change, we examined the rise of the state and its components. We then looked at the development of the welfare state, both internationally and in Canada. The welfare state provides many goods to citizens, particularly social programs. Through examining both universal and means-tested programs, we assessed how government programs can reduce social inequality and deal with particular social issues, such as poverty among the elderly and children. We also explored the role of reparation programs, particularly the TRC, as a means by which the state addresses social inequality. The chapter ended with a discussion of a key issue facing the modern state, the decline of social capital. This weaker connectedness between people can make the state's ability to engage citizens and effectively institute social change difficult.

Key Terms

civic engagement 381
civicness 379
economic perspective 360
generational replacement 376

Guaranteed Income
    Supplement (GIS) 364
life-cycle effect 376
managerial perspective 359

For Further Reading

Evans, Peter B., Dietrich Rueschemeyer, and Theda Skocpol. 1985. *Bringing the State Back In*. New York: Cambridge University Press.

Inglehart, Ronald. 1997. *Modernization and Postmodernization: Cultural, Economic and Political Change in 43 Nations*. Princeton, NJ: Princeton University Press.

Putnam, Robert D., with Robert Leonardi and Raffaella Y. Nanetti. 1993. *Making Democracy Work: Civic Traditions in Modern Italy*. Princeton, NJ: Princeton University Press.

Stanbridge, Karen, and Howard Ramos. 2012. *Seeing Politics Differently: A Brief Introduction to Political Sociology*. Don Mills, ON: Oxford University Press.

Tilly, Charles. 1992. *Coercion, Capital, and European States (990–1992)*. Cambridge, MA: Basil Blackwell.

References

Barnes, Andre, and Erin Virgint. 2013. "Youth Voter Turnout in Canada." Publication No. 2010-19-E. 7 April 2010. Revised 9 August 2013. Ottawa: Library of Parliament.

Blais, André, and Peter Loewen. 2011 (January). *Youth Electoral Engagement in Canada*. Working Paper Series. Ottawa: Elections Canada.

Bradley, D., E. Huber, S. Moller, F. Nielson, and J.D. Stephens. 2003. "Determinants of Relative Poverty in Advanced Capitalist Democracies." *American Sociological Review* 68(3): 22–51.

Briggs, Asa. 2000. "The Welfare State in a Historical Perspective." In C. Pierson and F. Castles, eds, *The Welfare State Reader*, 1–31. Cambridge: Polity Press.

Coleman, James S. 1990. *Foundations of Social Theory*. Cambridge, MA: Belknap Press.

Fleury, Dominique. 2008. "Low-Income Children." *Perspectives on Labour and Income* 9(5): 14–23.

Frenette, Marc. 2007. *Why Are Youth from Lower-Income Families Less Likely to Attend University?* Ottawa: Statistics Canada.

Geertz, Clifford. 1962. "The Rotating Credit Association: A 'Middle Rung' in Development." *Economic Development and Cultural Change* 10: 240–63.

Gerth, H.H., and C. Wright Mills, eds and trans. 1946. *From Max Weber: Essays in Sociology*. New York: Oxford University Press.

Government of Canada. 2017. "Do You Have Children? The New Child Care Benefit May Affect Your Family." https://www.canada.ca/en/revenue-agency/news/newsroom/tax-tips/tax-tips-2016/you-have-children-new-canada-child-benefit-may-affect-your-family.html.

Jones, Allison. 2012. "Anti-Poverty Group Urges End of Child Tax Benefits." ctvnews.ca 21 November. http://www.ctvnews.ca/canada/anti-poverty-group-urges-end-of-child-tax-benefits-1.1047052.

Kenworthy, L. 1999. "Do Social-Welfare Policies Reduce Poverty? A Cross-National Assessment." *Social Forces* 77(3): 1119–39.

McPherson, Miller, Lynn Smith-Lovin, and Matthew Brashears. 2008. "The Ties That Bind Are Fraying." *Contexts* 7(3): 32–6.

Marx, Karl, and Friedrich Engels. 1964. *The Communist Manifesto*. New York: Modern Reader Paperbacks.

Osberg, Lars. 2001. "Poverty among Senior Citizens: A Canadian Success Story." In Patrick Grady and Andrew Sharpe, eds, *The State of Economics in Canada: Festschrift in Honour of David Slater*, 151–81. Ottawa: Centre for the Study of Living Standards and John Deutsch Institute.

Peoples, Clayton D. 2012. "Welfare State." In George Ritzer, ed., *The Encyclopedia of Globalization*, 2218–21. Malden, MA: Wiley-Blackwell.

Perry, J.H. 1989. "A Fiscal History of Canada: The Post War Years." Canadian Tax Paper no. 85. Toronto: Canadian Tax Foundation.

Poggi, Gianfranco. 2004. "Formation and Form: Theories of State Formation." In Kate Nash and Alan Scott, eds, *The Blackwell Companion to Political Sociology*, 95–106. Malden, MA: Blackwell Publishing.

Putnam, Robert D., with Robert Leonardi and Raffaella Y. Nanetti. 1993. *Making Democracy Work: Civic Traditions in Modern Italy*. Princeton, NJ: Princeton University Press.

——— 2000. *Bowling Alone: The Collapse and Revival of American Community*. New York: Simon & Schuster.

Stanbridge, Karen, and Howard Ramos. 2012. *Seeing Politics Differently: A Brief Introduction to Political Sociology*. Don Mills, ON: Oxford University Press.

Statistics Canada. 2017. "Children Living in Low-Income Households." 13 September. http://www12.statcan.gc.ca/census-recensement/2016/as-sa/98-200-x/2016012/98-200-x2016012-eng.cfm.

Strayer, Joseph R. 1970. *On the Medieval Origins of the Modern State*. Princeton, NJ: Princeton University Press.

Tilly, Charles. 1985. "War Making and State Making as Organized Crime." In Peter Evans, Dietrich Rueschemeyer, and Theda Skocpol, eds, *Bringing the State Back In*, 169–87. Cambridge: Cambridge University Press.

Van den Berg, Alex, Claus-H von Restorff, Daniel Parent, and Anthony Masi. 2008. "From Unemployment to Employment Insurance: Towards Transitional Labour Markets in Canada." In Rudd J. Muffels, ed., *Flexibility and Employment Security in Europe: Labour Markets in Transition*, 308–35. Cheltenham, UK: Edward Elgar.

Veenhof, B., B. Wellman, C. Quell, and B. Hogan. 2008. "How Canadians' Use of the Internet Affects Social Life and Civic Participation." Catalogue no. 56F0004M—no. 016. Ottawa: Statistics Canada. http://www.statcan.gc.ca/pub/56f0004m/56f0004m2008016-eng.htm.

Watters, Haydn. 2015. "Education 'Only Way Forward,' Says Gov. David Johnston as TRC Ends." cbcnews.ca 3 June. http://www.cbc.ca/news/politics/education-only-way-forward-says-gov-gen-david-johnston-as-trc-ends-1.3098297.

14 Social Movements

Chapter Outline

Photo Credit: Rob Walsh/flickr

Introduction

In 2017, a series of serious sexual assault and harassment accusations came out against Hollywood producer Harvey Weinstein. These accusations set off a cascade of other accusations against powerful men in Hollywood, politics, and the corporate world. They also spawned the #MeToo movement. Social activist Tarana Burke created #MeToo to empower women to tell their stories of sexual abuse and harassment to support other women who were experiencing similar things and to raise awareness about the widespread nature of these issues. Actress Alyssa Milano encouraged others to use #MeToo, and it has created a viral sensation and intense conversation about the nature and prevalence of sexual harassment and abuse in our society.

In Chapter 13, we learned how social change occurs through the state. For example, we can elect leaders who will pass laws and policies that create social change. However, not all social change happens in this way. Sometimes social movements, such as #MeToo, arise through other means without the state's active involvement. In this chapter, we will learn about social movements, specifically how people come to participate in them and how they can lead to social change.

PHOTO 14.1 #MeToo has been a powerful movement that brings attention to sexual harassment and assault in the workplace and beyond. By saying that they have also been victims of sexual harassment or assault, women and men are raising the profile of this issue in our society as a whole.

Sam Wordley/Shutterstock

Social Movements

Social movements are sustained challenges to existing holders of power in the name of a wronged population. This population could be a group who feels that its rights have not been respected, such as women, LGBTQ people, ethnic minorities, immigrants, Indigenous people, individuals with disabilities, the young, or the homeless. Their members engage in activities such as **protesting** in the streets, occupying buildings, sending emails to political leaders, striking, and **boycotting** products. Through these actions, the wronged population and/or sympathetic allies work to demonstrate that they are worthy of being listened to, united in their cause, numerous, and committed to social change (Tilly 1997).

In many ways, social movements are similar to routine politics, such as elections. Groups use both to gain public support for their opinions and interests. For example, a social movement group might work to increase public support for legalization of marijuana. In election campaigns, political leaders sometimes also discuss laws around marijuana use; they try to convince the electorate that their perspective on this issue matches voters' opinion and therefore merits votes. In addition, the interests of social movement groups can be incorporated into party policy and government. For example, the Green Party has taken up many of the environmental movement's concerns. And the federal government has created large bureaucracies, such as Environment Canada, to deal with these issues, often after much pressure from the environmental movement.

There are also important differences between elections and social movements. Elections and political parties are often run by powerful political insiders. Social movements, however, tend to represent the interests of outsiders who have less power. Elections are also routine, occurring at set times. Engagement in social movements is less predictable and involves different strategies depending on the situation. Participation in elections is also low-cost, since going to the polls does not require risky behaviour or a great amount of time. Participating in social movements requires more energy and commitment from members and activists.

According to Charles Tilly (1997), social movements require five main elements. They must involve a sustained challenge; engage power holders; act on behalf of a wronged population; work to demonstrate worthiness, unity, numbers, and commitment; and participate in unauthorized action. Let's examine each of these components separately.

The first major component of a social movement is that it involves a sustained challenge. One protest event does not make a social movement. If there is a protest on your campus to reduce tuition fees but no other event ever materializes, it is not a social movement. However, once the issue of tuition fees is taken up by an organization such as the Canadian Federation of Students and/or is the source of repeated protests, email campaigns, and media advertisements, it fulfills Tilly's first requirement. This sustained challenge involves repeated collective claims to power holders, which demonstrate to the public that the movement is committed to the issue at hand.

As discussed, social movements tend to involve people with less power challenging those with more. For example, social movements can try to convince government leaders to change laws. Activists can also work to get business leaders to alter their practices, perhaps by paying their workers higher wages. Movements can encourage other institutions, such as churches, the media, or schools, to change how they operate. For example, activists could call for the media to be more inclusive of people from various ethnic and racial backgrounds. In all these examples, social movements focus their actions on trying to get power holders to change elements of society with which they disagree.

PHOTO 14.2 These protesters attended the Montreal Black Lives Matter march in 2016. This movement began on Twitter and focused on the disproportionate amount of violence perpetrated against black people by the police. It has expanded to a broader movement concerned with large-scale, systemic racism in society.

Josie Desmarais/iStockphoto

We mentioned at the beginning of this section that social movements represent a wronged population. For example, the women's movement fights for the rights of women, including the right to vote, to get equal pay, to be protected from physical and sexual violence, and to have access to daycare. Indigenous movements in Canada fight for treaty rights, better schools on reserves, social programs for Indigenous people, and reparation for past injustices.

Movements are composed of both the wronged population and **conscience constituencies**, other people who are sympathetic to the group's plight. Many men support groups such as Take Back the Night, a feminist organization that works to raise awareness of sexual assault against women. Many non-Indigenous people support the payment of reparations to those who were forced to attend residential schools. Conscience constituents do not directly benefit from the movement's success, yet they support the cause and efforts.

To gain attention, social movements have to disrupt daily routines. Holding a protest against clear-cut logging in the middle of an old growth forest far from any towns or cities will neither be seen by many people nor cause a disruption. As a result, it probably will not create social change. Conversely, the activists of the Greensboro sit-ins, a major part of the US civil rights movement, protested in busy stores. Because of this disruption, the sit-ins gained public attention and were instrumental in creating mass social change. In fact, they were a major reason that businesses in the American South were desegregated. Social movement activists must engage in action that is outside regular politics—not just voting or donating money to political parties. They must also protest, boycott, or do other unconventional activities to gain media and public attention.

Finally, the strength of a social movement is based on the worthiness, unity, numbers, and commitment (**WUNC**) of its members. Worthiness is showing that your group or interests are worth listening to—that you are important enough to deserve the attention of the public and those in power. Endorsements from moral authorities, such as religious or community leaders, can show worthiness. Having the pope or the Dalai Lama support your cause, for example, would be a sure demonstration of your worthiness! Groups exhibit unity by sharing similar values, interests, and goals. A group that seems fragmented will not be as strong as one that is united. Wearing the same shirts, having the same signs, or singing the same songs shows that the group belongs together and is unified in its cause. A group also needs to demonstrate that it has the support of a large number of people. Leaders and the public will be much more likely to care about social issues if they are brought forth by a large group instead of a small circle of friends. A group can show their numbers by holding large public demonstrations that fill the streets, sending **petitions** with many signatures, or having a large number of members in their organization. Finally, a group must show that their members are committed to the cause. When members are willing to persist in costly or risky behaviour, they show their commitment. For example, if your members are willing to be arrested, go to jail, or camp out in the cold for long periods, they are highly committed to the cause.

Tilly (1997) says that the strength of a social movement is the result of the formula W x U x N x C. If any of these numbers is zero, the movement will have no strength, even if it has a lot of the other three components. However, you can make up for less of one with more of another. If you do not have many people interested in your cause but the people in your group are highly committed, you might engage in a more radical tactic, such as having them chain themselves to a gate at a military base. Even though there are only 10 people at your event, you can still garner attention through this risky behaviour. If many people are interested in your cause but not intensely committed to it, you might want to launch a Facebook campaign. People do not have to be very committed to a cause to "like" it; if you can get a thousand people to respond, you can show that your issue is important.

Social media has been very important for social movements and activism. In the following reading, Alison Dahl Crossley examines the role of Facebook in feminist mobilizations on university and college campuses. How have social media, particularly Facebook, been important for this social movement? How is the online activism discussed in this article similar to, or different from, mobilization face-to-face?

READING

Facebook Feminism: Social Media, Blogs, and New Technologies of Contemporary U.S. Feminism*

Alison Dahl Crossley

Scholars from a range of academic disciplines have examined online mobilizing and opportunity structures, framing processes, and tactical repertoires (Almeida and Lichbach 2003; Bimber, Flanagin, and Stohl 2005; Tarrow 1998). Consensus has increased regarding the influence of the Internet on social movement participants and the dynamic interplay between online and offline organizing (Diani 2000; Earl and Kimport 2011; Earl, Kimport, Prieto, Rush, Reynoso 2010; Van Laer 2010). Debate about the nature of online mobilization has endured, however. While research on offline movements has highlighted the importance of preexisting networks as the mobilizing bases for social movements (Freeman 1975; McAdam 1986), recent studies have raised new questions and reached varying conclusions about the usefulness of social media and online friendship networks to social movements (Lewis, Gray, and Meierhenrich 2014; Maireder and Schwarzenegger 2012).

Given far-reaching webs of online friendship and social networks, the Internet is potentially of great utility to movement participants who emphasize community and interpersonal relationships. Feminist movements value such interpersonal networks. Gender and social movement scholars have extended theories of offline mobilization in order to understand the characteristically gendered forms of activism deployed by participants in feminist movements (Crossley and Taylor 2015; Reger 2012; Staggenborg 1996; Taylor 1989; Whittier 1995). Feminists have always employed cultural tactics and targeted cultural change to a greater degree than participants in other movements (Van Dyke, Soule, and Taylor 2004), relying on friendship networks, communities, and solidarity to promote movement goals. These tactics have made feminist mobilizations less visible than movements engaging in street protest (Staggenborg and Taylor 2005). Some scholars advocate for expanded views of feminist mobilization in an effort to highlight a spectrum of organizing (Taylor 1996). Thus far, there has been little scholarly attention devoted to online feminism, even though the Internet has become a major resource for feminists today. One report called the Internet the "new engine for contemporary feminism" (Martin and Valenti 2013: 6).

In this article, I use the case of college students' feminist organizing and networking on Facebook and blogs to examine the relationships between online social and friendship networks and social movements. The analysis focuses on whether activists' consumption and production of content on Facebook and blogs can nourish the interpersonal networks that are crucial to perpetuating a movement. I ask two primary questions about the role of online mobilization, feminism, and social movements more generally. Do activists' use of Facebook and feminist blogs aid feminist mobilization today? Is Internet activism capable of fostering the kinds of interpersonal networks and communities that are critical to mobilization and to the continuity of a movement? This research is based on interview and participant observation data gathered at three U.S. college campuses, and is part of a larger study of feminism among young women and men. I draw primarily on literature about online and offline social movements and feminist movements. Extending scholarship on offline social movements, I show how blogs and online friendship networks also provide important opportunities for movement participants to learn about inequality and movement ideology, and to declare allegiance to a movement. While previous analyses of online mobilizations have found discussion boards important in nurturing online communities, I find that blogs and Facebook

Crossley, Alison Dahl. 2015. "Facebook Feminism: Social Media, Blogs, and New Technologies of Contemporary U.S. Feminism." *Mobilization: and International Quarterly* 29(2): 253–68

create and sustain solidarity between mobilized individuals. Because online activism joins geographically disparate individuals, participants spread feminist ideologies to large networks of individuals, propelling the movement beyond local face-to-face connections. I also build on offline women's movement literature and demonstrate how online feminism preserves feminist traditions such as challenging hegemonic perspectives, cultivating oppositional cultures, and generating feminist solidarity.

Interpersonal Networks and Social Media

Movement participants spread ideologies, nurture individual and collective identities, and expand their organizational membership through offline interpersonal networks (Diani 1995; Diani and McAdam 2003; Freeman 1975; McAdam and Paulsen 1993; Snow, Zurcher, and Ekland Olson 1980; White 1989). Much of this research focuses on how networks predict involvement in high-risk (Della Porta 1988; McAdam 1986) and low-risk settings (Klandermans and Oegema 1987). Recruitment may occur, for example, between participants from different organizations within the same movement (Gerlach and Hine 1970), or between mobilized participants and nonmobilized individuals (Schussman and Soule 2005). While interpersonal ties are fundamental to organizational membership bases, additional dimensions such as contextual conditions and individual or movement identities also increase the salience of ties for recruitment and solidarity (Dixon and Roscigno 2003; Taylor and Whittier 1992).

Another approach to offline interpersonal networks and social movements focuses on the development of solidarity between mobilized participants (Fantasia 1988; Taylor 1989). Social networks "supply not only the social ties but the cultural context, the strategies, and the tactical repertoires that facilitate the construction of politicized collective identities" (Taylor 2013: 46). Diani (1995: 348) writes, "networks provide . . . areas of social interaction in which holders of specific world views reinforce mutual solidarity and experiment with alternative lifestyles." In his study of recruitment and commitment in a student social movement, Hirsch (1990: 245) found that consciousness raising was critical to motivating participants, teaching potential participants movement ideology, and creating solidarity: "Consciousness raising is facilitated in nonhierarchical, loosely structured, face-to-face settings that are isolated from persons in power. . . . [P]eople can easily express concerns, become aware of common problems, and begin to question the legitimacy of institutions." Hirsch (1989; 1990) calls such offline settings "havens" for mobilization.

Although there has been extensive examination of how friendship networks have facilitated offline organizing, there has been little empirical research about online friendship networks and their influence on movement networks and community. It has been suggested that collective identity may be strengthened online (Earl and Kimport 2011; Myers 1994). In one of the few empirical analyses of collective identities online, Nip (2004: 43) argues that involvement in an online bulletin board established a sense of solidarity and a culture of opposition among networked participants, but did not create collective consciousness or unifying interpretive frames (see also Wall 2007). Also based on an online web forum, but in a much different context than the women's movement, Caren, Jowers, and Gaby (2012: 167) found evidence of participation in a social movement online community (SMOC), which they define as "a sustained network of individuals who work to maintain an overlapping set of goals and identities tied to a social movement linked through quasipublic online discussions." Caren et al. (2012: 167) analyzed over six million posts of online white nationalist organization members, and, like some offline social movement participants who merge political and cultural change, found evidence that SMOCs "use the Internet not only for activism, but more importantly to create an identity and a distinct community within their virtual space." SMOCs include more geographically diverse participants than their offline counterparts (187), although the applicability of the SMOC concept outside online discussion fora is unexamined (Caren et al. 2012).

In the last few years, research has begun to examine the effectiveness of social movement participants using online social media and friendship networks such as Twitter (Earl,

Hurwitz, Mesinas, Tolan, Arlotti 2013) and Facebook (Maireder and Schwarzenneger 2012; Reger 2014). While such studies argue that social media use is helpful to street protest co-ordination, social media campaigns based solely on online friendship networks have been found to be less successful. Lewis et al. (2014) studied the recruitment and fundraising attempts of the large Facebook campaign, Save Darfur. They found "[n]either recruitment nor donation results were impressive: most individuals in our dataset recruited no one else into the cause and contributed no money to it." The authors concluded, "Facebook is less useful a mobilizing tool than a marketing tool" (Lewis et al. 2014: 4, 7). This raises questions about the salience and mobilizing potential of online friendship ties. Similarly, Polletta et al. (2013: 18) speculate: "Friendship in the Facebook era may mobilize less by levying emotional obligations on intimates to participate and more by providing information to weakly linked acquaintances." The topic is complicated by the nebulous definition of an online friend. A recent study found that Internet users have an increasing number of online friends who they have never met in person (Cole 2013), and Facebook users aged 18–24 have an average of 510 Facebook friends (Marketing Charts 2013).

It is increasingly difficult to research offline movements without considering their online dimensions. A significant number of texts address the relationship between online and offline movements (Diani 2000; Earl et al. 2010), although they nearly uniformly center on political organizing and street protest (Earl and Schussman 2003; Reger 2014; Van Laer 2010). This is exemplified in Earl et al.'s (2010: 429) definition of online facilitation of offline activism: "providing information on, logistical support for, and/or recruitment for offline protest events." To illustrate this concept, in his comparative study of activists who used the Internet for street protest and those who did not, Van Laer (2010) found that the Internet was primarily used by "super activists" and is thus skeptical of the claim that the Internet may provide long-term sustenance for social movements. Whether an emphasis on social movement community and friendship networks will reach similar conclusions remains to be seen. . . .

Data and Methods

College students are ideal participants in a study of Facebook, blogs, and social movement participation. They are in a stage of their lives when they are amenable to mobilization and part of a dense network of young people (Corrigall-Brown 2012; N. Crossley 2008). This age group is also highly engaged online. Not only are young adults highly likely to go online and use wireless Internet (Lenhart et al. 2010), but also 41 per cent of individuals aged 18–25 report having had a political discussion or taken political action on social media (Martin and Valenti 2013). Every day, two million blog posts are written, and 172 million Facebook visits occur (Martin and Valenti 2013). Given the vast amount of content generated online and young people's reliance on the Internet, there is a need for additional analysis about how such mobilized participants use blogs and online friendship networks.

This article is based on individual- and organizational-level data about online and offline activism collected at three different institutions of higher education in 2011: the University of California, Santa Barbara; the University of Minnesota, Twin Cities; and Smith College. The University of California, Santa Barbara (UCSB) is a public research university with approximately 21,000 undergraduate and graduate students in the coastal city of Santa Barbara, California. The University of Minnesota, Twin Cities (U of M) is a public research university with approximately 51,000 undergraduate and graduate students located in the metropolitan area of Minneapolis/St. Paul, Minnesota. Smith College is a women's private liberal arts college with approximately 2,600 undergraduates in the town of Northampton, Massachusetts. . . .

Interviewees were currently enrolled undergraduate college students, primarily between the ages of 18–21. Participants self identified as white (n = 42), Latina/o (n = 8), mixed race/other (n = 13), Asian American (n = 6), African American (n = 5), and American Indian (n = 1); heterosexual (n = 46), queer (n = 9), bisexual (n = 9), gay/lesbian (n = 7), queer and bisexual (n = 1), and nonspecified sexuality (n = 3); women (n = 68) and men (n = 7, including 1 transgender male). Many were first generation college students. Twenty-seven self-identified as poor, working class, or lower-middle class and 48 located themselves in the middle-class range. The respondents share a degree of educational privilege. However, this sample diverges from a number of studies that focus on the experiences of white feminists: 33 of the 75 respondents identified as Latino, mixed race, Asian American, African American, or Native American. UCSB, in particular, has attracted a diverse undergraduate student body and has been named a Hispanic-Serving Institution because of the high number of Latina and Latino students. . . .

Facebook Friendship: Unifying and Recruiting Feminists, Interacting with Adversaries

Facebook, too, has an array of "unique affordances" (Earl and Kimport 2011) for feminists. Feminist Facebook members circulate feminist news, blog links, petitions, and personal stories. Because Facebook users generally share personal information with a large network, Facebook provides a distinctive online setting to construct communities and facilitate interaction. Respondents used Facebook to expand mobilizing structures and enlarge recruitment bases. To begin, participants were involved in online feminist campaigns. During the period of this data collection, for example, Planned Parenthood was at risk of having their federal funding eliminated. This threat was a unifying issue for feminists across the three campuses, and served as a catalyst for feminist conversation and protest. Respondents attended rallies, adhered stickers supporting Planned Parenthood to their backpacks and water bottles, and spoke with me at length about the topic. Facebook was also an important venue for their mobilization. UCSB student Chelsea, a bisexual Asian American woman involved in a number of campus groups, told me about the importance of Facebook as a site of feminist discussion on the topic: "One thing that I'm seeing on Facebook is the Planned Parenthood issue. I love the solidarity I'm seeing on Facebook, all kinds of women. It makes me think feminism is inclusive." Respondents reported frequently updating their Facebook statuses with information about the proposed cuts to Planned Parenthood. Heterosexual African American UCSB student Summer, who was involved in a Greek and non-Greek student group, said her Facebook friendship network was especially busy during the Planned Parenthood campaign, and she posted status updates and videos in support of Planned Parenthood for her Facebook friends. Summer said, "Even if you didn't know about the Planned Parenthood issue, after going on Facebook you knew something. . . . I feel like Facebook is very powerful as far as social change." Elizabeth, a white bisexual Smith student active in off-campus social justice organizing, said in a serious and dry tone, "For a while my Facebook profile pic was from when I went to the march in Boston for Planned Parenthood, and I had a big sign in my profile pic that said 'Keep your patriarchal misogynist bullshit off my reproductive rights!' So that was a way of signaling my feelings." For Elizabeth, a picture of an offline protest declared her presence as an online feminist, and it signaled to her friendship network her assertions regarding reproductive rights. The Facebook campaign unified feminists by identifying a common cause and circulating feminist perspectives to their feminist and non-feminist Facebook friends, which is distinct from much of the literature that has focused on how online organizing facilitates offline activism (see Earl and Kimport 2011).

Feminist student organizations used their Facebook networks as a free organizational resource and as a tactic to expand the reach of their offline campaigns. UCSB student Camille, a heterosexual Armenian woman active in a number of organizations, said, "I think it's important to recognize that Facebook can be one of the best feminist resources in the world." Students spoke to me about their dependence on Facebook in the age of budget cuts and lack of institutional support for their feminist organizations. Members of a Smith feminist organization that was allocated only seventeen dollars for one semester told me with despair that they could not afford to copy fliers, make posters, or even chalk campus sidewalks with notices of an upcoming event. Instead, they relied on disseminating Facebook event pages to their friendship networks, using the Internet to counteract limited resources and support (Earl and Kimport 2011; Diani 2000).

All of the feminist organizations in this study used Facebook to advertise offline events and meetings, to communicate with existing members, and to recruit new members. The topic generated notable conversation in student group meetings and in interviews. During one feminist event at the U of M, I observed a workshop leader refer to using traditional paper posters to advertise events as nearly "obsolete." Anna C. is a white bisexual member of a Smith feminist organization, and reported recently using Facebook to advertise events for feminist coming out day and International Women's Day. Liz, also a Smith student, said, "People are using Facebook as a tool for activism especially for organizing events. It is very hard for groups to do it any other way." Rueben, a white queer transgender male Smith student, is a leader of a campus organization. He stated, "I use Facebook for social change events, it's incredible as an organizing tool, it's amazing." Students excitedly told me about their group's reliance on Facebook. Diana, a heterosexual Latina, was involved in several groups at UCSB. She said, "I'm always the one with a million Facebook events about my programs." UCSB student Summer reported being on Facebook for hours at a time. She said she used Facebook for advertising events of her feminist multicultural sorority "all the time!" She continued, "For events, my status will be 'come here at 7:00 pm.'" Students reported that leveraging their Facebook friendship networks was effective. For example, when Anne W. reported sending Facebook invitations for an upcoming meeting of the nationally affiliated pro-choice group that she led, "at least an additional eight people show up." If she forgot to send the invitation to the group's friendship network, attendance was more apt to be sparse. In fact, U of M student Zan, a lesbian of mixed ethnicity, said that rather than using Facebook for social purposes, she used the site primarily for keeping up to date on the events of the queer organization she leads, and those of other campus groups.

Dialogue with antifeminists was also a notable element of respondents' Facebook feminism. Respondents said that sexist content is commonplace on Facebook, so they had ample opportunities to disseminate feminist ideologies in their friendship networks. Research participants reported frequent Facebook interaction with friends who expressed antifeminist sentiments. Lauren, a U of M student, said, "I certainly have blocked a number of my friends who are posting conservative stuff that I really get frustrated with. I just delete them from my Facebook. . . . A lot of people just keep friends on Facebook so that they can get the word out to as many people as they want." Indeed, interview respondents reported keeping antifeminists or conservatives with whom they disagreed in their network of friends as a way to teach them about feminism. Anna P., a queer white Smith student who leads a campus feminist organization, gleefully told me about a conversation that unfolded on her Facebook page:

> I posted something about immigration in Iowa, which I view as a feminist issue. And there was a dialogue on my Facebook page between a peer in high school and my history professor at Smith. So we have this ignorant Iowan and this Smith professor going back and forth about immigration . . . and they went at it [laughter].

Smith student Vivica said, in an exasperated tone, that she was frequently compelled to show her Facebook network "how their privilege affects other people negatively" by confronting her Facebook friends about their sexist posts. She reported using course readings to bolster her responses. One male friend posted an offensive comment about a woman's body size, and she relayed a theory from a sociology text called, "Behind the Mask of a Strong Black Woman," linking individual experiences to structural racism. UCSB student Elsa is a queer Mexican American–African American who is not involved in student organizing because she works forty to sixty hours per week. She reported posting quotes from her feminist studies class readings on her Facebook page, and said, "I've had my cousin or my brother go on Facebook and say, she just likes to fight with guys, but I don't do it necessarily to argue, but to bring awareness." Respondents felt responsible for providing feminist perspectives to their Facebook friendship networks. Sharing feminist ideologies were valuable experiences, as was evident in their detailed and emotional retelling of such interactions.

Members of offline feminist organizations used their Facebook friendship networks for online campaigns. Participants reported experiencing reactions ranging from hostility to indifference related to their Facebook campaigns. For example, I observed a UCSB antirape organization's in-person meeting devoted to the topic of Facebook and text-message stalking.

It is worth underscoring that this was an online campaign facilitated by offline discussion, a twist on the more frequently documented offline campaign facilitated by online organizing. In the meeting, student leaders encouraged participants to post Facebook status updates describing the seriousness of stalking (posting: "It's not a joke, it's not okay"). Lisa, a heterosexual of mixed ethnicity and a member of the organization, told me later that she posted numerous status updates about Facebook stalking and the dangers it poses. She reported receiving mostly positive feedback, and many Facebook friends inquired further about the stalking and sexual assault awareness month:

> A lot of them were positive reactions but I do definitely remember a few reactions where it was not intentionally offensive, but very dismissive. At least those few said something so it gave me a chance to respond back, which was, I think, effective. I'm glad sometimes to have a negative reaction just because I take that as an opportunity to educate them.

Other students reported that they managed their feminist organizations' Facebook pages and forwarded news articles, feminist blog posts, and relevant current events to their networks. The respondents' commitment to feminism motivated them to express feminist ideologies in their Facebook friendship networks, creating feminist exchanges that were often prized moments.

Conclusion

I began this article by asking whether Facebook and blogs are capable of aiding mobilization and fostering the kinds of interpersonal networks and community that are critical to mobilization and the perpetuation of a movement. The data presented here support the argument that, among these respondents who were involved in the feminist movement, Facebook and blogs were used to create online feminist communities, nourish offline networks, expand recruitment bases, and provide opportunities for online interaction with adversaries. In contrast to those who argue that millennials use the Internet and social media to waste time (Warner 2013) or indulge in narcissistic behavior (Williams 2013), these data demonstrate that the Internet promotes feminist mobilization and is indicative of generational shifts within the movement.

Activists' blog and Facebook networks reinforced participants' dedication to feminist ideology and bolstered the level of emotional solidarity, allowing them to express pride and enthusiasm in their feminist beliefs and communities (Taylor 2013; Taylor and Leitz 2010). Just as patronizing coffee shops or music venues by like-minded individuals "reinforce[s] mutual solidarity" (Diani 1995: 348), this research illustrates how feminist blogs and Facebook created "havens" (Hirsch 1989) for feminism, in which participants learn about the movement, express concern for sexism, and foster connections with other feminists (Hirsch 1990; Keller 2012; Shaw 2012). . . .

Facebook provided activists access to larger networks of individuals than they had in their face-to-face lives. Online social networks were used for similar goals as offline networks—such as recruiting, disseminating information, creating solidarity, and raising consciousness (Ferree and Hess 1995; Hirsch 1990). However, this analysis illuminates how Facebook is a unique infrastructure for mobilization and recruitment, in that respondents had large and diverse friendship networks that were used to spread feminism and raise feminist consciousness. Previous understandings of Facebook friendship networks found them valuable for "providing information to weakly linked acquaintances" (Polletta et al. 2013: 18), and "less useful a mobilizing tool than a marketing tool" (Lewis et al. 2014: 7). The present article shows that strong friendship ties cultivate community and organizations, and weak ties created opportunities for activists to expand recruitment bases and reach a wide number of individuals with whom they would not come into contact in their offline lives (Granovetter 1973; Snow, Zurcher, and Eckland Olson 1980). More than simply providing information within their networks, activists taught feminism and spread feminist ideology, drawing in individuals who would not typically engage in feminist discussion (Dixon and Roscigno 2003; Taylor and Whittier 1992). Since one of the worst things that can happen to movement participants is that their grievances and perspectives are not heard, the multiplicity of ways that respondents employed their Facebook networks is not inconsequential.

This analysis presents similarities and variations in online mobilization according to type of ICT. Facebook and blogs allowed activists to span geographical distances. But, unlike blogs, Facebook provided opportunities for adversarial interaction with no offline component, as well as logistical support for offline mobilization. The way respondents' expressed feminist sentiments were not the same on Facebook and blogs. On Facebook, boundaries between feminists and non-feminists were clear-cut due to the polarizing nature of many conversations. When participants encountered an objectionable post or a sexist Facebook friend, their feminism was more direct and succinct, perhaps due in part to lack of space or the simplification of content that occurs online. In contrast, respondents were drawn to feminist blogs as venues to learn about and discuss varying approaches to feminism. Blogs allowed feminists to ruminate and reflect, and to consider how feminist ideologies applied to their own everyday, offline lives. Thus, online feminism was dynamic. It shifted according to type of Internet participation and presence of adversaries, providing additional insight into how mobilization varies by political and cultural context (Crossley 2010; Ferree 2012; Reger 2012). . . .

CRITICAL READING QUESTIONS

1.   Why are social media important for social movements? In what contexts are they most important?

2.   How do social media affect social networks? What types of people do we tend to engage with on social media—those similar to us or those who are different? Why might this matter?

3.   How can we create communities online? How are these communities similar to, or different from, communities offline?

4.   How are Facebook and other social media important for feminist mobilization on campuses? How might this be applied to other movements or settings?

REFERENCES

Almeida, Paul D., and Mark Irving Lichbach. 2003. "'To the Internet, From the Internet': Comparative Media Coverage of Transnational Protests." *Mobilization* 8(3): 249–72.

Ayers, Michael D. 2003. "Comparing Collective Identity in Online and Offline Feminist Activists." Pp. 145–64 in *Cyberactivism: Online Activism in Theory and Practice*, edited by Martha McCaughey and Michael D. Ayers. New York: Routledge.

Bimber, Bruce, Andrew Flanagin, and Cynthia Stohl. 2005. "Reconceptualizing Collective Action in the Contemporary Media Environment." *Communication Theory* 15(4): 365–88.

Caren, Neal, Kay Jowers, and Sarah Gaby. 2012. "A Social Movement Online Community: Stormfront and the White Nationalist Movement." Pp. 163–93 in *Media, Movements, and Political Change, Research in Social Movements, Conflicts and Change Volume 33*, edited by Jennifer Earl and Deana A. Rohlinger. Bingley, UK: Emerald Publishing.

Cole, Jeffrey I. 2013. *Digital Future Report*. Los Angeles, California: Center for the Digital Future, University of Southern California.

Corrigall-Brown, Catherine. 2012. *Patterns of Protest: Trajectories of Participation in Social Movements*. Stanford, CA: Stanford University Press.

Crossley, Alison Dahl. 2010. "When It Suits Me, I'm a Feminist: International Students Negotiating Feminist Representations." *Women's Studies International Forum* 33(2): 125–33.

Crossley, Alison Dahl, and Verta Taylor. 2015. "Abeyance Cycles in Social Movements." Pp. 64–87 in *Movements in Times of Democratic Transition*, edited by Bert Klandermans and Cornelis van Stralen. Philadelphia, PA: Temple University Press.

Crossley, Nick. 2008. "Social Networks and Student Activism." *Sociological Review* 56(1): 18–38.

Della Porta, Donatella. 1988. "Recruitment Processes in Clandestine Political Organizations: Italian Left-Wing Terrorism." Pp. 155–72 in *From Structure to Action*, edited by Bert Klandermans, Hanspeter Kriesi, and Sidney Tarrow. Greenwich, UK: JAI Press.

Diani, Mario. 1995. "Networks and Participation." Pp. 339–59 in *The Blackwell Companion to Social Movements*, edited by David A. Snow, Sarah A. Soule and Hanspeter Kriesi. Malden, MA: Blackwell.

———. 2000. "Social Movement Networks: Virtual and Real." *Information, Communication, and Society* 3(3): 389–410.

———— and Doug McAdam, eds. 2003. *Social Movements and Networks: Relational Approaches to Collective Action*. Oxford, UK: Oxford University Press.

Dixon, Marc, and Vincent J. Roscigno. 2003. "Status, Networks, and Social Movement Participation: The Case of Striking Workers." *American Journal of Sociology* 108(6): 1292–327.

Duncan, Barbara. 2005. "Searching for a Home Place: Online in the Third Wave." Pp. 161–78 in *Different Wavelengths*, edited by Jo Reger. New York: Routledge.

Earl, Jennifer, Heather McKee Hurwitz, Analicia Mejia Mesinas, Margaret Tolan, and Ashley Arlotti. 2013. "This Protest Will Be Tweeted: Twitter and Protest Policing during the Pittsburgh G20." *Information, Communication, and Society* 16(4): 1–20.

Earl, Jennifer, and Katrina Kimport. 2011. *Digitally Enabled Social Change: Activism in the Internet Age*. Cambridge, MA: MIT Press.

Earl, Jennifer, Katrina Kimport, Greg Prieto, Carly Rush, and Kimberly Reynoso. 2010. "Changing the World One Webpage at a Time: Conceptualizing and Explaining Internet Activism." *Mobilization* 15(4): 425–46.

Earl, Jennifer, and Alan Schussman. 2003. "The New Site of Activism: On-Line Organizations, Movement Entrepreneurs, and the Changing Location of Social Movement Decision-Making." *Research in Social Movements, Conflicts, and Change* 24: 155–87.

Ferree, Myra Marx. 2012. *Varieties of Feminism*. Stanford, CA: Stanford University Press.

Ferree, Myra Marx, and Beth B. Hess. 1995. *Controversy and Coalition: The New Feminist Movement across Four Decades of Change*. New York: Routledge.

Freeman, Jo. 1975. *The Politics of Women's Liberation*. New York: David McKay.

Gerlach, Luther P., and Virginia H. Hine. 1970. *People, Power, Change: Movements of Social Transformation*. New York: MacMillan Publishing Company.

Granovetter, Mark S. 1973. "The Strength of Weak Ties." *American Journal of Sociology* 78(6): 1360–80.

Hirsch, Eric L. 1989. *Urban Revolt: Ethnic Politics in the Nineteenth Century Chicago Labor Movement*. Berkeley: University of California Press.

————. 1990. "Sacrifice for the Cause: Group Processes, Recruitment, and Commitment in a Student Social Movement." *American Sociological Review* 55(2): 243–54.

Keller, Jessalynn Marie. 2012. "Virtual Feminisms: Girls' Blogging Communities, Feminist Activism, and Participatory Politics." *Information, Communication, and Society* 15(3): 429–47.

Klandermans, Bert, and Dirk Oegema. 1987. "Potentials, Networks, Motivations, and Barriers: Steps toward Participation in Social Movements." *American Sociological Review* 52(4): 519–31.

Lenhart, Amanda, Kristen Purcell, Aaron Smith, and Kathryn Zickuhr. 2010. *Social Media and Young Adults*. Pew Internet and American Life Project. Washington D.C.: Pew Research Center. Retrieved February 3, 2012 (http://pewinternet.org/Reports/ 2010/Social-Media-and-Young-Adults.aspx).

Lewis, Kevin, Kurt Gray, and Jens Meierhenrich. 2014. "The Structure of Online Activism." *Sociological Science* 1: 1–14.

Maireder, Axel, and Christian Schwarzenegger. 2012. "A Movement of Connected Individuals: Social Media in the Austrian Student Protests 2009." *Information, Communication, and Society* 15(2): 171–95.

Marketing Charts Staff. 2013. *18–24-Year-Olds on Facebook Boast an Average of 510 Friends*. Retrieved on November 1, 2013 (http://www.marketingcharts.com/wp/direct/18-24-year-olds-onfacebook-boast-an-average-of-510-friends-28353/).

Martin, Courtney E., and Vanessa Valenti. 2013. *#Femfuture: Online Revolution*. New York: Barnard College. Retrieved May 30, 2013 (http://bcrw.barnard.edu/publications/femfuture-online-revolution/).

McAdam, Doug. 1986. "Recruitment to High-Risk Activism: The Case of Freedom Summer." *American Journal of Sociology* 92(1): 64–90.

McAdam, Doug, and Ronnelle Paulsen. 1993. "Specifying the Relationship between Social Ties and Activism." *American Journal of Sociology* 99(3): 640–67.

Myers, Daniel J. 1994. "Communication Technology and Social Movements: Contributions of Computer Networks to Activism." *Social Science Computer Review* 12(2): 251–60.

Nip, Joyce Y. M. 2004. "The Queer Sisters and Its Electronic Bulletin Board: A Study of the Internet for Social Movement Mobilization." *Information, Communication, and Society* 7(1): 23–49.

Polletta, Francesca, Pang Ching, Bobby Chen, Beth Gharrity Gardner, and Alice Motes. 2013. "Is the Internet Creating New Reasons to Protest?" Pp. 17–36 in *The Future of Social Movement Research: Dynamics, Mechanisms, and Processes*, edited by Jacquelien van Stekelenburg, Conny Roggeband, and Bert Klandermans. Minneapolis: University of Minnesota Press.

Reger, Jo. 2005. *Different Wavelengths: Studies of the Contemporary Women's Movement*. New York: Routledge.

————. 2012. *Everywhere and Nowhere: Contemporary Feminism in the United States*. New York: Oxford University Press.

————. 2014. "Micro Cohorts, Feminist Generations, and the Making of the Toronto Slutwalk." *Feminist Formations* 49(1): 49–69.

Schussman, Alan, and Sarah A. Soule. 2005. "Process and Protest: Accounting for Individual Protest Participation." *Social Forces* 84(2): 1083–108.

Shaw, Frances. 2012 "'HOTTEST 100 WOMEN' Cross-platform Discursive Activism in Feminist Blogging Networks." *Australian Feminist Studies* 27(74): 373–87.

Snow, David A., and Robert D. Benford. 1992. "Master Frames and Cycles of Protest." Pp. 133–155 in *Frontiers in Social Movement Theory*, edited by Aldon D. Morris and Carol McClurg Mueller. New Haven, CT: Yale University Press.

Snow, David A., Louis A. Zurcher, Jr., and Sheldon Ekland-Olson. 1980. "Social Networks and Social Movements: A Micro-Structural Approach to Differential Recruitment." *American Sociological Review* 51(4): 464–81.

Staggenborg, Suzanne. 1996. "The Survival of the Women's Movement: Turnover and Continuity in Indiana." *Mobilization* 1(1): 143–58.

Staggenborg, Suzanne, and Amy Lang. 2007. "Culture and Ritual in the Montreal Women's Movement." *Social Movement Studies* 6(2): 177–94.

Staggenborg, Suzanne, and Verta Taylor. 2005. "Whatever Happened to the Women's Movement?" *Mobilization* 10(1): 37–52.

Tarrow, Sidney. 1998. "Fishnets, Internets, and Catnets: Globalization and Transnational Collective Action." Pp. 228–44 in *Challenging Authority: The Historical Study of Contentious Politics*, edited by Michael P. Hanaganm, Leslie Page Moch, and Wayne Te Brake. Minneapolis: University of Minnesota Press.

Taylor, Verta. 1989. "Social Movement Continuity: The Women's Movement in Abeyance." *American Sociological Review* 54(5): 761–75.

———. 1996. *Rock-a-by Baby: Feminism, Self-Help, and Postpartum Depression*. New York: Routledge.

———. 2013. "Social Movement Participation in the Global Society: Identity, Networks, and Emotions." Pp. 37–57 in *The Future of Social Movement Research: Dynamics, Mechanisms, and Processes*, edited by Jacquelien van Stekelenburg, Conny Roggeband, and Bert Klandermans. Minneapolis: University of Minnesota Press.

Taylor, Verta, Katrina Kimport, Nella Van Dyke, and Ellen Andersen. 2009. "Culture and Mobilization: Tactical Repertoires, Same-Sex Weddings, and the Impact on Gay Activism." *American Sociological Review* 74(6): 865–90.

Taylor, Verta, and Lisa Leitz. 2010. "From Infanticide to Activism: Emotions and Identity in Self-Help Movements." Pp. 446–75 in *Social Movements and the Transformation of American Health Care*, edited by Jane Banaszak-Holl, Sandra Levitsky, and Mayer N. Zald. New York: Oxford University Press.

Taylor, Verta, and Nancy Whittier. 1992. "Collective Identity in Social Movement Communities: Lesbian Feminist Mobilization." Pp. 104–29 in *Frontiers in Social Movement Theory*, edited by Aldon D. Morris and Carole McClurg Mueller. New Haven: Yale University Press.

Van Dyke, Nella, Sarah Soule, and Verta Taylor. 2004. "The Targets of Social Movements: Beyond a Focus on the State." Pp. 27–51 in *Authority in Contention, Vol. 25*, edited by Daniel J. Myers and Daniel M. Cress. Oxford, UK: JAI Press.

Van Laer, Jeroen. 2010. "Activists 'Online' and 'Offline': The Internet as an Information Channel for Protest Demonstrations." *Mobilization* 15(3): 405–17.

Wall, Melissa A. 2007. "Social Movements and Email: Expressions of Online Identity in the Globalization Protests." *New Media and Society* 9(2): 258–77.

Warner, Russ. 2013. *Who Wastes More Time at Work: Millennials, Gen X'ers or Boomers?* New York: AOL. Retrieved July 3, 2014 (http://www.huffingtonpost.com/russ-warner/who-wastes-more-timeat-w_b_2618279.html).

White, Robert W. 1989. "From Peaceful Protest to Guerilla War: Micromobilization of the Provisional Irish Republican Army." *American Journal of Sociology* 94(6): 1277–302.

Whittier, Nancy. 1995. *Feminist Generations: The Persistence of the Radical Women's Movement*. Philadelphia, PA: Temple University Press.

Williams, Ray B. 2013. *Do Facebook and Other Social Media Encourage Narcissism?* New York: Sussex Publishers. Retrieved July 3, 2014 (http://www.psychologytoday.com/blog/wired-success/201306/do-facebook-and-other-social-media-encourage-narcissism).

The Collective Action Problem

Early work on social movements argued that participation is irrational. If you think about the costs and benefits of participating, it is clear that the former are relatively high and the latter relatively low. The costs of participating include finding information about a cause, a group involved in that cause, and an event that the group is putting on. In addition, you have to spend the time and energy to go to the protest event, sign the petition, or boycott the product. All these activities are pretty costly in terms of time and energy. If you believe that there is a relatively small chance that you will help the group be successful, perhaps it does not make rational sense to participate in social movements.

This sort of reasoning is very familiar. Everyone has heard the argument that people do not vote because they feel that it will not make a difference. Even if they care about the cause, people might not go to a protest event because they think that their individual participation will not contribute to the group's success. This perspective, first articulated by Mancur Olson (1965), is called the **collective action problem** (or the **free-rider problem**). Olson argued that people tend to avoid participating in collective action (e.g., social movements) because they still benefit from whatever is gained whether or not they contribute to the cause. Therefore, collective action is unlikely to occur even when large groups of people have common interests.

Social movements often fight for **public goods**, things that are non-excludable (one person cannot reasonably prevent another from consuming the good) and non-rivalrous (one person's consumption of the good does not affect another's). Clean air is a public good that illustrates the collective action problem. Environmental activists lobby the government to pass laws restricting pollution, and they boycott companies that pollute. If these tactics are successful, we will have cleaner and better-quality air. Once the air is cleaner, I (as an environmental activist) cannot stop you (a free rider) from breathing my clean air, even though you never went to any of my protest events to fight for it. Voting rights is another example of a public good. Once women got the right to vote, all women—those who fought for it and those who did nothing—can enjoy this right.

Olson's argument makes some intuitive sense, but it also poses some important problems. If everyone sat at home and waited for others to push for social change, nothing would ever happen. (You need someone fighting for clean air and voting rights!) Also, if Olson's theory is true, how do we explain all the social movement events and campaigns that have occurred? Are all social movements simply a bunch of irrational people getting together? The next section considers the variety of reasons that someone might join a social movement.

HIGHLIGHT

Taking a Knee as Protest

AP Photo/Marcio Jose Sanchez

Protest can take make forms. Colin Kaepernick of the San Francisco 49ers began kneeling during the singing of the national anthem in the pre-season games of the 2016 season of the NFL as an act of protest. He was showing his solidarity with the Black Lives Matter movement and trying to highlight the issues of police brutality and racial inequality. His protest actually went unnoticed for two weeks before the media began asking him why he was kneeling. Once the media began covering his protest and the cause behind it, however, this act garnered a lot of attention. By the first week of the 2016 season, 11 other players had joined in the protest (Jacobson 2017).

This act of protest was received in very different ways across the political spectrum. Many thought it was brave to highlight these important issues in such a public way. Others argued that it was unpatriotic to kneel during the national anthem when it is the usual custom to

Continued

stand. US President Donald Trump was particularly offended by NFL players "taking the knee" during the anthem. He called for the players who were protesting to be fired by the NFL. This criticism of the protesting players angered many in the NFL who felt that these comments were an attempt to stifle the free speech of the professional athletes. Two days after Trump's comments, more than 200 players, coaches, and owners joined the protests and knelt during the anthem (Jacobson 2017).

Kneeling to highlight issues of police brutality and racial inequality gained a lot of attention for the Black Lives Matter movement and the issues at hand. However, it also caused backlash against the movement from those who did not understand the connection between kneeling and the cause. Activists always struggle with the need to select a tactic that is innovative and dramatic in order to get attention while still being understandable and appealing to the public. How do other movements and activists try to balance these two, sometimes conflicting, needs?

Trends in Social Movement Participation

Many people participate in social movements, and they do so in various ways. Some are members of social movement organizations (SMOs). Others never join groups but go to social movement events, such as protests or marches. Still others simply do things that support social movement causes. For example, composting and biking to school both support the environmental movement.

These different methods of engaging in social movements vary along two main dimensions that have already been introduced—the risk associated with the activity and the cost of engaging (Corrigall-Brown 2013). Most activism in Canada is not particularly risky. For example, there is little danger in attending a peaceful protest or signing a petition. Some Canadian activists do participate in risky activities, such as occupying a building or breaking into military bases, which can lead to jail time or social stigma. Engaging in social movement activities in other contexts (particularly non-democratic countries) can be quite dangerous. Participation can also be more or less costly in terms of how difficult the activity is for an individual. If you have to travel a far distance or take time away from work or school to engage, the activity has a higher cost than other, easier activities.

Risk and cost are usually related. Signing a petition is both low-risk and low-cost. Camping out at an Occupy protest for weeks is both risky (in that you could be arrested) and costly (in terms of time and energy). However, quitting your job to volunteer for Greenpeace is costly but not very risky. Attending a protest event in a country that does not permit protest is not very costly (does not take a lot of time) but is extremely risky (could lead to a jail sentence).

Using World Values Survey data, Table 14.1 compares three social movement activities: protesting, signing a petition, and boycotting a product. Protesting is the most contentious of these activities, although it is legal in all the countries listed (the survey does not ask about protest participation in countries where it is illegal, such as China). Boycotting is the least contentious of the three acts because it requires only that you avoid doing something. For example, if you are concerned with sweatshop labour, you might refuse to buy clothing from companies that use sweatshops. If you are an advocate of animal rights, you might not buy products from companies that engage in animal testing.

You can see from the table that in most countries, people are more likely to sign a petition or boycott a product than attend a protest event. And they are also usually more apt

TABLE 14.1 Participation in social movement activities by country, 2010–14 (per cent)

Country	Protested	Signed a Petition	Boycotted a Product
France	38	67	14
Germany	31	50	9
Canada	26	73	24
Netherlands	20	46	14
Austalia	20	79	15
India	19	29	15
Great Britain	17	68	17
Mexico	16	21	3
United States	15	70	20
Rwanda	14	9	4
South Africa	13	12	10
Japan	10	60	7
Turkey	6	12	5

Source: Data from World Values Survey Data analysis tool, Wave 6 (data collected from 2010–2014), http://www
.worldvaluessurvey.org/WVSOnline.jsp

to sign a petition than boycott a product. This is partly because signing a petition is a one-time activity while boycotting requires a sustained commitment not to buy something.

In comparison with the other countries in the chart, Canadians are fairly active in social movements. Over the past 50 years, the character of protest in modern industrial democracies, such as Canada and the United States, has changed radically. Since the 1960s and 1970s, the frequency of protest events and the levels of individual participation in protest activity have increased (Meyer and Tarrow 1998). This trend is evident in Canada—Canadians, as a group, have increased their propensity to participate in social movements (see Table 14.2). In the United States, the percentage of people who have attended a demonstration has also increased, from 11 per cent in 1975 to 15 per cent in 2014. Over the last quarter of the twentieth century, most advanced industrial democracies saw a rise in protest participation (Inglehart 1997; Norris 2002).

TABLE 14.2 Social movement participation, Canada, 1982–2008 (per cent)

	1982	1990	2000	2008
Demonstration	14	21	20	25
Petition	62	77	73	58
Boycott	15	22	21	16

Source: Data from World Values Survey Data analysis tool, http://www.worldvaluessurvey.org/WVSOnline.jsp

Explaining Social Movement Participation

The survival and success of social movements is based on the participation of individuals. With this in mind, what predicts who will participate in a social movement? What leads certain individuals to participate in social movements while others do not? Participation requires four main elements: ideology, resources, biographical availability, and social ties and identity.

Ideology

Individuals need to be committed to the goals of a movement in order to participate in a social movement (Klandermans 1997). Not all individuals who believe in a cause become activists. However, it is equally true that individuals who are not sympathetic to the cause are highly unlikely to join a movement. Ideological commitment is important because it makes people at least cognitively available to participate in a movement.

Ideology is also a very significant part of why many people participate in protests. We mostly think of a protest as something in which liberals engage. Research supports this argument, showing that leftists are more apt to attend protests (Dalton, Van Sickle, and Weldon 2010). However, protest is clearly no longer just for people on the political left. The prominence of conservative movements in Canada and the United States has brought people from across the political spectrum into social movements.

Religious ideologies are also important predictors of engagement. Religious beliefs can motivate individuals to come together to create social change. Belonging to and participating in a religious institution can lead individuals to develop social networks, political knowledge, and resources. Such factors make these individuals more prone to join social movements than those not tied to religious institutions (Diani 2004; McAdam 1986).

However, ideology alone is not enough to predict engagement. Individuals must also feel that their participation will yield results. This sense of **efficacy** is the belief that one is capable of the specific behaviours required to produce a desired outcome in a given situation (Gecas 2000). Individuals who are efficacious are self-confident and feel that they can produce the changes in the world that they desire. Not surprisingly, these individuals are more likely to participate in protest activities (Rosenstone and Hansen 1993).

Resources

Along with ideologies, individuals must have the resources that allow them to engage in social movements. For example, individuals with more money are much more apt to protest than people with less money. This difference is not because those with more money believe more strongly in social movement goals but because money helps individuals to translate their beliefs into action.

Socio-economic status (SES) is one of the most important predictors of an individual's propensity to protest (Verba, Schlozman, and Brady 1995). Individuals with high SES tend to have other resources, such as free time and certain skills that enable them to participate in social movements. As a result, they are more likely than other people to engage in groups of all kinds, including social movement organizations (see also Rosenstone and Hansen 1993).

Other non-financial resources, such as education and political knowledge, also predict engagement (Wilkes 2004). Putnam's (2000, 35) work on political participation and general group membership finds that political knowledge is a "critical precondition for active forms of participation" and that those who know more about politics are more disposed to engage in protest.

PHOTO 14.3 The Raging Grannies, who started out as anti-nuclear campaigners in the late 1980s, are activist groups comprised of older women. Older people are less likely to be targets for arrest—if you were a police officer, would you want to be seen arresting these women? Why or why not?

Biographical Availability

When individuals are **biographically available** to participate in social movements, they have the opportunity to convert their ideology and resources into action (Beyerlein and Hipp 2006). Life changes make individuals more or less available to participate. For example, if you are married or have children, you might be less inclined to attend protests because you have less free time to engage and you might be more fearful of the risks of participation (McAdam 1986, 70). Students are often considered particularly biographically available because many do not have spouses, children, full-time jobs, or other constraints on their time (Wiltfang and McAdam 1991). Older people are also frequently biographically available because they are usually retired and do not have children living at home (Nepstad and Smith 1999).

Social Ties and Identity

Having social ties to other activists is another central component of participating in social movements. If you have many close friends who are active in social movements, you are much more likely to join (McAdam 1986).

One of the main reasons that social ties are so important is that they can help to create identities that facilitate and encourage social movement engagement. **Identities** are the names that people give to themselves and others in the course of social interaction (Snow 2001). Some sociologists argue that a collective identity, a sense of "we-ness" that comes from shared attributes or experiences among a group (Melucci, Keane, and Mier 1989), is a prerequisite for collective action (Klandermans and de Weerd 2000). By participating in social movements, individuals can come to change their identities, sometimes adopting an "activist identity" (Taylor and Raeburn 1995).

Political Context/Critical Events

Social movement participation is also shaped by the context in which it happens. Some contexts are more facilitative to the growth of social movement mobilization than others. These facilitative contexts are called **free spaces**, the small-scale settings within a community or movement that are removed from the direct control of dominant groups, are voluntary, and generate the cultural challenge that precedes or accompanies political mobilization (Polletta 1999). These free spaces protect activists from those in power who might oppose them. Student lounges, union halls, and neighbourhood groups are examples of free spaces (Fantasia and Hirsch 1995).

In his research on Beijing's pro-democracy student movement, Zhao (1999) conducted 70 interviews with student activists. He found that free spaces were critical to the movement's success. In particular, universities acted as safe places that allowed students to meet and organize.

RESEARCH METHOD
INTERVIEW

Consequences of Participation

Participating in a social movement or protest activities can have long-term transformative effects for individuals. A group of studies (e.g., Whalen and Flacks 1989) that interviewed people who were active in social movements of the 1960s found that participating in protest had important consequences for the later lives of individuals. Activists tended to maintain the same ideology over the course of their lives and to remain politically active. There were many interesting personal consequences to their participation as well. Former activists are concentrated in teaching and other helping professions; have lower incomes; are more likely to have divorced, married later, or remained single; and are more apt to have experienced an episodic or non-traditional work history than non-activists (Giugni 2004).

The Media and Social Movements

Most of what we learn about social movement causes and campaigns comes from the media, which work to frame social movements. **Frames** are ways of interpreting the world that allow individuals to understand and label occurrences in their daily lives. There are simply too many things happening in the world "out there"; we need frames to condense the world into a smaller set of ideas designed to attract and mobilize potential participants. The process of framing is about selecting certain parts of the world to emphasize and others to de-emphasize. Think of a photograph. When you take a picture, you capture some of what is happening, but some elements are left out. In the same way, a frame focuses on some aspects of reality to promote a particular interpretation of an event or issue. Activists use frames to inspire and legitimate social movement activity. The media might pick up these frames and make them available to the public.

Frames have three key parts: diagnostic, prognostic, and motivational. First, the social movement and activists "diagnose" the problem. In terms of the environmental movement, a group could argue that environmental problems are the result of weak laws that do not prevent or restrict pollution. Second, a social movement tries to propose a solution to the problem. If we think that the government's environmental laws are too weak, the prognosis is that we should lobby the government to pass firmer legislation. Third, social movement activists try to get individuals to do something to solve the problem. Perhaps we should start a petition, go to a protest event on Parliament Hill, or create a Facebook page for environmental protection. A different group might argue that individual consumers cause environmental problems by buying too much stuff and using too many resources (diagnosis). It might suggest that consumers should buy less or recycle/reduce/reuse (prognosis) and start a campaign such as Buy Nothing Day or a campaign to encourage recycling (motivational). Even though both groups are interested in protecting the environment, their different diagnostic frames lead to different solutions and calls to action.

Selection and Description Bias

One way for the public to be exposed to social movements' frames is by attending their events or going to SMOs' websites. We can also learn of social movement activities and causes through media coverage of protests and campaigns. Because so many events occur every day, the media must select which are the most "important" to cover. Many social movement groups stage events that get no coverage at all!

Media editors must pick a limited number of events to observe and report because there is only so much space in the paper, on the website, or in the broadcast. **Selection bias** involves media editors' choices of a small number of protest events from a much larger pool. Media agendas can influence this selection, independent of an event's characteristics. With the exception of size, objective matters such as the form of the protest or its timing are unrelated to whether an event is reported in the mass media (Smith et al. 2001).

Events are more likely to be reported if their substantive focus can be used to illustrate an issue that is already on the media's radar. A group concerned with gun control has a better chance of getting media attention after a large-scale incident of gun violence. Such **issue attention cycles** are the specific times when the public is more apt to become concerned about a problem and attempt to solve it. Once the public realizes the cost of addressing a problem, however, enthusiasm for solutions often dampens. Eventually, the decline in public interest is followed by (as Staggenborg says) a post-problem phase.

Once a group has secured media coverage (no small feat!), activists become concerned with **description bias**, or how they and their actions are depicted. We can make sense of how the media select what to cover and how they frame that coverage in a variety of ways. These explanations are generally based on either organizational or ideological models (Smith at al. 2001).

From the perspective of **organizational models of the media**, the media act as gatekeepers. These gatekeepers do not just choose the most important events to cover. Instead, they also give more coverage to events that are seen to be changing. For example, in the last chapter we learned about the very serious problem of child poverty in Canada. Getting coverage for this issue is difficult because it is relatively stagnant over time (i.e., the rates remain high and unchanging). Why would the media cover child poverty today or tomorrow instead of something that is considered more current? For social movement activists to get this issue covered, they must connect it to some event or matter that is seen to be increasing, spreading, or intensifying to make it sufficiently interesting. A UN report stating that child poverty in Canada is higher than in most other Western countries or a story of a particular child and his plight can capture the public's interest and therefore draw media attention to the larger issue.

Economics also shape what is covered in the media. Newspapers, television stations, and news websites are experiencing budget cuts. Consequently, editors tend to favour generalist reporters rather than specialists. Generalists can write a story on transit today, education tomorrow, and health the next day, which eliminates the need to have one reporter (who might not have anything to cover on a given day) for each area. Generalists are cheaper and easier to hire; however, by their very nature, they do not know as much about each area that they cover because they are forced to move from one to another. As a result, they are more reliant on official government sources for information. A reporter who covers a transit strike, the education system, and health care wait lines can call up a government contact and get a quote to include in the article on any of these topics. She is less apt to contact social movement activists or others (such as bus drivers, teachers, or nurses) because she lacks contacts in all these different areas. This means that the news is more likely to represent the interests and perspectives of officials and those in power than of challengers.

The organizational perspective does not argue that journalists and editors conspire against coverage of social movements and other critical groups. Reporters and editors want to get the best and most accurate story out to the public. The structure and organization of news collection simply makes it so that reporters write and editors choose stories that tend to support the status quo and undermine activists.

The **ideological model of media coverage** argues that there is a more concerted effort on the part of the media, political, and corporate elites to control the information in the news. This model says that broader structures of power relations in society affect the portrayal of social movements and protest. Such structures lead to increased privatization, commercialization, and concentration of ownership, which severely limits the range of ideas conveyed in the media (see Chapter 7).

The media make money through advertising; therefore, they tend to cover issues that will get the most attention, regardless of their importance. Articles about Kim Kardashian having a baby or Taylor Swift dating someone new are not really "important," but they attract many readers. As a result, the news outlet can charge more for advertisements. Publishing sensational stories in order to draw the public's attention is also the basis of the saying "If it bleeds, it leads." News coverage of crime often focuses on particularly gruesome murders. Such articles frequently appear on the front page or as the top item on a broadcast or website and include dramatic photographs of the accused killer or innocent victim. Despite the fact that the overall crime rate in Canada is declining, coverage that emphasizes these dramatic crimes is selected because it attracts attention and makes money for the news outlet.

Because of the importance of advertising revenue, journalists must be very aware of advertisers' interests. Thus, from the perspective of the ideological model, the media work to reproduce broader power relationships. For example, they tend to focus on individual responsibility for social problems and neglect social causes. Instead of reporting on the overall reasons that crime rates are higher in some areas or groups, the media tend to centre on one individual criminal or victim. This approach encourages a shallow understanding of these issues and discourages the critical engagement of audiences.

As our discussion has indicated, media framing is important because the media play a powerful role in educating the public about social issues. It sends signals about who is legitimate and sympathetic and to whom we should listen. Consequently, the media can affect public opinion and government policy. In terms of social movements, the media coverage of protests generally tends to be limited and, when it does occur, negative. These findings are consistent with both the organizational and ideological perspectives: the media tend to emphasize officials' views at the expense of activists' and other challengers' and centre on individual-level explanations instead of the social explanations most movements try to convey. In addition, because the media try to attract attention and emphasize drama in order to increase circulation and revenue, they tend to focus on the violence, drama, and "wackiness" at a protest event.

ACTIVITY

Media Images of Protest—The Oka Crisis and Black Lives Matter

To see how the media depict protest events, let's look at two examples—the Oka Crisis and Black Lives Matter.

The Oka Crisis

The **Oka Crisis** is Canada's largest and longest standoff between First Nations people and the government. On 11 July 1990, several dozen Mohawk people from Kanesatake, Quebec, set up a barricade to stop the town of Oka's plans to expand a golf course in the area. The development included land that was supposed to be held in trust for the Mohawks, who had a symbolic and spiritual connection to it. Oka's mayor responded to the protest by calling in the provincial police, who stormed the barricade. In the ensuing conflict, one police officer was killed, and the police retreated. The barricade continued, and the event received extensive media coverage in Canada and around the world. Protest events supporting the Mohawks were held across Canada, and a peace camp was set up at Oka Park.

Frustrated by the long standoff, Prime Minister Brian Mulroney called in 2500 Canadian soldiers to replace the Quebec police. On 26 September, the remaining Mohawks burned their weapons and walked away. Most of the protesters were charged with various offences, although only two were convicted of any crime. In 1997, the Canadian government purchased the land and "gave" it to the Mohawk people.

With this background in mind, do an Internet image search for the Oka Crisis. Use the photos you find to answer the following questions:

1. How do the images represent the Mohawks, the Quebec police, the Canadian military, and others? Do the photos reflect a positive or negative view of these groups? How is the relationship between these various groups depicted?
2. Why would these images have been selected for publication? Answer this question using the organizational model, then the ideological model.
3. The following image, "Face to Face," appeared more than 100 times in Canadian newspapers, becoming the most reprinted image of the Oka Crisis. How does it depict the Canadian soldier and the Mohawk protester? Who elicits more sympathy? How would the image affect public opinion about this event?

THE CANADIAN PRESS/Shaney Komulainen

4. The following two images were also taken during the Oka Crisis but did not appear in newspapers. How do these photos depict the protesters and the officials? Do they convey a different message about this event and

Image provided courtesy of DND

Continued

THE CANADIAN PRESS/Tom Hanson

the participants from the others you've seen? How would the organizational and ideological models explain why these other images were not shown in the media?

Black Lives Matter

1. Now look online for images of the Black Lives Matter protests. How are the protesters depicted in these images? How are officials depicted (if they are shown)?
2. Why were these images selected? How do they relate to the organizational or ideological theories of the media? Do these images support or challenge the idea of the protest paradigm?
3. Are the depictions of protesters and officials the same as or different from those in the Oka Crisis? If so, why?

The specific way that the media tend to cover protest events is known as the **protest paradigm** (McLeod and Hertog 1999). This template uses a particular framing and relies on official sources. Together, these elements lead to the delegitimization, marginalization, and even demonization of protesters.

A major modern movement in Canada has been Idle No More. We have learned about this movement in various sections of this book. In the following reading, Indigenous scholar Angela Semple examines the roots of Idle No More and considers how it has been experienced by Indigenous peoples in Canada. When reading the article, consider the movement taking into account what we know about participation in social movements, tactical choices, and media coverage.

On Idle No More

Angela Semple

Kisukyukyit, hu qak‡ik Angela Semple. I am a member of the Ktunaxa nation located in Southeastern British Columbia, and a status Indian according to section 6.2 of Canada's Indian Act. I choose to open this review by positioning myself as an "insider" when it comes to Indigenous people in Canada: an important starting point, as it has become well-accepted practice within Indigenous studies to acknowledge our positionality as writers, activists, scholars, and community members. I will focus strongly on this concept of positionality throughout my discussion of the three texts reviewed.

Following the footsteps of many of the authors under review, I'd like to share a bit about my own experience with the Idle No More movement. When I was approached to write this essay, I was immediately brought back to the winter of 2012/2013, where I followed and participated in the movement in various ways, from attending gatherings (Park Royal Mall, Vancouver) and marches (Elsipogtog Rally, Vancouver), speaking at events (Idle No More Rally, Simon Fraser University), all the while tweeting and Facebooking the hashtag along with thousands of people across the world over the past three years. Never in my lifetime have I experienced this kind of Indigenous pride and unity, and I am eternally grateful for the experience, which will follow me through a lifetime of being "idle no more."

But what is "Idle No More?" While the social media posts and gatherings that happened worldwide were life-changing for myself and many other Indigenous people in Canada, the majority of Canadians still have little to no understanding of the events that took place, or of their continued impact on our communities. Often, not surprisingly given the historical coverage of Indigenous resistance, the media "went wrong" (*Winter*, 294) in regards to Idle No More. This illustrates a necessity for literature such as the three books in review. "Idle No More" as a catch phrase was coined by four women in Saskatchewan: Jessica Gordon, Sylvia McAdam, Sheelah McLean, and Nina Wilson. In 2012, these women found themselves "fed up" with the Canadian government's omnibus Bill C-45, a "massive piece of impenetrable federal legislation" (Coates, XIII), taking particular issue with proposed changes in environmental protections and Indian Act legislation. Gordon, McAdam, McLean and Wilson decided to hold a "teach-in" on November 10 to garner support in their protest. They advertised the teach-in through a Facebook event under the title "Idle No More" as a "grassroots movement for solidarity which welcomes all community members!" (Coates 3). The women also took to Twitter, with Jessica Gordon using the hashtag (#idlenomore) for the first time on October 30, later tweeting it to Sean Atleo, then Chief of the Assembly of First Nations (4). The response was immediate, as Indigenous people from all over Canada began sharing the Idle No More hashtag and planning their own events, from teach-ins to round dances to a "National Day of Solidarity and Resurgence" held on December 10, 2012 (Kino-nda-niimi Collective 391).

I cannot remember the first moment I heard about Idle No More, though I do remember an early conversation where a friend of mine shrugged it off "oh, right, we shouldn't leave our cars idling . . ." (many cities and towns have "Idle-Free zone" signs posted in parking lots and pick-up zones, an almost unattainable goal during Canadian winters). I giggled, wondering myself about the title. I echoed the sentiments shared in some of the works under review that we, as Indigenous people, had never been "idle," and I questioned the connotations that "Idle No More" had when thinking about our Elders and their own fights and movements (ie. Oka or AIM). But as time went on, I came to view it as an immediate call to action rather

Semple, Angela. 2015. "On Idle No More." Transmotion 1(2). https://journals.kent.ac.uk/index.php/transmotion/article/view/198/740.

than a reflection on the history of Indigenous protest. As Coates explains, "Gordon, McAdam, McLean, and Wilson decided to do something. This, among all the things that happened over the coming months, was the most radical step" (Coates, 3). And that is the heart of "Idle No More": Of course, we, as Indigenous people have been doing good work in our communities since time immemorial, but with this current (2012) federal government and their secretive and destructive omnibus bills, it simply wasn't enough. "Idle No More" became our rallying cry.

What is truly fascinating, though, is how Idle No More grew to encompass much more than a specific protest about a specific piece of legislation. As the events spread through cities, small towns, and Indigenous communities, it was clear that Indigenous peoples and our allies had simply been waiting for a spark to start the forest fire that became Idle No More. This metaphorical forest fire spread far and wide in the milliseconds it took to click thousands of "retweet" and "share" buttons. It burned in our hearts as we sang, drummed, and danced together. It left any sense of apathy behind in its ashes, clearing a path for a renewed empowerment of Indigenous voices within Canada. At each Idle No More event I attended, and every time I logged in to check the progress of the hashtag on Twitter, I was inspired and uplifted by the connections Idle No More was making all over the world. I was born more than a decade after the height of the American Indian Movement, and was only two years old when Oka happened. For me, Idle No More created a sense of Indigenous community that I had never been a part of before, and it did so through social media. Known in Indian country as our newest form of the "moccasin telegraph," social media has transformed the way Indigenous communities across North America are able to communicate with each other, connecting our Elders, children, aunties, and uncles from all different nations in mere seconds, and allowing us to find solidarity on issues we care about, as seen through Idle No More.

Here I want to return to the discussion of positionality. As I mentioned, I have placed myself in the role of the "insider": someone who participated in the Idle No More movement as a status Indian in Canada. I've identified myself by sharing my nation with you (Ktunaxa). This is protocol within Indigenous communities. In certain settings, for example at a community gathering, I would follow this up by naming my grandmothers (Patricia Sam and Sabina Cote) in order to situate myself further within the community. Because this protocol is so well established, it is a natural progression for Indigenous scholars to continue this form of introduction through our academic work. It is important to note here that Indigenous Studies is a relatively new field within the academy, and to also acknowledge that Indigenous-authored scholarship within the field is an even more recent advancement. I point this out, as until 1960 it was illegal for a status Indian in Canada to obtain a university degree unless they were willing to give up their status.

Under those conditions, non-Indigenous people created virtually all research done about Indigenous people. This concept of control over representation is not a new one, but I want to stress it to the context of the three books being reviewed here, at a time when thousands of Indigenous academics, writers, artists, filmmakers, Elders, teachers, community leaders, and even politicians have emerged to tell our stories from our point of view. This is inherently important when it comes to Idle No More, as each of the texts explains issues with media coverage of Indigenous resistance and resurgence. When, for a century or more, we've seen non-Indigenous people continuously get it wrong, it is important that we share our own stories, and that those stories get heard. This is not—I repeat, firmly, *not*—to say that non-Indigenous people cannot participate in Indigenous Studies. Instead, I am arguing for a careful examination of work on or about Indigenous people that includes awareness of the positionality of the author or editors. To explain this further, I want to draw upon Ken Coates' description in *#IDLENOMORE and the Remaking of Canada*:

> In fact, Idle No More was not meant for non-Aboriginal Canadians. It was not an attempt to persuade, convince, or direct political change. Idle No More, it seemed clear as time went on, was by Aboriginal people, for Aboriginal people, and about

Aboriginal people. For the first time in Canadian history, non-Aboriginal Canadians were relegated to the sidelines (xxi).

So, if the movement was by us, for us, and about us, who better to look to for an explanation than the "insiders"?

CRITICAL READING QUESTIONS

1. What is Idle No More? How did it originate?
2. What different tactics did this movement use? Why do you think that these tactics were chosen?
3. How did Idle No More change over time, according to Semple?

Success in Social Movements

Social movement groups often call for large-scale social changes. A women's group that calls for equality between the sexes will find that the goal is pretty hard to achieve. How can full equality be attained? If men and women make the same salaries, is that equality? What about access to education or depictions in the media? When groups have large and broad goals, it is frequently hard to determine if they have been successful. Moreover, groups with a variety of goals tend to achieve only some of them.

Another reason that success is hard to measure is that politicians, business leaders, and others in power are often reluctant to admit being influenced by social movement groups. Leaders might feel that doing so makes them seem weak and easily swayed by public opinion. They often do not want to encourage more protest or campaigns. A very active and engaged population is certainly harder to govern than one that sits at home and only comes out to vote once every four years. With these issues in mind, how can we measure social movement success?

William Gamson has created a typology of outcomes for social movements. He examines two markers of social movement success. First, groups are looking for **acceptance**, being seen as a valid spokesperson for a legitimate set of concerns. Second, groups are looking for **new advantages**, like laws, policies, or other gains (Gamson 1990). We can see that these two dimensions may overlap, but this is not always the case. In fact, when we combine these two dimensions, there are four distinct outcomes (see Table 14.3).

If a group gets full acceptance and many new advantages, this is full response. This is exactly what a challenger wants—to be seen as a legitimate spokesperson and to get the law or policy that you want. The other end of the spectrum is when you get no acceptance or new advantages. In this situation, your group is in collapse—you have not won anything and may not survive as a group. The final two combinations are more complex.

TABLE 14.3 | Outcome of challenges

		Acceptance	
		Full	**None**
New	Many	Full response	Pre-emption
Advantages	None	Co-optation	Collapse

Source: Based on William Gramson, 1990, 1975, *The Strategy of Social Protest*, 2nd edn, pp. 28–37, Belmont, CA: Wadsworth Publishing Company.

If you get full acceptance but no new advantages, this could be a case of co-optation. Perhaps the government senses that public opinion in on your side, so they allow your group to sit on government boards without giving your group the policies or laws they seek. Or, if the there is no acceptance but many new advantages, this could be a case of pre-emption. The government could quickly respond to your policy requests but undermine the existence of your group as a whole (Gamson 1990). Measuring social movement success is a challenge because all of these outcomes are ideal types—no group will fall neatly into any of these boxes. However, this work highlights the complex factors involved in measuring whether social movements have "won."

Public Sociology and Using Our Sociological Imagination

Recently, there have been calls for sociologists to engage more with the public and bring sociological ideas to the larger community. **Public sociology**, a term introduced by Herbert Gans in 1988, uses the sociological imagination to engage with wider audiences outside traditional academic circles. Promoters of public sociology have sought to encourage sociologists to engage with social issues in explicitly public and political ways. This movement uses the theories and findings of sociology in debates about not just what is or what has been in society but also what could be.

ACTIVITY

Using Our Sociological Imagination for Social Change

Patricia Hill Collins, an important feminist scholar, has long been concerned with her work's impact on different communities of people. She and many other sociologists hope that their work and a sociological understanding of the world can be used to improve society. Collins (2013) discusses intellectual activism and how it can help us use our sociological imagination to improve society and the lives of individuals. This idea is similar to public sociology. She argues that, as sociologists, we should both "speak truth to power" and "speak truth to people." The former uses the power of ideas to confront existing power relations in order to change the foundations of social hierarchy—the less powerful take on the ideas and practices of the powerful, often armed solely with their ideas. The latter means talking to the masses and is based on the idea that sociologists should communicate how sociological knowledge can help to improve individuals' daily lives (Collins 2013).

To learn more about public sociology, go to this book's companion website to read an excerpt from Herbert Gans. Then answer the following questions:

1. What is public sociology, according to Gans? What four kinds of public sociology should academic sociologists undertake?
2. How can sociology students engage in these activities? Is it possible to be a public sociology student? Why or why not?
3. Take one of the main theories or research findings that you have learned about in this book. How could you use this information to engage in public sociology?
4. Who would you want to know about your public sociology research? How would you try to get this information to them? How could it create social change and a more equitable world?

Summary

In this final chapter, we examined social change as it can occur through social movements. We began by learning about the core features of social movements. The collective action problem helped us to understand why we might not expect individuals to engage in social movements. Despite this problem, Canadian participation is relatively high and is increasing. Therefore, it is important to know why some individuals might take part in protest and social movement events. We discussed the media's importance in social movements, particularly regarding issues of selection and description bias. We also considered how to measure success for social movements. We ended this chapter, and this book, by thinking about public sociology and intellectual activism.

Key Terms

acceptance 415
biographical availability 407
boycott 391
collective action problem (or free-rider problem) 402
conscience constituency 393
description bias 409
efficacy 406
frames 408
free spaces 407
identities 407
ideological model of media coverage 410

issue attention cycles 409
new advantage 415
Oka Crisis 410
organizational model of media coverage 409
petition 393
protest 391
protest paradigm 412
public good 403
public sociology 416
selection bias 409
social movement 391
WUNC 393

For Further Reading

Klandermans, B. 1997. *The Social Psychology of Protest*. Oxford: Blackwell.
McAdam, Doug. 1988. *Freedom Summer*. New York: Oxford University Press.
McCarthy, J., and M. Zald. 1973. *The Trend of Social Movements in America: Professionalization and Resource Mobilization*. Morristown, NJ: General Learning Press.
Meyer, David S., and Sidney Tarrow, eds. 1998. *The Social Movement Society: Contentious Politics for a New Century*. Lanham, MD: Rowan and Littlefield.
Staggenborg, Suzanne, and Howard Ramos. 2016. *Social Movements*, 3rd edn. Don Mills, ON: Oxford University Press.

References

Beyerlein, K., and J.R. Hipp. 2006. "A Two-Stage Model for a Two-Stage Process: How Biographical Availability Matters for Social Movement Mobilization." *Mobilization* 11: 299–320.

Collins, Patricia Hill. 2013. "Truth-Telling and Intellectual Activism." *Contexts* 12(1): 36–41.

Corrigall-Brown, C. 2013. "Participation in Social Movements." In D.A. Snow, D. della Porta, B. Klandermans, and D. McAdam, eds, *The Wiley-Blackwell Encyclopedia of Social and Political Movements*. Oxford: Wiley-Blackwell.

Dalton, R.J., A. Van Sickle, and S. Weldon. 2010. "The Individual–Institutional Nexus of Protest Behaviour." *British Journal of Political Science* 40: 51–73.

Diani, M. 2004. "Networks and Participation." In D.A. Snow, S.A. Soule, and H. Kreisi, eds, *The Blackwell Companion to Social Movements*, 339–59. Malden, MA: Blackwell Publishing.

Fantasia, R., and E.L. Hirsch. 1995. "Culture in Rebellion: The Appropriation and Transformation of the Veil in the Algerian Revolution." In H. Johnston and B. Klandermans, eds, *Social Movements and Culture*, 144–62. Minneapolis: University of Minnesota Press.

Gamson, William. 1990. *The Strategy of Social Protest*, 2nd edn. Belmont, CA: Wadsworth.

Gecas, V. 2000. "Value Identities, Self-Motives, and Social Movements." In S. Stryker, T.J. Owens and R.W. White, eds, *Self, Identity, and Social Movements*, 93–109. Minneapolis: University of Minnesota Press.

Giugni, Marco G. 2004. "Personal and Biographical Consequences." In D.A. Snow, S.A. Soule, and H. Kriesi, eds, *The Blackwell Companion to Social Movements*, 489–507. Malden, MA: Blackwell.

Inglehart, Ronald. 1997. *Modernization and Postmodernization: Cultural, Economic and Political Change in 43 Nations*. Princeton, NJ: Princeton University Press.

Jacobson, Louis. 2017. "A Short History of the National Anthem, Protests, and the NFL. Politifact." http://www.politifact.com/truth-o-meter/article/2017/sep/25/short-history-national-anthem-and-sports.

Klandermans, B. 1997. *The Social Psychology of Protest*. Oxford: Blackwell.

——— and M. de Weerd. 2000. "Group Identification and Political Protest." In S. Stryker, T.J. Owens, and R.W. White, eds, *Self, Identity, and Social Movements*. Minneapolis: University of Minnesota Press.

McAdam, D. 1986. "Recruitment to High-Risk Activism—The Case of Freedom Summer." *American Journal of Sociology* 92: 64–90.

McLeod, D.M., and Hertog, J.K. 1999. "Social Control, Social Change and the Mass Media's Role in the Regulation of Protest Groups." In D. Demers and K. Viswanath, eds, *Mass Media, Social Control and Social Change: A Macrosocial Perspective*, 305–30. Ames, IA: Iowa State University Press.

Melucci, A., J. Keane, and P. Mier. 1989. *Nomads of the Present: Social Movements and Individual Needs in Contemporary Society*. Philadelphia: Temple University Press.

Nepstad, S.E., and C. Smith. 1999. "Rethinking Recruitment to High-Risk/Cost Activism: The Case of the Nicaragua Exchange." *Mobilization* 4: 25–40.

Norris, Pippa. 2002. *Democratic Phoenix: Reinventing Political Activism*. Cambridge: Cambridge University Press.

Olson, Mancur. 1965. *The Logic of Collective Action: Public Goods and the Theory of Groups*. Cambridge, MA: Harvard University Press.

Polletta, F. 1999. "'Free Spaces' in Collective Action." *Theory and Society* 28: 1–38.

Putnam, R.D. 2000. *Bowling Alone: The Collapse and Revival of American Community*. New York: Simon & Schuster.

Rosenstone, S.J., and J.M. Hansen. 1993. *Mobilization, Participation, and Democracy in America*. New York: Macmillan.

Smith, Jackie, John D. McCarthy, Clark McPhail, and Boguslaw Angustyn. 2001. "From Protest to Agenda Building: Description Bias in Media Coverage of Protest Events in Washington, D.C." *Social Forces* 79(4): 1397–423.

Snow, D.A. 2001. "Collective Identity and Expressive Forms." In N.J. Smelser and P.B. Blates, eds, *The International Encyclopedia of the Social and Behavioral Sciences*. Oxford: Elsenier Selpin.

Taylor, V., and N.C. Raeburn. 1995. "Identity Politics as High-Risk Activism: Career Consequences for Lesbian, Gay, and Bisexual Sociologists." *Social Problems* 42: 252–73.

Tilly, Charles. 1997. "Social Movements as Political Struggle." Working Paper, Center for Advanced Study in the Behavioral Sciences at Stanford University. https://www.ciaonet.org/wps/tic03.

Verba, S., K.L. Schlozman, and H.E. Brady. 1995. *Voice and Equality: Civic Voluntarism in American Politics*. Cambridge, MA: Harvard University Press.

Warner, Kris. 2013. "The Real Reason for the Decline of American Unions." *BloombergView* 23 January. http://www.bloombergview.com/articles/2013-01-23/the-real-reason-for-the-decline-of-american-unions.

Whalen, J., and R. Flacks. 1989. *Beyond the Barricades: The Sixties Generation Grows Up*. Philadelphia: Temple University Press.

Wilkes, Rima. 2004. "First Nation Politics: Deprivation, Resources, and Participation in Collective Action." *Sociological Inquiry* 74: 570–89.

Wiltfang, G.L., and D. McAdam. 1991. "The Costs and Risks of Social Activism—A Study of Sanctuary Movement Activism." *Social Forces* 69: 987–1010.

Zhao, D. 1999. "Ecologies of Social Movements: Student Mobilization during the 1989 Pro-democracy Movement in Beijing." *American Journal of Sociology* 103: 1493–529.

Glossary

ableism A term for discrimination against a person with a cognitive or physical disability on the basis of stereotypes about their limitations.

acceptance According to Gamson, a measure of social movement success in which a movement is considered a valid representative for a legitimate set of interests.

achievement-based stratification system A system that ranks individuals based on their accomplishments.

agents of socialization The various societal groups that help us learn to become members of society (e.g., family, peer groups, the education system, the mass media, and religion).

alienation Generally, the separation of things that naturally belong together. According to Marx, workers become alienated from the product they make, the process of production, other workers, and themselves.

alternative media Media that are non-profit, anti-establishment, and creative and are based on a two-way relationship between the producer and the consumer.

anticipatory socialization The process of individuals rehearsing roles that they may have to perform in the future.

arranged marriage A marital union in which a third party selects the bride and groom. Arranged marriage was common in certain cultures and areas throughout history and remains so in South Asia, Africa, the Middle East, Latin America, Southeast Asia, and parts of East Asia.

ascription-based stratification system A system that ranks individuals based on a person's ascribed features (e.g., race or sex).

authoritarian personality Adorno's term for a personality that is more likely to develop prejudicial attitudes. People with this type of personality tend to see the world in terms of good and evil and strictly follow rules and orders.

automation The operation of equipment with minimal or reduced human intervention.

biographical availability A main predictor of social movement engagement. Individuals with fewer responsibilities and constraints, such as young people, students, single people, and those without children, are more likely to have the time, energy, and inclination to engage in contentious political activity.

bourgeoisie (capitalist) One of the two primary classes in Marx's theory; the owners of the means of production.

boycott The minimally contentious act of withdrawing from commercial or social relations with a country, organization, or person as a form of protest.

breaching experiments Experiments that intentionally break a social rule or norm in order to reveal the common work done by individuals to maintain social order in day-to-day life.

bureaucracy Literally, "the rule of the office or desk," an organizational form that predominates in modern society and focuses on rationality. Weber described bureaucracies as human machines.

Canada Pension Plan (CPP) A universal social program available to all Canadians over the age of 59, regardless of financial means.

cash crops Crops that are sold for profit. This type of agriculture contrasts with subsistence farming in which farmers grow crops for their own consumption.

census The systematic collecting and recording of information about members of a given population.

chronic disease prevalence A measure of the health of a population that assesses how common chronic diseases are within a group.

civic engagement The individual and collective actions designed to identify and address issues of public concern. The decline of civic engagement is the core concern of Robert D. Putnam's work.

civicness Putnam's term for the values, norms, institutions, and associations that allow and foster civic commitment, solidarity, mutual trust, and tolerance.

class consciousness An awareness of what is in the best interests of one's class. Marx argued that this awareness is an important precondition for organizing into a "class for itself" and advocating for class interests.

class struggle The conflict between those who own the means of production (bourgeoisie) and those who own only their labour power (workers).

cohabitation The state of a heterosexual or homosexual couple living together and having a sexual relationship without being legally married.

collective action problem (free-rider problem) The idea, posited by Olson, that people tend to avoid participating in collective action (e.g., social movements) because they will benefit from whatever is gained whether or not they contribute to the cause.

commodification The process of reducing social relations to an exchange relation (i.e., assigning them with a monetary value).

commodity An item of value and uniform quality produced in large quantities by many producers. Consumer goods, such as clothing, cars, and food, are commodities.

commodity chain A process used by companies to gather resources, transform them into goods or commodities, and distribute them to consumers; the connected path from which a good travels from producers to consumers.

companionate marriage A marriage based on the satisfaction of the couple, the family as a whole, and the different roles each person plays in the family. Companionate marriages include a clear division of labour between the breadwinner (usually the husband) and the homemaker (usually the wife). Husbands and wives are seen as friends and confidants who need and rely on one another to perform the roles that each cannot.

conflict theory The idea that human behaviour and social relations result from the underlying conflicts that arise from the power differences between competing groups in society.

conscience constituency A sympathetic ally who is outside the "wronged population" represented by the social movement.

consensus crimes Deviant acts that are illegal, perceived to be very harmful to society, and have a high level of public agreement regarding their severity. Murder and sexual assault are examples of consensus crimes.

contact theory Allport's theory that increasing contact between antagonistic groups can reduce prejudice, lead to a growing recognition of similarities, and alter stereotypes about the other group.

control theory Hirschi's theory that weak social control contributes to an individual engaging in deviant or criminal acts. Weak controls can be the result of having few social connections and relationships.

core countries The most economically diversified, wealthy, and powerful nations in the world. Core countries are highly industrialized and tend to produce manufactured goods rather than extract raw materials for export.

corporate concentration The extent to which an industry, such as the media, is increasingly owned and controlled by fewer large corporations and conglomerates.

corporatization The process of using business or management techniques to transform institutions and services previously managed by government. Corporatization occurs in universities with the naming of buildings and scholarships after major donors and the signing of exclusive contracts with companies.

costs of masculinity Messner's concept that there are rules to masculinity and what men can be and do. For example, masculinity is defined by external success; men must avoid everything feminine and are expected to be aggressive and show little emotion.

counterculture A group, such as an anti-consumerist organization, that rejects certain elements of the dominant culture.

credentialing Collins's term to describe an authority, such as a university, issuing a qualification or competence to an individual. This practice is used to exclude some people from certain jobs or opportunities.

Crime Severity Index (CSI) A measurement of the severity of police-reported crime, calculated by assigning each offence a weight based on its perceived seriousness (as measured by the sentences handed down by the courts).

cultural capital Bourdieu's term for the non-financial social assets that promote social mobility. For example, individuals can gain degrees, learn a more refined style of speech, or adopt elite social tastes, which can make them appear to belong to a higher social class than the one they were born into.

culture A system of behaviour, beliefs, knowledge, practices, values, and materials that shape how we act and the physical elements of our society.

curriculum The standardized content, materials, resources, and processes used to teach students. Each province in Canada outlines a specific curriculum for each grade.

cyberbullying The use of technology, such as the Internet, to deliberately harass, intimidate, or threaten a person.

cycle of poverty The causes and elements of poverty that trap people in this situation and require outside intervention.

deep acting Based on Hochschild's work on emotional labour, the modification of an employee's inner feelings to match the expressions required by the employer.

defensive credentialing The process of attending college or university and/or enrolling in graduate and professional programs in order to avoid losing job opportunities to degree holders and to gain an advantage in employment.

deinstitutionalization of marriage The term used by Cherlin to describe the weakening of social norms concerning marriage and people's resulting doubt of their actions, and those of others, within this institution.

demographic diversity The extent to which the media represent and address the interests of people from a variety of groups, such as races, ethnicities, genders, and classes.

dependent variable A variable that is affected by other variables.

description bias In terms of social movements, the media's positive or negative depiction of a protest event or activist.

deterrence The process of dissuading someone from committing future wrongdoings by making the "cost" of punishment outweigh the "benefit" of the offence. The idea is based on the assumption that individuals conduct a rational cost–benefit analysis before committing a crime.

deviance The act of breaking a social norm.

different expectations The different values and outlooks that families have, based on their social class. The different education expectations of low-income and high-income families could explain why individuals from the former are less likely to perform well in schools or earn degrees than people from the latter.

differential association The idea that children from the lower class are less likely than other children to have role models who have achieved at school or attended university. As a result, these children lack the knowledge of how to work within the system and are less successful in it.

differential preparation The various ways that individuals can be prepared for an aspect of society, depending on their social class. For example, children from families with more money probably have more access to private tutors, educational trips, educational toys, and books and newspapers than do poorer children. These resources help to prepare them for school and to do well in the educational system.

digital divide An inequality between groups' ability to access, use, or learn about information and communication technologies. Within countries, this term refers to inequalities between individuals, households, and geographic areas at different socio-economic levels. The global digital divide examines the gap in digital access across countries.

disability A mental or physical condition that limits a person's daily activities.

discrimination The unfair treatment of an individual based on his actual or perceived membership in a certain group or category.

disenchantment of the world The term used by Weber to describe the change from explaining phenomenon through magical or other-worldly forces to using rational thought and science.

division of labour A focus of Durkheim's work, the specialization of cooperating individuals who perform specific tasks and roles.

dominant culture The culture that, through its political and economic power, is able to impose its values, beliefs, and behaviours on a given society.

double shift (second shift) Hochschild's concept that women in heterosexual dual-income households often spend significantly more time on household tasks and caring work than their partners do in addition to their work in the paid workforce.

dramaturgical perspective Goffman's theory that social life is like a stage and individuals are actors on it, performing roles for others.

ecological footprint A measure of a person's or community's impact on the earth's ecosystems; the amount of land and sea area required to sustain the use of natural resources and to process the associated waste.

economic perspective Based on Marxist theory, the argument that the state is needed to regulate economic interests and the clashing of those interests between groups. Marx argued that the state usually "resolves" these conflicts by siding with capitalists.

efficacy The belief that one is capable of the specific behaviours required to produce a desired outcome in a given situation. Efficacy is an important predictor of social movement engagement.

emotional labour Work, especially in the service sector, that requires emotional performances from employees. This labour is commodified and controlled by management.

essentialism The theory that some "essential" element makes a person part of a particular race or ethnic group. From this perspective, ethnic groups and nationalities are based on biological factors (similar appearance, skin colour, or eye colour) and a territorial location (region or country).

ethnicity The shared language, religion, customs, and history of a particular group. The core difference between race and ethnicity is that race is based on perceived biological traits and ethnicity is based on cultural differences.

experiment A process that allows researchers to examine a specific factor's effect on individual behaviour by comparing two groups: the experimental (which is exposed to the factor) and the control (which is not exposed to it).

extended family Two or more generations of a family living in the same household or in close proximity to one another; often contrasted with the nuclear family.

fair trade certification An official certification that tells consumers that a product is produced in a way that is consistent with principles of ethical fair trade.

false consciousness A willingness among the working class to support ideologies that are advantageous to the ruling class but disadvantageous to working-class interests. Marx argued that false consciousness is part of the reason that the working class does not unite and overthrow the capitalist system.

family A group of people who are related by birth, affinity, or cohabitation.

family household A residential unit of people who are related by blood, marriage, or adoption.

family violence Any abuse, mistreatment, or neglect in which the victim and perpetrator are related or have an intimate relationship. Types of family violence include physical, sexual, emotional, and financial abuse.

feminism The various movements and ideologies that seek to define, confirm, and protect equal political, economic, and social rights for women. Feminism is sometimes understood as occurring over three waves of activism.

feminization The process of a particular job, profession, or industry being dominated by or predominantly associated with women (e.g., nurses, secretaries, teachers, and family doctors). Feminized jobs tend to lose prestige, wages, required skill levels, and opportunities for promotion.

fertility rate The average number of children born to a woman over her lifetime.

First Nations A term of ethnicity that refers to the Indigenous people in what is now Canada who are neither Inuit nor Métis.

frames Interpretation schemes that enable individuals to understand and label occurrences in their daily lives. Framing is composed of three parts: diagnostic, prognostic, and motivational.

free spaces The small-scale settings of a community or movement that are outside dominant groups' direct control, are voluntary, and create the cultural challenge preceding or accompanying political mobilization. Social movements need free spaces so that activists can have some protection from authorities.

gender A social concept that includes all social patterns associated with being male or female and that ranges from masculine to feminine. Gender focuses on differences that are social and cultural, not biological.

gender reversal in educational outcomes The trend, which seems to have stabilized, of more women than men obtaining post-secondary degrees. In the past, men were much more likely than women to attend and graduate from university or college.

gender roles The behaviours and mannerisms that people learn as being appropriate to their respective genders and that are reinforced by cultural norms.

gender socialization The process of learning how to behave consistently with society's gender rules and norms.

general deterrence A type of deterrence that makes examples of deviants in order to discourage others from committing crimes.

generational replacement A main theory in voter turnout research that seeks to explain declining voting rates by examining how the emergence of new generations of voters (who vote less) are replacing older generations of voters (who vote more).

Gini index A measure used to compare income inequality across countries. The index ranges from zero (perfect equality) to one (total inequality).

globalization The increasing interconnectedness of people and places that results from advances in transport, communication, and information technologies and causes political, economic, and cultural convergence or integration of different people and places around the world. Globalization has three major dimensions: physical, spatio-temporal, and cognitive.

Guaranteed Income Supplement (GIS) A Canadian means-tested program that provides money to seniors whose income is below a certain level.

health A state of physical, mental, and social well-being.

health care systems The organizations of people, resources, and institutions that provide and deliver health care to a population.

health disparities The differences in health status linked to social, economic, or environmental conditions.

health policy The decisions and actions that are undertaken to achieve specific health care goals.

healthy life expectancy The average number of healthy years one can expect to live if current trends remain.

heteronormative The social institutions, practices, and norms that support the assumption that people are or should be heterosexual.

Heterosexual–Homosexual Rating Scale Kinsey's seven-point scale of sexual inclinations. Instead of thinking of people as either gay or straight, Kinsey argued that they simply have life histories that express different desires. People can have more or less homosexual or heterosexual desires and more or less homosexual or heterosexual experiences, but these things are not always related.

hidden curriculum Marx's term for lessons that are not normally considered part of the academic curriculum and that schools unintentionally or secondarily provide. These lessons teach students to be submissive, punctual, and hard-working—all the traits that make "good" workers in the capitalist system.

high culture The culture of the elite, which may generally be difficult to appreciate without having cultivated a palate for it. High culture is often juxtaposed with popular culture, the culture of the majority.

homophily The propensity of individuals to make friendships and other social ties with people who share their characteristics, such as race, class, or religious beliefs.

homophobia The negative attitudes and feelings, ranging from antipathy to hatred, toward homosexuality or people who identify as or are perceived to be LGBTQ.

honorifics A form of address or reference that shows esteem or respect toward a person.

human capital model The argument, related to Durkheim's theory, that schools are organized largely to nurture productive skills needed in the economy.

Human Development Index (HDI) A number that combines a variety of measures (e.g., life expectancy, education, and income) regarding the health and quality of life in a country.

idea diversity The diversity of viewpoints expressed in the media.

identities The names that people give to themselves and others in the course of social interaction. Identity is central to social movement participation as both a cause and outcome of engagement.

ideological model of media coverage The perspective that media, political, and corporate elites make a concerted effort to control the information released through the media. This model argues that broader structures of power relations in society affect the portrayal of social movements and protest.

ideology A system of conscious and unconscious ideas that shape a person's or group's objectives, expectations, and actions. Marx argues that a society's dominant ideologies come from the dominant class and serve to perpetuate the capitalist system.

imagined communities Anderson's term to describe members of a nation feeling a sense of community even though they will never know most of their fellow citizens.

immigration The movement of people around the world. Canada has three major categories of immigrants: economic, family class, and refugees.

independent variable A variable that affects other variables.

individualized marriage A marriage that focuses on the individual's satisfaction and ability to develop and express a sense of self. These marriages are more flexible than other types because they attempt to meet the varied needs of each spouse.

infant mortality rate A common measure of health in a country; reflects the number of deaths in the first year of a child's life, per thousand live births.

institutional marriage A marriage that is less concerned with whether spouses are in love or are good companions to each other and more focused on how the marriage solidifies family and community ties and benefits society as a whole.

intergenerational income elasticity The statistical relationship between a parent's and child's economic standings; the higher the elasticity, the less social mobility a society offers. In this situation, childhood upbringing plays a larger role than individual talents and capabilities in predicting later income.

intersectionality Crenshaw's term for the study of how various dimensions of inequality can combine.

intersex People who are born with both male and female sexual organs.

interview A qualitative research technique whereby a researcher asks subjects questions, records their answers, and then analyzes the responses. Interviews allow the researcher to ask questions that require longer answers and to follow up by asking for more detail.

invisible knapsack Coined by McIntosh, an unseen collection of unearned assets that white people use in their daily lives but about which they are expected to remain oblivious.

irrationality of rationality Weber's concept that rationalized systems can create negative outcomes.

issue attention cycles The idea that the public is more likely to become alarmed about a problem and concerned with its amelioration at certain times. Learning the cost of addressing the problem can quash this enthusiasm, followed by a "post-problem phase" of sporadic recaptured interest.

Kinsey Reports The name given to Kinsey's two books on human sexuality, *Sexual Behavior in the Human Male* (1948) and *Sexual Behavior in the Human Female* (1953).

labelling theory Becker's theory on how we label and think about individuals who engage in deviance. Becker argues that the important element is not the behaviour but the label of being deviant, which can create a deviant or criminal identity and produce a self-fulfilling prophecy that leads to more deviance.

latent functions Unintended functions.

learning theory Developed by Sutherland, who argued that different environments or social milieu, such as a jail, provide opportunities to learn to engage in crime. This theory claims that we are socialized into deviance and criminality through learning from others.

legitimation A major function of the education system, aimed at legitimating certain kinds of knowledge and divisions in society. This process is consistent with Marx's conflict theory.

lesser crimes Acts of deviance that are illegal; however, their perceived harmfulness and severity of public response are moderate. An example of a lesser crime is speeding.

LGBTQ Lesbian, gay, bisexual, transgender, and queer/questioning.

life-cycle effect A main theory in voter turnout research that seeks to explain turnout by illustrating that there is usually an increase in the propensity to vote among older people.

life expectancy The average number of years a population at some age can expect to live.

looking-glass self Cooley's theory that we refine our sense of self over time in light of how others react to us.

low-income cut-offs (LICOs) Income thresholds, created by Statistics Canada, below which a family will likely spend more than the average amount of its income on basic necessities (i.e., food, shelter, clothing).

lumpenproletariat The lowest layer of the working class, according to Marx, including criminals and the chronically unemployed.

managerial perspective One of the major lenses used to understand the rise of the state. This perspective argues that the state was established to politically administer increasingly large territories more effectively.

manifest functions Obvious and intended functions.

marriage The legal union of two people in an intimate relationship.

mass media A message that originates from one source but is intended for many people.

McDonaldization Ritzer's term to describe the movement from traditional to rational methods of thought. Where Weber used the model of the bureaucracy to represent this change, Ritzer sees the fast-food restaurant as representing this transformation.

means-tested program A type of social program that bases eligibility for government assistance on whether an individual or family possesses the means to do without that help. In Canada, means tests are used for student finance (for post-secondary education), legal aid, and welfare (direct transfer payments to individuals to combat poverty).

mechanical solidarity The type of solidarity that involves societies being held together by similarities among people. Durkheim argued that in early societies, people shared a collective consciousness that created solidarity, despite the fact that each unit (such as a family) basically provided for its own production and consumption needs and subunits could survive in isolation from one another.

media The technological processes facilitating communication between a sender and a receiver.

media literacy The framework used to access, analyze, and evaluate media messages and thus create an understanding of the media's role in society.

"medium is the message" Marshall McLuhan's famous statement that argues that the content of the medium is less important than the physical or psychological effects of that medium.

mental health State of well-being in which one can realize one's own potential, cope with the normal stresses of life, work productively, and make a contribution to one's community.

meritocracy The idea that people will achieve based on their own merit.

micro-financing A system of offering financial services to individuals who are not served by the traditional financial system. These services provide small amounts of start-up capital to assist people with their entrepreneurial projects and thus help to lift individuals, families, and communities out of poverty.

militaristic perspective One of the main lenses used to understand the rise of the state. From this perspective, the state was instituted to create a monopoly on the legitimate use of violence, particularly in relation to the ability to wage war.

modernization theory One of the main theories of globalization, which contends that countries are poor because they cling to traditional and inefficient attitudes, technologies, and institutions. Modern societies embrace industrial capitalism, modern technologies, and modern institutions. This theory predicts that, given enough time and with the "correct" behaviours, all societies can become modernized and develop like Western societies.

monocropping The agricultural practice of producing high yields by growing a single crop on the same land each year. Corn, soybeans, and wheat are three common monocrops.

monogamy An exclusive relationship between two people (one man and one woman, two women, or two men).

multiculturalism Based on the idea of pluralism, support for having various cultural or ethnic groups in a society; the belief that conflict is a central feature of societies and that ethnicity is an essential aspect of individual identity and group behaviour.

nation A group of people united based on shared language, ethnicity, or history.

nation-state A group of people who share a physical territory and government.

new advantage According to Gamson, a measure of social movement success in which a group gains benefits, such as a new policy or law, during a challenge and its aftermath.

new media On-demand access to content, interactive user feedback, and creative contribution on any digital device. New media technologies are digital and interactive and can be manipulated, networked, and compressed.

normality of crime Durkheim's argument that crime is necessary, functional, and even good for a society. According to Durkheim, all societies have crime and deviance, which allow groups to define and clarify their collective beliefs.

nuclear family A family consisting of two adults living with one or more children.

obesity A body mass index (BMI) of more than 30.0.

Oka Crisis A standoff, occurring in 1990, between the Mohawk First Nations and the Quebec police/Canadian army over the contested use of an area of land called the Pines.

one-child policy A policy enacted in China in 1979 to reduce population growth by restricting part of the population to having only one child. Exemptions include families with twins, rural couples, ethnic minorities, and couples who were both only children.

organizational model of media coverage The perspective that the media acts as a gatekeeper that determines what events are newsworthy and, because of the way it is set up, tends to rely on official sources and generalist journalists, leading to a particular type of coverage of protest.

outsourcing Contracting work, usually manufacturing or supporting processes, to another country.

parole The supervised early release of a prisoner for such things as good behaviour. Parolees work with parole officers to adjust to life outside prison and to ensure that they do not violate the conditions of their release. If they do, their parole can be revoked, and they can be sent back to prison.

participant observation (ethnography) A qualitative research method in which a researcher attempts to deeply understand a given group of individuals and their practices by becoming intensely involved in their cultural environment, usually over an extended period of time.

party In Weber's theory, organizations that attempt to influence social action and focus on achieving some political goal.

patriarchy The system of male domination in society.

people first philosophy An approach that focuses on the individual and her abilities rather than her limitations

performativity Judith Butler's term to describe the repeated rituals that create and sustain gender through performance.

periphery countries The world's least economically diversified and industrialized nations. These countries focus on one type of economic activity (mostly extracting and exporting raw materials to core nations).

personal troubles Problems that individuals face in their personal lives.

petite bourgeoisie Small-scale capitalists, such as shopkeepers and managers.

petition A document signed by many people, requesting an authority (usually a government official or public entity) to do something in regard to a particular cause.

polygamy The practice of having multiple spouses. Polygamy is illegal in Canada and the United States.

popular culture The culture of the majority or the masses; often juxtaposed with high culture, the culture of the elite.

poverty A condition in which material or cultural resources are lacking. Relative poverty describes the deprivation of some people in relation to those who have more; absolute poverty is a life-threatening deprivation of resources.

power According to Weber, the chance that a person or group can realize its own will in a communal action, even against the resistance of others participating in the same action. The idea is based on a person's or group's economic class, social status, and party.

power elite C. Wright Mills's name for the interwoven interests of society's military, corporate, and political leaders.

precarious employment Employment in dead-end, low-paying, and insecure jobs (sometimes called McJobs). In this area, employers have full control over the labour process; they are able to hire and fire employees with ease and frequency because that kind of work makes them readily replaceable.

prejudice A negative attitude toward someone, based solely on her membership in a particular group.

primary deviance In labelling theory, early acts of deviance. Isolated acts of primary deviance rarely lead to the successful application of a deviant label.

primary sector The economic sector concerned with extracting or harvesting products from the earth. Agriculture (both subsistence and commercial farming), mining, forestry, and fishing are primary sector activities.

primary socialization The earliest stage of socialization, in which we learn how to be a member of society and what attitudes, values, and actions are culturally and socially appropriate.

probation A community release that can be granted to individuals convicted of less serious crimes. Probation entails supervision and certain conditions, such as being involved in and completing a substance abuse program. If the offender does not adhere to these conditions or is re-arrested, the probation can be revoked.

proletariat (worker) One of the two primary classes in Marx's theory. Proletariats own only their capacity to labour, which they must sell to the capitalist.

property Any resource that can be used to produce things of value and to generate wealth. In Marxist theory, property is owned by the capitalist.

protest An organized and public demonstration against an event, policy, or action.

protest paradigm The particular way that the media tend to cover protest events, which works to delegitimate and marginalize protesters and focuses on the spectacle by highlighting sensational details such as violence, visible drama, and deviant or strange behaviour.

public good Things that are non-excludable (a person cannot reasonably prevent another from consuming the good) and non-rivalrous (a person's consumption of the good does not affect another's). Clean air is an example of a public good.

public issues Social problems that a society faces as a whole.

public sociology A sociological approach that attempts to interact with audiences outside academia by encouraging sociologists to engage publicly and politically with issues concerning public policy, political activism, and the institutions of civil society.

punishment The penalty (e.g., denial of certain privileges, abilities, or rights) inflicted on someone for committing a transgression. In criminal law, a judge and/or jury decide punishments.

qualitative research A set of research techniques, including interviews and participant observation, in which the researcher intensively studies a smaller number of cases. This research tends to focus on process questions, including how and why certain things happen, and to look at how actions affect individuals and groups.

quantitative research A set of research techniques that focus on things that can be counted, examine how variables relate to one another, and test relationships with statistical models. This type of research explores what, where, when, how often, and how long social phenomena occur.

race A social distinction based on perceived physical or biological characteristics.

racism The systematic belief, which operates at every level of society, that races have particular characteristics or abilities that make them inferior or superior to others.

rationalization According to Weber, rationalization and rationality are ways of solving problems by focusing on the optimal means toward an end. The process is based on predictability, calculability, efficiency, and control.

realistic conflict theory Based on the work of Bobo, the theory that prejudice originates from social groups competing over valued resources or opportunities.

recidivism rate The rate at which individuals recommit crimes after an initial offence.

rehabilitation The attempt to reform (or "heal") an offender so that she will not commit further offences.

religiosity A measure of how religious a person is, sometimes based on attendance at religious services or intensity of belief.

reparation programs Measures taken by the state to redress gross and systematic human rights violations through some form of compensation or restitution to the victims. Governments enact these programs to deal with injustices on a societal level.

research question The first stage of research. These questions focus on the relationship between two variables.

resocialization The process in which individuals take on new roles and discard former behaviours, attitudes, and values.

restoration An aspect of restorative justice that requires offenders to accept their guilt and to restore the moral order by compensating or fixing the injustice they caused.

retribution Based on "an eye for an eye," punishment that makes offenders undergo suffering that is comparable to that which they have inflicted.

roles The associated behaviours, beliefs, and norms that individuals perform and/or display in social situations.

rotating credit association An example of social capital, a cooperative association that operates in Southeast Asia. In these organizations, people pool their resources and then take turns drawing on the general fund of credit.

Sapir–Whorf hypothesis Developed by Edward Sapir and Benjamin Whorf, the idea that language influences thought.

schooled society A term used by Davies and Guppy to describe the education system in modern society, particularly how mass education has expanded from elementary to high schools and to high post-secondary enrolment in Canada; how schooling has become increasingly integral to modern life; and how the forms and functions of education are increasing and diversifying.

scientific management (Taylorism) The application of scientific principles and methods to the management of labour. These practices were popularized by Frederick Taylor in order to rationalize work and make it more efficient by dividing it into increasingly smaller tasks.

secondary deviance In labelling theory, deviant acts that persist, become more common, and eventually cause people to organize their lives and identities around their deviant status.

secondary sector The economic sector that manufactures finished goods. Metalwork, automobile production, textile production, and engineering industries are part of this sector.

secondary socialization The second stage of socialization in which people learn the appropriate behaviours and attitudes of a smaller group—a subculture—within larger society.

secularization A process whereby society as a whole moves away from religious explanations, institutions, and values to secular ones.

selection A major function of the education system; the sorting, differentially rewarding, and certifying graduates of elementary, secondary, and post-secondary schools. According to Weber, schools use this function to confer status and prestige.

selection bias In regard to the media and social movements, the gatekeepers' (editors') choice to report on a small number of protest events. Media agendas can influence this selection, independent of the events' characteristics.

self-fulfilling prophecy Defined by Merton as a strongly held belief that a person thinks of as true, regardless of whether it actually is, which so influences the person that his reactions ultimately fulfill the prophecy.

semi-periphery countries Countries that are moving toward industrialization and a more diversified economy. During this transition, such countries are not usually dominant in international trade.

sex A biological identity that is based on physical or biological differences and that can be divided into the main categories of male and female.

sexuality Feelings of sexual attraction and behaviours related to them.

sexual orientation A person's sexual identity, expressed in terms of whom a person desires, wants to have sex with, and feels a sense of connectedness with.

sick role Based on the work of Talcott Parsons, the patterns of behaviour that a sick person adopts in order to minimize the disruptive impact of illness.

significant others Key individuals, such as parents, whom young children imitate and model themselves after in the process of socialization.

social capital From the work of Bourdieu, Coleman, and Putnam, the collective value of all social networks. Social capital is essentially about whom you know and the "norms of reciprocity" that develop between people who know one another.

social change The alteration of culture and social institutions over time.

social construction According to Berger and Luckman, a process that involves two steps: 1) people categorize experience and then act on the basis of those classifications; 2) they eventually forget the social origins of the categories and come to see them as natural and unchangeable.

social determinants of health The larger social factors that shape the kind of lives we lead and the health of those lives.

social fact Larger structures of society and norms that shape individuals' actions.

social inequality According to Grabb, the result of social differences that have consequences for individuals. This inequality shapes the rights individuals enjoy, their opportunities, and the privileges that they can exercise in society.

social institutions The norms, values, and rules of conduct that structure human interactions.

socialization The lifelong process of developing a sense of identity and self, as well as of inheriting and transmitting norms, customs, and ideologies that provide the skills and habits required to participate in society.

socialization (function of education) A major function of the education system that helps children to learn the specialized tasks that they will perform in society as well as the values and behaviours required to fit into the mainstream.

social media Websites and other means that allow users to create, share, and/or exchange information and ideas.

social mobility The upward or downward movement in a stratification system, such as the class system. Social mobility can be intergenerational (occur between generations) or intragenerational (occur within a single generation).

social movement An organized and sustained challenge to existing power holders on behalf of a wronged population.

societal protection An element of punishment that protects members of a society from harm. For example, we can limit a criminal's ability to commit crimes by placing the offender in prison.

society Human groupings that are based in a defined geographic area and share common institutions.

socio-economic status (SES) A measure of a person's or family's income, educational attainment, and occupational prestige that is used to determine one's social and economic position in relation to others'.

sociological imagination A world view that sees the connections between our individual lives (and personal troubles) and the larger society (with its public issues) in which we live.

sociology The systematic study of human society.

specific deterrence A type of deterrence that aims to discourage the specific individual by convincing him that engaging in crime has no benefits.

stages of role-taking Outlined by George Herbert Mead, the four stages that occur in socialization and teach people to take the role of the other. The stages are preparatory, role-taking, game, and taking the perspective of the generalized other.

standards for health care in Canada The first pillars of health care in Canada as set out in the Canada Health Act: universality, accessibility, portability, comprehensive coverage, and public administration.

state A set of institutions that include four groups of people: political decision-makers, who can be either elected or appointed; administrative units or bureaucracies; a judiciary or legal system; and security services. States are attached to a geographic territory and maintain a monopoly on rule-making, coercion, and violence within that area.

status group Weber's term for a group that is based on social honour or prestige and that has a "style of life." Honour refers to any distinction, respect, or esteem that is accorded to an individual by others.

strain theory Merton's theory that some individuals experience a poor fit between cultural goals and opportunities for success. For example, these individuals might want to earn enough money to support themselves but cannot get a well-paying job. Thus, they turn to illegitimate means (i.e., crime) to make money.

streaming (tracking) The placing of students with those of similar skills or needs, such as in specific classes or groups within a class.

structural functionalism A theory that, by looking at how societal structures or institutions work together to create consensus and social cohesion, focuses on explaining how society functions effectively.

subculture A group that differs from the dominant culture in some way but is not necessarily critical of it.

subcultural theory A theory that focuses on the role of culture in crime. Cohen argues that gangs and other criminal organizations are subcultures with norms and values different from those of the larger culture.

surface acting In Hochschild's theory of emotional labour, the situation of a worker presenting emotions without actually feeling them.

surplus value In Marx's theory, the new value created by workers that is in excess of their own labour-cost and is available to be appropriated by the capitalist. This value is the amount of money that the capitalist keeps after paying the workers' wages.

survey research A major tool of quantitative research that involves learning about people's characteristics, attitudes, or behaviours by having a large group complete a questionnaire.

symbolic ethnicity Waters's term for the individualistic type of ethnicity that some people can adopt with little social cost.

symbolic interactionism A theory that argues that meanings do not naturally attach to things—we derive meaning from and come to understand our society and our role in it through interacting with other people.

tertiary (service) sector The economic sector that provides services to the general population and to businesses. Retail sales, transportation and distribution, entertainment, banking, health care, and law are part of the tertiary sector.

Thomas principle Thomas and Thomas's theory that if we define a situation as real, it is real in its consequences.

trade union density The percentage of a population's wage earners who are members of a union.

transgender (or trans) umbrella A term used to encompass the variety of different sexual expressions in modern society.

Truth and Reconciliation Commission of Canada (TRC) Part of Canada's reparation program for Indigenous people who were forced to attend residential schools. By examining school records and collecting thousands of personal testimonies, the commission sought to learn the truth about what happened in the schools. Its six years of work culminated in the release of its final report in June 2015.

types of suicide According to Durkheim, suicide has four variations, which differ based on the level of integration or regulation in society as a whole. The types are egoistic (low integration), altruistic (high integration), anomic (low regulation), and fatalistic (high regulation).

UN Convention on the Rights of People with Disabilities (CRPD) A UN convention that sets out a list of rights that people with disabilities have and how the state should work to protect these rights.

Uniform Crime Reporting (UCR) Survey Conducted by Statistics Canada since 1962, a survey that records information on all criminal incidents reported to and confirmed by Canadian police services.

universal program A type of social program available to all citizens regardless of income or wealth. The Canada Pension Plan (CPP) is a universal program.

variable A construct that can take on different values. Examples include age, gender, height, and nationality.

vertical mosaic John Porter's term that describes a society, such as Canada, that contains different ethnic, language, regional, and religious groups with unequal levels of status and power.

victimization survey A survey that asks respondents if they have been victims of crimes and other related questions. In Canada, the General Social Survey is such a survey.

visible minority A Canadian term used to designate a person or group that is visibly not of the majority race in a given population.

welfare state A system in which the state provides a range of social services, including a minimum income and economic assistance to the ill, elderly, and unemployed, to ensure the health and well-being of its citizens. Canada became a welfare state after the passage of social welfare reforms in the 1960s.

white-collar crime A type of crime that occurs in a work setting and is motivated by monetary gain but does not involve intentional or direct acts of violence.

world society theory A main theory of globalization that emphasizes the significance of institutions and culture in forming the structure and behaviour of nation-states, organizations, and individuals worldwide. This theory seeks to explain global change (especially the dispersion of Western policies) as a result of the post–World War II emergence of global institutions and international organizations, as well as an increasingly shared world culture.

world systems theory A main theory of globalization that views the world as a transnational division of labour, which classifies countries as core, semi-periphery, or periphery.

WUNC (worthiness, unity, numbers, commitment) According to Tilly, the criteria that determine the strength of a social movement.

Index